WOMANHOOD MEDIA SUPPLEMENT:

Additional Current Resources About Women

by
HELEN RIPPIER WHEELER

The Scarecrow Press, Inc.
Metuchen, N.J.   1975

Library of Congress Catalog Card No. 72-7396
ISBN 0-8108-0858-7

Copyright © 1975 by Helen Rippier Wheeler
Manufactured in the United States of America

CONTENTS

Foreword	v
Aviso Latinas	vi
Introduction	vii

A BASIC BOOK COLLECTION
000 Generalities	1
100 Philosophy	8
200 Religion	15
300 Social Sciences	17
400 Language	45
500 Pure Sciences	46
600 Technology--Applied Sciences	47
700 Arts	56
800 Literature	59
900 General Geography, History, Biography	69
Individual Biography	72
Fiction	85
Short Stories	94

NON-BOOK RESOURCES
Pamphlets	97
Movement Periodicals	131
Audiovisual Resources	144

DIRECTORY OF SOURCES
The Directory	297
Speakers & Consultants	371
Status-of-Women Commissions, Councils, etc. (Governmental)	402
Women's Liberation Groups & Centers	405
Rosters for Employment and Other Affirmative Action	439

Index to "A Basic Book Collection"	459

FOREWORD

Since 1969, when work on Womanhood Media (Scarecrow, 1972) began, the conditions of woman's life have not generally improved. There are tokens displayed in the media, but the male establishment is digging in: "strident" and "militant" are terms assigned to nonsubmissive women; lesbianism and questions of health are used to discredit; terms like "women's lib" and "libber" have been passed off on feminists by the same non-thinkers who rise up in righteous indignation when an Oriental male is referred to as a "little Jap." Attempts to divide women along racial, class, age, educational, socio-economic and other lines are belied only occasionally by such things as the CLUW founding conference in 1974 (3000+ women members of 58 labor unions from across the U.S.A., officially on the record for the ERA). Women in academia who file charges with the agencies provided by the system to implement the Civil Rights Act typically cannot survive (no woman has filed without tenure and remained on the job--indeed, some with tenure have become unemployable). Non-discriminatory affirmative action employment, especially in higher education, is a fraud--women on faculties have decreased.

For a variety of reasons, this will be the only supplement to Womanhood Media. For one thing, since work on it began circa 1969, Movement-related media have proliferated. Many of these publications and activities should be eschewed as byproducts of sexist corporate activity, but some publisher-producers have succeeded in capturing a share of the market with fair products, and feminists and feminist groups have struggled to begin such projects as Women Studies Abstracts, The Women's Rights Almanac, Women's Organizations and Leaders, The New Woman's Survival Catalog, the Boston Women's Health Book Collective, etc., etc. These tools should be perfected, expanded, and used. Womanhood Media has served an interim need.

1975

AVISO LATINAS

El termino "Latinas" es usado en este Suplemento para referirse e incluir a todas las mujeres del hemisferio del Nuevo Mundo nacidas en paises latinos en donde son más oprimidas las mujeres.

Los factores que caracterizan a una mujer como "Latina" son los siguientes: su origin, su nacionalidad, su lugar de nacimiento, su religión y su idioma, aunque sea el español, portugués o cualquier otro idioma latino su segundo idioma. A veces se refieren a la mujer Latina como perteneciente a un "Tercer Mundo," como Chicanas, Puertoriqueñas, Cubanas, Indias o Negras. Sepan todas las "mujeres Latinas" lectoras de este Suplemento que nosotras las tenemos por nuestras hermanas, y por lo tanto nos preocupamos por vosotras y deseamos brindarles una hermandad mundial.

E. R. W.

INTRODUCTION

The <u>Womanhood Media Supplement</u> continues the media and other <u>resource parts of the 1972 volume</u>, i.e., its Part III, "A Basic Book Collection," IV, "Non-Book Resources," and V, "Directory of Sources." Explanations of arrangements, symbols, and directions for use provided in that work apply here as well and are not repeated.

It would be well to review in the basic volume pages 105-108 (introductory notes to "A Basic Book Collection"), page 197 (a note on pamphlets), page 200 (a note on Movement periodicals), and page 219 (a note on audiovisual resources) <u>before using material in the supplementary basic books and non-book resources,</u> as well as page 255 (introductory notes to Part V, "Directory of Sources") <u>before using supplementary sources.</u>

It is no longer necessary to list "relevant out-of-print titles." Many of those suggested earlier (1972 volume, Appendix no. 3, pp. 328-30) have been reprinted, and works by and about our foremothers and sisters are being made available for research and reading. Some areas of concern which receive more consideration in the <u>Supplement</u> are affirmative action, the arts, Canadiana, Latinas, Lesbiana, and the media. As a resource, the <u>Womanhood Media Supplement</u> can nonetheless be used independently of the basic volume.

A BASIC BOOK COLLECTION*†

000 GENERALITIES

010 Bibliographies & Catalogs (SEE ALSO "Pamphlets" part of Non-Book Resources section, under Bibliographies)

(319) Aldous, Joan and Reuben Hill
International bibliography of research in marriage and the
    family, 1900-1964.
Minnesota Family Study Center & Institute of Life Insurance
    1967 508p Univ. of Minnesota Press $17.50
Considered the most exhaustive bibliography on the topic to date, indispensible for research on women in the family. (Stara Stauffer Whaley with Margrit Eichler, 'A bibliography of Canadian and United States Resources on Women,' Women Studies Abstracts, Fall 1973, v2 #4: page i ff.)

(320) American Library Assoc., Social Responsibilities
    Round Table, Task Force on Alternatives in Print, comp.
    (SRRT Task Force on AIP 1973-4: Sanford Berman, co-
    ordinator Jackie Eubanks, Alice Jacoby, Rossella Mo-
    cerino, Susan Novick, Mimi Penchansky).
Alternatives in print, '73-74; the annual catalog of social
    change publications [3d ed.].
Glide 1973 375p bib index 74-634967 $6.95 (+35¢
    handling)/pap 912078-34-0
For information about AIP's previous editions, SEE Womanhood Media (1972), page 101. The Task Force describes this as "a guide to publications available from non-profit, anti-profit, counter-culture, Third-World and movement

---

*HS = suitable for Jr. & Sr. high school students and adults;
S = also available in Spanish.
†An author and title index to this collection is at the end of the book.

groups--the free press. We hope this directory will provide librarians, booksellers and movement-involved individuals far greater access to much needed but hard-to-locate material." A publisher's note requests corrections and suggested additions; send them to the Task Force c/o Glide. Note the "How to use ..." section carefully. A sampling of subject headings utilized to organize the material (pamphlets, books, posters, audiovisuals, buttons, periodicals, etc.): Abortion, Birth control, Childbirth, Feminism, Lesbians, Rape, Sexual revolution, Women's Liberation.

(321) Astin, Helen S., et al
Women; a bibliography on their education and careers.
Human Service Press 1971 243p $5.95/pap. Also available as ERIC Document # ED 056-271.
Et al = Nancy Suniewick and Susan Dweck. An annotated list of 352 items, with an overview of their findings and an essay on interpretation of the information covered by this project. While now several years old, it is important to get information on women's education and career development into a data base. Seek out subsequent documents, especially if this is your first encounter with ERIC.

(322) Bickner, Mei Liang
Women at work; an annotated bibliography.
Manpower Research Center, Institute of Industrial Relations, Univ. of California, Los Angeles 1974 unpaged index $6.00
Although a review of the literature of womanpower utilization, there is considerable selectivity and, fortunately, a contemporary emphasis. Minority and nonprofessional women are considered. (Let's begin to refer to "employed women.")

(323) Floyd, Mary K., comp.
Abortion bibliography for 1970....
Whitson 1972 125p 72-78877 $7.50 0-87875-024-X; for 1971: 1973 268p $11 0-87875-030-4
Announced as the first in an annual series. Emphasis is on periodical literature. A variety of indexes have been searched: Canadian Periodical Index, Cumulative Index to Nursing Literature, Index to Legal Periodicals, Index Medicus, as well as more "popular" tools such as Readers' Guide.... Material is then well organized via such feminist-relevant subject headings as Hospitals and abortion, Induced abortion, Mortality, Nurses and abortion, Physicians and abortions, Potassium permanganate, Psychiatry, Septic Abortion and Septic Shock, Statistics, Students, Women's Liberation, Youth.

Basic Book Collection 010

(324) Goode, Stephen H., comp.
Venereal disease bibliography; 1966-1970.
Whitson 1972 613p 71-189843 $22.50 0-87875-023-1
Announced as the first in an annual series. Emphasis is on periodical literature. Material is organized via such woman-relevant subject headings as Gonorrhea, Gonorrhea + 33 subheads, Pregnancy, Prostitution. There is little overlap with Floyd's "Abortion bibliography" (# 323).

(325) Hughes, Marija Matich
The sexual barrier; legal and economic aspects of employment.
Ms. Hughes 1970 43p 74-151298 $5.00 0-91256-01-0
Also available as ERIC Document # ED 065-703, 65¢/microfiche 0-91256-01-0
   Supplement I 1971 79p $3.00. Also, ERIC # ED 065-701 65¢
   Supplement II 1972 85p $3.00. Also, ERIC # ED 065-702 65¢
   Supplement III In process
A variety of types of materials on discrimination against women in employment, 1959- . Areas considered include legal aspects of employment, pay differentials, professional opportunities, general employment information, discrimination itself. This work grew out of Ms. Hughes' "Women's rights in employment."

(326) Indiana University. Institute for Sex Research. Library.
Catalog of the Social and Behavioral Sciences Monograph Section.
G. K. Hall 1974 4v $300.00 0-8161-1141-3
The Institute was founded in 1947 by Dr. Alfred C. Kinsey (SEE #'s 170 and 171). This first publication of the holdings of the Institute Library consists of books from the behavioral and social sciences section cataloged up to September 1973. Areas include history of marriage, early sex education, women's rights, sex ethics and religion, abortion, venereal disease, contraception, laws regulating sex behavior. Works from Western cultures of the 19th and 20th centuries predominate, although the Library collects materials in all languages. While the monographs themselves are primarily of interest to researchers, such a catalog has a variety of potential uses.

(327) Jacobs, Sue-Ellen
Women in perspective; a guide for cross-cultural studies.

Univ. of Illinois Press 1974 299p index 72-93987 $10.95
   00299-7; $3.95/pap 00345-4
This is a revised, expanded, and corrected version of her
"Women in cross-cultural perspective; a preliminary sourcebook," published by the University's Department of Urban and Regional Planning in 1971. It can be used to complement Bullough's "Subordinate sex" (# 841).

(328) Krichmar, Albert, et al
The Women's Rights Movement in the United States, 1848-
   1970; a bibliography and sourcebook.
Scarecrow Press 1972 436p 72-4702 $13.50 0-8108-
   0528-6
Et al = Barbara Case, Barbara Silver, Ann E. Wiederrecht. An important tool, the largest such bibliography published at the time. Partially annotated; scope: since 1848. Variety of media: books, periodical articles, doctoral dissertations, pamphlets, selected state and federal government publications. Special features are a list of relevant manuscript collections and the biography section, which includes living women. In Scarecrow's "Issues of the seventies" series.

(329) Schlesinger, Benjamin, ed.
The one-parent family; perspectives and annotated bibliography,
   2 ed.
Univ. of Toronto Press 1970 $6.00
Much of his "The Jewish family; a survey and annotated bibliography" (Toronto, 1971, $7.50) of socio-psychological studies in English is also relevant.

(330) Seruya, Flora, et al
Sex and sex education; a bibliography.
Bowker 1972 336p indexes 72-8333 $15.75 0-8352-0544-4
Et al = Albert Ellis, Susan Losher. Vast sexology list having utility because of author, title and analytical-subject indexes, inclusion of guide for parents and teachers, complete bibliographical data, and brief annotations.

(331) Soltow, Martha Jane, et al
Women in American labor history, 1825-1935; an annotated
   bibliography.
Michigan State Univ. School of Labor & Industrial Relations
   1972 150p indexed $2.50/pap
A selective bibliography; appended are lists of significant archival collections in the U.S.A. on women and labor and publications of the U.S. Dept. of Labor Women's Bureau through 1935.

Basic Book Collection 020   5

(332)   Strugnell, Cecile
Adjustment to widowhood and some related problems; a selective and annotated bibliography.
Health Sciences   1974   185p   73-5781 $6.50/pap
This is the first in a series of three based on research done
in the Widow-To-Widow Program, Laboratory of Community
Psychiatry, Harvard Medical School, where Strugnell is a
research assistant.   Books and articles in English.   Relevant
also to research re older women.

(333)   Waldrip, Louise and Shirley Ann Bauer
A bibliography of the works of Katherine Anne Porter and of
   the criticism of the works....
Scarecrow Press   1969   219p $6.00
The only female in Scarecrow's "Author Bibliographies Series."

(334)   Walstedt, Joyce Jennings
Psychology of women; a partially annotated bibliography.
KNOW   1973   76p $2.25/pap   #K2310   0-912786-23-X

(335)   Williams, Ora, 1926-
American Black women in the arts and social sciences; a
   bibliographic survey.
Scarecrow Press   1973   141p   73-4560 $6.00   0-8108-0615-0
An expanded revision of an article published in the March
1972 California Library Assoc. Journal.   Audiovisuals and
Black periodicals and publishing houses are listed.   Almost
all references are to work by Black women, and the women
themselves are mostly contemporary.   Basic.

020   Library & Information Science

(336)   Ash, Lee, ed.
Subject collections, 4th ed.
Bowker   1974   908p   74-19331 $38.50   0-8352-0435-9
About 65,000 collections devoted entirely to or of unusual
strength in specific subject-matters are listed.   Most are
libraries or parts of library programs; also manuscript collections and those of libraries in museums in the U.S.A.
and Canada.   In many ways a decidedly non-feminist product.
Under each subject-heading, libraries are arranged alphabetically by state.   Feminists must arm themselves with the
basic fact-of-life that our language reflects and reinforces
the status quo--viz. subject-headings, thesauri, descriptor
systems, all potentially sexist.   (SEE Dickinson's "Statement
to the RTSD CCS Subject Analysis Committee on sex-biased

subject-headings..." in "Pamphlets" part of Non-Book Resources section, under Sexism in Education & Media.) Ash employs Woman and Women subject-headings; what's the difference?

030 040 General Encyclopedic Works

(337) The Encyclopedia of the American woman.
McGraw-Hill 1975 720p bib
Editors: Gail Berson, Miriam Blankstein, Cindy Cohen, Nancy Evans, Betsy Gehman, Louise Knight, Shelley Richtmyer, Elizabeth Smith, Freya Sonenstein, Sheila Tobias, Sue VanVoorhees. Suggestions for 20th-century women biographees and ideas for articles under headings, male culture and female culture, are welcomed by the collective. A prospectus is available; contact The Encyclopedia at Box 2600, East College, Wesleyan University, Middletown, CT 06457. 203-347-9411, x 669.

(338, 339) North American Reference Encyclopedias: Reference encyclopedia of Women's Liberation 1972: The new woman, vol. 1.
North American Pub. Co., 134 N. 13, Philadelphia, PA 19107. 1972 bib $27.50 #7210
William White, editor. Contributors include Bella Abzug, Caroline Bird, Shirley Chisholm, Bernice Sandler, Gloria Steinem. 25+ "major articles" on law, science, sexism, occupations, history, literature. Also in this series, "Reference encyclopedia of abortion, 1972, volume 5" ($27.50 #7213.)

050 General Periodicals

(340) Barrer, Myra E., ed.
Women's organizations and leaders directory, 1975 ed.
Today publications 1975 index 73-86473 $40.00/pap
  discounts available
A feminist directory of individuals and organizations furthering equal opportunity for women. Ms. Barrer publishes the national newsletter, Women Today. Alphabetical, geographical, and subject-area indexing to U.S.A. women. Entries are complete even to telephone numbers. Information based on questionnaires returned by persons widely selected by the publisher-editor. Has potential in implementation of non-discriminatory affirmative action programs, as just one example. Basic.

Basic Book Collection 080

(341) Gager, Nancy, ed.
Women's rights almanac, 1974 [vol. 1].
Elizabeth Cady Stanton Pub. Co. 1974 624p bib index
  74-77527 $6.95; $4.95/pap
The introduction to this annual states "our goal was to give at least a timely summary of every subject and places to go for further information and aid with every problem." 4 sections: lists-by-state of 'almanac' information (statistics, officials, voting record, organizations, etc.) about women; more general information on women in elected office, women's organizations, publications; essays on important issues (abortion, lesbiana, health, etc.); and a 4th section, "Women in time," includes a 1973 article, calendar, landmarks, history, international overview, periodicals. Appendix of bibliographies, glossary, and 'legal assistance.' Good paper and legible print. Ms. Gager is a feminist who founded the Elizabeth Cady Stanton Publishing Company in 1973.

(342) Women; their changing roles.
Arno 1973 556p bib index 72-5020 $35.00 0-405-04164-0
Elizabeth Hall Janeway, advisory editor. "Great Contemporary Issues" series. These articles appeared in the Arno-related New York Times from late 19th century to the present. Thus material consists largely of obituaries and articles, as opposed to news stories. At least Women are classed by the New York Times Company on this occasion as great and contemporary. Ms. Janeway's introduction is as useful as any part of the volume itself. There are deficiencies in the overall product, but it is nonetheless basic at this time for a variety of reasons: the real world of changing roles conveyed in primary sources, the need for publications at least overseen by feminists.

080 General Collections

(343) American women; images and realities [series].
Arno Press 1972 44v $765.00/set, library price; individual books from $9.00 to $30.00.
Annette K. Baxter and Leon Stein, advisory editors. Books about women, selected, edited and introduced by Baxter and Stein. Great variety of style, reading level, subject-matter, view-point through 19th and 20th centuries, written by men and women. The thing they have in common is that the authors were writing at that time about themselves, thus

avoiding what is being ground out today--history by hindsight. Several of the books from which the selections have been taken are included elsewhere here in the Basic Book Collection in their in-print complete editions.

090   Manuscripts and Book Rarities

(344)   Schlesinger, Arthur & Elizabeth, Library on the History of Women in America; The manuscripts inventory and the Catalogs of the manuscripts, books and pictures. Radcliffe College.
G. K. Hall   1973   3v $215.00   Books catalog 0-8161-1053-0; Manuscripts catalog 0-8161-1069-7
Vol. 1 Book Catalog A-L
Vol. 2 Book Catalog M-Z, Etiquette, Periodicals.
Vol. 3 Manuscripts Catalog, Manuscripts Inventory, Picture Catalog.
Offset reproduction of approximately 40,000 cards to Summer 1973, on durable, acid-free paper, Class A Library Binding; a supplement is planned.   The contents of the collection are especially valuable because they include newsletters, underground newspapers, flyers, ephemera, task force reports, research data, even television scripts ... women from the past, as well as the papers of such persons as Betty Friedan.   U.S. Library of Congress subject headings are generally used, providing (only) consistency.   Even here we find the sub-suming subject headings: Women as this and that's.

100   PHILOSOPHY

150   Psychology

(345)   Aldrich, Ann, pseud.
Take a Lesbian to lunch.
MacFadden-Bartell   1972   Manor Books   #125-118 $1.25/pap
Has been out-of-print but now being reprinted.   Aldrich has been referred to (Synergy issue #37) as "the Uncle Tom of the Lesbian world"; keeping in mind that she has been writing since the turn of the century, why might even a gay person react thusly to "Take a Lesbian to lunch?"   On the other hand why is it included in the ALA SRRT Task Force on Gay Liberation's "A Gay Bibliography, 3d revision" (SEE Pamphlets: Lesbiana) and being reprinted?   Food for thought: Are Lesbians sick?

Basic Book Collection 150   9

(346) Bengis, Ingrid
Combat in the erogenous zone.
Knopf   1972   260p   72-2248 $6.95   0-394-47550-X
One of the cleverest titles around. Most Establishment reviewers summarize with something like "analysis of her relationships with men and women," which, while not inaccu-
rate, does not convey the reason for our needing to know
about this combat ... human sexuality via Bengis' lesbian
experience and self-knowledge. Her reasoning has produced
a work which is being frequently quoted by both men and
women.

(347) Freeman, Lucy
Farewell to fear.
Putnam   1969   339p   69-18173   Ballantine $1.25/pap
   0-345-02090-1-125
Freeman is not a feminist, i.e. she does not see, for example, sexist language, despite her skill in writing. The
story of her "journey to maturity" comes 18 years after her
first book, best-seller "Fight against fears" (1952), the "sensational, pioneering account of her five years in psychoanalysis." "In one way analysis had freed me from enough fear
that I could at least try to live with a man.... As I found
myself on my knees soaping bathroom and kitchen floor,
waxing bedroom floor, dusting and vacuuming, as both my
husband and I believed a 'proper' wife should do, I thought,
I am a slavey. ... He claimed I should find time for both
housework and writing. But the housework alone exhausted
me, physically and emotionally. I never would have dreamed
of seeking a woman for help when I first started analysis....
I could now look on a woman as equal to a man rather than
hold contempt for her (for myself, really--and unreally) ..."
(preliminary pages, 53-4, 92). A good example of a book
which may not be entirely appealing, with its tiresome Freud,
too much H. S. Sullivan School, etc., but well worth reading.

(348) Friday, Nancy
My secret garden ... women's sexual fantasies.
Trident   1973   361p   72-96815 $7.95   671-27101-6

(349) Garskof, Michele Hoffnung, ed.
Roles women play; readings toward Women's Liberation.
Brooks-Cole   1971   210p   index   75-146974 $4.50/pap
   0-8185-0009-3
Contemporary Psychology Series. Garskof explains that she
attempted to bring together important material about women
when starting to teach a course on psychology of women; she

wanted to stress inter-relationship of economic and social factors to the evolution of the psychology of women as is, and as could be. An anthology of three sections: Woman's place in society (includes Caroline Bird); Psychology, sociology and women (includes Jo Freeman); and Toward the liberation of women (e.g. Alice Rossi). This needs a "further reading"-type bibliography, which would be a good exercise for Women's Studies students and feminist librarians. Above all, these are articles by living vibrant females. Check out the index, with its entries under abortions, advertising, birth control, Black women, childbearing, childless women, childlessness, consumer, consumerism, double standards, Galbraith, J. K., male chauvinism, myths, orgasm, psychotherapy, religion, stereotypes, Tiger, L. Put this on almost any undergrad psychology course bibliography!

(350) Hegeler, Inge and Sten Hegeler
An XYZ of love; frank answers to every important question about sex in today's world; tr. by David Hohnen.
Crown 1970 216p 72-127513 $10.00
The Hegelers really take women seriously.

(351) Hite, Shere, comp.
Sexual honesty; by women for women.
Warner 1974 294p $1.50/pap
Hite is a member of the New York NOW Chapter's Feminist Sexuality Project. Her questionnaire circulated among 2000 women from 14 to 74; 45 sample responses belie the sexist contention of women's unvaried sexuality. Hite is involved in a research project, with this report an interim document confirming what feminists have known right along.

(352) Jung, Carl Gustav, 1875-1961
Civilization in transition; collected works, volume 10, 2 ed.; G. Adler, et al., editors; R. F. Hull, tr.
Bollingen Series, volume 20 1964 52-8757 Princeton Univ. Press $10.00 0-691-09762-3
Jung is much cited in contemporary feminist theory (e.g. Abbott #374). This is not to say that Jung, Jung Foundation publications, and Jungian psychologists are feminist. See for examples, Irene Claremont DeCastillejo's "Knowing woman; a feminine psychology" (Putnam for the Jung Foundation, 1973, $7.50); Robert Johnson's "He! a contribution to understanding masculine psychology" (Religious Pub. Co., 1974, $4.95).

Basic Book Collection 150

(353) Kaye, Harvey, M.D.
Male survival; masculinity without myth.
Grosset 1974 224p 73-15129 $8.95 0-448-01306-1
Psychiatrist Kaye sees that the masculine mystique is as impossible as the feminine. Using role stereotypes--superman, sexual athlete, achiever, etc.--he shows the conflict between what is expected in the contemporary system of a male and what he can survive and deliver. Notable that he has carefully used the word, "male," in the title, rather than "man."

(354) Kochansky, Hanja
Freely female; the sexual fantasies of women.
Ace 1973 $1.25
Relate to Nancy Friday's "My secret garden ..." (#348).

(355) McFadden, Michael
Bachelor fatherhood; how to raise and enjoy your children as a single parent.
Walker 1974 192p bib 73-90390 $7.95 0-8027-0456-5
Will disappoint the people who assume it's a handbook for/about unwed fathers, for the main-title is a come-on! The sub-title is what McFadden's talking about and from chosen experience. He did have a wife, the mother of his still-young children, and they do still "see" her.... NBC TV's Tomorrow host Tom Snyder seemed fixated by just how much went on during her visits, snicker. Besides his awareness and concern for women and children, McFadden is also aware of and concerned about the responsibilities of parenting. Many insights for feminist non-parents as well, e.g. his realization come-by the hard way of the housework racket, with subsequent application of reorganization principles which would put most media commercials and products out of biz!

(356) Mitchell, Juliet, 1940-
Psychoanalysis and feminism.
Pantheon 1974 456p index 73-18717 $8.95
Mitchell's point of departure is her belief that most feminist writers misunderstand Freud's theories, that they deny the unconscious. She is right in contending that an extention of such an assumption would be a damaging psychology. She contends that psychoanalysis is not an advocacy for patriarchal society but an analysis of one. Useful for more advanced college psychology majors and Master's-level students, Women's Studies personnel willing and able to attack the Establishment contention that Women's Studies are not "excellence," substantive, "solid like Black Studies" and areas

studies, or challenging. Having read the book, relate the contributions of Deutsch (#15), Horney (#14), Johnson & Masters (#209), Laing (#206), Reich (#213), Sherfey (#424), Thompson (#11), et al; SEE ALSO Miller's "Psychoanalysis and women" (#546).

(357) Mannoni, Maud
The backward child and his mother; a psychoanalytic study.
 Tr. from French by A. M. Sheridan Smith.
Pantheon 1973 242p 72-3417 $8.95
World of Man Series. Mannoni is a French children's psychoanalyst. Freudian, she sees the backward child victimized, engulfed by mother, mentally handicapped. This, of course, is the traditional mother, a captive herself. How might feminists have titled the series and translated the title?

(358) Pleck, Joseph H. and Jack Sawyer, eds.
Men and masculinity.
Prentice-Hall 1974 184p bib 74-13395 $6.95; Spectrum
 S-347 $2.95/pap 0-13-574319-2 ($3.25 in Canada)
Patterns of Social Behavior Series. Psychologists Pleck and Sawyer have gathered recently-published articles mostly by men, some feminists, into seven prefaced-groups: Growing up male, Men and women, Men and children, Men and men, Men and work, Men and society, Men's Liberation. Some of these have appeared in Ms. magazine, and will not bring news to feminists; many of the others, while in the literature, are brought forward for the first time, e.g. Michael Silverstein's "The history of a short, unsuccessful academic career," constituting with two others the Men and work group, was previously printed in two journals. It is a stunning analysis of a gay male's evolution in the politics of academia--his recognition of the politics of the environment, application of theory, recognition of reality--his tremendous self-knowledge and above all, his perception of oppression of women and men. There are several "personalities," e.g. Marc Fasteau ("Why aren't we talking?" a Ms. reprint); I. F. Stone, ("Machismo in Washington"). This is not a "feminist" anthology; Pleck and Sawyer have been aroused to awareness of the status quo's damaging effect on men and boys, but they seek what they term "human liberation" (the new old refrain). They do not see clearly that Women's Liberation must have a high priority--analogous to the difference between equal opportunity and affirmative action employment--responsibility and action must be stressed.

(359) Sheehan, Valerie Harms, ed.
Unmasking; ten women in metamorphosis.
Swallow Press 1973 286p 72-96163 $8.95 0-8040-0330
The record of consciousness-raising sessions of ten women artists.

(360) Sherman, Julia A.
On the psychology of women; a survey of empirical studies.
Thomas 1971 304p bib $10.75; $6.75/pap
A biological-bibliographical approach to the female life cycle.

(361) Sorensen, Jane and Edythe Cudlipp
The new way to become the person you'd like to be; the complete guide to consciousness-raising.
McKay 1973 312p index 73-79948 $6.95
The jacket claims everything you can think of for this (and misleads a bit). What does it have for feminists re CR? Part 2, CR step-by-step, how-to outlines for starting, leading, topics, questions. See also Chapter 3, "Women and leadered CR: 'And a woman shall lead them'." CR is not rapping, therapy, counseling, confessional, whining, unloading.... The authors' "pocket dictionary definition: CR is the exploration of individual oppression through examining personal, cultural, social, sexual, and religious roles with the options of keeping some roles, dropping others, and modifying still other roles in an effort to increase personal functioning and potential" (p. 5). This means structuring a situation (know-how, qualified leader, group members' agreement in advance to ground rules) in which no one will be interrupted and will be further supported by the rest of the group. Important. Perhaps the lack of a further-reading type bibliography reflects the lack of such material.

170 Ethics (Moral Philosophy)

(362) Daly, Mary
Beyond god the father; toward a philosophy of Women's Liberation.
Beacon 1973 256p index 73-6245 $8.95 0-8070-4164; $3.95/pap
Although the author's background is Roman Catholic, her credentials clearly qualify her to develop "a metaphysical basis for the feminist revolution." She is most critical of the sexism in the Catholic Church, but cognizant of its presence throughout organized religion. Perhaps her hope for "psychic androgyny" threatens people. Don't be put off

by so-called independent reviewers' use of the old "shrill, arrogant, and clichéd--but nonetheless well reasoned and carefully documented"-type admission. Daly is a feminist leader in theory and action, and must be heard. In the opinion of Dorothy Curzon reviewing for the excellent Canadian feminist magazine, Emergency Librarian!, Daly with this book becomes "a giant in the Women's Movement." "Mary's transformation from reformist to revolutionary takes her from the musty confines of the confessional to the heady 'Cosmic Covenant of Sisterhood.' She stresses throughout the importance of language to oppression." (v2 #1:14-15, October 1974). She has changed, progressed much since "The church and the second sex" (#25; now available in paperback with a "New postchristian introduction" by Dr. Daly; Harper, 1975, $2.95).

(363) Degen, Marie Louise
The history of the Woman's Peace Party.
Johns Hopkins Univ. Press 1939 266p B. Frank repr.
 $15.00 0-8337-5275-8
The Johns Hopkins University Studies in History & Political Science. Series 57, #3. The Woman's Peace Party was founded in 1914 by Jane Addams and eventually affiliated with the Women's International League for Peace and Freedom.

(364) Mannes, Marya
Last rights.
Morrow 1974 160p 73-9881 $5.95
Why is a book about philosophy of death included among womanhood media? Because seemingly women are most often expected to grin and bear it, (want to) be kept in the dark, and sustain others in same!

(365) Perkins, D. M. (Lovelace, Linda)
Deep throat; a novel.
Dell/Quicksilver c1973 by Gerard Damiano Film Productions
 190p $1.50/pap Based on the filmscript and film,
 "Deep Throat."
The Womanhood Media Basic Book Collection was introduced via a list of a few obscenely mysogynous-but-nonetheless standard books--some even classics, chic (see pp. 105-6 of the basic volume). Everyone should experience first hand the boredom and sexism of pure porno, and Linda Lovelace's masterpiece is timely and multi-media! The story is, according to the cover, "of a modern girl with an unusual Problem and how, through the wonders of medical science and her own zest for life, she was able to find a

Solution for it." Consider Ms. L's perception of Dr. Young
(page 35): "He had to be a real doctor, she thought, looking
at the framed diplomas on his walls. His office was decorated in dark wood paneling, modern paintings, and strange
and expensive furniture. He couldn't be a quack." In case
you don't get it, deep throat is "so that they could swallow
a man's penis during the act of fellatio with no trouble at
all" (page 46). Mr. Polo: "You're like the rest of them!
You're nothing but a woman, with a mouth, breasts, and
cunt. Give me a man any day! Men are closer to whatever
secrets there are in life. Women are things, another race
men have to deal with. The first Martians." This is classic usury of women--merely more blatant than what is acceptable in everyday life.

200 RELIGION

230 Christian Doctrinal Theology

(366) Tavard, George H.
Woman in Christian tradition.
Univ. of Notre Dame Press   1973   257p   index   72-12637
   Harper $9.95   0-268-00490-0
Tavard is a Catholic priest-scholar. He carefully reviews
women/church, including other religions, winding up by rejecting the traditional church view of woman: symbol of evil
ipso facto equality's meaning.

240 Christian Moral and Devotional Theology

(367) Henderson, Nancy
Out of the curtained world; the story of an American nun
   who left the convent.
Doubleday   1972   276p   74-171297 $6.95
Ms. Henderson came back after six years ... another socalled personal narrative, but hers clearly points up the discriminatory hierarchal patriarchal authoritative inhumaneness,
which after all, in other forms is imposed on all women.

(368) Russell, Letty M.
Human liberation in a feminist perspective--a theology.
Westminster   1974   224p   bib   74-10613 $3.95/pap
Dr. Russell has coined the term, "Fourth World," to describe today's female. By making this kind of analogy as
well as others--Black Liberation, for example--she evolves

a model for progressing. She, like others, sees the problem of "language," among the problems. This is not just another WL religion book. It is theoretical, complex--but possible. She is attempting to evolve a theology, a relationship between "God" and women.

(369) VanDerMeer, Haye
Women priests in the Catholic Church?; a theological-historical investigation, tr. by Arlene and Leonard Swidler.
Temple Univ. Press 1974 199p index 73-79480 $10.00 0-87722-059-X
Like other writers, Mr. VanDerMeer goes back over history and the Catholic position on women, especially re the priesthood. He concludes (only) that the past discriminatory regulations have not been legitimate, and, in addition, questions whether the rulings made in the past are "relevant" today.

260 Christian Social and Ecclesiastical Theology

(370) Arisian, Khoren
The new wedding; creating your own marriage ceremony.
    Photography by Ingbet.
Knopf 1973 bib 72-11029 Random $7.95; $3.50/pap
Arisian is associated with the Ethical Culture movement. Most "new" wedding ceremonies include a portion of tradition, e.g. Rhoda Morgenstern's "As long as we both shall love." But the new ceremony does provide an opportunity to consciously move towards honesty in human relationships and the making of contracts which are feasible for both parties. These relate to growing together, spiritual freedom, and, as one Establishment reviewer put it, "Even the precepts of anarchofeminism!" Western and Eastern rites, suggested poems, musical selections.

270 History and Geography of Church

(371) VanVuuren, Nancy
The subversion of women as practiced by churches, witchhunters, and other sexists.
Westminster 1973 192p 73-5874 $5.95
VanVuuren, a member of the Association of Feminist Consultants, maintains that the Judeo-Christian tradition was responsible for establishing men as the wielders of religious power. "The Roman Catholic Church, and later the Protestant Church, imposed its convictions of male supremacy and

Basic Book Collection 300

superiority on the entire Western world, and subverted women into the roles that men most feared, and so perhaps desired: sex and magic-witchcraft." While some women chip away at prejudices, gaining ordination, being honored with election to high posts and winning other recognition, others are posing questions that are shaking the fathers of the organized church. Westminster Press is the publishing arm of the United Presbyterian Church in the U.S.A.

(372) Lebeson, Anita
Recall to life; the Jewish woman in America.
T. Yoseloff 1970 $7.60 0-498-07480-3
The emergence of the American Jewish woman as a social force; the history which produced her.

290 Other Religions and Comparative

(373) Ruether, Rosemary Radford, ed.
Religion and sexism; images of women in the Jewish and
    Christian traditions.
Simon & Schuster 1974 360p index 74-2791 $9.95;
    $3.95/pap
Religions have been largely responsible for "the images that have degraded and suppressed women." This collection portrays this responsibility throughout history. Doley has already edited a collection (#26) which shows this manifest in the role of today's church-woman.

300 THE SOCIAL SCIENCES

(374) Abbott, Sidney and Barbara Love
Sappho was a right-on woman; a liberated view of Lesbian-
    ism. HS
Stein & Day 1972 251p bib 77-160348 $7.95
    0-8128-1409-6; $1.95/pap 0-8128-1590-4
A readable book which should be read and then studied by all persons, for information and for enlightenment. Should be translated into Spanish. The sub-title makes a good after-reading discussion topic. "Those Feminists, at least whose interest is limited to specific issues, seem to want only a little bit of independence, defined as relief from housework, a day-care center, promotion on the job. What the lives and writings of Lesbians tell them is that real independence means fundamental, even drastic societal change, and that this change begins with their own lives and the way

they see themselves" (p. 138, paperback). Read especially
Chapter 6, "Lesbianism and feminism"; be able to identify
"the Lavender Menace" and to dissociate yourself. Basic.

(375) Adams, Elsie and Mary Louise Briscoe, eds.
Up against the wall, mother; a Women's Liberation reader.
Glencoe Press 1971 521p bib $4.95 #47020; $2.95/pap
   #47021
An anthology of essays by Freud, Mill, Merriam, Engels,
Bird, Sinclair Lewis and others. Each is followed by questions and discussion by scholars Adams and Briscoe. Four
sections: traditional view of women, nature of women, adjustment for survival, toward freedom.

(376) Babcox, Deborah and Madeleine Belkin, eds.
Liberation now!
Dell 1971 $1.25/pap 440-04787-125
A collection of writings by a variety of women who are all
part of the WL Movement. The self-knowledge of the enervated housewives. You won't scan this!

(377) Banks, Olive and Joseph Ambrose Banks
Feminism and family planning in Victorian England.
Schocken 1964/1963 bib $4.50 0-8052-3071-8
The Banks' books are often cited by contemporary feminist
scholars and theoreticians, e.g. Millett, Morgan. Women's
protest, the rights they had, and attitudes toward them were
their subjects. A bibliography of pamphlets on The Woman
Question in Britain, 1792-1880 is included; pamphlets have
always been a vehicle for change. (Today we have pamphlets and reprints, from KNOW, for example.) Their "Prosperity and parenthood; a study of family planning among the
Victorian middle classes" is also in print (Humanities, 1954,
$6.00).

(378) Beard, Mary Ritter, 1876-1958, ed.
America through women's eyes.
Greenwood Press c1933/1969 558p bib 68-54772 $18.70
   0-8371-0301-0

(379) Beard, Mary Ritter, 1876-1958
On understanding women.
Greenwood Press c1931/1968 541p bib $18.25
   0-8371-0302-9

(380) Beauvoir, Simone de, 1892-
The coming of age; tr. by Patrick O'Brian.

Basic Book Collection 300

Putnam 1972 585p index 75-189871 $10.00
 0-399-10911-0; $2.25/pap 0-446-72182-4. S
Beauvoir's consideration of society's abuse of the old, stemming from a faulty value system. Ageism is sexist. (The original, French title, "La Vieillesse," was translated exactly for the British edition--"Old Age"--but became "The coming of age" in the U.S.A.!)

(381) Bernard, Jessie Shirley, 1903-
The future of marriage.
World 1972 367p bib index 77-183085 $9.95
 0-529-04521-4
Traditional marriage will have to be modified into a mutuality.

(382) Bernard, Jessie Shirley, 1903-
The future of motherhood.
Dial 1974 352p index 74-13391 $10.00 0-8037-2747-X
"The motherhood instinct" is another myth--"parenting," a better role definition. Current literature survey including day-care and cohabitation (guilty if you do; odd if you don't).

(383) Billings, Victoria, 1945-
The womansbook. HS
Wollstonecraft 1974 266p bib 73-82723 $7.95
 0-88381-006-9
The publisher's material disclaims this as "... neither militantly feminist nor ardently status quo; it is for all those who say, 'I'm not really a women's liberationist, but...'." Claims it's "an enlightened guide to achieving self-awareness and independence...." Despite all of this built-in, our time-wasting marketing, Billings can write, and really knows where she's at. She has a one-two-three style which is pragmatic and readable. A good gift for the fully grown but immature adult female.

(384) Caine, Lynn
Widow.
Morrow 1974 224p 73-23124 $6.95
It took her husband's unexpected death to force Missus Martin Caine to stand on her own two feet. Now Ms. Lynn Caine is giving advice--actually on how to catch/grow up. Among the best of several similar books, hers protests the status she finds herself in, her realization that she should be concerned with security, her learning to communicate, resort to therapy. Most of these books have relevance for divorced and older women. They include: Harriet LaBarre's

"Life of your own" (McKay, 1972, $6.95); Theresa A. Morse's "Life is for living" (Doubleday, 1973, $4.95); Phyllis Rolfe Silverman's "Helping each other in widowhood" (Health Sciences, 1974, $8.95); and Cecile Strugnell's "Adjustment to widowhood and some related problems" (Health Sciences, 1973, $6.50; #332).

(385) Carden, Maren Lockwood
The new feminist movement.
Russell Sage Foundation 1973 73-83889 Basic Books
  $8.95 0-87154-196-3
"By accepting available opportunities to broaden their roles (basically by joining the paid work force) they are trying to trade off despised parts of the traditional feminine role for admired parts of the traditional male role. Yet, at the same time, they fear that they may, in fact, also lose admirable parts of the traditional role and adopt what they consider to be unacceptable parts of the traditional male role." How do we survive in the predatory male world, without becoming partners ourselves?

(386) Casler, Lawrence
Is marriage necessary?
Behavioral Publications 1974 240p bib 73-18236 $8.95
  0-87705-132-1
This is an important work for us. Casler documents his case against traditional monogamous marriage. He is not particularly feminist. In fact his condemnation is based on several things, e.g. its damage to children (which leads to a changed attitude towards day-care). Monogamous marriage was perhaps once logical in its context; it is not now. His contentions extend to suggestions for needed change--monogamy is among the several alternatives, but even so it must be different in that it will be by real choice and coexist among several equally socially-acceptable choices. (At present, there is no choice among nice people.)

(387) Chafe, William Henry
The American woman; her changing social, economic, and
    political roles, 1920-1970.
Oxford 1972 351p bib 72-77496 $7.95 501578-9
As feminist readers know, female suffrage did not alter the status of women. Chafe has done some reading and agrees. He supplements this with the fact of World War II, which inadvertantly provided women with the chance to get outside of the house, earn a better wage, and thusly led to some political change as well. He realizes that sexual inequality is

Basic Book Collection 300   21

perpetuated by the social structure which condones and condems "roles" (Janeway's "place")--thus his opinion that a new social system is needed, and what every feminist knows: there is no such thing as modifying the status quo to provide equality. A comparison of media and reviewer perceptions is always interesting and can be productive: Rose Laub Coser writes in Dissent that the book "combines the rigorous scholarship of the historian with social sensitivity and superb writing ... [and] must be read not only for the information it presents, but as a model of how to combine ideological sophistication with objective writing." Choice's academician-reviewer states that this "book is neither analytic nor polemical. Because it is essentially a chronicle, not an analytic study, the historian and general reader will find it more interesting than the sociologist or anthropologist ..." (Feb. 1973:1628). Booklist's librarian-staff annotator describes it as "judicious and thought-provoking.... The principal assumption of the book is that sexual inequality is rooted in the social structure through allocation of different spheres of responsibility to men and women ..." (Jan. 1, 1973:413).

(388) Dash, Joan
A life of one's own; three gifted women and the men they
  married.
Harper 1973 388p $10.00
The three gifted women are Maria Goeppert-Mayer, Edna St. Vincent Millay, and Margaret Sanger. Ms. Dash questions whether self-realization is possible for women if they continue to live with men. Actually it is the marriages of these women which she considers.

(389) Davidoff, Leonore
The best circles; women and society in Victorian England.
Rowman & Littlefield 1973 127p bib index 73-10386
  $12.00 0-87481-428-1
A study useful for students seeking topics in sociology and history.

(390) Davis, Angela Y., et al
If they come in the morning; voices of resistance.
Signet 1971 281p 71-169154 Third press $6.95
  89388-022-1; $1.25/pap #4999 NAL
Davis argues that most people confined in prison are political prisoners. Although not feminist, Davis is a Black woman communist intellectual. In her notes for court arguments on the issue of self-representation, Davis wrote that

she considered herself--as a Black woman--at an enormous disadvantage.

(391) Decter, Midge
The new chastity and other arguments against Women's
   Liberation.
Coward 1972 188p 72-26668 $5.95 698-10450-1
"The childishness of the Libbers is one of the main points made.... Midge Decter writes well, presses hard and persuades a good deal of the time.... The sisters will yowl" (Virginia Kirkus Reviews). "The liberated woman and other Americans" (Coward, 1971, $6.95) ripped off the Movement, with its come-on partial-title, quoted from Daniel P. Moynihan. Such publications as this and Arianna Stassinopoulos' "The female woman" (Random, 1974, $5.95) and their handling by the media should have our attention.

(392) Dreifus, Claudia
Woman's fate; raps from a feminist consciousness-raising
   group.
Bantam 1973 320p bib $1.25/pap
Another good and needed work on CR how-to, with demo. (Rapping, however, is different.) As a handbook, its bibliography is a reading list. Several chapters, each devoted to one session and topic via transcript format, e.g. adolescence, adult sexuality, love.

(393) Dworkin, Andrea
Woman hating.
Dutton 1974 217p bib 73-17308 $7.95 0-525-23595-7
The book has as an avowed purpose the destruction of partiarchal power at its source, the family, the nationstate.... This is "strident" and may turn off sexist persons (the opposite of feminist). Congratulate any library in which you find it and don't give it to an "emerging" feminist. It is, nonetheless, right on target.

(394) Fasteau, Marc Feigen
The male machine.
McGraw 1974 225p 74-9858 $7.95 0-07-019985-X
A male reviewer, having conceded that Fasteau indentified "hurtful consequences of stereotyping," had to conclude that Fasteau "unfortunately finds nothing positive to say about maleness." The male machine is "programmed to tackle jobs, override obstacles, attack problems, overcome difficulties, and always seize the offensive." The sexually stereotyped hero's concept of women, thusly, is one of

pleasing things to "service him with love and devotion induced by recognition of his superior design and the importance of his functions...." Fasteau includes an excellent discussion re the irrelevance of most analogies with primates (p. 44) made by such persons as Tiger (#433). Publication of George Gilder's propatriarchal "Sexual suicide" (Quadrangle, 1973, $6.95) was followed by his fiancee's breaking their engagement. Late addition: Warren Farrell's "The liberated man: beyond masculinity; liberating men and their relationships with women" (Random, 1975, $10.00).

(395) Gettleman, Susan and Janet Markowitz
The courage to divorce.
Simon 1974 228p bib index 74-945 $7.95
For two of the numerous how-to books in this area, see Lynn Forman's "Getting it together; the divorced mother's guide" (Berkeley, 1974, $1.50) or Mary Ann Singleton's "Life after marriage; divorce as a new beginning" (Stein, 1974, $7.95). But for an approach to the gutsy fact-of-life that divorce is better than dragging on and on in a bad marriage, notwithstanding the good-of-the-children myth, advisors, and sacrilege, read Gettleman and Markowitz.

(396) Goldstein, Rhoda L.
Indian women in transition; a Bangalore case study.
Scarecrow 1972 172p 72-4627 [out of print]
    0-8108-0527-8

(397) Huber, Joan, ed.
Changing women in a changing society.
Univ. of Chicago Press 1973 bib 72-96342 $7.95
    0-226-35644-2; $2.95/pap 35645-0
Although originally a special issue of the American Journal of Sociology, this anthology is for popular reading. For information on issues of out-of-the-field periodicals devoted to the Women's Movement, SEE Women Studies Abstracts.

(398) Huyck, Margaret Hellie
Growing older.
Prentice-Hall 1974 192p 74-8061 $6.95; $2.65/pap
Huyck's recognition of the fact that sex-role stereotyping also damages older persons is important.

(399) Janeway, Elizabeth Hall, 1913-
Between myth and morning; women awakening.
Morrow 1974 279p 74-7176 $8.95
After reading Janeway's "Man's world, woman's place" (#69),

one should progress with her to the specifics of her contentions. This collection since written--for feminists and others.

(400) Jenness, Linda, ed.
Feminism and socialism; an anthology.
Pathfinder 1972 160p 72-82948 $5.95; $1.95/pap
Socialist women active in the WL Movement discuss specific oppression of Black women and Chicanas, debate Norman Mailer (SEE #178), investigate the relationship between socialism and feminism, support the Equal Rights Amendment, strategize.

(401) Johnston, Jill
Lesbian nation; the feminist solution.
Simon & Schuster 1973 283p bib 72-83934 $7.95. Also available in Touchstone paperback
An important personal narrative from both feminist and sexist perspectives.

(402) Kahn, Kathy
Hillbilly women. Photographs by Al Clayton; Migrant photographs by Frank Blechman, Jr.
Doubleday 1973 288p index 72-96246 $6.95. HS 0-385-01411-2
Appendix lists related organizations and publications (not all feminist) in Southern mountains. These women of Appalachia and beyond are themselves crippled and scarred--too many of the nineteen are wives and daughters suffering because of their connections with men. Reviewers may comment on their quiet strengths, courage, endurance--even on the exploitation by mine-owners, managers, politicos--but rarely do they recognize this as sexism. Ms. Kahn is a community organizer, actively involved with the struggles of poor and working people in the north Georgia mountains, and has recorded an album, "The working girl; women's songs of mountains, mines and mills."

(403) Klein, Carole
The single parent experience. HS
Walker 1973 241p bib 72-80536 $7.95 0-8027-0371-2
Not a widows', widowers', or divorced persons' how-to, this guidebook is for those who choose to parent. Appendix of state sources for counseling, legal issues, adoption sources.

(404) Koedt, Anne, et al, eds.
Radical feminism.

Quadrangle 1973 424p 72-91380 Harper $10.00
0-8129-0316-1; $3.95/pap
45 classic articles on feminism which were significant influences on the politics of the Women's Movement.

(405) Lemons, J. Stanley
The woman citizen; social feminism in the 1920's.
Univ. of Illinois Press 1973 266p 72-75488 $9.50
0-252-00267-9
A distinction between the women of the 1920's who devoted themselves to women's rights, i.e. emancipation and suffrage and those who viewed social reform as the primary feminist need. Messrs. O'Neill (#82) and Lemons have used this priority dichotomy, still seen today, with Lemons here concerned with the "social feminists." He refers to the extreme feminists concerned with women's rights as "hard core."

(406) Little, Kenneth
African women in towns; an aspect of Africa's social revolution.
Cambridge Univ. Press 1974 242p bib index 73-77175
$14.95; $4.95/pap

(407) Martin, Del and Phyllis Lyon
Lesbian/Woman.
Glide 1972 281p 72-76532 $7.95 0-912078-20-0.
 Bantam paperback
Lesbianism and Feminism. Winner of the 2nd Annual Gay Book Award of the Gay Task Force of the ALA-SRRT.

(408) Mitchell, Juliet, 1940-
Woman's estate.
Pantheon 1972 182p 77-164419 $5.95 (London: Penguin Books)
The family mystique: "The family is a stronghold of what capitalism needs to preserve but actually destroys: private property and individuals. The housewife-mother is the guardian and representative of these. She is a backward, conservative force--and this is what her oppression means. She is forced to be the stone in the stream" (p. 161).

(409) Moreno, Dorinda de Gladden
¡La mujer--en pie de lucha! y la hora es ya! (S)
Women of La Raza 1973 $8.00 Contact the author at
 California State University, La Raza Studies, 69 Campus Circle, San Francisco, CA 94132.

Collection of articles, poetry, artwork and historical information on La Raza women, in Spanish and English.

(410) Myrdal, Gunnar
An American dilemma; the Negro problem and modern democracy, 20th anniversary edition.
Harper   1962   2v $16.50   0-06-034590-X; $3.95/pap each
    0-06-131443-9, 0-06-131444-7
Appendix 5 (p. 1073-9): A parallel to the Negro problem.

(411) Nunes, Maxine and Deanna White
The lace ghetto.
Toronto: New Press   1972   152p $7.95   0-8870-049-7;
    $3.95/pap   0-88770-075-6
New Woman Series #3; General editor, Adrienne Clarkson. Intended to be about Canadian women, and it is, but it is universal too.

(412) Oakley, Ann
Sex, gender and society.
London: Temple Smith   1972 $3.25/pap
"Compiles in one place all the major sex-role research" (Sherrill Cheda).

(413) O'Brien, Patricia
The woman alone.
Quadrangle   1973   288p   bib   72-94650   Harper $7.95
About and for older and single women, as well as all the other lone women. Self-reliance. In our society the woman living alone is without power, suspect.

(414) O'Neill, Nena Dross and George O'Neill
Open marriage; a new life style for couples.
M. Evans   1972   287p   bib   75-164550   Lippincott $6.95
Anthropologists researching to avoid the "closed marriage," which stifles individual creativity and fulfillment. Guidelines for role-free behavior. See also #417.

(415) Peck, Ellen and Judith Senderowitz, eds.
Pronatalism; the myths of mom and apple pie.
Crowell   1974   224p   bib   74-6087 $5.95
Pronatalism is the sum of social policies and informal pressures that reward parenthood and stigmatize childlessness. Antiwoman. Anthology of articles examining pronatalist biases in government, business, education, media, society in general, challenging the myths that "all women have a biological urge for motherhood," and "children keep marriages together."

(416) Phipps, Joyce
Death's single privacy; grieving and personal growth.
Continuum   1974   192p   73-17881   Seabury $5.95
Once again the stranded widow who finally reaches personhood through tragedy.   See also #364.

(417) Rogers, Carl Ransom
Becoming partners; marriage and its alternatives.
Delacorte   1972   243p   bib   72-3868 $7.95
Personal narratives by men and women experiencing open-ended marriages, or other relationships, which have lasted at least three years.   Bibliography is annotated and includes references to audiovisuals.

(418) Rossi, Alice S., ed.
The feminist papers; from Adams to DeBeauvoir.   HS
Columbia Univ. Press   1973   600p   bib   73-8828 $12.95
   0-231-03795-3.   Bantam paperback.
Rossi introduces each writer and provides historical, biographical and sociological background.   "... one of its first offerings in a new Woman Book Club ... which will make appeal through general women's magazines, and therefore to reach an adult audience of many non-college educated women ... even if some of the abridgements themselves are difficult for many non-historical students.   I have found many college students who just read the biographic sketches and were tremendously involved and excited by reading of so many women of note in the past" (Rossi).

(419) Rover, Constance
Love, morals, and the feminists.
Routledge   1970   illus   166p $7.50   0-7100-6693-7

(420) Rowbotham, Sheila
Women, resistance, and revolution; a history of women and
   revolution in the modern world.
Pantheon   1973   287p   bib   72-3404 $7.95
Social revolution and feminism's interrelationship is the history of the idea that "the liberation of women necessitates the liberation of all human beings."   As an historical work, many pamphlets and journals were used.   The 24-page bibliography was published in 1972 as "Women's Liberation and revolution" (Falling Wall Press).   Her latest is "Hidden from history; rediscovering women in history from the 17th century to the present" (Pantheon, 1975, $7.95).

(421) Ruitenbeek, Hendrik Marinus, 1928-
The male myth.
Dell 1967 68-63150 $.75/pap

(422) Seaman, Barbara
Free and female; the sex life of the contemporary woman.
Coward 1972 288p index 70-172633 $6.95
Feminist Seaman surveys 100 high-achieving women and reports on women's sexual needs. Relate to Johnson & Masters (#209), which it clarifies.

(423) Shaw, Nancy Stoller
Forced labor; maternity care in the United States.
PhD diss. "So you're going to have a baby..."; institutional
   processing of maternity patients. 1972. Pergamon Press
   017834-9, 017835-9/pap prices not set
"Powerful sociological analysis of how women are treated by hospitals, doctors, and nurses during pregnancy and childbirth" ("Our Bodies, Ourselves," #529). Dehumanizing and humanizing factors in the birth process identified.

(424) Sherfey, Mary Jane, M.D.
The nature and evolution of female sexuality.
Random 1972 188p 69-16458 $5.95 0-394-46539-3
"A theory of female sexuality," which appeared in Morgan's "Sisterhood is powerful" (#81), expanded. This volume, the first of two, is a biological study of female sexual evolution. Attacks Freudian view of female sexuality which equates maturity with vaginal orgasm.

(425) Silverman, Anna and Arnold Silverman
The case against having children.
McKay 1971 218p index 74-159821 $5.95
Questions so-called maternal instinct and the motivations of many persons who want to have children. (A demonstration of how book evaluators can accept parts of books with which they personally agree and put down others can be seen in Library Journal 96:2756--this reviewer rejects the Silvermans' contention that many people have children for the wrong reasons, but accepts the ecological argument against overpopulation.)

(426) Sochen, June
The new woman; feminism in Greenwich Village, 1910-1920.
Quadrangle 1974 175p 70-190125 $7.95 0-8129-0257-2
Five feminist women writer-activists who struggled for equal rights in a unique political era and place: Neith Boyce,

Susan Glaspell, Crystal Eastman, Ida Rauh, and Henrietta Rodman.

(427) Sommers, Tish and Genny Guracar (Bulbul)
The not-so-helpless female.
McKay 1973 240p 72-86968 $7.95
"... an extremely useful guide to activism for women. Countless examples detail strategy and tactics for successful individual and group action. The philosophy is very Alinskyesk and should be appreciated by readers of his 'Rules for radicals' " (Michelle Rudy).

(428) Staples, Robert
The Black woman in America; sex, marriage, and the family; foreword by Joyce Ladner.
Nelson-Hall 1973 269p bib index 72-95280 $8.95
0-911012-55-9
Material documenting the stereotyping and role assigning by racist/sexist Americans, including Black males, of Black females is needed. Unfortunately this leaves something to be desired. Ms. Ladner's "Tomorrow's tomorrow; the Black woman" (Doubleday, 1971, $6.95 and $1.95/pap) is a sociological study of Black womanhood in relationship to White middle-class standards.

(429) Stephenson, Marylee, ed.
Women in Canada.
Toronto: New Press 1973 331p bib $4.95/pap
0-88770-728-9
Scholarly articles in the social sciences, including material on Indian women and women in prison, and a lengthy bibliography by Margrit Eichler and Lynne Primrose. What does it mean to be a woman in Canada? "Canada does not generally evidence the same degree of misogynic and conservative reaction as the United States.... Masculine discrimination in Canada has usually, but not always, been justified in terms of female peculiarities rather than of outright inferiorities ..." (p. 287f). Why this difference?

(430) Sullerot, Evelyne
Woman, society and change, transl. from French by Margaret Seatford Archer.
McGraw 1971 256p bib index 78-90234 $4.95 062335-X; $2.45/pap 062336-8
Status of women world-wide. Sullerot is a gung-ho sociologist.

(431) Sullivan, Judy
Mama doesn't live here anymore.
Arthur Fields 1974 Dutton $6.95 0-525-63011-2
Ms. Sullivan left her husband and 11-year-old daughter, moved to New York, and then chose to publicize this as a "political" supportive act. Many women have never been able to recognize the situation as part of the double standard; even Ms. magazine's reviewer asked "What if my mother had done that to me?" (Oct. 1974:28).

(432) Szalai, Alexander
The situation of women in the United Nations.
UNITAR 1973 49p $2.50
It's not good. George St. George's "Our Soviet Sister" (McKay, 1973, $7.95) describes progress.

(433) Tiger, Lionel, 1937-
Men in groups.
Random 1969 254p bib index 69-16459 $6.95
    0-394-43592-3; $1.95/pap 0-394-70588-2
Tiger contends there is a biological basis for differences in male and female roles, that the biological necessities of early people produced social patterns which were "programed" through the ages into the life cycles of the two sexes. He has coined the term, "male bond"--the tendency for males to group together, and women not to. He concedes that "male bonding will make it more difficult, if not impossible, for ambitious females to reach the posts they wish. Dependent as most women still are on the earnings of men, they break ranks very soon." It is important to understand this concept whether or not one agrees with Tiger's theory of its evolvement. Elaine Morgan's "The descent of woman" (#521) and other thinkers make frequent reference to it.

(434) Trotsky, Leon, 1877-1940
Women and the family; intro. by Caroline Land.
Pathfinder 1973 78p 72-92457 $3.95; $1.25/pap
"In order to change the conditions of life, we must learn to see them through the eyes of women."

(435) Willing, Martha Kent
Beyond conception; our children's children.
Population Dynamics 1974 241p bib index 76-160416
    Gambit $6.95 0-87645-044-3; $2.95/pap
Biologist negates the medical profession and drug industry handling of pill, IUD. Stop at two!

Basic Book Collection 320

(436) Wolff, Charlotte, M.D.
Love between women.
St. Martin's Press 1971 230p bib $6.95
"Straight" psychiatrist posits her own theory that human nature is intrinsically bisexual and surveys female homosexuality research.

(437) Womanpower Project
The New York Woman's Directory.
Workman Pub. Co. (231 East 51, New York 10022) 1973
    262p bib $2.95/pap 0-911104-13-5
A coalition of New York women put together this sourcebook for women in New York. Women in other areas can use it as a model, but add an index. The "Chicago Women's Directory" is available from Inforwomen ($2.25).

320 Political Science

(438) Abzug, Bella S.
Bella! Ms. Abzug goes to Washington, ed. by Mel Ziegler.
Saturday Review Press 1972 314p 72-182486 $7.95

(439) Chamberlin, Hope
A minority of members; women in the U.S. Congress. HS
Praeger 1973 374p 73-151950 $10.00
Brief sketches of the 85 female United States Congresspersons since 1917, from Jeanette Rankin to Bella Abzug.

(440) Chisholm, Shirley Anita St. Hill, 1924-
The good fight.
Harper 1973 206p 72-10680 $6.95; $1.50/pap Bantam
Like so many women who have also attempted to fight the good fight, Chisholm has (1) become alarmed at the increasingly closed nature of the political process, (2) experienced betrayal, and (3) been financially wiped out.

(441) Harper, Ida Husted, ed.
The life and work of Susan B. Anthony.
Women Suffrage in America Series 1969 repr. of 1908 ed.
    3v Arno $55.00 0-405-00102-9
Based on primary source material.

(442) Jaquette, Jane S., ed.
Women in politics.
Wiley 1974 367p bib index 74-1037 $14.95
A collection of essays conveys the problems of women participating in politics.

(443) Moffett, Toby
Nobody's business; the political intruder's guide to everyone's state legislature, intro. by Ralph Nader.
Chatham 1973 191p 73-83355 Viking $6.50
 0-85699-080-9; $2.95/pap 0-85699-081-7
How-to handbook.

(444) Murphy, Irene L.
Public policy on the status of women; agenda and strategy for the 70's.
Heath 1974 129p bib index 73-9658 $11.00
 0-669-90316-7
The failure of public policy in behalf of the feminist movement.

(445) Reid, Inez Smith
"Together" Black women--Black women speak out.
Third Press 383p 73-83156 $6.95 89388-114-7;
 $3.45/pap 89388-115-5

330 Economics

(446) Alexander, Rodney and Elisabeth Sapery
The shortchanged; women and minorities in banking.
Dunellen 1974 186p bib 73-79033 $12.50
 0-8424-0066-4; $5.95/pap 0-8424-0067-2
Hiring and lending policies of commercial banks in Atlanta, Chicago, Detroit, New York, Philadelphia, and Washington confirm employment sex-discrimination, and further more, its perpetuation by Federal law, policy, and complacency.

(447) Galbraith, John Kenneth
Economics and the public purpose.
Houghton Mifflin 1973 $10.00 0-395-17206-3; $4.50/pap
 text 0-395-17864-9
"... much information solemnly imparted as social wisdom is, in fact, in the service of some influential economic interest. I concluded this was true of the education of women, and resolved to explore...."

(448) Galenson, Marjorie
Women and work; an international comparison. HS
Cornell 1973 120p bib 72-619725 $4.50 0-87546-049-6;
 $3.25/pap

(449) Gilman, Charlotte Perkins Stetson, 1860-1935.
The man-made world; Or, our androcentric culture.

Basic Book Collection 330   33

Johnson repr. of 1911 ed.   260p $13.50   0-384-18560-6
Also: Library of the Women's Movement 1970 reprint:
    Collector's Editions $10.00   0-87681-085-7
Early feminist's case against male supremacy.

(450) Henry, Alice
The trade union woman.
Lenox Hill repr. 1915/1972   73-2799 $14.50
Her 1923 "Women and the labor movement" has also been reprinted (Arno, $10.00).

(451) Madden, Janice F.
The economics of sex discrimination.
Heath 1973   160p   73-12103 $12.00   0-669-90506-2
Wharton School's Madden shows in this important work that traditional economic theory should not be applied to the problem of sex-discrimination.

(452) Penny, Virginia
How women can make money, married or single, in all
    branches of the arts and sciences, professions, trades,
    agricultural and mechanical pursuits.
Arno repr. of 1870 ed.   1971   552p   75-156439 $22.00
    0-405-02937-3
Herta Hess Levy's "What every woman should know about investing her money" (Pocket Books, 1969, $.95) a century later.

(453) Ralston, Mary and Wilbur Cross
How to return to work in an office.
Harper 1973   239p bib   73-79689 $6.95
If you must....

(454) Ross, Donald K.
A public citizen's action manual.
Grossman 1973 $5.95 $1.95/pap
Primer for organizing consumer projects and groups.

(455) Teitz, Joyce
What's a nice girl like you doing in a place like this?   HS
Coward 1972   285p   77-172627 $6.95   0-698-10437-4
A collection of interviews of 11 women who have been "successful" in non-traditional ways.

(456) Thomas, Sarah M. and Bernadine Weddington
A guide to sources of consumer information, foreword by
    Virginia H. Knauer.   HS

Information Resources Press 1973 177p bib index
73-77342 Herner $10.50 0-87815-010-2 HS
Not particularly feminist but a much-needed reference book
for information and organizations; brief annotations, addresses.

(457) Thomson, Dorothy Lampen
Adam Smith's daughters.
Exposition 1973 140p 72-97724 $6.00 0-682-47675-7
Contributions of six women to economics, including summaries of their writings. Millicent Fawcett, Rosa Luxemburg, Jane Marcet, Harriet Martineau, Joan Robinson, Beatrice Webb. The same approach needs to be taken to women in other "men's fields."

340 Law

(458) Beserra, Sarah Senefeld, et al
Sex code of California; a compendium, ed. by Elizabeth R. Gatov.
Kaufmann 1974 197p $3.95 0-913232-12-2
Daniel deJ. Benedictis' "Legal obligations and rights of married men" (Cornerstone, 1971, $1.50/pap) also.

(459) Cleverdon, Catherine L.
The Woman Suffrage Movement in Canada, 2d ed.
Univ. of Toronto Press 1974 73-82587 $17.50
"Social History of Canada" Series, no. 18; first published in 1950, with an introduction by Ramsay Cook.

(460) DeCrow, Karen
Sexist justice; how legal sexism affects you.
Random 1974 329p 73-15835 $7.95 0-394-48403-7
For what Random is getting out of this, busy attorney and national NOW President DeCrow should have stipulated indexing. She has put all areas of the legal system on the spot. A serious book.

(461) Ford Associates
Directory of women attorneys in the United States, 1st ed.
Ford Associates 1973- . $10.00
Any profits to be used "in the promotion of women's legal rights." Reference tool-list of 6000 names and addresses of professionally qualified women attorneys in U.S.A.

(462) Ford Associates
Women's legal handbook series on job and sex-discrimination.

Basic Book Collection 340   35

Ford Associates: all vols. $10.00 each.
(Vol. 1) Civil Rights Act, 1974, (2) At federal level,
    (3) Title VII & Cases, (4) Equal pay, (5) Equal Rights
    Amendment, (6) State commissions on women, and
    (7) Government administrative agencies.

(463)   Hardin, Garrett
Mandatory motherhood; the true meaning of "right to life."
Beacon   1974   164p   bib   74-4880   Harper $4.95; $1.95/
    pap

(464)   Jongeward, Dorothy and Dru Scott
Affirmative action for women; a practical guide.
Addison   1973   334p   73-10592 $8.95   0-201-03293-7
Anthology organized by "key questions." A how-to in re
business and industry, religion, etc., i.e. not education.
(Another such book re academic affirmative action is needed;
meantime, see #474.) If its TA (transactional analysis)
orientation appeals to you, then your group may want to refer to Thomas A. Harris' "I'm ok--you're ok; a practical
guide to transactional analysis" (Harper, 1969, $5.95).

(465)   Kanowitz, Leo
Sex roles in law and society; cases and materials.
Univ. of New Mexico Press   1973   706p   72-94656 $20.00
    0-8263-0254-8
Mainly, but not exclusively, for a 2-3 hour course.

(466)   Lader, Lawrence
Abortion II; making the revolution.
Beacon   1973   242p   bib   index   72-6228 $7.95
    0-8070-2180-6
Abortion I = #205.

(467)   Ross, Susan C.
The rights of women; the basic ACLU guide to a woman's
    rights.   Special editor, Ruth Bader Ginsburg, Coordi-
    nator, ACLU Women's Project.
Discus   1973   384p   bib   73-84702   Avon   #17285
    $1.25/pap + $.15 by mail from Avon, 250 West 55th
    Street, New York, NY 10019
Should be included in the "literature kit" which almost every
feminist women's organization provides workshop partici-
pants.   A copy is included with ACLU membership; if not
available locally--which is fraught with implications--contact
ACLU Literature Department, 22 East 40th Street, New York,
NY 10016.   See also #468.

(468) Series
American Civil Liberties Union Handbooks:
The rights of women. (See #467)

   The rights of students; the basic ACLU guide to a student's rights, by Alan Levine. Discus 1973 160p 73-84703. Avon $.95/pap.

   The rights of mental patients; the basic ACLU guide to a mental patient's rights, by Bruce J. Ennis and Loren Siegel. Baron 1973 336p bib 72-96829. Dutton $5.95 0-877-770-39-5

   The rights of teachers..., by David Rubin. Baron 1973 175p 72-87846. Dutton $4.95.

   The rights of prisoners ..., by David Rudovsky. Baron 1973 128p 72-96828. Dutton $4.95.

   (The rights of servicemen ..., by Robert S. Rivkin. Baron 1973 154p 72-87844. Dutton $4.95.)

Norman Dorsen, general counsel to the editors of this ACLU series, edited "The rights of Americans; what they are-- what they should be" (Random, 1970, $12.95); the portion re women (p. 521f) was prepared by Pauli Murray.

(469) Sickels, Robert J., 1931-
Race, marriage, and the law.
Univ. of New Mexico Press 1972 167p 72-86815 $6.95 0-8263-0256-4
History of the legal status of interracial marriage in U.S.A.

(470) Stannard, Una
Married women v. husbands' names; the case for wives who keep their own names.
Germainbooks (81 St. Germain Ave., San Francisco, CA 94114) 1973 55p bib index 73-87334 $4.95 0-914142-00-3; $2.00/pap 0-914142-01-0 (add $.25 postage-direct)
The Center for a Woman's Own Name (see "Directory of Sources") and Ms. magazine Dec. 1973:97f may also be of interest. Sam Ervin and Birch Bayh oppose wives' keeping their own names. This is a serious matter relating to personhood and personal rights. Ms. Stannard is the author of a novel of a woman who rejects the sexual stereotype, "The new Pamela" (Ballantine, $.95).

(471) Stimpson, Catharine R., ed.
Discrimination against women; Congressional hearings on

Basic Book Collection 340   37

equal rights in education and employment.
Bowker 1973   558p   index   72-13703 $13.50   0-8352-0608-4
These, in 1970, were the first hearings on the subject of
sex-discrimination ever held by a Congressional committee.
Stimpson, with the Congressional Information Service, has
edited the material, making it more usable than the government document.

(472) Stimpson, Catharine R., ed.
Women and the "Equal Rights" Amendment; Senate Subcommittee hearings on the Constitutional amendment, 91st
   Congress.   With preface by U.S. Rep. Martha W. Griffiths.
Bowker   1972   538p   77-39745 $12.95   0-8352-0532-0

(473) Theodore, Athena Rentoumis, ed.
The professional woman.
Schenkman   1971   769p $12.50   0-87073-9662; $5.95/pap
   0-87073-965-4
"An excellent collection of articles ranging from the sexual
structure of professions to female professionalism and social
change and including socialization, career patterns and cultural definitions of the female professional. It leaves little
doubt that there is still men's work and women's work, both
in people's minds and in reality" (Sherrill Cheda). See also
her outstanding report on "Academic women in protest"
("Pamphlets" part of Non-Book Resources, under Sexism in
Education & Media).

(474) U.S. Department of Health, Education, and Welfare.
       Office of the Secretary.   Office for Civil Rights.
Higher Education Guidelines: Executive Order 11246.
U.S. HEW.   1972   17p + ten multi-paged tabs.   US GPO:
   1973   735-686/2105.   HEW-391
Why is it not possible to obtain this U.S. Government paperback publication from the Supt. of Documents, Government
Printing Office...? Obtain from one's regional office for
civil rights (see "Directory of Sources"), or from Public Information Office, Office for Civil Rights, Dept. of HE&W,
Washington, DC 20201. I:Legal provisions; II:Personnel
policies & practices; III:Development of affirmative action
programs.

(475) Wheeler, Michael
No-fault divorce.
Beacon   1974   194p   index   73-17421 $7.50
   0-8070-4482-2

(476) Zuker, Marvin A. and June Callwood
Canadian women and the law.
Toronto: Copp Clark 1971 100p bib 72-79735 $2.50/pap

350 Public Administration

(477) Schur, Edwin M.
Crimes without victims; deviant behavior and public policy:
   abortion, homosexuality, drug addiction.
Prentice-Hall 1965 180p 65-12304 $2.45/pap
   0-13-192930-5
"The deviant is one to whom that label has successfully been applied; deviant behavior is behavior that people so label." Although old, sad to say not enough change has occured to make this work stale, e.g. in the year 1974 the New Orleans Delta Women's Clinic must close while the Right to Life continues to "counsel" as a "united fund" agency! Nicholas N. Kittrie's "The right to be different; deviance and enforced therapy" also deserves thought here (J. Hopkins, $4.50/pap).

360 Welfare & Association

(478) Allen, Herb, ed.
The bread game; the realities of foundation fundraising, rev.
   ed.
Glide 1974 96p bib 74-3094 $2.95/pap 0-912078-40-5
Includes how to form tax-exempt organization, what books to keep, how to report. Also check out "The Grants Index."

(479) Amir, Menachim, 1930-
Patterns in forcible rape.
Univ. of Chicago Press 1971 394p 79-140222 $15.00
   0-226-01734-6
Of 646 rape cases, 71% were premeditated crimes--planned--thus not the result of so-called, excusable "uncontrollable urge." Only 3% of all sex offenders could be considered psychotic.

(480) Authors' Collective
Storefront day-care centers; the Berlin experiment.
Beacon 1973 $9.95

(481) Bernstein, Rose
Helping unmarried mothers.

Association Press 1971 187p $6.95 0-8096-1782-X
Potential psychological and social hazards of bearing a child
out-of-wedlock and the factors determining what social services the mother will receive are her two areas of main
concern.

(482) Breitbart, Vicki
Every mother's child; the why, what, and how of day care.
Knopf 1974 224p 73-7294 $7.95; $3.95/pap

(483) Burkhart, Kathryn Watterson
Women in prison. HS
Doubleday 1973 465p bib 72-92195 $10.00
   0-385-04674-X
Prison reform and feminism. Especially good on why women
commit crimes. Edna Walker Chandler's "Women in prison"
is for younger readers (Bobbs, 1973, $4.95).

(484) CWLA Standards for child protective service, rev. ed.
Child Welfare League 1974 $2.50 0-87868-113-2

(485) California Conference on Abortion, San Francisco,
   1969.
Abortion and the unwanted child, ed. by Carl Reiterman,
   California Committee on Therapeutic Abortion.
Springer 1971 181p 74-146659 $7.50 0-8261-1221-82-6;
   $4.95/pap

(486) Csida, June Bundy and Joseph Csida
Rape; how to avoid it, and what to do about it if you can't.
Books for better living 1974 238p 74-75574 $1.50/pap
   0-87056-361-0
Ms. Csida is the author of "The second feminist revolt"
article in the World Book Encyclopedia. Carol V. Horos'
"Rape" (Tobey, $2.95/pap) includes a directory of U.S.A.
crisis centers. Diana E. H. Russell's "The politics of
rape; the victims' perspective" (Stein & Day, 1975, $10.00)
came to my attention at the last minute.

(487) Evans, E. Belle and George E. Said
Day care for infants; the case for infant day care and a
   practical guide.
Beacon 1972 216p 72-75537 $6.95
Sequel to her "Day care; how to plan, develop, and operate
a day care center" (#136).

(488) Evans, E. Belle, et al
Designing a day care center; how to select, design and

develop a day care center.
Beacon   1974   176p   bib   73-16886 $7.95

(489)   The Health Policy Advisory Committee (Health-PAC)
American health empire; power, profit and politics, by
   Barbara Ehrenreich.
Random   1970   279p   79-127539 $7.95; $1.95/pap   Vintage
   0-394-76453-9
An important book on who controls American medicine today.

(490)   Maxtone-Graham, Katrina
Pregnant by mistake; the stories of seventeen women.
Liveright   1973   435p   73-82425   Dutton $8.95
   0-87140-572-5

(491)   Medea, Andra and Kathleen Thompson
Against rape.
Farrar, Straus & Giroux   1974   bib   160p $6.95; $2.25/pap
   Women's groups sales discounts.   Canada: Doubleday
An outstanding work providing much handbook type information but also important material on the subject itself--women will be better able to cope with the fact of rape in all of their lives if they come to grips with its meaning: rape affects every woman in this country.   The little rapes. Rape is not the isolated act of an aberrant individual but a crime against women that is encouraged by a sexist society, for women are seen in our culture not as whole human beings, but as objects and authorized victims of male aggression. Ms.'s M and T are available as speakers, especially in Chicago area; contact via Katherine Parker of Farrar editorial staff.

(492)   Norman, Eve
Rape
1973 $6.95
"The crime of rape has no parallel.   It is the only crime in which the victim is treated like a criminal by the police, hospital personnel, and the courts."   Norman is available as an experienced speaker.

(493)   Parker, Tony
In no man's land; some unmarried mothers.
Harper   1972   159p   72-79684 $5.95
Interviews of six unwed mothers, none of whom is "typical."

(494)   Roby, Pamela, ed.
Child care--who cares?   Foreign and domestic infant and

Basic Book Collection 360   41

early childhood development policies, foreword by Shirley
Chisholm.
Basic books 1973 456p index 72-89179 $16.00
0-465-00983-2
Collection of experts' opinions. Roby's editorial work provides relationship to sex-discrimination.

(495) Sarvis, Betty, 1943- , and Hyman Rodman
The abortion controversy, 2d ed.
Columbia Univ. Press 1973 209p bib index 74-794
   $8.95 0-231-03871-2; $3.95/pap 0-231-03865-9
Revised to survey the implications of the Supreme Court Jan.
1973 ruling. The "issues" researched and discussed for the
rather unusual reader--non-specialist but well-informed
thinker. Comprehensive. Includes reference to Nixon's
letter to Cardinal Cooke. Suggests "birth planning" as a
preferable term (discussion p. 134). Unfortunate final (no.
10) Chapter title; "Black genocide" is actually about what
Black women really want and need. Regardless of the differences (and there are differences--see p. 155) in desire
and ability to use contraceptives, "Once women make contact with a family planning clinic they tend to become effective contraceptive users."

(496) Sheehy, Gail
Hustling; prostitution in our wide-open society.
Delacorte 1973 273p 73-6771 $7.95

(497) Sidel, Ruth
Women and child care in China; a firsthand report. Photos
   by Victor W. Sidel.
Hill & Wang 1972 207p bib 72-81286 $6.95; Penguin
   $1.25/pap
Changing attitudes toward child-raising and women, by psychiatric social worker. She sees similar problems in China
and United States of America, although China's Women's
Liberation is part of their ideology.

(498) Steinfels, Margaret O'Brien
Who's minding the children; the history and politics of child
   care in America.
Simon 1974 281p bib index 73-14093 $8.95
   0-671-21597-3

370 Education

(499) Chabaud, Jacqueline
The education and advancement of women.
Paris: UNESCO 1970 155p illus UNIPUB $2.00/pap
Advancement of women through access to education, UNESCO's part in this. In referring to family planning, Ms. Chabaud states that "if the birth rate is to be really reduced, governments must make women understand specifically and in detail the significance of the protective measures to be taken and the procedures to be followed."

(500) Cohen, Selma Jean, et al, eds.
A sampler of Women's Studies, ed. by Dorothy Gies McGuigan.
Center for Continuing Education of Women, Univ. of Michigan 1973 116p bib index $2.50/pap Sales benefit Center's Scholarship Fund
Papers from a lecture series reflect commitment to scholarship and feminism.

(501) Feldman, Saul D.
Escape from The Doll's House; women in graduate and professional school education.
Carnegie Commission on Higher Education 1974 207p bib index 73-12829 McGraw $8.95 0-07-010069-1
Contention: the mere presence of women in graduate school is no testimony that they have escaped The Doll's House. Consider: status, prestige, attitudes, research, financial rewards, power, beliefs, behavior. Betty Richardson's "Sexism in higher education" (Continuum: Seabury, 1974, $7.95) goes into the gamesmanship practiced by the male establishment to keep women in their place in academia; all of the devices used to delay, divide and discredit them are examined: dossiers, promotion, tenure, etc.

(502) Frazier, Nancy and Myra Sadker
Sexism in school and society.
Harper 1973 215p bib 72-11496 $2.95/pap 06-042172-X
Critical issues in education. Could be used as a "text book." Built around main issues or themes.

(503) Furniss, W. Todd and Patricia Albjerg Graham, eds.
Women in higher education.
American Council on Education 1974 336p 72-22230 $10.00
The women are faculty, students, and administrators. Affirmative action, Equal Employment Opportunity Commission,

Basic Book Collection 370   43

child care, quotas, maternity leave, credentialism, etc. A
collection of suggestions.

(504) Gersoni-Stavn, Diane, ed.
Sexism and youth. S
Bowker 1974 468p bib index 73-21651 $9.95
  0-8352-0710-2
49-article anthology of four sections: socialization, in general, schools, books (including text, fiction, nonfiction,
winners), and other media (including motion pictures, television, games). Sex-role stereotyping of American children
pre-school through high school.

(505) Harrison, Barbara Grizzuti
Unlearning the lie: sexism in school; a blueprint for action
    for those who want an alternative to sexist education.
Liveright 1973 176p 72-97486 Dutton $6.95
  0-87140-560-1
The story of the sex roles committee of a Brooklyn school.

(506) Johnson, Willis L., ed.
Director of special programs for minority group members,
    1974: career information services, employment skills
    banks, financial aid; with an additional section on employment assistance services for women.
Garrett Park Press 1974 384p 73-93533 $7.95/pap
  0-912048-12-5
Employment services and educational assistance. Part 3:
Women's Career Counseling and Job Assistance Programs.
The U.S. Dept. of Commerce Office of Minority Business
Enterprise has "Directory of minority media" (1973, $1.25,
411-327/296). These are both useful in affirmative action
employment procedures. (12% of the population = Black;
17 minority groups; 53% women.)

(507) LaCrosse, E. Robert, Jr., ed.
Early childhood directory; a selected guide to 2000 preschool
    educational centers, 1st ed.
Bowker 1971 455p index 77-126012 $20.25
  0-8352-0408-1

(508) Schiller, Patricia
Creative approach to sex education and counseling; foreword
    by David R. Mace.
Association Press 1973 255p bib index 73-4033 $12.00
  0-8096-1862-1
Includes material on model training programs for teachers

and curricula for students; annotated core collection on sex
education. A source book for educators, rather than sex
information.

(509) Woody, Thomas, 1891-1960
A history of women's education in the United States.
Octagon 1966 2v 643, 608p 66-17495 $32.50
Such a book has much insight about "woman's place" in early
U.S.A.

380 Commerce

(510) Johnson, Nicholas
How to talk back to your television set.
Little 1970 228p $5.77 0-316-46937-8
Do! to the FCC, the sponsors, and ad agencies especially.

(511) Kaye, Evelyn
The family guide to children's television; what to watch,
 what to miss, what to change and how to do it.
Pantheon 1974 224p bib 73-18726 $8.95; $2.95/pap
Sponsored by Action for Children's Television. Includes resource directory. Useful for discussion but mainly for
action. National Association for Better Broadcasting's 1974
"Comprehensive Guide to Family Viewing" included. Women
should monitor all TV--soap-operas, talk-shows, commercials.

390 Customs & Folklore

(512) Braxton, Bernard
Women, sex and race; a realistic view of sexism and racism.
Verta Press (15 Randolph Pl. N.W., Washington, DC 20001)
 1973 227p index 72-91049 $6.95; $2.95/pap
The similarities of myth-making about women and Blacks.

(513) Lewinsohn, Richard
A history of sexual customs, tr. by Alexander Mayce.
Harper 1956/1971 repr. $1.25/pap

(514) Riegel, Robert Edgar
American woman; a story of social change.
Fairleigh Dickinson Univ. 1970 bib $12.00 0-8386-7615-4

(515) Schafer, Edward H.
The devine woman; Dragon ladies and rain maidens in T'ang
   literature.
Univ. of California Press 1974   200p   73-78543 $10.00
   0-520-02465-6

(516) Seligson, Marcia
The eternal bliss machine; America's way of wedding.
Morrow 1973 304p bib 72-126 $7.95
Aptly titled. Mainly about the ritual, consumerism--but some consideration of new ceremonies, homosexual weddings, and group marriages. See also #370.

(517) Waugh, Norah
Corsets and crinolines, illus.
Theatre Arts 1954/1969 repr. 176p $11.95; $4.95/pap
Her "The cut of women's clothes, 1600-1930" (Theatre Arts, 1968/73, $21.00) and "... of men's clothes, 1600-1900" (1971, $11.50) are also available.

400   LANGUAGE

410   Linguistics

(517a) Key, Mary Ritchie
Male/female language; with a comprehensive bibliography.
Scarecrow Press 1975 200p indexes bib 74-19105 $7.00
   0-8108-0748-3
About linguistics and communication, this is a remarkable combination of "good reading," documented utilitarian material, and bibliographic support. Basic.

420   English & Anglo-Saxon Languages

(518) Todasco, Ruth Taylor, ed.
Feminist English dictionary. Volume I: An intelligent
   woman's guide to dirty words; English words and phrases
   reflecting sexist attitudes toward Women in patriarchal
   society, comp. by The Feminist Writers Workshop.
YWCA of Metropolitan Chicago Loop Center (37 S. Wabash
   Ave., Chicago, IL 60603) 1973 76p bib $1.50
Arranged according to usage and idea. Class I = Patriarchal epithets. Sections: 1 Woman as whore; 2 as whorish; 3 as body; 4 as animal; 5 as -ess; 6 as -ette. Class II = Patriarchal stereotypes.

460 Spanish & Portuguese Languages

(519) Martínez Sierra, Gregorio
Mamá, comedia en tres actos, ed. with Notes, Intro. and
    Vocab. by Margaret S. Husson.
Norton   1937   156p   38-19594 $1.95/pap   0-393-09456-1
Spanish version of Ibsen's "A doll's house."

500   PURE SCIENCES

570   Anthropology & Biological Sciences

(520) Levi-Strauss, Claude
Tristes tropiques, tr. by John and Doreen Weightman.   S
Atheneum   1974   432p   illus   79-162975 $12.00; $3.95/pap
Women in other countries.

(521) Morgan, Elaine, 1920-
The descent of woman
Stein & Day   1972   280p   bib   index   76-186494 $7.95
    0-8128-1458-4;   1973 Bantam $1.75/pap
Check out the tape, "Me Jane, you Tarzan," in "Audiovisuals" part of Non-Book Resources section. This is scintilating anthropological feminist theory. Numerous references to Tiger (#433) and his "male-bonding."

(522) Murphy, Yolanda and Robert F. Murphy
Women of the forest.
Columbia Univ. Press   1974   256p   bib   74-9912 $12.50;
    $3.95/pap
Anthropologists look at women, finally.

(523) Rosaldo, Michelle Zimbalist and Louise Lamphere,
    eds.
Woman, culture and society.
Stanford Univ. Press   1974   346p   bib   index   73-89861
    $12.50   0-8047-0850-9; $3.95/pap   0-8047-0851-7
Scholarly anthropology collection which originated in Rosaldo's Stanford University course, "Women in cross-cultural perspective." Carolyn Matthiasson's "Many sisters; women in cross-cultural perspective" (Free Press, 1974, $15.00) may be used with this.

Basic Book Collection 610   47

600 TECHNOLOGY (APPLIED SCIENCES)

610 Medical Sciences

(524) Anthony, Catherine Parker, 1907- , & Norma Jane
Kolthoff
Textbook of anatomy and physiology, 8th rev. ed.
Mosby 1971 580p 78-138467 $10.25 0-8016-0253-X
Readable, well illustrated, basic nursing text. Elsie Fitzpatrick's "Maternity nursing, 12 ed." (Lippincott, 1971, $10.00) is also in print and has a caring attitude. Nancy A. Lytle's "Maternal health nursing" (Brown, 1967, $3.50/pap) is an anthology which is unique in that it discusses no-no's like pro/con of induced labor, baby abnormalities.

(525) Bean, Constance A.
Methods of childbirth; a complete guide to childbirth classes
   and the new maternity care.
Doubleday 1972 210p bib 78-187123 $6.95 0-385-06220-6

(526) (527) Bing, Elisabeth D.
Six practical lessons for an easier childbirth. Illus.
Grosset 1967 128p 67-10527 $4.95 0-448-01181-6;
   Bantam $1.00/pap
American Lamaze Method. Bing is co-founder of the American Society for Psychoprophylaxis in Obstetrics. Irwin Chabon's "Awake and aware; participating in childbirth through psychoprophylaxis" (Dell, 1969, $.95/pap) is similar, but has more photographs.

(528) Bluford, Robert & Robert E. Petres
Unwanted pregnancy; the medical and ethical implications.
Harper 1973 116p 72-78064 $4.95
Gynecologist and clergy believe legal therapeutic abortion may be a responsible principled humane act.

(529) Boston Women's Health Book Collective
Our bodies, ourselves; a book by and for women.
Simon & Schuster 1971 276p bibs illus 72-83220 $8.95
   671-21434-9; $2.95/pap 671-21435-7 Clinic rates
The spirit and title convey the philosophy of more and more women today. This wonderful book has utility for coursework, Women's Studies, gift-giving. The Chronicle of Higher Education reported it seventh in "what they read on campuses in 1973," and Mlle. gave a special group award to the 12 women of the Collective. Can you define Women's Health Movement, and control of our bodies? A little prog-

ress has been made in kids' so-called sex books, e.g. Siv Widerberg's "The kids' own XYZ of love and sex" (Stein & Day, 1972, $4.95).

(530) Burack, Richard, 1926-
New handbook of prescription drugs; official names, prices, and services for patient and doctor, rev. ed.
Pantheon 1970 362p tables 76-15606 $7.95; Ballantine $1.25/pap
A good guide to prescription drugs and prices. See also #536. The medical establishment would prefer that patients not be aware of "The Physician's Desk Reference," and often libraries find it necessary to ask patrons to request it....

(531) Chesler, Phyllis
Women and madness.
Doubleday 1972 359p index 72-76136 $8.95 0-385-02671; Avon $1.95/pap
A basic, important, fully documented, and readable work. Dr. Chesler has written, "We need not stop being tender, compassionate, or concerned with the feelings of others. But when will we start extending this tenderness and compassion to other women--and to ourselves?" (Ms., October 1972:86f). Women who are victims of mental illness are also victims of a double standard in treatment. If a woman overplays the female role, she's called neurotic; if she underplays it, she's called schizophrenic.... The Los Angeles Times has called "Women and madness" "a stunning book ... absolutely fascinating and ... necessary to every woman in America."

(532) Crile, George, Jr., M.D.
What women should know about the breast cancer controversy.
Macmillan 1973 160p 73-7142 $4.95
Includes "Breast cancer: A patient's Bill of Rights."

(533) Dalton, Katharina Dorothea
The menstrual cycle.
Pantheon 1969 $4.95 0-394-46867-8; $.95/pap Paperback Books
Good for premenstrual tension syndrome and treatment by hormones.

(534) Demarest, Robert J. & John J. Sciarra
Conception, birth, and contraception; a visual presentation.
    Intro. by Mary S. Calderone, M.D.
McGraw 1969 129p 69-13667 $8.95 0-07-016252-2
Well illustrated, including male anatomy.

Basic Book Collection 610   49

(535) Dickinson, Peter
The fires of Autumn; sexual activity in the middle and later
    years.
Drake   1974   192p   73-18403 $8.95
His message is "whatever you do, it doesn't matter, if you
don't mind, " but he is considerate of the older woman and
the lone woman.

(536) DiCayan, Erwin & Lawrence Hessman
Without prescription.
Simon & Schuster   1972   77-171603 $7.95   0-671-21137-4
Basics of over-the-counter drugs; use with #530 and Morton
Mintz's "By prescription only" (Beacon, 1967, $3.95), which
portrays the drug industry's power and control of regulatory
bodies.

(537) Frankfort, Ellen
Vaginal politics; intro. by Mary Constanza, M.D.
Quadrangle   1972   288p $6.95   0-8129-0284-X
Frankfort is to gynecologists as Chesler to psychiatrists,
and both to all specialties, because we are persons. It's
good news that more and more women are recognizing the
political aspects of the sexist set up. Frankfort is Village
Voice health columnist. An ad claims the book is "forcing
doctors to be more accountable to women medically, financially and psychologically ... " which is still a great goal.

(538) Fried, John J.
Vasectomy; the truth and consequences of the newest form
    of birth control--male sterilization.
Saturday Review   1972   148p   bib   73-186429 $5.95
    0-8145-0169-6
Fried is a "science writer" by trade, a former police reporter, M.S. in journalism. Of the numerous "popular"
treatments on the market, his book, aside from the unfortunate subtitle, comes across with a substantial amount of
readable and useful facts. In addition, he makes a good
case for the fact that family planning and population once
again (like the pill) have not been well thought out and researched. It is an indictment of our refusal to make a political and public commitment to priority development of a
national population policy and to finance well-coordinated research programs. Even so, his information and message
often convey those built in sexist assumptions which contami-
nate so many otherwise useful media. Lawrence Lader's
"Foolproof birth control; male and female sterilization"
(Beacon, 1972, $6.95) is useful.

(539) Gray, Madeline
The changing years; the menopause without fear, rev.
Doubleday 1967 279p 67-10366 $4.95; $.95/pap Q4251
   SigNAL

(540) Green, Thomas H., Jr.
Gynecology; essentials of clinical practice, 2 ed.
Little 1971 $8.50/pap
Gynecology textbooks are typically written by males whose decrees are to be unquestioned by students and women and expressed in often unnecessarily complex jargon. Pauline Barth and colleagues have prepared several papers on the whole put-hold-strap down (see "Pamphlets" part of Non-Book section, under Health). Jacob P. Greenhill's "Office gynecology, 9th ed." (Yearbook Publications, 1971, $21.50) is less difficult to comprehend but still dubious. And Edmund R. Novak's "Textbook of Gynecology, 8th ed." (Williams & Wilkins, 1970, $22.50), which is considered the text ("I take my text from ...") is also chauvinistic.

(541) Group for the Advancement of Psychiatry
Humane reproduction.
Scribner's 1974 128p bib index 73-11574 $6.95
   0-684-13639-2; $2.95/pap 0-684-13641-4
The Group recommends career opportunities for women, neighborhood family health care centers, abortion until contraception is perfected.

(542) Gutcheon, Beth
Abortion; a woman's guide.
Abelard-Schuman 1973 147p index 72-9549 $5.95
   0-200-04003-5; $2.95/pap 0-200-04008-1
Sponsored by Planned Parenthood of New York City, Inc. Comprehensive, responsible.

(543) Guttmacher, Alan F., M.D.
Pregnancy, birth, and family planning; a guide for expectant
   parents in the 1970's.
Viking 1973 72-79006 $10.00 0-670-57311-6
Continues to be a basic guidebook. New revision has additional interesting information, e.g. whose chromosomes determine the baby's sex? (the father's).

(544) Loebl, Suzanne
Conception, contraception; a new look. HS
McGraw 1974 bib index $6.95
Many illustrations provide facts and help dispel hearsay.

Basic Book Collection 610   51

(545) Lutzker, Edythe
Women gain a place in medicine. HS
McGraw   1972 $5.95   0-07-039115-7
Careers of five pioneer 19th-century English women physicians. The author was 46 when she entered New York City College.

(546) Miller, Jean Baker, M.D., ed.
Psychoanalysis and women.
Penguin 1973 415p bib 72-95634 $2.95/pap
   0-14-02-1729-0
Freud's long-standing, phallocentric view of women is unrealistic. "An assemblage of some of the history and the present state of knowledge among psychoanalysts who have worked at developing new starting points for a more valid understanding of women" (p. xiv) should help. This is not a collection of reprints bound together in paperback and associated with a reputable name to get yet-another oar into the ocean of Women's Lib (!) profits, to use the male mass-media term. It is an anthology of 15 physician-authors and one co-author (8 are men) of 21 readings, each introduced and some (especially the older ones) edited by M.D. female Miller, who has also provided biographical material where needed, and a substantial "Conclusion" of new issues and approaches. She approaches her mission via three sequential parts: (1) pertinent pioneers, e.g. Karen Horney, Alfred Adler, Clara Thompson; (2) the emergence of new evidence, e.g. Mary Jane Sherfey; (3) present problems and some future possibilities, e.g. Alexandra Symonds. The collection is a guide, and the reader is urged to consult the original papers, as well as the additional references. All of the points of view are not necessarily agreed with, but are included for perspective and history. Adversaries of the feminist movement will find little or nothing here to help with their perpetuation of myths and evasion of realities.

(547) Neumann, Hans H., M.D., & Sylvia Simmons
The straight story on VD; a doctor answers 201 of the most
   common questions about venereal diseases. HS
Warner 1973 261p index $1.25/pap
Can someone have gonorrhea and syphilis at the same time? (yes). Appendix lists 325 local clinics.

(548) Olds, Sally Wendkos & M.S. Eiger
The complete book of breastfeeding.
Workman 1972 208p 72-191822 $6.95
Karen Pryor's "Nursing your baby" rev. ed. (Harper, 1973,

$6.95) is advertised as a "companion" for women rediscovering "the womanly art"; Dana Raphael's "The tender gift; breastfeeding" (Prentice Hall) uses a new word--matrescence: transition of a woman into a mother.

(549) Robbins, June & John Robbins, comps.
An analysis of "Human Sexual Inadequacy."
New American Library 1971 317p 77-169832 $6.95
Summarizes Masters & Johnson's "Human sexual inadequacy" (Little, 1970, $12.50; see also #209). Also provided are a couple's experiences at the Reproductive Biology Clinic, descriptions of related types of therapies, articles on homosexuality, ghetto sexual mores, and psychoanalytic views.

(550) Rush, Anne Kent
Getting clear; body work for women.
Random 1973 290p 72-12532 $7.95; $4.95/pap
Female energy and how to use it, exercises included.

(551) Seaman, Barbara
The doctor's case against the pill.
Wyden 1969 279p 75-96788 $5.95

(552) Sloane, R. Bruce, M.D., & Diana Frank Horvitz
A general guide to abortion.
Nelson Hall 1973 265p index 72-90556 $8.95
    0-911012-35-4

(553) Speert, Harold, M.D.
Iconographia gyniatrica; a pictoral history of gynecology and
    obstetrics.
F. A. Davis 1973 540p index 71-167953 $40.00
    0-8036-8070-8

(554) Strouse, Jean, ed.
Women and analysis; dialogues on psychoanalytic views of
    femininity.
Grossman 1974 416p 73-7313 Viking $12.50
Classic essays by such as Abraham, Bonaparte, Deutsch, and Freud, with contemporary comments by such as Coles, Erikson (on Erikson), Mead, and Mitchell. Very useful.

(555) Szasz, Thomas Stephen, M.D., 1920-
The manufacture of madness; a comparative study of the In-
    quisition and the mental health movement.
Harper 1970 383p 71-83626 $8.95 0-06-014198-0; Dell
    paperback

Basic Book Collection 620   53

"Excellent attack on the concept of mental illness and institutional psychiatry. Compares the situation of the homosexual in today's society as scapegoat to the situation of witches during the Inquisition and Jews in Hitler's Germany" (Emergency Librarian! Feb. 1974:15). Szasz sees our society's tendency to diagnose mental illness in any person whose behavior deviates from the majority, or is nonconformist, with the 17th-century's accusation of witchcraft.

(556) Wilson, Robert Arthur, M.D., 1895-
Feminine forever.
M. Evans 1966   224p   66-11166 $5.95; $.75/pap Paperback Books
A different (positive) view of menopause by a male medico.

620   Engineering & Allied Operations

(557) Adams, Florence
I took a hammer in my hand; the woman's build-it and fix-it
     handbook.
Morrow 1973 $9.95
Not condescending. Illustrated. Kay B. Ward's "Feminine fix-it handbook" (Grosset, 1972, $5.95) demystifies tools. Paul & Aileen Weissler's "Woman's guide to fixing the car" (Walker, 1973, $3.95/pap) is useful too.

640   Domestic Arts & Sciences

(558) Harrison, Molly
The kitchen in history.
Scribner's 1973   142p   bib   72-11323 $7.95

(559) Paolucci, Beatrice and Patricia Thompson
Personal perspectives; a guide to decision-making. HS
McGraw-Hill 1973   466p $9.16 text edition 0-07-048437-6;
     teacher's manual $3.24   0-07-034859-6
The first home economics textbook addressed to senior high school boys and girls that presents both in home and family-related activities, e.g. women carpenter and men care for babies.

650 Business & Related Enterprises

(560) Basil, Douglas C.
Women in management; performance, prejudice, promotion.
Dunellen 1971 bib 78-148697 $6.95 0-8424-0047-8
   See also #565

(561) Benet, Mary Kathleen
The secretary; a new look at the female ghetto.
McGraw 1973 $5.95 0-07-004536-4 Not available for sale in the British Commonwealth, but available in Canada

(562) Bird, Caroline
Everything a woman needs to know to get paid what she's worth.
McKay 1973 304p 73-79946 $8.95
Bird defines a woman's job as anything that pays less than a man will do it for. Question-and-answer format. There is a surprising similarity of obstacles met by women workers of all types (professional, business, blue-collar, clerical) in seeking equal pay; this is important in these times when efforts are being made to divide women along all possible lines. See especially the 40-page Resource Section on jobs, publications, nonprofit commercial services, government agencies, women's organizations and caucuses. Although Bird advises women on how to handle themselves in a male-dominated job-world, this isn't another book advocating "adjustment to the status quo," nor is it for the woman who is trying to decide whether to go (back) to employed work. She recognizes that many women have no choice and tries to help us cope.

(563) Ginzburg, Eli & Alice M. Yohalem, eds.
Corporate Lib: Women's challenge to management. Policy Studies in Employment & Welfare, 17.
Johns Hopkins Univ. Press 1973 153p bib 72-12371
   $6.50 0-8018-1475-8; $2.50/pap 0-8018-1474-X
1971 Conference on Women's Challenge to Management sponsored by the Executive Programs of the Columbia University Graduate School of Business. Unfortunate title. Original papers by six men and five women.

(564) Loring, Rosalind and Theodora Wells
Breakthrough; women into management.
Van Nostrand 1972 $7.95
"A comprehensive and readable book written for the execu-

Basic Book Collection 650   55

tive, usually male, who must respond to pressures requiring
equal treatment of women and men in executive circles, this
book should be read and understood by all women determined
to enter organizational power centers. After reviewing the
legal, social and economic factors resulting in demands for
the end of sex discrimination, the authors explore manageri-
al climate, work-role and culture-role stereotypes and male
managers' expectations of working women for their effect on
corporate policy and practice. Innovations and guidelines
for immediate and future changes in attitudes, practices and
beliefs are detailed. A supplement describes Revised Order
4, affirmative action programs, sources of management and
professional women, and media sources for awareness training materials" (Michelle Rudy).

(565) Lyle, Jerolyn R. & Jane L. Ross
Women in industry; employment patterns of women in cor-
    porate America.
Heath   1974   164p   bib   index   73-1012 $10.00
    0-669-86124-3
Important, serious book, but the recognition of the fact that
all corporations discriminate is a refreshing starter! Surveyed were 246 varied companies to determine the degrees
of discrimination and its organizational characteristics. A
section on federal laws since 1960. Useful for Women's
Studies too.

(566) Lynch, Edith M.
The executive suite--feminine style.
AMACOM (div. of the Amer. Management Assoc.) 1973
    258p   73-75674 $10.50   0-8144-5320-1
"Behind this provocative title is a work that is partly a re-
cruitment brochure and partly a report of the findings of a
survey made among ninety plus women employed in top management and executive positions. While it succeeds in its
stated purpose 'to prove that there are capable women
around and that they deserve a place in management's sun,'
the author is equivocal about the feminist movement. Thus,
her interpretation of survey results often reinforces worn
out stereotypes about management women--'must think like
a man,' 'must not be emotional,' rather than calling for a
change of values in these areas. As a result, the book's
value lies in identifying and characterizing successful women
executives, their work and home problems and how they deal
with them" (Michelle Rudy).

(567) Seidenberg, Robert, M.D.
Corporate wives--corporate casualties?

American Management Association 1973 177p 73-77954 $10.00 0-8144-5331-7
Psychiatrist Seidenberg documents the findings of his examination of the victims of "corporate machismo," which have much application to humanizing for many types of employment structures. See also "Identities and affinities ..." in "Audiovisuals" part of Non-Book Resources section.

660   Chemical & Related Technologies

(568) Stevens, Paul
I can sell you anything; how I made your favorite TV commercials with minimum truth and maximum consequences.
Wyden 1972 245p 72-85996 $5.95
Stevens has been an ad agency writer since 1961. What are the implications for women of such a title?

700   THE ARTS

(569) Woman in art series: Sachs, Hannelore
The Renaissance woman; tr. from German by Marianne Herzfeld, rev. by Prof. D. Talbot Rice.
Edition Leipzig 1971 60p + 32 color plates and 80 black & white illustrations bib 79-154549 McGraw Hill $12.95 0-07-054374-5
Also: "The woman in Indian art," by Heinz Mode and "The woman in Egyptian art," by Stefeen Wenig.

720   Architecture

(570) Cole, Doris
From tipi to skyscraper; a history of women in architecture.
HS
i Press 1973 136p bib 73-80932 Braziller $8.95
   0-913222-01-1; $3.95/pap 0-913222-02-X
Scope is actually limited to North American architecture. The author who justifies women beginning to be involved in a heretofore "man's field" by pointing out how their unique qualities can improve it is usually a foggy thinker. And this is not what Cole, an architect, does; rather, she faces the fact that the men haven't done too well! Architecture has the smallest proportion of women--less than 2%. Gloria and Esther Goldreich's "What can she be?" children's series includes "an architect," Susan Brody, who "successfully com-

bines motherhood with an exciting career" (Lothrop, 1974, $4.50) and others: newscaster, lawyer, veterinarian.

740   Drawing, Decorative & Minor Arts

(571)   Levine, Ellen
All she needs...; a book of drawings.   Intro. by Naomi
    Weisstein.
Quadrangle   1973   73-79920 $1.95/pap   0-8129-6221-4
The Women's Movement is serious, but Levine can show up the ridiculous positions women are placed in by the system. "Think of all the comic strips you've read. Now think of all those that didn't ... include a silly club lady, a domineering mother-in-law, a wife who can't drive a car or balance a checkbook, a sex-starved spinster, a spendthrift wife, a chorus girl trying to trap a rich man, a teenager trying to trap a boyfriend, a fat Mexican or Indian woman trailing behind her man, a maid who dominates her employers, a dumb blonde, a dumb Sapphire, or a big-breasted wide-eyed nurse/stewardess/secretary/victim. Are there any left? Are you laughing?" (Weisstein). See also "Audiovisuals" part of Non-Book Resources section under Cartoons.

770   Photography & Photographs

(572)   Lange, Dorothea & Margaretta K. Mitchell
To a cabin.   IIS
Grossman   1973   127p   73-6359   Viking $15.00
    0-670-71627-8
Photographer Lange's diary of the California Coast.

(573)   Tucker, Anne, ed.
The woman's eye.
Knopf   1973   169p   bib   73-7283 $15.00   0-394-48678-1;
    $6.95/pap   0-394-70626-9
Anthology of work of ten major photographers, including Bourke-White, Dater, Kasebier, Lange. Title is not quite right.

790   Recreational Arts

(574)   Boslooper, Thomas & Marcia Hayes
The femininity game.
Stein & Day   1973   256p   bib   index   72-96603 $7.95

0-8128-1545-9
Sexism in sports (and a marketable title).

(575) Famous American athletes of today (repr. series)
1st series: by Charles Haven Ladd Johnston.
Books for Libraries 1928 70-142648 $15.75 -2168-2
Chapters on Helen Wills, Gertrude Ederle.
2nd series; by Johnston; chapters on Glenna Collett, Amelia Earhart.
5th series: by Leroy Atkinson, et al; chapters on Helen Stephens, Hazel Hotchkiss Wightman.
6th series: by Harold Kaese, et al; chapter on Katherine Rawls.
7th series: by Jerry Nason, et al; chapters on Patty Berg, Alice Marble.
8th series: by Kaese, et al; chapters on Evelyn Chandler, Sarah Palfrey Cooke.

(576) Gerber, Ellen W., et al
The American woman in sport.
Addison Wesley 1974 562p bib index 74-2849 $8.95
0-201-02353-9
In publisher's series, The Social Significance of Sport. Et al = Drs. Jan Felshin, Pearl Berlin, Waneen Wyrick. Focuses on American females of college age and older.
Sport = activities which involve specific administrative organization, historical background of rules and customs which define. A needed and usable book, organized into four sections: Chronicle of participation (Gerber); Social view (Felshin); Woman athlete (Berlin); Biophysical perspectives (Wyrick), each with its own bibliography. Felshin's "The dialectics of woman and sport" is especially good. The Project on the Status and Education of Women (of the Association of American Colleges) published a 21-page pamphlet-newsletter in April 1974, "What constitutes equality for women in sport?--federal law puts women in the running," which should be mentioned here.

(577) Haney, Lynn
The lady is a jock. HS
Dodd 1973 224p 73-11548 $5.94 0-396-06870-7
Interviews of women riders. A good start, but feminists may not consider it a winner. Why? See last chapter.

(578) Haskell, Molly
From reverence to rape; the treatment of women in the movies.
Holt 1974 400p 72-91580 $10.00 0-30-007606-4

Basic Book Collection 800

(579) King, Billie Jean & Kim Chapin
Billie Jean. HS
Harper 1974 196p index 73-4099 $6.95 0-06-012392-3
Also available as a recording from Voice Over Books
(#01774 at $6.95). They have also authored "Tennis to win"
(Harper, 1970, $5.95), and Ms. King with Joe Hyams,
"Billie Jean King's Secrets of winning tennis" (Holt, 1974,
$6.95).

(580) Lichtenstein, Grace
A long way, baby; behind the scenes in Women's Pro Tennis.
Morrow 1974 256p 74-1166 $6.95

(581) Mellen, Joan
Women and their sexuality in the new film.
Horizon 1974 255p 73-88659 $10.00 0-8180-0704-4;
    $4.95/pap 0-8180-0705-2
A collection of essays about contemporary foreign films.

(582) Rosen, Marjorie
Popcorn Venus; women, movies and the American dream.
Coward 1973 416p bib index 73-78740 $9.95
    0-698-10545-1

(583) Smith, Sharon
Women who make movies.
Hopkinson & Blake 1974 $8.00; $4.50/pap
Includes a directory of 600 current women filmmakers.

800 LITERATURE & RHETORIC

(584) Cornillon, Susan Koppelman, ed.
Images of women in fiction--feminist perspectives.
Popular Press (Bowling Green State University, OH 43403)
    1972 400p $10.00; $4.00/pap
Anthology of women as writers and in fiction. Especially
useful for Women's Studies.

(585) Ferguson, Mary Anne, ed.
Images of women in literature.
Houghton 1973 437p $4.95/pap
Collection of stories, poetry, and a playlet by modern
American women and men writers, organized around female
stereo- and archetypes. Barbara Warren's "The feminine
image in literature" (Hayden, 1973, $3.99) traces images
of women through classical and modern literature.

(586) Foster, Jeannette Howard, 1895-
Sex variant women in literature; a history and quantitative
  survey.
Vantage 1957/1974 412p 56-9038
Surveys lesbianism from earliest records on Sappho and Ruth
through 20th-century writings in English, German and French.
Received the 1974 SRRT Task Force on Gay Liberation's 3rd
annual Gay Book Award. First published at Dr. Foster's
own expense; now reprinted by Diana Press.

(587) Goulianos, Joan, ed.
By a woman writt; literature from six centuries by and about
  women.
Bobbs 1973 496p $14.95 0-672-51616-0; Penguin
  $2.45/pap 0-14-003786-1
Literature of six centuries, including a number of 'firsts,'
e.g. 17th-century Aphra Benn, first Englishwoman to write
for money. Anthology of forms most available to women--
letters, diaries, autobiography.

(588) Hardwick, Elizabeth, 1916-
Seduction and betrayal; women in literature.
Random 1974 208p 73-3982 $6.95 0-394-49069-X
Essays from New York Review of Books on psychology and
social history of mostly, but not entirely, 19th-century
women as writers and subjects of literature. Valuable as a
source of demonstration of the effect on women of patriarchal society's damaging roles.

(589) Legman, George Alexander, 1917-
Rationale of the dirty joke; an analysis of sexual humor.
Grove 1968 811p 68-29924 $15.00
Numerous references are made to this work by such thinkers
as Millett and Morgan. The relationship between the dirty
joke and folklore, with the dirty joke functioning as a safety
valve, is no laughing matter. Note the categories considered: children, fools, animals, the male approach, the
sadistic concept, women, premarital sexual acts, marriage,
adultery, homosexuality, prostitution, VD, castration, dys-
phemism and cursing, scatology.

(590) Murray, Michele, comp.
A house of good proportion; images of women in literature.
Simon & Schuster 1973 379p bib 72-93509 $9.95;
  $3.95/pap Touchstone
Anthology of lesser known short stories, poems, and novel
excerpts from American and European male and female au-

thors, compiled by Murray to demonstrate the depiction of stages and roles assigned women.

(591) Schneir, Miriam, ed.
Feminism; the essential historical writings.
Random 1972 360p 70-159371 $7.95 0-394-47191-1;
    Vintage $2.45/pap 0-394-71738-4
Contents: 18th century rebels; Women alone; An American Woman's Movement; Men as feminists (John Stuart Mill, Henrik Ibsen, Friedrich Engels, August Bebel, Thorstein Veblen); 20th century themes.

(592) Sullivan, Victoria & James Hatch, eds.
Plays by and about women; an anthology.
Random 1973 425p 72-13524 $8.95
Although the editors renounce any feminist responsibility in their selections ("plays first, not polemics"), it is a useful collection of eight Western World plays with biographical material on the authors.

810   American Literature in English

(593) Birkby, Phyllis, et al, eds.
Amazon Expedition; a Lesbian feminist anthology.
Times Change 1973 93p 73-79902 Monthly Review $4.95
    0-87810-526-3; $1.75/pap 0-87810-026-1
Ten varied articles by such authors as Ti-Grace Atkinson, Bertha Harrison, Jill Johnston, and Rebecca Patterson.

(594) Chester, Laura & Sharon Barba, eds.
Rising tides; twentieth century American women poets; intro. by Anais Nin.
Washington Square 1973 410p index Simon & Schuster
    $1.95/pap 0-671-148753-3
Most of these 70 women are still living. Use with #'s 596 and 606. Biographical material included.

(595) Heilbrun, Carolyn G.
Toward a recognition of androgyny.
Knopf 1973 $6.95 0-394-46175-4
Essays by an Associate Professor of English at Columbia University. The concept of androgyny is vital to an understanding of sexism and resistance to feminism.

(596) Howe, Florence & Ellen Bass, eds.
No more masks; an anthology of poems by women.

Anchor 1973 396p 72-89675 Doubleday $3.95/pap
0-385-02553-X
Contemporary American poets introduced via an excellent
essay. Chronologically presented. A Women's Studies basic.

(597) Jong, Erica
Half-lives.
Holt 1973 $6.95 0-03-007426-6; $3.95/pap 0-03-007411-8

(598) Klagburn, Francine, ed.
The first Ms. Reader.
Warner 1973 $1.50/pap Independent News Co. (75 Rockefeller Plaza, New York, NY 10019) $1.50/pap
An original paperback collection of articles (some excerpted)
reprinted from Ms. magazine's Spring 1972 preview issue
mainly. The writers are all concerned with changing a system that hobbles women. The concept of sisterhood must
be understood by any feminist, and it comes across here.
A history of the magazine and form of address is included.
Ms. is also responsible for the book, "Wonder Woman"
(Holt, 1972, $12.95).

(599) Lorde, Audre, 1934-
From a land where other people live.
Broadside Press 1974 $1.50
A nominee for a National Book Award. Lorde, a Black
woman poet, has two earlier books, "The first cities"
(Poets' Press, 1968) and "Cables to rage" (Riverside, 1970),
both limited editions.

(600) Lowell, Amy, 1874-1925
Complete poetical works.
Cambridge editions 1955 Houghton $10.00 0-395-07489-4

(601) Morgan, Robin
Monster; poems.
Random 1972 86p 72-5809 or 72-5810 $5.95; Vintage
$1.95/pap 0-394-71841-8
Thirty poems attack the damagers of lives of so-called liberated women. "Arraignment" has had to be revised by Ms.
Morgan because of the publisher's fear of being sued by Ted
Hughes, husband of Sylvia Plath, whom she accuses of
Plath's murder (only Feminist Art Journal was willing to
publish it). See also Morgan's "On the Watergate women"
poem in Ms. magazine April, 1974:69.

(602) Parker, Gail, ed.
The oven birds; American women on womanhood, 1820-1920.

Basic Book Collection 810   63

Anchor 1972 387p 72-171338 Doubleday $2.50/pap
Anthology of the writings of some important American women, e.g. Jane Addams, Lydia Marie Child, Charlotte Perkins Gilman, Harriet Beecher Stowe, Angelina Weld). Although Parker's emphasis is on literature, it is not as a pseudo-feminist, but rather to further understand the women via its socializing effect.

(603) Rich, Adrienne Cecile, 1929-
Diving into the wreck; poems 1971-72.
Norton 1973 $5.95; $1.95/pap
Ms. Rich was 1974 National Book Awards poetry co-winner for this book, but by pre-arrangement with two other nominees, Audre Lorde (#599) and Alice Walker (#824), she accepted "in the name of all the women whose voices have gone and still go unheard in a patriarchal world." The money will go to women's rights organizations. Their full statements appear in Spokeswoman August 15, 1974:8 and Ms. Sept. 1974:21.

(604) Sanchez, Sonia
A blues book for blue Black magical women.
Broadside 1974 62p 72-77309 $1.95/pap

(605) Segnitz, Barbara & Carol Rainey, eds.
Psyche; the feminine poetic consciousness. HS
Dial 1973 256p 73-13786 $10.00 0-8037-7207-6
Collection of modern women poets' work.

to the memory of ANNE SEXTON (1928-1974)
The awful rowing toward God (Houghton Mifflin, 1975, $3.95/pap)

(606) Stanford, Ann, 1916- , comp.
The women poets in English; an anthology.
Herder & Herder 1973 374p 72-4145 McGraw $9.50
    0-07-073223-X
Comprehensive collection of poetry by women, from A.D. 800 to the present; with biographical material. Basic.

(607) Stanford, Barbara Dodds, 1943- , ed.
On being female; an anthology. HS
Pocket books 1974 $1.25/pap 671-48134-7
A reader which conveys, via writings of men (e.g. Thorsten Veblen) and women (e.g. Stanford), the destructive effects traditional roles have had on women. For consciousness-raising—a list of some United States groups is appended. Any library should have all of these writings.

(608) Stein, Gertrude, 1874-1946
The previously uncollected writings ..., ed. by Robert Bartlett Haas.
Volume I: Reflection on the atomic bomb. (1914-46)
Black Sparrow 1973 164p 73-13730 $10.00; $4.00/pap
Volume II: How writing is written. (1928-1945)
Black Sparrow 1974 161p 73-17266 $10.00
 0-87685-200-2; $4.00/pap 0-87685-199-5

(609) Terry, Megan
Approaching Simone; a play. HS
Feminist Press 1972 144p $2.75 0-912670-11-8
Won Obie Award for Best Play of 1969-70. Simone Weil (1909-43), French mystic philosopher on whose life play is based. See also #628.

(610) Wakoski, Diane, 1937-
Greed, Parts 8, 9, 11.
Black Sparrow 1973 50p 68-4425 $15.00 0-87685-156-1;
 $3.00/pap
Wakoski is considered by many to be the foremost poet of the day; she is a feminist. Part 1--Of polygamy. Part 2--Of accord and principle. Part 3--The greed that is not greed. Her "The motor cycle betrayal poems" (Simon & Schuster, 1972, $5.95) was considered shrill!

820 English & Anglo Saxon Literature

(611) Adburgham, Alison
Women in print; writing and women's magazines from the Restoration to the accession of Victoria.
Allen & Unwin 1972 302p bib index Humanities $15.00
 0-04-070005-4
Ms. Alison is a journalist. Included is a chronology of women's periodicals.

(612) Bazin, Nancy Topping
Virginia Woolf and the androgynous vision.
Rutgers 1973 251p bib 72-4198 $9.00 0-8135-0735-9
Also of interest may be Alice VanBuren Kelley's "The novels of Virginia Woolf; fact and vision" (University of Chicago Press, 1973, $8.95) and Jean Alexander's "The venture of form in the novels of Virginia Woolf" (Kennikat Press, 1974, $9.95).

(613) Browning, Elizabeth Barrett, 1806-1861
Sonnets from the Portuguese and other poems. S

Basic Book Collection 820   65

Funk & Wagnalls   1967 $.95/pap
Series of poems of which the underlying theme is that love--
human love--effectively replaces the love of Christ as a redemptive force.

(614) Colby, Vineta
Yesterday's woman; domestic realism in the English novel.
Princeton Univ. Press   1974   269p   index   73-2469 $12.50
Recommendation of reduced expectations of domestic virtue
and effort over Romantic aspirations in Victorian novels by
women.

    Many novels of the Victorian period, especially the
popular and subliterary ones, reflect the belief that love was
a variety of religious experience, but they do not create this
belief.   This is a very big subject--one that lies at the
heart of any real understanding of Victorian and modern culture.   Some examine this belief critically and reject it
("The awakening," most Henry James and Thomas Hardy
novels).   De Beauvoir in "The second sex" describes and of
course rejects this idea in the chapter on "The woman in
love."   Of course it is still with us in the 20th century:
Hemingway subscribes to a form of it: Robert Jordan and
Maria in the sleeping bag, Frederick and Catherine in the
hospital bed; Norman Mailer and his apocalyptic orgasm;
Eugene O'Neill, D. H. Lawrence, Sherwood Anderson in
"Many marriages."   In fact the whole Freudian tradition as
it finds expression in literature tends in this direction.   Regardless of Freud's personal attitude toward sexuality, the
literary imagination in assimilating Freudian ideas comes to
view sexuality as a potent mystery, one having redemptive
potential--another way of saying sex is a variety of religious
experience!

(615) Eckley, Grace
Edna O'Brien
Bucknell Univ. Press   1974   88p   bib   79-168806 $4.50
Progressive exploration of feminine consciousness in O'Brien's
fiction.   Chronology included.

(616) James, Henry, 1843-1916
The portrait of a lady.
Many editions and formats in print.
His "The Bostonians" (Modern Library, $1.25/pap) is usable
with young people; the "Fiction Catalog, 7th ed." lists it
under the subject-heading, Woman--Social & Moral Questions.
His "The speech and manners of American women," ed. by

E. S. Reggs (Lancaster House, 1974, $3.45/pap) may prove useful in viewing his women.

(617) Johnson, Diane
The true history of the first Mrs. Meredith and other lesser lives.
Knopf 1972 232p bib 72-2227 $7.95
Unusual biography of 19th-century "daring" Englishwoman, Mary Ellen Peacock Nicolls Meredith (1821-1861), daughter of novelist Thomas Love Peacock and first wife of writer George Meredith. Great reading.

(618) Livesay, Dorothy
Forty women poets of Canada
Ingluvin 1972 $7.00; $3.00/pap
Ingluvin, a so-called women's press, anthology.

(619) Manley, Seon & Belcher, Susan
O, those extraordinary women! Or, The joys of literary lib. HS
Chilton 1973 330p bib index 72-8061 $8.95
0-8019-5636-1
Well-illustrated collection of writings of over thirty women authors.

(620) Middleton, Thomas, 1580-1627
Women beware women, ed. by Charles Barber.
Univ. of California Press 1969 136p bib $6.50
0-520-01494-4; $1.80/pap 0-520-01495-2
Fountainwell Drama Texts Series (critical editions of English dramatists in which the original spelling and punctuation are normalized but not modernized). 1657 play about the double standard of morality current in Renaissance society--women as commodities. "Men buy their slaves but women buy their masters"--Isabella. Performed in London by the Royal Shakespeare Company in 1962 and in 1968 at Edinburgh.

(621) Schreiner, Olive, 1855-1920
A track to the water's edge; the Olive Schreiner reader, ed. by Howard Thurman.
Harper 1973 198p 72-78068 $6.95 0-06-068076-8
Extracts from "The story of an African farm," "Thoughts on South Africa," "Dreams," "Woman and labour," "Trooper Peter Halket of Mashonaland," "Stories, dreams and allegories," and "From man to man."

(622) Wagner, Geoffrey
Five for freedom; a study of feminism in fiction.

Basic Book Collection 840 67

Fairleigh Dickinson Univ. 1973 234p index 73-8284
  $10.00 0-8386-1423-X
Heroines in "Les liaisons dangereusex," "Jane Eyre,"
"Madame Bovary," "Tess of the D'Urbervilles," and "Buddenbrooks."

(623) Whissen, Thomas R.
Isak Dinesen's aesthetics.
National Univ. 1974 130p bib index 73-83272 Kennikat
  $7.95 0-8046-9059-6

830 Literatures of Germanic Languages

(624) Böll, Heinrich, 1917-
Group portrait with lady, tr. from German by Leila Vennewitz.
McGraw 1971 405p 72-8835 $7.95 0-07-006423-7
Böll is 1972 Nobel Literature prize-winner. Edwin Newman, interviewing him in December 1973, looked surprised and amused when Böll declared that he sees Women's Liberation as "not having had much effect."

(625) Strindberg, August, 1849-1912
Getting married, tr. and ed. by Mary Standbach.
Viking 1974 384p 72-11063 $7.95 670-33760-9
Thirty stories by the author of "The stronger," currently being shown as part of Vivica Lindfors' program. Women's studies.

840 Literature of Romance Languages

(626) Beauvoir, Simone de, 1908-
A very easy death, tr. by Patric O'Brian.
Putnam 1966 106p 66-15581 $3.95
Day-by-day account of the death of her mother, autobiographical.

(627) Blais, Marie-Claire, 1939-
The day is dark. Three trouble. Two novellas, tr. from
  French by Derek Coltman.
Farrar 1967 183p 67-18971 $4.95
First published in Canada in French. "A season in the life of Emmanuel..." (Grosset, $1.95/pap) and "The manuscripts of Pauline Archange, a novel..." (Farrar, 1970, $5.95) are also well known.

(628) Weil, Simone, 1909-1943
First and last notebooks, tr. by Richard Rees.
Oxford Univ. Press 1970 $9.75 0-19-213945-2
Several of her works are in print. See also #609. 20th-century intellectuelle de gauche.

(629) Wittig, Monique
Les guérilleres, tr. from French by David LeVay.
Viking 1969 144p 70-158521 $4.95
Published in France just before the first action of the Mouvement de Liberation des Femmes, in which Wittig has been totally involved. She has evolved the word, "feminary."

860 Spanish & Portuguese Literatures

(630) DaCosta, Maria Velho, et al.
The three Marias: new Portuguese letters; tr. by Helen R. Lane
Doubleday 1975 432p 74-2826 Doubleday $10.00
"The Three Marias" are novelists DaCosta and Maria Isabel Barreno, and poet Maria Teresa Horta. The title derives from 17th-century "Letters of a Portuguese nun." The Portuguese censor declared that their collection of feminist essays, stories, and poems was an outrage to public morals, and the women were jailed in 1972. The book details the psychological, political and economic oppression and sexual exploitation in manifestos, fiction, etc., which the government charged with "eroticism." One part of a poem reads, "In Portugal, the majority of women are not only and simply 'slaves' of men, but act out, cheerfully, with conviction their role of woman-object, and it is not necessary to be stoned, to be annihilated.... It is enough that she emerges and speaks as 'a man'." A French edition of the book has been printed. Contact Arlie Scott of the New Portuguese Letters Assoc., 1594 Manning Ave., Los Angeles, CA 90024 for information. Document #33 of the 1973-4 American Library Assoc. Council resolutions expressed distress with the censorship of "Novas Cartas Portuguesas" and concern for the three women and urged that the United Nations Human Rights Commission give all possible consideration to the petition of the International Feminist Planning Conference. Since the April 25, 1974 coup, several women's organizations have been dissolved. See Ms. January 1975:86f for update.

890 Literatures of Other Languages

(631) Akhmatova, Anna Andreevna, 1888-1966
Poems of Akhmatova. Selected, tr., intro. by Stanley
   Kunitz and Max Hayward.
Atlantic Little   1973   173p   72-13856 $7.95; $3.95/pap

(632) Benson, Ruth Crego
Women in Tolstoy; the ideal and the erotic.
Univ. of Illinois Press   1973   140p   bib   72-92631 $6.95
   0-252-00287-3
"War and Peace," "Anna Karenina," "Family happiness."

(633) Rexroth, Kenneth & Ling Chung, trs. and eds.
The orchid boat; women poets of China.
Seabury   1973   180p   72-6791 $7.50
From B.C. to mid-20th century.

900 GENERAL GEOGRAPHY, HISTORY, BIOGRAPHY

(634) Fogarty, Michael, et al
Sex, career and family; including an international review of
   women's roles.
Russell Sage   1971   582p   70-158823 $17.50
   0-8039-0121-6; $7.50/pap
et al = Rhona Rapoport and Robert N. Rapoport.

(635) Kane, Paula & Christopher Chandler
Sex objects in the sky.
Follett   1974   160p   74-80327 $5.95
Ex-stewardess documents well this sexist job.

(636) O'Faolain, Julia & Lauro Martines, eds.
Not in God's image; women in history from the Greeks to
   the Victorians.
Harper   1973 $12.50; $3.45/pap
Anthology of European women.

910 General Geography

(637) Pitseolak
Pictures out of my life.   From recorded interviews by
   Dorothy Eber.
Univ. of Washington Press   1972   95p   72-4111 $9.95
Pitseolak is an old Eskimo woman on Baffin Island who narrates, and whose art work is shown.

920 General Biography (Collections)

(638) Crane, Louise
Ms. Africa; profiles of modern African women. Illus.
   with photographs. HS
Lippincott 1973 160p $4.95 0-397-31446-9

(639) Dannett, Sylvia Gwendolyn Liebovitz, 1909-
Profiles of Negro womanhood.
Educational Heritage, Inc. (733 Yonkers Ave., Yonkers, NY
   10704) 1964 v1: 1619-1900; 1966 v2: 20th century
   [out-of-print]
In Library of Congress collection: E185.96

(640) Dexter, Elizabeth Williams Anthony, 1887-
Career women of America, 1776-1840.
Marshall Jones 1950 262p bib 51-812 Kelley repr.

(641) Dexter, Elizabeth Williams Anthony, 1887-
Colonial women of affairs; a study of women in business and
   the professions in America before 1776, 2d ed. rev.
Houghton Mifflin 1931 223p bib 31-5314 Gale repr.
   1972 $8.50; also Kelley repr.

(642) Majors, Monroe Alphus, 1864-
Noted Negro women; their triumphs and activities.
Donohue & Hanneberry c1893 365p 20-20515 Books for
   Libraries repr. $14.50 -8733-0 73-138341
Illustrated sketches of many women. Then as now it's possible to infer (but not assume) much from the way in which the names were listed--an approximately equal distribution among Miss, Mrs., and no prefix; with a scattering of Dr., Mrs. Rev., Madam, Queen, and née.

(643) Merriam, Eve, 1916-
Growing up female in America; ten lives.
Doubleday 1971 308p 79-157611 $7.95
Lives of a variety (races, religions, ethnicity, economics) women from the past, from diaries, journals, correspondence, etc. Ms. Merriam is perhaps best known for her children's books--e.g. "Boys and girls, girls and boys. Pictures by Harriet Sherman" (Holt, 1972, $4.50) and of course, "Mommies at work" (Knopf, 1961, $4.50). See also her "Catch a little rhyme" in "Audiovisuals" part of Non-Book Resources section.

(644) Moffat, Mary Jane & Charlotte Painter
Revelations; diaries of women.

Basic Book Collection 920   71

Random 1974 448p bib 74-8040 $10.00
Diary selections organized around love, power, and work
themes.

(645) Nathan, Dorothy
Women of courage (Landmark Series). HS
Random 1964 $1.95 0-394-80407-4; $.75/pap
Jane Addams, Susan Brownell Anthony, Mary McLeod
Bethune, Amelia Earhart, Margaret Mead.

(646) Osen, Lynn M.
Women in mathematics.
MIT Press 1974 185p 73-19506 $5.95 0-262-15014-X

(647) Overton, Grant Martin, 1887-
Women who make our novels, rev. ed.
Dodd 1928 352p bib 28-6114 Books for Libraries repr.
    $10.25 -0758-2 67-23257
Authors.

(648) Peacock, Virginia Tatnall, 1873-1918
Famous American belles of the Nineteenth Century.
Lippincott 1901 297p 1-29226 Books for Libraries repr.
    $11.50 -1893-2 73-128284

(649) Ross, Nancy Wilson, 1905-
Westward the women.
Knopf 1944 199p bib 44-8939 Books for Libraries repr.
    $8.75 -1846-0 76-117832
Women who went with and followed men to settle the West,
including missionaries.

(650) Ross, Pat, comp.
Young and female; turning points in the lives of eight young
    women--personal accounts. HS
Random 1972 128p bib $3.95

(651) Sickels, Eleanor Maria, 1894-
In calico and crinoline; true stories of American women,
    1608-1865; drawings by Ilse Bischoff.
Viking Press 1935 274p bib 35-9452 Books for Libraries
    repr. $11.25 -2474-6 70-167418
Useful with this is her "Twelve daughters of democracy;
true stories of American women, 1865-1930; illus. by Doro-
thy Bayley," published in 1941 and reprinted by Books for
Libraries for $9.75.

(652) Ungherini, Aglauro, 1847-
Manuel de bibliographie biographique et d'iconographie des
femmes célèbres....
Turin, Roux; Paris, Nilsson 1892-1905 3v Z-207-8
Availability: United States Library of Congress, University
of Notre Dame, Columbia University, and other major libraries for reference use. Should be reprinted. Main work
and two supplements constitute a "useful index to material
about women of all countries and all periods. Gives an
identifying phrase with dates of birth and death, lists monographic biographies in various languages, and cites portraits,
autographs, etc. A cumulated index in the second supplement" (Constance M. Winchell. "Guide to reference books,
8th ed.," American Library Assoc., 1967).

(653) Who's who and where in Women's Studies, ed. by
Tamar Berkowitz, Jean Mangi and Jane Williamson.
Feminist Press 1972- 256p $12.50 0-912670-36-3;
$7.50/pap

(654) The world who's who of women. Vol. I: 1973, ed.
by Ernest Kay.
Rowman & Littlefield 1973 976p $49.50
This great rip-off on the Movement is listed here because
of the scarcity of worthy tools of the scope the above title
claims and possibly as raw material for an exercise in
feminist book review-evaluation! Good news is the paperback edition of #256, "Notable American women, 1607-1950;
a biographical dictionary," Janet Wilson James, assoc. ed.,
$25.00!

Individual Biography/Autobiography
(Arranged Alphabetically by biographee, whose surname is
underlined)

(655) Davis, Allen F.
American heroine; the life and legend of Jane Addams.
Oxford Univ. Press 1973 339p index 73-82664 $10.95
Helen Stone Peterson's "Jane Addams; pioneer of Hull House"
(Garrard, 1965, $2.50) is recommended for children.

(656) Jones, Enid Huws
Mrs. Humphry Ward [Mary Arnold].
St. Martin's Press 1973 180p bib index 73-80643 $7.95

(657) Langhorne, Elizabeth
Nancy Astor and her friends.

Basic Book Collection 920

Praeger 1974 328p index 72-83006 $10.00
0-275-50520-4

(658) Atkinson, Ti-Grace, 1938-
Amazon odyssey; illus. by Barbara Nessim.
Link Books 1974 226p 73-80394 Quick Fox $15.00;
 $4.95/pap

(659) Randall, Mercedes M.
Improper Bostonian; Emily Greene Balch.
Twayne 1964 $6.00

(660) Beauvoir, Simone de, 1908-
All said and done; tr. by Patrick O'Brian.
Putnam 1974 450p 73-93772 $8.95

(661) Bogan, Louise
What the woman lived; selected letters of Louise Bogan,
 1920-1970, ed. & intro. by Ruth Limmer.
Harcourt 1973 385p index 73-9737 $14.50
 0-15-195878-5

(662) Noble, Iris
Cameras and courage; Margaret Bourke-White.
Simon 1973 191p 72-11927 $4.95 Messner
 0-671-32577-9; 0-671-32578-9/lib binding

(663) Peters, Maureen
An enigma of the Brontës.
St. Martin's Press 1974 185p bib index 73-82236
Tom Winnifrith's "The Brontës and their background; romance and reality" (Barnes & Noble, 1973, $12.75) may also be of interest.

(664) Lupton, Mary Jane
Elizabeth Barrett Browning. HS
Feminist Press 1973 112p $2.25 0-912670-02-9

(665) Woods, Lucia, et al
Willa Cather; a pictorial memoir; text by Bernice Slote.
Univ. of Nebraska Press 1973 134p index 72-91511
 $15.00 0-8032-0828-6
Barbara Bonham's "Willa Cather" (Chilton, 1970, $4.25) is recommended for older children.

(666) Hicks, Nancy
The Honorable Shirley Chisholm; Congresswoman from

Brooklyn. HS
Lion 1971 118p $5.95 0-87460-236-X
Susan Brownmiller's "Shirley Chisholm; a biography" (Doubleday, 1970, $3.50) is recommended for younger readers.

(667) Colette, Sidonie Gabrielle, 1873-1954
The evening star.
Bobbs 1974 144p 73-11793 $5.95
Margaret Crosland's "Colette; the difficulty of loving--a biography, with an introduction by Janet Flanner" (Bobbs, 1973, $8.95) is also recommended.

(668) Sprigge, Elizabeth
The life of Ivy Compton-Burnett.
Braziller 1973 191p bib 72-96072 $7.95 0-8076-0685-5

(669) Cooper, Anna Julia Haywood, 1859-
A voice from the South, by a Black woman of the South.
Aldine 1892 304p 12-2877 1969 repr. $11.50
   0-8371-1384-9; also Negro Univ. Press 1970
   $12.00 0-8411-0032-2

(670) Davis, Angela Y.
Angela Davis: an autobiography.
Bernard Geis Assoc. & Random 1974 320p 73-20580 $8.95
Regina Nadelson's "Who Is Angela Davis? The biography of a revolutionary" (Wyden, 1972, $5.95) is useful.

(671) Wood, James Playsted
Emily Elizabeth Dickinson; a portrait. HS
Nelson 1972 190p 72-5903 $4.95
Aileen Fisher and Olive Rabe's "We Dickinsons" (Atheneum, 1965, $4.50) is recommended for middle grades and junior high school age.

(672) Hardwick, Mollie
Mrs. Dizzy; the life of Mary Anne Disraeli, Viscountess
   Beaconsfield.
St. Martin's 1973 218p bib 72-89422 $7.95

(673) Flynn, Elizabeth Gurley, 1890-
I speak my own piece; autobiography of the rebel girl.
1935 International 384p $12.50; $3.95/pap 0-7178-0343-0
International has also published her "My life as a political prisoner; the Alderson story" (1973, $2.25/pap).

(674) Ford, Laura May
Bittersweet; the autobiography of a lesbian.

Basic Book Collection 920

Exposition Press   1969   144p $4.00   0-682-46958-0

(675) Deiss, [Joseph] Jay
The Roman years of Margaret Fuller; a biography.
Crowell   1969   338p   70-81941 $6.96   0-690-71175-1

(676) Bhatia, Krishan
Indira Gandhi; a biography of Prime Minister Gandhi.
Praeger   1974   320p   bib   72-92880 $10.00   0-275-19900-2
Emmeline Garnett's "Madam Prime Minister; the story of Indira Gandhi" (Farrar, 1967, $3.95) is recommended for older children.

(677) Rubenius, Aina
The woman question in Mrs. Gaskell's life and works.
Russell & Russell   1973   396p   bib   72-90568 $20.00
   0-8462-1717-1
Originally published in 1951 by Harvard.   Essays & Studies on English Language and Literature, #5.

(678) Gilman, Charlotte Perkins Stetson, 1860-1935
The yellow wallpaper.
Feminist Press   1973   64p $2.50   0-912670-09-6

(679) Giovanni, Nikki
Gemini; an extended autobiographical statement on my first
   twenty-seven years of being a Black poet.
Bobbs   1971   149p $5.95

(680) Fetherling, Dale
Mother Jones, the miners' angel.
Southern Illinois Univ. Press   1974   263p   bib   index
   73-12444 $11.85
Irving Werstein's "Labor's defiant lady; the story of Mother Jones" (Crowell, 1969, $4.50) is recommended for children.

(681) Friedman, Myra
Buried alive; the biography of Janis Joplin.   HS
Morrow   1973   333p   78-189274 $7.95   0-688-00160-2;
   also available from Voice Over Books (#00274 at $6.95)
Peggy Caserta's "Going down with Janis" (Lyle Stuart, 1973, $7.95) is also on the market.

(682) Julie.
My nights and days.
Putnam   1974   73-93729 $6.95

(683) Wright, Constance
Fanny Kemble and the lovely land.
Dodd   1972   242p   72-3699 $7.95
John Anthony Scott's "Fanny Kemble's America" (Crowell, 1973, $4.50) is junior-senior high school level; Winifred Wise's "Fanny Kemble; actress, author, Abolutionist" (Putnam, 1966, $3.95) is recommended for older children.

(684) Klasner, Lily Casey, 1862-1946
My girlhood among the outlaws; ed. by Eve Ball.
Arizona Univ. Press   1972   336p   77-165206 $7.50
0-8165-0328-1; $4.95/pap   0-8165-0354-0

(685) Kearns, Marty
Kaeth Kollwitz.
Feminist Press   1973   320p $5.00   0-912670-15-0
Mina C. Klein's "Kathe Kollwitz; life in art" (Holt, 1972, $11.95) is recommended for young people.

(686) Beecham, Justin.
Olga [Korbut].   HS
Two Continents   1974   128p   73-15022 $2.95/pap
0-8467-0018-2

(687) Wilson, Dorothy Clarke
Bright eyes; the story of Susette LaFlesche, an Omaha Indian.
McGraw   1974   324p   bib   73-15636 $8.95   0-07-070752-9
Margaret Crary's "Susette LaFlesche; voice of the Omaha Indians" (Hawthorn, 1973, $5.95) is recommended for older children.   Marion E. Girdley's collection, "American Indian women" (Hawthorn, 1974, $5.95), is also useful, for children.

(688) Turney, Catherine
Byron's daughter; a biography of Elizabeth Medora Leigh.
Scribner's   1972   320p   bib   79-37206 $8.95

(689) Ross, Ishbel
The president's wife; Mary Todd Lincoln; a biography.
Putnam   1973   378p   bib   72-97309 $8.95

(690) Lindbergh, Anne Spencer Morrow, 1907-
Bring me a unicorn; diaries and letters, 1922-1928.
Harcourt   1972   259p   71-182329 $6.95   0-15-114180-0
"Hour of gold, hour of lead; diaries and letters of Anne Morrow Lindbergh, 1929-1932" (1973, $7.95) and "Locked rooms and open doors; diaries and letters of Anne Morrow Lindbergh, 1933-1935" (1974, $7.95) also.

Basic Book Collection 920   77

(691) Dunnahoo, Terry
Before the Supreme Court; the story of Belva Ann Lockwood.
HS
Houghton 1974 $4.95 0-395-18520-3

(692) Loud, Patricia Russell, 1926-
Pat Loud; a woman's story.
Coward 1974 224p 73-88543 $6.95 0-698-10578-8

(693) Luxemburg, Rosa, 1870-1919
Reform or revolution.
Pathfinder 1973 79p 73-79783 $3.95; $1.25/pap (Repr.
 of "Rosa Luxemburg speaks; ed. & intro. by Mary-Alice
 Waters," 1970.)

(694) McCarthy, Abigail Quigley
Private faces, public places.
Doubleday 1972 448p 70-171305 $8.95
Her former husband is Senator Eugene McCarthy.

(695) Graver, Lawrence
Carson McCullers.
Univ. of Minnesota Press 1969 $.95/pap 0-8166-0546-7

(696) Dykeman, Wilma
Too many people, too little love; Edna Rankin McKinnon,
 pioneer for birth control.
Holt 1974 304p 73-3746 $6.95 0-03-010801-2

(697) VanVoris, Jacqueline
Constance DeMarkievicz. HS
Feminist Press 1973 140p $2.50 0-921670-04-5

(698) Kapp, Yvonne
Eleanor Marx. Vol. 1: Family life (1855-1883).
International 1973 319p bib 72-92771 $12.00
 0-7178-0390-2

(699) Mead, Margaret, 1901-
Blackberry winter; my earlier years.
Morrow 1972 305p 72-7187 $8.95 0-688-0051-7

(700) Millett, Kate, 1934-
Flying.
Knopf 1974 546p 73-20766 $8.95
Also available from Voice Over Books (#00674, $6.95).

(701) Morris, Jan
Conundrum.
Harcourt (a Helen & Kurt Wolff book) 1974 174p 74-525
   $5.95 0-15-122563-X
Having made the transition, she states, "I can only report that having, in the second half of the twentieth century, experienced life in both roles, there seems to me no aspect of existence, no moment of the day, no contact, no arrangement, no response, which is not different for men and for women. The very tone of voice in which I was now addressed, the very posture of the person next in the queue, ... constantly emphasized my change of status.... Men treated me more and more as a junior--my lawyer, in an unguarded moment one morning, even called me 'my child'; and so, addressed every day of my life as an inferior, involuntarily, month by month I accepted the condition. I discovered that even now men prefer women to be less informed, less able, less talkative, and certainly less self-centered than they are themselves; so I generally obliged them.... I have seen life from both sides, and I know what prejudice survives. I know that by the very fact of my womanhood, even in so urbane a city as Bath, I am treated in many petty situations as a second-class citizen--not because I lack brains, or experience, or character, but purely because I wear the body of a woman. Nothing infuriates me more than to see a woman brushed aside or scorned by some dullard man; for I know for absolute certainty how nonsensical this bigotry is, and I boil to think of it applied to greater affairs of life.... But I do not for a moment regret the act of change...." Canary Conn's "Canary; the story of a transsexual" (Nash, 1974, $8.95) is also in print.

(702) Sokoloff, Alice Hunt
Hadley, the first Mrs. Hemingway.
Dodd 1973 111p 72-11253 $6.95
Hadley Richardson Hemingway Mowrer.

(703) Nin, Anaïs, 1903-
Diary.
Harcourt v5 The diary of..., 1947-1955; ed. & with preface by Gunther Stuhlmann. 1974 275p 66-12917
   $7.95 0-15-125593-8
See also #273. "Celebration! with Anaïs Nin, ed. by Valerie Harms" (Magic Circle Press, 1973, $6.95) is recommended; Benjamin V. Franklin has prepared "Anaïs Nin; a bibliography" (Kent State Univ. Press, 1974, $6.50).

Basic Book Collection <u>920</u>

(704) Sergio, Lisa
A measure filled; the life of Lena Madesin <u>Phillips</u>, drawn from her autobiography.
Luce 1972 246p 71-190073 McKay $5.95

(705) Aird, Eileen M.
Sylvia <u>Plath</u>.
Barnes & Noble 1973 114p bib 73-3267 Harper $5.25 0-06-490038-X
Plath's "Winter trees" (Harper, 1972, $5.95) includes poetry and her radio-play, "Three women"; Nancy Hunter Steiner's "A closer look at Ariel; a memory of Sylvia Plath..." (Harper, 1973, $5.00) is also in-print.

(706) Josephson, Hannah
Jeannette <u>Rankin</u>.
Bobbs 1974 224p 74-22674 $8.95

(707) <u>Rivers</u>, Caryl
Aphrodite at mid-century; growing up Catholic and female in post-war America.
Doubleday 1973 288p 73-79706 $6.95 0-385-05632-X

(708) <u>Robinson</u>, Jill
Bed/Time/Story.
Random 1974 320p 74-8578 $7.95

(709) <u>Rose</u>, Madeline Belkin
The life and times of my mother and me.
Feminist Press 1973 160p $2.50 0-912670-16-9

(710) James, Bessie Rowland
Anne <u>Royall</u>'s USA.
Rutgers Univ. Press 1972 447p 72-1796 $15.00
Anne Newport Royall (1769-1854) wrote a novel, "The Tennessean...," considered "one of the worst ever written in America" by "The Dictionary of American Biography" (Volume 16:204-5), which also characterized her as "Godless" ... because she was an articulate widow forced to earn a living as a journalist! Johnson has reprinted her "Sketches of history, life and manners in the United States by a traveller" (1826/1971, $12.50). See also #343.

(711) Gallant, Mavis
The affiar of Gabrielle <u>Russier</u> [1937-1969], tr. from French.
Knopf 1971 176p 75-154931 $5.95 0-394-46924-0;
  Popular Library $.95/pap 445-00354-095

(712) Bluemel, Elinor
Florence Sabin; Colorado woman of the century.
Colorado Association 1959 238p 59-1235 Univ. of Colorado Press $5.50 0-87081-016-2
Mary Kay Phelan's "Probing the unknown; the story of Dr. Florence Sabin" (Crowell, 1969, $4.50) is recommended for middle grades and junior high school age readers.

(713) Nicolson, Nigel
Portrait of a marriage.
Atheneum 1973 256p 73-80754 $10.00 0-689-10574-6
Vita Sackville-West, 1892-1962.

(714) Sanger, Margaret Higgins, 1883-1966
My fight for birth control.
Farrar c1931 360p 31-28223 Pergamon $17.50
Pergamon has made available most of the writings of Ms. Sanger.

(715) Gerson, Noel Bertram
Daughter of earth and water; a biography of Mary Wollstonecraft Shelley.
Morrow 1973 280p bib 76-182976 $6.95
William Walling's "Mary Shelley" (Twayne, 1973, $5.50) is also useful. Margaret Leighton's "Shelley's Mary: a life of Mary Goodwin Shelley" (Farrar, 1973, $5.95) is suitable for high school readers.

(716) Reyher, Rebecca Hourwich, 1897-
Zulu woman [Christina Sibiya]
Columbia Univ. Press 1948 Signet 1970 repr. $.95/pap

(717) Sitwell, Edith, 1887-1964
Taken care of; the autobiography of Edith Sitwell.
Atheneum 1965 239p bib 65-10912 $5.95 0-689-10253-4

(718) Oakley, Mary Ann B.
Elizabeth Cady Stanton. HS
Feminist Press 1973 160p 72-80249 $2.50
   0-912670-03-7
See also #343. Doris Faber's "Oh, Lizzie!; the story of Elizabeth Cady Stanton" (Lothrop, 1972, $4.95) is recommended for juvenile reading.

(719) Mellow, James R.
Charmed circle; Gertrude Stein and Company.
Praeger 1974 530p bib index 73-7473 $12.95

Basic Book Collection 920   81

Richard Bridgman's "Gertrude Stein in pieces" (Oxford Univ.
Press, 1973, $12.50) is another current imprint. Young
people's books are also useful: Ellen Wilson's "They named
me Gertrude Stein" (Farrar, 1973, $5.50); Howard Green-
feld's "Gertrude Stein; a biography" (Crown, 1973, $5.95);
and W. G. Rogers' "Gertrude Stein is Gertrude Stein is
Gertrude Stein..." (Crowell, 1973, $4.50).

(720) Blackwell, Alice Stone
Lucy Stone; pioneer of women's rights.
Little Brown 1930 313p index Gale repr. $14.50
   77-164111; also Kraus repr. $13.75.

(721) Clarke, Robert
Ellen Swallow; the woman who founded ecology.
Follett 1973 288p index 73-82198 $7.95 0-695-80388-3

(722) Sanders, Marion K.
Dorothy Thompson; a legend in her time.
Houghton 1973 428p index 72-9013 $10.00

(723) Toklas, Alice B.
Staying on alone; letters of Alice B. Toklas, ed. by Edward
   Burns.
Liveright 1973 272p 73-82424 Dutton $11.95
   0-87140-569-5

(724) Truth, Sojourner [orig. Isabella VanWagener], 1797?-
   1883.
Sojourner Truth; narrative and book of life; foreword by
   Sterling Stuckey.
Johnson 1972 240p $4.50
Jacqueline Bernard's "Journey toward freedom; the story of
Sojourner Truth" (Norton, 1967, $5.25) is recommended.
Victoria Ortiz's "Sojourner Truth; a self-made woman"
(Lippincott, 1974, $5.50) is a juvenile book.

(725) Viva, fl. 1970
Superstar.
Putnam 1970 317p 78-129959 $6.95
Autobiographical novel.

(726) Kempf, Beatrix
Woman for peace; the life of Bertha Von Suttner; tr. from
   German by R. W. Last.
Noyes 1973 200p 72-87475 $8.95 0-8155-5013-8

(727) Blackett, Monica
The mark of the maker; a portrait of Helen Waddell.
Constable 1974 256p 73-161815 Harper: Barnes & Noble
   $13.00   0-09-459100-8

(728) Fritz, Jean
Cast for a revolution; some American friends and enemies,
   1728-1814.
Houghton 1972 400p bib 72-515 $7.95
Mary Otis Warren.

(729) Weaver, Harriett E.
Frosty; a raccoon to remember. With line drawings by
   Jennifer Owings Dewey.
Chronicle 1973 156p 73-77331 $5.95

(730) Webb, Beatrice Potter, 1858-1943
Beatrice Webb's American diary, 1898, ed. by David A.
   Shannon.
Univ. of Wisconsin Press 1963 181p 63-8436 $6.50
   0-299-02851-8

(731) Willard, Frances Elizabeth, 1839-1898
Glimpses of fifty years; the autobiography of an American
   woman.
Women's Temperance Publication Assoc. 1889 2v 724p
   27-14734 $26.00 and $31.00 Source Library repr.

(732) Flexner, Eleanor, 1908-
Mary Wollstonecraft; a biography.
Coward 1972 307p 72-76664 $8.95 698-10447-1; Pen-
   guin books $2.50/pap
See also #103.

(733) Tomalin, Claire
The life and death of Mary Wollstonecraft.
Harcourt 1974 316p bib index 74-14816 $8.95
Margaret George's "One woman's situation; a study of Mary
Wollstonecraft" (Univ. of Illinois Press, 1970, $6.50) is in
print.

(734) Noble, Joan Russell
Recollections of Virginia Woolf. Ed. and with introd. by
   the author.
Morrow 1972 207p 72-5595 $6.95

(735) Zassenhaus, Hiltgunt
Walls: resisting the Third Reich--one woman's story.

Beacon 1974 $7.95
"I was haunted by fear [but] once you start it's like an avalanche. You find you are stronger and stronger. You learn to have the courage of your own convictions. If only a few people do this, they can make an enormous difference in a society ..." (from an interview).

940 General History of Europe

(736) Serebriakova, Galina Losifovna
Nine women, drawn from the epoch of the French Revolution ...; tr. by H. C. Stevens, with intro. by Mrs. Sidney Webb.
NY: J. Cape & H. Smith 1932 287p 32-30385 Books for Libraries repr. $9.25 -1314-0 71-93375
Chapters on Theroigne de Mericourt, Charlotte Corday, Manon Roland, Madame DuBarry, Claire LaCombe, Lucile Desmoulins, Elisabeth Lebas, Madame Tallien, and Josephine Bonaparte.

(737) Thompson, Roger
Women in Stuart England and America; a comparative study.
Routledge 1974 276p index 73-93638 $11.25
Why 17th century Virginia and Massachusetts women were able to fill greater roles (status) than women in England.

950 General History of Asia

(738) Dayan, Ruth & Helga Dudman
And perhaps ...; the story of Ruth Dayan. HS
Harcourt 1973 236p 72-79920 $6.95

(739) Meir, Golda Mabovitz, 1898-
A land of our own; an oral autobiography, ed. by Marie Syrkin. HS
Putnam 1973 251p 72-87630 $6.95

(740) Serebrennikov, Georgii Nikolaevich
Position of women in the U.S.S.R.
London: Gollancz 1973 288p 37-15327 Books for Libraries repr. $9.75 -5585-4 72-137384
Chapters entitled "Soviet laws on the rights of women and for the protection of the woman workers," "Women in the intellectual professions and administrative work," "Women in the national republics."

970 General History of North America

(741) Bullough, Vern L. & Bonnie Bullough
The subordinate sex; a history of attitudes toward women.
Univ. of Illinois Press   1973   72-91079 $10.95
    0-252-00320-9
Source book, early history-20th Century.   See also #327.

(742) Cott, Nancy F., ed.
Root of bitterness, documents of the social history of American women.
Dutton   1972 $4.95/pap   0-525-47328-9
Anthology of primary-source documents.

(743) Ellet, Elizabeth L. F.
The women of the American Revolution.
Haskell   1969 $37.50   0-8383-0197-5
Americana Series #37.

(744) Fowler, William Worthington
Woman on the American frontier; a valuable and authentic history of the heroism, adventures, privations, captivities, trials, and noble lives and deaths of the "Pioneer mothers of the Republic."
Hartford: S S Scranton Co.   1878   527p   Gale repr. $16.50
    73-152915
Gale has recently made a number of historical titles available, e.g. Maturin M. Ballou's "Notable thoughts about women" (1882, $15.00); Charles F. Carter's "The wedding day in literature and art" (1900, $8.50); Elizabeth Cooper's "The harim and the purdah" (1915, $15.00); Ernest Crawley's "The mystic rose" (1927, $24.00); Cicely Mary Hamilton's "Marriage as a trade" (1909, $9.00); Carl Holliday's "Woman's life in colonial days" (1922, $12.50); Dorothy Margaret Stuart's "The girl through the ages" (1933, $7.00); Helena Swan's "Girls' Christian names"; and Thomas F. Thiselton-Dyer's "Folk-lore of women" (1906, $9.50).

(745) Leonard, Eugenie Andruss, 1888-
The dear-bought heritage.
Univ. of Pennsylvania Press   1965 $15.00   0-8122-7436-9
Many consider this the best general survey of women in Colonial America.

(746) Lerner, Gerda, ed.
Black women in White America; a documentary history.
Pantheon   1972 $12.95; $3.95/pap

Basic Book Collection fiction   85

Anthological collection of documents demonstrating double invisibility. Late 19th- and 20th-century history.

(747) Noyes, Ethel J. R. C.
The women of the Mayflower, & Women of Plymouth Colony.
Gryphon 1921 197p 75-145709 Gale repr. 1971 $10.00

(748) Robertson, Constance Noyes, ed.
Oneida Community; an autobiography, 1851-1876.
Syracuse Univ. Press 1970 364p 75-115417 $11.50
    8156-0069-0
Commune, 1848-1881

(749) Sochen, June
Movers and shakers: American women thinkers and activists, 1900-1970.
Quadrangle 1973 320p index 73-76290 Harper $8.95
    0-8129-0360-9
Her "Herstory; a woman's view of American history" (Alfred, 1974, $5.95/pap) is a chronological survey, 1600-1974. These are both extremely useful.

(750) Spruill, Julia Cherry
Women's life and work in the Southern Colonies.
Univ. of North Carolina Press 1938 426p bib 38-33672
    Norton 1972 repr. $3.45

(751) Wharton, Anne Hollingsworth, 1845-1928
Colonial days and dames
Lippincott 1895 248p 2-5482 Gale repr. $9.50

(752) Woman's Rights Convention, Seneca Falls & Rochester, NY, 1848.
July-August Proceedings Arno repr. 1969 $3.50
    0-405-00117-7
Women Suffrage in America Series. Lenox has reprinted the Proceedings of the Women's Rights Convention held at Akron, Ohio, May 28, 1851 ($8.50).

FICTION

(753) Atwood, Margaret Eleanor, 1940-
Surfacing.
Simon & Schuster 1973 224p 72-86983 $6.96 (Canada:
    McClelland & Stewart)
"... as much as they hate their second class citizenship

(along with the Indians, DPs and mongoloids) women are defined by the reality of the world around them. Even though all the female characters in Margaret Atwood's novels have had a college education and have connections (!) with the CBC, they are still realized in a way which clearly marks them as objects. Think of the heroine (anti-heroine) of <u>Surfacing</u>. She goes to her parents' Northern Ontario wild wood home with a girlfriend and two finks who subject the women to the most disgusting assaults for the sake of some film footage. The men have no real appreciation of the human dimensions of the women, or anyone else. The women are there to be manipulated. But the difference here is that the manipulation is seen by a woman novelist with a woman's sensibilities and her heroine recoils from the assault into almost complete withdrawal. She gradually loses all feeling of relationship with these men and even the other woman because she cannot stand any more of this kind of reality. She has come North to find her identity again, thinking she can find it with her parents who created her being. But they are no longer there for her to find herself. Whether she does find herself or not is not clear, but Atwood shows us the modern woman's nightmare dilemma clearly. The novel is a pilgrim's progress to a final acceptance of dehumanized society. The woman makes her way in it all alone ..." (<u>Emergency Librarian</u> Oct. 1974:7. "Does sex make a difference?!?!?!?; some propositions on Canadian novelists" by Freya Geirsson).

(754) Austen, Jane, 1775-1817
Emma.
Many editions and formats are in-print, including some for children. Emma Woodhouse, spinster-heiress who did not have enough to do, kept house for her father and interfered in others' affairs ... is the way her situation is usually described. Unspoiled and not contaminated by the great world, too. Austen's "Mansfield Park" has the theme of feminine dependence (and independence), is available in Spanish.

(755) Beauvoir, Simone de, 1908-
Les belles images, tr. by Patrick O'Brian.
Putnam 1968 224p 68-12095 $7.50; $3.95/pap
The dust-jacket on this occasion is accurate: this novel reveals the hollowness of life based on the pursuit of the glitter of "les belles images." A sophisticated woman saves her daughter by helping her to find the strength she needs to rise above them. "The problems which plague Laurence must be confronted by every thinking woman who has been

Basic Book Collection fiction   87

dazzled by our consumer civilization"--even if not living in
Paris, employed in the business world and "young and attractive, married to a successful architect; herself an established advertising executive."

(756) Beresford-Howe, Constance
The book of Eve; a novel.
Little 1974 176p 74-5416 $5.95 (Macmillan of Canada)
Eva, in her 60s, leaves her husband to begin living.

(757) Bowen, Elizabeth Dorothea Cole, 1899-1973
Eva Trout; or, changing scenes. S
Knopf 1968 302p 68-12685 $6.95

(758) Brown, Rita Mae
Rubyfruit jungle
Daughters, Inc. 1973 $3.35/pap
Hilarious novel of a female Huck Finn named Molly Bolt.
Her "The hand that cradles the rock" is also well known
(New York Univ. Press, 1971, $4.50).

(759) Bryant, Dorothy
Ella Price's journal; a novel. S
Lippincott 1972 227p $5.95 0-397-00894-5
Middle-aged housewife goes to junior college to discover why
she isn't as happy and satisfied as everyone tells her she
should be.

(760) Buchanan, Cynthia Dee, 1942-
Maiden. S
Morrow 1972 212p 70-163446 $5.95; $1.25/pap Pocket
    Books 0-671-78255-X
Novel being made into a movie by Lily Tomlin; 30-year old
virgin living in a singles apartment says "Our lives are full
of claptrap, and we rarely see ourselves."

(761) Calisher, Hortense, 1911-
Standard dreaming.
Arbor 1972 127p 72-82176 $5.95 0-87795-043-1
A not particularly feminist tale.

(762) The Carpenter (Pseud. for June Arnold)
The cook and the carpenter.
Daughters, Inc. 1973 $3.35/pap
Uses interesting neuter pronouns: "na" signifies either male
or female, and all characters have names that preclude
gender identification. The novel itself was inspired by the

1970 takeover of a building on Fifth Street in New York City's Lower East Side and is the story of a women's commune in Texas.

(763) Cather, Willa Sibert, 1875-1947
A lost lady. HS
Knopf   1973   73-4265 $7.50
Her 1923 novel of "a woman who had a big capacity for love in its physical aspect" has been reissued to commemorate the centennial of her birthday (See #234:355-64).

(764) Colette, Sidonie Gabrielle, 1873-1954
Retreat from love, tr. & intro. by Margaret Crosland.
Bobbs   1974   256p   73-16804 $7.95
The first novel Colette wrote completely on her own; now available in English, it was first published in 1907 as "La Retraite."

(765) Davis, Rebecca Harding
Life in the iron mills, with a biographical interpretation by
    Tillie Olsen.
Feminist Press   1974   176p $2.50   0-912670-05-3
Originally written for the April 1861 issue of Atlantic Monthly, this novella constitutes about half of the book.

(766) Defoe, Daniel, 1661?-1731
Roxana, the fortunate mistress, ed. with an intro. by Jane
    Jack.
Oxford Univ. Press   1964   333p $6.25   0-19-255304-6;
    $2.50/pap   0-19-281046-4
Subtitle: "Or, history of the life and vast variety of fortunes of Mlle de Beleaux, afterwards called the Countess de Winselsheim in Germany, being the person known by the name of the Lady Roxana in the time of Charles II."

(767) Dunn, Nell, 1936-
Talking to women.
International   1965   223p   66-2184 $5.25

(768) Gaines, Ernest J., 1933-
The autobiography of Miss Jane Pittman; a novel.
Dial Press   1971   77-144380 $6.95; $1.25/pap   Bantam
    Q7181
See also "Audiovisuals" part of the Non-Book Resources section. In the Bantam paperback edition on the page following author-biographical information there is a list of Bantam's "Black Studies" books "which deal with various aspects

Basic Book Collection fiction 89

of the Negro and his life": Soledad brother, Adventures of the Negro cowboys, Notes of a native son.... Gaines was raised in Louisiana by a crippled aunt until he was 15 and went out into the world--San Francisco; his agent is a woman. His "Of love and dust" (Dial, 1967, $5.00) says basically that a Southern White male may love a Black woman, but no Black man may under any circumstances make love to a White woman and survive.

(769) Gould, Lois
Necessary objects.
Random 1972 271p 72-26996 $6.95 0-394-46847-3; $1.75/pap 440-06688-175 Dell

(770) Hardy, Thomas, 1840-1928
Tess of the D'Urbervilles; pure woman. HS
Published in 1891; many editions and formats--including high school, critical annotated, college classics, and paperback--are in print.

(771) Hochman, Sandra
Walking papers.
Viking 1971 211p 78-148149 $6.95 0-670-74892-7
A feminist novel of "the wife's side of divorce madness" (Phillip Roth). See also her "Year of the woman" in "Audiovisuals" part of Non-Book section.

(772) Jong, Erica
Fear of flying.
Holt 1973 320p 73-3697 $6.95 0-03-010731-8
Jong's third book, this is her first novel and a good place to start for someone who hasn't read anything by her. She doesn't apologize! It's your loss if you're fussy about language (fearful about flying).

(773) Kaufman, Sue
Falling bodies.
Doubleday 1974 270p 73-83644 $7.95 0-385-05132-8

(774) Klein, Norma
Give me one good reason. HS
Putnam 1973 246p 73-82020 $6.95 0-399-11234-0
A 32-year-old unmarried female decides to have a child. Klein's numerous children's books are useful. Her conversion to novel form of a journal is outstanding: "Sunshine" (Avon, 1974, $1.50/pap).

(775) Lagerlof, Selma, 1858-1940
The treasure.
Daughters 1973 repr.
First published in 1904; author a Nobel Prize winner in literature.

(776) Laurence, Margaret Wemyss, 1926-
A jest of God.
Knopf 1966 240p $5.95; $2.25/pap
Canadian author of several books, this made into the movie, "Rachel, Rachel."

(777) Lawrence, David Herbert, 1885-1930
Women in love.
Viking 1920 $5.75 0-670-77849-4; $1.95/pap
   0-670-00065-5; also Modern Library $2.95
Joyce Carol Oates' "The hostile sun; the poetry of D. H. Lawrence" (Black Sparrow, 1973, $3.00/pap) may be of interest to Lawrence and Oates fans.

(778) Lessing, Doris May, 1919-
Children of violence.
Simon & Schuster 2v 1964-6 64-22405 v1 $7.50, v2
   $6.95
A series of novels which includes "Martha Quest," "A popular marriage," "A ripple from the storm," and "Landlocked," this is often referred to as Lessing's masterwork.

(779) Mertz, Barbara Gross
Greygallows [by] Barbara Michaels.
Dodd 1972 279p $6.95
A gothic novel.

(780) Moore, Brian, 1921-
I am Mary Dunne; a novel.
Viking 1968 217p $4.95 0-670-38966-8
Canadian writer sensitive to the need to portray independent female characters in his novels.

(781) Mortimer, Penelope
The home.
Random 1971 258p 77-179305 $5.95 0-394-47306-X;
   $.95/pap Curtis
When a middle-aged woman's marriage breaks up and she thinks she's going to become an autonomous person ... she finds it's just not possible.

Basic Book Collection fiction   91

(782) Munro, Alice, 1913-
Lives of girls and women; a novel.
McGraw 1972 250p 72-1124 $6.95 0-070044043-3
Growing up in the 40's.

(783) Nin, Anaïs
Ladders to fire.
Swallow 1959 $3.50; $2.00/pap

(784) Oates, Joyce Carol, 1938-
Do with me what you will.
Vanguard 1973 563p 73-83039 $7.95 0-8149-0750-4
Novel won National Book Award.

(785) O'Brien, Edna
Night.
Knopf 1973 179p 72-2257 $5.95

(786) O'Donnell, Lillian
Dial 577--R-A-P-E.
Putnam 1974 182p 73-93739 $5.95 399-11317-7
O'Donnell is a woman writer of mysteries about strong women. See also her "The phone calls" and "Don't wear your wedding ring" (Putnam, $4.95).

Perkins, D. M. "Deep throat; a novel" SEE #365.

(787) Phillips, David Graham
Susan Lennox; her fall and rise (a novel).
Several repr. of this 1910 novel are in print, for example, a 2v American Authors Series set ed. by Abe C. Ravitz, pub. by Garrett Press in 1970. ($41.95 0-512-00565-6.)
Phillips was honored as a leading feminist fiction writer, assassinated in 1911 by a man who thought he was out to destroy the ideal of gracious womanhood. Reviews of his books provide fascinating extracts of contemporary comment --his "Husband's story" (1910) was branded as "... incurable vulgarity ..." (Dial 49:289). See "Book Review Digest" volumes circa 1910.

(788) Piercy, Marge
Small changes.
Doubleday 1973 562p 72-96253 $8.95 0-385-05666-4
An interesting exchange took place on the occasion of Lucy Rosenthal's Ms. review (September 1973:29-31), which was contested by Phyllis Chesler (November 1973:8, 12):
"... powerful and wonderful combination of poetry, passion,

and politics. It is the first novel about the lives of American feminists." She then analyzes the reasons for a negative review, even in Ms. "We are too used to 'weak, tragic' women in fiction. Piercy's heroines are experienced as threatening. Female heroines portrayed with sympathy are always better received." She points out that "women's books"--like Blacks, Puerto Ricans, Indians--are all seen the same, they look alike, interchangeable.

(789) Quist, Susan
Indecent exposure.
Walker 1974 176p 73-90378 $6.95 0-8027-0441-7

(790) Radcliffe, Ann, 1764-1823
Gothic romance novel genre was established by Ms. Radcliffe. In print is her "Novels," a 1971 repr. of the 1824 ed. (Adler, $30.80).

(791) Roiphe, Anne
Long division.
Simon & Schuster 1972 72-83905 $5.95 671-21363-6;
    $1.25/pap Crest

(792) Roy, Gabrielle
The road past Altamont ...; tr. from French by Joyce
    Marshall.
Harcourt 1966 146p 66-22286 $3.95 0-15-177868-X
Originally published in French in Canada; four chapters in a woman's life, linked by the philosophical theme of the meaning of change.

(793) Schreiner, Olive, 1855-1920
From man to man; or, Perhaps only ...; with introd. by
    S. C. Cronwright-Schreiner.
New York and London 1927 463p $22.50 repr. by John-
    son 0-384-54278-6
Schreiner has long been recognized as the first major South African writer exploring the experiences of young women in a world dominated by men. Another of her novels now made available by Johnson reprint is "Undine ..." (1928/1972, $17.50).

(794) Schweitzer, Gertrude
Before honor.
Doubleday 1974 312p 73-83669 $6.95
Deborah Fletcher, assistant minister.

Basic Book Collection fiction

(795) Shockley, Ann Allen
Loving her; a novel.
Bobbs-Merrill 1974 187p 73-13226 $6.95 0-672-51835-X
Black & White lesbiana.

(796) Shulman, Alix Kates
Memoirs of an ex-prom queen; a novel.
Knopf 1972 274p $6.95 0-394-47156-3

(797) Smedley, Agnes
Daughter of earth.
Feminist Press 1973 432p 72-14442 $8.00
    0-912670-10-4; $3.00/pap 0-912670-11-8
A semi-autobiographical chronicle, first published by Coward-McCann in 1929, in novel-like form accompanied by material by Paul Lauter.

(798) Spark, Muriel
The prime of Miss Jean Brodie. S
Lippincott 1962 187p 62-7182 $3.95; $.75/pap Dell
Ms. Spark is probably best known for this story whose title translated into Spanish becomes The spring of an old maid.

(799) Stead, Christina
The man who loved children; intro. by Randall Jarrell.
Holt 1940 527p 65-10128 $1.25/pap Bard. Avon.
Cisler describes this as an "excruciating portrait of a family in pre-War Washington--the bullying child-father is a negative archetype, the mother one awful extreme to which a woman can be brought."

(800) Stern, Richard Gustave, 1928-
Other men's daughters.
Dutton 1973 244p 73-79545 $6.95 0-525-17245-9

(801) Uhnak, Dorothy
Law and order.
Simon & Schuster 1973 512p 72-14250 $8.95
    671-21505-1
Best-selling novel by ex-policewoman and winner of New York Police Department honors.

(802) Wilson, Ethel
Swamp angel.
Toronto: McClelland & Stewart 1954 158p. NY: Harper
    215p 54-9003. $1.95/pap New Canadian Library

(803) Zola, Emile, 1840-1902
Nana. S
Many editions and formats, including high school level and paperback, are in print, e.g. pocket edition French and English Classics Series (Penguin, 1970, $2.65/pap).

SHORT STORIES (COLLECTIONS)

(804) Bambara, Toni Cade
Gorilla, my love.
Random 1972 177p 72-4091 $5.95

(805) Dinesen, Isak, pseud. (Karen Blixen), 1885-
Seven Gothic tales. S
Smith & Haas 1934 Modern Library $2.95; $1.95/pap
   Vintage
See also "Portrait of a modern woman" in "Audiovisuals" part of Non-Book section.

(806) Freeman, Mary Wilkins
The revolt of mother and other stories, with an Afterword
   by Michele Clark.
Feminist Press 1973 224p $3.50 0-912670-18-5

(807) Grau, Shirley Ann
The wind shifting west.
Knopf 1973 247p 73-7290 $6.95

(808) Katz, Naomi and Nancy Milton, eds.
Fragment from a lost diary and other stories: women of
   Asia, Africa, and Latin America.
Pantheon 1974 352p 73-7014 $10.00 0-394-48475-4
Short stories and poems.

(809) Lessing, Doris May, 1919-
The habit of loving.
Crowell c1957/1974 311p $6.95 0-690-00501-6
17 reprinted stories first collected in 1957.

(810) Lispector, Clarice
Family ties (Lacos de familia), tr. & with intro. by Gio-
   vanni Pontiero.
Univ. of Texas 1973 156p 72-412 $5.75
Originally published in Brazil in 1960.

(811) Manley, Seon and Gogo Lewis, comps.
Mistresses of mystery, two centuries of suspense stories by

Basic Book Collection fiction   95

   the gentle sex. HS
Lothrop 1973 220p 72-12377 $4.95
Companion volume to their "Ladies of horror; two centuries of supernatural stories by the gentle sex" (Lothrop, 1971, $5.95).

(812) Mansfield, Katherine, 1888-1923
The short stories of Katherine Mansfield; intro. by J.
   Middleton Murry. S
Knopf 1937 688p $6.95
Murry was her husband.

(813) Oates, Joyce Carol, ed.
Scenes from American life; contemporary short fiction.
Vangard 1973 73-83040 $6.95
Her "Wheel of love and other stories" (Vangard, 1970, $6.95) and "Marriages and infidelities; short stories" (Vangard, 1972, $7.95) are also recommended.

(814) O'Brien, Edna
A scandalous woman & Other stories.
Harcourt 1974 168p 74-7366 $6.95

(815) O'Neill, William Laurence, comp.
Women at work, including The long day; the story of a New
   York working girl, by Dorothy Richardson, & Inside the
   New York Telephone Company, by Elinor Langer.
Quadrangle 1972 $10.00; $2.95/pap

(816) Owens, Rochelle
Futz and What came after.
Random 1961 235p 68-18263 $2.45/pap 0-394-42592-8
The string game, Futz, Belch, Istanboul, and Home.

(817) Paley, Grace, 1922-
Enormous changes at the last minute.
Farrar 1974 208p 73-87691 $6.95 0-374-14851-1

(818) Parker, Dorothy Rothschild, 1893-1967
Collected stories.
Modern Library 1942 $2.95

(819) Rascoe, Judith
Your, and mine.
Atlantic-Little, Brown 1973 $6.95

(820) Schneiderman, Beth Kline, ed.
By and about women; an anthology of short fiction.

Harcourt 1973 337p 72-96987 $3.95/pap 0-15-505665-4
Modern short stories in English.

(821) Schulman, L. M.
A woman's place; an anthology of short stories. HS
Macmillan 1974 264p 73-8575 $5.95 0-02-781420-3

(822) Spinner, Stephanie, ed.
Feminine plural; stories by women about growing up. HS
Macmillan 1972 264p 76-187798 $5.95
Each author details an aspect of a girl learning "her place" in a man's world. Carson McCullers, Doris Lessing, Colette, Shirley Ann Grau, Katherine Anne Porter, R. Prawar Jhabvala, Edna O'Brien, Kay Boyle, Tillie Olsen, and Flannery O'Connor.

(823) Stein, Gertrude, 1874-1946
Fernhurst, Q.E.D., & other early writings. S
Liveright 1971 214p 71-148663 $7.95 0-87140-532-6

(824) Walker, Alice
In love and trouble; stories of Black women. HS
Harcourt 1974 160p 73-7607 $6.50 0-15-144405-6
See #603.

(825) Wharton, Edith Newbold Jones, 1862-1937
The ghost stories of ...; illus. by Laszlo Kubinyi.
Scribner's $8.95
Last issued as a whole in 1947 with the title, "Ghosts."

(826) Women; feminist stories by nine new authors, with a
    photographic essay. Hand & Leaf Book 4.
Eakins Press 1972 146p 70-183717 $5.95; $2.50/pap
Mildred Barker, Sylvia Berkman, Elizabeth Fisher of Aphra, Susan Griffin, Margaret Lamb, Helen Neville, Irini Nova, Mary Rouse, May Swenson; photographs by Mariette Ollier.

NON-BOOK RESOURCES

PAMPHLETS

The following publications have been grouped in a category called "pamphlets," which will be undefined. They have been arranged within the following subject areas, within which they are alphabetical by author or sponsor when known, otherwise by title:

Abortion see CONTRACEP-
TION
AFFIRMATIVE ACTION
Ageism see OLDER WO-
MEN, AGEISM
Athletics see SPORTS, ATH-
LETICS, SELF-DEFENSE
BIBLIOGRAPHY
Black Woman see RACE
BUSINESS MANAGEMENT--
WOMEN IN
CANADIANA
Chicana see LATINA
CHILD CARE
CONSCIOUSNESS-RAISING
CONTRACEPTION (incl.
Abortion)
Day Care see CHILD CARE
Equal Employment see AF-
FIRMATIVE ACTION
DIRECTORIES
HEALTH
INTERNATIONAL
LA LATINA
THE LAW
LESBIANA
LIBRARIANS, LIBRARIAN-
SHIP
MEDIA
MISCELLANEOUS
OLDER WOMEN, AGEISM
POLITICS
RACE
RELIGION, BIBLES, THE
CHURCH
Self-defense see SPORTS,
ATHLETICS, SELF-
DEFENSE
SEXISM IN EDUCATION &
MEDIA (including Re-
sources as well as docu-
mentation)
SONGBOOKS, MUSIC,
SONGS
SPORTS, ATHLETICS,
SELF-DEFENSE
U.S. GOVERNMENT AS A
SOURCE
WOMEN'S STUDIES

Sources of pamphlets can be identified by references to the sources listed in both <u>Womanhood Media</u> and this <u>Supplement</u>. Feminist groups rely on pamphlets and newsletters to communicate in print, and the pamphleteer has historically been a movement leader. Some pamphlet-sources within or close to the Movement are:

"Alternatives in Print, 3d ed." (#320, Basic Book Collection)
Feminist Press
Green Mountain Series (Feminist Press)
KNOW
National Organization for Women
New England Free Press
New Moon Communications
Pathfinder Press
Public Affairs Committee
Shameless Hussy Press
Times Change Press
U.S. Dept. of Labor Women's Bureau
Women's Health & Abortion Project Pamphlet Series.

AFFIRMATIVE ACTION

Betsy Hogan Associates. "Step by step; affirmative action for women." $2.50

City University of New York. Chancellor's advisory committee on the status of women at the CUNY. "The status of women at the City University of New York; a report to the Chancellor by Katherine M. Klotzburger. Dec. 1972." $2.50 (535 East 80 St., New York, NY 10021). Available from KNOW, #X1000, $3.00.

McAllester, Susan, ed. "A case for equity: women in English departments." #00652 1971 $1.75 National Council of Teachers of English.

Morgan, Ellen. "Comfort me with apples; a hard-core action handbook on achieving equity for women in academe" 1973 Contact national NOW office. $2.00 non-members. ("Neo-feminism and modern literature" is Ms. Morgan's as yet-unpublished dissertation; 28 Cranbury Rd., Princeton Junc., NJ 08540.)

Municipal Women's Project, Boston. "Sex discrimination; how do you know when it's happening to you?"

National Council of Administrative Women in Education. "Wanted--more women." 1973 $2.50 from the Council; also available from ERIC.

National Council of Teachers of English, Committee on the Role and Image of Women in the Council and the Profession. "Guidelines for confronting attitudes that penalize women," free.

National Federation of Business & Professional Women's Clubs, Inc. "BPW Highlights," e.g. information sheet on Talent Bank (1970).

Pamphlets

National Organization for Women, E. Mass. Chapter. "Sex discrimination in employment; what to know about it, what to do about it, 2nd ed." 1973 $3.00

Shulman, Carol. "Affirmative action; women's rights on campus" 1973 $2.00 from ERIC.

U.S. Citizens' Advisory Council on the Status of Women. "Women in 1970" March 1971. 0-1971-420-805 $.40 / "Women in 1971" Jan. 1972. 0-484-789 $.40 / "Women in 1972" March 1973. 0-543-757(23) $1.10.

U.S. Equal Employment Opportunity Commission. "7th annual report, (1972)." 1973 0-506-531 $.70 @ GPO Bookstore; $.95.

──────. "Affirmative action and equal employment; a guidebook for employers." 2v 1973-729 517/1068 & 1069 I-3. Request from EEOC Office of Voluntary Programs in Washington, D.C. or your regional office.

Women's Action Alliance. "Tools for the elimination of sex discrimination in state and local governments" $1/individuals; $3/institutions.

BIBLIOGRAPHY (see also each individual subject section)

Barabas, Jean. "Women; their educational and career roles; an annotated bibliography of selected ERIC references." Urban Disadvantaged Series #31. August 1972. ERIC ED 067 123; MF $.65 HC $3.29 [note: these ERIC documents are more fully described and abstracted in the Fall 1973 issue of Women Studies Abstracts].

Business & Professional Women's Foundation. "Career counseling: new perspectives for women and girls; a selected annotated bibliography." 1972 $.50

Cheda, Sherrill, comp. "Women; a selected annotated bibliography. Prep. for Women's Day, Canadian Library Assoc. Annual Conference, Winnipeg, Manitoba, June 1974." Canadian Library Assoc., 151 Sparks, Ottawa, Ont., KIP 5E4, or Ms. Cheda.

Cisler, Lucinda. "Women; a bibliography, 6th ed." 1970 KNOW.

DuPont, Julie A. "Women--their social and economic status; selected references." Dept. of Labor Library. 1970 ERIC ED 049-371; MF $.65 HC $3.29.

Eichler, Margrit. "An annotated selected bibliography of bibliographies on women." 1973. $1.00 prepaid from Publications

Office, Assoc. of Universities & Colleges of Canada, 151 Slater, Ottawa, Ontario KIP 5N1.

Freeman, Leah. "The changing role of women; a selected bibliography, revised edition." 1972 California State University, Sacramento 95819, Library's Bibliographic Series #9.

Harmon, Linda A. "Status of women in higher education, 1963-1972; a selective bibliography." 1972. #2 Iowa State University Series in bibliography #2. ERIC ED 070-384; MF $.65 HC $6.58. (Also The Library, Att. Photo Duplication Center, Ames, IA 50010.)

PM2 Women's Liberation; a bibliography. c/o B. Broedel, 308 S. McComb, Tallahassee, FL 32301. Florida Free Press.

Rowbotham, Sheila, comp. "Women's liberation and revolution; a bibliography." Published by Falling Wall Press. $1.00 from Feminist Press.

Salzer, Elizabeth & Hannah B. Applebaum. "A selected bibliography of books on women in the libraries of SUNY @ Albany." 1972. $1.00 Bibliographic Services, Reference Dept., Library, SUNY, Albany, 2400 Washington Ave., Albany, NY 12222. Also ERIC ED 072-795; MF $.65 HC $9.87.

Sense and Sensibility Collective. "Women and literature; an annotated bibliography of writers, 2nd rev. ed. expanded." c1973. $1.25 From the Collective.

Sociologists for Women in Society. "Current research on sex roles, 3d ed." 1973. $1/students, $2/others. From Carol S. Weisman, 505 W. University Pkwy., Baltimore, MD 21210.

Witterberg University Information Services. "Women; a selected bibliography, rev." 1973. $2.00 (Springfield, OH 45504).

Wollter, Patricia. "50 years after the 19th Amendment; a bibliography on the elusive struggle for Women's Liberation." 1971. Sonoma State College Library, Rohnert Park, CA 94928.

Women's History Research Center. "Bibliographies on women; indexed by topic." 1973 $2.00.

BUSINESS MANAGEMENT--WOMEN IN

Bellevan, Margareth. "Women executives and managers--a present and future challenge." 1971 Fairleigh Dickinson University thesis. Ms. Bellevan, H2, The Meadow, Clifton, NJ 07012.

Pamphlets

Business & Professional Women's Foundation. "Women executives; a selected annotated bibliography." 1970 $.50

Council on Economic Priorities. "Shortchanged; women and minorities in banking." Elizabeth Sapery, co-director of study. 1972. Ms. S., 456 Greenwich St., New York, NY 10013.

Durkin, Jon J. "The potential of women." c1971 Human Engineering Laboratory, 347 Beacon St., Boston, MA 02116.

Kahne, Hilda. "Women in management: strategy for increase." 1974 $.50. From Business & Professional Women's Foundation.

CANADIANA (see also: Marylee Stephenson's "Women in Canada" [#429 Basic Book Collection], Items beginning with Canada..., and Status of Women Commissions, both within Directory of Sources section)

Canadian Association for Adult Education. "What's in it; a study guide for nation-wide circulation and discussion." 1971. National Council of Women, Ottawa.

Canadian Government Bibliography of Royal Commissions on the Status of Women in Canada, December 1968. Desjarins and Kaplansky.

Communique: Canadian Studies, Volume 1, no. 2, December 1974. 18-page issue devoted to Women's Studies. Association of Canadian Community Colleges. Association des Colleges Communautaires du Canada, 1750 Finch Ave. E., Willowdale, Ontario M2N 5T7.

Harrison, Cynthia. "Women in Canada 1965 to 1972; a bibliography." 1972 $2.00 McMaster University Library Press, Mills Memorial Library, Hamilton, Ontario.

Status of Women in Canada, 1973. #CP32-1 7/972. Information Canada, Ottawa. [Ways in which the federal government is implementing recommendations of the Report of the Royal Commission on the Status of Women.]

Whaley, Sara Stauffer & Margrit Eichler. "A bibliography of Canadian and United States resources on women." $1.50 from Women Studies Abstracts.

CHILD CARE

Bergstrom, Joan. "A model for quality day care [; a summary of research by Dr. Bergstrom]" 1972 $.25 Business & Professional Women's Foundation.

Greenleaf, Phyllis Taube. "Liberating young children from sex roles; experiences in day-care centers, play groups, and free schools." $.40 New England Free Press.

Hallett, Kathryn J. "Single parent manual" 1973 $1.25 From Ms. H., 1005 Dunn Rd., Florissant, MO 63031.

League of Women Voters. "Day care; who needs it?" $.35 The League.

U.S. Dept. of Labor. Women's Bureau. "Day care facts, pam 16 (rev) 1973 USGPO: 1973 512-378-1304. By Annie L. Hart and Beatrice Rosenberg, with assistance of Pearl G. Spindler."

Women's Action Alliance. "How to organize a child care center." Individuals/$1.00, institutions/$3.00.

CONSCIOUSNESS-RAISING

Allen, Pamela. "Free space; a perspective on the small group in Women's Liberation, 2d ed." 87810-006-7 c1970 $1.25 Times Change Press.

Center for a Woman's Own Name. "Booklet for women who wish to determine their own names after marriage." And supplements. $2.00

Dempewolff, Judy. "56 item-scale to measure attitudes toward the Women's Movement." Ms. Dempewolff, 210 Hullihen Hall, University of Delaware, Newark, DE 19711.

Image. "The answers [what to say to male-chauvinist putdowns]." $1.00. Box 76M, Ms. Magazine, 370 Lexington Ave., New York, NY 10017.

Katz, Linda Sternberg & Anne Roberts. "The rhetoric of the Women's Liberation Movement; consciousness-raising." 1972 ERIC 074-545 MF $.65 HC $3.29

Moberg, Verne. "Consciousness razors." 1973 $.20 each, or $1.00/10+SASE. Feminist Press.

Pamphlets

New York Women's Law Center. "Report on women's right to retain their own names." $.50+SASE from Women's Law Center.

O'Sullivan, Elizabeth. "The relationship of reference groups and self-esteem to women's political interest and opinion leadership." PhD dissertation in progress. Ms. O'Sullivan, School of Public Service, Grand Valley State College, College Landing, Allendale, MI 49401.

Women's Action Alliance. "Guidelines for consciousness-raising." $.50

CONTRACEPTION (including Abortion)

Abortion Rights Association, Inc. "Abortion: A physician's rights and responsibilities." $.25

———. "Abortion: A woman's right." $.25 (Also available in Spanish: "Aborto: Un derecho de la mujer.")

———. Listing of selected New York State Abortion Clinics. $.25

American Public Health Association. "Recommended program guide for abortion services, rev." 1973 Gratis from Director, Population Projects, the Assoc.

Cherniak, Donna, ed. "Birth control handbook." KNOW #236 single copy gratis (include $.16 postage). Also available from the Birth Control/VD Handbook Collective.

Geijerstam, Gunnar K. "An annotated bibliography of induced abortion." 1969 University of Michigan, Center for Population Planning, Ann Arbor, MI 48104.

Gray, J. J. "How to make love, not babies; an egg and sperm handbook." $.45 from the author, Box 7024, Berkeley, CA 94704.

Health organizing collective of New York. Women's Health and Abortion Project. "Vacuum aspiration abortion." KNOW $.20

Liebman, Jan. "How to deal with Right-to-lifers." PO Box 40542, Palisades Station, Washington, DC 20016.

National Organization for Women. New York (City) Chapter. Reproduction & Its Control Committee. "Contraceptive rip-off male-female; a study of comparative prices of contraceptives in

New York area researched and published by the Committee." 47 East 19 St., New York, NY 10003.

Planned Parenthood Federation of America, Inc. "Basal temperature record chart." #900 $.25

_____. "Facts and figures on legal abortion." gratis copy, cost quantities.

_____. "How to take the worry out of being close."

_____. "Modern methods of birth control" #401. $.25 (Also available in Spanish: "Métodos anticonceptivos modernos" #943. SEE ALSO Pamphlets under LATINA for other Spanish-language titles.)

_____. "The safe period" #404. 1965 $.25 (Also available in Spanish: "Método del ritmo" #955.)

_____. "To be a mother ... to be a father" #590. 1967 $.25 (Also available in Spanish: "Ser padre ... ser madre" #951.)

_____. "Voluntary sterilization for men and women" #1108. 1970 $.25 (Also available in Spanish: "Esterilización voluntaria para hombres y mujeres" #1149.)

_____. "What every man should know about birth control" #1041. 1969 $.25 NOTE: Request latest revisions and editions from PPFA.

Planned Parenthood--World Population. "Family planning library manual." 1970 gratis.

_____. "Guide to information sources." 1970 gratis.

_____. "A small library in family planning for the general reader." 1970 gratis.

Smith, Mary. "Birth control and the Negro Woman." #967 1968 $.25 Planned Parenthood Federation of America.

Venceremos Publications. "Birth control; your right to choose." gratis 1969 University Ave., East Palo Alto, CA 94303.

Women's Health & Abortion Project. "Abortion in New York City, 1970-71." (Ask for latest.)

_____. Pamphlets Series.

_____. "Saline abortion."

_____. "Vacuum aspiration abortion."

Pamphlets

DIRECTORIES

Association of Feminist Consultants. "Directory of members, 3d ed." January 1975. Directory coord. Vicki Wengrow.

Barnett, Jean D. "Women; a bibliography of materials [with] Women's groups in Los Angeles, a list comp. by Ann Pettingill." March 1973. J. F. Kennedy Memorial Library, California State University, Los Angeles, CA 90032. SASE.

Beare, Nikki. "Feminist directory of services, first ed. comp. for NOW." 1974 $2.00 From Ms. Beare, 7200 SW 16 Ct., S. Miami, FL 33143 or Judith Meuli, 1126 HiPoint, Los Angeles, CA 90035.

Boston Women's Collective, Inc. "Women's Yellow Pages, 1974 edt." $1.64 includes postage.

Byerly, Carolyn M. "A guide to women's educational opportunities at Western colleges and universities." June 1973 $3.50/pap Western Interstate Commission for Higher Education, PO Drawer P, Boulder CO 80302.

Community Communications Communautaire. "Montreal Women's Yellow Pages" (annual). PO Box 1238, Place d'Armes, Montreal 125, Quebec.

Changes Project. Women's Directory; Changes issue #23, March-April 1973 $.50 2314 Elliot Ave. S., Minneapolis, MN 35404 or The Amazon Bookstore.

Grimstad, Kirsten, et al. "New woman's survival catalog, first edition 1973." PO Box 90, Planetarium Station, New York, NY 10024. $5.00 Also from Coward, McCann & Geohegan.

Modern Language Assoc. Commission on the Status of Women. "Directory of women scholars in the modern languages." $2.50 MLA Publications Center, 62 5 Ave., New York, NY 10011.

HEALTH (see also Contraception)

American Cancer Society. "A breast check ... so simple ... so important." 71-2R-2MM 4/73 No. 2088-LI c1971 Contact local office of ACS or national office, 219 East 42 St., New York, NY 10017. 212-867-3700.

American Nursing Home Association. "Thinking about a nursing home?" gratis ANHA, Box C, 1200 15 St., N.W., Washington, DC 20005.

Barry, Kathleen. "The cutting edge; a look at male motivations in obstetrics and gynecology; a paper." $.75 New Moon Communications.

Bart, Pauline & Diana Scully. "A funny thing happened on the way to the orifice: women in gynecology textbooks." Also "A hard day at the orifice; women in gynecology texts." (Professional papers 1972 and 1973.) Send SASE to Bart, School of Medicine, University of Illinois Medical Center, Chicago, IL 60680, Box 6998.

Birth Control Handbook/VD Handbook Collective. "VD handbook." $.25 The collective, PO Box 1000, Station G, Montreal 130, Quebec.

Campbell, Margaret A., M.D. "Why would a girl go into medicine?"; medical education in the United States: a guide for women. 1973 $3.50 0-912670-339 Feminist Press.

Cargill, Jennifer, comp. "Ohio's women medical specialists." 1973 $.50 10/$4.50 NOW Butler County Chapter. From Cargill, PO Box 15, Oxford, OH 45056.

Cherniak, Donna & Allan Feingold SEE Birth Control Handbook/VD Handbook Collective's "VD handbook" above.

Circle One. "Self-health handbook--guide to beginning gynecological self-help." 1973 $.75 and bulk-rates. From CO, 409 East Fontanero, Colorado Springs, CO 80907.

EdU Press. Adult comic books:
"VD Claptrap," by Sol Gordon. 1972 $.25
"10 heavy facts about sex"
"The eater's digest"
"Protect yourself from becoming an unwanted parent," by Sol Gordon. c1973
"Drug youse survivor's handbook," by Roger Conant. c1972
From EdU Press, 760 Ostrom Ave., Syracuse, NY 13210.

Ehrenreich, Barbara and Deirdre English. "Complaints and disorders: the sexual politics of sickness." 1973 0-912670-20-7 $1.50 Feminist Press.

_____. "Witches, midwives, and nurses--a history of women healers." 1972 $1.25 0-912670-13-4 Feminist Press.

Feminist Women's Health Centers. "How to start your own self-help clinic." $2.50

Gilden, Dorothy. "Fact sheet on breast surgery." Feminist Women's Health Center, Los Angeles.

Pamphlets

Haire, Doris. "The cultural warping of childbirth." $.75 from her at 251 Nottingham Way, Hillside, NJ 07205. (Also ask about her publication, "Implementing family-centered maternity care with a central nursery.")

Joint Commission on Accreditation of Hospitals. "An accredited long-term care facility." Gratis from JCAH, 875 North Michigan Ave., Chicago, IL 60611.

_____. "Standards for long term care facilities, revised edition." $1.75

Kitzinger, Sheila. "Intercourse during pregnancy and in the puerperium." National Childbirth Trust Teacher's Broadsheet #2, 1967. Distributed in U.S.A. by Boston Assoc. for Childbirth Education, Box 29, Newtonville, MA 02160.

_____. "An approach to antenatal teaching." National Childbirth Trust.

Lang, Raven. "Birth book." $5.00 Genesis Press, PO Box AJ, Cupertino, CA 95014.

New Moon Communications. "The witch's OS." (History of the self-help movement.) $2.00

Reynard, Muriel Joyce. "Gynecological self-help; an analysis of its impact on the delivery and use of medical care for women." (Thesis). Health Sciences Center, School of Allied Health Professions, SUNY, Stonybrook, NY. Xerox copy $6.00 from Reynard at Nassau/Suffolk Regional Medical Program., Inc., 1919 Middle Country Rd., Centereach, NY 11720.

Santa Cruz Home Birth Center. "The birth book; a feminist childbirth manual; with references to clinics and MD's offering 'enlightened woman-centered care'." $4.20 Box 142, Orinda, CA 94563.

Student Assoc. for the Study of Hallucinogens (STASH) Library. "Women and drug use; an annotated bibliography." $.50 Susan Christenson, STASH Librarian, 638 Pleasant St., Beloit, WI 53511.

U.S. Dept. of Health, Education & Welfare. "Report of the Women's Action Program." GPO 922-425 Jan. 1972. Foreword by Eliot Richardson. Not available from U.S. Government Printing Office; demand direct to issuing agency: Washington, DC 20201.

_____. National Institute of Mental Health. "Facts about: group therapy." HE20.2402.T34 S/N 1724-0256. 1972 $.10

_____. Public Health Service, Communicable Disease Center, VD Branch, Atlanta, GA. "Syphillis; a synopsis."

Weiss, Kay. "DES and the epidemiology of vaginal cancer and adenosis." $2.25 from Advocates for Medical Information, 2120 Bissonet, Apt. B, Houston, TX 77005.

West Coast Sisters. "How to start a self-help clinic." $2.50 from Feminist women's health center, Los Angeles.

Women in Psychology. "Feminist therapist roster, comp. by Annette M. Brodsky." #17007 $.70 from KNOW.

Women's right to health; phases of her life packet--for audience of 150 persons on low budget; kit including sample letters, program, content, moderator's role, publicity, refreshments.... $2.50 from Baltimore County NOW Health Task Force, PO Box 21, Sunshine Ave., Kingville, MD 21087.

INTERNATIONAL (see also Canadiana)

Center for Women's Studies and Services, San Diego. "International Women's Day." $.10

Indochina Peace Campaign. "Women under torture." 1973 $.25. The Campaign, 181 Pier Ave., Santa Monica, CA 90405.

UNITAR. "The situation of women in the United Nations; research report no. 18." $3.00 801 UN Plaza, New York, NY 10017.

United Nations Declaration on Women's Rights. (Text) SEE New York Times Nov. 8, 1967:24; Reference Shelf Jan. 1972 (p. 217 of Womanhood Media), and other reference sources. Known as Declaration on the Elimination of Discrimination Against Women.

UNESCO. Commission on the Status of Women, 25th session. "Influence of mass communication media on the formation of a new attitude towards the role of women in present-day society; report of the Secretary-General (Item 7 on the provisional agenda. Original; English)." 74-00755, Jan. 10, 1974. (Note: Only Austria stressed need for more action-oriented resolution!)

United States. Dept. of Health, Education & Welfare. "Women and social security; law and policy in five countries, by Dalmer Hoskins and Lenore E. Bixby." Social Security Adm. Research rep. no. 42. S/N 1770-00108. HE.3.49:42. 1973 $.75 (Belgium, Federal Republic of West Germany, France, Great Britain, and the U.S.A.)

Pamphlets

Whaley, Sara Stauffer. "A cross-national review of studies on the status of women; prepared for delivery at the 1973 annual meeting of the American Political Science Association. New Orleans, LA, Jung Hotel, Sept. 6, 1973 [with bibliography]." c1973 A.P.S.A. Contact Ms. Whaley, c/o Women Studies Abstracts.

Women. "Women [; a collection of articles by women around the world on women's movements in their countries]." 1973 $1.50 from Women.

Women's International Network (WIN). "International women's directory, Fran P. Hosken, coordinator." In process circa Summer 1974. Contact Ms. Hosken, 187 Grant, Lexington, MA 02173.

LA LATINA

Abortion Rights Association, Inc. "Aborto: Un derecho de la mujer." $.25

American Library Association. Adult Services Division. Subcommittee on Spanish Materials. "Suppliers of Spanish-Language materials, compiled under a Title II-B grant of Higher Education Act, with cooperation of the Dept. of Library Science, Library Materials for Minority Groups Institute, Queens College, Flushing, New York." nd. Queens College, Flushing, NY 11367.

Castro, Fidel and Linda Jenness. "Women and the Cuban Revolution." 87348-177-1 1970 $.35 Pathfinder Press.

Duran, Pat Herrera. "The Chicana; a bibliographic study." 1973 ERIC 076-305 $.65 MF, $3.29 HC.

National Organization for Women. Central New Jersey Chapter. Employment Task Force. "La discriminación sexual en el trabajo." The Task Force, Box 2163, Princeton Junction, NJ 08540. $.50 to help cover costs; indicate Spanish, or English, or both versions.

Women's Action Alliance. "Directory of national women's organizations." (Includes Spanish-speaking women.) $.50

THE LAW

Boalt Hall Women's Association. "Guide to California law schools."

———. "How to apply to law school."

———. "Wanted by the law: Women (general information)." Boalt Hall Women's Association, University of California, Berkeley, School of Law, Berkeley, CA 94720. $.50 each or $1.25 for the above pamphlets.

Boyer, Gene. "Are women equal under the law?" $1.00 218 Front St., Beaver Dam, WI 53916.

Eisenberg, Sue & Pat Micklow. "The assaulted wife: 'Catch 22' revisited." 1974. University of Michigan Law School, Ann Arbor, MI 48104.

Epstein, Cynthia Fuchs. "Women and professional careers; the case of the woman lawyer." PhD dissertation, Columbia University 1968.

Greene, Roberta. "Til divorce do you part, 2d ed." $1.75 KNOW.

Knowles, Marjorie Fine. "Cases and materials on women and the law." $2.50 Feminist Press. (Updates and supplements #131, Basic Book Collection.)

Michigan Women's Task Force on Rape. "Rape Law Reform" (subject-packet). $2.00

National Lawyers Guild. "How to do your own divorce." $.10

———. "Marriage? You lose." $.05

National Organization for Women, San Francisco, CA Chapter. "Women and credit; NOW's Credit Discrimination Committee research." $.55, 12/$6.00. From Michelle D. Stratton, 546 11 Ave., San Francisco, CA 94118.

Penne, Mary Jo. "Women's rights booklet [; legal rights for women in Minnesota--rights they have and do not have]." Ms. Penne, 1926 Nicollet Ave., Minneapolis, MN 55403.

Sherman, Charles E. "How to do your own divorce in California, with the forms you will need to do it." 1971. $4.95. Nolo Press, Box 2147, Station A, Berkeley, CA 94709.

Women in Transition, Inc. "Women's survival manual; a feminist handbook on separation and divorce." 1972 $3.00 KNOW.

Women United. "Is a woman a person?"

———. "Women and the draft; what does 'equal rights' mean?"

Women's Organizations for Employment. "The women's job rights handbook." c1974 $1.50.

Pamphlets

LESBIANA

ALA SRRT Task Force on Gay Liberation. "A gay bibliography, 3rd revision." 1974.

ALTA. "Burn this and memorize yourself; poems for women. Photographs by Ellen Shumsky." 87810-012-1 $.50 Times Change Press.

_____. "Letters to women." Shameless Hussy Press.

_____. "Poems." 1971 $.65 KNOW.

American Civil Liberties Union. "ACLU Statement on homosexuality, August 31, 1967."

Copely, Ursula Enters, ed. "1973 directory of homosexual organizations and publications, 2nd rev. edition." $2.00 from Homosexual Information Center.

Daughters of Bilitis. "Gay is good for us all." Also: "Who will set the female homosexual free?" $.10 each from Boston DOB.

"The girls' guide--1974 [700 listings, 20 countries]." $5.00 The Girls' Guide, 115 New Montgomery, San Francisco, CA 94105. By mail only.

Homosexual Information Center, Los Angeles. "A selected bibliography of homosexuality, 5th edition." Gratis. SEE ALSO Copely, above.

Hunter, Rebecca. "Proud 'n queer; a collection of poems by Lesbians." $.45 from Hunter at 411 Lathrop, River Forest, IL 60305.

The Ladder (serial). "The Lesbian in literature (a bibliography)." $4.25. New edition in 1975: $7.50.

Martin, Del & Phyllis Lyon. "Lesbian love and liberation." 1973 $1.95 Multi media resource center.

National Institute of Mental Health. "Final report of the Task Force on Homosexuality." 1969. SEE U.S. Dept. of Health, Education & Welfare, National Institute....

National Organization for Women. "NOW literature--sexuality and Lesbianism. Resolution 144 of NOW national conference, Feb. 1973." $.15 from National NOW Gay Task Force, 80 5 Ave., New York, NY 10011.

U.S. Dept. of Health, Education & Welfare. National Institute of Mental Health Task Force on Homosexuality. "Final report and background papers, ed. by John M. Livingood" 1972 S/N 1724-0244 HE20.2402:H75/2 $.75. Includes the final report of the Task Force, which was released in 1969, and 7 specially-prepared background papers, 5 of which are published for the first time. Some of the Task Force members were outstanding behavioral, medical, social, and legal scientists. Single courtesy copies of NIMH publications may be requested from Publications Distribution Office, Room 1, B 64, 5600 Fishers Lane, Rockville, MD 20852.

Winant, Fran. "We are all Lesbians; poetry anthology." 1973 $2.00 Violet Press.

LIBRARIANS, LIBRARIANSHIP (see also Dickinson's "Statement..." in Sexism in Education & Media, Planned Parenthood-World Population Contraception pamphlets; and "Women in Library management" in Audiovisual section of this book).

Blake, Fay M., PhD., an Instructor for several years at the University of California, Berkeley, School of Librarianship, Berkeley, CA 94720, has offered a Women's Studies-type course. Contact her for information.

Cheda, Sherrill. "That special little mechanism; paper presented at the Canadian Library Association. Annual conference Theme Day, June 20, 1973. Mount Allison College, Sackville, N.B."

_____. "Women in the library profession [; a bibliography]." Seneca College Library, June 1973.

Hammerstein, Gretchen. "Bibliography on women in library management." Contact her c/o Connecticut Women in Libraries.

Lipow, Anne, et al. "A report on the status of women employed in the Library of the University of California, Berkeley, with Recommendations for affirmative action." Library Affirmative Action Program for Women Committee, December 1971. ERIC ED 066-163, MF $.65. (For a report relating to the University of Washington libraries, contact (Ms.) Lynne Rhoads, 4004 Whitman N., Seattle, WA 98103.)

Myers, Margaret, Jennifer Blythin, and Bonita Dawson. "Women in librarianship; a bibliography" orig. comp. by the Women's Liberation Task Force of the Philadelphia SRRT, Nov. 1970; rev. & updated for the ALA-SRRT Task Force on Women, June 1973; updated May 1974 by Margaret Myers and Sara Chrisman; rev. & updated again May 1975. $1.00 + SASE to Ms. Myers, American Library Assoc., 50 E. Huron St., Chicago, IL 60611.

Preconference on the Status of Women in Librarianship; SRRT Task Force on the Status of Women. "Women in a Woman's Profession: strategies; July 4-6, 1974." American Library Assoc. Contact Betty-Carol Sellen, Brooklyn College Library, Brooklyn, NY 11210 for possibility of 6-page list of registrants and Proceedings.

Rhoads, Lynne. SEE Lipow, Anne, above.

Schiller, Anita R. "Characteristics of professional personnel in college and university libraries, revised." 1969. #16 in University of Illinois Graduate School of Library Science Misc. Publications. NOTE: This is one example of Ms. Schiller's several publications in this area; check <u>Library Literature</u>, <u>Women Studies Abstracts</u>, etc. etc.

Swaim, Elizabeth A. (Special Collections Librarian & Archivist, Wesleyan University, Middletown, CT 06457). Untitled testimony re The Grolier Club of New York City before City Commission on Human Rights' public hearing on discrimination by exclusionary-membership, November 13, 1973.

Whaley, Sara Stauffer. "Women & Librarianship," the title of a course which Ms. Whaley has offered at the State University of New York's School of Library & Information Science, Geneseo. Contact her c/o <u>Women Studies Abstracts</u>, Box 1, Rush, NY 14543.

Wheeler, Helen Rippier. "Placement services in accredited library schools; Report of the ALA-SRRT Task Force on the Status of Women in Librarianship. May 1973." MF $.65, HC $3.29. ERIC ED 078-847. NOTE: Other action research areas undertaken by the Task Force during Michelle Rudy's tenure as coordinator, 1972-3, included nepotism; contact Ms. Rudy at 401 Waldron, West Lafayette, IN 47906.

Women's National Book Assoc. New York Chapter. Has carried out action research re sex-discrimination in publishing. See Eastman, Ann Heidbreder under the "Sexism in Education" heading (below) of "Pamphlets."

MEDIA

Adams, Whitney M. "Women in the wasteland fight back; a content analysis study of the image of women in TV programing." Contact Ms. Adams via Association of Feminist Consultants.

American Civil Liberties Union. "Your right to government information; how to use The Freedom of Information Act." $.25 from New York ACLU, which also has "The Bill of Rights"

($.05), "Public television; a question of survival" ($1.00), and "What is the A.C.L.U.?" ($.05).

Association of American Colleges. Project on the Status and Education of Women. "Women and film; a resource handbook" 1973 The Project.

Directory of Women in Media. 1974 Millicent Hodson, Special Events Coordinator, University of California, Berkeley, CA 94720.

Foley, K. Sue & Leeda Marting, comps. "Directory of women in media education [1st edition, 1974]." Gratis. Broadcast Education Assoc., 1717 N St., N.W. Washington, DC 20036, is distributing this and a new edition.

Hart, Lois B. "A feminist looks at educational software materials." c1973 Continuing Education Press of University of Massachusetts, distributed by Everywoman's Center, or contact Ms. Hart, RD 1, Box 627, Belchertown, MA 01007.

Mendenhall, Janice. "Films on the Women's Movement; a list of feminist films for Federal Women's Day." Contact Ms. Mendenhall, General Services Administration, Office for Civil Rights, Washington, DC 20405.

Radio Free People. "The people's tape guide [including a summary of how to make good tape recordings]." $.25

United Methodist Church, Women's Division, New York. "Films on women." 1972.

U.S. Dept. of Labor. "Information, please; a guide to acquiring information from the Department of Labor." L1/7/1: in 3 S/N 2900-00168 1972 $.20.

_____. Women's Bureau. "A guide to sources of data on women and women workers for the United States and for regions, states, and local areas." 1972.

Women's Action Alliance. "How to make the media work for you." $1.50/individuals, $3.00/institutions.

Women's History Research Center, Inc. "Directory of films by and/or about women, 1972; Directory of filmmakers, films, and distributors--internationally, past and present." c1972 $5.00/pap.

MISCELLANEOUS

Borun, Minda, et al. "Women's Liberation; an anthropological view...." 0-912786-19-1 $1.25 KNOW.

Brown, Judith and Beverly Jones. "Toward a female liberation movement ('The Florida Paper')." $.40 New England Free Press.

Carnegie Commission on Higher Education. "Opportunities for women in higher education; report." 1973.

Chicago Women's Liberation Union. "Socialist feminism; a strategy for the women's movement (a position paper adopted by the membership at third annual conference)" (reprinted in The Spokeswoman, Nov. 1, 1972).

Citizens Advisory Council on the Status of Women. "Women" 1973. $1.10.

Cook, Barbara Ivy Wood. "Role aspiration as evidenced in senior women." 1967 Doctoral dissertation, Purdue University. University Microfilms 67-16, 627.

Cornell Conference, Jan. 1969 [on the status of women] ed. by Sheila Tobias. $2.75 KNOW.

DePauw, Linda Grant. "Herstory 1776." American Revolution Centennial Administration.

_____. "Women of New York in the era of the American Revolution." 1974. Produced under the auspices of New York (State) Bicentennial Commission. $1.00. KNOW--part of profits go toward women's Bicentennial activities.

Dodson, Betty. "Liberating masturbation, illustrated." $3.00 Ms. Magazine.

Eclectic Eve; illustrated interviews with Tor women artists. $3.50 from Sharon Snitman, 9 Caines Ave., Willowdale, Ont.

Flexner, Eleanor. "Women's rights--unfinished business." PAIS Pamphlet #469, 1972. $.25 from New York Public Affairs Committee, Inc.

Fontana, Gloria. "An investigation into the dynamics of achievement motivation in women." University of Michigan, Ann Arbor 48104.

Ford Foundation, Office of Reports. "That 51%; Ford Foundation activities related to opportunities for women." 74-79495 April 1974 320 East 43 St., New York, NY 10017.

Fought, Carol Ann. "The historical development of continuing education for women in the United States: Economic, social and psychological implications." Doctoral dissertation, Ohio State University, 1966. University Microfilms Publication no. 67-2444.

Goldman, Emma, 1869-1940. "The traffic in women; & Other essays on feminism. Foreword by Alix Shulman." 0-87810-001-6 1971 $1.25 Times Change Press.

Gyne, Jocasta. "To Oedipus from Mother." $1.95 Box 377, Piermont, NY 10968.

Hall, Ann Nuree. Thesis will test hypothesis that 'logic of collective action' theory is applicable to a study/explanation of the lack of collective action in the Women's Liberation Movement. An American National Election Study, Virginia Polytechnic Institute and State University. Contact Ms. H, 6200 F. Terrace View Apts., Blacksburg, VA 24060.

Hallet, Kathryn J. "People in crisis." $1.25. Ms. H, 1005 Dunn Rd., Florisant, MO 63031.

Harkness, David J. "Southern heroines of the American Revolution." 1973 $.25/in TN, $1.00/outside TN. Extension Library, University of Tennessee, 420 Communications Blvd., Knoxville, TN 37916.

Hawley, Marjorie Jane. "The relationship of women's perceptions of men's views of the feminine ideal to career choice." Doctoral dissertation, Claremont Graduate School & University Center, 1968. University Microfilms 68-18, 269.

Hayden, Trudy. "Punishing pregnancy; discrimination in education, employment and credit." For the Women's Rights Project of the American Civil Liberties Union. $1.00. From ACLU, New York.

Hedges, Elaine, ed. "Women writing and teaching." #39782, October 1972 College English, $1.50. National Council of Teachers of English.

Heide, Wilma Scott. "A feminist perspective of manipulation of woman (Woman includes man)." Presented at November 8, 1973 Symposium of The Genetic manipulation of man, University of Wisconsin, Stevens Point. From NOW Public Information Office, New York.

Jacobsen, Josephine. "From Anne to Marianne; some women in American poetry [a lecture at the US Library of Congress, May 1972, looking at the atmosphere in which American women poets worked]." $.35 U.S. Supt. of Documents, (NOTE: Pub-

lished with another lecture, 'Leftovers.') 1973. LC 1.14:st 1
S/N 3016-00019.

John Hay Whitney Foundation. "Project Second Start." 1973?
Gratis from The Foundation, Time-Life Building, New York, NY
10010.

Loesch, Juli. "Tis the season to be." 0-912786-15-9 $.50
KNOW.

McCormick, Pat. "Volunteerism; what it's all about." $.50
1973 From NOW Task Force on Women & Volunteerism.

Michigan. University. Center for Continuing Education of Women.
"New research on women." 1973. The Center.

Miller, Ruthann, et al. "In defense of the Women's Movement."
#87348-186-0 1970 $.25 Pathfinder Press.

National Lawyers Guild. "Bibliography: Women in prison." $.10

Niland, Janet. "12 steps to non-sexist masculinity; how to be a
lover, husband, and father without fouling up women." $2.00
From Ms. N., 812 Kenyon La., Newark, DE 19711.

Novack, George. "Revolutionary dynamics of Women's Liberation."
#87348-120-8 1970 $.25 Pathfinder Press.

Petesch, Natalie. "The Odyssey of Katinou Kalokovich." 1972.
A novel of which several chapters have been published; author
seeking publisher. Contact her at 3520 Beech Ave., apt. B,
Baltimore, MD 21211.

Political Science Women's Caucus. University of Chicago. "Statement." $.15 from University Women's Association.

Prescott, Suzanne. Survey on the "battered wife syndrome."
From her at Governors State University, Women's Advisory
Board, Park Forest South, IL 60466.

Professional Women's Caucus. "16 reports on the status of professional women, April 1970; reports presented at the organizing conference of the Professional Women's Caucus." $2.75 KNOW.

Rettew, Roslyn. "12 steps to non-sexist masculinity." SEE Niland, Janet.

Seifer, Nancy. "Absent from the majority; working class women in America." Middle America Pamphlet Series. 1973 $1.25.
From National Project on Ethnic America, Institute on Human
Relations, 165 East 56 St., New York, NY 10022 (The American
Jewish Committee).

Shinder, Dorothy. "Mayhem on women." $2.95. San Francisco: Ombudswoman.

Somerville, Mollie, comp. "Women and the American Revolution." 1974. $1.50 from National Society of the Daughters of the American Revolution, 1776 D St., N.W., Washington, DC 20006.

Withers, Jean. "Prostitution--fact and fiction; report based on a three-year study in Seattle." $1.25 ERA Enterprises.

Women's Action Alliance. "An introduction to the Women's Movement; a packet." $2.00/individuals, $4.00/institutions. Includes Reading List, Directory, and Consciousness-raising guidelines, each of which can be ordered separately @ $.75.

Women's Crisis Center, Ann Arbor. "Freedom from rape" gratis for 2 $.10 stamps. Also have an organizing manual: How-to, for $2.00 donation towards their expenses; 5/$7.50.

Women's History Library. Vicki Lynn Hill, Female Artists Project coordinator. "Female artists--past and present, 2nd ed." c1974 $5.00/individual women, $6.00/men, groups, institutions. Women's History Research Center.

Women's Liberation (Detroit, MI). Stop rape. 1973 $1.00 Room 516, 2230 Witherell, Detroit 48201.

Women's Photo Co-Op. "Image nation eleven; photographs by women about women." Published, in Canada, by Coach House Press, $2.00. Distributed in U.S.A. by Light Impressions, Box 3012, Rochester, NY 14614, $2.50.

OLDER WOMEN, AGEISM

Institute of Gerontology. "Women: life span challenges, 26th Annual Conference on Aging (theme), Sept. 10-12, 1973." The Institute, 543 Church, Ann Arbor, MI 48104.

Nader, Ralph Study Group. "Old age: the last segregation-- Ralph Nader's Study Group Report on nursing homes." Citizen Publisher, Inc., P.O. Box 19404, Washington, DC 20036.

National Organization for Women. Task Force on Older Women. "Growing older female." Tish Sommers, 434 66 St., Oakland, CA 94609.

Randolph, Kathryn Scott. "The mature woman in doctoral programs." Doctoral dissertation, Indiana University, 1965. (University Microfilms Publication no. 65-14, 060.)

U.S. Dept. of Health, Education & Welfare. "Facts on aging." 1970 $.30   HE 17.309/A:F   119   S/N 1762-00007.

_____. "Menopause and aging [; summary-report & selected paper from a research conference, Hot Springs, AR, May 23-26, 1971]." 1973 $.85   HE 20.3352:M   52   S/N 1746-00015.

POLITICS

Bibliographic Information Center for the Study of Political Science. "Women in politics; toward a bibliography of bibliographies" #2 in Series of staff bibliographies. $.35 from Robert B. Harmon, Librarian of the Center, 2570 Sue Ave., San Jose, CA 95111.

Center for the American Woman & Politics. "Women state legislators; report from a conference, May 18-21, 1972."   1973 $1.00.

Crater, Flora. "The woman activist campaign handbook, 1973. August 26th commemorative issue."   1974. $1.00 from The Woman Activist (Serial).

Elshtain, Jean Bethke. "Women and politics; a theoretical analysis." (Dissertation). Dept. of Political Science, University of Massachusetts, Amherst, MA 01002.

Hammond, Nancy & Mary Hellman. "The Michigan legislative report, 1971-72." From Michigan Women's Political Caucus.

Hightower, Nikki V. "Women politicians; social backgrounds, self-concepts and sex-role stereotypes." (PhD dissertation in progress).   50 Norwood Rd., Northport, NY 11768.

Kayden, Xandra. "A handbook for women entering politics." $1.00   1572 Mass. Ave., Cambridge, MA 02138.

Lee, Marsha M. "Women in politics and local government." (A paper.) Dept. of Political Science, Rutgers University, New Brunswick, NJ 07102.

Levenson, Rosaline. "Women in government and politics; a bibliography of American and foreign sources."   1973   Council of Planning Librarians' Exchange Bib. #491, PO Box 229, Monticello, IL 61856.

The Majority Wins. "The majority wins; How to build a program for legislative change."   1974 $2.10   Box 954, Lansing, MI 48901.

Paizis, Suzanne. "The political woman's handbook." $2.50. PO Box 943, Aptos, CA 94003.

Waters, Mary-Alice. "The politics of Women's Liberation today." 87348-158-5 1970 $.25 Pathfinder Press.

Women's Action Alliance. "Tools to eliminate discrimination in state and local government." $2.00/individuals, $4.00/institutions. The Alliance.

Women's Organizations for Employment. "Women's job rights handbook." $1.60.

RACE

The Black woman and the Black family. 1972 $1.75. Indiana University Bookstore Mail Order Dept., Bloomington, IN 47401.

Civil Rights Digest. "Sexism and racism: feminist perspectives." Spring 1974 (issue). Gratis, from U.S. Commission on Civil Rights, Washington, DC 20425.

Davis, Lenwood G. "Black women in the cities, 1872-1972; a bibliography of published works on the life and achievements of Black women in cities in the United States." 1972 $5.00 Council of Planning Librarians, PO Box 229, Monticello, IL 61856. Exchange bibliography no. 336.

Indiana University. Library Staff and Afro-American Studies Department. "Black family and the Black woman; a bibliography [of materials in the library]." 1972 $1.74. Indiana University Bookstore Mail Order Dept., Bloomington, IN 47401.

Murray, (Ms.) Jocelyn, comp. "A preliminary bibliography; women in Africa." 1974 gratis. Published under the auspices of Graduate Women in History, University of California, Los Angeles, CA 90024.

Newman, Pamela and Maxine Williams. "Black woman's liberation." Pathfinder Press.

Russell, Valerie. "Racism and sexism, a collective struggle; a minority woman's point of view." 1973 United Church of Christ Task Force on Women in Church and Society. KNOW #231.2.

U.S. Department of Labor. "A study of black male professionals in industry (Manpower research monograph no. 26)." 1973 $.50 L1.39/3:26 S/N 2900-00172.

Pamphlets 121

_____. Women's Bureau. "Facts on women workers of minority races, rev." 1972 $.15 L 36:102:M 66 S/N 2916-0001.

"Women and employment; an annotated bibliography." 1974 SASE to D.C. Public Library, Communications Dept., Room 422, 901 G. St. NW, Washington, D.C. 20001.

RELIGION, BIBLES, THE CHURCH

American Academy of Religion. Working Group on Women and Religion. "Women and religion; 1972, Papers of the Working Group...." $2.00 from Council on the Study of Religion, Waterloo Lutheran University, Waterloo, Ontario.

American Civil Liberties Union, New York. "The military chaplaincy system." $1.00

_____. "The case against parochial aid." $.20

_____. "Public funds for parochial schools?" $.50

Bontrager, Frances. "The church and the single person." 0-8361-1575-9 1969 $.50 Herald Press.

Brit Ha-Nerot (Covenant of Candles); Ceremony for the naming of a Jewish baby girl, created by (Ms.) Mickey and Rabbi Paul Swerdlow. $1.00 to cover postage and printing, from the Swerdlows, 12 Selwyn Dr., Broomall, PA 19008.

Champagne, Emily ed., "N.O.W. Packet: Women and religion." 745 Walker Ave., Oakland, CA 91761.

Church Women United. "The Woman Packet." $1.50.

Farians, Elizabeth. "The double cross: women and religion." Set of her pamphlets $2.50: Justice; the hard line. Phallic worship: the ultimate idolatry. Exorcising the sexual demon. The true myth. The coming of woman; the Christa. Women in the Church NOW (Canon law). Human dignity of women in the Church (recent Papal statements). Status of women in the Church. Women, religion and the law (Civil). Women, ethics and ecology.

_____. "Selected bibliography on women and religion, 1965-1972, 5th rev. ed." 1973. $1.00.

_____. "Women and religion...." SEE her "Selected bibliography...."

Gilliam, Dorothy, comp. "Women and the church; a selective bibliography. Prepared for the Consultation on Women in Theological Education, March 31-April 1, 1973. Union Theological Seminary, Richmond, Virginia." $.50 from The Library, UTS, 3401 Brook Rd., Richmond, VA 23227.

Grailville Conference on Women Doing. "Theology Packet." From Church Women United.

Habonim. "Sisters of exile; sources on the Jewish woman." $2.00. 200 Park Ave., S., New York, NY 10003.

Kirby, Ellen. "Women; over half the earth's people; guide to resources and processes." 1973. $.85. Women's Division, Board of Global Ministries, United Methodist Church, New York.

Kirby, Kathryn. "The status of women in the Church, Vatican II--1968. [Annotated bibliography, unpublished paper]." Department of Library Science, Catholic University of America, Washington, DC 20017.

Koltun, Liz, ed. "The Jewish woman; an anthology." Summer 1973 issue of Response; a contemporary Jewish Review. $2.00 from Response, Box 1496, Brandeis University, Waltham, MA 02154.

Mumaw, Evelyn King. "Woman alone." 0-8361-1620-8 1970 $1.95/pap Herald Press.

National Council of Jewish Women. "Guide to study and action on the juvenile justice system." $1.00

United Church of Christ, Southern California Conference. Task Force on Women. "Workshop resource packet for women, Pasadena, 1972."

Women's Campus Ministry Caucus. Kit.

SEXISM IN EDUCATION & MEDIA (including Resources) (see also numerous titles in Audiovisual Section beginning with word Sex...)

Ad hoc committee for women and girls in education. "Eliminating sexism from the public schools of Washington state." 1973 $1.00 from Georgie Kunkel, 3409 S.W. Trenton, Seattle, WA 98126.

Ahlum, Carol & Jacqueline M. Fralley, eds. "Feminist resources for schools and colleges; a guide to curriculum materials." 0-912670-14-2 1973 $1.25 Feminist Press.

Pamphlets 123

——————. "High school feminist studies, with Intro. by Florence Howe." 0-912670-24-X 1974 $5.00 Feminist Press.

All of Us. "Sex stereotyping in children's literature; documented research." $1.00.

American Association of University of Women, Status of Women Committee, San Fernando Branch. "Jack and Jill." 1972 $1.00 Box 403, Livermore, CA 94550.

American Federation of Teachers. "Policy resolutions on women's rights adopted by annual conventions." AFT, 1012 15 N.W. Washington, DC 20005.

——————. "Women in education; changing sexist practices in the classroom, edited by Marjorie Stern." 1973. $1.00.

——————. "Women and higher education; an AFT special conference, May 11-13, 1973..., by Virginia Mulrooney."

American Library Assoc. Children's Services Division. Discussion Group on Sexism in Library Materials for Children. Booklists, guidelines, etc. $1.00/mailing list postage: Janet Dellaria, Northbrook Public Library, 1201 Cedar Ln., Northbrook, IL 60062.

Child's Play (Bookstore). "Child's Play catalog." 1974 $.25

Clearinghouse on Women's Studies. "Non-sexist curricular materials for elementary schools, edited by Laurie Olsen Johnson." 0-912670-25-2 $5.00 Feminist Press.

Czaplinski, Suzanne M. "Sexism in award-winning picture books." 0-912786-21-3 1973 $2.00 KNOW.

Davis, Enid A. "156 good books for girls." $.75 from Ms. Davis.

——————. "20 tales a feminist could tell." 1973 $.40.

Dickinson, Elizabeth. "Statement to the RTSD CCS Subject Analysis Committee on sex-biased subject-headings; presentation before the American Library Assoc./Resources and Technical Services Division/Cataloging and Classification Section/Subject Analysis Committee at the 1974 ALA Conference. Ad hoc committee of the Social Responsibilities Round Table Task Force on Women, headed by Joan K. Marshall." SASE + $.50 to partially cover printing. From Ms. Dickinson, Hennepin County Library, York Ave. S. @ 70, Edina, MN 55435.

Eastman, Ann Heidbreder. Contact Ms. E. for her analysis of the "Guidelines for equal treatment of the sexes in McGraw-Hill

Book Company publications" and her "Survey of sex discrimination in publishing." 5G, Hampton House, 166 N. Dithridge St., Pittsburgh, PA 15213.

Eaton, Cynthia. "Dick and Jane as victims; sex stereotyping in children's readers." From Ms. Eaton, 25 Cleveland Ln., Princeton R.D. 4, NJ 08540.

———. "Sexism in schools, in K-8." 1972. from Ms. Eaton.

Emma Willard Task Force on Education. "Sexism in education; resources." 1972 $3.50/individuals; $5.00/institutions. University Station Box 14229, Minneapolis, MN 55414.

Federbush, Marcia. "Let them aspire; a plea and proposal to eliminate sex discrimination in the public schools, 4 ed." 1973 $3.00 KNOW.

Feminist Book Mart. "Girls and boys together [a bibliography/catalog of non-sexist books for children]." 1974 $.75.

Feminist Press. "Bibliography on the treatment of girls in schools." Free to teachers and students. Suggestion: Send SASE.

Feminists on Children's Media. "Little Miss Muffett Fights Back, rev. ed., August 1974; recommended non-sexist books about girls for young readers." #X0600 $1.25 KNOW.

Kannenberg, Susan. "Sex-typed depictions on toy boxes; a study of 800 toys." 1973 $2.00 from Ms. Kannenberg, 279 Winter, Weston, MA 02193.

Kaylen, Sharon & Florence Howe, eds. "Women's Studies for teachers and administrators: a packet of in-service education materials." 1974 $7.50 Feminist Press.

Lucido, Corrine. "Community workshops on children's books." 0-912670-41-X 1974 $2.00 Feminist Press.

Macleod, Jennifer S. & Sandra T. Silver(wo)man. " 'You won't do'; what textbooks on United States government teach high school girls." 0-912786-25-6 1973 $2.25 KNOW.

Mason, Bobbie Ann. "The girl sleuth; a feminist guide to Nancy Drew and her sisters." 1973 $2.00 Feminist Press.

Minnesota Library Assoc., Children & Young People's Section. "Little Miss Muffett hangs in there, 1973." $.15 + SASE. The Association, 5511 27 Ave. S., Minneapolis, MN 55417. (SEE ALSO "Little Miss Muffett fights back..." of which this is an update, page 197, Womanhood Media, as well as Feminists on Children's Media entry, this section.)

Pamphlets

Minnesota Resource Center for Social Work. "Sex role stereotyping; implications for the human services." 1973 $3.00 The Center, 731 21 Ave. S., Minneapolis, MN 55405.

Moberg, Verne. "A child's right to equal reading; exercises in the liberation of children's books from the limitations of sex role stereotypes." 1974 $.45 Feminist Press.

Montaperto, Nicki. "Report on sexism in toys." 1973 $.25 Ms. Montaperto, 483 3 Ave., Roselle, NJ 07203.

National Organization for Women. New York Chapter. Education Committee. "Report on sex bias in the public schools." Annual update, $3.00. 47 E. 19, New York, NY 10003.

_____. St. Louis Chapter. "Sex bias in junior high school literature anthologies." $1.50 PO Box 16132, St. Louis, MO 63105.

National Council of Teachers of English. Committee on the Role & Image of Women in the Council and the Profession. "Guidelines for publications." Gratis.

Ottawa. Advisory Council on the Status of Women. "Improving the image of women in textbooks." Gratis. The Council, Box 1541, Sta. B. KOP 5RP.

Rosenfelt, Deborah Silverton, ed. "Strong women; an annotated bibliography of paperbacks for the high school classroom." 0-912670-40-1 $1.50 Feminist Press.

Rothchild, Nina. "Sexism in schools; a handbook for action." c1973 $2.00 postage paid. From Ms. Rothchild, 14 Hickory, Mahtomedi, MN 55115.

Stephens, Elizabeth Lucas, et al, comps. "What can they be? prepared by the Education Task Forces of the Westchester Professional Women's Caucus and Southern Westchester NOW." SASE + $.50 coin. 424 Pelham Manor Rd., Pelham Manor, NY 10803.

Stern, Marjorie Stern, ed. "Changing sexist practices in the classroom." #600 1974 American Federation of Teachers.

Syracuse University. College for Human Development. "Sex in a plain brown wrapper." 1973 $1.00 EdU Press.

Theodore, Athena Rentoumis. "Academic women in protest [and Counter stratagems used by the victims]." 1974 $3.00 contribution to the Victims' Defense Fund. From Dr. Theodore, 27 Turning Mill Rd., Lexington, MA 02173; also available as ERIC Document # ED 091989.

Tiedt, Iris M., ed. "Women and girls" #39773 1973 $1.50 National Council of Teachers of English.

Women on Words and Images. "Dick and Jane as victims; sex stereotyping in children's readers." 1972 $2.00 PO Box 2163, Princeton, NJ 08540.

Zimmerman, Bonnie. "Jack and Jill; a booklist for teachers, counselors, community organizations, parents and students aimed at arousing awareness of sex-role stereotyping in all phases of life." 1972 $1.00 Ms. Zimmerman, 36 Castledown Rd., Pleasanton, CA 94556.

SONGBOOKS, MUSIC, SONGS (see also Audiovisual section)

Busch, Judy & Laura X., comps. "Women's songbook." 1971 $1.16/women, $3.16/men, institutions, libraries. From Women's History Research Center. Includes 'Heaven help the working girl,' 'The un-fair affair,' 'We don't need the men,' and 'Male supremacy' and others, old and original.

Dobson, Alix, feminist songwriter. $.25 each from her at 330 East 70 St., New York, NY 10021: 'The woman in your life is you,' 'Her precious love,' 'A woman's love,' 'My kind of girl.'

Feminist Party Songbook. 10 songs, including 'Abortion rap,' by Diane Schulder; 'Women's time is here,' a new song about F. Kennedy by Jeanette Kah. Cover is Feminist Party poster. $.25 5/$1.00.

Joplin, Janis. "Women is losers" is a 'song she wrote at a time when that realization had barely begun to dawn on most women, and, in her painful struggle to come out on top, she often seemed like a composite of a generation of women trying to do the same.' (Ms. Nov. 1973:39.)

Liggera, Lanayre. "Woman is my name." Feminist songbook 1973 $.75. From Ms. Liggera, 66 Teel, Arlington, MA 02174.

MacNeil, Rita. "Born a woman; the Rita MacNeil songbook, with guitar chords and illustrated by Pat Bourque." 1974. Women's Press.

Maginnis, Patricia T. "The abortees' songbook." $1.00 Society for Humane Abortion.

Pfaehler, Phoebe & Lynne Leslie. "Equality road and other songs." 5 feminist songs with music, lyrics, guitar cues, piano arrangements. $2.50, 2 or more $1.50 each. KNOW.

Purple Honey; feminist music for flute and guitar. Women's Folk Song Project.

Silverman, Jerry, comp. "The liberated woman's song book." 74-165563 1971 Macmillan $3.95 Melodies with chord symbols.

Woman's Soul Publishing, Inc. SEE Sources section.

SPORTS, ATHLETICS, SELF-DEFENSE

Association of American Colleges. Project on the Status and Education of Women. "What constitutes equality for women in sport? Federal law puts women in the running." Includes 'Resources'--Newsletter issue.

Conroy, Mary. "Personal defense for women; a practical manual for teachers and students." c1973 $3.40 from Trident Shop, California State University, Los Angeles, 5151 State University Dr., Los Angeles, CA 90032.

The Female Runner. $1.25 from World Publications, Box 366, Mountain View, CA 94040.

Harris, Dorothy V., ed. "DGWS research reports: Women in sports." 2v., 1971 and 1973. $3.00 American Association for Health, Physical Education & Recreation. From Association for Intercollegiate Athletics for Women.

Hoepner, Barbara J., ed. "Women's athletics; coping with controversy. 1974. $3.25. AAHPER. From AIAW.

Short, Pauline M. & Paula Short. "Fight back! [; a self-defense training program for women]." $2.25. From PMS, Inc., 724 E. Burnside, Portland, OR 97214.

U.S. GOVERNMENT AS A SOURCE

"Birth expectations and fertility: June 1973" (Series P-20, #254). U.S. Dept. of Commerce. Bureau of the Census. For the National Institute of Child Health and Human Development. $.25 from Supt. of Documents or Commerce District Offices.

"Careers for women in the 70's." 1973 U.S. Dept. of Labor. Women's Bureau. S/N 2916-00012 L36:102:C18. $.35

"Dual careers." Manpower Research Monographs #21, Vol. 2.
U.S. Dept. of Labor. 1973. L 1.39/3:21/v.2 S/N 2900-00176. $2.10.

"Education directory." U.S. Dept. of Health, Education & Welfare. Office of Education. $5.30.

"Earnings by occupation and education." Bureau of the Census. 1970 Census of population, subject reports PC (2)-8B S/N 0301-03622 C3.223/10:970 /v.2/pt. 8B. $4.50.

"Equal rights for men and women 1971." Hearings before Subcommittee No. 4, House Committee on the Judiciary, 92d Congress, 1st sess., 1971. Y 4.J 89/1:92-3 S/N 5270-01730 $3.95.

"Expanding opportunities ... Women in the federal government." 1973 CS 1.2: W 84/6 S/N 0600-00689. $.40

"Facts about women heads of households and heads of families." U.S. Dept. of Labor. Women's Bureau. 1973, April.

"The federal women's program; a point of view." 1972 U.S. Civil Service Commission $.20 Supt. of Docs. stock #0600-0627.

"The myth and the reality, May 1974 revised." $.25 Supt. of Docs. stock #2916-00015. U.S. Dept. of Labor. Women's Bureau.

"Review and synthesis of research on women in the world of work, by Mary Bach Kievit." 1972. U.S. Office of Education $.55 S/N 1790-0918. HE 5.2:W84.

"Sex discrimination." U.S. Dept. of Health, Education & Welfare. Office for Civil Rights. HEW-391 DHEW Publ. No. (OCR) 74-6. Inside back cover has addresses of regional offices.

"Study of the employment of women in the federal government, 1971." U.S. Civil Service Commission. $2.35 from Supt. of Docs.

"We, the American women." 1973. Bureau of the Census. We the Americans ser. no. 4 $.40 S/N 0324-00122. C56:234:4.

"Women in apprenticeship--why not? By Norma Briggs." 1974. Dept. of Labor, Manpower research monograph no. 33. $.75 L1.39/3:33.

"Women in forest service." 1972 $.10 Supt. of Docs. Order # S/N 0100-92641.

"Working woman's guide to her job rights, prepared by Rose Terlin." June 1974. Leaflet 55 $.60 U.S. Dept. of Labor. Women's Bureau. 0-553-180 GPO.

WOMEN'S STUDIES (See also #'s 500 and 653, Basic Book Collection)

Center for Women's Studies & Services, San Diego, CA. "Current trends in feminist organizing; sisterhood can be powerful!" $.10. "Feminist counseling and Center for Women's Studies & Services radical services concept" $.25. "Job development fact sheet" $.10. "Rainbow snake, by Barbara Miles" $2.00. "Selected bibliography of women writers" $.50. "Women of the convicted class" $.75.

Cheda, Sherrill, comp. "Women Studies resources handbook." Published by "Research on women in Canada" newsletter. Contact Margrit Eichler, Dept. of Sociology, University of Waterloo, Waterloo, ON N2L 3G1.

Farians, Elizabeth. "Women's Studies; a program for colleges and universities." $2.25 from Dr. Farians, 6125 Webbland Pl., Cincinnati, OH 45213.

Female Studies (Series). From KNOW and Feminist Press.
Vol. I, 0-912786-01-0, 1970, $2.25; Vol. II, 0-912786-02-7, 1970, $4.25; Vol. III, 0-912786-03-5, 1971, $4.50: Vols. I, II, III associated with Florence Howe, Carol Ahlum, Sheila Tobias, et al as editors; Vol. IV, 0-912786-04-3, 1971, $2.25, Elaine Showalter, Carol Ohmann, eds.; Vol. V, 0-912786-05-1, 1972, $4.75, Rae Lee Siporin, ed.; Vol. VI, 0-912670-26-6, 1972, $5.00, Nancy Hoffman, et al, eds.; Vol. VII, 0-912670-27-4, 1973, $5.00, Deborah Silverton Rosenfelt, ed.; Vol. VIII, 1974, $5.50, Sarah Slavin Schramm, ed.; Vol. IX, 0-912670-38-X, $5.00, Sidonie Cassirer, ed.; Vol. X, 0-912670-39-8, $5.00, Deborah Silverton Rosenfelt, ed.

Kaylen see SEXISM section of "Pamphlets."

Kirsten, Drake, et al. "Women's work and women's studies." Annual bibliography $7.50, $4.50/pap Barnard College Women's Center, New York, NY 10027.

Massachusetts Institute of Technology, Humanities Library. "Human Studies bibliographies." $1.50.

Michigan. University. Center for Continuing Education of Women. Numerous Women's Studies publications. The Center, 330 Thompson, Ann Arbor, MI 48108.

Project on the Status & Education of Women. "Women's centers; where are they?" Assoc. of American Colleges.

Robinson, Lora. "Women's Studies: courses and programs for higher education." $2.00 from ERIC.

Tobias, Sheila. "History of the family" bibliography for term papers $1.50. Also, "Social, cultural and educational factors of women in higher education" $2.00. Dr. Tobias, Wesleyan University, Middletown, CT 06457.

U.S. National Student Assoc. Source Collective. "Women on campus; articles on women's studies programs and women's health care services, compiled for the 26th National Student Congress." $2.75 from the Association, 2115 S St., N.W., Washington, DC 20008.

Westervelt, Esther Manning, et al. "Women's higher and continuing education; an annotated bibliography with selected references on related aspects of women's lives." c1971 $1.50 from College Entrance Examination Board, Box 592, Princeton, NJ 08540.

Wexford, Mary, et al. "Women's work and Women's Studies, 1971." 0-912786-18-3 1972 $4.25 KNOW. Also "1972" 0-912786-24-8 1973 $5.00.

Wisconsin. University Extension Women's Resource Center. Edited transcriptions of noncredit classes offered over statewide educational telephone network, $1.00 each, 12/$10. "Women's Liberation; what does it mean to you?" "Men and masculinity." "Feminism and the family."

(NON-BOOK RESOURCES, cont.)

MOVEMENT PERIODICALS

New Women's Movement periodicals have again been included, with some repeats where there has been a known address or other change. See also <u>Audiovisual</u> section of Non-Book Resources for older periodicals available only or mainly in microform. Listing of "Special Issues on the Woman" has been discontinued. With the establishment of <u>Women Studies Abstracts</u>, which regularly lists such special issues of non-Women's Movement periodicals, there is no longer need for even a sampling. Patricia O'Connor's bibliography, "Women and the Human Revolution; Guide to Special Issues of Magazines" (Wittenberg University, Springfield, OH 45501) and "The Index to Women's Periodicals" (Box 2382, Eugene, OR 97402) are also useful.

ALA SRRT Task force on women [in librarianship] newsletter: "Women in Libraries"
Kay Cassell, ed., 1F, 150 E 30
New York, NY 10016

AT&T Alliance for women newsletter
Mary Delle Stelzer
212-393-2249

Affirmative action register
Warren H. Green, ed.
10 South Brentwood Blvd.
St. Louis, MO 63105

Albatross
82 S. Harrison St.
East Orange, NJ 07017

Alert: Women's legislative review
Box 437
Middletown, CT 06457

Amazon quarterly
554 Valle Vista
Oakland, CA 94610

American Negro woman
Box 99007
Cleveland, OH 44199

Aphra
Box 893 Ansonia Station
New York, NY 10023

As we see it now
Box 1455
Detroit, MI 48231

Aurora; prism of feminism
24 DeBraun Ave.
Suffern, NY 19101

Battle acts
Women of youth against war and fascism, 46 West 21
New York, NY 10011

Before Eve
Katie Houston, c/o Hannah
 Middle School
East Lansing, MI 48823

Berkeley women's newsletter
2801 Ellsworth
Berkeley, CA 94705

Big mama rag
1635 Downing
Denver, CO 80218

Black women's log
Sisterhood Alliance Media, Inc.
Box 398, Forest Park Station
Springfield, MA 01108

Body politic
4 Kensington Ave.
Toronto 2B, Ontario

Booklegger
72 Ord
San Francisco, CA 94114

Bookwoman
Mary Ann O'Brian Malkin
PO Box 1100
Newark, NJ 07101

Branching out; Canadian magazine for women
11015 89 Ave.
Edmonton, Alberta T6G OZ7

Breakthrough; official publication of the Interstate Association of Commissions on
 the Status of Women
14 & E Streets N.W., District
 Bldg., Room 204
Washington, D.C. 20004

Broadside
PO Box 4190
Berkeley, CA 94704

Broadside
Dartmouth Women's Caucus,
 Women's Center
Hanover, NH 03755

Brother; a forum for men
 against sexism
PO Box 4387
Berkeley, CA 94704

Brothers; a Men's Liberation
 newsletter
c/o Rising free, 197 King's
 Cross Road
London, WC1, England

Building blocks
Hyde Park-Kenwood Community
 Conf. Child care task force
1400 East 53
Chicago, IL 60615

Bulletin board of the Task Force
 on women [in librarianship]
 SEE Rosters in Directory of
 Sources Section

Canadian newsletter of research
 on women
c/o Dept. of Sociology, University of Waterloo
Waterloo, Ontario N2L 3G1

Canadian Women Studies newsletter SEE Canadian newsletter ...

Change; a working woman's
 newspaper
968 Valencia
San Francisco, CA 94110

Changes magazine
2314 Elliot Ave. S.
Minneapolis, MN 55404

Changing woman
705 S.E. 46 Ave.
Portland, OR 97215

Chatelaine
Maclean-Hunter
481 University Ave.
Toronto 2, Ontario

Movement Periodicals

Children's Television Workshop
 newsletter
1 Lincoln Plaza
New York, NY 10023

Chomo-Uri; a collection of
 women's expressions
506 Goodell Hall
Univ. of Massachusetts
Amherst, MA 01002

Chronicle of Higher Education
 (non-profit)
1717 Massachusetts Ave., N.W.
Washington, D.C. 20036

Cleveland feminist
10206 Clifton
Cleveland, OH 44102

Cold day in August
3028 Greenmount Ave.
Baltimore, MD 21218

Coming out
PO Box A-22, Oberlin College
Oberlin, OH 44074

Comment
1 Dupont Circle
Washington, D.C. 20036

Common cause report from
 Washington
2100 M St., N.W.
Washington, D.C. 20037

Compliance newsletter
NOW Compliance and Higher
 education task forces

Congress votes/how your congress(wo)man voted this week
PO Box 9695
Washington, DC 20016

Connections
Toni Zimmerman, apt. 15E
100 W 94
New York, NY 10025

Connections magazine
Bell Hollow Road
Putnam Valley, NY 10579

Consciousness up
Box 453
Smithtown, NY 11787

Country women
PO Box 51
Albion, CA 95401

Cowrie
359 E 68
New York, NY 10021

Cries from Cassandra; the official newspaper of the Amazon
 Nation
2916 N Burling
Chicago, IL 60657

Day care & child development
 reports
2814 Pennsylvania Ave., N.W.
Washington, D.C. 20007

Day care & early education
Behavioral Publications
2852 Broadway
New York, NY 10025

Did You Know?
PO Box 5024, F.D.R. Station
New York, NY 10022

Distaff
Box 15639
New Orleans, LA 70175
(Also 4011 Magazines, 70115)

Dykes & gorgons
PO Box 840
Berkeley, CA 94704

EMKO Newsletter
7912 Manchester Ave.
St. Louis, MO 63143

Echo of Sappho
PO Box 263
Brooklyn, NY 11217

Effeminist
PO Box 4089
Berkeley, CA 94704

Elima
149 West 4th Annie Gottlieb, 5D
New York, NY 10012

Emergency librarian!
32-351 River Ave.
Winnipeg, Manitoba r#1 OB5

Essence
Box 2989
Boulder, CO 80302

Executive woman
747 3 Ave., 29th Floor
New York, NY 10017

Familia
Box 73
Kingston, NY 12401

Family planning digest
National center for family
  planning services
560 Fishers La., Rm 12A-33
Rockville, MD 20852

Federal regulations & the employment practices of colleges and universities; a guide to the interpretation of federal regulations affecting personnel administration on campus
National Assoc. of College &
  University Business Officers
1 Dupont Circle, Ste. 510
Washington, D.C. 20036

Federation Alert
4818 Drummond Ave.--Fed. of
  Organ. for Professional Women
Washington, D.C. 20015

Female state; a journal of female liberation
371 Somerville Ave.
Somerville, MA 20143

Feminine focus
Intercollegiate Assoc. of women
  students, 2401 Virginia Ave.,
  N.W. Box 2
Washington, D.C. 20037

Feminist art journal
41 Montgomery Pl.
Brooklyn, NY 11215

Feminist country survival manual SEE Country women

Feminist bulletin
Box 9, Westchester Women's
  Liberation Coalition
Hartsdale, NY 10530

Feminist Newsletter of Chapel Hill
PO Box 954
Chapel Hill, NC 27514

Feminist Party news
311 West 24
New York, NY 10011

Feminist Press News/Notes
Box 334
Old Westbury, NY 11568

Feminist quarterly journal
1520 New Hampshire Ave., N.W.
Washington, D.C. 20036

Feminist studies
417 Riverside Dr.
New York, NY 10025

Feminist Therapist Roster SEE
  Assoc. for Women in Psychology Sources

Feminist Voice
PO Box 1144, 22 East Ontario
Chicago, IL 60611

51%; a paper of joyful noise for
  the majority sex
25333 Oak
Lomita, CA 90717

Movement Periodicals

Focus
E.C. Brown Center for family
   studies, Univ. of Oregon
1802 Moss
Eugene, OR 97403

Freelance directory
201 East Walton, Ste. 301
Chicago, IL 60611

Full moon (ceased publication)
200 Main
Northampton, MA

Genesis III
Philadelphia task force on wo-
   men in religion
PO Box 24003
Philadelphia, PA 91939

Gidra; monthly of the Asian
   American experience
PO Box 18649
Los Angeles, CA 90018

Gold flower; a Twin Cities
   newspaper for women
PO Box 8341, Lake Street Sta.
Minneapolis, MN 55408

The Greene Sheet (X)
National Right to Life Com.,
   Inc.
200 15 St., N.W.
Washington, D.C. 20005

Guardian
33 West 17
New York, NY 10011

Health-PAC Bulletin
17 Murray
New York, NY 10007

Hecate
c/o Carole Ferrier, Eng. Dept.
Univ. of Queensland
St. Lucia, Brisbane 4067
QLD Australia

Hennepin County [Minn.] Library
   [system] Cataloging bulletin
Technical services division
7001 York Ave. S.
Edina, MN 55435

Her-self
225 East Liberty
Ann Arbor, MI 48108

Herstory SEE Audiovisual Sec.

Indian of all tribes news
4339 California
San Francisco, CA 94118

Ingenue SEE New ingenue

Issues in radical therapy
IRT Collective, Box 23544
Oakland, CA 94623

Journal of homosexuality
Haworth Press, 130 West 72
New York, NY 10023

Journal of the National association for women deans, administrators & counselors
1028 Connecticut Ave., N.W.
Washington, D.C. 20036

Ladder Index now available SEE
   ALSO Amazon quarterly

Lavender woman
c/o Betty Peters, 1434 W. Thome
Chicago, IL 60660

Lazette
c/o New Jersey DOB, PO Box 62
Fanwood, NJ 07023

La Leche League news
9616 Minneapolis Ave.
Franklin Park, IL 60131

Lesbian feminist
Box 243, Village Station
New York, NY 10014

Lesbian tide
373 North Western Ave.
Los Angeles, CA 90004

Lesbians come together
Contact Ms. Gill Tew,
#1 Gunyah Ct., Spencer Rd.
Chiswick, London W4 England

Letters
157 George
Saratoga, NY 12866

Libera journal
516 Eshlemann Hall
University of California
Berkeley, CA 94720

Liberator...
1404 Grand Ave.
Fort Worth, TX 76106

Light; a poetry review
Box 1105, Stuyvesant Station
New York, NY 10009

Lilith's rib; Jewish women's
 movement newsletter
PO Box 60142, 1723 W. Devon
Chicago, IL 60660

Long time coming
Box 161, Station E
Montreal 151, Quebec H2T 3A7

Mainely NOW
PO Box 534
Kennebunkport, ME 04046

Majority report
74 Grove, Sheridan Square
New York, NY 10014

Mano a mano
Chicano Training Center
3520 Montrose, Ste. 215
Houston, TX 77006

Marin women's news journal
PO Box 1412
San Rafael, CA 94902

Marriage & divorce
Abraxas Communications
874 Malcolm Ave.
Los Angeles, CA 90024

Matrix
PO Box 4218
North Hollywood, CA 91607

Media report to women
3306 Ross Pl., N.W., Women's
 inst. for freedom of the press
Washington, D.C. 20008

Michigan papers in Women's
 Studies
Univ. of Michigan Women's
 Studies program, 1058 LSA
Ann Arbor, MI 48104

Modern times
American Independent Movement
441 Chapel
New Haven, CT 06511

Momma; the newspaper/magazine
 for single mothers
PO Box 567
Venice, CA 90291

Monthly extract; an irregular
 periodical
New moon communications
Box 3488
Stamford, CT 06905

Moving out
169 Mackenzie Hall, Wayne
 State Univ.
Detroit, MI 48202

Ms.
123 Garden
Marion, OH 43302

Movement Periodicals

Ms.: an author & subject index; Spring 1972-Feb. 1974. (covers the time until Reader's Guide picked up indexing)
Rochester Inst. of Technology Library
1 Lomb Memorial Dr.
Rochester, NY 14623

NCAWE News
National council of administrative women in education
1815 Fort Myer Drive N.
Arlington, VA 22209

NCHE News
National Committee on household employment
1625 Eye St., N.W.
Washington, DC 20006

NLIS Newsletter
PO Box 15368
San Francisco, CA 94115

NOW Feminist products catalog
1126 HiPoint
Los Angeles, CA 90035

Native sisterhood
PO Box 515
Kingston, Ontario

New consultants; a periodic supplement to Consultants & Consulting Organizations
Gale Research, Book Tower
Detroit, MI 48226

New directions for women in Delaware
223 Planet Road
Newark, DE 19711

New directions for women in New Jersey
PO Box 27
Dover, NJ 07801

New Hampshire sisters
6 Rumford
Concord, NH 03301

New ingenue
635 Madison Ave., 21st century communications, inc.
New York, NY 10022

New lady
1335 A
Hayward, CA 94541

New York radical feminists newsletter
c/o Jean Grove, 80 Thomson
New York, NY 10012

News notes
Feminist Press, Box 334
Old Westbury, NY 11568

A newsletter about women in music and the music in women
4900 W Street, N.W.
Washington, DC 20007

Northern woman
318 South Marks
Thunder Bay F, Ontario

Notes
Women's Liberation, PO Box AA
New York, NY 10011

Notes on Women's Liberation; women speak in many voices
1900 East Jefferson
Detroit, MI 48207

Now or never [feminist newsletter]
Contact via Bibliotheque Feminine, Place du Pantheon
Paris 5, France

Off our backs; a women's news journal
1724 20 Street, N.W.
Washington, DC 20009

On campus with women
1818 R Street, N.W.
Project on the Status & Education of women
Washington, D.C. 20009

On our way
PO Box 4508
Edmonton, Alberta

On the way
7801 Peck Ave., Anchorage
   Women's Liberation
Anchorage, AK 99504

One-to-one
PO Box 397, Old Chelsea Sta.
New York, NY 10011

Other woman
Box 928, Station Q
Toronto 7, Ontario

Over the way
c/o 306 Herkimer
Hamilton, Ontario

Page one
PO Box 14015
Atlanta, GA 30324

Paid my dues
PO Box 5476
Woman's soul publishing
Milwaukee, WI 53211

The pedestal
704 Richards
Vancouver, British Columbia

Peer perspective
(Proj. on Equal Educat. Rights)
1522 Conn. Ave. N.W.
Washington, D.C. 20036

Phyllis Schlafley Report (X)
Fairmount
Alton, IL 62002

Playgirl (X)
PO Box 67567, Playgirl, Inc.
Los Angeles, CA 90067

El Popo Femenil
Chicano Studies Dept., California State Univ.
Northridge, CA 91324

Portcullis; a feminist/Lesbian
   publication
PO Box 65791
Los Angeles, CA 90065

Press censorship newsletter
1750 Pennsylvania Ave., N.W.
Room 1310, Reporters committee
   for freedom of the press
Washington, D.C. 20006

Prime time
Box 5C, 232 East 6
New York, NY 10003

Priorities
2803 Wall
Vancouver 6, British Columbia

Proud woman [formerly mother]
   (ceased publication)

Purple rage
c/o Women's Liberation Center
243 West 20
New York, NY 10011

Quebeçoises deboutte
3908 Mentana
Montreal, Quebec

Quest; a feminist quarterly
PO Box 8843
Washington, DC 20003

Rantings
11205 Euclid Ave., Nancy Wood
Cleveland, OH 44106

Movement Periodicals

Rape crisis center newsletter
PO Box 20015
Washington, DC 20009

La razón mestiza
Concilio Mujeres
2588 Mission, #201
San Francisco, CA 94110

Reaching out; Canadian magazine for women
11443 77 Ave.
Edmonton, Alberta T6G OL9

Redstockings (ceased publication)

Research action notes
Resource center on sex roles in education
1156 15 Street, N.W.
Washington, DC 20005

Response
7820 Reading Rd.
Cindinnati, OH 45237

Right-on, Sister
Isla Vista Women's Center
6504 Pardell Road
Isla Vista, CA 93017

SHER newsletter (Self-help for equal rights)
SHER-NIHEW, PO Box 30044
Washington, D.C. 20014

Santa Fe women's community magazine
520 Jose Street, #5
Santa Fe, NM 87501

Sappho
BCM/Petrel
London, WCIV 6xx, England

Saskatoon WL Newsletter
Women's Centre
147 2 Ave. S.
Saskatoon, Saskatchewan

Say it so it makes sense
Institute for family research & education, 760 Ostrom Ave.
Syracuse, NY 13210

Scientific, engineering, technical (wo)manpower comments
Scientific Manpower Commission
1776 Mass. Ave., N.W.
Washington, D.C. 20036

Second wave
74 Mt. Auburn
Cambridge, MA 02138

Sex discrimination in education Newsletter
Dept. of Psychology
Univ. of Michigan
Ann Arbor, MI 48104

Sex news
P.K. Houdek, 7140 Oak
Kansas City, MO 64114

Shameless Hussy review
Shameless Hussy Press, Box 424
San Lorenzo, CA 94580

Single
Steirman Communications, Inc.
545 Madison Ave.
New York, NY 10011

Siren--newsletter of Anarcho-Feminism
713 West Armitage Ave.
Chicago, IL 60614

Sister
PO Box 597
Venice, CA 90291

Sister
3438 Yale Station, New Haven
Women's Liberation
New Haven, CT 06520

Sojourner; a magazine of women's writing and visual art
336 Central Park West,
Florence Epstein
New York, NY 10025

So's your old lady
710 West 22
Minneapolis, MN 55405

Speakout
PO Box 6165
Albany, NY 12206

Sportswoman
PO Box 2611
Culver City, CA 90230

Status of women news
PO Box 927, Adelaide Street
Toronto, Ontario M5C 2K3

Sweet 'n Low magazine
Communications Publishing, Inc., 363 7 Ave.
New York, NY 10001

Television news index & Abstracts, January 1972- .
Vanderbilt TV News archive
Joint University Libraries
Nashville, TN 37203

Tell-a-Woman
4634 Chester Ave., Women's Liberation Center
Philadelphia, PA 19143

Texas Woman
1208 Baylor
Austin, TX 78703

13th moon
30 Seaman Ave.
c/o Embissert/Kathleen Chodor
New York, NY 10034

This magazine is about schools
PO Box 876, Terminal A
Toronto 1, Ontario

Tightwire
Box 515
Kingston, Ontario

Tres femmes
2250 B Street
Gay Center for social services
San Diego, CA 92102

Triple jeopardy
Third world women's alliance
346 West 20
New York, NY 10011

US
4213 West Bay Ave.
United sisters
Tampa, FL 33616

UVA URSI
R.F.D.
Robbinston, ME 04671

Union W.A.G.E.
2135 Oregon
Berkeley, CA 94705

Valley Women's Studies journal
Mt. Holyoke College
Marjorie Childers, ed.
South Hadley, MA 01075

Venus
154 South VanNess Ave.
San Francisco, CA 94103

Viva
155 Allen Blvd.
Farmingville, NY 11735

Vocal majority; NOW national Capital area
1736 R Street, N.W.
Washington, D.C. 20009

La voz de la mujer
111 Laguna Place, N.W.
N.O.W. Newsletter
Albuquerque, NM 87104

Movement Periodicals

"W"
Fairchild Publications, Inc.
7 East 12
New York, NY 10003

WEAL Washington report
1254 4 Street, S.W.
Washington, D.C. 20024

WICA: Ames feminist newspaper
Room 6S, Memorial Union,
Univ. of Iowa Women's Coalition
Ames, IA 50010

WONAAC Newsletter
150 5 Ave., Women's Nat'l.
Abortion Action Coalition
New York, NY 10011

West-East Bag (W.E.B.)
PO Box 539, Canal St. Station
New York, NY 10013

What she wants
1409 Marlowe, #8
Lakewood, OH 44107

Whole woman
1628 Winnebago
Madison, WI 53704

Windsor woman newspaper
1309 University Avenue W. &
76 Univ. Ave. W., Room 603
Windsor, Ontario

Woman
Campus Women's Forum
201 Sproul, Univ. of California
Berkeley, CA 94720

Woman
2621 Beachwood Drive
Los Angeles, CA 90068

Woman
PO Box 135
Kalamazoo, MI 49006

Woman
235 Park Avenue South
Reese Publishing Co., Inc.
New York, NY 10003

Woman becoming
6664 Woodwell
Pittsburgh, PA 15217

The woman CPA
University of Mass.
Dr. Ula K. Motekat
Amherst, MA 01002

Woman news
Contact Spokeswoman

Woman to woman
PO Box 50191
New Orleans, LA 70150

Womankind
852 West Belmont, Chicago
Women's Liberation Union
Chicago, IL 60657

Woman's place newsletter
31 Dupont
Toronto, Ontario

Woman's pulpit
International Assoc. of Women
Ministers, 3717 3
Des Moines, IA 50313

Womanspace journal
11008 Venice Blvd., Womanspace
Los Angeles, CA 90034

Women [annual]
Random House, Dept. of Information Sciences, Box 804
Madison Square Station
New York, NY 10010

Women and art
89 East Broadway
New York, NY 10002

Women and film
2802 Arizona Ave.
Santa Monica, CA 90404

Women and politics/Women's
　Caucus for Political Science
　newsletter
Carolyn L. Ball, Program in
　Social Ecology
Univ. of California, Irvine
Irvine, CA 92664

Women and religion [annual]
CSR Executive Office, Water-
　loo Lutheran University
Waterloo, Ontario

Women and revolution; journal
　of the Spartacist League,
　Central Committee Com.
　for Work Among Women
Box 1377, GPO
New York, NY 10001

Women and work
U.S. Dept. of Labor, rm. 2138
14th & Constitution Ave., N.W.
Washington, D.C. 20210

Women are human; an infor-
　mation sheet for women
Ohio State Univ. Libraries
1858 Neil Ave.
Columbus, OH 43210

Women employed
37 S. Wabash
Chicago, IL 60603

Women in public broadcasting
　newsletter
3435 Main (also 323 Norton)
Buffalo, NY 14214

Women in the arts
PO Box 4476, Grand Central
　Post Office
New York, NY 10017

Women writing
Polly Joan, RD #3
Newfield, NY 14867

Women's Abortion & Contracep-
　tion Group newsletter
105 Musters Rd., c/o Rose
　Knight
West Bridgeford, Nottingham,
　England

Women's action movement news-
　letter
Box 4770, Mississippi State Univ.
Starville, MS 39762

Women's advocate
Minnesota Women's Center
301 Walter Library, Univ. of
　Minnesota
Minneapolis, MN 55455

Women's Almanac
Armitage Press, 1430 Mass. Ave.
Cambridge, MA 02138

Women's Collection Newsletter
Special Collections Dept.
Northwestern Univ. Library
Evanston, IL 60201

Women's free press
1929 21 Ave. S.
Nashville, TN 37212

Women's guide to books
MSS Information Corp.
655 Madison Ave.
New York, NY 10021

Women's health & abortion
　project newsletter
37 West 22
New York, NY 10010

Women's information bulletin
PO Box 24344, Univ. Station
Baton Rouge, LA 70803

Women's International League
　for Peace & Freedom
201 West 13
New York, NY 10011

Women's Liberation Center
　newsletter
36 West 22
New York, NY 10011

Movement Periodicals

Women's literary magazine
  c/o Janet Heller
5110 South Kenwood Ave.
Chicago, IL 60615

Women's Lobby Alert SEE
  Women's Lobby Quarterly

Women's lobby quarterly
1345 G Street, S.E.
Washington, D.C. 20003

Women's newsletter
PO Box 1412
San Rafael, CA 94902

Women's rights law reporter
180 Union Ave.
Newark, NJ 07102

Women's Studies
Gordon Breach Science Pub.,
  Ltd., 41-42 William IV St.
London WC 2, England
(USA: 440 Park Ave., S.
  New York, NY 10016)

Women's Studies Newsletter
Clearinghouse on Women's
  Studies, Box 334
Old Westbury, NY 11568

Women's work
Washington Opportunities for
  Women
1111 20 NW
Washington, D.C. 20036

Women's work and Women's
  Studies SEE KNOW publications

WomenSports
PO Box 4963
Des Moines, IA 50306

(NON-BOOK RESOURCES, cont.)

AUDIOVISUAL RESOURCES

A LA MODE (mo pic)
Grove #003 5min S$50
By Stan Vanderbeek. "A witty satire on modern women, shaping girlie and glamour illustrations into a collage" (Grove).

A TO B (mo pic)
Nell Cox 1970 36min C Time-Life R$40 S$400
Adolescent female in contemporary American society; documentary of White middle-class person.

AFL-CIO WOMEN'S CONFERENCE (cassette)
Obtain from Union Women's Alliance 90min $5.
Union WAGE Conference--speeches, panelists, floor-discussion: negotiation, women's issues, employed women and the law, organizing the unorganized; "role" of women in the labor movement, employed women and the media.

ABORTION (mo pic)
Women's Film Coop 30min R$20
Besides being a strong film about the need for women to gain the right to control their own bodies, effectively portrays the horror of U.S. drug (contraception) experimentation on Third World and poor White women, in the South, ghettos, and Puerto Rico. Supreme Court's ruling does not make this out-of-date. Begins with the "story" of an illegal abortion undergone by one of the film-makers.

ABORTION (tape)
CBC 1 hour $14
#489L "a look at the legal aspects"; #132L "one girl's mental and physical reaction plus a discussion on abortion."

ABORTION AT WILL IN THE FIRST TWELVE WEEKS (mo pic)
Indiana Univ. 1971 57min Advocate Series Univ. of California
    Ext. #8545 R$17
"Shows advocates and opponents of legalized abortion as they dispute whether or not a woman has the right to have her pregnancy terminated during the first three months. Advocates assert that

ready accessibility to abortion would reduce the number of unwanted children, who, studies show, run a greater risk of being socially maladjusted or mentally ill. Those opposed claim that the embryo is a human being, even though it is unable to survive independently, and that most women only 'think' they want an abortion. Many awards" (California).

ABORTION; HOW IT IS (audio visual)
H. J. Willke   circa 1973   Hiltz   2 audio cassettes, 4 30min sides, illus. by 20 slides, S$19.95   Cassettes, filmstrip, S$15.95
"The medical and social aspects of development of the human baby in the womb and of the reality of abortion.... A scientifically accurate, fascinating story. Focus is largely on the unborn. Senior high-up" (Hiltz).

ABORTION; PUBLIC ISSUE OR PRIVATE MATTER (mo pic)
NBC   1971   25min   R$13/3days

ABOUT ME AND CHURCH (FS)
Women's Culture, producer.   28min   54fr   Snd: cassette or rec.
    C   Radio Free People, distributor #73-15.   S$25. $40. with slides instead of FS
"... created by 9 members of St. Clement's Episcopal Church women's group, ages 25 to 56, who were raised as Roman Catholic, Presbyterian, agnostic and Episcopalian. They each speak intimately about how the church and the women's group have affected their lives. Attitudes range from deep loyalty to the church to toal disillusionment. The filmstrip is composed of photographs of the speakers made during their weekly meetings. The first showing was for a feminist service at St. Clement's in New York. Several women confessed to being moved to tears. Another showing started a 2-hour unscheduled discussion of the Women's Movement at a church-and-arts national meeting" (W.C.).

ABOUT SEX (mo pic)
Herman J. Engel, producer-director.   Sarah Oakes, associate producer, editor.   1972   23min   C   Study guide, grades 7+   Texture   R$25   S$220   72-703340
"All in all, I would label ... 'about perfect'." Harriette Surovell, Students' Coalition for Relevant Sex Education.

THE ABUSE OF CHILDREN (tapes)
CBC #160-164   30min each $7 each, $35 set.   Series of 5 talks.

ACTOR (mo pic)
CCM   1968   54min   Univ. of California Ext. #8220   R$32. Narrated by Alec Guiness
"Lively examination of stage actors and their 'mystique,' ... by leading English actors, directors, and playwrights.... Actress Joan Plowright discusses male domination of the theater."

AN ACTOR WORKS (mo pic)
SEE Lindfors, Viveca in Directory of Sources section.

ADAM AND EVE (play)
Dallas Women's Coalition sponsored play about women in management, at state fair. Contact Dallas NOW.

ADOLESCENCE (mo pic)
Univ. of California Ext. #7954 1967 22min R$11
Fourteen-year old Sonia takes ballet lessons from Mme. Egorova, whose Paris school is famous. Many international awards.

ADRIENNE RICH READING HER POEMS (tape)
Pacifica #BC 0949.02 19min $8.50 reel or cassette
From two of her earliest books, "Snapshots of a daughter-in-law" and "Necessities of life."

ADVENTURES IN NEGRO HISTORY (rec series)
Pepsi-Cola Matrix #XVTV 90962
Contributions of a long list of persons, of whom five are women: Marian Anderson, Mary McLeod Bethune, Sojourner Truth, Harriett Tubman, Phillis Wheatley.

AFFAIR OF GABRIELLE RUSSIER (tape)
Pacifica
French school teacher who fell in love with a student in 1968 revolution, i.e. stepped out of her role. SEE ALSO #711 Basic Book Collection.

AFFIRMATIVE ACTION IN UNIVERSITIES (videotape)
Helene N. Guttman, Box 4348, Chicago, IL 60680 312-996-2211
   1975 C 30min BW R. S.

AFRICAN FOLK TALES (FS with sound)
Imperial 1970 4 sound filmstrips, with phonodiscs $44; with tape cassettes $51.80
"Five folk tales representing Africa's cultural legacy emphasize man's closeness to nature and his place in a tribal society somewhat akin to the pluralistic society of the U.S. Primary-Intermediate" (Booklist May 1, 1973:839). "The girl who loved danger" (a Congo folk tale, 39fr, 10:15 min) in the company of "The greedy man and the stranger," "The unbending king," and "The man with two wives"!

AFRO-AMERICAN HISTORY-MYSTERY (game)
Theme circa 1973 $5
Try F.A.O. Schwarz, 5th Avenue @ 58th Street, New York, NY 10022
Twenty-eight persons, of whom four are women, including dancer Katherine Dunham and Abolitionist Sojourner Truth.

AFTER THE REVOLUTION (FS) see WOMEN IN AMERICAN HISTORY SERIES

AFTER THE VOTE (mo pic)
Canadian filmmakers' distribution centre 1969 28min Bonnie

Audiovisual Resources

Kreps, director
"Fast moving comment on the current state of the position of women emphasizing what the socialization process does to us and how we haven't come a long way, baby."

AFTER THE VOTE; NOTES FROM DOWN UNDER (mo pic)
Univ. of California Ext. #8445 1972 21min Bonnie Kreps, dir.
    Alternate title: A report from down under.
"Opens with brief historical footage of women's suffrage movement, then examines current status of women, more than fifty years after they attained 'equality.' Considers the socialization of women into submissive and subordinate roles; job discrimination and lack of opportunities for advancement; and the treatment of women as sexual objects. Interesting historical footage, news clips, and interviews with women are intercut with a long interview in which a sympathetic male psychologist discusses a variety of aspects of the oppression of women. Good introduction to many of the ideas of the feminist movement. Canadian production, but readily applicable to the U.S." (California).

ALIVE ALMIRA 38 (mo pic)
Filmmakers coop. 20min Canyon cinema R$30 S$Apply
"... a dance poem, a tribute to a woman who sought freedom, an abstract film...."

ALIVE AND TRUCKING THEATER COMPANY
3316 10 Ave. S, Minneapolis, MN 55803 (for mail) 612-824-4477
Feminist theater company doing both street theater and full-length plays, workshops for gaining skills, book of scripts, photos. "Stage left"; "The welfare wizard of ours" is a musical take-off about a welfare mother's plight to find a home for her daughter and herself.

ALTERNATIVES (radio)
Sample 4-minute scripts from Education Committee, Los Angeles
    NOW, 8864 Pico Blvd. 90035
Feminist view toward education, weekly, program produced by Gladys Falken, KMET.

AMELIA EARHART (mo pic)
Wolper 1965 26min From Biography Series
Sterling. Uses actual footage to portray personal life as well as history-making.

AMERICAN FAMILY (TV series)
Public Broadcasting System 1973 Associate producer, Susan
    Lester
With Craig Gilbert, Lester also wrote proposal for what was possibly the most extensively written-about program in TV history.
SEE ALSO #692, "Pat Loud; a woman's story" in Basic Book Collection.

AMERICAN GIRL (The problems of prejudice) (mo pic)
Dynamic films 28min CCM #7-1027-501-1 R$10 S$165
Director, Lee R. Bobker. Writer, Howard Rodman. Junior high +
"Based on an actual incident [in which an] adolescent girl in a
small town tests the democratic tradition in which she has been
reared [that portrays] her experience with anti-Semitism ..." (CCM).

AMERICAN HISTORY (transparencies)
Civil Education Service 551 transparencies grouped in 31 units.
Separate teacher's guide with each.

first semester units	# of transps.	price
Indians before white man	14	$35.00
Women's duties: 1 transp. $2.50		
How colonists lived	27	67.50
Women's work: 1 transp. $2.50		
Social and economic changes, 1800-1860	29	72.50
Women's education: 1 transp. $2.50		
second semester units		
Social and economic changes, 1860-1917	28	70.00
Women's rights: 1 transp. $2.50		
Suffrage: 1 transp. $2.50		
Roaring twenties	14	35.00
Women: 1 transp. $2.50		

AMERICAN LEADERS (FS)
McGraw average length: 42 fr C $7.50 6/$41
Series of six persons, of whom two are women: Jane Addams,
Susan B. Anthony.

AMERICAN WOMAN'S SEARCH FOR EQUALITY (FS & sound)
Current affairs #358 1973 18min C 35mm Current Affairs
  Filmstrips Series
With discussion guide.
66fr with 1S 12" 33 1/3 rpm record, $17.50; with cassette, $19.50
Advisor, Manson VanB. Jennings 72-736131
Through interviews and examination of existing and proposed legis-
lation, analyzes the theoretical and actual standing of women in the
U.S. Explains that women's organizations are making progress in
the fight against job and pay discrimination. (U.S. L.C.) Unfor-
tunate use of "Women's Lib" in Company materials.

AMERICAN WOMEN IN HISTORY (tape)
Pacifica. Judy Chicago interviews Isabel Welch, University of
  California, Berkeley political scientist

AND IT IS PART OF ME (mo pic)
Elda Hartley 9min C R$15 S$100
Natalie Hammond's beautiful garden-self.

Audiovisual Resources 149

AND NOW MIGUEL (mo pic)
United world 1960 63min
Child-growth and life in Spanish-speaking family.

"AND ONE AND TWO" & OTHER SONGS (rec)
Folkways #FC 7544 Ella Jenkins

AND THEY LIVED HAPPILY EVER AFTER? Understanding teen-age marriage (mo pic)
Guidance associates. Discussion guide.
Part I: 106 fr/20min. Part II: 104 fr/21min.
2 filmstrips; 2 12" LPs/$37.50/9A-100 253
2 filmstrips; 2 cassettes/$41.50/9A-100 279
"Identifies major reasons for teenage marriage: pregnancy, escape from home, sexual guilt, the draft, group status, 'drifting into marriage'. Considers handicaps of early marriage: economic stress, educational limitation, financial and emotional dependence on parents. Explores influence of social custom, religion. Teenagers and marriage 'veterans' describe their experiences..." (Guidance).

ANGELA DAVIS; PORTRAIT OF A REVOLUTIONARY (mo pic)
Yolande DuLuart 60min New Yorker R$75 S$425
"A moving documentary, with footage of University of California and the Women's House of Detention in New York.... Angela Davis' strength and courage, her willingness to talk openly about ideas, provides us with the kind of role model women rarely see, and always need." A UCLA student crew filmed her writing, teaching, joking with her students....

ANGELA DAVIS; SOUL AND SOLEDAD (rec)
Flying Dutchman #FD 10141 IV-235 An430. Interviews by Art Seigner

ANNE FRANK; THE DIARY OF A YOUNG GIRL (tape cassette)
CMS #X4549 1971 52min $7.95
Narrated by Elinor Basescu. Entries from the diary are selected --some picture the awakening of the young girl to early womanhood. To supplement and draw to the book, "Diary of a young girl" ($.75, Pocket Books).

ANOTHER LOOK AT THE MIAMI CONVENTION (video tape)
Women's Video News Service 1972 The Kitchen

ANTHOLOGY OF NEGRO POETS (rec)
Folkways #9791 1954 50min $6.50
Six distinguished poets read from their own works, two of whom are Margaret Walker (For my people, Old Molly Means, Kissie Lee, Stackalee, John Henry) and Gwendolyn Brooks (Kitchenette, Song of the yard, The preacher ruminates, The children of the poor, Old laughter, Beverly Hills, Chicago).

ANTIGONE (mo pic)
Macmillan Audio Brandon 1962 88min R
Director-writer, George Tzavellas. Adapted from the text of
Sophocles' drama of woman vs. authority. Photographer, Dinos
Katsourides. Cast: Irene Papas. Greek dialog with English subtitles.

ANTONIA: A PORTRAIT OF THE WOMAN (mo pic)
Judy Collins, Jill Godmilow. Rocky Mountain Productions, distributor, PO Box 315, Franklin Lakes, NJ 07417
Feminist documentary of indomitable woman musician, Antonia Brico.

ANYTHING YOU WANT TO BE (mo pic)
Liane Brandon New Day 1971 8min R$17 includes handling
 S$100. Eccentric circle cinema workshop 1972 8min S$100
 (May have C version)
Society's "subtle indoctrination" of women to conform to certain roles while offering them illusion of free choice. This is usually referred to as a "light film," shorter and more fun than "Growing up female" for example. Suggestion: use both together ... ask is it funny?

APOTHEOSIS (mo pic)
Yoko Ono 25min C Genesis R$250 includes package of 3 others
 + 4 shorts totaling 95min
Closeup of Yoko and John.

APPALACHIAN SPRING (mo pic)
Rembrandt 1959 32min Univ. of California Ext. #5518 R$15
"Full-length Martha Graham ballet whose early American theme and strong folk flavor make it one of her outstanding works ... " (California).

APPROXIMATELY INFINITE UNIVERSE (rec album)
Yoko Ono Apple
"Hands down the finest female rock 'n roller since the Shangri-Las" (Mike Saunders in Phonograph Record Magazine).

ARABESQUE (mo pic)
Nancy Linde 1965 7min Children's cultural foundation. Apply
 for R. Youth films R$10.50 S$70
Series of vignettes follow a day in the life of a "different" girl who is also alone. Filmmaker Linde was sixteen at the time of production. SEE note in Directory of Sources section re Youth Film Distribution Center.

ARE YOU LISTENING? (series) see SHOP STEWARDS; WOMEN
 WHO HAVE HAD AN ABORTION

ARETHA FRANKLIN, SOUL SINGER (mo pic)
McGraw 25min R$25 S$325

ARROWS (mo pic)
Barbara Scharres 1973 4min C silent Canadian filmmakers
    distribution centre R$6
"Loving, playful, erotic, funny films by men about women they love &/or lust for, abound. This is a loving, playful, erotic, funny film about a man by a woman."

ART REGISTRY (slides)
PO Box 539 Gracie Station, New York, NY 10028 or c/o Lucy
    Lippart, 138 Prince, New York, NY 10012
SEE ALSO Women's Art Registry.

THE ARTIST (FS) see WOMEN IN AMERICAN HISTORY (Series)

AS LONG AS THE RIVERS RUN (mo pic)
Producer-director (Ms) Carol Burns. Survival of the American
    Indian Assoc. 1972 60min C. American Doc R$60 S$650;
    Impact R$65 S$600
Filmed by Ms. Burns. American Indian women strong central characters.

AS SEEN BY YOUNG WOMEN (mo pic program)
Youth Program #VIII 34min R$45 S$350
1. "Aspirations" by Peri Muldofsky; 2. "Young love" by Lind Rivera; 3. "Office Cinderella" by Lauretta Baker; 4. "Three in the park" by Bernadette Beekman; 5. "Trio at 19" by Judith Kurtz
"Recent years have witnessed increased independence, expression and self-identification by women. In this program, five young women give voice to some of the pleasures, conflicts and terrors of growing up female."

ASPIRATIONS (mo pic)
Youth 6min C R$12 S$90 Filmmaker, (Ms.) Peri Muldofsky

ASSERTIVE TRAINING FOR WOMEN (mo pics)
American Personnel & Guidance Assoc. 1974? C R$25 S$250
Part I 17min vignettes especially for high school and college women; Part II 18min for college age and older. Patricia Jakubowski-Spector's pamphlet, "Introduction to assertive training procedures for women," is also available from APGA (1973, $2.25).

AT FIRST THE INFANT (tape)
CBC #7811 1 hour $14
"A celebration of the phenomenon of birth--describing its meanings, fears, and moods."

ATTEMPT (mo pic)
Youth 1968 7min R$10.50 S$70 Filmmaker, Ivan Quiles
"Boredom, attempted rape, and police action in New York City."

AUGUST 26th, INSIDE THE MOVEMENT (tape)
Feminist women's health centers   30min   R$30   S$50
Video tape in the series, "Women in Control."

AUTOBIOGRAPHY OF MISS JANE PITTMAN (mo pic)
Robert Christiansen and Rick Rosenberg, producers   1974   110min
   C   Ernest J. Gaines' novel (SEE Basic Book Collection #768)
   adapted by Tracy Keenan Wynn.   John Korty director.   Cicely
   Tyson as Miss Jane.   Learning Corporation of America
   R$150   Lease $1,450
"... quite possibly the finest movie ever made for American television" (Pauline Kael).

AWAKENING OF RUTH (mo pic)
Univ. of California Ext.   circa 1922
"A good, clean photoplay starring Shirley Mason. The story of a young girl who found happiness through self-sacrifice" (from the UCB Film Supplement, Dec. 1922).

AWARENESS '73 ... WOMEN, AFTER 1920 (radio)
WFBM, PO Box 20167, Indianapolis, IN 46220
Writers-producers-directors Teri Moore and Connie Munro.
WFBM and WFBQ Indianapolis mini-documentary series portraying contributions of twenty-seven Indiana women in furthering progress of women's rights.

- B -

BACK TO SCHOOL, BACK TO WORK (mo pic)
American Personnel & Guidance Assoc.   1973?   20min   C   R$25
   S$250
"Vignettes relating to the decision to undertake dual roles." Is there an assumption that they must be dual? ... beware "roles."

BALINESE FAMILY (mo pic)
New York Univ.   1951   17min   Character formation in different
   culture Series   Univ. of California Ext.   #8086   R$10
Producers, Gregory Bateson and Margaret Mead
"Portrays how a Balinese father and mother treat their three youngest children--the lap baby, knee baby, and child nurse. Shows the father giving the baby his breast, the behavior of the knee baby during the lap baby's absence, and the difficulties the small child nurse has in caring for the younger baby" (California).

BANDS   see   details under individual entries: Jenny & The Roseberries; Lavender Jane; The New New Haven Women's Liberation Rock Band; Songs & Rituals: Kay & Jeriann;   see also Women's Music Network, Inc. (Kay Gardner, 212-799-0020).

BARBARA'S BLINDNESS (mo pic)
Filmmaker's coop   1967   17min   C(hand-tinted)   Canadian filmmaker's distribution centre   R$15   Filmmakers, Betty Fergu-

son and Joyce Wieland
"A collage film. We started out with a dull film about a little blind girl named Mary and ended up with something that made us go crazy" (Wieland).

BARD AT LARGE (tape)
Pacifica #BC0935 44min $10 reel or cassette Producer, KPFA, 207 Shattuck Ave., Berkeley, CA 94707
Rae Lake Costos is the "bard at large" of KPFT, Pacifica Houston. She defines a bard as a person who travels about carrying the news of heroes from place to place. In this age, the heroes are those who help us define what spiritual freedom is....

BARNET THE CHILD (mo pic)
International Film Bureau 1971 48min C Univ. of California Ext. #8175 R$48 Swedish production (Svensk tonfilm, Stockholm) with British narrator. 72:712667
Presents the story of a young couple having their first baby and provides a complete account of the conception, gestation, and birth of the child. Uses animation to explain conception; provides actual photographs to trace the development of the fetus. Shows the delivery process in detail and includes an account of post-natal hospital care [L.C. summary].

BASIC HISTORY PORTFOLIOS (prints)
Afro-American publishing co., inc., 1727 S. Indiana Ave., Chicago, IL 60616. 6 social science studies portfolios, $4.95 each, package AT-4P $42.50. Each portfolio contains 24 2-color 11x14" plastic-coated prints with large portrait, short bio sketch, and source-references for all grades.
#1 Negroes in our history (women included: Mary McCleod Bethune, Blanche K. Bruce, Mary Church Terrell, Harriet Tubman, Maggie Walker, Phillis Wheatley). #2 Modern Negro contributors (women included: Gwendolyn Brooks, Katherine Dunham, Leontyne Price). #3 Negroes of achievement (women: Miss Maria Louise Baldwin, Mrs. Cora L. Burgan, Mrs. Mary Ann Shadd Cary, Mrs. Katie Chapman Davis, Mrs. Frances Ellen Watkins Harper, Mrs. C. A. Johnson, Madam Elizabeth Keckley, Miss Mary E. P. Mahoney, Mrs. W. E. Matthews, Mrs. Josephine St. Pierre Ruffin, Miss Gertrude J. Washington, Miss Ida B. Wells). #4 Science and invention. #5 Business and professions (woman included: Madam C. J. Walker). #6 Education and religion. #7 Fighters for freedom (women included: Charlotte L. Forten, Sojourner Truth, Harriet Tubman). #8 Champions of human rights (women included: Mary Pleasant, Mary Barnett Talbert). #9 Government and judicial (women included: Patricia R. Harris, Constance B. Motley).

I BASILISCHI see THE LIZARDS

BATHING BABIES IN THREE CULTURES (mo pic)
New York Univ. 1954 9min Character formation in different culture Series. Univ. of California Ext. #8087 R$7

Producers, Gregory Bateson and Margaret Mead. "Comparative study of the interplay between mother and child in three different settings--the Sepik River in New Guinea, a modern American bathroom, and a mountain village in Bali" (California).

BATTERED CHILD (mo pic)
Indiana Univ. 1969 58min Univ. of California Ext. #8021 R$16
Doctoral study shows team of psychiatrist, pediatricians, and social workers at the University of Colorado Medical Center studying causes and effects of child abuse. Points out that more children die each year from parental abuse than from all commonly known diseases. Based on the book of the same title edited by Drs. Ray E. Helfer and C. Henry Kemp (Univ. of Chicago Press, 1968, $12.50).

BECOMING A WOMAN/BECOMING A MAN (Revised) (FSs and sound)
Guidance associates With discussion guide. Part I: 56 frames/8
    min. Part II: Band 1: 50 fr/7min; Band 2:45 fr/7min. 2
    filmstrips; 2 12" LPs/$40.00/9A-100 543. 2 filmstrips; 2
    cassettes/$44.09/9A-100 550.
"Details male and female reproductive systems, comparative development during puberty, physical changes and their reasons. Focuses on emergence of male and female sexuality: 1) male physical and emotional sexual response, masturbation, responsibility, understanding of female needs and expectations; 2) changing views of female sexuality, physical and emotional responses, sex role and sexuality as part of total and continuing adjustment to life" (Guidance associates). Words to check out: needs, role, adjustment.

THE BEGINNING (script)
Bev Stager, YWCA, 571 Jarvis, Toronto, Ontario M4Y 2J1.
A multi-media presentation prepared by the Toronto YWCA. 1973. Request assistance re slides, music, production of the script.

THE BEGINNINGS OF A LONG AND REAL REVOLUTION (slide
    documentary)
Toni Carabillo 1972 200 slides with tape narration, script. NOW
    Public Information Office R$15 for NOW Chapters; $25 other
    groups S$150
Historical perspective on the history of feminism, 1868-present, with emphasis on NOW's accomplishment.

BEHIND THE VEIL (mo pic)
Impact 1972 50min C R$95/60 S$600 Writer-director, Eve
    Arnold. Nourma's voice narration, Janet Suzman
From the Impact catalog: "The Crown Prince of Dubai in the oil-rich Trucial States is taking a wife.... For the first time in film history we are taken inside a harem, with Nourma, a servant-woman as hostess. But we also see some remarkable things happening ... inside the Bank of Dubai women handling their own money and property; high-bred women learning to read and write, and accepting the benefits of modern medicine and birth control ..."

Two other films useful in re international women: Fear woman, From 3 A.M. to 10 P.M.

BEING ME (mo pic)
Univ. of California Ext. #7410 1969 13min R$8 S$75
"Documents a creative dance class of nine Black and White girls, aged 8 to 13, conducted by Hilda Mullin at the Pasadena Art Museum. Spontaneous movements, evolved in a series of explorations, reveal the dancers' total physical, mental, and emotional involvement ..." (California).

BELLE DE JOUR (mo pic)
Luis Bunuel 1967 102min 35mm in French with English titles
   International Film Dist., Ltd. (NTA Int.), 20 Bloor St. W
   Toronto
"Any woman who feels she is deprived of joy because she has never had the chance to be a call girl should see the movie.... That will fix her fantasy. The need for both physical and psychic beatings that go with this profession--the woman must punish herself for indulging unconsciously in incest--is clearly portrayed in some superb sadistic scenes, both of the fantasies that preceded this woman's prostitution and her actual experiences with men as she lives out the fantasy of gaining pleasure through pain" (page 201 of the paperback edition of Lucy Freeman's "Farewell to fear." SEE Book collection #347).

BETTY TELLS HER STORY (mo pic)
New Day 1972 20min R$25 S$200 Filmmaker, Liane Brandon
Betty recalls a simple incident: she needed "the perfect dress" for a special occasion. She describes in amusing detail how she found just the right one, spent more than she could afford for it, modeled it, felt absolutely beautiful, and then never got to wear it ... a delightful anecdote. Then she retells the story, revealing how she really felt. The contrast between the stories raises serious questions about self-concept, beauty, social values. A truly useful film.

BEYOND RUFFLES AND RESTRAINTS (slide show)
Circa 1973 1 1/2 hours C S$18.50 From: Marilyn Elias, NOW
   Center, 8864 W Pico Blvd., Los Angeles, CA 90035
Illustrates how typical socializing influences at home and school damage the self-esteem of girls.

LES BICHES (mo pic)
Macmillan Audio Brandon 1968 97min C R Director, Claude
   Chabrol; producer, Andre Genovese; writers, Chabrol and Paul
   Gegauff; photographer, Jean Rabier. Cast: Stephane Audran,
   Jacqueline Sassard.
French dialog with English subtitles. Two women, one man in menage-à-trois lead into violence.

BIG TOWN (mo pic)
Texture 1973 25min C Director-photographer-editor of parts,

Claudia Weill
5 pieces about big-city life: Mannequin, Marriage, Commuters, Yoga, Lost and found.

BIGAMIST (mo pic)
Ivy Film/16 1953 Director, Ida Lupino. Cast: Edmund O'Brien, Joan Fontaine, Ida Lupino.
"Ida Lupino, famed Hollywood actress, directed several features. This film ... is about a man who is married to two women and tormented by guilt. Joan Fontaine plays his career-minded wife, who is anxious to adopt a baby, while Ida Lupino enacts the other woman" (First International Festival of Women's Films).

BILLIE HOLIDAY STORY (mo pic)
Third world cinema
Dramatization of the career of the late blues stylist by the late Diana Sands.

BIOGRAPHY OF MARGARET SANGER (mo pic)
1966 15min In the collection of the Washington, D.C. Public Library

BIOGRAPHY OF SUSAN B. ANTHONY (mo pic)
1951 19min In the collection of the Washington, D.C. Public Library

BIRTH (mo pic)
Filmmakers 1968 72min Univ. of California Ext. #7539 R$19
  Arthur Barron Production. Producer, NET Public Broadcast Laboratory
"Warm, candid cinéma-vérité documentary of a young couple who are about to have their first child.... Includes a compelling 20-minute sequence of Debbie's labor and delivery, with Bruce helping" (California). Included as one example of the many motion pictures on the current scene about childbirth; it is certainly not feminist in viewpoint or presentation. Contrast with The Birth Film.

BIRTH CONTROL: HOW? (mo pic)
N.B.C. 1965 32min Films #33-0007 S$160. Human growth and reproduction series. R$7.60 from Florida State Univ.

BIRTH FILM (mo pic)
Susan Kleckner, filmmaker 35min C New Yorker R$60/classroom, $100/unrestricted use S$395
"No matter whether you've seen films about births already; this is one to see. The birth takes place at the home of the parents. The father is intimately involved, and both parents begin the film by talking about the difficulties and joys of having a child at home. A feminist and a lawyer, the mother says that the decision was a natural outgrowth of controlling her own life. The actual moment of birth is intensely moving" (Ms August 1973:97).

BLACK CONTRIBUTORS TO AMERICAN CULTURE (rec)
Society for visual education   1970   4 albums, 2 phonodiscs per album, each album $11.50; each cassette album $15.50
Brief historical biographies dramatizing contributions of Black Americans to U.S. culture.   #1 Blacks in science; #2 Blacks in government and human rights (57:20 min #IR-31.   Cassette #IC-31), includes Mary C. Terrell; #3 Blacks in music (60:05 min #IR-32. Cassette #IC-32), includes Marian Anderson; #4 Blacks in art.

BLACK FANTASY (mo pic)
Impact 1972 78min C R$75/$135 S$750 Producer-director, Lionel Rogosin. Venice Film Festival, Whitney Museum, New American Filmmakers Series
From the Impact catalog, where it was not listed in Women's Studies: Growing up in Arkansas under the supervision of his grandparents, abandoned by his parents at an early age, Collier recalls how he always wanted a white woman because she seemed to have "all the things the Marlboro man gets." Now that he has one, the illusions fostered by his early lust and envy have been replaced by a bitter struggle to maintain a love relationship capable of withstanding the anger, fear and resentment of friends and foes, both black and white.

BLACK FORUM (rec)
Motown #H1725   Langston Hughes and Margaret Danner's "Writers of the revolution."

BLACK HERITAGE (tapes)
Imperial international learning   1973   28 audiotapes, each approx. 20 min reel-to-reel 3 3/4 ips, with 35 student activity booklets for each tape and teacher's manual, $231.   On tape cassettes, $231.   Each tape or cassette with 35 booklets, $8.75. Writer, Kenneth Richards
Includes women Sojourner Truth, Marian Anderson, Harriet Tubman, Mary McLeod Bethune, Althea Gibson.

BLACK IS A BEAUTIFUL WOMAN (program)
Margo Barnett, performer.   TV version won two Emmy awards; for TV production information, write Sam Johnson, WETA TV, 3620 27 St., Arlington, VA 22206.   Demonstration cassette-tapes available.   Howard University, PO Box 345, Administration bldg., Washington, DC 20001.   301-773-8386 or 202-735-7104.

BLACK ON BLACK (mo pic)
Time   1971   60min R$7.50 S$50
Individual films on Shirley Chisholm, Coretta Scott King, and others.

BLACK PIONEERS IN AMERICAN HISTORY (recs)
Caedmon 1968 V1 19th century V2 19th-20th centuries
V1 Eartha Kitt and Moses Gunn reading the autobiographies of Charlotte Forten, Frederick Douglass, Susie King Taylor, Nat

Love. 1 12" LP $6.50, cassette $7.25. V2 Diana Sands and
Moses Gunn reading the autobiographies of Mary Church Terrell,
W. E. B. Dubois, Josiah Henson, William Parker. 1 12" LP
$6.50, cassette $7.95. Each reading accompanied by biographical
sketch of the author.

BLACK POLITICAL POWER (FS with sound)
Doubleday 1969 6 sound filmstrips, with phonodiscs, $93.50;
   with tape cassettes $105.50. Julian Bond, John Conyers, Jr.,
   Carl Stokes.
Yvonne Brathwaite: black and white together (147fr, 18 1/2min).
Shirley Chisholm: elect your own (133fr, 18 1/2min). Summary.

BLACK WOMAN (mo pic)
Indiana Univ. 1971 52min Black journal series. Univ. of Cali-
   fornia Ext. #8337 R$17 Producer-director, Stan Latham,
   Photographer, Chester Higgins, Jr. 77-714823
"Examines role and problems of Black women in U.S. society.
Includes interviews and discussions with many prominent Black
women, among them Lena Horne, Bibi Amina Baraka (wife of
Imamu Amiri Baraka, formerly LeRoi Jones) and poetess Nikki
Giovanni; they comment on the relationship of Black women to
Black men, to White society, and to the Black liberation struggle.
Shows a photographic essay on the Black woman, and includes
songs by Novella Nelson and Roberta Flack and dancing by Loretta
Abbott" (California).

BLACKLIST: A FAILURE IN POLITICAL IMAGINATION (tape)
Center for the study of democratic institutions #260 29:09 $7.50
"Although blacklisting is no longer practiced as it was in the 1950's,
an insidious and subtle form, far more dangerous, remains today.
So say two once-blacklisted artists--Millard Lampell, film writer,
and entertainer-commentator John Henry Faulk. Dale Minor of
WBAI-FM asks the questions" (Center catalog).

BODYSCAPE (mo pic)
Multi Media Center 10min C R$15 S$50 Laird Sutton, filmmaker
Semi-abstract film of a woman's body, closely shot, incredible
detail.

LE BONHEUR/HAPPINESS (mo pic)
Janus non-commercial R 1965 85min C France, subtitled
   Director-writer, Agnes Varda
"... one of the most beautiful films that I think you will ever see"
(Judith Crist). "... personal happiness as a force both self-grati-
fying and pathetically destructive" (Janus).

BOY BABY (toy)
Hans Gotz non-sexist toy 1973 $10 Age range 4+ Order from
   Bloomingdale's, Lexington Ave. @ 59 St., New York. NY 10022
German import with infant genitals anatomically correct, wets;

girl baby doll with suggestion of labia. Unfortunately "girl" comes dressed in pink, "boy" in blue, both blond and White only.

BOY TO MAN (mo pic)
Perennial C R$17 Churchill companion film to "Girl to woman" "An authoritative treatment, for boys, that deals candidly with the primary and secondary sexual changes in the male. JH-SH." Listed for discussion and reaction only....

BOYS AND GIRLS--ALIKE AND DIFFERENT (mo pic)
ABC Media #27402 9min C R$15 S$125
"You do many things because you're You, not because you are a boy or a girl...."

BOYS ONLY IS FOR GIRLS TOO (mo pic)
Xerox Corp., Advertising div., PO Box 1540, Rochester, NY 14600 1971
Kinescope about a Soviet girl who plays soccer better than her brother.

BREAK AND ENTER/ROMPIENDO PUERTAS (mo pic)
Newsreel 1971 42min R$50
The people of Operation Move-in in 1970 occupied 38 Manhattan apartment buildings. Most were Black and Latin, 80% were women with large families fighting to control their homes and build a community. / En marzo de 1970 un grupo de trabajadores, la mayoría de mujeres latinas, protestaron contra la ciudad de Nueva York; transformaron los apartamentos "inhabitables" en hogares; formaron una organizacion llamada Operation Move-In (abstracted from Catalog).

THE BREAKFAST DANCE (mo pic)
David Wilson 6min C Women's Film Coop R$10 Also available from New Haven Women's Film Coop.
"Portrays a woman serving breakfast to her family. You see her feelings about her role in a slow-motion, dance-like portrayal. A surprise ending packs a wallop!" (Women's Film Coop). Boredom, resentment; see if you "understand" the conclusion.

BREAST SELF-EXAMINATION (mo pic)
Cancer society 15min

BRIDAL SHOWER (mo pic)
Canadian filmmaker's distribution centre 1972 22min C R$25
  Filmmaker, Sandy Wilson
"The North American, premarital fertility ritual, complete with humiliations, party games and fright masks. Wilson is a filmmaker with some experience; among other things, she helped Sylvia Spring make "Madeleine Is ..." (Centre catalog, "Films by women").

BRIEF INTERLUDE (mo pic)
National sex & drug forums 6min silent C Multi media research

center R$15 S$50 Laird Sutton, filmmaker
Masturbation technique by a young woman.

BRONTE SISTERS (mo pic)
International Film Bureau 1970 19min C Univ. of California
Ext. #7877 R$16
"The somber beauty of the Yorkshire landscape appears here much as it did in the early 19th century when it influenced the Brontë sisters' writings. In these locations young people casually stroll in 19th century dress as Eric Portman describes details of the lives of the Brontë family and examines the personality of each sister. Actresses read from Emily's poem, 'Often rebuked,' Charlotte's letters, and Anne's poem, 'Self-communication' " (California).

BUMPER STICKERS see STICKERS & LABELS

BUNNY (mo pic)
U.S. Government National AV Center 1971 16min C In Social
  seminar series Univ. of California Ext. #8145 R$7
"A typical junior at UCLA. Casual drug usage is just one part of her life" (California).

BUT FIRST THIS MESSAGE (mo pic)
Action for children's television 15min C R$25 S$100
"An analysis of what is on commercial TV for children, with excerpts from TV shows and commercials, comments from professionals working with children and reactions from children themselves." Provides a basis for discussion about TV for children; ACT sends film with a kit containing statistics, clippings and background information, and an ACT newsletter. Aside from the excellent film content, feminists can learn from the ACT organization!

"... BUT THE WOMEN ROSE." (recs)
Compiled & edited by Susan Kempler and Doreen Rappaport.
Folkways 1971 2 phonodiscs, each approx. 45 min, with notes,
  each $5.98
V1 FD 5535: Anne Hutchinson, Abigail Adams, Judith Sargent Murray, Emma Hart Willard, Sarah and Angelina Grimke, Frances Watkins Harper, Margaret Fuller, Elizabeth Cady Stanton, Elizabeth Blackwell, Sojourner Truth, Lucy Stone, Harriet Beecher Stowe, Susan B. Anthony. V2 FD 5536: Anna Howard Shaw, Carrie Chapman Catt, Jane Addams, Mother Jones, Emma Goldman, Dorothy Day, Elizabeth Gurley Flynn, Margaret Sanger, Eleanor Roosevelt, Betty Friedan, Redstockings, Shirley Chisholm, Margaret Mead, Eleanor Holmes Norton. Readings from the writings and speeches of women prominent in American history since 1700. "Voices of women in American history" inserted in slipcases (79-752830).

BUT WHAT CAN A GIRL DO? (multi-media series)
Westinghouse Learning Press, 100 Park Ave., New York, NY 10017

4 C Filmstrips, 7 audio tapes
Eight women and their individual solutions to the problem of women's status in the working world: Judith Viorst, Eleanor Holmes Norton, G. G. Michelson, Janice Goodman, Gloria Santiago, Mary Woodward, Cecile Dickey, Marlene Sanders. Narrator, Julie Harris. Unfortunate versus-bit: NOW vs the Pussycat League, Rep. Martha Griffiths of Michigan vs Senator Sam Irvin of South Carolina, Kate Millett vs Lionel Tiger, but not devisive within the Movement.

BUT WHAT IF THE DREAM COMES TRUE? (mo pic)
Carousel 1971 52min C Produced by CBS News Univ. of California Ext. #8300 R$33
"revealing portrait of the goals and problems of an upper-class family whose dreams of affluence in the exclusive suburb of Birmingham, MI, are realized. Examines with insight the distinctly different pressures on each member of the family, consisting of Sam and Jane Greenawalt, their daughters aged 12 and 14, and their son aged 10. Shows that the pursuit of 'the American Dream' may mean an exchange of material problems for psychological ones ..." (California).

BUTTON, BUTTON (mo pic)
Suzanne Bauman, filmmaker and source 1969 13min C R
Animated documentary humorous investigation of people who make and wear buttons!

BUTTONS
SEE ALSO "Button, button" (mo pic). Jo Freeman's "Say it with buttons" (Ms August 1974:48-53, 75) which includes "where to buy" and information on a "starter set." Ms. Freeman suggests Ted Hake's "The button book" (Dafran House, 25 West 39 St., New York, NY 10018, $5.95) for additional general information on history, buying, selling and trading. SEE details under individual entries in Directory of Sources section: Beahive; Checkers Enterprises; Chicago Women's Liberation Union; Cisler, Lucinda; Farians, Elizabeth; Feminist Party; Know, Inc.; NOW, N.Y. Chapter; Torrez, T., 145 W. 45, #902, New York, NY 10036; Women's National Abortion Action Coalition.

- C -

CLUW (tape)
Video-tape of Coalition of Labor Union Women conference, Chicago, April 1974--3,200 strong!
Much of the taping done for the Amalgamated Clothing workers and the Amalgamated Meat Cutters to use for organizing and labor history archives.

CR-1 (script)
1 hour musical satirical revue, which needs six persons and piano accompaniament From Fresno NOW, Pat Bradley, 114 North Wood Duck Dr., Sanger, CA 93657

THE CABINET (mo pic)
Filmmaker, Suzanne Bauman 1972 14min C Carousel R$25
   S$175
Producer reflects upon her life via family memorabilia. Animated
sequences and life-action. Consider: Why is this listed under
"Women's films" in catalog?

CAFETERIA (mo pic)
Judith Wardwell, filmmaker Canadian filmmaker's distribution
   centre 1971 1min BW/C R$3
The story of a girl and her 26 cows. (Centre catalog, "Films by
women").

CALENDARS, ALMANACS, & DATE-BOOKS
   Colorado Democratic Women's Caucus.
   Diana Press
   Loercher, Donna, 162-11 9 Ave., Whitestone, NY 11357.
   Universe Books, 381 Park Ave. S., New York, NY 10016.
      (Lynn Sherr and Jurate Kazickas' "The liberated woman's
      apointment calendar, 19___")
   Virginia Slims, PO Box 7115, Westbury, NY 11590. ("Book
      of days.")

CARDS see GRAPHICS

CAREER MOTHERS (FS series)
Audiovisual Instructional Devices (AIDS) 1971 Range: 36-47 fr, 4:
   22-6:18 min C 6 strips with 6 discs or cassettes, automatic
   and manual. Teacher's guide. Gr K-6 AIDS-recommendation.
   $85 series. Advertising agency executive; Retail clerk; Nurse;
   Teacher; Commercial artist; Factory worker
From the catalog: "... different occupations in which women are
employed. They are all narrated by a child, who tells the story
of what his or her mother does in her job ... from a child's point
of view, what each occupation is like, and where and how it fits in
to the general structure of society.... Children will understand
and take pride in the fact that a mother can work, and still manage
her home and children." A learning experience may be provided
by searching the literature systematically for professional reviews,
e.g. Helen W. Cyr (Head, AV Dept., Enoch Pratt Free Library,
Baltimore) in LJ SLJ Previews, Oct. 1972: "... Prototype mothers
are shown in atypical occupational settings: the retail clerk is
seen in a chic shop; the teacher works in a school with no racial
minorities visible. Pictures do not match script in visual terms:
the cloth cutter's technique is shown with a long shot; described
hospital patients are not seen. The voices of the child narrators
are annoyingly over-expressive; words are swallowed and regional
accents (Northeastern U.S.) abound...."

CAREERS: CLERICAL (mo pic)
Doubleday #61625 1970 9min $98.50
From the catalog: "Clerical careers require basic secretarial

skills. This film traces the steps of a young girl who was unprepared and unable to find a job. We follow her through her training to the office where she is employed as a key punch operator. She speaks openly of her feelings during the search for work, the high school training she could have had, the difficulties of her key punch job and what makes it rewarding. Through her eyes, the duties of the other clerical workers are also shown." Junior high level.

CAREERS: COMMUNICATIONS (mo pic)
Doubleday #61545 1970 12min $98.50
"The communications industry encompasses a myriad of jobs.... A printing salesman discusses his feelings of satisfaction.... An advertising executive talks about his deep involvement in the industry.... Finally, a commercial photographer is shown on the job, photographing a road race. His excitement and love for his job are obvious...." Junior high level. Award-winner! For consciousness-raising!

CAROLINE (mo pic)
National Film Board of Canada 1964 27min S$170 Georges Duffaux and Clement Perron, writers, directors, editors
One of three NFBC films about women which are not produced with feminist ideas in mind but which nonetheless show women and their daily lives realistically; for sparking discussion and CR. Caroline is a "working mother" employed in a telephone business office helping customers.

CARTOONS, COMICS, COLORING BOOKS--SOURCES (see also
  #571 Basic Book Collection, and "Sexism in cartoons" slide-documentary).
  Feminist Press
  Golden West Publishers, 4113 N. Longview, Phoenix, AZ 85014.
  KNOW
  Last Gasp Eco-Funnies
  Lollipop Power
  Mama's Press
  Multi Media Resource Center (San Francisco): Lora Fountain's "Facts O'Life Funnies, 1972"
  New Seed Press
  Philadelphia Women's Political Caucus, 640 Rodman (19147).
  Planned Parenthood Federation of America: "Escape from fear/Amor sin temor" #326/942 English/Spanish color-comic book love-story.
  Rainbow Institute, Box 13907, UC, SB, Santa Barbara, CA 93017.
  Super Samantha...
  Woman's Soul Publishing Co.
  Women's Press Collective
  Zizi Press

CATCH A LITTLE RHYME; poems for activity time (rec)
Caedmon 1971 Stereo, 47:05min $6.98 #TC1339. Cassette $7.95 #CDL 51339 Read by Eve Merriam, from her 1966

illustrated book (Atheneum) for children.
These poems encourage participation and listeners are invited to respond!

THE CATS (mo pic)
Macmillan Audio Brandon 1964 93min R Director, Henning
  Carlsen; writer, Sigyn Sahlin. Based on a play by Valentin
  Chorelle. Cast: Eva Dahlbeck, Isa Quensel. Swedish dialog
  with English subtitles
The story of a group of women who work within the depressing confines of a commercial laundry.

THE CEILING (mo pic)
Vera Chytilova, director Impact 1962 40min R$40 In Czech
  with English sub-titles. Also available in 35mm
This motion picture was Ms. Chytilova's graduation work for the Film Faculty of the Academy of Performing Arts, Prague. It is the drama of a young woman who discovers she has set herself a low "ceiling" of attainment by dropping out of school to become a model.

A CHANCE TO CHOOSE (FS)
Producer, Sex Equality in Guidance Opportunities Project
SEGO also has a multi-media kit.

CHANGING (mo pic)
Univ. of California Ext.   31min   C   R$10
"Shows problems of a young family attempting to create an alternative life-style that stresses openness and spontaneity and includes marijuana. Focuses on parent-child relationships."

CHANGING LIFESTYLES FOR WOMEN--their significance to families (tape)
American Home Economics Assoc. 1970 60min Tape #7157
  $7.50; Cassette #7158 $8.50
Sociologist Jessie Bernard and psychologist Catherine Chilman attempt to answer some questions: Why are single women happier than married women? Is it psychologically better for a small child to have two "working" parents? etc. etc.

CHANGING ROLE OF WOMEN (FS)
Social studies school service   C   With teacher's guide: 2 FSs 2 LP
  recs $35.   With cassettes $37
Explores questions including why women are treated as a minority group.

THE CHANGING WORLD OF WOMEN (radio-TV)
Phyllis Sanders comments on the news from a woman's point of
  view, WNYC TV Channel #31, New York City, 7:30 PM, Mon.
"Changing world ..." is her weekly interview series on WNYC-AM radio, Sundays at 3 P.M.

Audiovisual Resources 165

CHARITY BALL (rec)
Fanny's second album.

CHARLIE CO. (mo pic)
Filmmaker, Nancy Edell   Canadian filmmaker's distribution centre
    1972   8 1/2min   C   R$12
From the Centre's catalog, "Films by women": "A procession of
creatures of the mind from the worlds of Bosch, R. Crumb and
Jim Dine. 'One of the most delightfully sexist films I've seen'--
Bob Fothergill."

CHECKMATE/STALEMATE (mo pic)
Lester Berman, Arden R. Ynew, Robert J. Phillips   1972   20min
    Cinesound   72-700315
Story of a young married woman's conflicts--explores her feelings,
thoughts, memories. Subject-headings assigned by the U.S. Library of Congress are (1) Wives, and (2) Woman--psychology.
The subject of subject headings assigned to women is vast and significant; for further information: Hennepin County Library [system]
Cataloging Bulletin (SEE Movement Periodicals section); ALA-SRRT
Committee on Sexist Subject Headings, Joan K. Marshall, chairperson (in Directory of Sources section); and Elizabeth Dickinson's
"Statement to the RTSD CCS Subject Analysis Committee
on Sex-Biased Library of Congress Subject Headings" (in Pamphlets).

CHELSEA INFANTS OF THE MARTIAL ARTS (tape)
Women make movies   1973   1/2" videotape   EIaj 1/2hr reel
    10min
By Jane Warrenbrand, a former youth worker who is presently
teaching young people filmmaking. The Chelsea Infants of the
Martial Arts, ages 3-13, demonstrate an amazing energy and discipline, as they show off their karate skills.

A CHILD IS BORN (FS)   see   NACE UN NIÑO

CHILDREN OF CHANGE (mo pic)
International film bureau   1960   31min   Univ. of California Ext.
    #5744   R$14
"Discusses the stresses on both child and mother when the mother
works outside the home and must adjust to two full-time jobs.
Suggests day care centers as one solution to the problem" (California).

THE CHILDREN'S HOUR (mo pic)
Lillian Hellman's play (In her "Six plays," Modern Library), available from United Artists 16   1962   107min
"The film adaptation of Lillian Hellman's fine first play concerning
society's victimization of lesbians. A woman's life is destroyed
by the rumor of her lesbianism spread by a vicious student and by
her own consumptive guilt about her love for another woman. In
our optimism about the new consciousness we would like to think
of this film as outdated--in reality we must understand that Hell-

man's view of institutionalized intolerance is contemporary. She does however deal only with the destruction of this woman as inevitable because of the cruelty of society and its instinctive fear of difference, rather than allowing her character any real positive feelings, or even truly ambivalent feelings about her sexuality. 'The Children's Hour' is an essentially sympathetic as opposed to political view of the lesbian dilemma and in this way will fail us all as a film for self-affirmation. Hellman is skillful and has no trouble depicting how society treats lesbians but portrays the struggle as an isolated one without the possibility of a community. We are not requiring a rewrite from Ms. Hellman, as the play is powerful, moving, and shows us the kind of anguish that lesbians are still suffering--but if you are looking for a film on the real joy of women who love women, this is not the one. Try 'Home Movie'." This statement by a feminist film coop member clearly conveys the relevance at several levels of the book and motion picture.

THE CHILDREN'S SCHOOL (mo pic)
Filmmaker, Deborah Dickson-Macagno 1969 17min R from Ms.
    Dickson-Macagno
A moment in the life of an experimental school for children, an educational alternative.

CHOICE CHANCE WOMAN DANCE (mo pic)
Ed Emshwiller, filmmaker 1972 44min C Distributed by Vision
    quest and Canyon Cinema R$50
Electronic music by David Borden, Steve Drews performed by Mother Mallards Portable Masterpiece Co. featuring Susan Lazarus, John Friedman, Carolyn Carlson, Becky Arnold; songs by Joan Friedman. Choices available to the middle-class woman of today.

CHRISTOPHER STRONG (mo pic)
RKO 1933 77min Films, Inc. R$50 Lease$500 Director,
    Dorothy Arzner. Cast includes Katherine Hepburn and Billie
    Burke.
From Homer Dickens' "The films of Katherine Hepburn" (Citadel Press, 1970): "Under the astute direction of Dorothy Arzner, one of the few successful female directors in films, Hepburn began to develop her screen image as the independent woman of the twentieth century. She was persuasive and vivid as the career-minded aviatrix...."

THE CHURCH RESPONDS TO MINORITIES, Part 1, #1--Women
    (cassette)
United Methodist Church Board of Education, Division of the local
    church, Nashville, TN 37212 1972 Young culture lifetime
    service, #5

CIRCUS: SERRINA BECOMES AN ACROBAT (mo pic)
Encyclopaedia Britannica #3051 1972 11min S$135 R$6.50
    74-715518
For grades 4-8. Because she yearns to be a circus performer,

Serrina spends the summer working with circus acrobats. In voice over, she tells of her experiences and the endless work which leads to success.

CIVIL LIBERTIES: contemporary case studies (series) (FS + snd series)
Guidance associates Disc or cassette, automatic and manual. C 6 programs with 1 strip with 1 disc or 1 cassette each with student manuals, teacher's guide. Grade 9+. With disc $19.50, with cassette $21.50.
"A controversial film" #415-742; "The student press" #415-743; "Juvenile thief" #415-784; "Marijuana possession" #416-105; "Open housing" #416-121; "Pregnancy in high school" #416-147.

CLASS (tape series)
Feminist Radio Network.
A series of programs in the Spring of 1973 exploring the effects of one's cultural and economic background on women in general and how it is incorporated into the Women's Movement. Karen Kollias, organizer of the Washington Women's Center and Rape Crisis Center; Dolores Bargowski, feminist activist originally at Wayne State and New York City and presently on Quest staff; and Beverly Fisher, political activist, participate in the discussions. Includes: #373-4, Class in the Women's Movement, 29 3/4min.; #473-6, Self-concept and group identity, 35min. How self-concept and group identity relate to leadership and class. Also with Rita Mae Brown, poet, author of "Rubyfruit Jungle" and political activist; #573-9, Class visions, 29min.

CLEO FROM 5 TO 7 (mo pic)
Contemporary
"France. World-renowned film director, Agnes Varda wrote and directed this story of a beautiful young singer, played by Corinne Marchand. We share Cleo's life one evening from 5 to 7 P.M. as she wanders about Paris, anxiously awaiting the results of a cancer examination. The film unveils the girl's utter loneliness, confronted by the possibility of death" (First International Festival of Women's Films).

CLOISTER (mo pic)
Filmmakers' coop 19min silent R$40
Gretchen Langheld's documentary on the Women's House of Detention.

COCK ROCK (tape)
Radio free people #71-48 $4.00 13min
The Women's Movement forces a woman to take a second look at rock music.

CODE BLUE (mo pic)
U.S. Gov. National AV Center 1972 26min C Univ. of California Ext. #8518 R$17
"Designed to motivate minority students to consider medical and

health professions as a career, as well as to answer typical questions asked by such students who are thinking about entering medical schools. Includes scenes of Black and Chicano professionals in varied medical and allied health fields. Excellent production, combining sincerity, encouragement, and a light, entertaining approach. Award winner." Why is this included here?

THE COLONIES (FS) see WOMEN IN AMERICAN HISTORY (series)

COLORING BOOKS see CARTOONS...

COMICS see CARTOONS...

COMMUNITY HELPERS (Photographs)
Feminist Resources for Equal Education 1972 $2. set
#1 8 black and white photographs 8 1/2x11" of women including pediatrician, orthodontist, policewoman, milkwoman, mechanic, mailwoman, farmer, bus driver. "These pictures are focused around the theme of community helpers for use with young children, but may also be used with older children to illustrate women in non-traditional jobs." Also: "Professional women," "Men in non-traditional roles" (e.g. homemaker, secretary, nurse).

CONFLICTS BETWEEN MOTHERS AND DAUGHTERS (tape)
CBC #313L 1 hour $14
Communication between mother and daughter.

CONGRESSWOMAN BELLA ABZUG (tape)
Center for cassette studies 36min $12.95
Speech to National Press Club.

CONSUMER POWER: CREDIT (mo pic)
J. Gary Mitchell Films, prod. BFA #1104 1973 20min With
    Guide R$22 S$275 73-703309

CONSUMER POWER: WHISTLEBLOWING (mo pic)
J. Gary Mitchell Films, prod. BFA #1537 1973 23min With
    user's notes R$25 S$310 83-803310
These films have their flaws, but "whistleblowing" is still on a par with rocking the boat and people who engage in it are often "blacklisted." Until social responsibility is acceptable, this area must be sought out.

CONTINUOUS WOMAN (mo pic)
Twin Cities women's film collective 25min C Optical sound R$50
"a positive film about the strengths and alternatives of women through the eyes of five women who recognize their own strenghts (includes a three generational study)."

CORETTA SCOTT KING READS FROM "My life with Martin Luther
    King" (rec)
Caedmon TC 2060-2 12" LP's $13

COUNSELING: TODAY AND TOMORROW (cassette, tape)
American personnel & guidance assoc. In series, "Occupational
 futures for women" being prepared in cooperation with U.S.
 Dept. of Labor Women's Bureau.
A new counseling media series. Main message to counsellors is
to encourage girls and young women to think in terms of long-term
planning and preparation for careers, to consider the full gamut of
career possibilities, and to seek as much education as possible
consistent with their energies and talents. (Women's Bureau
"Plans for widening women's educational opportunities.")

THE COUNTRY DOCTOR (mo pic)
Macmillan Audio Brandon 1953 113min R Director, Sergei
 Gerasimov. Cast: Tamara Markarova. Russian dialog with
 English subtitles.
"Intimate drama about a woman doctor in a remote Siberian town
... her personal and professional problems. She must win the
confidence of her superior and of her patients, who are reluctant
to be treated by a woman."

COURAGEOUS SISTERS (tape)
Pacifica #BC 0933 60min $12 reel or cassette Producer, KPFA
 San Francisco radio, in honor of the 52nd anniversary of
 Women's Suffrage Day.
Program takes a look at some of the vibrant and exciting women
of the 1800's who were, in many ways, responsible for the beginnings of the Women's Movement in the U.S.A. Dramatized versions of speeches and diaries are used, as well as live and recorded music, and a discussion with Isabel Welsh, a specialist in
women's history. A marvelous montage which brings the early
feminist movement to life" (Pacifica).

COVER GIRL; A NEW FACE IN FOCUS (mo pic)
Director, distributor, Frances McLaughlin Gill 1968 28min C R
Model-of-the-Year contest winner, Elaine Fulkerson, comes to
New York to be trained for a career in the fashion world. International Films & TV Festival of New York, 1969, Gold Medal
Award.

CRAFTS see GRAPHICS, POSTERS

CRISIS INTERVENTION: BOY-GIRL RELATIONSHIP (mo pic)
Producer, Fiorelli films Magus Films 10min C R S$125
A 15-year old woman is considering using sex to keep her boyfriend; the Listener enables her to examine her feelings and to
verbalize many of her concerns.

CRISIS INTERVENTION: PREGNANCY (mo pic)
Producer, Fiorelli films Magus Films 10min C R S$125
A pregnant teen-age woman is confused and frightened, does not
know where to turn or what to do and calls the "hotline" for help.

CRISIS INTERVENTION: RUNAWAY (mo pic)
Producer, Fiorelli films Magus Films 10min C R S$125
A teenage woman is tired of being a pawn between her separated parents and is considering running away as the only solution; the Listener tries to assist her in thinking out other alternatives.

CRISIS OF IDENTITY (FS) see WOMEN IN AMERICAN HISTORY (Series)

CRISIS: WOMEN IN HIGHER EDUCATION (mo pic)
Dr. Konnilyn Feig Contact U.S. Office of Education 30min C

CROCODILE TEARS see YEAR OF THE WOMAN (mo pic)

CROCUS (mo pic)
Filmmaker, Susan Pitt Kraning New Line Cinema 1973 7min
   C R and S
An animated film of a couple going to bed and making love, interwoven with real and surreal details of family life: the baby needs a glass of water, a giant cabbage floats through the room and out the window (Ms August 1973:95).

CULT OF TRUE WOMANHOOD--male and especially female, 1800-
   1860 (FS set)
Multi-media productions # 7-07053 Cassette, automatic and manual
   C & BW 2 strips with 1 cassette 40 fr 14min each with
   teacher's guide Gr 7-12 $16.95 set Catalog kits
"The background for many of the unconscious beliefs held today about woman and her place in society. PreVictorian concepts of woman as exemplified by Piety, Purity, Submission and Domesticity" (LJ SLJ Previews September 1972:87).

CYCLES (mo pic)
Filmmaker, Linda Jassim Creative film society 1971 10min C
"Rape and return to the womb."

- D -

DAEMON LOVER & THE LOTTERY (rec)
Folkways 12" LP with Notes 1962 $6.98
Shirley Jackson reading her "The Daemon lover" and "The lottery" (1971, Avon $.95/pap).

DANCER'S WORLD (mo pic)
Rembrandt 1957 33min Univ. of California Ext. #4676 R$15
"Martha Graham, noted choreographer and modern dancer, discusses the dancer as a creative artist. She explains the dancer's craft simply and clearly as members of her company illustrate her theories in a beautifully executed dance choreographed by Ms. Graham specially for the film ..." (California).

DARLING (mo pic)
Audio film center 1965 122min R$75 John Schlesinger, film-
maker
Story of a female model who remains unsatisfied although "successful." The film is a powerful look at our society's definition
of and response to "beauty."

DAVID AND HAZEL (mo pic)
National film board of Canada Perennial 28min R$16.50
"Concentrates on how lack of communication in a family is detri-
mental to the development of a healthy emotional climate in a
home. Sex roles of husband and wife are seen by each partner
in quite different ways, leading to conflict" (Perennial catalog,
which suggests this for high school, college and adult levels.
Check out the use of word "role").

THE DAY BEFORE TOMORROW (mo pic)
Airlie Foundation for the International Planned Parenthood Foundation. Association-Sterling 1971 52min C S$100 English
and Spanish. Also available in 28min version
Annotation from IPPF Library Bulletin VIII:#1:72: "... brings to
the audience ample proof of the part overpopulation plays in hunger,
poverty, and environmental deterioration.... Throughout Asia,
Africa, and Latin America family planning workers are seen giving
lectures, working in maternal-child health care programs, and
making contraceptive advice available to those who so desperately
want it.... Population is not, however, a spectre that menaces
only developing countries; the United States, in spite of vast wealth
and resources, has not escaped its threat...." Appearing in the
film are C. P. Snow, Robert McNamara, U Thant, Paul Ehrlich,
Allan F. Guttmacher, and the (male) executive director of Colom-
bia's Profamilia.

DAY CARE; CHILDREN'S LIBERATION (mo pic)
Newsreel 15min R$35 S
"Beginning with images of the loneliness of an isolated mother, this
documentary shows how a group of women in Canarsie, New York
found unused space in their community and started a day care
center. We see parents (fathers as well as mothers) teaching,
setting up a food co-op and a clothing exchange. Best of all is the
sense of shared community and the commitment to use day care
not as a way to dispose of children but to draw the family closer,
changing the way of life of all concerned. Excellent for organizing"
(Ms August 1973:97).

A DAY OFF (mo pic)
Awareness Films 1973 25min
"Two men take a day off together, embark on a series of male
adventures which end badly, and part, without ever really making
contact" (Pleck).

DEAD BIRDS (mo pic)
McGraw 1963 83min C Univ. of California Ext. #6606 R$37

"Intensive two-year ethnographic study documents the way of life of the Dani people ... of New Guinea. The Dani base their values on an elaborate system of intertribal warfare and revenge.... Wars also keep a sort of terrible harmony in a life that otherwise would be hard and dull" (California).

DEBATE ON ERA AND PROTECTIVE LAWS (cassettes)
Anne Draper of Union WAGE vs Diane Watson, former president
   of San Francisco NOW.   Cassette/$5 from Union WAGE

DECALS   see   STICKERS;   see also   GRAPHICS

DELIVERANCE (mo pic)
Univ. of California Ext.   7-reel, 35mm film
"An epoch-making three-act photo-drama featuring Helen Keller. Her message to the world. The highlights in the life of this remarkable woman are shown in this film. It is divided into three parts, the first showing her childhood, the next maidenhood, and the last as she is today (From our catalog of Sept. 1922)."

DESTROY, SHE SAID (mo pic)
Grove #415   100min   R$150   S#550   French with English subtitles
"Marguerite Duras, the French novelist and playwright who gained fame in the world as the author of 'Hiroshima, Mon Amour,' has created a hypnotic and haunting film about five alienated people isolated in an unworldly hotel.... With Catherine Sellers ..." (Grove).

DEVIL WOMEN (tape)
CBC #687L $14/1hour
"Throughout the ages women were believed to have contacts with evil and supernatural forces ..." (CBC).

DIANE (mo pic)
Filmmaker, Mary Feldhaus-Weber   Source, David Westphal   1969
   25min   C   R
Struggles of a would-be actress from South Dakota.

DIARY OF A YOUNG GIRL (rec)
Produced and distributed by Spoken Arts   2 phonodiscs, 92:17min,
   with notes, $13.   #SA1116.   2 tape cassettes $15.90.
   #SAC7201/7202.   73-750405
Julie Harris reads thirty-one entries in Anne Frank's famous diary, edited for this occasion by Alma Reinecke. Passages relate to her parents, her self-awareness, problems she has in growing up as an adolescent female; epilog is a statement of what happened to the family. SEE ALSO "Anne Frank; the diary of a young girl" (Audiovisuals) and the book itself.

DIARY OF CONNIE McGREGOR (mo pic)
Produced and distributed by New York University College of Medicine, 550 First Avenue, New York, NY 10016   1963   28min   R

Documents a student nurse's experience in a chronic disease hospital, including physical and psychological responsibilities.

DICK AND JANE AS VICTIMS (slide-tape show)
1973 140 slides arranged in one carousel tray, script, tape containing narrating comments 30min R$35 + postage and handling S$300
Based on research described in the publications of the same title by Women on Words and Images. See Pamphlets under Sexism.

DICK AND JANE RECEIVE A LESSON IN SEX-DISCRIMINATION (slide show)
Corrine Perkins, 815 Oakcrest Ave., Iowa City, IA 52250

DIRTY BOOKS (mo pic)
Filmmaker-distributor, Linda Feferman 1971 17min C
Would-be novelist mixed up with pornography.

DISCRIMINATION AGAINST WOMEN IN EDUCATIONAL TEXTBOOKS (slide show)
1 hour 26 slides R$15 includes postage Contact Education Committee, San Fernando Valley NOW, PO Box 20, Canoga Park, CA 91303.
Elementary textbooks used in California and other states.

DISTINGUISHED WOMEN WRITERS (tape)
Spoken arts $47.50 Series of 6 cassettes
Diary of Anaïs Nin, v 1-2; Informal hour with Dorothy Parker; Strange Fruit; Our faces, our words; The loves of Charles II.

DO BLONDS HAVE MORE FUN? (mo pic)
Universal Kinetic 1 1/2min C Women's Film Co-op R$5
Use of blondes from magazine advertisements ... media impact on our image of women.

DODSWORTH (mo pic)
Macmillan Audio Brandon 1936 101min R Director, William Wyler. Based on Sidney Howard's play of the Sinclair Lewis novel. Cast included Ruth Chatterton, Mary Astor, and Maria Ouspenskaya
Macmillan Audio Brandon catalog: "... Lewis' story of a self-made American businessman adrift in Europe was chosen as Wyler's first ambitious drama for Samuel Goldwyn.... Dodsworth, a builder and a man of direct action. Sam is yanked from his roots by a childish wife who succumbs to the gigolos and fortune hunters of a Continent.... Sam forges an inner steel that leads up to the statement: 'People have to stop loving sometime--short of suicide.' Wyler's portrayal of marital intimacies and small wounds, so important for the credibility of the drama, are refreshingly innovative even for our frank times...." Much raw material in this as well as Lewis' books.

DOLL'S HOUSE (mo pic) #1
Encyclopaedia Britannica 1968 Humanities Series C Part 1
33min Destruction of illusion; Part 2 28min Ibsen's themes
Univ. of California Ext. Part 1 #7166 R$22; Part 2 #7167
R$21
Part 1: Scenes ... here set in a modern American suburban home--show the play to be startlingly ahead of its time. First produced in 1879, it created a furor with its commentary on the social position of women.... Prof. Norris Houghton, Vassar, comments. Part 2: ... a number of questions emerge: Which of Nora's illusions about herself and her family have been shattered, and how? Has she betrayed her duty to her family and herself? What elements of an apparently idyllic life cannot be trusted? Prof. Norris Houghton examines these recurring themes: the supreme importance of the individual personality and the difficulty of establishing "right" and "wrong" when there is serious conflict of ideas (California).

DOLL'S HOUSE (mo pic) #2
Joseph Losey, producer-director. Jane Fonda, Delphine Seyrig
    1974 109m C Learning Corp of America R$110 Lease
    $1,150
"She is a rich version of most women--most women, except for those who have developed a new consciousness, spend most of the time lying. Lying to ourselves, to the men we live with, lying to society in order to survive, in order to be accepted. It's very difficult to be a whole person if one is always lying"--Jane Fonda.

DOMESTIC TRANQUILITY (mo pic)
Harriet Kriegel, filmmaker. Chelsea Picture Station Women make
    movies 1973 7min R$12.25 S$70
Kriegel is a thirty-nine year old housewife working on MA degree in drama. A wife and mother is haunted by her one-time ambition to be an artist. SEE ALSO "Toward new life-styles."

DONNA AND GAIL; A STUDY IN FRIENDSHIP (mo pic)
National Film Board of Canada McGraw 1968 49min Univ. of
    California Ext. #8473 R$22
Character study of two young women who come from the provinces to work in Montreal, showing how they meet at work, become friends, decide to share an apartment, have personality differences which drive them apart.

DON'T SIT ON THE SIDELINES (tape)
American home economics assoc. #7155 tape $7.50 #7156 cas-
    sette $8.50 1972 60min
Elizabeth Carpenter, former press secretary and staff director for Ms. Lady Bird Johnson, discusses the new involvement of women and politics, traces her own involvement in the Women's Movement.

DOROTHEA LANGE; CLOSER FOR ME (mo pic)
Indiana University 1966 30min Photography Series Univ. of
    California Ext. #6817 R$10

Many of Dorothea Lange's photographs are presented.... To the present generation of photographers she proposes a new project: the cities of America--to be done on a scale comparable to that of the Farm Security Administration Photographic Project of the 30's. She also describes her own difficulties in photographing "What is really there--the underpinnings--the human conditions" (California).

DOROTHEA LANGE; UNDER THE TREES (mo pic)
Indiana University 1965 30min Photography Series Univ. of
   California Ext. #6818 R$10
... While she looks over the accumulation of a lifetime of photography, she comments on the reasons and emotions that have moved her to photograph particular scenes... (California).

DORY PREVIN LIVE AT CARNEGIE HALL (rec)
United Artists

"DOWNWARD PATH TO WISDOM" see WOMEN IN LITERATURE

DREAM POWER (tape)
Pacifica #BC 0928 43min $10 reel or cassette Producer, KPFA
Betty Roszak interviews Dr. Ann Faraday about her book, "Dream power." (1972, Coward, $6.95; $1.50/pap, Medallion) Dr. Faraday discusses how her early childhood dreams, her career as a psychologist, and her experience with analysts led to the writing of this book. She agrees with the Freudian theory that dreams contain meaningful messages, but she takes issue with the idea that every dream is a fulfillment or disguise for sexual or aggressive tendencies. Both book and tape suitable for young adults.

- E -

ERA: PRO AND CON (tape)
Center for Cassette Studies $15.95 53min cassette
Views expressed for/against final ratification of ERA by the states.

EACH CHILD LOVED (mo pic)
Airlie Foundation 1971 40min C International Planned Parent-
   hood Foundation R$44 S$225 Narrator, Candice Bergen
Illegal abortion is contrasted with medical, safe abortion filmed in an authentic clinic; authorities briefly explain medical, legal aspects. A plea for educating men and women on abortion, contraception, and voluntary sterilization. Good title.

ECOLOGY LADY (mo pic)
Stuart Finley, Inc., 3428 Mansfield Rd., Falls Church, VA 22041
   11min C S$150
"Our ecology lady, Mary Karraker, who runs the Tysons Corner Recycling Center, tells how to do it in her own words." Volunteer (of course) Debbie picks twist-cap metal closure rings off bottles before recycling (picky picky aptitude).

THE EDGE (cassette)
Teleketics $5.95   Also available as part of Kit on Women.
Interviews with Erma Bombeck, columnist-"humorist"; Dr. Mary
Daly, theologian; Rosemary Reuther, Harvard Divinity School;
Rosemary Haughton, author-lecturer. Dr. Daly's books include
"The Church and the second sex" (#25 in Basic Book Collection)--
basic.

EDITH HAMILTON (mo pic)
Films, Inc. #33-0044   30min   NBC $150
Teacher, writer, international authority on ancient Greek and Roman cultures talks with friend Huntington Cairns of the National Gallery of Art on the Maine coast.

EEYORE'S BIRTHDAY (video tape)
West Side Video Collective, producer   Distributor, The Kitchen

THE EFFECTIVE TEACHER: Family life and sex education (FS/
   sound series)
Deryck Calderwood, author. Guidance Associates. Part 1:
   112 fr/19min; Part 2:   89 fr/15min; Part 3:   87 fr/18min.
   3 filmstrips; 3 12" LPs/$49.50/9A-105 013.   3 filmstrips;
   3 cassettes/$55.50/9A-105 021. Discussion guide. Stop-
   banded records for discussion pointing
Discusses need for sex education from elementary school level up, stresses need for teachers to build mastery of all facts, self-awareness, professional objectives, realistic communication with students. Examines methods of stimulating discussion, relating material to individuals and groups, subordinating bias, using school and local referral procedures. Parts 2 and 3 illustrate these points in action.

80 MILLION WOMEN WANT? (mo pic)
Univ. of California Ext.'s bulletin, "Lifelong Learning" (March 5, 1973:1), describes this "sympathetic American film, made in 1913, ... scheduled to keynote a woman's film series presented by the University of California Extention at Berkeley, this year, sixty years after it was made."

THE ELEANOR ROOSEVELT WE REMEMBER (mo pic)
NBC-TV, producer   1963   30min   R   Source: National Academy
   for Adult Jewish Studies, United Synagogue of America, 218
   East 70 Street, New York, NY 10021
Helen Gahagan Douglas, author of "The Eleanor Roosevelt We Remember" (1963, Hill & Wang, $5.95), observes the first anniversary of the death of Ms. Roosevelt.

EMERGENCY CHILDBIRTH (mo pic)
U.S. Navy, producer   1961   21min   C   Univ. of California Ext.
   #7554   R$7
"Designed to prepare lay persons psychologically and technically to render necessary assistance in emergency delivery of a baby. Use

restricted to educational programs conducted by doctors or nurses"
(California). Is this restriction imposed by the U.S. Navy or the
University of California? Our bodies, ourselves!

EMERGENCY; THE LIVING THEATRE (mo pic)
Gwen Brown, filmmaker 1969 28min C Source: Quest productions
An attempt to bring the viewer inside the Living Theatre.

EMERGENCY TRAINING FOR STEWARDESSES (videotape)
Women make movies 1973
Consciousness-raising tape made in cooperation with Stewardesses for Women's Rights, Inc.

THE EMERGING WOMAN (mo pic)
Film Images 1974 40min R$45 up S$350 Director, Helena Solberg-Ladd; Photographer, Lorraine W. Gray; Script and research, Roberta Haber, Melanie Maholick; Editor, Jane Stubbs; Narration, (Ms.) Leslie Cass. Produced collectively by the Women's Film Project, with partial financing by grants from the National Endowment for the Humanities and Calvin Cafritz.
This "film about the history of women in the United States" was exhibited by Film Images during the 1974 annual American Library Assoc. conference in New York; instead of a bar or a booth, the distributor provided this preview-opportunity in a hotel room! (Would that all AV companies would experiment with such approaches to salesmanship.) "The emerging woman" is a film about women by women, for everyone. Approximately the first half is devoted to the usual dead woman-and-suffrage, albeit well done. But this film keeps right on going ... living women shown as active healthy feminist persons ... abortion, demonstrations, Lesbiana ... all come across as part of what it's all about, rather than a dab and a dart off before anything is really said. Presentation of the women who are responsible at the conclusion is logical. There is hardly a film collection (possibly one serving children through approximately sixth-grade level) which should not have "The Emerging Woman."

EMOTIONAL ILLNESS (mo pic)
Indiana Univ. 1963 30min About people series Univ. of California Ext. #7015 R$10
"About a young husband whose wife has suddenly had a nervous breakdown and must be hospitalized. Dr. Maria Piers discusses his reactions of fear and guilt and also explodes some of the destructive myths about mental disturbance and psychiatry. She answers such questions as: Can a psychiatrist change your personality? Is sex the main concern of psychiatry? Is insanity hereditary? Are psychiatrists racketeers? Does psychiatric treatment ruin artistic creativity? She defines neurotic, psychotic, and psychosomatic disorders and discusses psychosomatics in terms of the interrelationship of mind and body" (California).

EMPLOYMENT OF WOMEN (transparencies)
Lanford Publishing Co.   10 transparencies $49.95 Distributor:
    Baker & Taylor #T001 (recommended by them for grades 7-12)
"Overall view of working women--why women work, which women
are working and at what jobs, incomes as compared with those of
men" (B&T).

ENCOUNTER (mo pic)
Filmmaker, Amy Greenfield 1971 10min Silent C Filmmakers'
    Coop R$10
"... it is between two women or two parts of the same woman.
Some of the movement was improvised. Sometimes we rehearsed
a set phrase and then I changed it just before we started shooting."

THE ENCOUNTER; A TRAGICOMEDY (mo pic)
Written, directed by David Campbell 1972 10min Distributed by
    Perennial Education S$130 72-701257
A student-made film containing insights into human pretentions and
barriers. Described in the literature as "an 'almost' boy-girl
relationship that never occurs because of shyness."

THE END OF AUGUST AT THE HOTEL OZONE (mo pic)
Jan Schmidt, Czech filmmaker 85min New Line Cinema
Although this is the story of nine women who survive a nuclear
holocaust, it is not a feminist film. It does, however, provide
some insights for women. One of these is that women who have
never been socialized into sex roles can be as strong and daring
as men without being self-conscious about it. ("Films by and/or
about women" page 3, Women's History Research Center, 1972.)

ENGAGEMENT ITALIANO (mo pic)
Macmillan Audio Brandon 1964 85min R Italian dialog with
    English sub-titles.   Annie Girardot, Rossano Brazzi
Woman rebels against male chauvinist boyfriend.

"EQUAL EMPLOYMENT OPPORTUNITY IS THE LAW" (poster)
Combined English/Spanish   From EEOC Publications Unit, 1800 G
    St. NW, Washington, D.C. 20506

THE EROGENISTS (mo pic)
Filmmaker, Laird Sutton 12min C Multi-Media Resource Center
    R$30 S$175
A male gives a female a body massage.

ESPECIALLY FOR BOYS (FS, Rec)
Wexler Set of teaching materials (elementary-junior high levels):
    47 fr C FS, 33 1/3 rpm rec, 12p study guide Perennial
    #182 S$15
"This sex education program was designed to help boys in grade 6
and up develop basic understanding and wholesome attitudes about
human growth and reproduction. The concepts include (1) an overview of the pubertal changes which are a normal part of growing

up, (2) the processes by which egg and sperm cells function in the continuation of human life, and (3) the development of a human being" (Perennial).

ESPECIALLY FOR FATHERS (mo pic)
San Jose Unified School District, Adult Education, CA 1962 21min C Univ. of California Ext. #6022 R$14
"Shows the important role of the father in supporting his wife in labor. The couple in this story have trained for a 'participating childbirth,' and their portrayal is natural, convincing, and interesting. Directed to expectant parents, especially fathers, but also valuable in training nursing and medical students and for hospital orientation for expectant parents. Close-up delivery room scenes" (California).

ESPECIALLY FOR GIRLS (FS, Rec)
Wexler Set of teaching materials (elementary-junior high levels):
  60 fr C FS, 33 1/3 rpm rec, study guide Perennial #183 S$15
"By means of specially prepared art work, this filmstrip presents an exceptionally clear picture of the functioning of a girl's reproduction system, and its relation to growth and maturity. Illustrated are the development of the egg cell into a baby after fertilization and the delivery of the baby from the mother's womb. The development of a boy into a man is also described" (Perennial). Comparison of these two products is a useful experience ... begin with these annotations.

EUGENIE GRANDET (mo pic)
Macmillan Audio Brandon 1960 99min R Directed, written by
  Sergei Alexeyev, based on the novel by Honore de Balzac.
  Russian dialog with English subtitles.
From MAD catalog. This is a handsomely mounted version of Balzac's classic novel (see below). Eugenie Grandet (Ariadna Shengelaya) is a sensitive, idealistic young woman who tries to fight the restrictions of her narrow middle class society. Eventually, however, she succumbs to the materialism of the world of the Grandets.
  Numerous editions of the novel are in print, including the original in translation (New American Library), young adults' (Houghton Mifflin), text (Regents), and Penguin's 1969 paperback.

EVA PERON (mo pic)
Wolper 1963 26min R Sterling

EVE'N US; women and the Judeo-Christian tradition (FS, rec)
Developed by Betty Strathman Pagett, lecturer, Union Theological
  Seminary, with help of other women. Availability: Not available for purchase; Rental inquiries to Ms. Pagett, 46 Rockledge Ave., White Plains, NY 10601. Inquiries re cut version of 20min FS: Service Center, 7820 Reading Rd., Cincinnati, OH 45237. S$7.50 45min 80 fr C Sound
Designed for use in local churches--music, dialogue, resource

packet. Produced with grants from the United Methodist Board of Missions and the Auburn program in continuing education at Union Theological Seminary. On women in the church, made from a feminist viewpoint and to encourage reflection and action. History and present status of women in the church--i.e. the lack thereof! Packet contains much non-copyrighted material. Consciousness-raising. Script: Elaine Magalis; Guide: Ellen Kirby. This was originally a longer slide show developed by a group of church-women. Photography: Ms. Pagett, Toge Fujihira, Jacque Gill. Guide provides preparation, resources, follow-up.

EVENING WITH ANAIS NIN (tape)
Pacifica

EVENUS see EVE'N US...

EVERYTHING YOU'VE ALWAYS WANTED to know about sexual
 therapy (tape)
Pacifica #BC0979.01 55min $10 reel or cassette Producer, WBAI
A documentary on the sexual therapy clinic in New York modelled after the Masters & Johnson Clinic in St. Louis ... contains a series of interviews with sexual therapists who use techniques which focus exclusively on sexual problems. They discuss the use of the man-woman therapist team...; the three major sexual dis-functions and how they are treated; the use of surrogate partners, prescribed sexual tasks, sensate focus in therapy; use of group sexual therapy as a way of branching out to reach lower socio-economic groups ... manages to transcend the clinical, mechanis-tic approach to sexual problems (Pacifica).

EVOLVING TOWARD WOMAN (mo pic)
Deidre Walsh, producer-distributor 60min
The struggle of women to redefine themselves in the midst of the changes that are happening in our culture via an introduction to the issues, rather than concentration on any one specific. Rap ses-sions, interviews.

EXHIBITS see GALLERIES AND EXHIBITS

EYES (band)
Box 11056, Oakland, CA 94611 415-652-0959
Female rock band available for West Coast dances, concerts, etc.

- F -

FABIENNE (mo pic)
National Film Board of Canada
One of three NFBC films about women which are not produced with feminist ideas in mind but which nonetheless show women and their daily lives realistically; for sparking discussion and for CR. See also "Caroline" and "Françoise."

Audiovisual Resources

FAHRENHEIT 451 (mo pic)
Directed by Francois Truffaut. Based on the novel by Ray Bradbury. With Julie Christie 1966 112min C R from Macmillan Audio Brandon and Universal/16 #26702-A-2
Bradbury depicts a society in which possession or reading of books is prohibited, and anyone who disobeys the state is punished. All individualism is supressed. "Fahrenheit Four Fifty-One" is available in paperback (Ballantine) and hard-back (Simon & Schuster) formats.

THE FALL (mo pic)
Macmillan Audio Brandon 1961 86min R Original title, "La Caida." Screenplay by Torre Nilsson and Beatriz Guido, based on Ms. Guido's novel. Spanish dialog with English subtitles; from Argentina.
Innocent young girl (Elsa Daniel) who has been raised in a repressive environment has tragic first affair, according to MAB catalog, which continues about "the explosive nature of virginal emotions!"

THE FAMILY IN CRISIS (tape)
Center for the Study of Democratic Institutions. #478 38:24 $7.50 70-765726
"Like every other institution, the family is today in a state of crisis. Discussion of the history, literature and quality of family life leads to speculation about whether the family is disintegrating or only in transition and what its future form and strengths may be. Stewart Sutton, Canadian social worker, joins Center Fellows for this discussion" (Center catalog).

FAMILY LIFE; A KIBBUTZ (mo pic)
BFA 1970 14min C EFLA 72-7806

FAMILY PLANNING (Disc/tape series)
Producer, Classroom world. Distributor, Associated Educational Materials #TB-1 $33 mono. 6 open reel tapes (7 1/2 ips) or 6 cassettes. Range 12-15min. Suggested for gr 7-up.
Includes What is family planning; Counseling ... birth control; Parental understanding; Reproduction ... fact and fallacy; Counseling ... abortion; The responsibility of decision making. Interview form with Public Health officials, physicians, and clinic directors.

FAMILY PLANNING AND SEX EDUCATION (mo pic)
Oxford films 18min C Teachers guide R$20 S$250 Suggested for gr 9-up
Includes Methods of family planning.

FAMILY PLANNING; MORE THAN A METHOD (mo pic)
Filmmaker, Phyllis Johnson 1971 27min R Distributed by Planned Parenthood World Population
Paraprofessionals succeed with a personal approach.

FAMILY PLANNING TODAY (mo pic)
Guidance associates Part I: 87 fr/12min. Part II: 63 fr/11min.

2 FSs; 2 12" LPs/$40/9A-101 426. 2 FSs; 2 cassettes/$44/
9A-101 442. Discussion guide.
"Part I begins with a poor Mexican woman's description of unregulated childbearing under physically, economically and emotionally destructive circumstances; surveys worldwide history of birth control, newer health and psychological concepts, economic factors, impact of population explosion. Part II reviews current chemical, natural, mechanical and surgical methods, forthcoming 'mini-pill, ' advanced intrauterine devices, implants, the 'morning-after' pill. Stresses importance of medical consultation in selecting birth control method" (Guidance associates). And then there's choice, responsibility....

FAMILY TEAMWORK AND YOU (mo pic)
Aims #1210 13min C R$20 S$165 Primary--middle grades
    suggested
"Almost free of narration, this film provides a comparison of two families. One family works successfully as a team--the other has a 'let Mom do it' attitude. Original musical score helps provide an experience to affect students' attitudes" (Aims).

FANNIE LOU HAMER (mo pic)
Rediscovery Productions 1970 10min C EFLA 72-7834
Rated +- by Audiovisual Instruction November 1972:MMR:61.

FANNY (record album)
Fanny 1971--all-woman rock group's first album Reprise Others:
    Fanny Hill, Charity Ball, Mother's Pride

FAT FIGHTERS (mo pic)
Brigham Young Univ. 1971 20min C
8 overweight females going through a course of weight loss therapy which seeks to discover psychological reasons for their obesity in order to improve self-image and bring about permanent weight control.

FEAR (mo pic)
Women make movies 1973 7min R$12.25 S$70 Filmmaker,
    (Ms.) Jean Shaw, a typist in a neighborhood settlement house, working on her second movie.
A sequence of harsh events culminates in a triumphant confrontation with a rapist, as a young woman is led to a birth of courage. Made at Chelsea Picture Station, a neighborhood media center administered by WMM and open free to residents of the multi-racial Chelsea Community in Manhattan. SEE ALSO "Toward new life styles...."

FEAR WOMAN (mo pic)
United Nations 1971 29min C Elspeth MacDougall, filmmaker
    Contemporary/McGraw release #408620-0 R$11 S$260
    73-714857
Summary: A documentary about the status of women in Ghana, noting their reputation for independence. Points out that the women

Audiovisual Resources

run a large part of the retail trade of the country, and that they are beginning to enter into areas which have power and influence (U.S. L.C.). Includes interviews with three prominent women: a businesswoman, a judge, and a hereditary tribal chief. SEE ALSO "Film program."

FEELING THE SPACE (rec album)
Yoko Ono   Apple
"This album is dedicated to the sisters who died in pain and sorrow and those who are now in prisons and mental hospitals for being unable to survive in the male society."

FEMALE CYCLE (mo pic)
Institut fur Film und Bild   Films, Inc. #101-0010   Human growth
   & reproduction series   8min   C   S$100
Animated "story of menstruation."

FEMALE STEREOTYPES AND SOCIAL CHANGE (tape cassette)
By Cornelia B. Flora, PhD.   Behavioral Sciences Tape Library
   #85609   3 1-hour tapes S$21.   1. Women's magazine fiction, 85610; 2. Women's magazine fiction, cont., 85621; 3. Organizing women: professional women and housewives, 85632.
   72-751083
A trio of creative commentaries illuminating the most popular issue of the contemporary scene: the emerging liberated woman. Dr. Flora addresses herself to the fantasies of women's magazine fiction and the realities of organizing Woman-Power in today's world (BSTL catalog).

FEMINISM AS A RADICAL MOVEMENT (FS)
Produced and distributed by Multi-Media Productions   1972   2 snd
   FSs.   35mm   Pt 1: 40 fr 10:40min.   Pt 2: 34 fr 9;54min.
   With phonodisc & guide $14.95.   Order #7-97063R.   With tape cassette $16.95.   Order #7-97063C.
Another survey of the historical antecedents of the current Feminist Movement; comes up to the 1960's. Consider the American Library Association periodical, Booklist (January 1, 1973:432-3) need to point out that it is "vociferous," with "somewhat strident narration," and its use of the term, "women's lib."

FEMINIST CHURCH SERVICE
Contact Kathryn Lemmel, 107 Westbourne Ter., Brookline, MA
   02146

FEMINIST FORUM; SELLING WOMEN SHORT (tape)
Pacifica #BC0869   28min   reel or cassette
Interview with Colette Nijhof about the image of women in advertising media, discussing the techniques of selling and illustrating the "sexual sell" and the "psychological sell" used to exploit and oppress women.

FEMINIST PARTY STREET WALKS (mo pic)
Feminist Party with Herstory Film Co.   1972   7min   R   BW   with

optical sound   Pat Bartozzi, Marion Hunter, Marta Vives
New York City summer street demonstrations: Feminist Party
members in street scene protest at N.B.C., Time-Life, C.B.S.,
Y.M.C.A., New York Times, St. Patrick's Cathedral, singing
feminist protest-songs.

FEMINIST THERAPY IN WASHINGTON, D.C. (video tape)
Made by Melanie Maholick, filmmaker of "The emerging woman."
  Contact via Film Images.

UNE FEMME DOUCE (A gentle creature) (mo pic)
New Yorker Films   1969   87min   C   R$150
Based on Dostoevsky's novella of a man whose wife has suddenly
committed suicide.

LA FEMME FLEUR (mo pic)
Directed and animated by Jan Lenica   Contemporary #406497-5
   11min   C   R$16   S$160
Woman depicted as a flower, ranging from "an ethereal bloom in
a tree to a sterile virgin to a threatening Salome." Tour de force
camera exploration of turn-of-the-century Art Nouveau, typified in
the analogy.

FESTIVAL OF WOMEN'S FILMS, First international
June 5-21, 1972: 15 programs of short films, 4 feature-length
   documentaries.
Several of these films are included in this Section and are pointed
out as such.   SEE ALSO information about the Festival ... in
Directory of Sources.

LA FIANCEE DU PIRATE...   see   A VERY CURIOUS GIRL

51% (mo pic)
Drucker   1972   28min   C   Univ. of California Ext.   #8452   R$14
   S$200 from Drucker
Contrasts two "upper-level" business-women and the characteristic
difficulties they must overcome to advance in management positions.
3 dramatized episodes designed to convince (male) management that
females should be afforded equal opportunity to get in there! "Each
episode portrays a different aspect of prejudice and discrimination
against women, and shows managers how they can help correct
existing inequities and ensure that all corporate personnel are used
to their full potential.   Stresses need to evaluate each woman on
her individual merits, and challenges managers to question their
own stereotyped attitudes toward women employees" (California).

LES FILLES DU ROY (mo pic)
National Film board of Canada: En tant que femmes Project
"A search for the identity of the Quebec woman in the guise of a
love letter."   Production of twenty-eight women.   (Shooting had
been completed as of 1973.)

FILM FOR DISCUSSION (mo pic)
Sydney Women's Film Group   Distributed by Sydney (Australia)
    Filmmakers Coop.

FILM PROGRAM (s)
Just as most publishers have their "women's lib" books, most author-lecture bureaus now have a "woman's program" which purports to be Movement! The Author Lecture Service of Doubleday & Co., Inc. (277 Park Ave., New York, NY 10017. 212-TA6-2000), for example, offers a $1,000 package designed to run four days, accompanied by a feminist lecturer to benefit women filmmakers and including Fear woman, Growing up female, Gertrude Stein..., Woman's film, and A very curious girl.

FINNISH FRUSTRATIONS (mo pic)
Filmmaker, Eila Kaarresalo-Kasari 1969 7min
A Finnish film about the Finnish woman's life of paradox; considered independent, they remain yet the objects in the sexual arena. Contact Finnish-American Chamber of Commerce, 540 Madison Ave., New York, NY 10022, 212-832-2588.

FIRST LOVE (tape)
Feminist Radio Network #1173-25   31min
A reading of an original short story about lesbianism by Lynn Farley.

FIRST STOP (mo pic)
Planned Parenthood, San Francisco
A woman in Chicago tries to get an abortion and the problems she encounters.

FIVE (mo pic)
Produced by Silvermine Films 1971 28min Teacher's guide
    Distributed by West Glen Communications S$195 70-13414
The five are black artists, two of whom are women: Barbara Chase-Riboud and Betty Blayton. Each, in voice-over, talks about her life work.

THE FLAME (mo pic)
Macmillan Audio Brandon 1957 74min R Swedish dialog with
    English subtitles Director and star, Arne Ragneborn
Sympathetic portrayal of a prostitute who challenges the integrity of "respectable" society. Written by an official of Stockholm's Langholmen Prison, the film exposes the hypocrisy and smugness of citizens who self-righteously condemn all prostitutes as immoral criminals.

FLICKORNA see THE GIRLS

FOOD AND MATERNAL DEPRIVATION (mo pic)
New York Univ. 1961 20min Univ. of California Ext. #4849
    R$11

Part of the record collected by a French research unit studying effects of maternal deprivation on child development. Indicates that feeding difficulties are often linked with maternal deprivation and that a child's attitude toward food is frequently an expression of his/her attitude toward adults willing to give him maternal care. Intended for professional audiences.

FOR BETTER, FOR WORSE (mo pic)
ACI Productions   1967   25min   Methodist Church, Nashville, TN
NEGATIVE

FOR BETTER OR WORSE (mo pic)
By Judith Shaw Acuna   7min   1973   Women makes movies
    R$12.25   S$70
Professional by day and domestic by night, a newly-wed pediatrician finds herself working a double-shift. Her solution? SEE ALSO Toward new life styles.

FOR SALE (mo pic)
Youth   1970   10min   R$18   S$120   Ronald Kauffman, filmmaker
    (18 years old)
"A young woman who fulfills the stereotype of the 'doll-like-blue-eyed-blond' finds herself treated not as a person, but as just another 'advertised special'."

FOR THE CAUSE OF A SUFFRAGE (mo pic)
Univ. of California Ext. "Lifelong Learning" March 5, 1973:1 describes a 1909 motion picture which "portrayed the movement (women's voting rights) sympathetically."

FOR WOMEN ONLY (TV programs)
National Broadcasting Co. Community Affairs Dept., NBC News.
    Aline Saarinen.   30 Rockefeller Plaza, New York, NY 10020
Misnomer--topics are general, not "for women only," e.g., The problem gambler, Music and the community, Sleep, Sex and the law, Water pollution, Fertility. Panels loaded with males.

FOR WOMEN TODAY (TV programs)
Westinghouse Broadcasting Co., producer   Hour-long TV programs.
    WBZ-TV #4, 1170 Soldiers' Field Road, Boston, MA 02134.
    617-254-5670

FOUR CHOSEN WOMEN (stage production)
A Fine Art Service Production, 104 Lincoln Ave., Stamford, CT
    06902, 212-583-8676
Program: Anaïs Nin, Suzanne Benton, Joan Stone, Vinie Burrows.

FOUR PLUS TWO (mo pic)
Pat Saunders, filmmaker and source   1971   4min
Experimental film about a woman and her horse.

FOUR WOMEN (mo pic)
Filmmaker Ilanga Witt (Age 18)   Youth Films   1970   5min   C

Audiovisual Resources   187

   R$15 S$75
Nina Simone's song interpreted in dance by students at the Harlem
Preparatory School; film in counterpoint with images of women in
the community.

FRAGILITY AND FORCE IN THE "ETERNAL FEMININE" (art print
set)
Bro-Dart, 1609 Memorial Ave., Williamsport, PA 17701   #87-308
   Group A8   20 prints   "Commentaries," catalog cards available.
A few examples of the male artists and their works from this truly
corny-title series: Goya's Señora Sabasa Garcia, Toulouse-Lau-
trec's Portrait of Madame Lucy, VanGogh's Woman rocking a
cradle, Picasso's Classical head, and Cezanne's Madame Cezanne.

FRANCES FLAHERTY: HIDDEN AND SEEKING (mo pic)
Werner, producer 1972 56min Contemporary/McGraw #408655
   R$35 S$350 72-701805
Although most reviewers record documentary in terms of Frances
Flaherty, "the widow of filmmaker Robert Flaherty as well as an
energetic, alert, and active eighty-seven-year-old...," it is about
Ms. Flaherty, who speaks about her filming experiences and her
work as a photographer.

FRANCOISE (mo pic)
National Film Board of Canada
One of three NFBC films (Caroline, Fabienne) about women which
are useful to spark discussion and consciousness-raising, although
not produced with feminist motivation; this utility is basically due
to their showing women and their daily lives realistically.

"FREE THE SECRETARY" (Labels)
Compliments of Redactron Corp., makers of typewriters.
For walls and things....

FREE TO BE ... YOU AND ME (rec)
Bell Disc #110 $5.98. Cassette #M-51110 $6.95. Album
   can also be ordered from Ms, Dept. R, 370 Lexington Ave.,
   New York, NY 10017 ($6.50) which also has information re
   16mm film of the TV show.
A portion of the proceeds go to the Ms. Foundation for Women,
which will support more projects such as this one. Marlo Thomas
and friends (including Mel Brooks, Diana Ross, Alan Alda, Harry
Belafonte, Carol Channing, Tom Smothers, Rosey Grier, Dick
Cavett, Jack Cassidy, Shirley Jones, Bobby Morse, Billy DeWolfe,
and the New Seekers) present songs, stories and poems designed
to keep a child's mind open to all the possibilities life affords.
The same title in book form is available from Ms. Dept. MH,
published by McGraw ($5.50/pap, $8.50) for elementary school
age children. These are worthy self-conscious efforts which seem
to be screened through what adults think appeal to children.

FREEDOM TO LOVE (mo pic)
Grove #436 90min C R$150 S$725 By Drs. Phyllis and Eber-

hard Kronhausen
Archer Winsten, New York Post: "Avoids for the most part any taint of lewd thinking.... It has the European accent and scientific approach of ... a Paris-based team of psychotherapists, who bring to their commentary the prophylaxis of total sincerity.... Gives intellectual body to what might otherwise seem grossly exploitational material.... Educational material from the sex files that proves its own thesis. What used to be pornography turns out, after all, to be nothing but sex without the shame based on Victorian standards of behavior. And no one seems the worse for it.... Always is good for you." Grove catalog: about the irrationality of common sexual prejudices and traditional sex laws ... advances the point of view that sexual freedom is not inimical to the interests of society. The film suggests, in fact, that official and unofficial suppression of sexuality and the resultant sexual frustrations are actually a contributing factor in social ills, such as juvenile delinquency, crime, family breakdown, and divorce. To illustrate the effect of sexual bigotry, the Drs. K. have dramatized three case histories from their own files...: the prosecution of a "minor" involved in a sexual adventure; the encounter of a lesbian couple and two young girls; and the participation of an unhappily married couple in a group sex party.

FRIENDS (mo pic)
Churchill 1972 18min C
A story about the friendship between Nancy, an extroverted, impatient girl, and her vulnerable best friend; about what happens to feelings when Nancy goes off to play with another girl.

FROM THE INSIDE OUT (mo pic)
Film images 13min R$15 S$125
Six 15-year old girls express their thoughts and feelings through movement in creative dance choreographed by the girls themselves.

FROM THE MIXED-UP FILES of Mrs. Basil E. Frankweiler (media kit)
Miller-Brody #3010 kit: 12 paperbacks, record $17.90; with cassette $19.35.
E. L. Konigsburg's 1967 Atheneum book for children. Claudia maps out a careful running-away plan which leads her and her little brother from their suburban home to the Metropolitan Museum of Art in New York City.

FROM 3 A.M. to 10 P.M. (mo pic)
Contemporary #408062-8 15min R$12.50 S$115 Written and directed by Kreso Golik. Photography by Ivica Rajkovic. Produced by Zagreb Films.
Without narration or dialogue, Yugoslavian documentary describes the long day of a "working mother."

FRUIT OF PARADISE (mo pic)
Film Images 1970 98min C 16mm and 35mm
Vera Chytilova's analysis of the temptation of Eve. Czech dia-

logue with English subtitles. Award winner at Toronto 1973 Women & Film Festival, 1972 Women's Film Event at Edinburgh Film Festival. Can one live with the truth? Comedy and successful use of symbolism and abstraction which tell a story.

A FULL LIFE (Mitasareta Seikatsu) (mo pic)
New Yorker 1962 102min R$150
Story of a young woman who leaves her husband to find fulfillment outside her marriage role. She rejoins her old acting company and becomes involved with its director, a fellow defector from the bourgeoisie. Although a sympathetic portrait of the heroine, the film does slightly resemble more conventional Japanese "women's pictures"; however, the real focus is on two related themes: the oppression of women in modern consumer/capitalist society, and the need for men and women to harmonize their personal lives with the mass currents of social change. Ineko Arima as the heroine.

THE FURIES (tape)
Feminist Radio Network # 672-1 29min Cassette: $20; Reels: 7 1/2ips $25, 3 3/4ips $20
"An interview with women from the collective that published the Furies newspaper; discussion on lesbianism and feminism. Summer 1972" (FRN).

- G -

GALLERIES FEATURING THE WORK OF WOMEN; EXHIBITS
  Ailanthus
  A. I. R. Artists in Residence
  A. R. C.
  Artemisia
  Baldwin Street
  Central Hall Artists
  Not in New York...
  Penelope & Sisters
  Phyllis Kind Gallery
  Picture Post Gallery
  Planned Parenthood World
     Population (exhibit)
  Powerhouse Gallery
  Show of Hands
  Soho 20
  Womancraft
  Womanspace
  Women's Art Center
  Women's Coop. & Craft Store
  Women's Interart Center

THE GAME (mo pic)
Producer, director, photographer, editor: Abigail and Jon Child
  1972 38min R$30 S$300
Cinéma vérité "story" of a Black hooker and her pimp; reviews by males typically refer to Tina's having chosen her work. Distributor suggests this for use in sociology, psychology, Black studies, Women's Studies, urban problems studies. See if you agree. Consider Psychology Professor Leigh Marlowe's comments: "When I first saw the Child's documentary, Game, at the Women's Film Festival in New York, I decided I must have it for the Psychology of Women course I teach.... From the perspective of a feminist psychologist, Tina's story is a modern variation on an ancient

theme: women can do/become only what exploitative men permit
for their egocentric lifeways...."

THE GAMES MEN PLAY (rec)
New York Chapter of the National Women's Book Assoc. 1974
    Anti-Defamation League $12.00 album

GARDERIES (mo pic)
National Film Board of Canada En tant que femmes Project 1973
    1 hour scheduled for broadcast on CBC French network.
Production of twenty-eight women--"Less a study of day care for
children than it is a reflection on the child and the commitment of
adults to him. Editing is being completed."

GENESIS 3:16 (mo pic)
Maureen McCue and Lois Ann Tupper, filmmakers 20min R$30
Made by an all-woman crew, this documentary is about the alternative lifestyles women have created for their own growth. Focusing on life in a women's commune, includes sequences on self-defense and gay women. Contact Ms. Tupper, 60 Chilton, Cambridge, MA 02138.

GENETICS: MAN THE CREATOR (mo pic)
Document Associates, 211 E 51 St., New York, NY 10022 1971
    22min C Towards the year 2000 series Univ. of California
    Ext. #8384 R$25
Surveys current research and explores possibilities for "human genetic engineering," or the science of eugenics. Shows and discusses a sperm bank, an embryo transplant in a goat, and a lamb embryo growing in an artificial womb ... explains the concept of cloning, or forming many identical twins from one cell ... moral issues involved. Award winner.

A GENTLE CREATURE see UNE FEMME DOUCE

GERMAINE GREER MEETS THE NATIONAL PRESS CLUB (tape)
Pacifica Tape Library

GERRITSEN COLLECTION OF WOMEN'S HISTORY, 1543-1945
    (microfiche)
Microfilming Corp. of America; a New York Times Co., 21 Harristown Rd., Glenrock, NJ 07452; 201-447-3000, Jean Reid.
    4x6" microfiche collection, printed Guide, and "Catalog Card
    System" $18,000.
4,000+ volumes of books, periodicals and pamphlets from the Kenneth Spencer Research Library, University of Kansas.

GERTRUDE STEIN; when this you see, remember me (mo pic)
Producer-director Perry Miller Adato 1972 90min total C
    Contemporary R$50 up S$850. Also rent from Univ. of California Ext. #8435 $47 Contemporary Complete #408560-3.
    Part 1 408561-1 31min S$350. Part 2 408562-X 30min

S$350. Part 3 408563-8 28min S$300
Written by Mariana Norris. Shown at First International Festival
of Women's Films in New York, 1972, in whose bulletin it was
described as follows: The Stein home in Paris was a mecca for
artists, writers and composers of the '20s and '30s ... captures
the spirit of Stein's genius in a visual collage of old photos, excerpts from her novels, paintings from her famous collection,
candid interviews with friends and playful home movies with Alice
B. Toklas. Produced for NET.

GHETTO GODDESS (audiotape)
Women Make Movies 1973 1/4" audiotape 7 1/2ips 5" reels
    40min By Angela Lifsey, Lisa Methfessel, Denise Wragg--
    three teenagers interested in sports and drama.
A dramatic serial in four episodes, the story of Lorna Anderson,
teenage runaway who becomes super heroine dedicated to helping
people. Final episode--her decision to return home and face her
own family problems.

EL GHORBA see THE PASSENGERS

GIBBOUS MOON (mo pic)
Filmmaker, Nancy Ellen Dowd 1970 22min R Available from
    Canadian Filmmaker's distribution centre (R$30), Dowd (PO
    Box 523, 2708 Topanga Skyline, Topanga, CA 90290 and Mule
    Movies, same address: R$35, S$250). Also New Line Cinema.
Ms. magazine: "A lyrical portrait of an unmarried young woman
who decides to become a mother. While women may have varying
reactions to her poetical maternalism, it is impossible not to be
deeply moved by the death of her baby and by the simple beauty of
the film."

GIFT OF CHOICE (mo pic)
Indiana Univ. 1965 60min Population problem series Univ. of
    California Ext. #6616 R$14
Reports on experiments carried out to determine factors controlling
pregnancies, both to aid those who want children and to control
fertility for those who want to limit family size. Details scientific
research on why the egg is released, the ovulation process, passage
of the egg through the Fallopian tubes, and chemical changes that
occur to make conception and implantation possible (California).

GIRL BABY (toy) see BOY BABY (toy)

THE GIRLS/FLICKORNA (mo pic)
Mai Zetterling, director 1972 100min Sweden (Sandrews). New
    Line Cinema
Ms. Zetterling's fourth feature film ("Night games," "Loving
couple," "Doktor Glas"). Three actresses depart on a provincial
tour with "Lysistrata," Aristophanes' comedy about women who end
a war by refusing to sleep with their husbands. They begin to see
parallels with their own lives and continue their roles off-stage,

denouncing feminine apathy and male chauvinism. With Bibi Andersson, Gunnel Lindblom, Harriet Andersson.

GIRLS AND WOMEN (mo pic series)
University Television Center, Ann Arbor, MI 48104 Filmmakers Selma Odom, Margo Shackson
A series of 10 programs, 30min each, focusing on the physical and sociological differences between the sexes, the psychology of women, variations of life styles, women's "place" in history, stereotypes of women and women's rights. Contact Ms. Odom at Barbour Gymnasium, Univ. of Michigan, Ann Arbor 48104 and/or <u>Ann Arbor News</u>.

GIRLS ARE WEAK (slide show)
San Bernardino/Riverside, CA NOW 140 slides Contact Nancy White, 616 East Citrus, Redlands, CA 92373

THE GIRLS' CORNER; textbooks and options (slide shows)
Lenore Weitzman 6 shows: Introduction to sex roles in textbooks; Sex roles in mathematics, reading, science, social studies, spelling textbooks. 30min each tapes included R/S not yet determined
Contact Ms. Weitzman, University of California, Davis Sociology Dept., Davis, CA 95616.

GIRLS OF MOUNTAIN STREET (mo pic)
National Film Board of Canada
Not a feminist film per se, but shows women in their daily lives realistically.

GIVE TO GET (mo pic)
Filmmaker, Laird Sutton 11min C Multi Media R$30 S$175
A woman massages a man, they move to a water bed, and engage in intercourse.

GLORIA STEINEM (tape)
Center for Cassette Studies 59min cassette $16.95
A conversation with Gloria Steinem, who discusses the women's social revolution, its accomplishments and failures.

GLORY OF NEGRO HISTORY (rec)
Folkways #7752 1960 50min $5.98
"African chants and American Negro folk songs accompany Langston Hughes' discussion of triumps and tragedies of Negroes in America. Voices of Ralph Bunche and Mary McLeod Bethune are featured in this documentary. Intermediate-Upper" (<u>Booklist</u> May 1, 1973:843).

GOODBYE IN THE MIRROR (mo pic)
Written and directed by (Ms.) Storm deHirsch 1964 80min Impact R$50 up
A dramatic feature filmed on location in Rome, centered around the adventures and illusions of three young women living abroad.

It explores the restless nature of these "girls and their personal involvements in assuming the role of woman as hunter," as Impact puts it.

GOODBYE LYNN (mo pic)
Centron 1972 21min C S$280
A teenage, unwed, pregnant woman tells about her ordeal of facing family, school friends, teachers, physicians and her boyfriend. Focuses on the social reactions to Lynn's plight and the accompanying emotional stresses she must endure. Should help others experience the victim's desolation and understand how insensitivity on their part can cause anguish.

GOODMAN (mo pic)
Filmmakers, Laurie Lewis, Barbara Linkevitch Canyon cinema Coop
A film about two women with separate capacities for laughter, utilizing mime to the slight extent that we all do.

GOT TO PUSH (mo pic)
Ellen Calmus and Liss Jeffrey, filmmakers 1973 11min Women's Film Co-op R$15
About women garment workers in Boston, their perceptions of themselves and their work, their struggles with internal racism, their realizations about the system in which they live. Good animated photography, sound track is simply the women speaking without other analysis. Good for discussion.

GRANDMA MOSES (mo pic)
Radim 1950 22min C Univ. of California Ext. #5246 R$18
Grandma Moses, 90 in 1950, was America's best-known, best-loved primitive painter, although she started to paint only during the last years of her life. Includes a visual study of a Grandma Moses exhibition. Written and narrated by poet Archibald MacLeish. Music ("Grandma Moses Suite") by Aaron Copland.

THE GRANDMOTHER FILM (mo pic)
Ann Popkin 15min Available from Ms. Popkin, 3 Lamson Pl., Cambridge, MA 02139
Combines old silent footage from the 20's, 30's and 40's with present-day sync-sound footage in a compassionate, unsentimental portrait celebrating the strength, resilience and creative resourcefulness of an older woman. Ms. Popkin is a Boston area filmmaker who teaches a course in sex role at the University of Massachusetts, Boston and created this tribute to her grandmother.

GRAPHICS [e.g., postcards, crafts, prints, greeting cards] (see also: POSTERS, CARTOONS).

Aenjai
Aldridge, Adele
Alert
Andromeda Press
Boccaccio, Shirley

Catlett, E. (IN #335 in Basic Book Collection)
Cee-Jay Enterprises
Diana Press
ERA Enterprises

Feminist Book Club
Feminist Party
Graphics for Women
Hathaway, Virtue
International Portrait Gallery
 (in Audiovisuals)
Joesting, Joan
KNOW
Liberation Enterprises
New Feminist Bookstore
New York City Women's
 Center
New York NOW
NOW: Seattle
NOW: Albuquerque

New Moon Communications
Penelope & Sisters
Rainbow Institute
Sisterhood in Solidarity
Smith, Sophia Collection
Society for Individual Rights,
 83 6 San Francisco, CA
 94103
Wollstonecraft, Inc.
Women Enterprises
Women's Graphics Collective
 of the Chicago WL Union
Women's Press Collective
Zero Population Growth

GREAT AMERICAN WOMEN'S SPEECHES (rec)
Caedmon 1973 2 stereo phonodiscs, each approx. 35min, with jacket notes, $13.96 #TC2067. Tape cassettes, $15.90 #CDL52067. Read by Eileen Heckart, Claudia McNeil, Mildred Natwick. 72-750999
14 speeches from the era of women's first attempts to gain political and social equality: Lucy Stone, Sojourner Truth, Ernestine Potowski Rose, Elizabeth Cady Stanton, Susan B. Anthony, et al depict range of early feminists' goals, concerns, disappointments. Late 19th and early 20th centuries.

GREAT NEGRO AMERICANS (rec)
Sands Matrix #GNA 111.
Stories of Negro success and achievement. (Men and) women: Marian Anderson, Mary McLeod Bethune....

THE GREAT ONES (disc rec series)
Westinghouse Broadcasting Co. OSS 4223
Excerpts from a series of radio programs broadcast by Group W.... Famous American Negroes and their Achievements: (Men and) women: Harriet Tubman. 5 discs.

GREAT WOMEN ARTISTS, PAST AND PRESENT (slides)
Slide show and commentary 1 1/2hour fee negotiable C Karen
 Petersen and J. J. Wilson, Women's Studies Program, California State College, Sonoma, Rohnert Park, CA 94928.
 707-795-2495.

GREAT WOMEN OF AMERICA (FS with sound)
Elinor T. Massoglia, writer. Series #425. $135.70
Classroom World. Unit I (426) "Women in business & education": Mary McLeod Bethune, Lillian Gilbreth, Helen Keller, Elizabeth Koontz, Dorothy Shaver, Mary Wells. Unit II (427) "Women in medicine & social reform": Jane Addams, Susan B. Anthony, Clara Barton, Evangeline Booth, Dorothea Dix, Dr. Helen Taussig. Unit III (428): "Women in politics & history": Amelia Earhart, Clare Boothe Luce, Frances Perkins, Eleanor Roosevelt, Betsy

Ross, Margaret Chase Smith. Unit IV (429): "Women in the arts": Louisa Mae Alcott, Marian Anderson, Pearl Buck, Helen Hayes, Edna St. Vincent Millay, Dorothy Thompson. Unit price $34.80 Individual tape/cassette $6.20.

GREETING CARDS see GRAPHICS

GWENDOLYN BROOKS (mo pic)
Indiana Univ. 1967 30min Creative person series Univ. of California Ext #7493 R$10
Introduction to the personality and poetry of Gwendolyn Brooks, a Pulitzer Prize-winning Black woman poet, and a view of the Chicago that provides the source for most of her material. She describes her method of working, how she approaches poetry, and the things in life that she finds most pleasant (California).

GWENDOLYN BROOKS reading her poems with comment (cassette/tape)
LC 109 LW 3237 1961

GYNECOLOGICAL SELF-HELP PRESENTATION
Lolly & Jean Hirsch, New Moon Communications, Inc. For women only $500 Slide/film

- H -

H+2, CONCERNING TWO HEROINE ADDICTS (mo pic)
Holt 1970 22min C Univ. of California Ext. #8587 R$17
Documents the retrogression--from prison to "freedom" and back to prison--of two California heroine addicts over a two-year period. Both Alvin, a Black male, and Marilyn, middle-class White female, have undergone "rehabilitation" and are determined to stay away from drugs and build new lives for themselves and their families. The pressures and responsibilities prove too difficult: neither is able to find employment; Marilyn becomes pregnant, is arrested for parole violation, her child taken from her, although she has kept away from drugs.... Narrated by Burt Lancaster (Calif.).

HALF MILLION TEENAGERS (mo pic)
Churchill 1971 16min C Univ. of California Ext. #7586 R$14
Vivid yet unemotional film about syphilis and gonorrhea, aimed at teenagers.... Details progress of gonorrhea, consequent tissue damage, sterility, infection of baby during childbirth. Emphasizes disease can be cured if treated (California).

THE HAND THAT ROCKS THE BALLOT BOX (mo pic)
Nell Cox, producer 1972 30min ABC
Women in politics.

HAND TINTING (mo pic)
Joyce Wieland, filmmaker 1967 5 1/2min C Silent (24 FPS) Canadian filmmaker's distribution centre R$8. Also available

from Filmmaker's Co-op
Wieland's description: "A study of poor black and white girls at a Job Corps centre; brought from rural areas to be 'educated' in typing. Here you see displaced creatures ... swimming lesson, sitting, and mostly dancing, (who express what's happening to themselves through their bodies, their hands, their faces, in my film)."

HANDVOICE (mo pic)
Filmmaker, Laird Sutton   7min   C   Multi Media R$20 S$85
Several maturbatory techniques demonstrated by a woman in her thirties.

HANG IN THERE (rec album)
Holly Near Redwood Records, 564 Doolin Canyon, Ukiah, CA 95482
Songs of peace and freedom including "No more genocide," and "Wedding song."

HAPPY FAMILY PLANNING (mo pic)
Pharmaceutical Manufacturers Assoc., 1155 15 St. NW, Washington, D.C. 20005   free loan

HAPPY MOTHER'S DAY (mo pic)
Richard Leacock and Joyce Chopra, filmmakers 1964 26min
    Pennebaker, 56 West 45, New York, NY 10036 S$150
Booklist Jan. 1, 1973:431 "... the stunned and overwhelmed mother, who is the center of attention, seems to remain in the background as she is obscenely manipulated by the town which glorifies ... her unusual biological achievement. A telling comment on modern society and its ideal of woman's greatest accomplishment. An interesting accompaniment to 'Sometimes I Wonder Who I Am'." Also available on loan from Women's Film Coop, which describes "a documentary about Mary Ann Fisher of Aberdeen, South Dakota, who became the mother of quintuplets (on top of five other children). The film shows the aftermath from beauty treatments to quint souvenirs. The chamber of commerce banks on increased tourist trade, and Gerber's deposits a ton of baby food at the Fishers' door. Even George McGovern gets in an appearance."

HAROLD AND CYNTHIA (mo pic)
Eccentric circle 1971 10min C
An exploration of the impact of advertising on two ordinary people, whose attempts at establishing a relationship are clouded by the contrived ideals encouraged by Madison Avenue.

HARRIET BEECHER STOWE (kinescope/play)
90min shown on KQED, February 1972.
Original play written by Florence Ryerson and Colin Clements; TV adaptation of the 1943 Broadway drama, "Harriet."

HARRIET TUBMAN (mo pic)
Society for visual education

HARRIET TUBMAN AND THE UNDERGROUND RAILROAD (mo pic)
McGraw 1964 54min C Ruby Dee, Ethel Waters Univ. of California Ext. 21min version R$20 BFA Educational media: S. You are there series.
Produced by CBS for "The great adventure" series originally.
Dramatic portrayal of the first 19 trips into the South made by Tubman before the Civil War to lead runaway slaves along the underground railroad to freedom in the North.

HARRISON & TYLER: TAKE TWO (rec album)
20th century records 1973 release
Patti Harrison and Robin Tyler's second album. Reviewed by Helen Koblin (Ms Nov. 1973:116-7) "The first feminist comedy team" 's first label was "Try it, you'll like it." Contact them via William Morris Agency.

HEAR THE BIG CHAKRA (mo pic) see NEAR THE BIG CHAKRA

HEARTS IN HARMONY (mo pic)
Filmmaker, Judy Steed 1973 80min C Canadian filmmaker's distribution centre R$90
Female filmmaker Joyce Wieland has written about this film: "... we see symbolized the coincidence of her development as a human being and her political being ... what it is like to be a Canadian without any corn ... love story in Newfoundland, depictions of childhood, to gradual awakening to responsibility to the society in which we live...."

HEIDI (rec)
Caedmon #TC1292 $4.30. Cassette $7.95 #CDL51292. 1969 Stereo, 63:57min. Johanna Spyri's book for children, read by Claire Bloom, abridged.
This is an example of Caedmon's recordings of children's books which are classics but nonetheless convey positive images of girls for both boys and girls, i.e. the type of title included in "Little Miss Muffet Fights Back" (page 197 Womanhood Media). Other companies reproducing such books in recordings and filmstrips are BroDart, Millder-Brody, and Weston Woods.

HELEN KELLER AND HER TEACHER (mo pic)
Contemporary-McGraw #101463-2 1969 27min C R$29 S$350 Univ. of California Ext. #8211 R$22
Produced by McGraw in collaboration with Project 7 Films, Inc. for the McGraw-Hill Biography Series. An expanded version of the film, "Helen Keller," exploring the relationship between Helen Keller and Anne Sullivan, herself partially blind.

HELP WANTED--WOMEN NEED APPLY (slides)
61 slides with script Jim Farron, Dallas Regional Office, Civil Service Commission, Dallas, TX 75202 S$20
Designed to be shown to high school and college classes and women's clubs; shows women in a variety of jobs.

HERSTORY (microfilm)
Herstory 1 Update. Herstory 2. Herstory 3. Women's History
    Research Center
Herstory 1 Update: update to original Herstory published by Bell
& Howell from the Women's History Library collections. 175
titles of Women's Liberation, civic, religious, professional, peace
newsletters, newspapers, and journals covering October 1971-June
1973. 20 reels. S$480 set.
Herstory 2: 359 new titles of women's newsletters, newspapers,
and journals which began after the Bell & Howell film. Dates
through June 1973. 20 reels. S$480 set.
35mm silverhalide base positive film Reduction ratio 15:1 to
18:1 (depending on original) Diazo copies may be ordered at $440.
per 20 reel set.
The original Herstory 317 titles available at $623/23 reels from
Bell & Howell, Wooster, OH 44691. Note: For those who already
own the Bell & Howell film, the Center has one additional reel
($30) containing issues of the period before October 1, 1971, do-
nated after the Bell & Howell film was made. A comprehensive
reel guide, with addresses of publications, is being compiled.
October 1, 1971-June 1973 guide $3.00/individuals, $10/others.
Herstory 3 will update the entire collection and add new titles.
To be released fall 1974; standing orders accepted. Prices do not
include handling.

HIGH SCHOOL (mo pic)
Frederick Wiseman, filmmaker 60min OSTI Films, 264 3 Ave.,
    Cambridge, MA 02143 R$100
Documentary looks at a large high school in Philadelphia: teachers
oppressing students in a variety of ludicrous situations adding up to
a systematic programing of "all-American values."

HILDA CONKLING READING HER POETRY (rec)
Caedmon #TC1387 1 12" LP $6.50

HINDU FAMILY (mo pic)
Encyclopaedia Britannica 1952 11min Univ. of California Ext.
    #5331 R$7
"Family preparations for the marriage of young girl in the province
of Gujarat illustrate important aspects of Hindu life including school,
home, clothing, preparation of a meal, religious ceremonies" (California). Is this outdated?

"HIRE HIM. HE'S GOT GREAT LEGS" (ad)
6x9" newspaper ad mat 1973 NOW Chapters can order this from
    Campaign coordinator Midge Kovacs, 100 West 12 St., New
    York, NY 10011

HIS GIRL FRIDAY (mo pic)
Howard Hawks, filmmaker 1940 Brandon R$20
A movie everyone thought very funny at the time; in fact, it was a
movie "type"--almost a genre. Newspaper woman Rosalind Russell
tries to convince herself that what she really wants is marriage to

a nice insurance salesman. And then there's the brief marriage to her editor Cary Grant.

HOLDING (mo pic)
Filmmaker, Constance Beeson 15min C Multi Media R$30 S$200
Useful in a variety of situations, e.g. sex education courses where materials that include portrayal of same-sex love-making are needed. "Holding" and "Winterlight" (female).

HOME BORN BABY (mo pic)
Video film and baby produced by Sally Pugh and Ralph Diamant.
    Vision Quest 1972 47min 16mm film R$60 S$350 1/2" video tape R$25 S$175
A film completely demystifying childbirth made by a couple at home. Good for high school age people although there is no glossing over.

HOME FILM (mo pic)
Sydney women's film group Sydney (Australia) filmmakers co-op
    R$12
Documentary with re-enactment as two women who spent their childhood in the "homes" of the child welfare system reveal what happens when young women are incarcerated in these prisons. The child welfare system buttresses the patriarchal family--if the family of a working class girl should "fail, " she is liable to be locked up in a "home, " forced to undergo "virginity" tests and other indignities, sentenced to hard labor and deprived of all affectionate contact with other human beings. Deprived of all rights to education, freedom, or love, the girls who then rebel are sent through a system of increasingly punitive jails, ultimately emerging with only one prospect for survival--prostitution. This film is part of a campaign to abolish the "homes." (For information about the campaign itself, write 25 Alberta Street, Sydney, Australia.) What relevance or utility would such a film have to women in the United States and Canada...?

HOME MOVIE (mo pic)
Jan Oxenberg, filmmaker 1973 11min BW & C Women in control Series. Multi Media R$20 S$100 Also available as
    video tape.
Also available from Feminist women's health centers, Twin cities women's film collection, Women's film coop, which described it as follows: "A combined personal and political statement about growing up gay in America. Scenes of a Gay-in, Christopher Street West march, lesbians playing football, and old home movie footage of the filmmaker as a child mimicking her mother's roles. The narration is a personal history with which most lesbians can identify--and feel good about themselves...."

HOMOSEXUALITY IN MEN AND WOMEN (mo pic)
NET 60min R$12
Reporter Bryan Magee interviews in England and Holland.

HONOR THY WOMANSELF; songs of liberation, by the Arlington Street Women's Caucus
Rounder Records 186 Willow Ave., Somerville, MA 02144
1973 record of old and new Women's Movement songs, 2 sides.

HOPE OF THE MORNING (mo pic)
Cokesbury Regional Service Center, 1600 Queen Anne Rd., Teaneck, NJ 07666
Women's Liberation a la religion.

HOW ABOUT YOU? (mo pic)
Bonnie Friedman, Deborah Shaffer, Marilyn Mulford, filmmakers
   25min Texture R$35 S$290 Produced by FSM/Pandora Films and partially-funded by the Creative Artists Public Service program.
How female body functions, major methods of birth control ... conveyed via rap sessions of women counselors with high school age boys and girls. Free of the usual pussyfooting, feminist. Good for high school age people and people who work with them.

HOW DO I LOVE THEE? (mo pic)
Perennial 28min C R$30
Brigham Young University produced this film which Perennial describes thusly: "Have the moral standards of the past become outdated? This question is the basis of a realistic story involving two college couples."

HOW ON EARTH DO WORKING WIVES MANAGE? (kit)
Changing Times Jobs and careers Series Baker & Taylor distributes #064616 $8 Kit includes 40 reprints, 1 transparency,
   1 Dup master, 1 teachers' guide. Grades 7-12 suggested.
A devious message that not all wives "work" also goes with this.

HOW TO FIGHT FAIR IN LOVE AND MARRIAGE (tape)
By George Bach Superscope C104
In reality a fight between lovers is a plea for understanding. Bach's "training" tapes for intimate adversaries "show you how to turn fights into constructive, rewarding experiences." By the author of "The Intimate Enemy; How to Fight Fair in Love and Marriage" (1969 Morrow).

HOW TO MAKE A WOMAN (mo pic)
Polymorph 1972 58min C Univ. of California Ext. #8499 R$34
"Adaptation of feminist play that dramatically and symbolically depicts the difficulties facing a woman who tries to create her own identity in a male-supremacist society. Uses a fast-paced, overtly propagandistic, 'Marat-Sade-like' style to show how two men use typical manipulative strategems and put-downs to mold a pair of women into various submissive roles, such as 'big mama,' 'sweet little girl,' 'happy housewife,' 'sexual tigress,' and 'nagging shrew'. Extraordinary illumination of the mechanisms of personal and sexual relationships. A satirical, penetrating, and at times shrill statement that will outrage some viewers but will be revelatory to

others. Excellent for provoking discussion on the reason for the goals of the Women's Liberation movement" (California).

HUMAN LIBERATION (slide show)
Stanislaus County NOW, 912 Hackberry, Modesto, CA 95350 45min
    7pp script Not for R or S.
Reader's theater-type production tracing sexism from infancy through adulthood.

HUMAN REPRODUCTION 100, REVISED (slides)
Guidance Associates 80 slides packaged in Kodak carousel cartridge #9A-102-085 $55 C A daylight blackboard projection "slide system" ie. series. Teacher's manual.
Structure and function of male and female reproductive systems: processes of conception, pregnancy, birth; principles of sex determination and multiple births.

HUMAN REPRODUCTION SERIES (FS)
McGraw #626100 6 FSs C $59 Individual FS S$11 Average lengths 32 fr Adviser, Marion E. Purbeck. Advertised as senior high level but also junior high.
The male reproductive system, The female reproductive system, The menstrual cycle, Fertilization, Development in pregnancy, and Labor and birth.

HUMAN SEXUALITY IN RETIREMENT AGE (video tape)
Interview by Bonnie Geneway. Contact Seattle-King County NOW Chapter, Washington state.

HUNGER (mo pic)
Perennial 1972 20min
A woman biologist in an isolated cabin and her relationship with a rough woodsman.

HUSBAND AND WIFE COACHED CHILDBIRTH (graphics)
Feminist Resources for Equal Education 1972 set of 8 BW photographs 8 1/2x11" #3 $2.
Pictures show a couple working together in the labor and delivery rooms and the birth of their child. F.R.E.E. also has "Community helpers" and "Professional women."

HYPNOSIS IN OBSTETRICS (tape)
Behavioral sciences tape library #90414 1 hour $7.95 By Dr. E. E. Rawlings of Manchester, England.

- I -

"I AM A WOMAN" (dramatic readings)
Viveca Lindfors' one-woman show of forty dramatic readings from Anne Frank, Marilyn Monroe, etc. Manhattan Showcase production.

I AM SOMEBODY (mo pic)
McGraw 1970 28min C S$360 Madeline Anderson, filmmaker
   University of California Ext. #8433 R$22
How a relatively small group of underpaid black women hospital workers took on the white establishment in Charleston, South Carolina and won recognition as well as improved wages and conditions. Captures their growing confidence and sense of their own worth in the face of a fanatically determined opposition by local and state agencies, police, Southern patriarchal establishment. When Ms. Anderson went to Charleston to make the film, several stations refused her newsreel footage they had on the strike itself ... one night it appeared mysteriously at her door. This film has great meaning for any Southern woman, if she will look for it.

I AM WOMAN (rec)
Music by Ray Burton; lyrics by Helen Reddy c1971 Recorded by
   Ms. Reddy Irving Music, Inc. & Buggerlugs Music (BMI)
   Capitol album 1972

"I BET AN ATTRACTIVE YOUNG MAN LIKE YOU HAS A GIRLFRIEND" (skit)
Role reversal in the employment process 1972 Written by employees of the Quaker Oats Co., Personnel Department, Chicago, IL. Contact Feminist Voice (newspaper).

I DON'T KNOW (mo pic)
Penelope Spheeris, filmmaker 1971 27min Canadian filmmaker's
   distribution center R$30
A love story between a boy who wishes he were a girl and a girl who wishes she were a boy, reports Ms. Spheeris.

I LOVE YOU ... GOODBYE (mo pic)
Screenplay by Diana Gould. Hope Lange as Karen 1974 74min
   C Learning Corp. of America R$60 Lease $600
Karen--thirty-six, wife and mother--has spent half of her life cooperating in her own sublimation. The advertising for this film "balances" with such things as "justified or not (take your pick)...."

I LOVE YOU, I THINK (mo pic)
Filmmaker, Archie Woodard, age 17. 1966 10min Youth films
   R$15 S$100
Young Black man's disastrous attempt to parlay two extremely strong-willed women.

I LOVE YOU ROSA (mo pic)
Macmillan Audio Brandon 1972 84min C R Director-writer,
   Moshe Mizrahi. Hebrew dialog with English subtitles.
"... nostalgic but unsentimentalized drama based on the life of Mizrahi's mother. Suffused in an ancient religious tradition, but alive with modern concerns over women's rights and Jewish-Arab coexistence ..." (Macmillan).

I WISH I KNEW HOT IT WOULD FEEL TO BE FREE (tape)
Radio free people #70-11 31min S$6
Includes a group rap about how women have to fake orgasm, some history of a struggle with the San Francisco Chronicle, relevant news and music.

IBSEN: A DOLL'S HOUSE (tape)
CBC #556-558 30min $21/set $7 each
"radio adaptation of the play which has as its central theme the emancipation of women."

IDENTITIES AND AFFINITIES; the problem of justice in marriage and other unions (tape cassette)
By Robert Seidenberg, M.D. Behavioral sciences tape library
#13004 $72 for 12 1-hour tapes 72-751062.
1. Introduction, #13015.
2. Is marriage moral?, #13026.
3. Beyond sexual identity, #13037.
4. The Oedipus complex and sexism, #13048.
5. Can love and sex survive the elimination of sexism?, #13059.
6. Affinities out of desperation: The "Mrs. Robinson" syndrome, #13060.
7. Still-unacceptable affinities: Older women-younger men liaisons, #13071.
8. The trauma of eventlessness, #13082.
9. Uprooting and role-transference: issues of identity crisis in wives, #13093.
10. Gay affinities and the helping professions, #13105.
11. Existential aspects of sexual jealousy, #13116.
12. The state of the union, present and future, #13127.

I'LL NEVER GET HER BACK (mo pic)
N.B.C. 24min Twyman Films, 329 Salem Ave., Dayton, OH 45401 R$20
The story of the unwed mother, who relates her experiences from the time of her arrival at the "maternity home" through the birth of her daughter and the signing of the adoption papers.

I'M A WOMAN (tape)
Women's Culture, producer. 36min From San Francisco Women's Liberation Media Workshop Radio Free People, distributor
#70-12 S$6
"This collage focuses on the personal torment of women divided and alone: rating our beauty, competing with each other, sacrificing ourselves for a man. It shows how small groups of women meeting together can improve our lives" (W.C.).

I'M FEMALE, I'M PROUD (tape)
Radio free people #79-10 29min S$6
How business and advertising create a totally unrealistic picture of women and their needs, and then exploit this to sell products.

IMAGE OF WOMAN AND GIRLS in the primary reader (slide show)
San Diego NOW Textbook Task Force, producer-distributor 60

slides 45min S$25. PO Box 22264, San Diego, CA 92122.

IMAGE OF WOMEN (slide show)
Long Island Feminist Coalition
Presents the distorted image of women, sexism in advertising.

IMAGE OF WOMEN IN THE MEDIA (slide presentation)
Joyce Snyder, comp. New York NOW production on the image of women in the media. Contact New York NOW Image of Women Committee.

IMAGE OF WOMEN IN THE MEDIA--sexist advertising (video tape)
Contact Lorraine Hoffman at 315-472-3602.

IMAGES (mo pic)
Monroe-Williams, producer 1970 17min C 70-713595
Explains the need for the suburban Jewish American housewife to contribute time and money to the support of the activities of the Jewish Federation. (U.S.L.C.) If you consider volunteerism relevant, contact Federation of Jewish Philanthropies of New York, 130 East 59 St., New York, NY 10022.

IMAGES OF MALES AND FEMALES in elementary school textbooks (slide-tape show)
From Lenore J. Weitzman, Dept. of Sociology, University of California, Davis, CA 95616. 40min R:minimal mailing charge S$150
With narrative and music. No-profit show.

THE INDEPENDENT FEMALE (play)
Feminist play from Long Island Coalition

THE INNOCENT PARTY (mo pic)
Perennial 18min C $10
Kansas State Board of Health produced this "simple, sincere document of the nature, recognition, cure and control of syphillis ... young man, in a moment of indiscretion, contracts venereal disease from a pick-up; we see what then happens to him and to his 'steady' girl."

THE INTERNATIONAL PORTRAIT GALLERY
Gale Research Co. Basic collection: 750 8 1/2x11" plates, 60 file folders. With Master Index $125. Supplemental collections: 500 plates, also covered in master index $75. Combined collections, file folders, index $200 1968 Black ink on creamy white antique cover stock. On approval.
Suitable for reproduction without fee or permission. Captions include nationality, vocation, dates of birth and death. Naturally, there are some women, e.g. Bernadette Devlin, Simone DeBeauvoir; worth sending for prospectus.

Audiovisual Resources

INTERNATIONAL WOMEN'S HISTORY PERIODICAL ARCHIVE
   (microfilm) see HERSTORY

AN INTERVIEW WITH ANAIS NIN (tape)
Pacifica #BC0919   24min $8.50 reel or cassette
Milton Hoffman talks with Nin, diarist and novelist, about her recently published fourth Diary, which covers the years 1944-7. (SEE Basic Book Collection: #273 in "Womanhood Media," and this Supplement #703.) She discusses how her stature as a mythical figure is both unrealistic and dehumanizing; traces her conception of the diary from what was to her original documentary form to a form which is currently replacing fiction as a way of getting back in touch with reality; talks about the fact that much of her work preceded the basic ideas of the feminist movement, what she learned from the politics of the Movement, the far-reaching impact it will have for men and women.

INTERVIEW WITH GARRETT HARDIN (mo pic)
King Screen, Producer 1972 10min With guide Holt, Rinehart
   & Winston, distributors S$140 Modern Film Rentals apply.
   Florida State Univ. also rents: $5. 73-701369
Professor Hardin theorizes on the significant ecological problems of modern society--population control, world health, women's rights....

INTERVIEW WITH JULIET MITCHELL (tape)
Pacifica S
Marxism.

INTRODUCTION TO BIRTH CONTROL (slide program)
Planned Parenthood World Population 1968 revision 15min C
   R$4 S$15 Available with Spanish record, $10 extra.
Includes physiology.

INTRODUCTION TO SELF-DEFENSE (kinescope)
Contact KQED   30min
10 part course to teach women of all ages, shapes and sizes to defend themselves against attackers.

THE INVISIBLE MINORITY; the homosexuals in our society (FS)
Unitarian Universalist Assoc. By Deryck Calderwood and Wasyl
   Szkodzinsky 1972 60min C 3-part sound FSs with 3 recs,
   approx. 20min each $60.
"The best general introduction to gay people and the gay liberation movement so far available in audiovisual. Remarkable for number and diversity of gay people portrayed. Parts dated. Heavily focused on East and West-coast cities. Poor treatment of drag, transexuals, and transvestism. Excellent sequence of a college student's dialogue with her hostile father. First two sections can be used without the third. Sound often hard to understand; effort should be made to get top-quality sound system for the recordings" (ALA-SRRT Task Force on Gay Liberation).

IS THIS LOVE ? (mo pic)
Univ. of California Ext.   15min   R$8
Contrasts the romances of two college roomates.

IT HAPPENS (mo pic)
Noel Nosseck, producer   1972   25min   C   Pyramid Films   R$25
    S$300
A sex-education film: Angie, a high school senior, is faced with
the problems of an unwanted pregnancy. The film tries to come-
on as current but there is misplaced responsibility, available options not portrayed, and anti-feminism. As three women students
of library science concluded in their review (LJ SLJ Previews
December 1972:28): "unacceptable."

IT HAPPENS TO US (mo pic)
Amalie R. Rothschild, producer-director-writer   1972   30min   C
    New Day   R$32   S$325.   Canadian filmmaker's distribution
    centre R$30.   Anomaly S$300
All-women crew made this outstanding film of all women--married
and single, Black and White, ranging in age from seventeen to mid-
sixties--frankly discussing their abortion experiences. This basic
is owned-used by New York Public Library, University of Missouri,
Toronto Public Library, Philadelphia Free Library, the District of
Columbia Public Library, and Bronx Community College; it was
previewed-for-possible-purchase by the state library of Louisiana,
which is also the source of films for the state university, and rejected. Here's a calm, serious and personal film. Almost as a
side-effect, the film conveys the liberating effect which may accompany abortion--the "our bodies ourselves" concept.

IT ONLY HURTS WHEN I LAUGH (slide documentary)
Carol Benson, 2717 Rutledge Wy, Stockton, CA 95207   209-478-7646.
    2hr presentation can be shortened according to program needs
    1974   R$20 to NOW Chapters $25 to other groups
Examines sex-stereotyping in the comics.

IT'S SO NICE TO HAVE A WOMAN AROUND THE HOUSE (tape)
Feminist Radio Network # 874-25   29 1/2min   Cassette $20;
    Reels 7 1/2ips $25, 3 3/4ips $20
"An interview with Florence Adams, author of 'I took a hammer in
my hand; the woman's build it and fix it handbook.' Ms. Adams
tells what kinds of tools every build-it and fix-it woman should
have; explains the workings of a tank toilet; and how to build a
bookcase" (FRN).

IT'S YOUR WEDDING (cassette)
Creative Resources, a division of World, Inc.   April 1974
"Detailed help in designing wedding ceremonies"--contemporary
"liberated" ones.

- J -

JACK AND JIM, CINDY AND KAREN; a special kind of love story (videotape)
Public Affairs Dept. of Ch. WCCO-TV, Minneapolis. Available through Univ. of Minnesota Media Resources, 510 Rarig Center, Minneapolis, MN 55455   25min
A Lesbian pair and a gay male couple share their relationships.

JANE ADDAMS/SUSAN B. ANTHONY (FS)
McGraw $7.50 each
Each FS traces the life of the person from early childhood, discusses factors influencing her, refers to her most important achievements.

JANE EYRE (rec)
Charlotte Bronte's novel read by Anthony Quayle, Claire Bloom, Cathleen Nesbitt, et al.   Caedmon 1969   3 stereo phonodiscs 190:59min $20.94   #TC3003.   3 cassettes $23.85 #CDL53003. "Women in literature" collection.
Entire book is read.   (SEE ALSO #283 in Basic Book Collection.)

JANE KENNEDY, ACTIVIST (tape)
CBC #728L   1hour   S$14
"An interview with a White nurse from Chicago involved in Black Panther clinics."

JANIE SUE AND TUGALOO (mo pic)
Centron   1971   9 1/2min   C   S$125
The ff. is the Centron catalog annotation in its entirety: "Without the use of narration, this documentary film presents insights into the life of eight-year-old Janie Sue, who lives on a horse farm. Though she has her own pony, Snowball, she dreams of becoming an accomplished rider on Tugaloo, her brother's national champion Arabian stallion. Janie Sue leisurely explores her environment on Snowball, takes a riding lesson from her grandfather on Tugaloo, and helps her brother 'cut' cattle in preparation for a rodeo. Excellent for use in primary units on man and his environment, citizenship and family relationships."

JAPAN; ANSWER IN THE ORIENT (mo pic)
Indiana Univ.   1965   Produced in Japan.   Population Problem Series   60min   C   Univ. of California Ext.   #6613   R$21
Shows how the Japanese have achieved zero population growth through legalized abortion, the interest of large industries in fertility control measures, and ... the trend to marry at a later age ..." (California).

JAPAN: PLANNED PARENTHOOD/PLANNED NATIONHOOD (mo pic)
NBC   1971   24min   C   EFLA 72-7813

JENNY AND THE ROSEBERRIES (band)
A Women's country-and-rock group. Contact Ms.

LES JEUNES FILLES (mo pic)
National Film Board of Canada En tant que femmes Project. 1hr.
  scheduled for broadcast first on CBC French network. Production of 28 women.
To be approved for production hopefully. "Will present a multiple portrait of the young woman of today--the real woman behind the image of beauty contests, fashion and advertising." Was being scripted in 1973.

JEWELRY:
  Amani
  Cee-Jay Enterprises
  ERA Enterprises
  Everywoman Feminist Book
    Service
  First Things First
  Franklin Silversmiths,
    Greenfield, MA 01301
  Graphic Communications
  Herald
  Greater Indianapolis Women's
    Political Caucus
  House of L. I. B.
  League of Women Voters
  Liberation Enterprises
  Nielsen, J.
  Struggling Woman
  That Uppity Woman
  Those Uppity Women
  Women Enterprises

THE JEWISH WIFE (mo pic)
Doubleday Multimedia #61015 1971 20min C S$225.50 Super 8
  sound. By German playwright Bertoldt Brecht.
The goodbye is that of a Jewish woman saying farewell to her Aryan husband before she flees in Hitlerian Germany. SEE ALSO Viveca Lindfors' film/lecture program in Directory of Sources section.

JOB INTERVIEW: WHOM WOULD YOU HIRE? (2 mo pics)
Three young women. Three young men. Churchill 17min C/BW
  Business Education Films, 5113 16 Ave., Brooklyn, NY 11204
  R$7.50
Three types of young women interview for a job--discussion centers on mistakes they make during the interview and how to correct them.

JOBS AND GENDER (FS)
Guidance Associates 1971 C 2 FSs pt 1 63fr pt 2 62fr 35mm
  2 phono discs (2 S ea) 12" 33 1/3rpm 9min each part Discussion guide 71-739901
Explains the influence of sexual barriers and stereotypes on woman's vocational choices. Discusses traditional concepts of masculine and feminine work role through interviews with a male kindergarten teacher, a male nurse, a female carpenter, and a female newspaper reporter.

JOBS IN THE CITY--WOMEN AT WORK (mo pic)
Centron 1972 11min C S$150 Real world series With guide
  73-715373

"Shows newspaper printers, physicians, computer key punch operators, bank-tellers, pilots, mathematicians, aircraft executives, realtors, TV commentators, fashion artists. For elementary grades" (U.S. L.C.). Female narrator.

JOCKEY (mo pic)
Gretel Ehrlich, producer-director 1973 25min C & BW Texture films R$30 S$300
About Penny Ann Early, first woman jockey.

JOJOLO (mo pic)
Grove 1968 12min Univ. of California Ext. #7570 R$8
Study of a young woman of Haitian parentage who works as a fashion and film model in Paris.

JOURNALS OF SUSANNA MOODIE (mo pic)
Marie Waisberg, filmmaker 1972 15min Canadian filmmaker's distribution centre R$15
An evocative re-creation of one woman's view of life in this country in the last century; based on the poems of Margaret Atwood.

JOURNALS OF SUSANNA MOODIE (rec)
CBE 12" LP $5
Written by Margaret Atwood and read by Mia Angerson--a cycle of poems invoking the life and thoughts of a female immigrant to Canada from England in the 1800's.

A JOURNEY (mo pic)
Wombat, 77 Tarrytown Rd., White Plains, NY 10607. 11min C S$155
Suggested by company for grades 7-12, "strangely haunting film from Yugoslavia ... the sportsman, the merchant, the nun, the young lovers, the worker, and the prostitute ... philosophic impact that has relevance in any examination of the values we all live by."

JOYCE AT 34 (mo pic)
Filmmakers Joyce Chopra, Claudia Weill also distribute (6 Follen, Cambridge, MA 02138) 1973 28min C S$335 New Day R$37 S$350
In the collections of the Boston Public Library, New York Public Library, Radcliffe College. Late pregnancy, the birth of a daughter, conflict between love for a child and demands of a career, erosion of male privilege that her husband struggles to accept ... working out of a life style by a woman filmmaker.

JUANITA (mo pic)
USIA, producer 1970 13min C Available in English and Spanish Contact USIA Film Dept., 1776 Pennsylvania Ave. N.W., Washington, D.C. 20006
Juanita is a young Latin American soon to be married and contemplating her future life by comparison of her own home with the family of her fiance, i.e. large number of children, hardships,

guilt because she enjoys being in his home, where there is time to enjoy life. Unfortunately, it doesn't succeed--the wedding ceremony, church, responsibility and parenthood are emphasized and contraception not even mentioned!

JUDY CHICAGO AND THE CALIFORNIA GIRLS (mo pic)
Judith Dancoff, 1118 10 St., #4, Santa Monica, CA 90403 27min C
"I am an artist and a feminist ... and the film is a personal vision by Judith Dancoff of the Fresno Art Program--a program to educate women as artists, using performance as a tool in that education, as a way to reach subject matter for art. This program is part of my aim of developing a female art community in Los Angeles where I and other women artists can be ourselves" (Judy Chicago).

"JUST LOOKING" (mo pic)
Women make movies, inc. 1974 6min R$10.50 S$60
A portrait by Suzanne Armstrong, a former army pilot, of an older woman's satisfying day in Chelsea. Made at the Chelsea Picture Station.

- K -

K THROUGH 12, CAREER EDUCATION (mo pic)
A racist-sexist film using public tax money to prepare. In the Career Education Program. For information, contact Anne Grant of NOW.

KQED (video tape show)
30min show comprised of 3-min. vignettes of a female political candidate and some of the attitudes and problems. From Kathryn Kingson, South Bay NOW, 1029 Portola Rd., Portola Valley, CA 94025.

KANOJO TO DARE see SHE AND HE

KATHLEEN CLEAVER ON BLACK PANTHER POLITICS & The Feminist movement (tape)
Pacifica 34min $10 reel or cassette
After three years in Algeria, Kathleen Cleaver returned to the United States to seek legal assistance for her husband. In an interview with Yolanda DeFreitas of KPFA, acknowledges the women's movement's validity but warns against "feminist politics"; instead, she emphasizes the importance of women becoming political and aware of the struggles of all oppressed people.

KATIE KELLY (mo pic)
Women Make Movies 1973 5min R$8.75 S$50 By Barbara Brown, Nancy Greiner, Lorraine McConnell, Ann Weiner, Helen Zaglen.

Audiovisual Resources 211

A portrait of Katie Kelly, professional writer (author of "Garbage; its history and future in America"), environmentalist and active community leader. SEE ALSO Toward new life styles....

KATIE'S LOT (mo pic)
Univ. of California Ext. 1961 18min C R$23
Tomboy Katie's world is shattered when she must shed her jeans for a party dress.

THE KIBBUTZ (mo pic)
Perennial #793 22min C R#24 S$240
Based on the work of Dr. Bruno Bettelheim.

KILLING TIME (mo pic)
Gloria Laskowich, filmmaker 11min BW & C Filmmaker's coop R$15
Laskowich: "In black and white and color, in reality and fantasy, a female relates ambivalently to the males around her."

KIRSA NICOLINA (mo pic)
Gunvor Nelson, filmmaker 1970 16min C Multi Media R$25 S$330 Also available from Canyon Cinema Coop.
The birth of a child at home, with father assisting with physician's guidance.

KITTENS ARE BORN (mo pic)
Hugh & Suzanne Johnston, producers McGraw #102078 1971 10min S$145 76-711916
An example of a good contemporary sex-education picture for small children: mother cat goes through labor, bears, cleans, and nurses three kittens.

KNOW YOUR BODY: SEXUAL RESPONSE IN WOMEN AND MEN (tape)
Pacifica #BC-0943 69min $12 reel or cassette
Produced by WBAI. Norin and Leslie Coheb of Community Sex Information, a New York organization providing counseling and therapy for sexual problems, describe male and female sexual anatomy, the four-stage sexual response cycle, sexual therapy, the contribution that Masters & Johnson have made to it, masturbation, and various facts about male and female orgasm and myths surrounding it.

- L -

LADY & IF IT WEREN'T FOR THE MUSIC (rec)
Meg Christian sings "Lady." Chris Williamson sings "If it weren't for the music." Olivia Records' first LP 45rpm $1.50 includes postage

LADY BEWARE (mo pic)
Pyramid 16min C R$20 S$200

Common-sense self-defense methods for women, with Shirley Jones narrating.

LADY FROM CONSTANTINOPLE (mo pic)
Judit Elek, director   1969 Hungarofilm
Wistful old lady lives in the past, decides to exchange her spacious apartment for a smaller, quieter one; her flat is innundated with boisterous guests.

THE LADY IN THE LINCOLN MEMORIAL (mo pic)
New York Times Co. Teaching Resources   18min   16mm and S-8
   Multi Media S: 16mm $200, S-8 $175
How Marian Anderson expressed her commitment for racial equality through her art; traces her career, tours, to her historical performance at the Lincoln Memorial in 1939 after she had been denied the use of Constitution Hall by women.

THE LADY WITH A LAMP (mo pic)
Macmillan Audio Brandon   R
Life of Florence Nightingale.

LAMPS IN THE WORK PLACE (mo pic)
Dept. of Labor Wage & Hour Division Information Office   28min C
Case-study approach to the Equal Pay Act.

LATE SPRING (BANSHUN) (mo pic)
Filmmaker, Yasujiro Ozu   1949   107min   New Yorker Films R$175
"... we see clearly how the social conventions of traditional Japanese domestic life limit the possibilities of personal freedom and choice, but also how they make human existence bearable ... a father and daughter live together. She is happy living with him; he fears his needs are keeping her from marriage" (New Yorker).

LAURETTE (mo pic)
National Film Board of Canada/Barrie Howells, producer   1969
   20min   Contemporary #408-429 S$120
Laurette is separated from her husband, employed as a secretary, raising their young daughter. She is afraid, confused ... but has learned the difference between needing help and being dependent. This is not a feminist film, but has validity. For discussion-purposes.

LAVENDER (mo pic)
Perennial 1972 13min C 16mm, but also available 8mm, video-
   cassette   R$17 S$170. Colleen Monahan, Elain Jacobs, filmmakers
Two young Lesbians play themselves. Dialogue consists of their own thoughts and feelings, e.g. realization of their lesbianism, how they met each other, position of homosexuality in our society. For young people and adults. As the heroines say, "It's the only way things are going to change--if people start being a little honest."

Audiovisual Resources

LAVENDER JANE (band)
Women's Music Network.

LAVENDER JANE LOVES WOMEN (rec album)
Women's Wax Works #A001 Alix Dobkin, Kay Gardner, Patches
    Attom/Barbara Cobb Women's music network LP $5.25
"A very sexy record album" (Cowrie).

THE LAWRENCE STRIKE (tape)
Pacifica #BC 0980 35min $8.50 reel or cassette
Produced by WBAI. 70 years ago, the textile workers of Lawrence, Mass. were on strike. This program, describing the great strike, is based on "The rising of the women," a history of women in the labor movement from 1890 to 1920, by Meredith Tax. The Lawrence Strike was fought over a pay cut of $.30, 2 hours pay, the cost of 5 loaves of bread, the difference between survival and starvation for textile workers. About 50% of the mill-workers were women and children, who labored hard and died young--the average at the age of 36. Mixed with songs of the early labor movement, this program is a solid and poetic presentation of an important moment in women's labor history (Pacifica).

LEADING AMERICAN NEGROES (FS)
Society for visual education 6 sound FSs, with phonodiscs $49.50;
    with tape cassettes $55.50.
Highlights the careers of 6 prominent American Negroes and relates personal accomplishments to the growth of the U.S. Intermediate-Upper grades. 2 of the 6 are women: Mary McLeod Bethune, 48fr 15min; Harriet Tubman, 45fr 14min.

THE LEARNED LADIES (Les femmes savantes) (mo pic)
McGraw-Hill #407062 100min 3 parts R and S $500
"A sparkling performance by the Jean Meyer Company brings to life Moliere's classic 17th century comedy, satirizing the intellectual pretentions of foolish ladies" (Contemporary Films for intramural use only). English sub-titles.

LEARNING ABOUT SEX (mo pic)
Writer, Deryck Calderwood 90fr 15min Discussion guide
    Guidance associates. 1 FS, 1 12"LP/$20/9A-102-507. 1 FS,
    1 cassette/$22/9A-102-523
"Prepares older elementary students to benefit from sex education classes by 1) understanding adult embarrassment more realistically; 2) gaining clear knowledge of their own bodies; 3) communicating honestly with the opposite sex; 4) mastering proper sex vocabulary; 5) discussing social implications of sexual behavior" (Guidance).

LEARNING FROM WOMEN'S EXPERIENCE--a discussion of menstruation/menopause (videotape)
Women's Design Program. 1/2" 45min

LEARNING THE LIBRARY; a skills and concepts series (media package)
Educational Activities 1975 Helen Rippier Wheeler. #FSR461:

4 C filmstrips, 4 recs, Guide. $48. #FSC461: 4 C film-
strips, 4 cassettes, Guide. $52.
While designed to provide library instruction at the elementary
school level, a specific conscious attempt is being made throughout writing, production, selection of illustrative media-titles, etc.
to produce a learning experience for students and teachers which
will be, among other positive things, non-sexist.

LEARNING TO FORGET (tape)
CBC #818   30min $7
A documentary focusing on the socialization process of children.

LEENYA--daughter of the noble Blacks of Surinam (mo pic)
IFB   10 1/2min   C   R$9   S$135
"Leenya, a young Bush Negro of Surinam, tells her own story ...
[the] history of her people, the occupations of her father who works
in a lumber mill and her mother who cares for home and garden,
her schooling, her hopes ..." (IFB).

LEFT SIDE, RIGHT SIDE (mo pic)
Joan Jonas, filmmaker and distributor   1972   7min
Differences between a mirror and monitor in relation to self-
perception.

LEONIE'S FILM (mo pic)
Filmmaker, Leonie Crennan   Sydney filmmaker's co-op
Feminist Leonie Crennan of the Sydney, Australia Women's Film
Group.

LESBIAN MOTHERS (video tape)
Queen Blue Light Video, producer
The kitchen

THE LIBERATED MAN (tape)
Center for Cassette Studies   27min $12.95
"A discussion concerning the need for society to liberate men from
rigid sexist roles" (Center).

LIBERATION NOW (FS)
Media Plus   1971   11min   C   96fr   sound FS and slide
"Considers the relationships of the women's movement to 19th
century suffrage campaign and civil rights movement of the 1960's;
also outlines the major issues of concern in the contemporary
movement for women's liberation." (Media Plus. SEE ALSO "The
silenced majority ..." p. 243, Womanhood Media.)

LIBERATION NOW! (recs, sheet music)
Claro Music Corp., 117 West 46 St., New York, NY 10036
Song was released on Decca Records in 1970. Use for activities
and fund-raising. Sheet music with piano/guitar chords; $.15
each can be sold for up to $.95. Record is 45rpm; $.20 each can
be sold for up to $1.00.

LIBRARY ISMS (tape) see SEXISM IN CHILDREN'S BOOKS (tape)

LIEBALALA (SWEETHEART) (mo pic)
Univ. of California Ext. #8440 1972 58min R$21 S$350
"Rare ethnographic document of life of the Lozi people of Barotseland, now part of Zambia, filmed in 1935. Native actors depict scenes from their daily lives, portraying all aspects of a courtship and concluding with an actual wedding ritual.... A sound track was recently added containing authentic Lozi music and a narration by filmmaker Margaret Hubbard ..." (California).

LIFE BEFORE BIRTH (FS/slides)
Time-Life Part 2: 52fr 1972 10min C
Using microscopic photography, the growth of a human enbryo is observed from the 6th week through birth. Photographs originally appeared in Life magazine.

LIFE, DEATH, AND THE AMERICAN WOMAN (mo pic)
Landsburg Productions, 2000 Nicholas Canyon, Los Angeles, CA 90046 1972 60min
Originally shown on ABC-TV. Explains that American women are more prey to certain medical problems than women in other parts of the world; treats the stages in women's lives when particular problems may surface.

LIFE OF O'HARU (SAIKAKU ICHIDA ONNA) (mo pic)
Kenji Mizoguchi, filmmaker 1952 133min New Yorker R$150
Based on a 17th-century novel by Saikaku, chronicles the decline of a beautiful court lady who ends as a prostitute. Kinuyo Tanaka plays the woman exiled for loving a commoner.

LITTLE GIRL'S PLACE, LITTLE BOY'S WORLD (audio tape)
Dr. Pat Campbell, member, Atlanta, GA. NOW, and Dr. Charlie
    Thompson of Georgia State University 1974 26min audio-tape presentation S$3 from Campbell, Educational Foundations Dept., GSU, Atlanta, GA 30303.
"Uses lecture, discussion, activities to sensitize people to the pervasiveness of sex-role stereotyping in years of infancy, early childhood, elementary school" (Do It NOW 6/74).

LIVIA MAKES SOME CHANGES (mo pic)
Women make movies, inc. 1974 7min R$12.25 S$70 By
    Kathleen Melanaphy, Anne Sandys, Sheelah Weaver.
This cooperative production brought together a student, housewife, and member of Liberation Support Movement. A middle-aged housewife goes out to work despite opposition of husband and son. Things take a turn for the better one night when she works late.

LIVING TOGETHER (mo pic)
Julie Gibson, feminist filmmaker of the Sydney, Australia Women's
    Film Group. Distributor: Sydney Filmmakers Co-op. BW opt
    snd.
"Using animation based on a classic revolutionary feminist cartoon,

this film depicts the struggle women go through in trying to discover themselves while in relationship with men." (Co-op bulletin.) Narrated by Jeni Thornley; music written and sung by Angela Giblin.

LIVING WITH PETER (mo pic)
Miriam Weinstein, filmmaker 22min C R$25 S$225 from Ms. Weinstein Disc. guide Also distributed by Canadian Filmmaker's Distribution Centre R$25.
People begin to talk about doubts, anxieties, conflicts that a woman faces in living with a man she's not married to, as well as the external pressures subtly at work on her and all women to formalize the relationship through marriage. A personal documentary on a couple together without "the contract."

THE LIZARDS [I BASILISCHI] (mo pic)
Galatea Productions 1963 Lina Wertmuller, director. Gianni di Venanzo, camera
"an aimless group of young men from a southern Italian town. Preoccupied with sexual fantasies, a provocative blonde girl from the North becomes the focus of their dreams" (First International Festival of Women's Films, New York, 1972).

THE LOLLIPOP PEOPLE; a case for child care now (slide show)
127 slides From Ms. Tery Zimmerman, NOW Child Care Task Force, 61 Capri Dr., Roslyn, NY 11576.

LONER (rec album)
Indra Allen, wrote music, plays and sings.
Cell 16 Her experiences as a female and a feminist: "Freedom coming," "Pregnant blues," "Ten-speed rider," and others.

LONG HARD CLIMB (rec album)
Helen Reddy 1973 Includes "Delta Dawn" Capitol

LOOKING FOR ME (mo pic)
Encyclopaedia Britannica 1970 29min Univ. of California Ext. #7782 R$13 S$175
A film about the delights of experiencing one's body, as well as a document supporting a talented young teacher's belief that movement awareness is essential for children, and that for psychotic or handicapped children body language is an important means of communication. Shows Janet Adler, a dance or movement therapist.

LOREN McIVER (mo pic)
Filmmaker, Maryette Charlton 1962 47min C&BW Film Images R
Study of intimate relationship between artist's environment and her work.

LORRAINE HANSBERRY ON HER art and the Black experience (rec)
Caedmon #TC1352 1 12" LP $6.50. CDL #51352 cassette $7.95

Ms. Hansberry discussing her work and philosophy, the theater, the Black experience, and the challenge of the artist in mid-century America.

LORRAINE HANSBERRY SPEAKS OUT: Art and the Black revolution (rec)
Caedmon #TC1352 1971 Selected and edited by Robert Nemiroff; Read by the author.
From interviews and speeches.

THE LOTTERY (rec) see THE DAEMON LOVER (rec)

LOUISE NEVELSON (mo pic)
Connecticut Films 25min C R$50 S$350
Environmental sculptor Nevelson herself appears.

LOVE AND MARRIAGE (mo pic)
Guidance Associates Part I: 87fr/16min. Part II: 73fr/13min
  2 FSs; 2 12" LPs/$40/9A-102-705. 2FSs; 2 cassettes/$44/ 9A-102-721. Discussion guide.
"Part I focuses on 3 couples trying to understand love in their lives: high school students going steady, an engaged college couple, a couple living together as if married. Part II introduces a young couple married for 3 years, another divorced after 9 years, a third married for 20 years. Professional counselor helps relate their experience to realistic concepts of love and married life, self-awareness, personal maturity, independence and flexibility, ability to adjust in matters of sex, money, inlaws, parenthood" (Guidance associates).

LOVING COUPLES (mo pic)
Macmillan Audio Brandon 1965 113min R Director, Mai Zetterling. Original title "Alskande Par." Screenplay by Ms. Zetterling and David Hughes, based on the novel, "The Misses von Pahlen," by Agnes von Krustentjerna. With Harriet Andersson, Eva Dahlbeck, Anita Bjork. Swedish dialog with English subtitles.
An attack on men's domination of women in marriage.

THE LUNATIC (mo pic)
Produced, distributed by Centron 1972 23min R$32.50 S$325
  With guide.
A dramatic film about the human implications and responsibilities of V.D. A girl learns that she has contracted a venereal disease; her reactions to herself, her boyfriend, the disease and her other friends should stimulate a discussion around a number of interpersonal relationships. Extremely well done and very useful; for young people and adults 72-702506.

- M -

MADALYN (mo pic)
Robert R. Elkins Film Production, 11309 Q Ranch Road, Austin, TX 78759 (512-258-5943) 1970 30min C optional sound R$40 S$350
The film was used as a master's degree thesis-project while Mr. Elkins was a graduate student at the University of Texas, Austin; he asks the questions of Ms. O'Hair in the interview sequences. A documentary of Madalyn Murray O'Hair of Austin, who heads an organization for separation of church and state. One of the major sequences deals with a speech before students at Tulane University, New Orleans. A print of the film is in the collection of the New York Public Library. When asked by this writer whether she endorsed the film, Ms. O'Hiar replied, "With one exception which matters only to me--generally I approve." When asked whether she considers herself a feminist, she replied, "... and my mother before me."

MADAME BINN (mo pic)
Kansas Media Project, 815 Vermont St., Lawrence, KS 66044
15min
Madame Binn addresses American women about the War and the shared-role Vietnamese and American women have in struggling to end it; her first filmed interview, November, 1970.

MADAME BOVARY (mo pic)
Films, Inc. 1949 (France, 1934) 102min R$60+ Contemporary #408445-3 Director Jean Renoir. With English subtitles. Flaubert's novel.

MADAME ROSINA LHEVINNE; pianist and master teacher (mo pic)
Univ. of California Ext. #6480 1964 40min R$16 S$240

MADELEINE IS (mo pic)
Sylvia Spring, filmmaker 1969 85min Canadian filmmaker's distribution centre R$100
"... the first feature film made in Canada by a woman since the 1930's, and it was Spring's first major directorial effort. Shot in Vancouver on a small budget which took years to raise.... Madeleine especially is a sympathetic figure, confused by the array of philosophies that her friends represent, and reluctant to give up a fantasy friend that she turns to whenever the going gets rough ..." (The Centre).

MÄDCHEN IN UNIFORM (mo pic)
Film Images 1931 Germany Leontine Sagan, director and actress. Hertha Thiele, actress.

MAGIC PRISON (mo pic)
Encyclopaedia Britannica 1969 36min C Humanities series
Univ. of California Ext. #7655 R$25
In this dramatized exchange of letters and poems, interspersed

with beautiful photography of the nature she wrote about, the genius of Emily Dickinson is movingly revealed. Corresponding with a stranger, Col. T. W. Higginson, the shy poet is able to speak her mind and heart almost as freely as she does in her poetry. Readings selected by Archibald MacLeish.

MAHANAGAR (mo pic)
Macmillan Audio Brandon 1964 122min R Bengali dialog with
  English subtitles. Title translation: "The big city." Screen-
  play by Mr. Satyajit Ray, based on short story by Ivarenda
  Mitra. Direction and music by Ray.
Explores role of "working wife" in patriarchal society.

THE MAID: CLEANING UP THE BATHROOM
THE MAID: MAKING UP THE ROOM (mo pics)
National Educational Media, Inc., 15250 Ventura Blvd., Sherman
  Oaks, CA 91403 #H201, 2. Available in Spanish and in French.
  10min S$133 each/8mm and Super-8mm cartridge $147. each.
  Study guide packets $11 C Accompanying tests available.
  Part of the "Professional hospitality program," of which "The
  Bellman" is another part....
Users of NEM's programs include American Airlines, Army and
Air Force Base Exchange Service, Bell Telephone Laboratories,
Brigham Young University, Brown Palace Hotel (Denver), Bureau
of Indian Affairs, Departments of Agriculture, Defense, and Health,
Education & Welfare, Disneyland, and the United States House of
Representatives. For CR (yours).

MAIS MOI (mo pic)
Filmmaker, 15-year-old Lois Greenfield 1968 5min Youth Films
  R$7.50 S$50
A lonely girl's fantasy about bold knights fighting for her charms.

MAKING A DIFFERENCE (mo pic)
Nashville TRAFCO (United Methodist Church), 1525 McGavock St.,
  Nashville, TN 37217

MAKING IT (mo pic)
Filmmaker, Lucy Ann Kerry 11min Blue Ridge Films, 9003
  Glenbrook Rd., Fairfax, VA 22030
A woman rebuilds her life after a divorce.

MALAWI; THE WOMEN (mo pic)
Max Red, producer 1971 20min C Study guide Churchill
  75-714773
Points out the varying life styles of African women of Malawi.
Shows at work in a village, in a city, and in the suburbs of the
city. Exemplifies the counter cultures of a society in transition.

MALE AND FEMALE (mo pic)
Miguel Sanchez, age 18 1968 8min Youth films R$12 S$80

A MALE CONDITION (mo pic)
Antioch Doc 1974 60min

MALE/FEMALE: CHANGING LIFESTYLES (tape)
EAV 4 strips with rec $56. 4 strips with cassette $60.
The roles of men and women are examined; theories of sex-role differentiation and social expectations are explored.

MAN ALIVE; GALE IS DEAD (mo pic)
Filmmaker, Jenny Barraclough 1970 50min C Anne Smith, BBC Enterprises, London W 12 R
About a woman, Gale Parsons, who was attractive, intelligent and had much to offer. But, aged 19 and a drug addict, she was found dead in the basement of a derelict house in Chelsea. A BBC Documentary.

MAN'S WORLD, WOMAN'S PLACE (cassette)
producer-distributor Center for Cassette Studies 1973 26min $12.95
Elizabeth Janeway, author of "Man's world, woman's place; a study in social mythology" (#69 Basic Book Collection: Womanhood Media), disputes the myths about the traditional role of women in a discussion with Casper Citron. A list of questions for discussion and interpretation and a Bibliography of related readings included. Outstanding.

MANUELA (mo pic)
Filmmaker, Humberto Solas 40min American Doc, San Francisco R
Cuban film-drama of a young peasant woman whose family is killed in a Batista police raid. She joins the guerillas in the Sierra Maestra and falls in love with a guerrillero as they fight for freedom. Rah.

THE MANY AMERICANS (film series)
Learning Corp. of America 8 films, of which 2 are about girls:
  Siu Mei Wong: who shall I be? 18min R$20 S$220
  Felipa: north of the border. 17min R$20 S$210
Of the series, LCA states that each "depicts a conflict in the life of an ethnic minority-child as he seeks to assimilate two worlds." Discussion guides provided....
Sui Mei Wong's consultant: Herbert Leong, University of Southern California. "Ballet dancers universally captivate young girls, and Sui Mei Wong is no exception...."
Felipa's writer-director: Bert Salzman. Supposedly about the "Americanization" of "the Mexican immigrant"--actually Felipa's devotion to her uncle.

MARCO (mo pic)
Kartemquin Films, Ltd. and InterMedia Foundation, producer 1970 83min Filmmakers, Vaile Scott and Lois Marrone. Photographer, Gordon Quinn. Music composed by Phillip Glass. Background, Catholic hospital. Cast: two males, one female/

Audiovisual Resources

    mother. Film Images R$50+ S$450
A documentary film on the birth of a child. This is not a feminist motion picture; it relates to Lamaze Method of prepared childbirth. Note title.

MARGARET SANGER (mo pic)
Herman J. Engel, writer-director-producer. Katherine Hepburn, narrator 1972 15min For Planned Parenthood--World Population Contemporary #407015-0 R$12 S$90 Univ. of California Ext. #8454 R$9

"Historic photographs and relevant early and contemporary motion picture footage is dramatically combined to present a portrait of Ms. Sanger, one of the great women of American history, and her courageous attempts to introduce the possibilities of family-planning to the women of America and the world. The film not only describes her personal trials and triumphs over the years of persecution and prejudice, but is a story of the times themselves--the struggles of women to achieve social and political equality, of family-planning's vital role in emancipating women and their children from a future of poverty and hopelessness. Finally, it is a study of the world population problem, how it came slowly to be recognized as one of the most urgent crises facing people today. (Adapted from PPWP.)

MARIA OF THE PUEBLOS (mo pic)
Centron 1971 15min C S$200
Coleman, producer "This inspiring motion picture centers around the life of Maria Martínez, who is probably the world's most famous and successful Indian potter ... gives an understanding of the culture, philosophy, art and economic condition of the Pueblo Indians of San Ildefonso, New Mexico" (Centron).

MARIANA (mo pic)
UN 1971 29min C Spanish with English translation Contemporary #408539-5 R$11 S$260 Univ. of California Ext. #8450 R$17
The heroine of this documentary film is a modern woman: 23-year old university student involved in the struggle of Chilean women to achieve dignity in their society, a campaigner for shared-responsibility with men in all aspects of life.

MARILYN (mo pic)
Films, Inc. 83min C R
The career of the late Marilyn Monroe, narrated by Rock Hudson and including clips from her motion pictures.

MARRIAGE (mo pic)
Macmillan Audio Brandon 1946 44min R$15 Director, Isador
    Annensky. Based on Anton Chekhov's play, "The wedding."
    Russian dialog with English subtitles.
"A sprightly satire on the hypocrisy and petty bargaining that precede a provincial wedding party" (MAB).

MARRIAGE (mo pic)
Produced by Wexler for E. C. Brown Trust Foundation 1971
17min C Distributed by Perennial R$23 S$230 Teacher's guide 73-12722
Supposedly for grades 7 and up, with animation. People conveyed as White, women in traditional roles, ideal marriage with hubby-breadwinner, marriage to have children, yeah team.

MARRIAGE AND CAREER (Preparing for work 1) (FS)
Denoyer-Geppert #66721 C $6.75
The "changing role" of women ... "women must now plan for both marriage and career, instead of choosing between ..." says Baker and Taylor Co.! Grades 7-12.

MARRIAGE PROBLEMS (mo pic)
Univ. of California Ext. #72012 1963 30min R$10
Dramatic-but-old vignette shows two sisters: one recently married, the other about to have her second child, neither happy. Dr. Maria Piers interprets.

MARRIAGE UNDER STRESS (mo pic)
BBC-TV, London 1969 40min Time-Life, U.S.A. release 79-714853
Examines the pressures in marriage that can cause separation and divorce and the problems which arise when a marriage is disolved. (U.S. L.C. summary.)

MARRIAGE; WOMEN SPEAK OUT (videotape)
Minda Bikman 50min From: Videowomen

MARRIED LIFE (mo pic)
BBC-TV, London 1970 45min C The Family of Man, #1 Time-Life, U.S.A. release 75-714844
Compares five different marriages in five different places. Shows a wife with three husbands in the Himalayas, a couple in an affluent English community, a man with three wives in New Guinea, a man with two wives in Botswana, and a young couple in Lancashire. (U.S. L.C. Summary.)

MARY POPPINS (rec)
Caedmon #TC1246, CDL#51246 Read by Maggie Smith, Robert Stephens, and cast. Music by Leslie Pearson. P. L. Travers' children's classic. 5 stereo phonodiscs, each $4.30; each cassette $7.95 1968 54:01min
Selections from another example of non-sexist children's literature.

MARY PRITCHARD (mo pic)
Indiana 1971 30min C Artists in America Series Univ. of California Ext. #8334 R$20
"Portrait of Samoan artist who is attempting to preserve the traditional Polynesian women's art form of tapa, a cloth material made from mulberry bark." Shows the process and examines forces causing this cultural tradition to die out (California).

MARY S. McDOWELL (mo pic)
NBC-TV 1964 50min I. Q. Films, 689 5th Ave., New York, NY 10022 R
A film portrait of a teacher who refused to take a loyalty oath prescribed by the Board of Education and as a result, suffered much public abuse.

MASCULINE/FEMININE (FS)
Scholastic Book Services, 904 Sylvan Ave., Englewood Cliffs, NJ 07632. #3901 Complete "teaching unit" (FS with sound, teaching guide) $15 10min
This item is listed in the Home Economics 7-12 section of the company's catalog, described as "a complete sound/filmstrip teaching unit on boy/girl relationships from a lively, youth-oriented point of view, for grades 7-10." It is the only "feminism" item in the 1973-4 Instructional Materials Catalog K/12, which generally is saturated with eye-catching references to such things as Art & Man units, Definition of Man, Images of Man (I and II), Better buymanship books, he-his-him, Courage literature unit, war heroes, and a Prejudice unit re race, religion, long-hair and age; of twenty "Great Issues," two on the Negro, one on Napoleon Bonaparte, zilch on woman or even women. The catalog annotation for "Masculine/Feminine": is designed to help students re-examine the terms "masculine" and "feminine." Since the words are part of every student's experience, the filmstrip serves as a rich take-off point ... and the youngsters themselves are their own resource for this unit.... The voices are those of real teenagers, discussing their own life experiences. The photographs are mostly documentary.

MASCULINITY (FS series)
Schloat Productions 4 part FS Series

MATCHSELLER (mo pic)
Lawrence Lewis, filmmaker 15min C Center Cinema Coop, 540 N. Lakeshore Dr., Room 240, Chicago, IL 60611 R
A dream-like depiction of a young English woman's fantasy of herself as a bride.

MAUDE IN HER HAT (mo pic)
Jeannie Youngson, filmmaker 1971 3min C Sussex Films
An old lady collects groovy sounds.

ME JANE, YOU TARZAN (tape)
Pacifica #BC0952 35min $10 reel or cassette Produced by KPFA
If you ask any school kid what pre-history was like, you're sure to hear about cave men, cudgels and pulling women by the hair. Until recently, neither children nor archeologist has attributed much importance to the role of cave women, not to mention that of she-apes, in determining the direction of prehistoric human development. Elaine Morgan, a Welsh woman, questioned the interpretations male archeologists have given to rather sketchy data in her 1971 book, "The descent of woman" (SEE #521 in the Basic Book Collection).

She proposes more logical theories concerning the prehistoric development and the present state of humanity (from Pacifica).

MEMBER OF THE WEDDING (mo pic)
Macmillan Audio Brandon 1952 91min R
Screenplay by Edna & Edward Anhalt, based on the book and play by Carson McCullers (SEE #300 in Basic Book Collection). With Julie Harris, Ethel Waters. "Carson McCullers' writing is one of the high points of literacy in American films: sharp and full of wit, yet with a lyricism rarely found on the screen. The theme is human isolation and the need to identify with something; the form is a fugue for three voices ..." (Pauline Kael, "Kiss kiss bang bang").

MEN AND WOMEN of our times series see MISS POKER FACE

MEN IN NON-TRADITIONAL ROLES (photos)
Feminist Resources for Equal Education

MEN OF THOUGHT, MEN OF ACTION (FS)
Doubleday 1969 9 sound FSs, with phonodiscs $135; with tape cassettes $153
Includes "The spirit of inquiry and the idea of liberty," "The slavery question," "Free at last?," "The whole man," and "Tides of change!"

MENSTRUAL EXTRACTION (video tape)
Feminist women's health centers 1 hour 2 30min tapes R$50 S$85
In series, Women in control.

MESHES IN THE AFTERNOON (mo pic)
Maya Deren and Alexander Hammid, filmmakers 14min Pacific Film Archive
Classic of American avant garde; a woman's surrealistic self-image.

MIKE AND ANN: A JOURNEY TO MATURITY (mo pic)
McGraw 1968 20min R$12.50 S$260
Teen-agers discuss their attitudes re sex and how society effects them.

THE MILKMAID (FS, rec)
Weston Woods $5.50 up
Randolph Caldecott's classic non-sexist kid-lit (Warne, 1882).

MINORITY YOUTH: ANGIE (mo pic)
BFA 10 1/2min C R$8 S$145
A Stuart Roe Film in which Angie relates her personal feelings about being a Mexican American. Suggested by BFA for elementary, junior and senior high.

MINORITY YOUTH: FELICIA (mo pic)
BFA 11 1/2min R$6 S$100

A Stuart Roe Film in which Felicia is concerned about the apathy of the adults in her Black community. Suggested by BFA for elementary, junior and senior high.

MISS AMERIKA (mo pic)
Kansas Media Project   6min   R$10
About the disruption of the Miss America Pageant of 1968. With raps, guerrilla theater, and original songs, women stress the (mis)use of their sisters by the Pageant as mindless sex-objects.

MISS HICKORY (rec)
Viking   1972   48:52min $6.95   #670-47942-X.   Cassette $7.95   #670-47943-B
An abridgement of the Newbery Award-winning book using intact excerpts presented in continuity with narration and dramatization. Miss Hickory, a resourceful scarecrow, survives a rough winter; the book (Viking 1946) is an example of a contemporary children's classic which is enjoyed by kids, conveys a strong female image, and also received a Newbery!

MISS JULIE (mo pic)
Janus   1950   90min   Subtitled in English   Non-commercial   R
Based on a play by mysogynist August Strindberg. The New York Times referred to this as "a major film"; Christian Science Monitor, "a brilliant film."

MISS POKER FACE (mo pic)
Staff Film Co., a division of Two Star Films, Inc., 79 Bobolink Lane, Levittown, NY 11756   15min   R
Produced by CBS-TV as the story of Helen Wills Moody, women's champion tennis player of the United States at age seventeen. From the Men and Women of Our Times Series.

"MRS. DALLOWAY" (rec)   see   WOMEN IN LITERATURE

MRS. SLATTERY'S STEW (mo pic)
Filmmaker, Phyllis Pigorsch   40min   C   Canyon Cinema   R$10
An allegory on women.

MOONBIRD (mo pic)
John and Faith Hubley, producers   1959   10min   C   animation
    Film Images   R$20   S$150
"Two small boys (the Hubley children) set out at night with a large cage to capture the mythical moonbird ... they do discover...."
Relate this to "Windy Day."

MOSORI MONIKA (mo pic)
Colin Young, Los Angeles Film Makers Coop. production   1970   20min   C   (Ms.) Chick Strand, filmmaker   Distributor: McGraw   R$24   S$275.   Also distributed by Canadian Filmmaker's Distribution Centre   R$25, Univ. of California Ext. #8256 etc. etc.   73-710255

U.S. Library of Congress assigned the subject-heading <u>Acculturation</u> to this motion picture and provided the following "<u>Summary</u>": "Shows acculturation of the Warao Indians of Venezuela as a result of the establishment of a Franciscan mission. Describes the manifestations of the contact from viewpoints of a young Spanish nun and an old Indian woman." "Mosori Monika" provides the educator, film-class, Women's Studies coordinator, librarian, feminist, social scientist with the opportunity to compare perceptions as manifest in film reviews, and hopefully, to realize the bases of these perceptions: Colin Young, Director of the London, England, National Film School and involved in the film's coming about, has written about it: "Strand's ethnographical film is a compassionate study of two women in a small Warao village in Venezuela. Through the innocent ignorance of the nun and the compliance of an old nostalgic Indian, we see the inevitable process of acculturation, presented as evidence of change, not as propaganda." Ernest Callenbach has written for <u>Film Quarterly</u> that it is "One of the best anthropology films" of which he knows. <u>LJ SLJ Previews</u> (Oct. 1972:12) assigned Robert E. Muller to review it and listed it among anthropological films; Mr. Muller summed it up as an "excellent film to use with young people to show how we project our own biases into what we see, as well as showing the impact of one culture on another." The Contemporary-McGraw-Hill catalog annotation: "Spanish Franciscan missionaries went to Venezuela in 1945 to 'civilize' the Warao Indians. This film is a compassionate study of two women in a small Warao village, an innocently ignorant nun and a compliant, nostalgic Indian. The inevitable process of acculturation is presented here as evidence of change, not as propaganda." The American Library Assoc. conference film presentation brochure characterized it as "ethnographic" and suggested it for use in "Area Studies." Landers' film reviews (March 1973:158), Filmmaker's Newsletter (July-August 1972:46), and the University of California, Extension media service catalog are other sources. And what does it have to say for and about women? feminists?

THE MOST (mo pic)
Gordon Sheppard, Richard Ballentine, filmmakers. A Janus film
    27min Pyramid R$25 S$290 Distributor suggests for Junior high up
"A candid and revealing <u>cinéma vérité</u> study of <u>Playboy Magazine</u> publisher Hugh Hefner. Director Sheppard unfolds some carefully-mounted contrasts that reveal the difference between 'Hef's' view of himself and what the viewer may consider. At one point, he puts it on the record: 'Genius? I suppose by definition I consider myself one.' A classic of its genre, one review said this: '... a document which allows its subject to speak for himself, giving him plenty of rope on which to hang himself. And Mr. Hefner does just that.' <u>Monthly Film Bulletin</u>." SEE ALSO "You worm" (page 253, <u>Womanhood Media</u> Audiovisuals).

MOTHER-INFANT INTERACTION #1: Forms of interaction at six
    weeks (mo pic)

MOTHER-INFANT INTERACTION #2: Forms of interaction at six
   months (mo pic)
New York University 1967-1968 49min-42min Produced by Sylvia
   Brody and Sidney Axelrad Univ. of California Ext. #'s 8312
   and 3 R$14-$13

MOTHER LOVE (mo pic)
Carousel 1960 26min Univ. of California Ext. #6661 R$11
"Dr. Harry Harlow, in his primate laboratory at the Univ. of Wisconsin, tests the reaction of a large colony of newborn rhesus monkeys to a variety of unusual and inanimate mother substitutes, which he calls 'mother surrogates,' in order to find the key to the bond between mother and child and to understand the effects of the denial of maternal love. He demonstrates that the single most important factor is body contact, holding, and nestling, and further concludes that deprivation of this can cause deep emotional disturbances, even death" (California).

MOUNTAIN MOVING DAY (rec)
Rounder Records (anti-profit collective) $3.50 New Haven Women's
   Liberation Rock Band and the Chicago Women's Liberation Rock
   Band.

Ms. (tape)
U.S. Library of Congress, Division for the Blind & Physically
   Handicapped has this magazine, among others, available on tape.

Ms. MAGAZINE (tape)
Feminist Radio Network #474-11 29 3/4 min Cassette: $20;
   Reels
Where it's been and where it's going; includes interview with Ms.
staff.

Ms. STARTER SET (buttons)
Dept. B, Ms. Magazine Corp., 370 Lexington Ave., New York, NY
   10017. 13 feminist buttons assorted $2. (Assortment pictured
   on page 75 of August 1974 issue.)

MS. ERY (cartoons)
"Ms. ery" by Anne Wittels and Ivy Bottini. c1973 0-88381-001-8
   $3 Wollstonecraft
Cartoon-style humor on the Women's Movement. More than just funny--as someone somewhere said, "perceptive, gotcha-click!"

LA MUCHACHA SOLITARIA (videotape)
Angelita Alberio, filmmaker, mother, active member of local school
   Parents' Advisory Committee 1973 12min 1/2" videotape
   BW 1/2hour reel EIAJ Women make movies
"A portrait of a young Puerto Rican woman alone in New York City who loses her job and forfeits her apartment. The happy conclusion of this Spanish love story reflects the important role played by the extended family in Spanish culture and beautifully conveys the director's commitment to a loving family life" (from WMM listings).

MUSIC: A SAMPLING OF TODAY'S WOMEN COMPOSERS, recorded:
Bacewicz, Grazyna: Music for Strings, Percussion and Celeste, recorded by Witold Rowicki and the Warsaw Philharmonic (Philips PHS 900).
Boulanger, Lili: recorded by Igor Markevitch and the Lamoreux Orchestra (Everest 3059).
Dlugoszewski, Lucia: A Space Is a Diamond (Nonesuch 71275).
Glanville-Hicks, Peggy: The Transposed Heads, an eerie opera based on Thomas Mann's short story, Louisville Orchestra (Louisville 545/6).
Kolb, Barbara: Trobar Klus & Solitaire for Piano and Vibes. A Fromm Foundation commission, recorded by Ralph Shapey and the University of Chicago Contemporary Chamber Players (Turnabout 34487).
Musgrave, Thea: Excursions for Piano (Argo ZRG-704).
Oliveros, Pauline: Outline for Flute, Percussion and String Bass; An Improvisation Chart (Nonesuch 71237).
Seeger, Ruth Crawford: String Quartet (Nonesuch 7142).

MY BODY IS MINE TO CONTROL (tape)
Radio Free People, producer-distributor.
Songs about women's struggle for liberation written by Beverly Grand and Lynn Phillips.

MY COUNTRY OCCUPIED (mo pic)
Newsreel, San Francisco 30min R$35
"Oaxaca de Mejia is a Guatemalan woman who speaks of her life on a United Fruit Co. plantation, and how this company has taken everything from the Guatemalans. She joins the guerillas in fighting to take back her country" (Newsreel).

MY FATHER THE DOCTOR (mo pic)
Filmmaker, Miriam Weinstein 1972 17min C Discussion guide
    Canadian Filmmaker's Distribution Centre R$20. Also from Ms. Weinstein, 27 Seymour, Concord, MA 01742 (617-369-5791) R$20 S$200
A study of the relationship, past and present, between filmmaker and her father.

MY LIFE IN ART (mo pic)
(Ms.) Freude Bartlett, filmmaker 1971-3 30min C Canadian
    Filmmaker's Distribution Centre R$35
"A series of short films mounted together on one reel to make up a programme documenting the growth of the filmmaker's art. In a home-movie style, she concentrates on herself and the camera, her friends, her surroundings, the birth of her child, her own fantasies. Includes 'The sacred heart of Jesus,' 'Promise her anything but give her the kitchen sink,' 'Shooting star,' 'Adam's birth,' 'Sweet dreams,' 'Bride & groom (folly),' and 'Women & children at large' " (Centre brochure, "Films by Women").

MY LIFE WITH MARTIN LUTHER KING, JR. (rec)
Coretta Scott King Caedmon #TC9300

Audiovisual Resources

MY NAME IS OONA (mo pic)
Filmmaker, Gunvor Nelson 1969-70 10min Canyon Cinema Coop
Fragments of the coming to consciousness of a girl child, the filmmaker's daughter.

THE MYSTERY OF AMELIA EARHART (mo pic)
BFA 22min R$20 S$330 "You are there" social studies series

MYTH AMERICA--HOW FAR HAVE YOU REALLY COME? (show)
Rosalie Gresser Abrams, writer-director. 2549 Runyon Pl.,
    Anaheim, CA 92804
Feminist show which has been performed for several years in California. Printed material and song ranging from biblical passages to commercials.

- N -

NOW FEMINIST CATALOG (products)
Judith Meuli, editor, 1126 HiPoint St., Los Angeles, CA 90035.
    V2 #1--Spring 1973. Graphics, posters, pamphlets, jewelry, audiovisuals, etc.
Feminist products financing the Revolution. NOW does not endorse any product/service; only requirement is that advertisers qualify themselves as feminists. Products can be used to raise funds.

NOW LEGAL DEFENSE & EDUCATION FUND Public Service Advertising Campaign (kit)
Midge Kovacs, campaign coordinator, 127 East 59 St., New York,
    NY 10022. Actual print ads, radio discussions, TV commercials on film.
These kits have been sent directly to radio and television stations and leading publications; local promotional efforts by NOW Chapters, which also received kits, are needed.

NACE UN NIÑO (A CHILD IS BORN) (FS)
Comisión de ayuda social y vecinos mundiales, Lima, Perú, producer. Distributor, Regional technical aids center, Mexico.
    1 FS, 31fr, silent. Spanish headlines and leaflet.
SEE International Planned Parenthood Federation Library Bulletin (V 7:68) for Spanish and English descriptions, from which the following is drawn: Reproduction process illustrated through the use of colorful, simplified drawings. Leaflet provides brief, easy to understand explanations of each frame. After showing the formation of sperm and ovum, the various stages of gestation are presented, as are the position of twins in the uterus, and finally the process of birth.

NANA (mo pic)
Macmillan Audio Brandon 1934 87min R Based on Emile Zola's novel. With Anna Sten, Mae Clark.
"Dorothy Arzner, the only female director to operate freely in the upper castes of the Hollywood system, places this free adaptation

of the Zola novel in the Paris of 1868 ... [and] conceived [it] as
a morality tale about the rise and fall of a notorious courtesan ..."
(MAB).

NANA, MOM AND ME (mo pic)
New Day Films 47min C
Amalie Randolph Rothschild's autobiographical film about her grandmother, Addye Goldsmith Rosenfeld.

NAUGHTY NURSE (mo pic)
By Paul Bartel 9min C Grove #420 R$30 S$125
"This sharply satiric film revolves around a compassionate and efficient nurse whose medical ministrations to ease the pain of her patients are relieved by her lunchtime frolics with the doctor in which she acts out a fantasy life of sadism and leather fetishism. Produced in the old tradition of the vaudeville sketch ... tops its gags and blackouts with a surprise ending" (Grove).

NEAR THE BIG CHAKRA (mo pic)
Anne Severson, filmmaker 15min C silent Multi-media R$35
  S$200
"A startling film that silently presents close-ups of what seem to be hundreds of vaginas in various stages of excitation. Neither clinical nor leering, its strange neutrality makes it possible for the viewer to be simultaneously fascinated, repulsed, awestruck at the diversity of women's genitals, and finally, at their universality. A difficult film, but worth it" (Ms. August 1973:98).

THE NEGRO AMERICAN CITIZEN (tape)
Produced under the personal direction of Elizabeth Duncan Koontz,
    past president of the National Education Assoc. and former Director, U.S. Dept. of Labor's Women's Bureau 1969 42 reel-to-reel audiotapes or tape cassettes, $198, from Valiant. Suggested for school-age and adults. Arranged chronologically from 450 B.C.

NEGRO POETRY FOR YOUNG PEOPLE (rec series)
Read by Arna Bontemps. Folkways #FC 7114 (Men and) Women:
    Josephine Copeland, Helene Johnson, Beatrice Murphy

NEGRO POETS (rec series)
Read by the poets themselves. Folkways #FL 9791 (Men and)
    Women: Margaret Walker and Gwendolyn Brooks

NEGRO POETS IN THE U.S.A.--200 YEARS (rec series)
Read by Arna Bontemps. Folkways #FL 9792 (Men and) Women:
    Angelina Weld Grimke, Helene Johnson, and Phillis Wheatley

THE NEGRO WOMAN (rec)
Read by Dorothy Washington. Folkways #FH 5523. Compiled and
    edited by Jean M. Brannon 1966 12" LP rec with Notes
    $5.98 Phillis Wheatley, Sojourner Truth, Harriet Tubman,

Frances Ellen Watkins Harper, Ida B. Wells, Mary Church Terrell, and Mary McLeod Bethune.

NEVER A BRIDE (mo pic)
Brigham Young Univ.   1969   20min   C   Univ. of California Ext.
   # 8492   R$15
"Dramatic portrayal in which a young woman works at her aunt's dude ranch for a summer in hope of finding romance with the 'right man.' A series of unexpected events forces her to reevaluate herself and makes her realize that she must become the sort of person the man she is searching for would want" (California).

NEVER UNDERESTIMATE THE POWER OF A WOMAN (mo pic)
Filmmaker, Norma Briggs, Dept. of Labor grant   1971   15min   C
   Walter Mieves, Dept. of Photography & Cinema, 45 N. Charter St., Madison, WI 53715   R$12.50   S$125
Discusses myths and facts about "working women." Designed for adults, it shows women in a variety of non-stereotypical blue-collar jobs.

NEW AMERICAN FEMALE FLIES HIGH (mo pic)
Pathe news for Milestones of the Century, producer   5min   Creative film society   R$4
Newsreel exemplifies members of Women's Liberations of the 20's and early 30's who defied their role as the "weaker sex" by performing daredevil stunts aboard high-flying airplanes, swinging by their teeth, tap-dancing on wings, etc. !

THE NEW AMERICAN WOMAN (FS)
New York Times Education Division # 320660   1972   65fr   35mm & phonodisc   2s   12"   33 1/3 rpm   15min   Current Affairs Series   Rec $9.   Cassette $10   Teacher's guide, script, duplicating master   72-733344
U.S. Library of Congress "Summary": "Explores the changing role of American woman--the home, on the job, and in politics--and points out the help that she is getting from the new Equal Rights laws, from the courts, and from the Women's Liberation Movement." And from the NYT catalog: "Here is a look backward at the American woman's place in history and a look forward to her long-range objectives. Junior and senior high school."
Functional perhaps in providing a take-off for researching the alleged "help": new laws (Civil Rights Act amendments), courts (E.E.O.C., H.E.W., etc.), and the W.L. Movement (sisterhood).

NEW CAREERS FOR WOMEN (mo pic)
American educational films, 331 N. Maple Dr., Beverly Hills, CA 92010   17min   C   R$25   S$235

THE NEW FEMINISM (tape cassette)
Behavioral sciences tape library # 85700   3 one hour tapes $21
   By M. Jane Pollock, Ph.D., Brandeis University   72-751084
1. History of the Women's Movement--Technological change--The immediate goals of the Women's Movement (# 85711). 2. Towards

an understanding of sexism (#85722). 3. Towards an understanding of sexism (contd.)--Some personal observations (#85733). An overview of the history and goals of the women's movement together with a penetrating analysis of sexism as found in today's society. A long-needed, balanced overview of women's struggle for equality (BSTL).

NEW NEW HAVEN WOMEN'S LIBERATION ROCK BAND
Jennifer Abod, 1504 Boulevard, New Haven, CT 06511 203-389-1971

A NEW LEAF (mo pic)
Filmmaker, Elaine May 1971 102min C Films, Inc. R S$150
May has written, directed, and starred in a comedy about a bachelor who runs through his inheritance and has a choice of working or marrying a rich wife.

NEW LIFE STYLES FOR WOMEN (cassette)
Cynthia Clark Wedel's thesis 1972 Theological cassettes, v3 #6.
  PO Box 11724, Pittsburgh, PA 15228

NEWBERY/CALDECOTT AWARD BOOKS-IN-PRINT (audiovisuals)
Some of the books receiving these awards are non-sexist children's literature. They can be obtained, often abridged or excerpted, in various audiovisual formats from such sources as Miller-Brody, Baker & Taylor, etc. Be sure to understand why some of these titles should be rejected and others recommended. SEE Ms. May 1973:99, School Library Journal Jan. 1971, etc.

NIKKI GIOVANNI READS RE: CREATION (tape)
Cassette/tape Broadside $5.00

NO LONGER A THING (tape)
CBC #297L 1 hour $14
A report on the liberation of women.

NO ROOM AT THE INN (tape)
CBC #134L 1 hour $14
An unmarried-mother's story plus an examination of attitudes towards single mothers.

NO TEARS FOR KELSEY (mo pic)
CCM #INS-407 27min C R $16.75 Lease $270
An Insight Film produced by the Paulist Fathers. Cast includes Geraldine Brooks. The Paulist Fathers have produced a Kelsey who has "escaped from the slums because he learned to squelch his emotions. Now his teenage daughter has run away from home, lost her virginity, used pot, totally rejected her parent's values and been taken to juvenile hall for truancy. But Kelsey is controlled. He asks 'Why?' She answers that they never listened to her, but the 'Beautiful People' did. Then she breaks and reveals all was not so beautiful. But Kelsey is sickened. He promises discipline within an inch of her life and slaps her down. He immediately

Audiovisual Resources

regrets this--but too late.   As feeling dies in her eyes--he learns to cry again."

NO TEARS FOR RACHEL (mo pic)
NET 1972 27min 74-702593 Indiana Univ. #CSC2449 R$12.50 S$315
A thorough, basic film about rape.   Useful at high school as well as adult level.

NOBODY WAVED GOODBYE (mo pic)
National Film Board of Canada 1964 80min Macmillan Audio Brandon R
"Two teenagers, Peter (Peter Kastner) and Julie (Julie Biggs), from affluent homes, are at odds with the values of their parents' generation. They have a love affair, and Julie becomes pregnant. Peter steals money and a car so they can run away, but Julie begs him to stay and face their problems. She is unable to persuade him, and he drives away without her" (MAB). Ten years ago this was an outstanding film; in many ways it still is, but....

NOBODY'S VICTIM (mo pic)
Vaughn Obern and Alan Barker, producers for Self-Protection Media for Women. Distributed by Film Fair Communications, 10820 Ventura Blvd., Studio City, CA 91604 1972 20min S$230. Also distributed by Univ. of California Ext. and Ramsgate Films.
Based on the rather naive premise that women need not feel helpless when faced with danger. Relevant to men too. Good demonstrations of self-defense.

NOON WINE (rec) see WOMEN IN LITERATURE

NOT SO YOUNG NOW AS THEN (mo pic)
Filmmaker, Liane Brandon 1974 film 18min C R$33 S$275
You are cordially invited to attend a 15th high school reunion.

NOTHING BUT A MAN (mo pic)
Macmillan Audio Brandon 1964 92min R With Abby Lincoln, Gloria Foster, Julie Harris, Helen Arrindell.
"... moving drama of the personal struggle of a Southern black man and his wife in a society hostile to them. A young railway worker gives up a good job to settle down and marry the preacher's daughter, a schoolteacher. ... the problem is intensified because the man is a Negro and will not play the expected Negro role ..." (MAB).

NOW, AT LAST, BETTER JOBS FOR WOMEN (Jobs and careers) (kit)
Changing times education service Gr 7-12 40 reprints, 1 transparency, 1 dup master, Teacher's guide $10. Distributed by Baker & Taylor.

NURSES TRAINING (FS)
Planned Parenthood World Population 14min S$15 FS and rec C
Nurses show ways they introduce concept of birth control to appropriate patients.

NURSING MOTHER (non-sexist toy)
Possum Trot: Soft cotton 18" woman with red hair, pink face, green calico dress. Unsnap her bodice and there are snaps on her breasts instead of nipples, $25. 9" baby doll, red-headed and diapered, snap on its mouth--a breast-feeding baby. Also from Possum Trot (an Appalachian coop): Mother Pig, 5 piglets suckle when snapped in place on the large orange flannel mother, or they play along, $15. Bear Threads: Mother Moo brown plush fur cow with green felt for the grass in her mouth and an udder with 4 snaps; the calf snaps on for feeding. (2519 Wilshire, Santa Monica, CA 90403.) Also: Children's Concepts, 2295 Broadway, New York, NY 10024.

- O -

O TANNENBAUM (tape)
Feminist videotape collective 5min

ODI (mo pic)
Macmillan Audio Brandon 1968 17min C R$20
"... portrait of a woman possessed by a sense of loss. The film explores her recollections, fantasies and kaleidoscopic experiences" (MAB).

OCCUPATIONAL OPPORTUNITIES & INFORMATION (Slides/cassette)
Feminist resources for equal education 1973 slides-cassettes series
FREE: "A series of slides and taped interviews with women in various occupations. These will be done on a vertical basis--e.g. the set on dentists might include a dental student, a practicing dentist, several dental specialists, a dental professor, etc. The purpose of this is to give students information about all aspects of a profession. In addition to general information about the profession, the problems, if any, that women face in this field will also be discussed."

OF WOMEN (mo pic, slides, songs)
Cassandra O'Gyla, filmmaker-distributor: 5507 Margaretta, Pittsburgh, PA 15206 6min
A production with slides, a film, and 2 songs by Nina Simone. It shows women on the streets of Pittsburgh, women in the roles of housekeeper and mother, women in art, women learning self-defense, women working, women as sex-objects, etc. In general, the myths of womanhood and how women can overcome them.

Audiovisual Resources 235

OFF WE GO...? (tape)
Pacifica #BC 0932   Produced by KPFA   52min $10 reel or cassette
"During World War II, 'Air-Wacs' performed a wide range of military duties which were unusual for women in those days. Today, there are 14,000 WAF; and, according to the Air Force, women 'are not organized as a separate corps, but form an integral part of that service.' They allegedly 'compete equally with men for promotion in each of the airman and officer grades, including general officer rank, and they are trained, assigned, and administered under essentially the same policies and procedures.' A lot of women in the air force don't think so. This documentary explores the role of WAF in the male-dominated military, with interviews with recruiting officers, enlisted women, and officers. A ... program which points to some rather obvious contradictions in military policy" (Pacifica).

OFFICE CINDERELLA (mo pic)
Filmmaker, Laurette Baker   3min   Youth Films   R$4.50   S$30
In a familiar work situation, a young Black woman unexpectedly rebels against the oppressive manipulations of her (male) boss.

OH! YOU SUFFRAGETTE (mo pic)
"Not all films were favorable [to the women's voting rights movement]; in 1911, ... was released in the United States...." Lifelong Learning March 5, 1973:1 catalog of the University of California Extension bibliographic essay re women/film.

(ON) OLDER WOMEN (slide show)
Seattle-King County NOW Chapter Task Force on Aging   1974
    Karla Williams, Ellen Kaline currently working on this.

OLYMPIA (PART II) (mo pic)
Leni Reifenstahl, producer-director   Contemporary
"The greatest sports film of all time" (First International Festival of Women's Films). Documents the 1936 Olympic Games in Berlin; Part II includes gymnastic and aquatic events, sailing and rowing, field hockey, polo and soccer, equestrian events, bicycling, marathon and decathalon.

ON MY WAY TO SCHOOL (tape)
CBC #145L $14   1 hour
"Story of an Indian girl who was beaten and raped by four white men on her way to school" (CBC).

OPEN FOR CHILDREN (mo pic)
Odeon   30min   C   R$25   S$350   1972
"A natural filming in day care centers provokes discussion of parent and teacher attitudes" (Odeon).

OPEN SECRET (rec)
CBC   12" LP Rec $5

Read and written by Gwendolyn MacEwen. Contains a selection from her poetry, short stories and novels.

L'OPERA MOUFFE (mo pic)
Filmmaker, Agnes Varda 1958 19min Grove R
"Ms. Varda explores the theme of pregnancy. It is an experiment in the abstract representations of the thoughts of a pregnant woman ... film that can be meaningful to other women" (Women's History Research Center).

ORAL CONTRACEPTIVES (mo pic)
U.S. Govt., National AV Center 29min Florida State Univ. R$5
An adult film in which "Dr. Garcia defends the use of oral contraceptives, stressing the superior efficiency of this method. Dr. Lasagna feels that there are other methods which are clinically more advisable and he stresses the now-emerging adverse consequences of contraceptive drugs" (FSU).

ORGANIZING WOMEN OFFICE WORKERS (tape)
Women's Culture, producer. 60min Radio Free People, distributor #74-2, S$6, 2 tracks. Single track version (2 reels) $10
"Taped at a conference held Oct. 1973, this program deals with the low pay, lack of security, and subordinate position of secretaries. Several solutions are presented: filing equal opportunity lawsuits, forming groups such as Chicago Women Employed--a central organization which supports women in a variety of workplaces--, union organizing, and CR on the job" (W.C.).

OTHER WOMEN, OTHER WORK (mo pic)
Churchill 20min C S$230
"Made by a man and woman crew. Available with study guide. Useful to raise consciousness about jobs considered traditionally male: truck driver, veterinarian, roof shingler, pilot, marine biologist, carpenter, woman who does a daily segment on a TV news program" (Women Studies Abstracts). Pilot with lacy blouse noted by everyone.

OUR FAMILY IS BLACK (FS)
Coronet 1970 6 sound FSs, each approx. 50fr, 10min, with
    phonodiscs, $55. With tape cassettes $70.
Pictures the daily life of a five-member family living in a middle-class city neighborhood. For intermediate and upper grades. Two out of six: "Mother works hard, too." "Rose is sixteen."

OUR NORTH AMERICAN FOREMOTHERS (slide show)
Anne Grant, producer "multi-media documentary slide presentation with narration and music."
Relates the histories of obscure American women through period portraits, drawings, cartoons, newspapers, original handwritten letters, and modern color photography. Ms. Grant, co-ordinator of NOW national Task Force on Education, after two years of research, produced this much-needed tool. Recognized by Mlle. magazine for this work and her feminism, she was interviewed

on Dec. 11, 1972 CBS-TV morning news by Nelson Bennett, who looked bored and amused, cut her off. (Ironically, at the conclusion of the newscast, it was necessary for him to comment on newscaster Michelle Clark's accident-death--seemingly ashamed of his humaneness, his voice waivered, the camera shifted from him, and did not return; he mentioned all of her feminine qualities, but was not allowed to cry!) Ms. Grant referred to the production as "touchstones of accomplishment," a NOW Project. Contact her at 617 49 St., Brooklyn, NY 11220.

OUT OF THE MAINSTREAM (FS)
Warren Schloat 1970 6 sound FSs, each approximately 15min, each with phonodisc, $92; with tape cassettes, $110. For intermediate and upper grades.
First-person account(s) of persons out of the mainstream (Third World?): Black male migrant worker, Black woman's account of her childhood with her father and as sharecropper's wife, Chicano farm-worker, Puerto Rican cafeteria baker, White Kentucky tobacco farmer, Sioux Indian woman.

- P -

PARANOIA BLUES (mo pic)
Filmmaker, Jane Warrenbrand 1973 5min Chelsea Picture Station
What the title suggests--the daily anxiety of city life for women.

PARENT TO CHILD ABOUT SEX (mo pic)
Perennial #401 Frederick J. Margolis and Stuart Finch, MD's.
  31min C R$28 S$280
Purports to show "parents how to teach their children important facts and wholesome attitudes about sex in a simple, direct fashion" (Perennial).

PARENTHOOD: MYTHS AND REALITIES (FS)
Guidance Associates 2 FSs; 2 12" LPs/$37.50/9A-103-786. 2 FSs; 2 cassettes/$41.50/9A-103-794. Discussion guide.
"Part I depicts daily parent-child interactions from the child's viewpoint; demonstrates the need for responsibility and commitment in parental behavior.... Part II features round-table discussion led by psychiatrist Robert Gould.... Finally, participants strongly emphasize the need for prospective parents to examine their motivations" (G.A.).

PASSAGES FROM FINNEGANS WAKE (mo pic)
Mary Ellen Bute, director 1965 Grove
"... has been hailed by literary and film critics alike for its enlightening treatment of Joyce's work. His imaginative composite words are doubly revealed: spoken by the Irish cast and simultaneously flashed on the screen as subtitles. Like the novel, the film presents Finn, the Irish hero, coming again (Finnegan), waking into cosmic consciousness" (First International Women's Film Festival).

THE PASSENGERS (El Ghorba) (mo pic)
Annie Tresgot, French director Third World Cinema Group
Cinema verite interviews of Algerians emigrating to France.

THE PASSION OF ANNA (mo pic)
Ingmar Bergman, Director 99min C Swedish with English subtitles United Artists R
A probe into the mysteries of why male and female find it so hard to reach each other.

PATRICIA HARRIS (FS)
McGraw With record and guide, $20. With cassette and guide, $22
The story of Ms. Harris who was born in a small Illinois town and became a lawyer, then dean of Howard University Law School, a U.S.A. Ambassador to Luxembourg, a delegate to the UN, and a member of the President's Commission on Violence.

PAUL'S FILM (mo pic)
Amy Taubin, filmmaker, source: 70 Riverside Dr., New York, NY 10024 1971 10min C R
A woman out on bail from the (New York City) House of Detention.

PEARL S. BUCK (mo pic)
Films, Inc. #33-0017 30min S$150 1960 Univ. of California Ext. #6887 R$11
N.B.C. interview at her home.

PEOPLE OF THE AUSTRALIAN WESTERN DESERT; a multi-part series (mo pics)
Univ. of California Ext. #7693 1969 13min R$8 S$80
"Spinning hair string. Getting water from well. Binding girl's hair": Part 9.

THE PERILS OF PAULA (videotape)
Univ. of Michigan Center for Continuing Education of Women's Arrow Program.
A trigger film for group discussion, depicting scenes of conflict in a young woman's life. Actresses: Mary Ellen Kazmark, Irene Connors. Hour-long programs in outreach program for undergraduate women.

PERIODICALS ON WOMEN & WOMEN'S RIGHTS (microform)
Greenwood Press 1974 microfiche or microfilm $415
Collection of periodicals from mid-19th century through World War I. Includes: Forerunner, Liberal Review, Lily, Lowell Offering, Lucifer the Lightbearer, Mother Earth Bulletin, The National Citizen and Ballot Box, The Revolution, Stiletto, Una, Western Woman Voter, Woman Voter, and Woman's Protest.

PERSONALITY PLUS (FS series)
RMI Film Productions 1972 One of a series of 6 Home Economics C FSs with cassettes or records, 30min, $30each. Grades 7-

Audiovisual Resources

14 suggested.
SEE ALSO their "Good grooming." "Jacqueline Skubal covers many helpful hints designed to aid girls in developing pleasing personalities without sacrificing individuality. Without preaching, emphasis is on cheerfulness, friendliness, confidence, honesty, consideration and purpose" (RMI).

PHEDRE (mo pic)
Macmillan Audio Brandon 92min C R French film with Marie Bell. French dialog with English subtitles.
Racine's classic drama in original alexandrine verse.

PIERRE VALLIERES (mo pic)
Joyce Wieland, filmmaker 1972 45min C French with English subtitles Canadian Filmmaker's Distribution Centre R$50
Ms. Wieland says "... he delivered 3 essays, without stopping, except for reel change and camera breakdown: 1) Mont Laurier; 2) Quebec history and race; 3) women's liberation. Everything which happened is recorded on film. It was a oneshot affair, I either got him on film or I missed. What we see on film is the mouth of a revolutionary, extremely close...."

PILLAR OF WISDOM (mo pic)
National Film Board of Canada 1970 9min Carousel
Fifty young freshmen, smeared with grease, try to get a cap on top of a twenty-foot pole (Pleck).

PINK AND PABLUM, SUGAR AND SPICE (slide program)
Sharon Tipton, Women's Center, Kalamazoo YWCA, Kalamazoo, MI 49007 20min R$50
On children's books.

PIPPI LONGSTOCKING (mo pic)
Based on Astrid Lindgren's series of kid-lit (Viking 1950, also available in Compass paperbacks), the movie will be distributed by G. G. Communications of Boston and will tour U.S.A. and Canada beginning 1974. Pippi's message has been "Don't worry about me; I'll always come out on top!" She has been translated (from Swedish) into 18 languages and audiovisuals. Sequels to the original book: "Pippi in the South Seas" (1959) and "Pippi goes on board" (1957).

PIPPI LONGSTOCKING (rec)
Read by Esther Benson. 1971 3 phonodiscs 150min with paperback book $17.50 #AA3311/13. Cassettes $22.50 #CX311/13 Listening Library
A reading of the complete book without musical background or sound effects.

PLASTIC BLAG (mo pic)
Judith Wardwell, filmmaker 1968 7min Canadian Filmmaker's Distribution Centre R$7
Consumer packaging takes the wrap.

PLAY WITH ME (FS, rec)
Weston Woods   FS $7.25   Also available from other companies
    and in various AV formats.
Marie Hall Ets' simple text portrays an inquisitive little girl who
finds many animal friends by a pond in the forest; the 1955 Viking
book is a non-sexist children's classic of fiction.

THE PLIGHT OF WOMEN IN BROADCASTING (tape)
Pacifica #BC0944   70min $12 reel or cassette
Lois Hansen, Ellen Dubrowin, Deborah Janone asked executives of 9
San Francisco Bay Area radio and TV stations about the status of
female employees at their stations. Discovering that women were
almost exclusively employed in clerical positions, the 3 women
from KPFA asked for the descriptions of technical and on-the-air
jobs and definitions of "talent" from the men who judge women
applicants. It became obvious that it would take years for women
to qualify for such positions as described/defined by men.
Recollections of "Catch-22" routine: You can't get the experience
unless you've had a job; you can't get a job unless....

POBLACIÓN: PROBLEMA EXPLOSIVO (Population Explosion problem) (FS)
Producer: Comisión de ayuda social y vecinos mundiales, Lima,
    Perú.   1 FS   37fr   silent   Spanish headlines and leaflet.
SEE International Planned Parenthood Federation Library Bulletin
volume 7:68,9 for Spanish and English annotations. Begins by telling audience that population growth is a phenomenon which is common to most Latin American countries. Brief history of population growth, photos re advances in fighting disease, demographic
charts showing population growth. By year 2,000 there will be in
Latin America ten people for each one of those who lived in 1900!
Ends by asking viewer how he could help his family and community
in the fight against malnutrition, poverty, unemployment, illiteracy.

POETRY IS ALIVE AND WELL and living in America (mo pic)
Media Plus   series of 3 short C films with sound on 3 contemporary American poets--2 are women. Director, Frances Ross
    R:terms

POETRY OF EDNA ST. VINCENT MILLAY (rec)
Valiant $6.98   Read by the author

POETRY OF MAYA ANGELOU (rec)
GWP recs

POETRY OF THE BLACK MAN (rec)
United Artists UAS #6693   Six men and: Gwendolyn Brooks. Read
    by Sidney Poitier and: Doris Belack.

POPULATION AND THE AMERICAN FUTURE (mo pic)
Producer, distributor: Fisher Film Group, 216 East 49 St., New
    York, NY 10017   1972, released 1973   60min   S$300   For
    free loan, contact Population Affairs Film Collection, National

Audiovisual Resources   241

   AV Affairs Center (GSA), Washington, DC 20409.   Ages 13-
   adult   73-701825
This film version of the "Official Report of the President's Commission on Population Growth and the American Future" is extremely conservative but does contain much data.

POPULATION CONTROL BEGINS AT HOME (tape)
Center for the Study of Democratic Institutions #489D 12:43min
   $3.75   72-764786
There are now more underqnourished people than there were people in 1875. Paul Ehrlich suggests a plan.

POPULATION EXPLOSION PROBLEM (FS) see POBLACIÓN:
   PROBLEMA EXPLOSIVO

PORTRAIT OF A LOST SOUL (videotape)
Twin Cities women's film collective 15min 1/2" R$5
Deals with women's search for identification through the media of dance and music.

PORTRAIT OF A MODERN WOMAN (tape)
CBC #713L 1 hour $14
A program about Karen Blixen, better known as Isak Dinesen, the author.

PORTRAIT OF MY MOTHER (mo pic)
Bonnie Kreps, filmmaker 1973   25min C Canadian Filmmaker's
   Distribution Centre   R$30
"With an all-woman crew, Ms. Kreps visited her mother in her Wyoming cabin-home and recorded the pleasures and challenges of a life lived quietly, independently and in harmony with nature. This is a film that avoids any hyped-up message or mystery; the camera is attentive rather than dictorial" (CFDC).

PORTRAITS (FS) see WOMAN (kit)

POST CARDS see GRAPHICS

POSTERS--SOURCES [see also "Alternatives in print, 3d ed.: 40-1]:
   Ann's   It's about Time
   Boccaccio, Shirley   KNOW
   Cell 16   National Foundation for the
   Chicago Women's Liberation   Improvement of Education,
      Union   1156 15 St., NW, Washing-
   Clitarists   ton, DC 20005. "Sexism
   Diana Press   in education."
   E.E.O.C.   Oracle
   Feminist Press   People's Press
   Feminist Women's Health   Planned Parenthood World
      Center   Population
   Graphic Communications   Society for Individual Rights
      Herald   Tree Toad Graphics
   Grey Falcon House   Women Enterprises

Women's Press Collective.

POTTER'S SHOP (tape)
Feminist videotape collective   20min

PREJUDICE! (FS)
Guidance Associates   1972   2 sound FSs, part 1: 100fr, 15min;
    part 2: 72fr, 14min; each with phonodisc, with discussion guide,
    for use with manual or automatic projector, $37.50; with tape
    cassettes $41.50.   35mm   C   72-733733
The Library of Congress subject heading assigned to this is Pre-judices and antipathies, from which Sanford Berman derived the title of his Scarecrow Press book (SEE page 85, Womanhood Media; and SEE ALSO Elizabeth Dickinson's "Statement ... on sex-biased Library of Congress subject headings" in the "Sexism in education and media" section of Pamphlets collection herein).   "Introduces a broad range of literary response to personal and social bigotry" (G.A.).

PREJUDICE: HARVEST OF HATE (FS)
Audio Visual Narrative Arts, PO Box 398, Pleasantville, NY 10570
    1972   2 sound FSs, part 1: 72fr, 13:44min; part 2: 71fr,
    12:35min, each with phonodisc, for use with manual or auto-matic projector, $35.   #110   72-7364110
Paintings, drawings, and photographs illustrate this set on preju-dice in the U.S.A. from a historical point of view; "Seeds of hate ..." is a psychological perception of prejudice; "Prejudice!" (above), literary.   All three have scant (but some) consideration of women.

PREMARITAL SEX BEHAVIOR (tape)
Perennial #313   S$10
Dialogue between two male doctors.

PRINTS   see   GRAPHICS

A PRISON FILM: STILL LIVING (mo pic)
Churchill   1971   27min   C   With study guide   78-714771
U.S. L.C. Summary: Inmates and staff members of a women's prison express their attitudes, concerns, doubts, and hopes. They describe their roles within the prison and discuss positive oppor-tunities available, the problems encountered but unsolved, and the desires unfulfilled.   Some will find this "too good to be true": California cottages, "campus," etc.   (Of course these are the people who have yet to be aware of what loss of freedom is.) Race and homosexuality are the two big problems brought out, and as such, will lose some non-feminists right from the start.   For some it will be reinforcement, however--the calling of the prison-ers by their first names, reference to them as girls, smirk re "Ernie."   Stop the machine at some points, and discuss; or show it through, and then ask them to remember How did it begin, How did it end?

THE PRIVATE WORLD OF EMILY DICKINSON (FS)
Guidance Associates   Part I: 66fr/13min, Part II: 73fr/12min.
   2 FSs; 2 12" LPs/$37.50/9A-520-559.   2 FS; 2 cassettes/
   $41.50/9A-520-567.   Discussion guide.
Shows what has been called her "liberating relationship" to nature
and art, touches on her early life, includes sensitive readings of
many key poems.

PROBLEM OF ACCEPTANCE (mo pic)
New York Univ.   1970   47min   Psychodrama in group processes
   series   Univ. of California Ext.   #8317   R$19
Psychodramatic exploration of a 17-year-old homosexual woman's
feelings of self-rejection.   Introductory and closing comments by
male psychiatrist Ira Pauly.

PROFESSIONAL WOMEN (graphics)
Feminist resources for equal education   Set #2   8 BW photos
   8 1/2x11" $2/set
All women, including: surgeon, judge, ornithologist, artist, potter,
architect, computer programmer, politician.   SEE ALSO "Community helpers," and "Husband and wife-coached childbirth."

PROMISE HER ANYTHING BUT GIVE her the kitchen sink (mo pic)
Filmmaker, Freude Bartlett   3min   C   Canyon cinema coop   R$5
Contrasts the closed "female" world of the kitchen sink in close-
ups with the spacious "male" world of the outdoors, seashore.

PRUDENCE CRANDALL (mo pic)
Robert Saudek Assoc., producer   2 parts: 25min each   1966   IQ
   films   Profiles in Courage Series.   Period: 1830's.
A school teacher who insisted on the right of every American child,
regardless of color, to be educated ... considers equal opportunity
in education and the status of women and Blacks in America.

PSYCHOMONTAGE (mo pic)
By Eberhard and Phyllis Kronhausen   10min   Grove   S$75   8mm:
   S$20
The Kronhausens are best known for their literary, artistic and
psychological research into sexual matters, having written other
books, "Pornography and the law," "The sexually responsive woman," and "Erotic art."   A witty and at times shocking discovery
of sexuality in humans and in the animal world... (Grove).

PSYCHOTHERAPY AND WOMEN'S LIBERATION (tape cassette)
Behavioral sciences tape library   1 hour tape $6.95   #90245.   By
   Stephanie Miller, psychiatric social worker.   72-751111

PURPLE HONEY (music)
Long Island Feminist Coalition.
Feminist music for flute and guitar; Women's folk song project.

PUT DOWN (mo pic)   see   WOMAN (kit)

QUARTER MILLION TEENAGERS   see   HALF MILLION TEEN-
AGERS

THE QUEEN (mo pic)
Filmmaker, Frank Simon 1967 68min C Grove #175 R$100
   S$625
Documentary about real people--female impersonators who compete
annually for the drag Miss All-American beauty contest, in 1967.
Judges on this occasion were Andy Warhol, Terry Southern, Edie
Sedgwick, Larry Rivers, et al. This is a serious film. With
Jack Doroshow (Flawless Sabrina) and Richard Finnochio as Harlow.
Robin Morgan suggested it in "Sisterhood Is Powerful" (#81 in
Basic Book Collection, Womanhood Media). Judith Crist in New
York Magazine pointed out that "its sensational and shocking sub-
ject matter is treated with such sensibility, taste and compassion
that what might have been a grindhouse movie emerges as an im-
pressive human document and a finely made film as well"; and
Playboy: "An authentic shriek of sociology...."

QUEENIE PEAVY (rec)
Viking 1972 approx. 45min $6.95   #670-5824-X.   Cassette
   $7.95   #670-58425-8
Robert Burch's 1966 Viking book-publication for children is about
roughneck Queenie. Narration combined with dramatization of
Queenie, the fighter.

QUEST: A FEMINIST QUARTERLY (tape)
Feminist Radio Network #674-17 28min Cassette: $20. Reels:
   7 1/2ips, $25; 3 3/4ips, $20
"An interview with staff members Charlotte Bunch and Beverly
Fisher. Discussion on the journal's plans to serve as a national
forum for debate around women's issues" (FRN).

- R -

RACE/SEX STEREOTYPING IN TEXTBOOKS (slide show)
Dr. Gwyneth Britton completed this study in the Oregon Schools.
Slides developed from it provide documentation of the representation of minorities and women, the career roles provided for boys
and girls, and the continuation of these stereotypes over a twenty-
year period of time. Contact Dr. B. at Dept. of Education, Oregon State University, Corvallis, OR 97331.

RACHEL, RACHEL (mo pic)
Paul Newman, producer-director 1968 101min C With Joanne
   Woodward, Macmillan Audio Brandon R$125 Twyman Films
   (320 Salem Ave., Dayton, OH 45401) also distributes.
Based on Margaret Laurence's novel, "A jest of God" (SEE #776
Basic Book Collection) of a 35-year-old elementary-school teacher
who has never been able to allow herself a full emotional involvement. At a revival meeting she discovers the intense emotions
which she is capable of experiencing. She rejects the romantic

Audiovisual Resources

overtures of a colleague (Estelle Parsons), and has her first love affair with an old schoolmate (James Olson). When she is abandoned by her love, Rachel lives with the hope that she is pregnant, but once again is let down. Determined not to regress to her former sheltered life, she decides to move to another town.

RADICAL MASTECTOMY (video tape)
Feminist women's health centers 30min R$30 S$50 Women in
    control series
Facts: Every year, 50,000 women in the U.S.A. undergo radical mastectomies. Most of these women have little information about the procedure before it is performed and receive little supportive aftercare. Women from the Menopause Self-Help Clinic share their knowledge and experience in this discussion which goes into research (lack of) and experimentation on women.

RADICALISM AND THE WOMAN'S MOVEMENT (FS)
Multi-media productions 2 C FSs 1 LP rec. Teacher's guide
    $14.95 2 C FSs 1 Cassette. Teacher's guide $16.95
The history of the Feminist Movement from the mid-19th century-present.

RADIO & TV PROGRAMS
    Adelante   Sanders, Marlene
    Alternatives   Second sex scene
    Awareness '73 ... women,   Woman's Choice
        after 1920   Woman's Place
    Changing world of...   Women's clearinghouse
    For women today   WCBN FM, Ann Arbor,
    Radio Free women/WGTB-FM,   Student Activities Build-
        Juanita Weaver, Founder-   ing, Ann Arbor, MI
        moderator, c/o National   48104
        Assoc. of Social Workers

RAISIN IN THE SUN (mo pic)
AV Film Center 127min R$25
Lorraine Hansberry's play.

RAISIN IN THE SUN (rec)
Caedmon 1972 3 phonodiscs 141:28min with Jacket notes $21.94
    #TRS355. Cassettes $23.85 #CDL5355. "Women in literature" Collection
The play's original production includes Claudia McNeil, Ruby Dee and Diana Sands.

RAMPARTS OF CLAY (mo pic)
Cinema V Distributing, Inc.
The story of a Tunisian village girl.

RAPE IN COURT (tape)
CBC #320 30min $7
A woman defending the rights of her body in court plus a psychiatrist's comments.

THE RAPE TAPE (video tape)
Under One Roof Video, producer 1972 Distributor, The kitchen

RAPPING WITH THE FEMINISTS (FS) see "THE SILENCED MAJORITY," p. 243 of Womanhood Media (Audio-Visual section)

RED DETACHMENT OF WOMEN (mo pic)
Newsreel 1:45min C S$200
This is the same film shown on national television; covers the journey of the peasantwoman, Wu Ching-Hua, who escapes from her master and joins the Red Army. The story is described through ballet and shows some of the effects of the Chinese Revolution on the rural social order. Requires special Rental procedure.

REFLECTION ON MARRIAGE (mo pic)
National Film Board of Canada 1973 En Tant Que Femmes Project scheduled for one hour broadcast on Canadian Broadcasting Network. A production of 28 women.
"Four women make different choices--conscious choices, yet not choices because 'it was the only thing to do'."

REFORMERS (FS) see WOMEN IN AMERICAN HISTORY

REPLAY (mo pic)
Contemporary #408590-5 8min C R$15 S$125 Produced by Concepts Unltd.; Robert Deubel, director
"History does not repeat itself, and change is often a 'replay' of past events ... designed to give lie to the Generation Gap by humorously documenting the existence of a Generation Link ... explores various aspects of 'modern' culture: women's rights, censorship, hero worship, fads, fashions, and the eternal battle between the young as wild, unprincipled and uncouth ..." (Contemporary).

REPRODUCTIVE HORMONES IN MAN (FS)
H. M. Stone Productions, 6 East 45 St., New York, NY 10017 1971 51fr 35mm & Phonodisc: 2 S 12" 33 1/3rpm 19min C Secondary Science Series Also issued with phonotape in cassette. Captioned version also issued with Guide and Manual. 76-739798
U.S. Library of Congress Summary: "Describes endocrine glands and hormones; illustrates the general relations between gonadotropic hormones, gonads, gametes, and sex hormone production; and explains the female reproductive cycle." Subject headings assigned to this filmstrip about reproductive hormones in humans: Hormones, Sex. Reproduction. Sexual cycle of women.

RESPECT (mo pic)
Filmmaker, Willette Coleman 1971 9min C NET Training School R:Apply
Just married!

Audiovisual Resources

RICH AND JUDY (mo pic)
Filmmaker, Laird Sutton 12min C Multi Media Research R$30
    S$175
A film of two young people very much in love. They have been married for several years. It is a film for the introductory study of human sexuality.

RIGHT NOW, IT'S A LOVE TRIP (slide/FS program)
Planned Parenthood World Population 15min C Record included
    R$5 S$25
Needs and attitudes of young people, filmed at counseling service run for/by teenagers.

THE RIP-OFF (play)
A Feminist comedy by Stephanie Caruana, 2405 Roscomare Road,
    Los Angeles, CA 90024. Full length $4.00. Florynce Kennedy has called this "instant classic." Useful for fund-raising.

ROBERTA FLACK (mo pic)
Indiana Univ. 1971 30min C Artists in America Series Univ.
    of California Ext. #8330

ROBIN MORGAN READS HER POEMS (tape)
Pacifica #BC0949.01 37min $10 reel or cassette
Ms. Morgan reads her poems, which are mostly feminist, and from her book, "Monster" (SEE #601, Basic Book Collection).

THE ROCKS CRY OUT (tape)
Nancy Arnez and Beatrice Murphy. Tape cassette Broadside $5

THE ROLE OF THE BLACK WOMAN IN AMERICA (video tape)
Pacifica 50min $10.50
Discussion by 4 Black women: Peachie Brooks, Verta S. Grosvenor, Florynce Kennedy, Elinor Holmes Norton.

ROLL OVER (mo pic)
Filmmaker, Marian Hunter 10min C Herstory Films Available
    for R and S
All-woman crew has produced a film depicting women's roles, stereotyping, employment, and a look at the future. Music by Lavender Jane.

ROMANCE (mo pic)
Contemporary #408422-4 15min C R$21 S$220 Writer-director,
    Bretislav Pojar
Animated Czech puppetry traces a frivolous doll's demise.

THE ROSE (mo pic)
Sheil-Kama Productions 25min C Human growth & reproduction
    series Films, Inc. #113-0003 S$300
Lawrence Booth's experimental film recording psychological reactions of his wife, Sheila, during pregnancy and childbirth. "A wo-

man, like a rose, is in full bloom when she gives birth ..."
quoted in the catalog!

ROSELAND (mo pic)
Royanne Rosenberg, filmmaker 12min Vision Quest R$25 S$200
Documentary used with professionals in mental health field. Adaptation of the unmarried mother stereotypes. Recommended by Peter Barglow, M.D., professor of psychiatry. Try to discover its use for feminists.

ROSIE THE RIVETER (mo pic)
Ivy Films, 120 East 56 St., New York, NY 10022 1941 75min R
"With the coming war, Hollywood mobilized. Among the rash of propaganda movies and war films produced were light farces encouraging the effort on the homefront, and somehow making it all seem a bit more bearable.... Rosie is one of the best of its type ..." (Women's History Research Center).

- S -

SALAZAR FAMILY: A LOOK AT POVERTY (mo pic)
Univ. of California Ext. #7844 1970 14min R$8 S$85
A large (children) Mexican family near Salt Lake City, one sterilized at 15 while institutionalized. Little of the mother.

SANDY AND MADELEINE'S FAMILY (mo pic)
Sherrie Farrel, et al, filmmakers 1973 39min C Multi Media
    Resource Center R$50 S$300
"A lesbian couple and their 6 children shown at home. The children's feelings are explored. The women are deeply religious and maintain close ties with the church. Interviews with a judge, a social worker, and a doctor involved in their divorce and custody cases. Interview with Margaret Mead commenting on nuclear family. Some confusing transitions." (ALA-SRRT Task Force on Gay Liberation's "A Gay Bibliography, 3rd revision." SEE Pamphlets section for fuller information, Lesbiana Section.)

SAPPHO WAS A RIGHT ON WOMAN (tape) (#1)
Pacifica #BC0954 59min $10 reel or cassette Produced by KPFA
"Gay Liberation like Women's Liberation affects white male-dominated society both fundamentally and peripherally. Both groups have been manipulated by the system they are trying to help. Lesbians are the human beings that have the greatest stake in the survival and success of these two movements, and they are the people who have been heard the least. 'Sappho was a right on woman' is a recently published book (SEE #374, Basic Book Collection) and it is the first non-fiction account of gay women as an oppressed group in our society. The authors are Sydney Abbott and Barbara Love, who are lesbians active in both the women's movement and the gay movement in New York. The book contains a careful and authentic description of what it is like to be a lesbian in America as well as a very important account of how the feminist movement

has evolved in its attitude toward gay women. It talks about the future of the lesbian movement in terms of curing society as opposed to the popular concept of curing the homosexual and it goes beyond the idea of finding a place for the gay system as it is without the rhetoric we have been taught to expect from any minority group that is emerging as a political force. This book thoroughly establishes the idea that being gay is a valid and non-deviant sexual orientation that in itself is not strictly a personal problem but a sociological problem that must be dealt with by a repressive and immoral social order. This program is a discussion of lesbians in America, their role in the women's movement, the gay movement, and other movements seeking to bring about major social change" (Pacifica).
(#2)
Feminist Radio Network #1273-27 29 3/4min Interview with Sydney Abbott. Cassette: $20; Reels: 7 1/2ips, $25; 3 3/4ips $20

SCHMEERGUNTZ (mo pic)
Gunvor Nelson and Dorothy Wiley, filmmakers 1966 15min
  Canadian Filmmaker's Distribution Centre R$15. Also available from Macmillan-Audio-Brandon, Univ. of California Ext. (#8446), Canyon Cinema Coop (R$15, S$210), and New York Filmmaker's Coop.
The reviewer's quote often associated with this is that of Film Quarterly's Ernest Callenbach: "... one long raucous belch in the face of the American...." The Univ. of California Ext. catalog is often reliable: "Celebrated, pioneering women's film anticipating the feminist movement of the '70's. Contrasts the romantic, stereotyped 'glamor girl' idea, prevalent in the media, advertising, and beauty contests, with the harsher, seamier aspects of women's commonplace role--the discomfort of pregnancy, the tedium of child care, house-cleaning and other unpleasant routines. In a skillfully executed montage of rapid-fire images, recurring and explicit flashes of morning sickness, garbage, diaper-changing, and menstruation are intercut with the glamor sequences, insipid music, and commentary to produce a powerful, sardonic effect. This memorable film may be found offensive by some viewers, despite its artistry, wit, and social value. Many, however, find it forthright and honest. As one viewer said: 'Beauty contests are revolting, and cleaning diapers, vomiting, and toilets are reality.' An independent production, created by women."

THE SECOND SEX SCENE (TV show)
Cable-TV show. Elizabeth McDonald, producer-host. Reaches
  Bay area. Contact c/o Women's Job Rights, 620 Sutter, #318, San Francisco, CA 91402

SECRET LOVE OF SANDRA BLAINE (mo pic)
Aims 1971 28min C Univ. of California Ext. #8543 R$19
"Follows the step-by-step progression into alcoholism of a middle-aged woman.... Examines extent of alcoholism among women ...

facilities and methods available for successful treatment ..." (California).

SEEDS OF HATE; AN EXAMINATION OF PREJUDICE (FS)
Warren Schloat Productions, 115 Tompkins Ave., Pleasantville, NY
   10570. 2 sound FSs, part 1: 85fr, 11min. Part 2: 94fr,
   12min. Each with phonodisc, with teacher's guide, for use
   with manual or automatic projector, $40. With tape cassettes
   $46. Order #326. 72-733692
Grades 8-12 suggested by producer-distributor. Further in <u>Prejudices and antipathies</u>, the U.S. Library of Congress subject heading; SEE ALSO "Prejudice!" and "Prejudice; harvest of hate."

SEIZE THE TIME (rec)
Vault SLP #131   Elaine Brown, Black Panther Party deputy Minister of Information, with instrumental accompaniment; songs sung by composer.

SELECTIONS FROM THE FIRST INTERNATIONAL Feminist Planning Conference (videotape)
Videowomen   25min   By Barbara Bunker

SELF-HELP CLINIC (Videotape)
Feminist Women's Health Centers   30min   R$30   S$50   Women in Control Series
"The innovation which inspired a worldwide women's health movement was the concept and practice of self-help, starting with self-examination of the cervix. For the first time a woman could see, and thereby begin to gain control, of that part of her body which has been the 'dark and mysterious' realm of mythical taboo and male gynecology ..." (FWHC).

SELF-HELP SLIDE PRESENTATION
Feminist Women's Health Centers   Includes 2pp suggestions for use
   $15, women's groups; $20, others

SELF-HELP/WOMEN'S HELP (slide & talk sessions)
New Moon Publications. Lolly & Jean Hirsch, of <u>The Monthly Extract</u> (serial).

SELF-PORTRAIT (mo pic)
Barbara Scharres, filmmaker   1972   3min   C   Silent   Canadian Filmmaker's Distribution Centre   R$5
A cyclical self-portrait, awards-winning.

SESAME STREET FILMS (mo pic)
Dorothy Tod, filmmaker   1969   7min   5 short films   Children's TV Workshop, 1 Lincoln Plaza, New York, NY 10023
Opening theme song, counting, geometric concept, animal movement, animal-baby names.

THE SEVEN SECRETS OF SELLING TO WOMEN (cassette)
SMI #2 $9.75   By Dottie Walters

"... Tells how to make buying customers out of every woman you meet."

70 SOUL SECRETS OF SAPPHIRE (cartoons)
Sapphire Publishing Co. Cartoon-style look at Black woman in
   America by Carolyn Jetter Greene. 1973 $3.25 includes
   postage
Described as a "humorous psychological-sociological perspective on Black woman in America" this serio-comic book is the product of a new all-woman company. Examples #4: ... the only woman in the world who is the mother of a 65-year old "BOY." #6: Sapphire never reports rape because she knows no one will ever believe she didn't just give it away!

SEX AND SOCIAL RESPONSIBILITY (tape)
American Home Economics Assoc. 1965 45min #7051 tape
   $7.50. #7052 cassette $8.50
Dr. Mary S. Calderone, executive director of SIECUS provides modern answers to such questions as "What is the purpose of sex?" and "How can our sexuality be managed rather than repressed?"

SEX DISCRIMINATION IN TEXTBOOKS (slide program)
Sharon Tipton, Women's Center, Kalamazoo Y.W.C.A., Kalamazoo,
   MI 49007 20min R$16.50
On elementary reading textbooks.

SEX EDUCATION IN AMERICA (revised) (mo pic)
Guidance Associates Part I: 16min/90fr. Part II: 14min/69fr.
   Part III: 11min/56fr. 3 FSs; 3 12" LPs/$45/9A-104-784.
   3 FSs; 3 cassettes/$51/9A-104-792. Discussion guide.
Program created in cooperation with Woodlands High School, Hartsdale, NY; the Evanston, IL Public School System; the Stockton, CA Public School System; and University of Washington.

SEX EDUCATION IN THE SCHOOLS; philosophy and implementation
   (mo pic)
Perennial 25min C R$25 S$250 #725.
Sally Williams and Pauline Iyenaga. An adult film.

SEX EDUCATION; organizing for community action (mo pic)
Perennial 23min C R$22.50 S$225 #726

SEX ETHICS, SEX ACTS, AND HUMAN NEED (tape)
Perennial #109 S$10.
Two male doctors discuss such "issues" as masturbation, contraception, abortion, and premarital sex.

SEX MIS-EDUCATION (mo pic)
Dimension Films, 733 N. LaBrea Ave., Los Angeles, CA 90038
   11min C
"Young people's candid observations on the follies of sex education by parents and schools. They call for open, reliable information

on intercourse, masturbation, human physiology, etc." (from the American Library Association 1973 conference media showing brochure).

SEX-ROLE CONFUSION (mo pic)
Maureen Orth, an Associate Editor at Newsweek (444 Madison Ave., New York, NY 10022) currently producing a full-length documentary film about sex-role confusion (May 1973).

SEX-ROLES AND SOCIALIZATION IN CHILDREN'S BOOKS (slide presentation)
SEX-ROLE SOCIALIZATION IN PICTURE BOOKS FOR PRE-SCHOOL CHILDREN (slide show with text)
Contact: Lenore Weitzman, 1100 Gough, #15C, San Francisco, CA 94109 and/or at Dept. of Sociology, University of California, Davis, CA 95616. Also involved are Deborah Eifler, Elizabeth Hokada, Catherine Ross. SEE ALSO May 1972 American Journal of Sociology.

SEX-STEREOTYPED TOY MARKETING (slide show)
Contact: (Ms.) Gail L. Weaver, South Hills NOW, 504 HiTor Dr., Pittsburgh, PA 15236 49 slides & script 1/2 hour
Study of sexist marketing practices of several toy distributors stressing those toys aimed specifically at one sex or the other as well as the implications of this practice; slides are views taken from catalogs.

SEX-STEREOTYPES IN CHILDREN'S BOOKS variously-titled
SEXISM IN CHILDREN'S MEDIA slide-tape
SEXISM IN KID-LIT show(s)
Produced by Boston Area Task Force of SRRT WIL (Social Responsibilities Round Table Women's Issues in Librarianship).
  Contact: Carole Wilson, 24 Fulton, Medford, MA 02155.
  Ms. Wilson and Diane Holzheimer involved in production, narration and graphics 22min R$5 S$75
91 Color slides illustrating the stereotyped roles and activities in which people are portrayed in children's books, accompanied by a cassette tape discussing these stereotypes. Slides intended to give those who are not familiar with children's books an idea of the kinds of role differentiation accorded to boys and girls, men and women; roles modelled on sex-stereotypes. The slides are not a set of carefully-culled exceptions; they represent the overwhelming majority of children's books. The presentation is therefore not an attack on the books used in it but an attempt to show the message these books convey to the young child.

SEX-STEREOTYPING IN CHILDREN'S READERS (slide program)
Women on Words & Images, 25 Cleveland Ln., Route 4, Princeton, NJ 08540; also at PO Box 2163 20min 140 slides R$40
  Based on "Dick and Jane as Victims."
Has been described as "one of the finest consciousness-raisers for educators and general audiences."

SEX-TYPING IN THE SCHOOLS (show)
Contact: Constance Thrinnen, 430 Lowell Hall, 617 Langdon, University of Wisconsin, Madison 53706.
Part of the Education Telephone Network, which has completed 4 broadcasts on: Feminism in the family; Men and masculinity; What Women's Liberation means to you; and Sex typing in the schools; with a fifth, Growing up liberated, available in 1974 or 1975. Available to teachers, administrators, school board members, parents. More than 50 listening stations are available for the course for Wisconsin residents.

SEXISM... (multi-media program)
Contact: Marilyn Ellas, Los Angeles Education NOW Committee coordinator, NOW Center, 8864 West Pico Blvd., Los Angeles, CA 90035. 35pp script 50 slides, S$18.50, with profits used by the Committee for action!
Consciousness-raising program about sexist education of youngsters at home and school, spans ages 3-18, illustrating how typical American socialization leaves girls with low self-esteem and builds sexist attitudes in boys. Appropriate for teacher, counselor, parent audiences.

SEXISM IN ADVERTISING (slide show)
Image of Women Task Force, San Diego Chapter. Contact Marilyn Corodermas, PO Box 22264, San Diego, CA 92122. 140 slides 14pp script 50min

SEXISM IN CALIFORNIA STATE READERS (slide show)
Contact: Nancy Carroll, 8441 Balboa Blvd., apt. 30, Northridge, CA 93124 25 slides

SEXISM IN CARTOONS (slide documentary)
R from Carol Benson, 2717 Rutledge, Stockton, CA 95207 209-478-7646

SEXISM IN CHILDREN'S BOOKS (audiotape)
Gretchen Hammerstein's appearance on New Haven's Ch. 8 TV. 30-min live interview re sexism in children's books. Send a cassette tape for a transcription copy plus $1 postage costs to her at Toad Ridge Rd., Middlefield, CT 06455. The CWILS (Connecticut Women in Libraries) will also send "Library Isms," a collection of infuriating anti-feminist clichés compiled by a member for the State Library Service Center Workshop, Oct. 1973 (or send SASE for script of latter).

SEXISM IN EDUCATION (tape)
Behavioral sciences tape library #87207 3 one-hour tapes $21.
By Myra and David Sadker of American University.
Explores sex biases in education that limit the options of children of both sexes. The authors explore in depth the negative impact of a male-oriented society on females leading to a loss of academic ability and self-esteem as they progress through school, and the consequences of sexism in higher education.

SEXISM IN THE SCHOOLS (slide-cassette presentation)
Univ. of Wisconsin--Extension Women's Education Resources 1971
$27 C Slide-cassette tape presentation 18min Written by
2 high school girls describing some of their school experiences.
Order from Univ. of Wisconsin Ext., Photo-Cinema Lab.,
45 N. Charter, Madison, WI 53706.
Covers sex-stereotyping in Kindergarten toys, in early texts, in
industrial arts, career counseling, sports, etc. etc.

SEXIST MAGAZINE AND NEWSPAPER CARTOONS (slide show)
Contact (Ms.) Carol Benson, San Joaquin NOW, 2717 Rutledge Way,
  Stockton, CA 95207.

SEXIST AD SLIDE-SHOW
A production of Seattle, WA NOW, conceived by the Image of Women Task Force. Narrative written by Linda Miller, photography by Marvin Gregory.

SEXUAL STEREOTYPING IN ADS (slide show)
Contact Fr. Charles Brady, SM, Dept. of Theological Studies,
  Univ. of Dayton, Dayton, OH 45469 10min Available for
  showings in Dayton/Cincinnati area.

SEXUAL STEREOTYPING IN TEXTBOOKS; people finish last (slide
  show)
Contact Andrea Mohn, 1405 Gladstone Dr., Sacramento, CA 95825
  96 slides 6pp script R$5 S$30 For NOW Chapters only.

SEXUAL VALUES IN SOCIETY (FS)
Guidance Associates Part I: 90fr/11min. Part II: 75fr/14min.
  2 FSs; 2 12" LPs/$40/9A-104-875. 2 FSs; 2 cassettes/$44/
  9A-104-891. Discussion guide. Author: Richard Hettlinger,
  Professor of Religion, Kenyon College.

SEXUALITY AND THE TEENAGER SERIES (mo pics)
Perennial #727 3 C films R$60 S$600 National Film Board of
  Canada Part 1 #728 28min, Part 2 #729 22min, Part 3
  #730 19min

SHE AND HE (mo pic)
Iwanmi Productions, Inc., Japanese dialog with English subtitles
  1963 110min (Also released under the title, "Kanojo To
  Kare.") Distributors: CCM Films and Macmillan Audio Brandon
Story of a young wife in a Tokyo suburb who becomes aware of the life outside her home--a life which in her comfortable security she has never imagined.

SHE SHALL BE CALLED WOMAN (mo pic)
Gerard De Boe, producer-director 1954 14min Spoken in English
  by Flora Robson Macmillan Audio Brandon
A Belgian film described by the New York Times as "A muted, fluid depiction of woman's place in primitive African society through selected Belgian Congo sculpture."

Audiovisual Resources

SHIP OF FOOLS (mo pic)
Director-producer, Stanley Kramer. Screenplay by Abby Mann, based on the novel by Katherine Anne Porter. With Vivien Leigh, Simone Signoret, Elizabeth Ashley. Macmillan Audio Brandon

SHIRLEY CHISHOLM (FS)
McGraw-Hill. With record and guide, $20. With cassette and guide, $22.
"Shirley Chisholm fought her way up the political ladder in a Black ghetto community to become the nation's first Black congresswoman" (McGraw).

SHIRLEY CHISHOLM; elect one of your own (FS, rec, etc.)
Doubleday 1969 133fr #16791 With record $15.50 15min

SHOP STEWARDS (mo pic)
Martha Stuart, producer Are you listening? Series 1972 28min C Impact R$40 S$325
"The men and women in this film have all experienced the tedium and psychic brutality inherent in assembly lines.... As one man says, 'If you would treat a man a little better, you wouldn't have to give him better machines' " (Impact).

"SILAS MARNER" (rec) see WOMEN IN LITERATURE

SINGLE WOMEN RAISING FAMILIES (video tape)
West Side Video, producer 1972 The Kitchen

SISTERS (mo pic)
Jill F. Hultin, filmmaker 21min C Women's Film Coop
A story of two sisters who embark on a journey which changes both of their lives. We see incidents which show women in a variety of roles. Each incident exposes the emptiness of a particular role--daughter, wife, mother, old woman, glamour girl.

SISTERS OF THE PALETTE (slide show)
Slide show on the history of women in art. Speakers available to present illustrated feminist lectures. Contact:
Women's Studies Program, Sonoma State College, Rohnert Park, CA 94928.

SKATER DATER; A FILM ABOUT GROWING UP (mo pic)
Writer-director, Noel Black Producer, Marshal Baklar 18min C Pyramid Films R$20 S$250 Released world-wide by United Artists. Awards include Grand Prix--Cannes.
Advertisements typically refer to this as "A classic boy-meets-girl story." Actually, there are many themes, including meaning of love, growing up, nature of change, peer group values and pressures, individual choice and group loyalty. Add to this the film's entertainment value and discussion utility.

SKIT
Enid Davis
$1.00 + SASE will bring you a skit used for fundraising by Palo Alto NOW about a mock political convention and the ERA!

SLAVERY AND SUFFRAGE see WOMEN IN AMERICAN HISTORY (FS)

SLIDES--SOURCES
    Art Registry
    Feminist Women's Health Center
    Schramm, Sara Slavin see "SPEAKERS" under "Directory of Sources" sect.
    Smith, Sophia Collection
    WAIT
    WEB
    West Coast Women Artists
    Women's Art Registry
    Women's Research Project

THE SMILING MADAME BEUDET (mo pic)
Germaine Dulac, filmmaker 1922 35min 16 and 35mm Silent
    Museum of Modern Art, Dept. of Film Circulating Programs, 11 West 53 St., New York, NY 10019.
This early feminist work portrays a woman haunted by her patriarchal husband. Trick photography expresses pictorially her psychological conflict.

SOPHIA SMITH COLLECTION (prints)
From the Picture Collection. "Pic cat" Feb. 1972 $6
Prints can be used to make slides and filmstrips ... notable people, places, events. To order prints, use catalog # for identification and state intended media or use; billing is at various rates. All photos are copyrighted by the Collection and may not be syndicated, rented, loaned, sold, or reused without permission. Each is black-and-white, with size stated, reproduced on glossy paper. Special sizes at additional cost.

SOCIOBIOLOGY; DOING WHAT COMES NATURALLY (mo pic)
Document Associates 1972 22min C Towards the Year 2000
    Series Univ. of California Ext. #8428 R$25
Surveys research on the biological origins of human behavior. Several biologists and anthropologists explain--citing their work with monkeys, rats, fish, insects, etc.--their theories about male competitiveness and aggression, whether female "sexual reticence" is social biological, the origins of warfare, and reasons for the current rebellion of young people.

SOME OF YOUR BEST FRIENDS (mo pic)
Univ. of Southern California, Division of Cinema, University Park,
    Los Angeles, CA 90007 R$25 S$325 1972 38min C Also distributed by Univ. of California Ext. #8266 R$21
"... shows some of the activities of the gay liberation movement. Includes candid interviews with male and female homosexuals, scenes from group meetings, demonstrations, and a gay parade. A homosexual lawyer amusingly recounts his entrapment by police and describes his subsequent trial" (California).

Audiovisual Resources   257

SOMETHING DIFFERENT (mo pic)
Vera Chytilova, filmmaker 1963 Czech with English subtitles
    65min Grove #405 Also distributed by Impact R$100 S$400
    and available in 16mm and 35mm.
"... concerning the dilemma of modern woman: the conflict between her social ambitions and the limitations imposed on her by society...." A feature film which won several major European awards.

SOMETIMES I WONDER WHO I AM (mo pic)
Filmmaker, Liane Brandon 1970 10min Distributed by New Day
    S$85; Women's Film Coop R$10
"Melancholy film which shows a woman in her kitchen. As she works, we hear her thoughts about her husband, baby, how she views her life" (Women's Film Coop). Use with young people or adults; possibly use with "Growing up female; as six become one."
"Sometimes...," however, is useful for the problem of the college woman's choice; what is the conflict and where is the frustration? Also for a lead into a discussion of an evolving, retaliation myth--the married woman who "dreams of the career she could have had."

SONGBOOKS, MUSIC, SONGS, etc. see SONGBOOKS ... in
    "Pamphlets" section

SONGS & RITUALS: Kay & Jeriann (Band)
Women's Music Network, Inc.

SONGS OF THE SUFFRAGETTES (rec)
Folkways 1958 Phonodisc, approx. 45min With notes $5.98
    #FH5281 Sung by Elizabeth Knight
Collection of 16 songs set to familiar folk melodies and patriotic tunes, sung with guitar or piano. Historical, righteous and sentimental in tone frequently, some out-of-date references. LC R 58-498 "The Suffrage flag," "Winning of the vote," "Hallelujah song," "Going to the polls," etc.

SONGS, SKITS, POETRY AND PRISON LIFE (videotape)
Women Make Movies, Inc. 1/2" video-tape EIAJ 1/2 hour reel
    26min 1974
"By the women at Bedford Hills Correctional Facility, the only minimum/maximum security prison for women in New York State. This is a compilation from 7 hours of videotape shot by about 80 women who participated in the 12-week summer project during 1973. They sing songs, read poetry, act out skits, discuss their grievances. The edited tape, put together by Ariel Dougherty, teacher of the program, presents a strong portrait of the women and for an audience begins to put into perspective the reality of a women's prison" (WMM).

SONIA SANCHEZ READS "HOMECOMING" (cassette tape)
Broadside $5

"SONNETS FROM THE PORTUGUESE" (rec) see WOMEN IN LITERATURE

SOON THERE WILL BE NO MORE ME (mo pic)
Churchill 1972 10min S$130 Also R
"The touching true story of the last few months of a 19-year old mother who learns she is dying of cancer. Her reactions, her feelings, her love for her daughter and her husband are moving and real without being overly sentimental. Useful for many program situations since it deals with life in general as well as with dying" (Booklist Sept. 1, 1973:30).

SOURIS, TU M'INQUIETES (mo pic)
National Film Board of Canada En tant que femmes Project 197?
    1 hour scheduled for broadcast on the Canadian Broadcasting
       Corp. French network. Production by 28 women.
"The daily life of a Quebec woman expressed in a film combining drama and segments of nonfiction." (In 1973 were in final print stage.)

THE SOVIET WOMAN (mo pic)
ABC News 53min McGraw R$25 S$270
"From Madame Khruschchev to a construction worker, from the woman-in-charge of Soviet satellite tracking stations to a Mother Heroine with eleven children, from students to fashion models, the film reveals how the women of the Soviet Union carry on the day's activities at home and in public" (McG).

A SPACE TO BE ME (mo pic)
Maureen Sherlock and David Weinkauf, producers 30min C Third
    World Newsreel
"... quality daycare is not a privilege but rather a basic necessity for both mothers and their children. Through the thoughts and feeling of young mothers, some raising children on their own, analyzes the need for daycare in terms of the positive effects on children and the possibilities it creates for women to function and develop in roles other than housewife and mother."

SPEAKERS see under "Directory of Sources" section

THE SQUEEZE (mo pic)
Director, Hilary Harris 1965 11min Source: British Film Insti-
    tute Distribution Library, 42/43 Lower Marsh, London SE 1.
In 1965 200 babies were born every minute, and this disturbing short film shows the effect they have on the population problems. A kaleidescope of faces and voices, shots from the world's most crowded cities.

STAGE LEFT see ALIVE AND TRUCKING THEATER COMPANY

STAND UP AND BE COUNTED (mo pic)
Producer, M. J. Frankovich 99min 16 or 35mm C Columbia

Audiovisual Resources 259

 Cinematheque, 711 5 Ave., New York, NY 10022 R/S
"The first Women's Liberation comedy."

STEWARDESSES (tape)
Feminist Radio Network #774-22 29 3/4 Cassette $20 Reels:
 7 1/2ips $25, 3 3/4ips $20
"Interview with Sandra Jarrell of Stewardesses for Women's Rights and excerpts from a group discussion of airline stewardesses airing their concerns about their occupations' image and working conditions" (FRN).

STICKERS & LABELS--SOURCES
 Bumper Wrappings   men's Political Caucus
 Checkers Enterprises   Grey Falcon House
 Equality Products/Shirley   KNOW
  Spalding   Meaningful Bumpers
 Free the Secretary   Redactron Corp.
 Greater Indianapolis Wo-

STICKY MY FINGERS, FLEET MY FEET (mo pic)
Time-Life 1970 23min
Deflates one of the classic American myths: the middle-aged male who clings to a youthful standard of physical prowess and virility (Pleck).

STILL LIVING; A PRISON FILM see A PRISON FILM: STILL
 LIVING (mo pic)

STRATEGY FOR CHANGE (mo pic)
Moira Armour, filmmaker 1972 30min C Canadian Filmmaker's
 Distribution Centre R$25
A film of the First National Status of Women Conference. Discussions included Women In Politics, Native Women's Rights, and Education. Speakers include: Florence Bird, Ex-chairperson of the Royal Commission on the Status of Women; Senator Therese Casgrain; Maryon Kantaroff; Laura Sabia; Elsie Gregor-McGill; Madeleine Parent; June Callwood; and Isobel LeBourdais.

STRAUSS, ANNA LORD & PERCY LEE (Oral History)
"Oral History 25th Anniversary Report" page 8: "Important memoirs by Anna Lord Strauss and Percy Lee, prominent in women's movements long before the present interest in them was dreamed." Columbia University new projects, Box 20, Butler Library, Columbia University, New York, NY 10027.

STRAWBERRY GIRL (audiovisuals)
A variety of audiovisuals are available to see and hear Lois Lenski's 1949 Newbery Medal-winning "Strawberry Girl" children's story (Lippincott and Dell paperback). A resourceful girl and her family face hard times in Florida cracker society during the 1930's, is the way "Little Miss Muffet Fights Back" describes this non-sexist classic (page 15). Miller-Brody, Baker & Taylor, etc.

STREET OF SHAME (mo pic)
Macmillan Audio Brandon 1956 85min R Original title: "Akasen Chitai" ("Red-light district"). Japanese dialog with English subtitles.
Deals with the lives of four Tokyo prostitutes.

STRIPPER (mo pic)
Sydney women's film group Distributed by Sydney, Australia Filmmaker's Coop.

THE STRONGER see VIVECA LINDFORS' film/lecture program in "Directory of Sources" section

STRUGGLE FOR WOMEN'S SUFFRAGE (tape/slide)
Feminist History Research Project 24min #1 in Series "Recovering Our Past" R$25 S$80

SUSAN (mo pic)
Laird Sutton, filmmaker C Multi Media Resource Center R$35 S$200
Susan demonstrates a variety of masturbatory techniques.

SUSAN AFTER THE SUGAR HARVEST (mo pic)
Peter Robinson, producer 1970 27min C Film Images S$300 72-702844
"U.S.--Social conditions" is subject heading assigned by the U.S. Library of Congress to this film, which is about a young woman talking about her trip from the U.S.A. to Cuba to cut sugar cane.

SUSAN B. ANTHONY (FS) see JANE ADDAMS

SWEET BANANAS (mo pic)
Women make movies 1972 30min C R$30 S$300 Ariel Dougherty, filmmaker. Stars Rita Francoeur, Victoria Larrain, Ann Taylor, with Selma Greenberg and Kitty LePerrier.
A documentary portraying the love/hate ambivalence of contemporary women. Triggers many unresolved feelings and provokes many directions for discussion. Includes go-go dance scene.

SWORDSWOMEN (mo pics)
Swordswomen are motion pictures in Chinese with English subtitles, mostly produced by Shaw Brothers. Some highly recommended (Ms. April 1973:32) ones are:
   The blade spares none   One-eyed swordsman
   Blood flower sword   Young Avengeress
   Jade dragon   The crackling whip
   Black butterfly   Temple of the red lotus
   Twin swords   Golden sword
   Lady with a sword   That fiery girl

SYLVIA, FRAN AND JOY (mo pic)
Churchill Films, producer-distributor 1973 25min R S$170 73-700794

Three young women talk about their feelings about the wife-mother-housekeeper role(s).

SYLVIA PLATH: POET IN RAGE (tape)
Center for Cassette Studies   2 parts.   Part I: 50min $14.95;
   Part II: 38min $12.95
Part I: Sylvia Plath reads from her collections of poetry, "Ariel" and "Colossus," and from her novel, "The bell jar." The pathos and irony of this writer, as these elements are revealed in her work, are discussed in Part II by Elizabeth Hardwick.

SYSTEM (play)
Elisa King, 15 Highbourne Rd., Toronto 7, Ontario
Easy to produce feminist play.

SZASZ, THOMAS STEPHEN, M.D. (tapes)
National NOW Board member (now President) Karen DeCrow interviewed psychiatrist Szasz in two programs televised in Syracuse, New York, with Dr. Szasz giving his first TV statement on the Women's Movement. R/S copies available. Contact Ms. DeCrow, 116 Benedict Ave., Syracuse, NY 13210. (SEE ALSO Basic Book Collection #'s 9, 10 and 555.)

- T -

"TAKE OFF"; A STRIPTEASE THAT DARES GO ALL THE WAY (mo pic)
Polymorph Films

TAKE THIS WOMAN (mo pic)
Producer-director, Michael Fox   1971   25min   Producer distributor,
   NBC Educational Enterprises   R$12   S$275   73-701828
An overview of women of the U.S.A. labor force.

TAKING OUR BODIES BACK (mo pic)
Margaret Lazarus, producer-director   30min   Cambridge Documentary Films, PO Box 385, Cambridge, MA 02139   617-354-3677   R$39   S$370
Covers important aspects of the women's health movement.

TAMING OF THE SHREW (mo pic)
Burton/Defirelli production   C   Franco Zeffirelli, director
Burton and Taylor version clearly conveys the economic transaction which is poor Kate's equation, the wealth of her father, the "asset" which passes from man to man.
The Learning Corp. of America (711 5 Ave., New York, NY 10022) markets a series product to schools on "Great Themes of Literature." Specially-edited versions of 6 films, including this "Taming of the shrew," which represents the "Man and woman" theme! (33min   C   R$30   S$360). Other great themes funneled to the school kids in package form are "Authority and rebellion" via "Caine Mutiny," "Conscience in conflict" via "A man for all sea-

sons," "Power and corruption" via "Macbeth," "Heroes and cowards" via "Lord Jim," and "Crime and the criminal" via "In cold blood." Of 6 full-page color photos in accompanying brochure, only 2 have women--1 as background, the other Taylor.

TAPES (kinescopes, casettes, videotapes, etc.)
- Sources

Alverno College
Applegate Books
Bartl, Joan, c/o WPST-FM, Box 9750, Trenton, NJ 08067
Behavioral Sciences Tape Library
British Columbia. University. Women's Information Office, Room 230. Student Union Building. Box 85, Vancouver
CBC Learning Systems
Center for Cassette Studies
Center for the American Woman & Politics, Rutgers University. Eagleton Institute
Femedia
Feminist Radio Network
Graphic Communications Herald

KQED
The Kitchen
Pacifica
Templeton, Mary Ellen, Perkins Library, Duke University, Durham, NC 27706
Turko, Sally, 2620 Buchanan, San Francisco, CA 94115 415-JO7-6156
Vision Quest
West Side Women's Video Collective
Women Make Movies, Inc.
Women's Culture
Women's History Research Center
Women's Interart Center
Women's Involvement Programme
Women's Media Group, San Francisco

TEACH YOUR CHILDREN WELL (mo pic)
Marta Ashley, producer   Nina Janowsky, associate producer   30min   C   Femedia R
Documentary about three women: a Black, a Chicana, and a White; comparison of how their parents educated them and the consequences today.

TEDDY BEAR YEARS (mo pic)
Perennial 25min C R$28
"A week of 'live-in' type shooting at a child welfare agency produces impressive coverage of the life of an orphan" (WKYC-TV).

TELL ME WHERE IT HURTS (mo pic)
1974   Fay Kanin, writer   Maureen Stapleton   78min   C   Learning Corp. of America   R$60   Lease $600
Motion picture made for television. "And now that your last kid has gone, what are you going to do for the next twenty-six years?" asks Connie's friend. It's her college student-daughter who has pointed out the triteness of the usual chit-chat and brought the women to a CR-like point. A tribute to enlightened youth's determination to end the double standard.

Audiovisual Resources

TENEMENT (mo pic)
CBS News 1967 40min Impact R$35
Portrayal of a Chicago slum dwelling. "Some of the residents ... are ground down, worn to dull stupefaction. Others are poignantly articulate as they express their dreams of a 'richer, sweeter life out there--beyond reach--beyond hope.' In a few there is nobility and tenacity; these are the mothers who daily war against despair and strive fiercely to keep their children in school ..." (Impact).

TERMINATION OF PREGNANCY (mo pic)
Lalor Foundation 20min C English and Spanish Recently revised film available with Lalor Foundation Blue Book
"Uterine aspiration procedures, 5th ed." "Highly technical film for instruction of medical personnel, demonstrates procedures used in abortion by vacuum (uterine) aspiration. Used in China since 1958; popular in Eastern Europe and later in England. A uterine aspiration is performed on an outpatient who is 8 weeks pregnant. Total time (administration of paracervical block, measurement of uterus, dilation of cervix, aspiration, examination of material evacuated = 3 minutes. Repeated twice in detail. Cannot be done after 13 weeks." Description and annotations in English and Spanish in International Planned Parenthood Federation Library Bulletin volume 7: 64, 5.

TESTING, TESTING; HOW DO YOU? (mo pic)
Women make movies 1969 4min C R$8 S$40 Sheila Paige, filmmaker. Also available from Film-makers' Coop, R$5.
Filmed at the 1969 Miss America Pageant, Atlantic City.

THAT'S A PLENTY (rec album)
Blue Thumb Records (Ampex Tapes) BTS 6009 $6.98
The Pointer Sisters

THEIR MOVEMENT (slide show)
IPC, 181 Pier Ave., Santa Monica, CA 90405 80 slides with script R$5 S$25
Slide show on Vietnamese women--history of struggle, culture, achievements, goals.

THESE THREE (mo pic)
Produced by Samuel Goldwyn 1936 92min Macmillan Audio Brandon R$30
Screenplay by Lillian Hellman, based on her play, "The Children's Hour." With Miriam Hopkins, Merle Oberon, Bonita Granville, Margaret Hamilton. Ms. Hellman's play suggesting latent lesbianism has since been made into another movie version. In doing the screenplay, it was necessary for her to substitute a conventional romance for the female liaison, but she also adapted a script that preserved the drama's scathing attack on busybodies and slanderers. (It was and is, of course, the story of a tender romance between a doctor and a teacher and of the youthful idealism of two female educators who establish their own school.)

THIRD WORLD WOMEN (mo pic)
Film Images has announced this in process by Helena Solberg-Ladd, one of the makers of their "The emerging woman." She is a Brazilian filmmaker who came to Washington, DC in 1970.

THIRD WORLD WOMEN (cassette)
New World sound series #4 $3.50 from Service Center, United
    Methodist Church.
40 minutes of interviews, music, ideas about the role of women around the world.   Produced by women.

THIS BOOK IS RATED "S"; a report on sexism in children's litera-
    ture (slide show)
Contact: Berry Bock, 2617 Hartwood Dr., Fort Worth, TX 76109.
    In nearby areas, the Fort Worth Education Task Force can
    provide speakers or panel for discussion following show. R$15
    Kit includes 117 C slides, carousel, cassette, copy of script
    keyed to slides.   18min
"A discussion of sex-role stereotyping in children's literature beginning with preschool picture books and continuing with novels for teen-agers ... reveals the subtle discrimination and limited role expectations for girls in much of children's fiction, and encourages development of full human potential in both women and men."

THIS IS THE HOME OF MRS. LEVANT GRAHAM (mo pic)
Claudia Weill   1970   15min   Pyramid   R$15   S$150   Also avail-
    able from Cyclops Films
Of this film, Pyramid states, "A lively and honest portrait of an urban black mother and the life that centers around her. The black production company that made this cinéma verité film of 'the large matriarchal black family' has given us a view of real people that is specific, immediate, and individual. The picture of crowded housing, unemployment, and other problems, is balanced by the way the film captures the richness and variety of the culture of this community in the Shaw area of Washington, D.C.
First Prizes at Ann Arbor, Foothill, Monterey festivals.   JH-up."
If you buy this biz about Black matriarchy, SEE #109, Basic Book Collection, <u>Womanhood Media</u> for starters.

THOUGHTS ON RAPE (tape)
Feminist Videotape Collective   12min

THREE FACES OF A WOMAN (mo pic)
Films, Inc.   5min
"French animator Peter Foldes uses his inimitable 'Metamorphis' animation, together with more recent electronic techniques in the psychedelic, beflowered and contented sides of women." (Annota-from June 1972 "Cinema Nightcap" at American Library Association conference, Chicago.)

THREE GRANDMOTHERS (mo pic)
McGraw   1963   28min   Comparisons Series   Univ. of California
    Ext. #6621   R$14

A Nigerian (Muslim), a Canadian (Protestant), and a Brazilian (Roman Catholic).

THREE IN THE PACK (mo pic)
Filmmaker, Bernadette Beekman   1971   7min   C   Youth Films
R$15   S$105
Girlfriends out for a day in the park meet a young man who creates an awkward triangle with racial overtones.

THREE R'S AND SEX EDUCATION (mo pic)
Indiana Univ.   1971   60min   Kinescope   Univ. of California Ext.
#8053   R$18
Shows Pennsylvania Quaker school that believes sex education helps students make moral and ethical decisions, and teachers being trained to teach sex education. Negative side shown: arguments against sex education by Dr. Billy James Hargis, head of Christian Crusade, and John Birch Society members and others; follows campaign against in Cedar Rapids, Iowa, including confrontations during PTA and school board meetings.

THREE SISTERS (mo pic)
Macmillan Audio Brandon   1964   115min   R
Based on the play by Anton Chekhov. Russian dialog with English subtitles. Three unhappy women in small provincial town.

THREE WIVES (tape)
CBC #715   30min $7
A discussion about their former marriages.

TO BE MARRIED (mo pic)
Billy Budd   1971   13 1/2min   R$17.50   S$175
New forms of wedding services and traditional ceremonies. Asks questions: What is marriage built on? How can society strengthen a marriage? How can in-laws help? How do partners "grow" in marriage? Shows how people can change after the initial novelty wears off.

TO BE SOMEBODY (mo pic)
Atlantis   1971   29min   C   Univ. of California Ext.   #8520   R$19
Unrehearsed documentary on the progress of a young Mexican-American woman who is searching for work in an unfamiliar, Anglo-dominated world. Includes a good relationship between the Chicana and her counselor, a woman.

TO BE YOUNG, GIFTED, AND BLACK (mo pic)
Univ. of California ext.   #8553   90min   C   R$37   Also from NET
"Sensitive adaptation of the stage production depicting the life and works of Black playwright Lorraine Hansberry, who died of cancer in 1965 at age 34.... Much of the script, by her husband, Robert Nemiroff, is drawn from her plays ..." (California).

TO BE YOUNG, GIFTED, AND BLACK (rec)
Caedmon #TRS 342   1971   3 discs $21.94.   #CDL 5342   3

cassettes $23.85
The complete play, adapted by Robert Nemiroff from the work of the author, Lorraine Hansberry. Performers include Barbara Baxley, Claudia McNeil.

TO SPEAK OR NOT TO SPEAK (mo pic)
IFB 1971 11min C
Belgian animated film looks at the information of public opinion in a rigid society.

"TO THE LIGHTHOUSE" (rec) see WOMEN IN LITERATURE

TOMORROW AGAIN (mo pic)
Pyramid 16min R$15 S$140
A lonely old woman in an ancient resident hotel.

TOMORROW'S CHILDREN (mo pic)
Henry Mayer, producer (945 Middlefield Rd., Redwood City, CA 94063) 15min C In English and in Spanish. SEE International Planned Parenthood Federation Library Bulletin v 7:62, 3. Also available from Perennial R$22 S$225

TOO MUCH AND TOO LITTLE; an indictment of the press (tape)
Center for the study of democratic institutions #297 26:59min $3.75 77-765298
Donald McDonald of the Center analyzes the reasons for the failure of the press to report public affairs adequately ... and the consequences.

THE TORMENT OF JOAN OF ARC (mo pic)
BFA 21min C R$20 S$330 "You are there" series

TOWARD BECOMING A PERSON (game) see WOMAN (kit)

TOWARDS NEW LIFE STYLES; a discussion package
Women Make Movies 26min R$30 S$200
A wife, free-lance writer, mother, and secretary are shown in their struggle to change their lives. Especially good for high school students. Discussion re sexism, social institutions, women's work-roles: For Better or Worse; Katie Kelly; Domestic Tranquility; and Fear.

TOYS see TOY LENDING LIBRARY in Directory of Sources section

THE TRANSITIONAL FAMILY (tape)
Center for the study of democratic institutions #491D 14:28min $3.75 75-764784
"The dislocation of the family in a runaway technological society is a certainty; its sphere of influence and design will be considerably altered. Mrs. Eulah Laucks, writer and Board member of the Center, speculates on the possible forms the family of the future may take" (Center).

Audiovisual Resources

TRIAL OF SUSAN B. ANTHONY (mo pic)
BFL 1972 22min C "You are there" Series study guide R$20 S$330 72-70016
U.S. Library of Congress summary: A reenactment of suffragette Susan B. Anthony's trial for the "crime" of having voted in a national election.

THE TRIALS OF ALICE CRIMMINS (mo pic)
Women Make Movies 1971 6min
Cooperatively made by women who feel that Alice Crimmins was convicted on the basis of her life-style. A dramatic reenactment based on the 1968 and 1971 trials of the divorced-mother who was convicted, in 1971, for the murder of her two children.

TRIO AT 19 (mo pic)
Filmmaker, Judith Kurtz 1970 110min Youth Films R$15 S$100
A young woman's alienation and struggle for identity triggers tensions between her and two friends--both boys.

THE TROUBLE WITH WOMEN (mo pic)
McGraw 1959 7min R$12.50 S$65
"Provides a useful discussion about the good points and drawbacks of women factory workers, in order to encourage an objective look at their role in industry" (Office for Civil Rights GSA list).

TRUE STORY (tape)
Pacifica #BC0951 60min $10 reel or cassette KPFA producer
You think weeping sounds bad/You should hear me laugh. Alta, a Bay Area feminist poet, reads and discusses her poetry and talks about the Fminist Movement with Ruth Rosen and Isabel Welsh.
SEE ALSO Lesbiana, in Pamphlets part of Non-Book Resources section.

TRUTH IS ON ITS WAY (rec)
Nikki Giovanni Right-on Recordings #15001

TRY IT--YOU'LL LIKE IT! (rec album)
Pat Harrison and Robin Tyler Dore LP
"First feminist comedy team" and their first recording. Some people didn't think it too funny; H & T respond that they laugh with feminism--not at it.

THE TWIST OF FEELING (tape)
CBC #755 30min $7
Margaret Atwood discusses the ideas and emotions behind her collection of poems, "Power politics."

TWO DAUGHTERS (mo pic)
Satyajit Ray, filmmaker 1964 114min Janus R$120
Two Asian Indian movies comprising a whole: the first tells about a young postmaster who teaches his servant girl, a child, to read and write in order to make her more like his younger sisters; the second tells about a "tomboy" who is forced into marriage.

201-203 (mo pic)
Krishna Shah, writer-director-editor 1966 20min Creative film society R$12 S$150 FiA68-373
Hotel room #201 is occupied by an Occidental male, 203 an Oriental female. Each fantasizes about the other, screening through Hollywood myths ... she is seen like a Sayonara geisha, he like a Shane sheriff.

TWO RIGHT, TWO LEFT, DROP ONE (mo pic)
Recha Jungmann, filmmaker 1973 4 1/2min C Canadian Filmmaker's Distribution Centre R$6
"It is a simple study of 'love' and possessiveness in the relationship between man and woman and woman and woman, and about the necessity to change the quality of personal relationships" (CFDC).

TWO WOMEN--20 YEARS (videotape)
Center for Continuing Education of Women at the University of Michigan, Ann Arbor 1974 30min. Available on loan to organizations, individuals, groups as an educational and training tool.
Two women, '54 and '74 alumnae, exchange views on aspirations and uncertainties in their lives.

- U -

UGLY TEENAGED GIRLS (tape)
CBC #525 30min $7
What do plain girls do in a society that demands model proportions and beauty?

UMBRELLA (audiovisuals)
Taro Yashima's children's book (Viking 1958; Seafarer paperback) is available as filmstrip, record, etc. Weston Woods.

THE UNANSWERED QUESTION (mo pic)
Macmillan Audio Brandon 1966 5min R$8.50
" 'What is Brotherhood?'--a question people in all walks of life are either unable to or refuse to answer--is the question posed in this brief but telling 'cinéma-vérité' gem. For an interview-style TV spot on Brotherhood prepared in 1965 for the National Conference of Christians and Jews, Amram Nowak Associates questioned people on the street...." You will probably recall having seen the "spot" referred to by Macmillan Audio Brandon in their catalog. This film was put together from outtakes of these street interviews. "The film-makers feel that this is in many ways a more truthful film than the later TV spot, since it presents the actual, candid responses given in the street. The confusion, vagueness, and willingness to offer what they thought was desired and instead of what they really might have felt make the responses ... an eye-opener."
And how about the title/concept itself? Personhood? Sisterhood?

Audiovisual Resources

UNDERSTANDING CONCEPTION AND CONTRACEPTION (slides)
Ortho Pharmaceutical Corp., Raritan, NJ 08869 Slide set 56
   slides C S$28
From the IPPF Library Bulletin VIII:1, p. 84: "drawings ... illustrate the female reproductive system, the mechanism of menstruation, conception and birth, and most popular methods of contraception.... [The slides] contain no written material and are not self-explanatory: the information must be supplied by knowledgeable medical or para-medical personnel."

UNTIL I DIE (mo pic)
Patricia Barey, Gloria Callaci, filmmakers 1970 29min C
   Video Nursing R
A study of work of woman psychiatrist, Elisabeth Kuebler-Ross, treating terminally-ill patients.

UNWED MOTHER (mo pic)
ABC-TV 1965 29min
Probes the problems of the rising number of illegitimate births. Analyzes the factors that contribute to the rise and examines the problems faced by the unwed mother.

UP AGAINST THE MATTRESS; DOWN IN THE VALLEY (tape)
Radio Free People # 69-19 10min S$4
A collage of the most irritating put-down clichés women must face in their daily lives. Music, raps, advertisement. For CR.

UPPITY PUPPETRY (videotape)
Contact: Pat Jensen, Media Task Force coordinator, Santa Barbara NOW, 162 Alpine Dr., Goleta, CA 93017 R$15 1" C
   1/2 hour
A NOW-produced puppet show dealing with sex-role stereotyping in elementary school books.

UPPITY WOMEN UNITE (Button)
KNOW # A1800 Black on day-glo pink $.25

URSULA LeGUIN; WOMAN OF SCIENCE FICTION (tape)
Center for Cassette Studies 54min $16.95
A discussion with Ursula LeGuin about her life, work, and literary world; she also hails the Women's Liberation Movement.

USE OF SEX IN HUMAN LIFE (tape)
Perennial # 526 S$10
Discussion by two male doctors contrasting liberal and permissive approaches to "sexual expression."

UTAMARO AND HIS FIVE WOMEN (Utamaro o Meguru gonin no onna) (mo pic)
New Yorker 1946 95min R
Utamaro was the master of Japanese woodcut print-making, a painter of "common women."

- V -

VD. There are numerous audiovisuals marketed and being produced on the subject of "social diseases." The following are some which may have utility for feminists as they discuss, evaluate media, CR, etc. They are representative of the products being marketed today at various "levels":

VD (mo pic)
Ealing 26min C With teacher's guide Gr 7+   Holt, Rinehart & Winston 0-03-091615-1 S$360
(SEE LJ-SLJ Previews Sept. 1972:81 and other periodicals.)

VD: A CALL TO ACTION (mo pic)
CCM 1969 27min C Call to Action Series Univ. of California Ext. #8003 R$19
"Documents a typical workday of an epidemiologist as she tracks down VD carriers through interviews and police files. Provides factual information on syphilis and gonorrhea, and shows how one community works to control these diseases" (California).

VD: A NEW FOCUS (mo pic)
American Educational Films, producer-distributor 16min C With teacher's guide. Gr 7+   Also available S8--optical or magnetic. 16mm: R$25 S$225. S8: S$200
(SEE LJ SLJ Previews Sept. 1972:81 and other periodicals.)

VD--A VERY COMMUNICABLE DISEASE (mo pic)
Charles Cahill & Associates, producer Gr 5+   With teacher's guide C Aims #3929
Gonorrhea and syphilis.

VD--ATTACK PLAN (mo pic)
Disney 1972 16min Discussion guide S$225 Short version R$12 S$215 73-700962
Animation, syphilis and gonorrhea. Ignorance, Fear, and Shame are characters.

VD BLUES (mo pic)
60min C R from Modern Film, 1212 6 Ave., New York, NY 10036
A popular "special" which was shown on Public Broadcasting System in 1973.

VD: EPIDEMIC (mo pic)
Contemporary 1965 24min ABC Univ. of California Ext. #6790 R$11

VD; EVERY THIRTY SECONDS (mo pic)
Perennial #10 17min C R$21 S$210
Syphilis and gonorrhea.

VD: MYTH AND REALITY (FS)
Westinghouse Learning Press   3-part series
#1: An overview; #2: A clinical look; #3: Beneath the surface. For students of all ages, parents, community groups. Emphasis on prevention and control through understanding rather than through guilt, mystery and fear.

VD? SEE YOUR DOCTOR (mo pic)
Sterling 1966 22min C Univ. of California Ext. #7359 R$15
"Dramatizes the case of one teen-age boy who contracted gonorrhea from his girl friend, and how she finally disclosed the name of the older man from whom she must have contracted the disease...."

VD: THE SILENT EPIDEMIC (FS)
Audio Visual Narrative Arts, producer-distributor 1973 3 sound
  FSs, each with phonodisc, with Guide, for use with manual or automatic projector, $44. With tape cassettes, $50. #201 73-733496
1. VD--the silent epidemic: the physical attack, 58fr, 13:15min;
2. VD--the silent epidemic: the emotional attack, 57fr, 13:12min;
3. VD--the silent epidemic: crisis and counterattack, 57fr, 12:12min.

VENEREAL DISEASE (mo pic)
John Wiley 1973 17min C S$200
Syphilis and gonorrhea.

VENEREAL DISEASE: A PRESENT DANGER (FS)
Guidance Associates Discussion guide. Part I: 85fr/16min.
  Part II: 77fr/15min. 2 FSs; 2 12" LPs/$40/9A-105-906.
  2 FSs; 2 cassettes/$44/9A-105-922.
Syphilis and gonorrhea.

VENEREAL DISEASE IN AMERICA (audio cassettes)
Westinghouse Learning Press 5 audio cassettes
Dr. Bergan Evans explores the cultural aspects of the VD explosion.

VENEREAL DISEASE; THE HIDDEN EPIDEMIC (mo pic)
Encyclopaedia Britannica #3156 1972 25min C S$296 Univ. of
  California Ext. #8460 R$19
Syphilis and gonorrhea.

VASECTOMY (mo pic)
Martha Stuart Productions 1971 18min Spanish. International
  Planned Parenthood Federation--Western Hemisphere Region
"Vasectomy (male sterilization) is a simple procedure that takes 15 minutes under a local anesthetic; however, cultural, religious, and personal fears often hinder its acceptance as one of the safest and surest methods of contraception known to people. To investigate these fears, filmmaker Stuart interviews a group of Colombian men who have undergone the operation and records their reaction on film. The participants are encouraged to discuss their personal

reasons for seeking a vasectomy, the reactions they experienced from others, and their private sexual fears concerning the operation. They all feel the operation has been a very significant step in their lives and show no regrets. The questions include: Is there a difference in the orgasm? How does it feel to have a vasectomy? How has your life changed? Although Ms. Stuart is present, she does not intrude on the conversation" (IPPF Library Bulletin VIII:1, p. 80).

VENTIHOSE
Ventilated pantihose, the invention of Sunya Arden Rosenberg, 2510 Virginia Ave., N.W., Washington, DC 20037.

A VERY CURIOUS GIRL (La Fiancee du pirate) (mo pic)
Filmmaker, Nelly Kaplan, France. 1969 107min C Universal/16
"Above all the story is of a young woman Mary. The film is one of revolt. In other times she would have been burnt at the public square. Because of her mysterious origins and strange behaviour she is rejected by the provincial community in which she resides. In order to survive, she must use whatever means are available-- without resorting to the fantastic or supernatural. For Mary does not ride on a broomstick to the witches' sabbath; she draws upon destiny. The spell she weaves might be defined as the magic of the extreme ... the girl is a modern witch. In the Middle Ages a witch was burned. Nowadays I wanted to tell a story in which witches burn the others" (Nelly Kaplan).

VIDEOTAPES see TAPES

VIETNAMESE WOMEN (slide program)
Women's Film Coop R$10. Script included C & BW
75 slides "taken over the long course of the Vietnam war, with slides from the history of Vietnam. Juxtaposition of slides of life and demonstration with murder and our 'leaders.' All that is moving and beautiful about the determination of Vietnamese Women should give us strength, all that we've done we should remember" (NARMIC).

VILLAGE SKIN (mo pic)
Macmillan Audio Brandon 14min R$10
Sexual and emotional frustration of a young Japanese woman.

VINNIE BURROWS (cassette tape)
Production Listening Library, Inc., 1 Park Ave., Greenwich, CT 06870

VIOLENCE AGAINST CHILDREN (slide presentation)
Adah Maurer, Vice President, Committee to End Violence Against the Next Generation, 9777 Keeler Ave., Berkeley, CA 94708
Available to groups large enough or numerous enough to raise expenses and lecturer's fee.

Audiovisual Resources

THE VIRGIN, THE TEMPTRESS AND THE REAL WOMAN (FS)
Women's Culture, producer 10min 63fr Snd: cassette or reel-to-reel sound tape C Radio Free People, distributor #73-14 S$25. $40 for slides instead of FS.
"... collage of music and images contrasts the stereotypes of virgin-mother and temptress-Eve with real women active in women's project in and out of church. It has been used very successfully for starting meetings, in worship services and for CR. The sound is entirely musical and includes 'Rise up oh men of God,' 'Baby, you're lookin' good,' a selection from Duke Ellington, and Ruthie Gorton's 'This bird is learnin' how to fly.' Some of the visuals included are photographs of the Presbyterian Women's Task Force at work, a WL worship service and several women's theater groups in action" (W.C.).

VIRGINIA WOOLF: SEEKER OF VOICES (tape)
Center for Cassette Studies 27min $14.95
Dr. Mitchell Leaske examines Virginia Woolf, her revolutionary life and her novels.

VIRGINIA WOOLF: THE MOMENT WHOLE (mo pic)
NET, producer 1971 10min C ACI S$150; Univ. of California Ext. #8448 R$12 72-702447
Selected passages from Woolf's writings convey her concept of woman and articulate the problems and pressures of being a woman writer. Scenes by Marian Seldes in settings of the time, including "A Room of one's own," and "The Waves," and her diary. "A quiet, evocative introduction to the artist and to her feminist ideas" (California).

VIRGO RISING (rec)
Thunderbird Records, 325 Flint St., Reno, NV 89501 $5.95. Cassettes $6.95. Tapes $7.95 + $.50 handling. Royalties to Women's Action Alliance--West.
Stereo album produced, engineered, written, sung by women: Malvina Reynolds, Janet Smith, Nancy Raven, Charley's Aunts, Kit Miller. 12 selections. Includes "Talking want ad" song. Songs of sisterhood.

VISABLE WOMAN (mo pic)
Peter Wallach (age 17) 1967 3min C Youth Films R$6 S$45
"This totally improbable anatomy lesson begins with a Visible Woman Plastic Kit. The model comes to life. Her surrealistic growth, in plasticine animation includes sprouting 4 arms and a tearful eye in her bellybutton" (Youth).

VISAGES DE FEMMES (mo pic)
Peter Foldes, filmmaker 1968 10min C Films, Inc. 77-713676
U.S. Library of Congress: "An animated film which uses the feminine gender as its subject matter. Shows the triadic nature of woman through the three different personality types."

VOICE OF LA RAZA (mo pic)
William Greaves, producer, director, writer (with José Garcia)
   53min   C   R$40   S$380
Documentary film report from El Barrio of Spanish-speaking America, with Anthony Quinn, and Rita Moreno briefly. "Made for the Equal Employment Opportunity Commission and deals with the Commission's role in helping to combat job discrimination against Spanish-speaking Americans and other minorities, as well as women." No digo nada.

VOICES INSIDE (mo pic)
NBC 1969 22min C Univ. of California Ext. #7939 R$18
Voices of men and women in U.S.A. prisons. Brief comments by psychiatrist Karl Menninger. Award winner.

VOYAGE TO ITALY (mo pic)
New Yorker Films 1953 85min R
"It was the third (and best) of 5 very personal features Rossellini made with Ingrid Bergman.... Bergman is the wife of George Sanders, and they are an English couple visiting Italy to sell a family mansion. The film is 'about' the disintegration and regeneration of their marriage: on a deeper level it is about the spiritual needs of modern men and women in a world in which men, due to their roles in capitalist society, are more alientated (and psychologically handicapped) than women" (NYF).

- W -

WAIT Slide Registry see Directory of Sources Section

WEB: Bay Area Slide Registry see Directory of Sources Section

WAITING (mo pic)
Flora Mock, filmmaker 12min C CFS S$150
Award-winning experimental collage film utilizing both live action and animation techniques to illustrate the frustration of individuals (particularly women) who wait from birth to death for the age of happiness that always seems to be just around the corner in time yet never arrives. A pioneer Women's Liberation film, excellent for discussion purposes.

WANDA (mo pic)
Distributed by Bardene International Films, Inc. in both 16 and
   35mm 1970 106min C Keedrick Lecture Bureau has package
   of Loden and film. Barbara Loden wrote, directed, plays
   title-role; Nicholas Proferes shot and edited film.
Barbara Loden: first American woman to write, direct, star in a feature film, awarded International Critics Prize as Best Film at Venice Film Festival, winner of Antoinette Perry Award for her acting in Miller's "After the fall." Rex Reed: "... a wonderful actress, has written directed and starred in a quietly haunting little low-budget movie..., which should nicely nullify the myth

that women should be seen in front of the camera and not behind it. About as touching and personal statement concerning humanity as I've ever seen captured on the screen. There is more honesty in WANDA than I find in nine out of ten studio-financed movies, and a great deal more quality." About a poor, lonely woman from a mining town, cast off by her husband, picked up by an itinerant thief who urges her participation in his exploits, trapped by her environment into passivity. See also New York Times II April 25, 1971:11 "Lights! Camera! Women!" by Marion Meade.

WANDA LANDOWSKA (mo pic)
Films, Inc. #33-0049 28min S$150
NBC production of the eminent harpsichordist.

WAR YES, SEX NO! (tape)
Center for the study of democratic institutions #546 28:58min $7.50
"While doing research for his biography of the Marquis de Sade, Guy Endore, author, screen-writer and pamphleteer, discovered that much research material on sex is carefully locked away in libraries, but anyone is free to read about the most horrendous obscenities of war. A long-time friend of the Center, Mr. Endore recorded excerpts from his talk for our series on Peace and War" (The Center).

WATCHA DOIN', MAMA? (mo pic)
Cornell University production 2-part series of TV programs based on Cornell research studies probing time-use factors and priorities involved in homemaking. Contact John Hersberger, ETV Center, Film Library, Roberts Hall, Cornell University, Ithaca, NY 14850.

WAY DOWN EAST (mo pic)
Macmillan Audio Brandon 1920 113min Sound music only Directed by D. W. Griffith. Screenplay by Anthony Paul Kelly based on the play by Lottie Blair Parker. With Lillian Gish.
Woman deceived by man, rejected by society!

WE SHALL OVERCOME (rec)
Broadside #BR592
Documentary on the march on Washington, D.C. August 28, 1963. Includes speeches by men and Marian Anderson and Odetta.

WE SHOULD LIVE SO LONG (videotape)
Contact Matilda Moore, 1733 Grant, Berkeley, CA 94705 R$10
28min 1/2" Sony tape can be reproduced on almost any helica scan. Pamphlet of same title is a how-to re TV programming on ageism ($.50).
For open meeting on what it means to grow older female. Buttons, bibliographies, packets, etc. from NOW Task Force on Older Women, 434 66 St., Oakland, CA 94609.

WELCOME TO THE BELTLESS PINLESS GENERATION (mo pic)
Twin cities women's film collective 3min optical snd R$10

"A short animated movie made from cutouts of magazine ads, focusing on the way women are degraded by most advertisements" (The Collective).

WELFARE (mo pic)
Univ. of California Ext. #6664 17min R$9 S$100
"Compiled from reflections of a new social welfare caseworker and a young Negro woman receiving aid, this documentary is designed to stimulate discussion of the social rehabilitation process" (California).

WELFARE: EXPLODING THE MYTHS (mo pic)
Thunderbird 18min C
Rebuttals to myths about welfare. Music by Nancy Raven and Malvina Reynolds.

WELFARE REVOLT (mo pic)
Indiana Univ. 1968 60min Univ. of California Ext. #7343 R$16
"Documents how women on welfare in some northern ghettos have tried organizing local unions to change what they consider intolerable conditions. Both Black and White recipients describe their grievances, and leaders of the movement discuss group pressure and organized demonstrations as a means of forcing change" (California).

THE WELFARE WIZARD OF OURS (Musical) see ALIVE AND TRUCKING THEATER CO.

WELL KEPT SECRETS REVEALED; learning from women's experience (videotape)
Subtitle: women's experiences with changes in life.
Feminist's studio workshop production 1 hr Distributed by Vision Quest R$35/day, $7/each additional day
7 women, most now single, all over 50, discussing the subjects "you don't talk about": menstruation, menopause, hysterectomy, sex--in the context of growing old in a culture that values only youth. CR and Gestalt-oriented.

WEST COAST WOMEN ARTISTS (slides) see Directory of Sources section

WEST SIDE WOMEN'S VIDEO COLLECTIVE (video tapes) see Directory of Sources section

WESTWARD THE WOMEN (mo pic)
Films, Inc. 118min R$25
About women who get a wagon train half way across the country after the men hired as guides have abandoned it. The women are at the beginning weak, but grow through the film into strong, decisive, unintimidatable people.

WHAT ABOUT MARRIAGE? (FS & recs)
Producer-distributor, Sunburst Communications, Hemlock Hill Rd.,

Pound Ridge, NY 10576. 1973 3 sound FSs, each with phonodisc, with guide, for use with manual or automatic projector, $60. #112 73-734006
Surveys origins, ideals, realities of marriage by examining first the anthropological and historical background of monogamous marriage. Does not gloss over the role confusions affecting modern marrieds, refers to some alternatives to traditional relationships.
What about marriage? 'Til death do us part. 75fr, 14min
What about marriage? Romantic love and dirty dishes. 75fr, 14min
What about marriage? Two case studies. 78fr, 15min.

WHAT ABOUT SEX? (mo pic)
Nett-Link Productions 24min Coronet S$146.25

WHAT DO THOSE WOMEN REALLY WANT?: A primer on feminism (tape cassette)
Mary C. Howell, M.D., PhD., Harvard Medical School 3 1-hour tapes Behavioral Sciences Tape Library $21
90156 Feminism and sex differences; Equal pay for equal work, and all that. 90167 Feminism and the family; Feminism and the sexual revolution; Feminism and politics. 90178 Feminism and mental health; "Sisterhood."

WHAT I WANT (mo pic)
Sharon Hennessey, filmmaker 1971 11min C Canadian filmmaker's distribution centre R$12. Serious Business Co. S$120.
Ms. Hennessey reads an endless list of "wants" in behalf of all humanity, with special emphasis on women's demands. Funny, useful for CR.

WHAT IN THE WORLD (mo pic)
Don Duga 5min C Grove #355 S$75
Comic-strip film in the manner of "Barbarella," takes his heroine, Susey Creamcheese on a wild cinematic journey--galloping in the nude on a horse with the face of a dog, splashing down to the depths of the ocean, etc. etc. (Grove).

WHAT SHALL I TELL MY CHILDREN WHO ARE BLACK? (rec)
Margaret G. Burroughs Sound-a-rama #SOR 101-2S-12

WHAT'S A NICE GIRL LIKE YOU doing in a place like this? (slide show)
Contact Anne Thornton, 1611 Baker, San Francisco, CA 92117, 1 of 3
Stanford University women-students who developed their own multimedia show describing the reactions of male students and faculty to their enrollment in a graduate business school. General purpose: to help others understand the problems women encounter in a male-oriented field and affirm their interest in a business career. Use in colleges and high schools.

WHAT'S THE MATTER WITH ALICE? (mo pic)
Newsfilms, USA, 21 West 46 St., New York, NY 10036 S$225
  1972   30min   C   Univ. of California Ext. #8453   R$22
A Civil Service Commission film designed "to stimulate thinking by
managers and executives about career advancement, upward mobility, and equal opportunity for minorities and women" (California).

WHEN A WOMAN LOVES (mo pic)
Zengo Sakai produced for Shochiku Co., Ltd., Tokyo from a novel
  by Yasushi Inoue. Japanese dialogue with English subtitles.
  97min   C   United Films
Film News V. 29 #5/1972: "... the story is universal, though
set in contemporary Japan--of which it gives an insight new to
most of us ... has many values other than as an entertainment
feature...."

WHERE AM I NOW WHEN I NEED ME? (multi-media show)
University Commission on Status of Women Students, 301 Walter
  Library, University of Minnesota, Minnesota Women's Center,
  Minneapolis, MN 55455.

WHERE IS JIM CROW? A conversation with Lena Horne (mo pic)
Univ. of California Ext. #6975   1967   30min   R$13   S$180
"Discusses herself as a symbol of the Negro pinup, the representative Negro woman, or 'this year's Negro,' and tells how she had
to conquer this image for her own sake" (California).

WHERE IS JIM CROW? A conversation with Nancy Wilson (mo pic)
Univ. of California Ext. #6978   1967   30min   R$13   S$180
"Singer Nancy Wilson discusses civil rights and the Negro in show
business. She says she has rarely felt discrimination personally
and has never had great problems because she does not assume
that there will be trouble" (California). The "Where is Jim
Crow..."-type films provide excellent raw material for discussion
and thinking; begin with the title of the series applied to two women, the nomenclature of the annotations, and the personalities in
the series. Consider the relativity of these two areas of discrimination (why 'areas,' rather than 'types'?). What questions would
you ask Wilson? And, as the discussion branches off, before
bringing it back into focus, the two questions which might be
thrown in: "What do some Black and White women mean when
they refer to woman as 'nigger of the world' and/or as 'university
nigger'?" and "What analogies are there between race and sex
discriminations?"

WHERE IS PREJUDICE? (mo pic)
Indiana Univ. 1968 60min   Univ. of California Ext. #7345   R$16
"12 college students of different races and faiths are shown participating in a weeklong workshop arranged to test their common
avowal that they are not prejudiced ... as the days pass, the students lose much of their composure. The seminar atmosphere
turns to confrontation and withdrawal, demonstrating that our convictions color our outlook on the convictions of others ..." (Cali-

Audiovisual Resources

fornia). Although an excellently produced and exceptionally candid film, it concentrates on only two of the areas of potential discrimination covered by the Civil Rights Act! How might this be redirected, re-produced?

WHITE SUSAN (mo pic)
Marjorie Prisadsky, filmmaker   6min   Canyon Cinema   R$6
On being alone and aroused.

WHO AM I? (FS) see WOMAN (kit)

WHO IS SYLVIA? (mo pic)
Univ. of California Ext.   1957   27min   R$11
Study of the dreams, fear and hopes of a 14-year-old female.

WILD PARTY (mo pic)
Paramount's first talkie Dorothy Arzner, director 1929 With Clara Bow   76min   Universal/16

WIMMENS COMIX (series)
c/o Last Gasp-Eco Funnies, Box 212, Berkeley, CA 94701 $.50 each, for adults mostly

WINDOW WATER BABY MOVING (mo pic)
Macmillan Audio Brandon   1959   12min   C   Silent   R$25
Experimental film showing natural childbirth. "Brakhage records the birth of his first child," says the distributor's catalog, which also refers to (his wife) "Jane"!

WINDY DAY (mo pic)
Faith and John Hubley, filmmakers   1968   time varies (12min)   C
   Distributors: Women's Film Coop, Film Images R$20 S$150
Animated film. SEE ALSO Hubleys' "Moonbird" in relation to this. A comparison of descriptions of this film is interesting. Film Images' information sheet quotes Judith Crist: "Lyrical, lovely, delightful, sophisticated and completely charming," and Joseph Morgenstern (Newsweek): "A midget masterpiece ... strong, funny, preposterous and then appallingly beautiful because the children's imaginations animated the animators' pencils from the start...." Women's Film Coop, on the other hand, points out re the two sisters acting out their fantasies, "Little sister rebels against the older's always casting her in female passive princess roles and goes into her own fantasy world full of animals, often portrayed as mommies and babies. The girls see women as brides and mothers: the only other situations they play with are old age and death. Since women are trained to spend their lives dreaming about being married (until they really are), it seemed natural that in a child's fantasy, marriage is followed by old age and death." "Moonbird," also on the other hand, is about the Hubleys' two small sons, who set out on an adventure ... at night.

WINTERLIGHT (mo pic) see "HOLDING"

WITCH OF BLACKBIRD POND (audiovisuals)
Elizabeth George Speare's Newbery Medal Winner-children's book
(Houghton, 1958; Dell paperback) is available in several audiovisual
forms, including a Miller-Brody kit (#3014 provides paperbacks,
record, cassette, etc.) Historical fiction useful in junior and
senior high school social studies, if justification need-be.

WOMAN (mo pic)
Macmillan Audio Brandon 1918 64min R$25
"Depicts woman's degraded status through history and her new
freedoms following World War I. Included are scenes of Adam
and Eve, Messaline and Claudius, Heloise and Abelard, Cyrene
and the Fisherman, a girl and an officer during the Civil War ..."
(MAB catalog) and and and....

WOMAN (kit)
Teleketics 2 FS's: "Who am I?," "Portraits," with records; a
    film; a cassette; a simulation game; poster; 32-page guide.
    $95. Various elements can be ordered individually, e.g.
    FSs are $17.95 each.
Billed as "a multi-media resource for human liberation," which
"approaches the controversial topic of women's role in society
from a perspective of Christian personhood." Simulation game is
"Toward becoming a person"; film, "Putdown."

WOMAN CHASES MAN (mo pic)
Macmillan Audio Brandon 1937 69min R$30 With Miriam Hop-
    kins, Ella Logan
"In Goldwyn's only screwball comedy, a starving woman architect
pursues a miserly millionaire and divests him of his money and
his bachelorhood. A zestful look at the battle of the sexes, in the
great tradition of 'Bringing up baby' and 'It happened one night' "
(MAB).

WOMAN CONTROLLED ABORTION (videotape)
Feminist women's health centers 30min R$30 S$50 Women in
    control series
Tape includes: 2 actual abortions performed at the Women's
Choice Clinic, demonstrating good abortion procedure, visual and
verbal material on the politics of population control, money, abor-
tion, and the Women's Movement.

A WOMAN IN THAT JOB? (slides)
U.S. Dept. of Labor Women's Bureau 1971 30min C Slides
    with script
Directed toward employers, their affirmative action plans and show-
ing them how to reengineer positions to encourage women to apply.

WOMAN IN THE UNITED STATES: Her story, a reclamation and
    reassessment (package program). SEE ALSO "Directory of
    Sources" section
Contact: N.J. Educational Media Consortium, 240 High, Newark,
    NJ 07102

4 historical segments. Secondary and collegiate level. Multimedia, procedural manuals, evaluation form. For curriculum development. Consultants-participants include Kirsten Amundsen, Emily A. Champagne, Virginia Kelley. Organization: Colonial Era to 1848; 1848-1920; 1920-1963; 1963-present. Production by December 1975.

WOMAN IS THE NIGGER OF THE WORLD (rec)
Written, recorded by Yoko Ono and John Lennon   Apple label

WOMAN OF CHAMULA; a film on the Indian family (mo pic)
Filmmaker, Elda Hartley   14min   C   Distributor, Hartley Productions
Film News: "... a beautiful presentation of the distaff side of life...."

WOMAN OF THE HOUSE (mo pic)
American Foundation for the Blind, producer-distributor (15 West 16 St., New York, NY 10011)   1943   13min
Shows how a blind housewife with the help of special aids and appliances available to blind persons performs such everyday tasks as ironing a shirt, preparing and serving a meal and cleaning the house.

WOMAN OF THE MONTH--INDIRA GANDHI (mo pic)
CBS-TV, producer-distributor   1966   28min

A WOMAN REBELS (mo pic)
Pandro S. Berman, producer   1936   Films, Inc.   R$50   Lease $500   88min
Katherine Hepburn. Based on Netta Syrett's novel, "Portrait of a rebel."

WOMAN, WIFE OR WHAT (mo pic)
Producer-distributor: KUON-TV, University Educational TV Station, 1600 R St., Lincoln, NE 68508   29min
Explains that in a modern world, many modern women have feelings of being trapped, their role confused. Describes the battle for intellectual recognition and need for creative achievement.

WOMANHOOD (FS)
Warren Schloat   1971   35mm
SEE U.S. Library of Congress Filmstrip supplement for 1971.

WOMAN HOUSE (mo pic)
Johanna Demetrakas   47min   C   Whitney Museum New American Filmmaker's Series   1974   R$60   Purchase: apply
In 1972 Judy Chicago and the California Girls took over an old mansion in Los Angeles and set about redesigning its interior--goal to dramatize through their individual artistic talents the essence of a house in CR terms.   All of the live performances relate to women's

passivity and psychological isolation.   Beverly O'Neill, art and cinema.

WOMANHOUSE (mo pic)
Done by a group of Los Angeles women connected with California
    Institute of the Arts   18min   C   Canyon Cinema   R$18
"Not a documentary in usual sense, but a more personal comment of how I related to Womanhouse" (Mako Idemitsu).

WOMAN'S AWAKENING; WOMAN'S FIGHT; WOMAN'S POWER (3
    mo pic)
Released 1914-17.   Contact Univ. of California Ext.

A WOMAN'S CHOICE (radio-TV program)
Oakland VHF Channel #2 KTVU, 1 Jack London Square, Oakland,
    CA 94607   Univ. of California Ext.   C
Radio and television program Sunday 1-1:30 PM, May 19, 1974: the 2 hostesses interviewed woman mayor of Hayward, with "volunteerism" to be considered next time.

WOMAN'S DAY (mo pic)
Sydney filmmaker's coop, distributor   Sydney, Australian Women's
    Film Group film.

WOMAN'S FILM (videotape)
Deirdre Walsh, director-distributor
This should not be confused with the San Francisco Newsreel "Women's Film." This is about men and women talking in separate groups.   Cost Ms. W $300 to get it onto film--donations appreciated.

A WOMAN'S PLACE (mo pic)
Midge MacKenzie, filmmaker   30min   Source: Impact Films   R$90
A current view of the women's movement in England.

WOMAN'S PLACE? (mo pic)
American Assoc. of University Women, 2401 Virginia Ave., NW,
    Washington, DC 20036   1972?   30min   R$3 to AAUW members,
    others R$15
An AAUW panel-discussion by 6 women, including Alice Beeman, on the status of women.   Condensation of "Frankly Female" TV show narrated by Betty Grobley.

WOMAN'S PLACE (FS)
Social Studies School Service   4 C sound FSs with 4 LP recs (or
    cassettes) and Teacher's guide, $66.   With the cassettes, $78.
"A satirical trip into the place of women in our society, discussing biological differences between the sexes, traditional beliefs about the consequences of these differences, and the modern feminist movement since 1966." Comment: This poor over-used title! Wilma Scott Heide makes the comment to the effect that all roles with three exceptions are learned; those three being wet-nurse, human incubator, and sperm bank.

Audiovisual Resources

WOMAN'S RIGHTS SERIES (microcard)
NCR/Microcard Editions (901 26 St., NW, Washington, DC 20037) 1972   79 titles   4x6" $550
"Source materials relating to woman's march toward equality. Books written by and about women concerning marriage, suffrage, work, education, opening up of professions, social status, and other topics relating to the history of the woman's rights movement" (NCR).

A WOMAN'S WORK (mo pic)
George W. Colburn Laboratory, source (164 North Wacker Dr., Chicago, IL 60606)   1967   15min   C
Shows work being done in Alabama by the cooperative extension service to assist young rural homemakers of low socioeconomic status to become more economically and socially secure.

WOMANSPACE   see   Directory of Sources section

WOMEN, AMEN! (mo pic)
Kay Henderson, producer for the Division of TV, Radio & Film Communications of the United Methodist Church Joint Committee on Communication   1973   15min   C   Guide by Beverly J. Chain   Distributed by AV Dept., Rm. 1331, 475 Riverside Dr., New York, NY 10027   R$15   S$195
All-women crew of professional filmmakers made this documentary. Dr. Nelle Morton, Professor Emeritus at Drew University, reports on her discovery that early Greek Biblical manuscripts used inclusive words such as "Let anyone ..." not "Let any man...." Also films the lives of women in contemporary setting in Plainfield, NJ area. Director-coproducer, Marianna Norris; cinematographer, Juliana Wang. Also available from Cokesbury Film Library.

WOMEN AND CHILDREN AT LARGE (mo pic)
Freude Bartlett, filmmaker   10min   C   Serious Business Co., PO Box 198, San Francisco, CA 94103   R$9   S$75
Also available from Canyon Cinema (R$9) which describes it as an "occasionally lyrical, occasionally hilarious, glimpse at the life and random feelings of a small bedraggled, occasionally heroic circle of women."

WOMEN AND EDUCATION (mo pic)
Producer-source: Indian Government Films Division, Ministry of Information & Broadcasting, Bombay   1957   14min
"Describes the opportunities available to Indian women for self-education and for playing a decisive role in national life. Portrays the experiences of a young girl who wants to enter college."

WOMEN AND GIRLS IN AWARD-WINNING CHILDREN'S BOOKS (slide program)
Feminists on children's media, Box 4315, Grand Central Station, New York, NY 10017   60min

WOMEN AND HEALTH (tape)
Feminist Radio Network # 773-12   35min   Cassette: $30   Reels:
    7 1/2ips $35, 3 3/4ips $30
"Discussion of the herstory of women as healers and today's self-help movement. Women involved in women's clinics and self-help groups cover subjects such as vaginal infections, birth control, the concept of self-help and women's clinics" (FRN).

WOMEN & HEALTH (microfilm)
Women's History Library $5 per file, $25 per reel.   Total collection is 20 reels   R also possible.
The Health microfilm is divided into 8 subject-sections, some samples listed below: I Physical and mental health of women; II Physical and mental illness of women; III Biology, women and the life cycle; IV Birth control/population control; V Sex and sexuality; VI Appendix: a) mass periodicals--special issues, b) pamphlets; VII Special films on rape/prison; VIII Black women (will join Black Women's Health film and other such sections for a planned Black Women's film).

WOMEN AND LAW (microfilm)
Women's History Library   30-page Table of Contents $3 for xeroxing and mailing

WOMEN AND MADNESS (videotape)
Twin Cities Women's Film Collective   25min   1/2"   Free
"Personal experiences exploring the idea that madness as defined by society is a political act and results from conflicting ideas of what accepted behavior is."

WOMEN--AND TEMPORARY JOBS (mo pic)
CCM Films   14min   C
Presents candid interviews with women holding temporary jobs and explores their reasons for working, their changing attitudes and the new attitudes of their families.   (Note: An older film, "Women ... and temporary jobs," was produced by Manpower, distributed by Association-Sterling, 14min   C.)

WOMEN AT LARGE (mo pic)
Filmmaker, Freude Bartlett   10min   C   Canyon Cinema
    R$10
A highly recommended comedy about Women's Movement in and out of Life and Art.

WOMEN CHOOSE WOMEN (exhibit)   see   WOMEN IN THE ARTS in
    Directory of Sources section

WOMEN FOR WOMEN FESTIVAL (videotapes, films, photographs)
By/for/about women's organizations, by the Amazon Media Project
    1974   Contact: Video Study Center of Global Village, 454
    Broome St., New York, NY 10013.

Audiovisual Resources

WOMEN FOR WOMEN (mo pic)
Herstory Films 1972? Prices available
A documentary about women's political actions in New York; depicts women supporting women as the essence of the Women's Movement (Sisterhood).

WOMEN GET THE VOTE (mo pic)
CBS News "20th Century" production 27min McGraw #618077
   R$10 S$150 FiA64-89 Walter Cronkite, narrator
NOTE: Film not recommended by many feminists for its point of view, but it does contain exciting documentary footage, 1848-1919 (a good "pair" of dates to use in high school social studies).

WOMEN IN AMERICAN HISTORY (media kit)
Educational Activities FSR#460 c1973 C Consists of: 6 sound-FSs (56, 57, 57, 54, 56, 63fr); 3 records (12", 33 1/3rpm) or cassettes; Teacher's guide; $51.95 with recs, $54.95 with cassettes. Complete set of catalog cards and circulation materials when sold with kit, $.49. Written by Susan Kempler and Doreen Rappaport; produced by Norma Harris; illustrations by Alice Meyer-Wallace; photography ("Crisis of Identity") by Eva Rubinstein. Company suggests for Junior and Senior High School, but it will be useful for many adults. (1) The Colonies, (2) After the Revolution, (3) Slavery and suffrage, (4) Reformers, (5) The artist, and (6) Crisis of identity.
"Women's struggle for justice and equality and their contributions to American life are presented through memorable vignettes from the lives of outstanding women and brief excerpts from their speeches and writings. Discrimination in law, politics, religion, education, work, etc. ... the inequities that still exist. Visuals combine colorful water color illustrations, period photography, documents, old paintings and drawings, modern art and color photography. Anecdotes are dramatized and music and sound effects bring the American women's struggle and accomplishments alive ..." (EA).

WOMEN IN AN ERA OF CHANGE (FS)
Visual education consultants #3017 1971 Suggested by the Company
   for Intermediate grades
"Just a little over 50 years ago, women were denied the basic right to vote. Those who campaigned for this right were cruelly ridiculed. Today that right is unquestioned but more subtle restrictions on women still exist. This filmstrip reviews women's fight for equality ... encourages the student to form his own opinions ..." (VEC).

WOMEN IN CAREERS (mo pic)
Doubleday #91640 1972 15min C S$190.50
"In 1960, 1/3 of all black women were still employed as domestics. 74% of today's female work force earns less than $7,000 a year. The largest group of working-age adults on welfare are 2.5 million mothers, most of whom head families with no able-bodied male present.... This film introduces 4 females in skiiled professions

who feel their work is important to others and rewarding to themselves. For female viewers, this film will be an incentive. For males, it will be an education. For all, it will destroy the myth that women are helpless" (Doubleday cat.). So how come that myth? Consider another annotation for this film, with commercial interest: "... introduced four women in skilled professions who feel their work is important to others and rewarding to themselves. These women don't want to be men; nor do they wish to intimidate the male population. What separates these women from others is that they have done something more with their lives. They have taken the initiative and have used their abilities. For female viewers ..." (American Library Assoc. Media program brochure, 1973 annual conference).

WOMEN IN CONTROL (videotapes)
Feminist Women's Health Centers series 1 tape R$30 S$50 All shot and edited by Jan Oxenberg 1/2" EIAJ standard. Order from MEDIA, Feminist Women's Health Center, 746 South Crenshaw Blvd., Los Angeles, CA 90005
See individual titles: "Self-help clinic," "August 26th, inside the Movement," "Radical mastectomy," "Menstrual extraction," "Woman controlled abortion," and "Home movie."

WOMEN IN FRANCE (exhibition)
Exhibitions Dept., French Cultural Services, 972 5 Ave., New York, NY 10021 58 C panels, including texts, complemented by films by and about women, panel discussions, seminars throughout U.S.A. Gratis for shipping costs and insurance, to USA community and women's organizations.

WOMEN IN HISTORY OF UNITED STATES labor Movement (mo pic)
This film in process of development by Lorraine W. Gray, filmmaker of "The emerging woman," photojournalist, and recipient of Virginia Press Association's First Prize in General News Photography. Melanie Maholick is also involved in this project. For addresses, etc., see Women's Film Project in Directory of Sources section.

WOMEN IN LIBRARY MANAGEMENT (videotape)
Contact (Ms.) Leigh Estabrook, Simmons College School of Library Science, 300 The Fenway, Boston, MA 02115
Ms. Estabrook is soliciting case study examples to contribute to a book, "Women in Library Management," to be equally cases, articles, and reaction-explanations. Initial videotapes of case studies were used for a "Humanism" conference.

WOMEN IN LITERATURE (recs)
Caedmon 17titles/21records $109.20 net price to schools for the collection
TC 3003 (3) Charlotte Brontë: "Jane Eyre" $ 20.94
    1244   Gwendolyn Brooks reading her poetry   6.98
    1071   Elizabeth Barrett Browning: "Sonnets from/
              Portuguese"   6.98

Audiovisual Resources 287

TC	2026	(2)	Emily Dickinson: "A Self Portrait"	$ 13.96
	1119		Poems & Letters of Emily Dickinson	6.98
	2024	(2)	George Eliot (Marion Evans): "Silas Marner"	13.96
	1352		Lorraine Hansberry on her art & the Black experience	6.98
	1133		Katherine Mansfield: "Stories"	6.98
	1123		Edna St. Vincent Millay reading her poetry	6.98
	1024		Poetry of Edna St. Vincent Millay	6.98
	1025		Marianne Moore reading her poems	6.98
	1136		Dorothy Parker: "Stories"	6.98
	1006		Katherine Anne Porter reading "Downward Path to Wisdom"	6.98
	1016		Edith Sitwell reading her poems	6.98
	1050		Gertrude Stein reading from her works	6.98
	1010		Eudora Welty reading	6.98
	1105		Virginia Woolf: Selections from "Mrs. Dalloway" and "To the Lighthouse"	6.98
	2010	(2)	Katherine Anne Porter reading "Noon Wine"	13.00
TRS	355		Lorraine Hansberry: "Raisin in the Sun"	21.94

WOMEN IN LOVE (mo pic)
Ken Russell, director   129min   C   United Artists/16   R
Based on the novel by David H. Lawrence (Viking paperback and hardback, 1920; also Modern Library, $2.95). Insight to the lives and sexual mores of two couples in a small British mining town. And insight to contemporary lives and mores when grotesquely violent "Valdez is coming" receives a GP (general audiences) rating, and "Women in love," with honest and tasteful nude scenes is rated R (restricted to adults)! Movie raters consider normal sexual curiosity in the young more reprehensible than sadism. Or as Lenny Bruce used to say, a naked body is permissible in the mass media only if it is mutilated (R. H. Gardner, April 16, 1971 Baltimore Sun).

WOMEN IN MANAGEMENT (course)
By Freda F. Clark   1974   6 cassettes, workbook, notebook format $97.50 each course.   Additional workbooks @ $3.75.
"Self-exploring course equivalent to 3-day seminar," says the ad. Mainstream International, Box 16175, Philadelphia, PA 19114

"WOMEN IN MEDICINE" EXHIBIT
Contact Doris Thibodeau, Librarian, Johns Hopkins University Institute of the History of Medicine, 1900 East Monument, Baltimore, MD 21205. 3rd floor Welch Medical Library, open to general public, but suggest telephoning Ms. Thibodeau: 301-955-3159.

WOMEN IN PRISON (mo pic)
Contact William Dennis, ABC-TV, 33 West 60, New York, NY 10021.   1974   52min   C
Film highlights personal discussions among women prisoners about their own pasts and about prison conditions. One of the best TV documentaries.

WOMEN IN PRISON (mo pic)
Michael Grigsby, director. Elaine Grant, producer 1965 32min
   Contact Ms. Grant, 42/43 Lower Marsh, London SE 1, England
An investigation into the effects of imprisonment on women, who talk here about themselves, their marriages, and their children, as well as the prison conditions in which they live.

WOMEN IN PRISON (tape)
Radio Free People, producer-distributor
Account of the Women's Bail Fund and women in prison.

WOMEN IN THE 70's (cassette)
Superscope Library of the Spoken Word, 455 Fox, San Fernando, CA 91340
Cassette anthology, "survival kit" by Drs. Linda Selzer Fidell and Jane Emery Prather, 1972.

WOMEN IN VIETNAM (mo pic)
Indochina Peace Campaign, 181 Pier, Santa Monica, CA 90405
   R$20 + shipping   Also available from Jane Barton 30min C
   East Germany
Describes women in different aspects of North Vietnamese life, both in war and after the peace agreement.

WOMEN IN VIETNAM (slide show)
Indochina Peace Campaign, 181 Pier, Santa Monica, CA 90405
116 slides, with script, "describing the history of Vietnam through the life and struggles of its women" (IPC brochure).

WOMEN IN WAITING (videotape)
Twin Cities Women's Film Collective 12min 1/2" R$5
"An intriguing statement by women becoming aware of the significance of waiting in their lives."

WOMEN IN WORDS AND IMAGES (slide show)
Contact Corrine Osiesk, Interlibrary Reference & Loan Section,
   New Jersey State Library, Trenton 08625 140 slides, prerecorded cassette
Presents argument that both the stories and illustrations in school books for young children serve to reinforce and encourage traditional sex-role concepts. Available to schools and public libraries in New Jersey through interlibrary loan.

WOMEN MAKE MOVIES, INC. (tape)
Feminist Radio Network #973-20 29 3/4min Cassette: $20;
   reels: 7 1/2ips $25, 3 3/4ips $20
"Interview with filmmakers Sheila Paige, 'Women's Happy Time Commune'; and Ariel Dougherty, 'Sweet Bananas,' on the working of their New York City-based organization" (FRN).

WOMEN OF AFRICA (FS)
UNESCO 1966 46fr C 35mm With English commentary; available in French, Spanish 70-740223 Released in USA by Unipub,

Box 433, New York, NY 10016
U.S. Library of Congress Summary: Traces the emancipation of
African women, and explores their role in the development of their
countries from tribal societies to modern states.

WOMEN OF DESTINY (tape)
Learning Arts   8 cassettes $36.80
Biographies of women "who dedicated their lives to scientific, medical, and humanitarian causes: Helen Keller, Florence Nightingale, Amelia Earhart, Clara Barton, Madame Curie, Elizabeth Blackwell, Betsy Ross."

WOMEN OF INDIA (mo pic)
Producer-distributor: Indian Government Films Division, Ministry
     of Information & Broadcasting, Bombay   1964   17min   R
A documentary tracing the achievements of women in various activities, arts and sciences in modern India; includes a brief historical sketch of women's role in Indian history and society.

WOMEN OF THE WORLD (mo pic)
Pepsi Cola   14min   C   Association-Sterling #2594
New women in the old world--5 countries.

WOMEN ON SEX; A CONVERSATION (videotape)
West Side Women's Video Collective, producer   1972   The Kitchen

WOMEN ON THE MARCH (mo pic)
McGraw-Hill   30min   Contemporary Films.   Also distributed by
     Women's Film Coop of New Haven, CT, which comments:
"Seeing this film brought two gut-level responses from us....
[The] first was a feeling of tremendous pride--pride that women
have been strong enough to do any work a man could do, pride
that women have not allowed political repression to stop them.
The second was one of anger--anger that a man was narrating our
history, anger that the film selected out a very narrow part of the
feminist movement--the fight for suffrage--without commenting on
all the other revolutionary demands of feminists. It is also sad
to see the feminist movement being co-opted by the war effort.
Had we lived in those times we might have done the same thing,
but after several historical lessons in co-optation we don't intend
to let that happen again. In short, we think the value of the film
lies in its documentary footage and not in its historical analysis."

WOMEN TALK ABOUT SEX (videotape)
By Minda Bikman   30min   From: Videowomen

WOMEN TALKING (mo pic)
Director, Midge Mackenzie   1971   80min   Impact   R$50/100
     S$650
"... features conversations with leading personalities in the forefront of the women's liberation movement": Betty Friedan, Laurie Zimmer and Susan Silverman, Kate Millet, Selma James.

WOMEN; THE EMERGING RESOURCE (program)
Advanced systems, inc.   Prepared by Barbara Boyle and Frederick
    Herzberg
3 unit program includes color videotape lectures, role-playing sessions, dramatizations, actual interviews, coordinator's Guide, materials for participants. A training "program for management which is predominantly male," designed "to help them understand the woman worker."

WOMEN: THE FORGOTTEN MAJORITY (FS set)
Denoyer-Geppert #69710   1971   Parts 1 and 2 (set); automatic and
    manual.   2 C FSs with 2 discs   15min   Teacher's Guide $34
The review of this set which appeared in LJ-SLJ Previews Sept. 1972:30 provides great raw material for an analysis of an analysis!

WOMEN; the hand that cradles the rock (mo pic)
Document Associates   1971   22min   C   Towards the year 2000
    series   Univ. of California Ext.   #8406   R$25
"Intercuts footage of advertisements that use stereotyped images of women with brief, occasionally superficial sequences in which members of the women's liberation movement discuss their ideas. Anne Kyle-Moderno, a former fashion model, explains why she is leaving her marriage, though not her husband, and is shown talking to a group of young women in a high school. Includes interviews with Dr. Phyllis Chesler, a psychologist, and Anselma Dell'Olio, director of a feminist theater.   Shows excerpts of panel discussion that includes Dr. Albert Ellis, noted sexologist.   Also interviews a woman who prefers being a housewife and mother, and who explains her reasons for rejecting the women's liberation movement" (California).

WOMEN UP IN ARMS (mo pic)
UN   28min   McGraw   R$8   S$130
Women's Liberation in Tunisia.

WOMEN vs. THE SYSTEM (rec)
New York Chapter of the National Women's Book Association   1974
    $12   album from Anti-Defamation League

WOMEN WHO CHANGED THINGS (FS)
AIDS   Series of 5 FS with rec or cassette, designed for grades 2-
    6.   Phillis Wheatley, Emma Lazarus, Jane Addams, Frances
    Perkins, Shirley Chisholm $75

WOMEN WHO HAVE HAD AN ABORTION (mo pic)
Martha Stuart, producer   Are you listening series   1972   29min
    C   Impact   R$40   S$325
"The consensus of opinion here was that this film is by far the best film on the subject" (Margaret Sanger Research Bureau). All of the women in this film faced the ordeal of deciding about having an abortion, subsequently had one, and were willing to talk about it.   These women, Black and White, represent a wide age range and varied socio-economic backgrounds.   Ms. Stuart's theory

is that the real experts on problems are the people who have the experience. These dignified and calm women are experts in the crisis of unwanted pregnancies.

WOMEN'S ART REGISTRY
Ad Hoc Women's Committee (on art), PO Box 539, Canal Street
    Station, New York, NY 10013
An international catalog of slides representing work of more than seven hundred artists.

WOMEN'S FILM (mo pic)
Filmmakers: Louise Alaimo, Judy Smith, Ellen Sorrin. 45min
    Newsreel, New York R$60 S negotiable Also available from
    Women's Film Co-op (R$50) which describes it as:
"a documentary which gives real insight into the guts of the Women's Movement as we see women of different races, backgrounds, jobs talk about their lives. The women are real--they are not idealogues, they do not rely on rhetoric rather than experience, they are political beings and they speak from their hearts. While each woman's awakening to her own past, present and future is distinct, the film gives a sense of how their history and ours are linked. A moving, brilliant and beautiful film, the best overall view of the Movement to date. However, this film was made a while back. Since then, the Women's Movement has grown in ways that make this amazing film seem a bit dated--the absence of lesbians is conspicuous" (Sometimes referred to as "The woman's film").

THE WOMEN'S HAPPY TIME COMMUNE (mo pic)
Sheila Paige, producer and director 1972 50min Women Make
    Movies, Inc. S$500
"Set in a fictional 1850, this all-woman Western is about one woman's attempt to recruit others for an all-woman commune. The story line hardly does justice to this film which allows a group of wonderfully idiosyncratic women to improvise characters close to their real and fantasy lives. Funny, ambling, offhandedly lyrical, the film also raises the issue of how women live without men. It is above all excellent for sharing warm feelings in a group and for stimulating discussions of reform vs. radical feminism" (<u>Ms</u>. August 1974:98).

WOMEN'S IMAGE IN ADVERTISING (slide program)
Women's Research Project 30 slides Script included R$10 C
Also available from Women's Film Co-op, which describes it as a "show of ads taken mainly from business magazines--magazines for men. Women are objectified and identified with the products they're used to sell, fear and perversion are documented as selling techniques."

WOMEN'S KIT (multi-media)
Ontario Institute for Studies in Education, 252 Bloor, Toronto.
"An attractive comprehensive multi-media kit containing over 250 items--print, records, slides, tapes, postcards, posters, film-

strips) on women which gets to the roots of the patriarchal system
by successfully presenting material on history, law, family life,
art, advertising, and achievement of Canadian women. Suitable
for high school students" (Emergency Librarian VI #3, Feb. 1974:
19).

WOMEN'S LIB (phonotape)
By Betty Friedan, Gloria Steinem, Bella Abzug Encyclopedia
　　Americana-CBS News Audio Resources Library 1972 55:59
　　min Vital History Cassettes #3 72-760717 Distributed by
　　Grolier Educational Corporation. 1 cassette 2 1/2x4"
Opening session in Washington, D.C., July 10, 1971 of the National Women's Political Caucus.

WOMEN'S LIBERATION (tapes)
San Francisco Women's Media Group 5 tapes running 15-30min
　　$4 each
Topics include abortion, male-chauvinism, small groups, sexism.

WOMEN'S LIBERATION (tape)
CBC #769L 1 hour $14
"A variety of women discussing Women's Liberation; its meaning, objectives, and social relevance."

WOMEN'S LIBERATION AND THE ARTS (tape)
Pacifica Millett, Nevelson, Ringgold, Paley, Lippard, et al

WOMEN'S LIBERATION DAY: New York, San Francisco, Berkeley
　　rallies of August 26, 1970 (tape)
Pacifica #BB2603 61min Available for school use $12 Customers
　　must specify whether they wish the program on reel or cassette; price same, program theirs to keep.
Includes speeches made and coverage of actions taken at the time
and places mentioned in title.

WOMEN'S LIBERATION ROCK BAND
1504 Blvd., New Haven, CT 00511

WOMEN'S RIGHT TO HEALTH; phases of her life (packet) see
　　Health, in Pamphlets part of Non-Book Resources section

WOMEN'S SCHOOL: Women's Liberation and Black civil rights (tape)
Pacifica #BC0981.01 72min reel or cassette $12
"In the first program in the Women's School Series from WBAI,
Catherine Stimpson, assistant professor of English literature at
Barnard College, discusses Women's Liberation and Black civil
rights. Her thesis is that serious tensions exist between feminism
and the Black movement as movements, and between White women
and Black women as people. Ms. Stimpson really knows what she's
talking about. Her position is drawn from a thorough analysis and
understanding of the history of both movements. This was a very
controversial talk in New York feminist circles, which is brought
out during the question-and-answer period, where a number of

well-known feminist theorists were present. Important because it addresses itself to one of the central questions in the feminist movement" (Pacifica).

WOMEN'S STREET THEATER (cartoon)
People's press $.30
"A paper movie (cranky) about women's history and oppression in cartoon form. If you buy two copies, you can build your own miniature cranky."

WOMEN'S STUDIES: Reaction & Evaluation (cassette)
Cleveland Women's Studies Research Group, Women's Center, Case Western Reserve University, 11111 Euclid Ave., Cleveland, OH 44106 1973 15min cassette tape with complete transcript $3/individuals; $5/institutions
Participants in a psychology-of-women course talk about themselves and the effects of the course.

WOMEN'S SUFFRAGE MOVEMENT (mo pic)
Dale Willard, producer 1971 3min silent super 8mm Throne Films, 1229 University Ave., Boulder, CO 80302 72-701304
U.S. Library Congress annotation: "... documents project, no. 335 Loop Film Cartridge. Film notes on case.... Includes arrests."

WOMEN'S WORK: AMERICA, 1620-1920 (FS)
Social Studies School Service 4C Sound FS 4 LP recs Teachers guide, $66; with cassettes, $78
Traces the history of women's rights from colonial America through the revolution of the 1920's.

WOMEN'S WORK IS NEVER DONE (slides)
From Pat Arnold, Cambridge-Goddard Graduate School, 5 Upland Rd., Cambridge, MA 02140
Extensive collection of slides about the work women have done throughout history.

WOMEN'S WORK IS NEVER DONE (dramatic reading)
From Ann Froines, Feminist Studies, Cambridge-Goddard address above a 12-p (with bibliography) paper 30min $.50
Written for a women's conference in Boston in 1972. The history of "working-women" has been neglected. This script for 4 women (narrator plus 1, 2, or 3) can also be illustrated with slides and/or music.

WONDER WOMEN (rec)
Harrison & Tyler 20th Century Records
"The world's first original floating female comedy team," represented by William Morris Agency.

WOO WHO? MAY WILSON (mo pic)
Amalie R. Rothschild, producer 1969 33min C Anomaly S$375; New Day R$37, S$375 Univ. of California Ext. #8449 R$23

Amalie R. Rothschild's first film; she has formed her own production company, Anomaly Films, 105 2 Ave., New York, NY 10003.
At 63, May Wilson, when her husband left her, moved from suburbs to New York City and--from "wife-mother-housekeeper-cook" syndrome--began to create a new life and identity. Art, which had previously been a hobby, became central. Her photo-booth portraits are well known to feminists; others will learn much from her and this portrait of a successful woman.

THE WORKING GIRL [women's songs from mountains, mines, and mills] (phonodisc)
Voyager VRLP 305's 1972 2s 12" 33 1/3rpm stereophonic 72-760786: Kathy Kahn with the Cut Cane Ramblers Fiddle Band. Notes principally by Ms. Kahn on slip case; textbooklet (12p) inserted.
SEE ALSO Ms. Kahn's "Hillbilly Women," #402, BBC.

THE WORKING WOMAN TODAY--AND TOMORROW (FS)
Visual Education Consultants #2896 BW silent FS, teacher's guide "American women are undergoing a 'quiet revolution.' Girls are no longer forced to choose between either marriage or the 'spinster life' as career women. Today, more women are working than ever before, including many millions who are married. 9 out of 10 modern girls will work sometime during their lives. This story shows and explains the changing role of women in our society. It encourages girls to prepare themselves for lives that can, and very likely will, include employment as well as marriage" (Visual Education Consultants, which suggests this for grade six through adult).

WRINKLE IN TIME (kit)
Madeleine L'Engle's 1963 Newbery Award-winning children's story (Farrar, 1962) is available from Miller-Brody: #3033 kit with 12 paperbacks and rec $17.90, with cassette $19.35.

WUTHERING HEIGHTS (mo pic)
Macmillan Audio Brandon 1939 104min R
Based on Emily Brontë's novel (SEE #284 in Basic Book Collection). Merle Oberon, Flora Robson, Geraldine Fitzgerald.

- XYZ -

THE X-FACTOR; WOMEN AS PEOPLE (videotape)
ETV Center, Cornell University, Van Renssalaer Hall, Ithaca, NY 14850 1" video tape 30min R$15
2 programs on the status and image of women, developed for a course at Cornell.

YEAR OF THE CANNIBALS (mo pic)
Liliana Cavani, Italian director 1970 Britt Ekland American International Pictures
A modern version of the Antigone legend.

YEAR OF THE WOMAN (mo pic)
Feminist Party   1973
Feature film produced, written, directed, and edited by an all-women staff, with exception of co-producer Porter Bibb. Poet-novelist Sandra Hochman (SEE her novel, "Walking papers," #771 Basic Book Collection) director.   Shot almost entirely at Democratic Convention in Miami Beach, but not really a documentary. "Stars" Hochman, lawyer Florynce Kennedy, stripper Liz Renay, columnist Art Buchwald. Also referred to by title, "Crocodile tears; the year of the woman."

YOU AND ME (rec album)
Send $6.50 check to Ms., Dept. R, 370 Lexington Ave., New York, NY 10017
LP children's record sponsored by Ms. Foundation. Marlo Thomas, et al. Bell Records, Inc.

YOU CAN (mo pic)
1967 3min Filmmaker-source: Rose Neiditch Sommerschield.

"YOU WON'T DO"; what textbooks on United States government
    teach high school girls (illustrated lecture)
SEE Women's Studies, in Pamphlets part (under Macleod), of Non-Book Resources section.

YOUNG LOVE (mo pic)
Linda Rivera, age 18, filmmaker 1972 8min Youth Films R$15 S$100
"The traditional rites of courtship and marriage are simply and beautifully evoked in this lyrical film," says the Youth Films brochure.

YOUNG, SINGLE AND PREGNANT (FS)
Guidance Associates   Part I: 52fr/7min.   Part II: 58fr/8min.   2 FSs; 2 LPs/$37.50/9E-102-226.   2 FSs; 2 cassettes/$41.50/ 9E-102-234. With discussion guide. Suggested for grades 6-8 by Guidance Associates.
"... Outlines basic rules for adoption, restrictions surrounding abortion; stresses the need to evaluate readiness for parenthood" (G.A.). It does, however, touch upon "advantages and disadvantages of forced marriage, single parenthood."

DIRECTORY OF SOURCES

ABC Media Concepts
1001 N. Poinsettia Pl.
Los Angeles, CA 90046
  Also: 1330 6 Ave., New
  York, NY 10019. 212-
  LT1-7777. Marlene Sanders,
  producer, at ABC News,
  7 West 66 St., New York,
  NY 10023.

AFL-CIO National Auxiliaries
815 16 St., N.W.
Washington, DC 20006

AIDS (Audiovisual Instructional
  Devices, Inc.)
209-14 41 Ave.
Bayside, NY 11361

ALA <u>see</u> American Library
  Assoc.

ARC (Artists, Residents of Chicago) Art Gallery
226 East Ontario
Chicago, IL 60611

Abortion & Family Planning Information Organization
1028 Connecticut Ave., N.W.
Washington, DC 20036
202-785-1077

Abortion-Birth Control Referral
  Service
4224 University Way N.E.
Seattle, WA 98105
206-ME4-3460

Abortion Coalition
Toronto, Ont.

416-863-9773

Abortion Counseling & Referral
  Service
1112 M St., N.W.
Washington, DC 20005
202-472-1358

Abortion Counseling for Free
1736 R St., N.W.
Washington, DC 20009
202-483-4632

Abortion Counseling Service
3100 W. 8 St.
Los Angeles, CA 90813
213-390-9450

Abortion Counseling Service
549 Turnpike Rd.
Golden Valley, MN 55427
612-515 8085

Abortion Counseling Service of
  Los Angeles
704 S. Spring St.
Los Angeles, CA 90014
213-627-6868

Abortion Counseling Services,
  Inc.
1835 I St., N.W.
Washington, DC 20006
202-293-9030

Abortion Education Committee
c/o Pat White
6731 Ridgeview Circle
Dallas, TX 75240
214-239-9054

Abortion Information & Central
  Appointment Service of the
  Problem Pregnancy Information Center
457 Kingsly Ave.
Palo Alto, CA 94301
415-329-9000

Abortion Information Institute &
  Referral Service
1420 K St., N.W.
Washington, DC 20005
202-628-7656 if no ans: 301-
  484-7424

Abortion Information Services of
  Washington, Inc.
1010 Vermont Ave., N.W.
Washington, DC 20005
202-628-5098

Abortion Institute of America
  see Abortion Information
  Institute...

Abortion Reform Association, Inc.
149 W. 93 St.
New York, NY 10025
212-663-3175

Abortion Reform Committee
515 Madison Ave.
New York, NY 10022
212-421-2155

Abortion Rights Association, Inc.
250 W. 57 St., Room 2428
New York, NY 10019
212-541-8887

Above It All
206 N. Lafayette
Macomb, IL 61455
  Sells posters by Women's
  Graphics.

Action Co-ordinating Council
  for Comprehensive Child Care
Betty Willett, Pres.
5889 W. Pico Blvd.
Los Angeles, CA 90019
213-388-5596, 380-3875

Action for Children
c/o Action Co-ordinating Council for Comprehensive Child
  Care

Ad Hoc Women's Committee
  [re art]
PO Box 539, Canal St. Station
New York, NY 10013
212-966-0288, Agnes Denes
  Maintains Women's Art
  Registry; publishes W.E.B.
  (West East Bag).

Adelante Mujer Project: Latino
PO Box 8257, Palma M. Knoll,
  Dir.
Detroit, MI 48213
  She produces "Mundo: His-
  pano" in Spanish, WBRB-FM.

Administrative Intern Program
  for Women in Higher Education
Cedar Crest College
Allentown, PA 18104
Amalie R. Shannon, Coord.
215-437-4471

Advanced Systems, Inc.
327 S. LaSalle
Chicago, IL 60604
312-427-7277

Advertising Women of New York
149 E. 37 St.
New York, NY 10016
  Affiliated with Advertising
  Women of New York Founda-
  tion.

Advocates for Medical Information
1156 McIntyre Rd.
Ann Arbor, MI 48105
  Kay Weiss, founder, is
  medical researcher.

Advocates for Medical Information
2120 Bissonnet, Apt. B
Houston, TX 77005

Directory of Sources

Advocates for Women
564 Market, Suite 218
San Francisco, CA 94104
   Dorothea Hernanez, dir. of
Women in Apprenticeship
program. Has "1973 San
Francisco Women's Business
Directory" ($2 contribution).
Employment roster, consult-
ing service, day care.

Aenjai Graphic Studio (feminist
professionals)
88 University Pl., 5 fl.
New York, NY 10003
212-989-6587

Affirmative Action Resource
Identification Program (form-
erly Minority Resource Identi-
fication Program)
WICHE, PO Drawer P
Boulder, CO 80302
303-449-3333
   Spike Adams. Has directory.

African American Women's
Assoc.
Nwanganja Shields
7704 Hamilton Spring Rd.
Bethesda, MD 20034

Ahrold, (Ms.) Kyle Warren
   Feminist book-reviewer
c/o Library Journal
1180 Sixth Ave.
New York, NY 10036
212-581-8800

Ailanthus (Gallery)
260 E. 10 St.
New York, NY 10003

Aldridge, Adele
31 Chapel Lane
Riverside, CT 06878
   Graphics source.

Alice James Books
138 Mt. Auburn
Marjorie Fletcher, Betsy Sholl
Cambridge, MA 02138
   New publishing cooperative
for poetry by women, e.g.:
J. Fletcher's "Us: Women."
C. Veenendaal's "The trans-
Siberian Railway."

Alive and Trucking Theatre Co.
c/o 3316 10 Ave. S.
Minneapolis, MN 55803
612-824-4477
   Has "Stage left; three plays"
($2).

All of Us
Rt. 2, Box 128
Monmouth, OR 97361
   Has brochure, "Children's
books," and documented
research, "Sex stereotyping
in children's lit" ($1).

Alpha Iota
1002 Grand Ave.
Des Moines, IA 50309
   Secretarial sorority supporting ERA.

Alpha Kappa Alpha
1751 New Hampshire Ave., N.W.
Washington, DC 20009
202-387-3103
   Black sorority-service
group; provides some em-
ployment referrals.

Alternative Press Centre
Bag Service 2500, Postal Sta. E.
Toronto, Ont.
   Published "Alternative Press
Index," which included Wo-
men's Liberation as a class-
ification but which ceases
with vol. 3 #2.

Altrusa Internationa, Inc.
332 S. Michigan Ave.
Chicago, IL 60604
   Pioneer women's service
club.

Alverno College Research
Center on Women

(cont.) 3401 S. 39 St.
Milwaukee, WI 53215
   Has audiotapes (R$3) and
   videotapes (R$5).

Alyssum
1757 Union
San Francisco, CA 94123
415-781-8390
   Women's group-alternative to
   male-dominated therapy.

Amani
Box 223N
Culver City, CA 90230
213-836-6155
   Jewelry source, fund-raisers,
   wholesale catalog.

Amazon Bookstore
(1) 3240 Cedar Ave. S.
Minneapolis, MN 55407
612-724-7163
   (2) 2607 Hennepin Ave. S.
   Minneapolis, MN 55408.

Amazon Media Project
454 Broome St.
New York, NY 10013

Amazon Nation
2916 N. Burling
Chicago, IL 60657
   Cries from Cassandra--the
   official newspaper of...

American Aging Association
Nebraska Medical Center
Omaha, NE 68105

American Assoc. for Affirma-
   tive Action
Betty Newcomb, Exec. Dir.
c/o Ball State University
Muncie, IN 47306
   Has newsletter.

American Assoc. of Retired
   Persons
1909 K St. N.W.
Washington, DC 20036
202-872-4700

American Assoc. of Women in
   Community & Junior Colleges
c/o Eileen J. Rossi
City College of San Francisco
50 Phelan Ave.
San Francisco, CA 94122
   Note: AACJC has no headquarters liaison, although
   this is "an affiliated council."

American Assoc. of Women
   Ministers
12 Sunset Rd.
Bowmanville, Ont.
   Supports ERA. Also: 202
   N. Harve, Oak Park, IL
   60302.

American Atheist Library &
   Archives, Inc.
4203 Medical Pky.
Austin, TX 78756
   Has a large atheist women's
   collection.

American Bar Assoc.--Law
   Students Div.--Women's
   Caucus
Idelle Anne Howitt, coord.
2109 Spruce
Philadelphia, PA 19103

American Business Women's
   Assoc.
9100 Ward Pky.
Kansas City, MO 64114
816-444-2886

American Civil Liberties Union
22 E. 40 St.
New York, NY 10016
212-725-1222

American Civil Liberties Union
6 S. Clark, Ruth Adams, Ill. Dir.
Chicago, IL 60603
312-236-5564

American College Health Assoc.
2807 Central
Evanston, IL 60201

Directory of Sources

American Council of Women
  Chiropractors
220 Grand Ave.
c/o American Chiropractic Assoc.
DesMoines, IA 50312
  Formerly, National Council
  of Women Chiropractors.

American Divorce Assoc. for
  Men
343 S. Dearborn #1505
Chicago, IL 60604

American Equal Rights Assoc.
NOTE: At its convention in
  1869 a formal split occurred,
  with the majority, the more
  conservative grouping, supporting the Boston abolitionist wing. Julia Ward Howe
  and Lucy Stone were among
  the majority, formed the
  American Woman Suffrage
  Assoc.; Susan B. Anthony
  and Elizabeth Cady Stanton,
  leading the radical minority,
  organized the National Woman
  Suffrage Assoc. The two
  groups remained separate for
  20 years.

American Federation of Teachers,
  Women's Rights Committee
1012-14 St. N.W.
Washington, DC 20005
202-737-6141

American Home Economics
  Assoc.
2010 Mass. Ave. N.W.
Washington, DC 20036
202-833-3100

American Library Assoc.
  Children's Services Div.
  Sexism in Library Materials
  for Children discussion group
Janet Dellaria, Northbrook Pub. Lib.
1201 Cedar Lane
Northbrook, IL 60062

ALA-SRRT (Social Responsi-
bilities Round Table) Task
Force on Gay Liberation.
Box 2383, Barbara Gittings,
Coord., Philadelphia, PA
19103

ALA-SRRT Task Force on the
  Status of Women see ALA-
  SRRT Task Force on Women
  (name changed 1973-4)

ALA-SRRT Task Force on Women
Elizabeth Futas, Coord. 1974-5
Rutgers School of Library Ser.
New Brunswick, N.J. 08903
  ALA-SRRT Task Force on
  Women Newsletter. Placement roster in serial form,
  called Bulletin Board...
  NOTE: The American Li-
  brary Assoc. itself has no
  headquarters and/or other
  organizational provision for
  the status-of-women in librarianship. SRRT also
  sponsors a Committee on
  Sexist Subject-Headings,
  chaired by Joan K. Marshall,
  Brooklyn College Library,
  Brooklyn, NY 11210, 212-
  780-5336. (SEE Dickinson
  in "Sexism in Education &
  Media," under Pamphlets
  part of Non-Book Resources
  section, for information on
  this concept: language reflects and reinforces society.)

American Management Associations
135 W. 50 St., AMA Bldg.
New York, NY 10020

American Personnel & Guidance
  Assoc., Inc.
1607 New Hampshire Ave. N.W.
Washington, DC 20009
202-483-4633
  654 E. Commonwealth Ave.,
  Fullerton, CA 92631: Film
  Dept.

(cont.) Sex Equality in Guidance Opportunities Project (SEGO) [of the Amer. Personnel & Guidance Assoc.], 1607 N.H. Ave. N.W., Mary Ellen Verheyden-Hilliard, Dir., Washington, DC 20009. 202-483-4633.

American Philological Assoc.
Women's Caucus (Classics)
Sarah Pomeroy
Box 1264 Hunter College
695 Park Ave.
New York, NY 10021
   APA Subcommittee on Status of Women in the Profession, Dr. Margaret D. Wilson, Chairperson, c/o 1879 Hall, Princeton University, Princeton, NJ 08540.

American Revolution Bicentennial Administration
736 Jackson Pl. N.W.
Washington, DC 20276
   Women's Participation director: Perdita Huston. "Open House USA" program developed by Carolyn Patterson of National Geographic. ARBA has materials, bibliography. SEE DePauw in "Miscellaneous," under Pamphlets part of Non-Book section; SEE ALSO Women's Coalition for the Third Century.

American Social Health Assoc.
1740 Broadway
New York, NY 10019
   Pamphlets, etc. on VD.

American Society for Engineering Education
Task Force on Women in Engineering
1 DuPont Circle, Suite 400
Washington, DC 20036
   Task Force has employment roster.

American Society of Women Accountants
327 S. LaSalle
Chicago, IL 60604
312-HA7-1989
   Supports ERA. SEE ALSO American Woman's Society of Certified Public Accountants.

American Woman Suffrage Assoc. "the more respectable" of two prominent organizations devoted to women's rights; the other, the militant National Women's Suffrage Assoc. (Morgan "Sisterhood...": 17-18).

American Woman's Society of Certified Public Accountants
327 S. LaSalle
Chicago, IL 60604
312-HA7-1989
   Supports ERA.

American Women in Radio & Television, Inc.
1321 Conn. Ave. N.W.
Washington, DC 20036

American Women Playwrights' Assoc.
Box A
New York, NY 10011
   Interested in plays reflecting feelings, attitudes, personal histories that have gone into making of the individual woman playwright's experience; send scripts to Florynce V. Hunt.

American Women's Hospital Service
50 W. 50
New York, NY 10020

American Women's Voluntary Services
125 E. 65
New York, NY 10021

Directory of Sources

Andromeda Press
PO Box 5246
San Diego, CA 92105
 Source of feminist greeting cards, etc.

Anemone Designs
PO Box 621, F.D.R. Station
New York, NY 10022

Ann's Enterprises
Box 228
Portland, CT 06480
 Posters.

Anomaly Films
105 2 Ave., Amale R. Rothschild
New York, NY 10003

Anti-Defamation League of B'Nai Brith
315 Lexington Ave.
New York, NY 10016

Antigone Books
710 S. Lehigh Dr.
Ms. Johnee Cunningham
Tucson, AZ 85710

Antioch Documentary Films
Yellow Springs, OH 54387

Apple Records, Inc.
1700 Broadway
New York, NY 10019

Applegate Books
Box 22124
San Francisco, CA 94122
 Source of tapes and other publications.

Aquarian Research Foundation
5620 Morton
Philadelphia, PA 19144

Arab League Committee on Status of Arab Women
Contact via Donald Allan of UNICEF staff in Beirut (U.S.A. UNICEF office, 331 E. 38, New York, NY 10016).

Aradia Clinic
4224 University Wy. N.E.
Seattle, WA 98105
206-ME4-2090
 Full line of information services, teaching, examinations, counseling. Coven is decision-making body for clinic.

Archive of Women in Architecture
41 E. 65
New York, NY 10021
 Involved in a major exhibition of work of women in architecture.

Ariel
Box 9183
Berkeley, CA 94709
 Feminist poetry

Arizona Men for ERA
1433 E. Broadway, Stuart Herzog
Tucson, AZ 85719

Art Registry
PO Box 539, Gracie Station
New York, NY 10028
 Or c/o Lucy Lippart, 138 Prince, 10012. Slides; activities to counter discrimination in schools.

Artemisia Gallery
226 East Ontario
Chicago, IL 60611
 Non-profit co-op of 20 women artists.

Artists-in-Residence (AIR)
97 Wooster
New York, NY 10012
 First all-women artists' co-op

Asian Women's Center
722 S. Oxford Ave.
Los Angeles, CA 90005
213-387-1347

Assoc. Women's Press
743 S. Grand View
Los Angeles, CA 90057
  Also: 1229 Princeton, Santa Monica, CA 90404. 5 publications: "Sister," "Womanspace Journal," "Lesbian Tide," "Momma," and "Women and Film."

Association for Abortion Reform
490 Alden Ave.
Columbus, OH 43201
615-228-1334

Assoc. for Education in Journalism. Ad Hoc Committee on the Status of Women in Journalism Education
College of Journalism & Communications. Ramona R. Rush
University of Florida
Gainesville, FL 32601
  Appointed to further improve the role of women in journalism.

Assoc. for Intercollegiate Athletics for Women
1201 16 St. N.W., c/o AAHPE&R
Washington, DC 20036
  AAIW Handbook ($1.50), Directory ($2), "Philosophy & standards for girls' and women's sports" ($2), "Guidelines for intercollegiate athletic programs for women" ($.10).

Assoc. for Vasectomy
14 W. 40
New York, NY 10018

Assoc. for Voluntary Sterilization, Inc.
14 W. 40
New York, NY 10018
212-524-2344
  Formerly Birthright, Inc. Has speakers.

Assoc. for Voluntary Sterilization International Project
708 3 Ave.
New York, NY 10017
212-867-3114

Assoc. for Women in Psychology. Has "Feminist Therapist Roster" (SEE "Health," under Pamphlets part of Non-Books section).

Assoc. for Women's Active Return to Education (AWARE)
5820 Wilshire Blvd., Suite 605
Los Angeles, CA 90036
213-WE3-8507

Assoc. of American Colleges Project on Status & Education of Women
1818 R St. N.W.
Dr. Bernice Sandler, Exec. Dir.
Washington, DC 20009
202-265-3137

Assoc. of American Foreign Service Women
PO Box 4931
Washington, DC 20008

Assoc. of American Women Dentists
33 Ponce de Leon Ave. N.W., Suite 204
Atlanta, GA 30308
  Supports ERA. Has Newsletter. Also 2950 S. Maryland Pky., Las Vegas, NV 89109.

Assoc. of Feminist Consultants
Betsy Hogan, coord.
222 Rawson Rd.
Brookline, MA 02146
617-232-0066
  Directory of Members. Newsletter.

Assoc. of Intercollegiate Athletics for Women see Assoc. for...

Assoc. of Married Women
1206 S. Buchanan

Directory of Sources

(cont.) Arlington, VA 22204
Actually, the Assoc. of
Married (and Formerly Married) Women. A new group
emphasizing issues, e.g. new
forms of marriage, happier
marriages, creating a women's legal research committee, implementing a Mental
Health Bill of Rights, protecting small children.

Assoc. of Mothers for Educated
Childbirth
1161 Beach 9 St. Dorothy Pereira
Far Rockaway, NY 11691

Assoc. of Women Business Owners, Inc.
1000 Conn. Ave., Suite 101
Washington, DC 20036
202-785-3760

Assoc. of Women in Architecture
PO Box 1
Clayton, MO 63105

Assoc. of Women in Mathematics
Julia Apter, Rush Medical College
1753 W. Congress Pky.
Chicago, IL 60612

Assoc. Residence for Women, Inc.
891 Amsterdam Ave.
New York, NY 10025
212-UN5-6500

Atlanta Lesbian Feminist Alliance
PO Box 7974, Station C
Atlanta, GA 30309

Audio/Brandon
Film Center/Films, Inc. Affiliated with Crowell Collier &
Macmillan
For outlet-addresses, SEE
Ideal.

Audio Film Center
34 MacQuestion Pky. S.
Mt. Vernon, NY 10550

Awareness Films
815 Murry Ct.
Ann Arbor, MI 48103

- B -

BBC
630 Fifth Ave.
New York, NY 10020
BBC Enterprises: London
W 12, Anne Smith.

Bach, Margaret
908 California Ave.
Santa Monica, CA 90403
Filmmaker and source.

Baker & Taylor Co.
PO Box 230, Audio Visual Services Div.
Momence, IL 60954
Inspection Center for Books
& [other] Media: 5820 Wilshire Blvd., Los Angeles,
CA 90036. 213-938-2925.

Baldwin Street Gallery of Photography
23 Baldwin
Toronto 180, Ontario
Co-op. Newsletter. Sales.
Darkroom available for use
by women.

Bambi
5650 Windsor Way, #303
Culver City, CA 90230
T-shirts.

Banks, Wanda J. Associates, Inc.
HE&W Women's Action Program has contracted with
Banks to conduct an evaluative study of women-owned
firms. Contact via WAP:
Rm. 3059, North Bldg.,
330 Independence Ave., S.W.,
Washington, DC 20201.

Bantam Lecture Bureau
666 5 Ave.

(cont.) New York, NY 10019
212-245-8172
  Susan Siem, Mgr. Catalog has "Human Liberation" section with Ellen Frankfort, Brenda Feigen Fasteau, Alix Kates Shulman, Nora Ephron, Margaret Sloan, etc.

Barbara's Emblem Co.
19 Alamo Sq.
Alamo, CA 94507
  T-shirts.

Barnard Bartending Agency
Barnard College
New York, NY 10027
212-280-2035

Barnard College "Job Exchange"
606 W 120
New York, NY 10027
212-280-2034
  Ms. Lynn Stephens, Placement Office. Free service to Barnard students and alumnae; listings of 50 words or less.

Barton, Jane
c/o American Friends Service Committee, 160 N 15
Philadelphia, PA 19102
  Speaker re women in Asia. Has copies of film, "Women in Vietnam" (AFSC, 2450 Lake, San Francisco, CA 94121).

Bassin, Amelia
12 W 55
New York, NY 10019
212-541-9340
  Speaker with slides re consumerism. President of Bassinova, Inc. Re ads offensive to women.

Bauman, Suzanne
25 Grove
New York, NY 10014
  Filmmaker and source.

Bay Area Transportation Corp.
Grove Way
Hayward, CA 94541
415-582-0625
  Reasonably-priced bus services on charter or contract basis, licensed drivers.

Beahive
PO Box 87, Williamsbridge Sta.
Gun Hill Rd.
Bronx, NY 10467
  Bea Barron

Beare, Nikki & Associates, Inc.
7220 S.W. 61 Ct.
South Miami, FL 33143
305-666-9804
  Compiler of "Directory of Feminist Services"

Before We Are Six
c/o Dept. of Sociology, University of Waterloo
Waterloo, Ontario
  Publishes non-sexist children's books.

Behavioral Sciences Tape Library
240 Grand Ave.
Leonia, NJ 07601
  On reels or cassettes.

Bellamy, Blank, Goodman, Kelly, Ross & Stanley
36 W. 44
New York, NY 10036
212-869-0020
  Feminist all-women law firm. SEE ALSO Lefcourt, Kiraft & Libow. Carol Bellamy, Diane Blank, Janie Goodman, Mary Kelly, Susan Ross, Nancy Stanley.

Benton, Suzanne
22 Donnelly Dr.
Ridgefield, CT 06877
  Artist, speaker-performer. Coord. NOW National Women & Arts Task Force.

Directory of Sources

Berg Collection see New York Public Library

Berkeley Women's Health Collective
2214 Grove
Berkeley, CA 94704
414-843-6194

Best Friends
c/o Sharon Barba
513 Jefferson St., S.E.
Albuquerque, NM 87108
Literature source.

Betsy Hogan Associates see Hogan...

Betty Owen Secretarial Systems
630 3 Ave.
New York, NY 10017
"Women in Office Work" Compliance Project/N.O.W.

Bibliographic Information Center
2570 Sue Ave.
San Jose, CA 95111

Bibliothèque Féminine
Place du Panthéon
Paris 5, France
Marguerite Durand's library. Said to be the best source in France today of information about women.

Billings Coalition for Women's Rights
Jeanette Vargo
Billings, MT 59103
Interested in all women-- Chicana, Indian, White. SEE ALSO Poppler & Barz.

Birth Control and Problem Pregnancy Counseling and Referral
2330 Guadalupe, The Univ. "Y"
Austin, TX 78705
512-478-0452

Birth Control Handbook/VD Handbook Collective
PO Box 1000, Station G
Montreal 130, Quebec

Birth Control Information & Centers
515 Madison Ave.
New York, NY 10022
212-572-2100
Margaret Sanger Research Bureau: 17 W. 16, New York, NY 10011. 212-929-6100. Birth Control Information--New York City: 377 Broadway, 212-233-3100.

Black Widow Publications
PO Box 3062
Berkeley, CA 94703
(Bay Area publishers)

Black Women Employment Program
Southern Regional Council
52 Fairlie N.W.
Atlanta, GA 30303
404-522-8764

Black Women Organized for Action
680 Beach, Room 346
San Francisco, CA 94109
Aileen Hernandez, co-founder. SEE ALSO Sapphire Publishing Co.

Black Women's Employment Project, NAACP--LEF (Legal Defense and Educational Fund, Inc.)
10 Columbus Circle
New York, NY 10019
Research-education program headed by Jean Fairfax will pinpoint areas of discrimination in employment suitable for class-action suits.

Black Women's Institute
National Council of Negro Women, Inc.
1346 Conn. Ave., N.W.
Washington, DC 20036
202-223-2363

Black Women's Liberation Committee
346 W. 20
New York, NY 10011

Black World Foundation
PO Box 908
Sausalito, CA 94965
Non-profit educational organization publishing The Black Scholar: Journal of Black Studies & Research, which has had several issues devoted to the Black woman, e.g. March-April 1973.

Boccaccio, Shirley
468 Belvedere
San Francisco, CA 94117
Posters.

Book and Cranny
27 W. Cassilly
Springfield, OH 45504
Feminist bookstore.

Book & Tea Shop
746 24 Ave. E.
Eugene, OR 97405
504-344-3422

Books Canada, Inc.
35 E. 67 Jack Jense, Marketing Director, New York City
New York, NY 10021
212-861-0877
Order dept.--warehouse:
33 E. Tupper, Buffalo, NY 14203.

Books for Libraries
1 DuPont
Plainview, NY 11803
516-938-8100
"Women: Parts I & II" 1974 catalog of 700 facsimile reprints of out-of-print books.

The Bookworks
1409 5
Berkeley, CA 94710
Childbirth literature, e.g. Janet Brown's "Two births"

($3.95).

Boston Area Task Force Women in Libraries (WIL)
Carole Wilson, 24 Fulton
Medford, MA 02155
617-391-2846
Affiliated with SRRT (Social Responsibilities Round Table). Has AV, "Sex stereotypes in children's books."

Boston Assoc. for Childbirth Education
Box 29
Newtonville, MA 02160
Distributed for National Childbirth Trust and others in U.S.A.

Boston Women's Task Force (Media)
22 Stowell Rd., Annalee Bundy
Winchester, MA 01890

Boston Theological Institute. Women's Inst. & Placement Service
Ms. Jean L. Williams
45 Francis Ave.
Cambridge, MA 02138

Boyle Kirkman Associates, Inc.
1385 York Ave.
New York, NY 10022
Founded in 70's by Barbara Boyle to do affirmative action consulting.

Bra Shop
139 Hill   Clara Hardin
Ann Arbor, MI 48104
SEE ALSO Businesswomen's Crafts & Business Guild.

Brandon, Liane
19 Langley Rd.
Brighton, MA 02135
Filmmaker and source.
Also: 2 1/2 Douglas, Cambridge, MA 02139

Breakaway

Directory of Sources

(cont.) 2801 Ellsworth
Berkeley, CA 94705
415-845-8854
  Also: 434 66, Oakland
  94609. Women's Free
  School, CR. Newsletter

Breast Cancer Screening Centers:
(Most centers serve residents;
for visitors in New York City,
Dr. Philip Strax, 1056 Fifth
Ave., 10028--212-EN9-2720,
will arrange complete breast
examination at his office at a
reduced fee. He can also
provide information on other
locations. Strax is Med. Dir.,
Guttman Institute.)
FL: St. Vincent's Hospital,
1800 Barrs, Jacksonville,
32204, 904-389-7751.
GA: Emory University &
Georgia Baptist Hospital,
1365 Clifton Rd. N.E., Atlanta, 30322, 404-377-2411,
525-7861.
ID: Mountain States Tumor
Institute, 151 E. Bannock,
Boise, 83702, 208-345-1780.
KS: Kansas University Medical Center, Rainbow Blvd. @
39, Kansas City, 66103, 913-831-5000.
KY: University of Louisville
School of Medicine Health Sciences Center, Louisville,
40217, 502-582-2211.
NJ: New Jersey College of
Medicine & Dentistry, 100
Bergen, Newark 07103, 201-877-4300.
NY: Guttman Breast Diagnostic Inst., Inc., 200 Madison
Ave., New York, 10016, 212-689-9797, 8, 9.
OH: University of Cincinnati,
Eden & Bethesda Aves., Cincinnati, 45229, 513-475-8000.
OK: University of Oklahoma
Health Sciences Center, PO
Box 26901, Oklahoma City,
73190, 405-271-4000.
WA: Virginia Mason Hospital,
1111 Terry Ave., Seattle,
98101, 206-624-1144.
WI: ACS Breast Screening
Project, 8700 W. Wisconsin
Ave., Wauwatosa, 53226,
404-257-5200.

Brigham Young University
Dept. of Motion Picture Prod.
Provo, UT 84601

British Information Services
845 3 Ave.
New York, NY 10022
212-752-8400

Bro-Dart, Inc.
1609 Memorial Ave. (Eastern
  Division)
Williamsport, PA 17701
  Western Division: 15255 E.
  Don Julian Rd., City of Industry, CA 91749.

Bronx Community Abortion
  Clinic
Bronx Community Center for
  Women's Health
60 E. 208
Bronx, NY 10467
212-920-4086

Brooklyn College Library
Liberation Library, Room 225
Brooklyn, NY 11210
212-780-5652
  User-built collection includes
  material on WL, among
  other subjects.

Brother
PO Box 4387
Berkeley, CA 94704
  Men against sexism. Serial
  is Brother; a forum...

Browner, Jacqueline
Gehring Associates, 18 Goodnow
Jaffrey, NJ 03452

Bryant, Barbara
School of Social Work, California State University

(cont.) Sacramento, CA 95819
Conducting research on Lesbian mothers.

Bumper Rappings
PO Box 456
Albuquerque, NM 87103
"make your own" and stick-on's

Bumper Stickers
PO Box 10573
Denver, CO 80210
I am woman! More than LIB service! MS driver! More than BRA-vado.

Businesswomen's Crafts & Business Guild
139 Hill
Ann Arbor, MI 48104
313-665-7162

- C -

CBC Learning Systems
Box 500, Station A
Toronto M5W 1E6, Ontario
"CBC tapes, records, and publications of interest to women."

CMS Records
14 Warren
New York, NY 10007

CUNY Caucus on Status of Women
320 Central Park West, 8 G
New York, NY 10025
CUNY = City Univ. of New York. SEE ALSO SUNY Caucus....

Cable TV Information Center
2100 M St. N.W.
Washington, DC 20037
202-872-8888
Nonprofit center set up to help local groups deal with the new technology. Notes. For FCC Regulations on Cable, contact FCC, Washington, DC 20554.

Caedmon Records, Inc.
505 8 Ave.
New York, NY 10018
212-594-3122

Calgary Birth Control Assoc.
223 12 Ave. N.W.
Calgary, Alberta
403-261-9821

California Committee for Sexual Law Reform
4040 13 Ave
Sacramento, CA 95820

Calif. Conference on Abortion
Box 526
Ross, CA 94956

Calif. State Dept. of Corrections
814 P St., Personnel Dept.
Sacramento, CA 95814
Employs women as guards ("correctional officers") in state prison system; must be 20-35, high school graduate; have 2 years' full-time paid working experience; emotionally mature, understand people under discipline, able to relate to prisoners; knowledge of firearms; and undergo 9-month trial period of supervision!

Calif. University
Extension Media Center
Berkeley, CA 94720
Rents, sells motion pictures. "Films 1973-1974" catalog. DonnaLee Smith, Sales Manager and member of editorial staff for bulletin; Elizabeth Buck, Rosia Davis, and Rosalinda DeVera are film reservation clerks.

Calif. Univ.
University Extension, 2223 Fulton

Directory of Sources

(cont.) Berkeley, CA 94720
Maria DelDrago, Coord.,
Continuing Education Programs for Women.

Calif. Univ., Los Angeles
Graduate Women in History
Los Angeles, CA 90024

Calif. Univ., Los Angeles
Manpower Research Center,
Institute of Industrial Relations
Los Angeles, CA 90024

Calif. V.D. Information
toll-free: 800-282-4896

"Call Me Ms." see Gellis, Audrey

CANADA. The ff. are individuals/organizations relevant to feminists which are not listed either in the Women's Liberation groups, which follows the "Directory of Sources" or among the Status of Women commissions within these "Sources."
Alberta Women's Bureau, Government of Alberta, 204 Legislative Building, Edmonton 6, Alberta, Catharine Arthur, Dir.
British Columbia Dept. of Labour, Women's Bureau, 411 Dunsmuir, Vancouver 3, British Columbia, Ms. C.K. Waddell, Dir.
Manitoba Dept. of Labour. Women's Bureau, 618 Norquay Building, Winnipeg, Manitoba R3C OP8, Mary Eadie, Dir.
New Brunswick: Gwen Black, Canadian Federation of University Women, PO Box 68, Sackville, NB. Marjorie Laws, Business & Professional Women's Club, 595 Shediac Rd., Muncton, NB.
Prof. Nancy Cook, Dept. of Economics, University of NB, Fredericton, NB. Lynda Gaw, Y.W.C.A., 2F Wellington Row, St. John, NB.
Nova Scotia: Halifax Women's Bureau, PO Box 3596, Halifax S. Postal Station, NS.
Margaret Colpitts, Provincial Council of Women, 72 Shore Dr., Bedford, NS.
Muriel Duckworth, Voice of Women/La Voix des Femmes, 6250 South St., Halifax, NS.
Mary Cutler, PO Box 1766, Antigonish, NS.
Dr. Lois Vallely, Dept. of History, Adadia University, Wolfville, NS.
Linda Bergstrom, 2915 Somerset Ave., Halifax, NS.
Ontario Ministry of Labour, Women's Bureau, 400 University Ave., Toronto.
La Voix des Femmes/ Voice of Women, 1554 Yonge St., Toronto 7, Ont.
Hon. John C. Munro, Minister Responsible for the Status of Women, House of Commons, Ottawa, Ont.
Québec: La Fédération des Femmes du Québec, Caroline Pestieau, 718 du Bocage, Pierrefonds.
Saskatchewan Dept. of Labour, Women's Bureau, Administration Building, Regina, Saskatchewan, Mary Rocan, Supervisor.
SEE ALSO: Entries throughout the "Directory of Sources," e.g. "International Women's Year."

Canadian American Women's Assoc.
40 Howe, c/o Dr. May Hall

(cont.) James
New Haven, CT 06511

Canadian Filmmaker's Distribution Centre
406 Jarvis
Toronto, Ontario M4Y 2G6
416-921-2259
"Films By Women," 15p catalog. Contact Kathryne Wing. Non-profit, educational corp. renting-selling.

Canadian Library Assoc. Task Force on the Status of Women
Dr. Sheila Bertram
School of Library Service
University of Alberta
Edmonton, Alberta T6G 2E1

Canadian Women's Educational Press
280 Bloor St., West, Suite 305
Toronto, Ontario
416-962-3904
"Women unite!" anthology of Canadian Women's Movement ($3.00); "The day care book" ($1.50); "Mandy and the flying map" non-sexist book; "Born a woman; the Rita MacNeil songbook."

Cancer Society of America
44 E. 53
New York, NY 10022
212-759-3500

Canyon Cinema Co-op.
Industrial Center Bldg., Rm. 220
Sausalito, CA 94965
415-332-1514

Card, Emily Watts
988 Noria
Laguna Beach, CA 92651
714-494-8331

Career Counseling for Women
755 New York Ave.
Huntington, NY 11743
516-421-1948

Career Planning Center
1623 S. LaCienga
LaCienga, CA 90035
Slide shows, audio cassettes on new careers, for guidance work.

Carnegie Library of Pittsburgh
C. C. Mellon Collection
Pittsburgh, PA 15230

Cassette House, Inc.
1030 E. Northwest Hwy.
Mt. Prospect, IL 60056

Catalyst
14 E. 60th St.
New York, NY 10022
212-759-9700
Barbara Jordan Moore, Dir. of Publications and PR. Contributions tax-deductible. Emily Rosenthal, Roster coord. "National non-profit organization that helps expand career opportunities for college educated women."

Catholic Women for the ERA
5545 Dunning Pl.
Cincinnati, OH 45227
Charlene Ventura, Spokeswoman.

Catholics for a Free Choice
140 E. 76
New York, NY 10021
New York State group; members organize nationally in defense of Supreme Court abortion decision and to counter 'right-to-life' forces. Pat Fogarty McQuillan, chairwoman.

Catholics for the ERA
1225 N. Bend Rd.
Cincinnati, OH 45524
Charlene Ventura, National Coordinator.

Caucus of Women Biophysicists
Julia Apter, Rush Medical

Directory of Sources

(cont.) College
1753 W. Congress Pky.
Chicago, IL 60612
   Has employment roster.

Cee-Jay Enterprises
6520 S.W. 45
Miami, FL 33155
   Graphics, jewelry. Tampa
   NOW has incorporated with
   Cee-Jay.

Cell 16
2 Brewer
Cambridge, MA 02138
   "No more fun and games...."
   Posters.

Center for a Woman's Own Name
261 Kimberley
Barrington, IL 60010
   "Booklet for women who wish
   to determine their own names
   after marriage" ($2). SEE
   ALSO Una Stannard's "Married women vs. husbands'
   names; the case for wives
   who keep their own names,"
   #470 in Basic Book Collection.

Center for Cassette Studies
8110 Webb Ave.
North Hollywood, CA 91605
213-768-5040

Center for Feminist Art Historical Studies
c/o Ruth Iskin and Arlene Raven
8330 Willis Ave.
Panorama City, CA 91402
213-994-8025

Center for Public Financing of
   Elections
201 Massachusetts Ave. N.E.
Washington, DC 20002

Center for the American Woman
   and Politics see Eagleton
   Institute...

Center for the Study of Democratic Institutions
The Fund for the Republic,
   Inc.
PO Box 4446
Santa Barbara, CA 93103

Center for the Study
   of Women in Higher
   Education & the Professions
Carolyn M. Elliott, Director
Wellesley College
Wellesley, MA 02181
617-235-0320

Center for the Study of Women
   in Society
4339 California,
San Francisco, CA 94118
415-752-7180

Center for Woman's Own Name
   see Center for a Woman's
   Own Name

Center for Women & Sport
Sports Research Institute. College for Health, Physical
   Education & Recreation,
   White Building
University Park, PA 16802
   Dorothy V. Harris, dir.

Center for Women Policy Studies
2000 P St. N.W., Suite 508
Washington, DC 20036
202-862-1770
   Jane Roberts Chapman, Margaret Jane Gates, attorney.
   "Equal employment opportunity and affirmative action
   for women; a selected bibliography" ($.50). J. Margaret Gates' "Statement Before the Advisory Council on
   the Status of Women re women in the military" ($.50).

Center for Women's Studies &
   Services
908 F
San Diego, CA 92101
   Will provide information/

(cont.) assistance in setting up similar centers. Has pamphlets.

Central Committee of Correspondence
3226 Powelton Ave.
Philadelphia, PA 19104
"Mailing List of Movement Organizations, 8th ed., rev." Oct. 1973 ($1). Also available on gummed labels ($3).

Central Hall Artists Gallery
402 Main
Port Washington, NY 11050

Central International
121 W. Santa Fe Ave.
Placentia, CA 92670
General counseling and referrals, gay and straight.

Centron Educational Films
1621 W. 9
Lawrence, KS 66044
913-843-0400

"Changing Woman"
Contemporary Features, Box 404
Chappaqua, NY 10514
Feminist column.

Checkers Enterprises
Box 8051F
St. Louis, MO 63108
Movement bumper stickers. Buttons.

Cheda, Sherrill
Seneca College of Applied Arts & Technology Library
1750 Finch Ave. E.
Willowdale 428, Ontario
491-5050
Librarian, active member of Canadian Library Assoc. Task Force on Status of Women. Feminist speaker: sex role stereotyping, radical feminism, women in librarianship, women in literature. Women's Studies expertise. Author.

Chelsea Picture Station, New York City see motion picture, "Women's happy time commune."

Chicago Economic Development Corp.
162 N. State, Suite 600. Women's Division
Chicago, IL 60601

Chicago, Judy see Womanhouse. An artist who in 1970 started class exclusively for women, at Fresno State College; moved to California Institute of the Arts in Valencia, joined forces with painter Miriam Schapiro to produce another feminist arts program, transformed building into Womanhouse. With Arlene Raven opening Feminist Studio Workshop.

Chicago Women Against Rape
Founded by Kathleen Thompson (co-author of "Against Rape." SEE #491 Basic Book Collection).

Chicago Women in Publishing
201 E. Walton, Suite 301
Chicago, IL 60611

Chicago Women's Liberation Union
852 W. Belmont Ave.
Chicago, IL 60557
312-348-2011
Large number of pamphlets, reprints, buttons, posters, periodicals; write them for catalog or see list in "Alternatives in Print."

Chicana Service Action Center
435 S. Boyle Ave.
Los Angeles, CA 90033
213-268-4141

Directory of Sources

(cont.) A service organization, established as a demonstration project by the Comisión Femenil Mexicana.

Chicana Welfare Rights Organization
A committee of the Chicana Service Action Center. SEE ALSO National Chicana Welfare Rights Organization.

Chicano Library and Education Researchers
1300 S. Wabash Ave.
Chicago, IL 60605
312-427-7080

Chicano Training Center & The Mexican Training Institute of Research and Training
3520 Montrose, Suite 215
Houston, TX 77006
  Serial, Mano a mano. A non-profit educational corporation.

Child and Parent Action (CAPA)
Contact at 2299 Market
San Francisco, CA 94114
  Pressure group: 200 people. Patricia Crawford, spokesperson.

Childbirth Education Assoc.
5340 Colfax Ave. S.
Minneapolis, MN 55419
612-825-2600
  9AM-7PM. Film rental phone #: 612-881-9194. Twin Cities area.

Children's Cultural Foundation
325 E. 57
New York, NY 10022
  Holly Hartley.

Children's Liberation Workshop
PO Box 207
Ancaster, Ontario

Children's Television Workshop
1 Lincoln Plaza
New York, NY 10023
Joan Ganz Cooney, president.
Children's Television Workshop Newsletter.

Child's Play
256 Atlantic Ave.
Brooklyn, NY 11201
212-237-2656
  Bookstore featuring nonsexist children's books for all ages. Mail order catalog, discount for schools.

Christian Women's Fellowship
222 S. Downey Ave.
Indianapolis, IN 46219

Church Women United
Box 134, Manhattanville Station
New York, NY 10027
  Packets: "The woman packet" ($1.50), "Women exploring theology" ($2). Order from Service Center. Also 1239 Vermont Ave. N.W., Washington, DC 20005.

Church Women's Collective
5821 Harrison, Marcella Womack
Kansas City, MO 64110

Cinema Feminina
New Feminist Talent
250 W. 57, Kristina Nordstrom
New York, NY 10019

Cinesound
1037 N. LaBrea Ave.
Los Angeles, CA 90028

Cisler, Lucinda
PO Box 240, Planetarium Sta.
New York, NY 10024
212-799-0620
  Has long list of literature available, buttons, postal/note cards. "Women; a bibliography, latest rev." ($.50 + postage).

Citizens for Abortion Rights and Religious Liberty

(cont.) 84 5 Ave., Room 300
New York, NY 10011

Citizens' Stamp Advisory Committee
U.S. Postal Service
Washington, DC 20260
  Action for commemorative stamps honoring women.

Civic Education Services
1725 K St. N.W., #1009
Washington, DC 20006

Clay, Vidal S.
8 Sturges Commons
Westport, CT 06880
  Menopause information.

Clearinghouse for Feminist Media
PO Box 207
Ancaster, Ontario
  Annual membership $1 for complete listing of feminists in media and feminist media in Canada; also has quarterly list of people writing/publishing feminist work or working for other media in that field.

Clearinghouse for Library and Information Sciences of the Educational Resources Information Center (ERIC/CLIS)
  Recently became NIE Clearinghouse on Information Resources. Contact ERIC.

Clearinghouse on Women's Issues
2401 Virginia Ave. N.W.
American Assoc. of University Women
Washington, DC 20037

Clearinghouse on Women's Studies
Box 334
Old Westbury, NY 11568
  Women's Studies Newsletter. An education project of the Feminist Press.

Cleveland Women Artists
11420 Fairchild Ave., #2,
  Karen Eubel
Cleveland, OH 44106
216-231-3595

Clitartists
1321 A Alcatraz
Berkeley, CA 94702
  Feminist art collective and studio. Posters. CR. Small exhibits. SEE ALSO Group One.

Club of Printing Women of New York
PO Box 5343, Grand Central Sta.
New York, NY 10017

Coalition for Freedom of Choice of San José
1119 El Prado Dr., c/o Diane Wisner
San Jose, CA 95120
  Coalition wrote, performed "Abortion Morality Play." NOW, Planned Parenthood, Zero Population Growth and other groups.

Coalition of Labor Union Women
(1:) 4859 S. Wabash, c/o Addie Wyatt
Chicago, IL 60615
(2:) 8731 E. Jefferson Ave
Detroit, MI 43214
313-926-524

Coalition of 100 Black Women
c/o Ms. Evelyn Payne Davis
Children's TV Workshop
1 Lincoln Plaza
New York, NY 10023
  Concentration on investigation of facilities used to house juvenile offenders, establishment of committee to study adoption procedure of Black children.

Coalition of Professional Organizations

Directory of Sources 317

(cont.) c/o Dr. Julia Apter
Rush Medical College
1753 W. Congress Pkwy.
Chicago, IL 60612
 Coalition = Assoc. of Women in Science, Assoc. of Women in Mathematics, Assoc. of Women in Psychology, Caucus of Women Biophysicists, NOW, Sociologists for Women in Society, and others. Have joint suit against National Institutes of Health.

Coalition of Women in Educational Sports Organizations
Rose Millevolte
c/o Memorial Junior High School
Valley Stream, NY 11582

Colorado Coalition of Women & Minorities
c/o Denver Chapter of NOW:
Jane Pechman
1289 Newark
Denver, CO 80010
 Denver NOW Chapter, Colorado Committee on Mass Media and the Spanish-Surnamed, Inc., Sundiata, Inc., Mass Media Task Force, etc.

Colorado Woman's College
Permelia Curtis Porter Library
7055 E. 18 Ave.
Denver, CO 80220

Come On In Shop
311 Columbus Ave.
New York, NY 10001
212-799-8243
 Between 74 and 75 Streets. Owned and operated by feminists.

Comisión Femenil Mexicana
4721 E. Olympic Blvd.
Los Angeles, CA 90022
 Established Chicana Service Action Center as demonstration project.

Commissions, committees, etc.

on STATUS of women see STATUS OF WOMEN

Commission on the Status and Role of Women of the United Methodist Church
2121 Sheridan Rd.
Evanston, IL 60201
 Permanent office location. Supports ERA.

Committee for Fair Divorce and Alimony Laws
509 5 Ave.
New York, NY 10017

Committee of Correspondence
345 E. 46
New York, NY 10017
 Bulletin. Not a membership organization.

Committee to Bring About Equal Opportunity in Athletics
University of Michigan
 Contact Marcia Federbush, Coord. for Committee, 39 Einstein Dr., Princeton, NJ 08540.

Committee to Defend the Right to Learn
210 W. 89
New York, NY 10024

Communications Network: Feminist Gynecological Self-Help Clinics of America
see The Monthly Extract, New Moon Communications, Inc., and Feminist Women's Health Centers, Inc.

Communications Workers of America
7460 N. Sheridan Rd.
Helga Nisbet
Chicago, IL 60626

Community Bookstore
2028 P St. N.W.
Washington, DC 20036

Community of Women
359 E. 68
New York, NY 10021

Community Sex Information
New York City
212-867-9044

Concilio Mujeres
2588 Mission, #201
Dorinda Moreno
San Francisco, CA 94110
415-826-1530, 755-6062 messages
 La razón Mestiza, newsletter.
 A Center for collecting and
 distributing cultural and educational materials which focus on Spanish-speaking women. Part of Raza Communications Network. Bibliog. ($2)

Conferencia Femenil: Bilingual women's conference held March 1973
 For information: Marian Lozano, Mexican-American Education, Sacramento State College, Sacramento, CA 94132.

Congress of Women's Organizations
Virginia
 Supports ERA.

Congressional Suffrage Union
 Split from NAWSA--emulated British sisters, holding vigils at the White House, picketing. Went to jail and on hunger strikes. Were force-fed, bringing new publicity and spirit to The Cause. Circa 1913.

Connecticut College Library
New London, CT 06320
 Collection has emphasis upon women in the state.

Connecticut Feminist Federal Credit Union
New Haven, CT
 c/o NOW or New Haven Women's Center. Susan Osborne, Karen Wynn, co-managers.

Connecticut Films, Inc.
6 Cobble Hill Rd.
Westport, CT 06880
203-227-2960

Connecticut Women in Library Science (CWILS)
c/o Gretchen Hammerstein
Toad Ridge Rd.
Middlefield, CT 06455
203-349-3135
 Has Newsletter. SRRT Affiliate.

Connecticut Women's Legal & Educational Fund
c/o K. Roth, 5 Hughes Pl.
New Haven, CT 06511

Conroy, Mary, EdD.
c/o Dept. of Physical Education
California State University
5151 State University Dr.
Los Angeles, CA 90032
 Resource person for workshops, courses, programs, clinics, personal defense. Her pamphlet, "Personal Defense for Women" under Athletics....

Consumer Cooperative Publishing Assoc.
4294 Wilkie Wy.
c/o Morris Lippman, apt. G
Palo Alto, CA 94306

Consumer Product Information
Washington, DC 20407

"Contact"
c/o Pat Adams, 1270 Sixth Ave.
New York, NY 10020
 NOW monthly columns reaching 100,000 Black readers.

Contemporary/McGraw-Hill Films

Directory of Sources

(cont.) 1221 6 Ave.
New York, NY 10020

Continuing Education for Women
   Workshop
George Washington University
2130 H St. N.W.
Washington, DC 20006

Controlled Parenthood
730 Hennepin Ave., Suite 507
Minneapolis, MN 55403
612-336-7797
   Nonprofit abortion referral
   service with offices in most
   major cities.

Cooperative College Registry
1 DuPont Circle N.W., Suite 10
Washington, DC 20036
202-223-2807
   Tena Cummings, Executive
   Officer.

Corea, Gena
c/o New Republic Feature
   Syndicate
1244 19 St. N.W.
Washington, DC 20035
202-331-7494
   Her "Frankly Feminist" is
   "first national weekly feminist column." 700-word
   weekly.

Cornell University
College of Arts & Sciences
Ithaca, NY 14850
   Women's Studies.

Council for University Women's
   Progress
University of Minnesota
68 Morrill Hall
Minneapolis, MN 55455
   News Service

Council of Women Citizens
322 S. Michigan Ave., Suite 440
Chicago, IL 60604

Council on Interracial Books
   for Children

1841 Broadway
New York, NY 10023

Council on the Status of Women
2130 Highland
Helena, MT 59701
   Natalie Cannon, co-chairwo-
   man.

Counseling Program for Gay
   Individuals and Couples and
   Families of Gay Men and
   Women
Los Angeles, CA
213-654-2420

Country Women
Box 51
Albion, CA 95410
   Working collective of six
   farms in Mendocino County,
   20 women. Magazine of
   same title.

Country Women's Council, U.S.A.
Greene Acres
Tutwiler, MS 38963
   Also: 307 N. Fulton, Keota,
   IA 52248.

Cox, Nell
150 W. 87
New York, NY 10024
   Filmmaker and source.

Coyote, San Francisco
   Prostitutes' action group,
   founded by Margo St. James,
   SEE Ms. Dec. 1973:17.
   Membership includes men
   and women of other occupations.

Craft Collective
406 1/2 Shirley Pl.
Beverley Hills, CA 90212

Creative Film Society
7237 Canby Ave.
Reseda, CA 91335
213-882-3887
   Teri Johnson, Dir. of sales.

Creative Funding
PO Box 19007
Oakland, CA 94619

Creative Women's Collective
250 W. 27
New York, NY 10001
  Workshops, silk-screen, etc.

Credit Women--International
2051 Railway Exchange Building
St. Louis, MO 63101
  Also: 611 Olive St.

Cronk, Caren
21250 Almar Dr.
Shaker Heights, OH 44122
  "It's all the same," play
  ($25-$35).

Crossing Press
Trumansburg, NY 14886
  John & Elaine Gill. Publishing house: Elaine Gill's
  "Mountain moving day..."
  ($3.95/pap), etc.

Culver, Cassee
  Feminist singer, musician, songwriter. For bookings:
  M. Spottswood, her womanger.
  217-12 St. S.E., Washington,
  DC. 202-547-5878.

Current Affairs
24 Danbury Rd.
Wilton, CT 06897

Current Affairs Films
527 Madison Ave.
New York, NY 10022

Cyclops Films, Inc.
1697 Broadway
New York, NY 10019
212-265-1375
  Claudia Weill, co-owner, of this independent film company.

- D -

D.C. Family Medical Center,
Inc.
919 18 St. N.W., Suite 121
Washington, DC 20006
202-785-3581, 3650; 833-3814, 3
  Contraception, abortion.

DES Information:
From: Robin Goodman
115 Jones Rd.
Englewood, NJ 07631

Dabney Co.
Box 31061-
Washington, DC 20031
  Old and new books on feminism and women.

Daly, Mary, PhD.
2018 Commonwealth Ave.
Brighton, MA 02135
  Business address: Boston College, Chestnut Hill, MA 02167, 617-969-0100, 787-3498.
  Speaker ($500 + expenses).
  Resource person in area of women and religion. (SEE #'s 25 and 362, Basic Book Collection.) Women's Studies.

Dartmouth Women's Caucus and Women's Center
Hanover, NH 03755
  Contact B. Hirschfeld re motion picture about their experience.

Data Bank of Information on Black [male and female] Librarians
Atlanta University
Atlanta, GA 30314

Daughters, Inc.
Plainfield, VT 05667
  Publisher of women's novels.
  Parke Bowman, June Arnold, Loretta Li. $3 paperbacks of 1974: Blanche M. Boyd's "Nerves," Pat Burch's "Early losses," Rita Mae Brown's "Rubyfruit jungle,"

Directory of Sources

(cont.) The Carpenter's "The cook and the carpenter," and Selma Lagerlof's "The treasure." See BBC.

Daughters of Bilitis; some examples of groups:
1910 S. Vermont, Los Angeles, CA 90007, 213-737-9159.
1005 Market, #208, San Francisco, CA 94103.
419 Boylston, Room 406, Boston, MA 02116, Focus; journal....
PO Box 244, Greenfield Station, Dearborn, MI 48126.
PO Box 62, Fanwood, NJ 07023, Lazette.
PO Box 5944, Dallas, TX 75222.

Davall, Irene
311 W. 24
New York, NY 10011
  Writer of column, "The Liberated Woman," and publisher of The Feminist Party News.

Davis, Dunlap & Williams
422 Turk
San Francisco, CA 94102
415-441-2618
  All-woman law firm.

Davis, Enid
1050 Newell Rd.
Palo Alto, CA 94303
  Speaker. Consultant. Resource person on sexism in kid-lit, children's librarian, story-telling expert. SEE SEXISM IN EDUCATION & MEDIA Pamphlets.

Day Care Council of America
1401 K St. N.W.
Washington, DC 20005
  List of publications issued by the Council and free from them.

University of Dayton

Albert Emanuel Library
Dayton, OH 45469

Deaconess Movement
1610 Vermont, Jeanne Barnes
Quincy, IL 62301

Defense Advisory Committee on Women in the Services
The Pentagon, Room 3D281
Washington, DC 20301
202-695-5153

Deitch, Donna
413 Howland Canal
Venice, CA 90291
  Filmmaker, source.

Del-Em
  Menstrual Extraction Kit, Lorraine Rothman, developer.
  Contact: New Moon.

Delos Records, Inc.
855 Via de la Paz
Pacific Palisades, CA 90272
  "A woman-managed company."

Delta Kappa Gamma Society, Internatl.
PO Box 1589
Austin, TX 78767
  Also. 416 W. 12

Delta Sigma Theta
1814 M St. N.W.
Washington, DC 20036
202-338-7727
  Black sorority-service group; some placement referrals.

Delta Women's Clinic
1406 St. Charles Ave.
New Orleans, LA 70130
  Contact C. Jackson, MD, 504-581-2250.

Democratic National Committee, Office of Women's Activities
2600 Virginia Ave. N.W.
Washington, DC 20037

Denver Feminist Bookstore

(cont.) 673 S. Pearl
Denver, CO 80209
  Free catalog, "The woman's voice."

DePauw, Linda Grant
c/o G. Washington University
Washington, DC 20006
  Operating a clearinghouse of American women in the Revolutionary Era as part of Bicentennial.

Dial-A-Bill Telephone Hot Line
Washington, DC
202-225-1772
  Provides information on bills going through legislature; you must be able to quote the #, author, or subject.

Diana Press, Inc.
12 W. 25
Baltimore, MD 21218

Dickson-Macagno, Deborah
310 W. 88
New York, NY 10024
  Filmmaker, source.

Distaffers, Inc.
1130 Western Savings Fund Building
Philadelphia, PA 19107
215-732-6666
  Experimental private employment service placing professional women.

Distaffers Research & Counseling Center, Inc.
3928 Legation St. N.W.
Washington, DC 20015
  "Career Planning for Women" ($1.50), extracted from their handbook has been used for college workshops.

Diuguid Fellowships; A Developmental Program for Mature Women
Council of Southern Universities, Inc.

795 Peachtree N.E., Suite 484
Atlanta, GA 30308
404-874-4891
  For residents of the South.

Divorce Anonymous
2704 N. Sawyer Ave.
Chicago, IL 60647

Doubleday Multimedia
Box 11607, 1371 Reynolds Ave.
Santa Ana, CA 92705

Douglas, Helen Gahagan Papers (Library)
DeEtte Turner (student)
University of Oklahoma, Graduate School
Norman, OK 73069

Dowd, Nancy Ellen
PO Box 523
2708 Topanga Skyline
Topanga, CA 90290
  Filmmaker, source.

Drucker, Robert & Co.
10718 Riverside Dr.
N. Hollywood, CA 91602
  AV Source.

Dyal, Susan
107 Rose Ave.
Venice, CA 90291
  Filmmaker, source.

- E -

EEOC see U.S. E.E.O.C.

ERA Enterprises
(1:) Box 1301 Capitol Hill
Seattle, WA 98112
(2:) PO Box 1280
Bellevue, WA 98009
  AV, labels, jewelry, etc.

ERIC see Educational Resources Information Center...

Ealing Corp.
2225 Mass. Ave.
Cambridge, MA 02140

Earth Onion:
Women's Theater Collective
Washington, DC
   Contact Lynn at 202-323-6174. Has workshops.

East Fifth Street Group
330 E. 5
New York, NY 10003

Eastport House
Eastport, ME 04631
207-853-9567
   For individuals or groups.

Eccentric Circle Cinema Workshop
Box 1481
Evanston, IL 60204

Economic Think-Tank for Women
Center for Policy Research
475 Riverside Dr.
New York, NY 10027
   Brainchild of Betty Friedan.

Ecumenical Task Force on Women & Religion (Catholic Caucus)
   Supports ERA.

Ecumenical Women's Centers
1653 W. School
Chicago, IL 60657
   Judy Thomas. Conferences.

Education Commission of the States
Women's Task Force
1800 Lincoln
Denver, CO 80203
   Task Force head, Constance Cook, Coy Glen Road, Ithaca, NY 14850.

Education Task Forces
424 Pelham Manor Rd.
Pelham Manor, NY 10803
   Of Westchester Professional Women's Caucus, South Westchester County NOW. Distributes "What can they be?"

Educational Activities, Inc.
1937 N. Grand Ave.
Baldwin, NY 11510
516-868-7460
   Norma Harris, Vice President.

Educational Day Care Services Assoc.
11 Day
Cambridge, MA 02140

Educational Foundation for Human Sexuality
Montclair State College
Upper Montclair, NJ 07043

Educational Resources Information Center (ERIC)
National Institute of Education (NIE)
Washington, DC 20202
   ERIC Processing & Reference Facility, 4833 Rugby Ave., Suite 303, Bethesda, MD 20014. Product information: 301-588-6180.

Effie's Book Series see Two Windows Press

Elizabeth Blackwell Women's Clinic
Blackwell Brigade. Contact: 1409 E. Maplewood
Bellingham, WA 98225
206-733-6344

Elizabeth Blackwell Women's Health Center
2000 S. 5
Minneapolis, MN 55404
612-335-7669

Elizabeth Cady Stanton Publishing Co.
5857 Marbury Rd.
Bethesda, MD 20034
301-229-7067

Elmira College. Hamilton Library
Washington & College Aves.

(cont.) Elmira, NY 14201
  Anne J. Morse, Special Collections Curator.

"The emerging woman in management; a confidence and skills-building workshop for women." Response & Assocs.
PO Box 333
Chicago Heights, IL 60411
312-758-4600

Emma Goldman Clinic for Women
715 N. Dodge
Iowa City, IA 52240
319-338-3289

Emma Goldman English Women
3694 Ste. Famillie
Montreal 130, Quebec

Emma Willard Task Force on Education
Box 14229, University Station
Minneapolis, MN 55414
612-333-9076
  Speakers, workshops, packet.

Emory University School of Medicine
Dept. of Gynecology & Obstetrics
69 Butler St. S.E.
Atlanta, GA 30303
  Family Planning Program.

En tant que femmes ... as women
National Film Board of Canada
PO Box 6100
Montréal 101, Quebec
  A Société Nouvelle Project by and for Women in the employ of the NFB. Challenge for Change/Société Nouvelle is an experimental program established by the Canadian Government.

Episcopal Churchwomen of the Diocese of New York. Committee of the Episcopal Churchwomen, Synod House
Cathedral of St. John the Divine
Amsterdam Ave. at 110
New York, NY 10025

Employher
Women's Center
286 Washington Blvd.
Oswego, NY 13126

Equal Rights Amendment Ratification Council
c/o Mary Gereau
1201 16 St. N.W., N.E.A.
Washington, DC 20036

Equal Rights Assoc.
960 Hall Ave
W. St. Paul, MN 55118

Equal Rights for Indian Women
c/o Celia Dare, 60 Stirling Ave.
LaSalle, Quebec
514-366-0019

Equality products
3014M Falmouth, Shirley Spalding
Louisville, KY 40205
  Stickers.

Equation Collection
PO Box 4307
Sunnyside, NY 11104
  "Feminist alternative to Avon."

Erewhon Books
PO Box 2807, Station A
Edmonton, Alberta
403-429-1887

Essex Institute Library
132-134 Essex
Salem, MA 01970
  Primarily non-circulating Salem witchcraft, including manuscripts.

Eugenics Society
69 Eccleston Sq.
London 01-838-3902
  Madeleine Simms headed abortion group for several

Directory of Sources 325

(cont.) years, now evaluating program.

Everywoman Feminist Book Service
7426 Orion Ave.
Van Nuys, CA 91406
  Nonsexist children's books, posters, jewelry.

Everywoman's Center see MA: Amherst

Ezrat Nashim
Apt. 2B, 250 W. 76
New York, NY 10025
  New York-based Jewish feminist organization which publicizes women's issues within the Jewish community.

- F -

FLIRT
2231 N.E. 34 Ct.
Lighthouse Point, FL 33064
  Samantha Potter. Female Liberationists for International Rights & Territories.

FMG Productions
49 E. 86
New York, NY 10020
  Frances McLaughlin-Gill, filmmaker, source.

Falling Wall Press
79 Richmond Rd.
Montpelier, Bristol BS6 5EP
  England
  "Women in industry" and other publications.

Family Medical Center, Inc.
919 18 St. N.W., Suite 121
Washington, DC 20006
202-785-3581, 3650

Family Planning Clinics
St. Paul Bureau of Health
555 Cedar
St. Paul, MN 55101

612-227-7741
  Contraception, vasectomy. Morning-after pill.

Family Planning Council of Western Mass.
16 Center
Northampton, MA 01060

Family Planning Information Service, Inc.
300 Park Ave. S.
New York, NY 10010
212-777-2015

Family Synergy
PO Box 30103, Terminal Annex
Los Angeles, CA 90030
213-324-3465
  Group advocating lifestyle alternatives, chiefly to monogamous marriage, for women and men.

The Family Tree
1599 Selby Ave.
St. Paul, MN 55104
612-645-0478
  VD clinic, Contraception, Abortion referral. Phone.

The Family Tree
Austin, TX
  Write c/o Ms., 370 Lexington Ave., New York, NY 10017. Robin and Joyce & their 4 children.

Fantastic Womanhood!
Winone Publishing Guild
Rt. 1, Box 71F
Plano, TX 75074
  A countercourse to Fascinating Womanhood. CR. Includes evidence revealing Christ as feminist ($3/pap).

Farians, Elizabeth, PhD.
6125 Webbland Pl.
Cincinnati, OH 45213
513-531-0393
  Buttons, Women's Studies, Literature. Religion resource person.

Farrell, Warren
Apt. 617, Crystal Plaza S.
2111 Jef. Davis Hwy.
Arlington, VA 22202

Fasteau, Brenda & Marc Feigen
5 Tudor City Pl.
New York, NY 10017
212-986-5177, 2400
  Feminist attorneys, speakers.

Feature & News
333 N. Michigan
Chicago, IL 60601
312-346-7037
  Colleen Dishon, editor.

Federal Aviation Administration
Kathy Vitek, Federal Women's
  Program Coordinator
Dept. of Transportation
Washington, DC 20591

Federal Communications Commission
1919 M St. N.W.
Washington, DC 20554

Federal Information Centers
General Services Administration/
U.S. Civil Service Commission joint venture
Washington, DC 20405
  "Federal Information Center" brochure lists. GSA DC 73-12648. For telephone-information especially; referrals also made. Non-English-speaking assistants. Often have state-local government information too. In 35 states.

Federal Trade Commission
Bureau of Consumer Protection
Washington, DC 20580

Federal Women's Program, U.S.
  Civil Service Commission
1900 E St. N.W.
Washington, DC 20415
  Helen S. Markoff, Dir. Federal Women's Program Speakers' List. Also: Mildred Marcy, at USIA, D.C. 20547.

Federation of American Women's Clubs
18 Avenue Kleber
75 Paris 16º, France

Federation of Jewish Women's Organizations
55 W. 42
New York, NY 10036
212-736-0240

Federation of Organizations for Professional Women
828 Washington
Wellesley, MA 02181
617-235-8624
  Has Roster, Clearinghouse.

Federation of Women's Organizations
  Phone Joyce in San Diego:
  714-295-5269

Feferman, Lind
42 Grove, Apt. 25
New York, NY 10014
  Filmmaker

Feldhaus-Weber, Mary
125 Western Ave.
Boston, MA 02134
  Filmmaker.

Fell Press
386 Park Ave. S.
New York, NY 10016
  "Natural childbirth of Tara," by Phillip and Ellen Thomas.

Female Liberation
639 Mass. Ave.
Cambridge, MA 02139
617-491-1071
  Tapes.

Female Revolutionary Front
62 Pleasant, Apt. 2
Cambridge, MA 02139

Femedia

Directory of Sources

(cont.) 2286 Great Hwy.
San Francisco, CA 94116

Feminist Airlines Project
c/o Lee Walker, 414 E. 52
New York, NY 10022
    Send tickets bearing your name, canceled or stubs (SEE Ms. July 1973:21).

Feminist Arts Program
California Institute of the Arts
Valencia, CA 91355

Feminist Astrologers
Box 142
Orinda, CA 94563
    Complete chart $10.

Feminist Book Club
2140 Westwood Blvd.
Los Angeles, CA 90025

Feminist Bookmobile
c/o 195 Seaton
Toronto 2, Ontario

Feminist Communication Collective
PO Box 455
Montreal 215, Quebec

Feminist Co-ordinating Council
Downtown Y.W.C.A.
Seattle, WA 98104

Feminist Federal Credit Union
Women's Resource Center
18700 Woodward Ave.
Detroit, MI 48203

Feminist Forge
686 S. Coast Hwy.
Laguna Beach, CA 92651
    Jewelry.

Feminist Health Center
746 Crenshaw Blvd.
Los Angeles, CA 90019
213-936-7466
    SEE ALSO: Self-Help Clinic.

Feminist History Research Project
218 S. Venice Blvd.
Venice, CA 90291
    Interested in 1910-1930, plans Digest. Box 1156, Topanga, CA 90290. Oral history project.

Feminist Invention Group, Inc.
333 E. 49, Box 8J
New York, NY 10017
    Elayne Snyder. "29 quick-witted answers to male-chauvinist putdowns" ($1.25).

Feminist Mailing Lists
    Contact: Spokeswoman.

Feminist News Exchange
Box 431, Planetarium Station
New York, NY 10024
    Nancy Borman. 11 publications.

Feminist Organization for Communication, Action & Service ("FOCAS")
c/o W. L. Center, 36 W. 22
New York, NY 10010
Majority Report.

Feminist Party, Main ofc.:
311 W. 24
New York, NY 10011
W. Coast ofc.:
699 Rhode Island, San Francisco, CA 94107. Feminist Party News. Posters. Audiovisuals.

Feminist Press
Box 334
Old Westbury, NY 11568
516-876-3086
    Non-profit, tax-exempt educational group interested in changing the books written about women and the education provided them. Media source. Clearinghouse on Women's Studies. Posters. Reprints. Ad infinitum.

Feminist Radio Network
PO Box 5537
Washington, DC 20016
202-332-8023
   Tax-exempt educational organization, formerly Radio Free Women, Inc. Produces broad range of hour and half-hour tapes aired twice weekly on WGTB-FM in Washington, DC and available in reel-to-reel form in 7 1/2 or 3 3/4 ips, as well as in cassettes. NOTE: This is a late entry and the many outstanding, useful tapes are not completely analyzed in the Audiovisuals part of the Non-Book Resources section; send for latest catalogue.

Feminist Resources for Equal Education (FREE)
Box 185, Saxonville Station
Framingham, MA 01701
   Media source.

Feminist Speakers Bureau
250 W. 47
New York, NY 10019
212-581-1066

Feminist Studio Workshop
2901 Waverly Dr.
Los Angeles, CA 90039
   Judy Chicago, Sheila de-Bretteville, Arlene Raven.

Feminist Theater see Woman's Building

Feminist Therapist Roster
Helen Copitka, National Coord.
4013 Lanark Ln.
Houston, TX 77025
   See also Pamphlets: Health for order information.

Feminist Videotape Collective
320 W. 87
New York, NY 10024

Feminist Women's Health Centers
746 S. Crenshaw
Los Angeles, CA 90005
213-936-7219
   Speakers. Clinics. Media source. Posters. Physician's Training Program in Early Abortion Techniques; Women's Choice Clinic; Women's Abortion Referral.
   429 S. Sycamore, Santa Ana, CA 92701, 714-836-1941.
   2930 McClure, Oakland, CA 94706, 415-444-5676.
   363 E. 6, Salt Lake City, UT 84404, 801-328-3032.
   18700 Woodward Ave., Detroit, MI 48203, 313-892-7790.
   Box 333, Boston, MA 02134, 617-787-3017.
   2411-112 Jackson Bluffs Rd., Coach Estates, Tallahassee, FL 32304, 904-575-3137

Feminist Writer's Workshop
769 Chelham
Santa Barbara, CA 93108
   "Child's nonsexist Xmas story" ($1.25).

Feminist Writer's Workshop
37 S. Wabash Ave.
Loop YWCA Center
Chicago, IL 60603
312-372-6600
   Cooperative network not limited to women.

Féministes pour la Vie see Feminists for life/Fém...

Feminists
4428 Mirada Dr.
Ft. Wayne, IN 46816
   Speakers, workshops.

Feminists
PO Box 10197
Pittsburgh, PA 15232

Feminists
120 Liberty

Directory of Sources

(cont.) New York, NY 10006
  Posters, buttons, packets,
  publications.

Feminists Cassette Library
606 W. Fairfax
Ft. Wayne, IN 46807
  Harriett Miller, Librarian.
  Tapes.

Feminists for life
PO Box 5631
Columbus, OH 43221
  "Toward a new Era in women's rights."

Feminists for life/Féministes
  pour la vie
159 Robert
Toronto, Ontario

Festival of Women's Films,
  1st Intl.
1582 York Ave.
New York, NY 10023
1972.

Field Enterprises. Library
  Services Div.
Merchandise Mart Plaza
Chicago, IL 60654

Fifth Street Women's Building
300 E. 5
New York, NY 10003

Fight Against Dictating Designers (FADD)
7609 Exeter Rd.
Bethesda, MD 20014
301-656-6172
  Non-profit membership group.
  Bumper stickers.

Film Images
17 W. 60
New York, NY 10023
212-279-6653

Filmmakers Corp.
175 Lexington Ave.
New York, NY 10016

Films for Social Change
PO Box 7143
St. Louis, MO 63177
  Non-profit filmmakers' coop.
  Abroad through Leonard
  Henry, Sociological Institute,
  University of Utrecht, Neth.

First Things First-er (Bookstore)
23 7 St. S.E.
Washington, DC 20003
202-546-4951, 7292
  Walk-in and ordering house.
  Posters, Jewelry. See
  also KNOW.

First Women's Bank
111 E. 57
New York, NY 10022
212-644-0670

Flatt, Carolyn
27 Greenway Circle
Sacramento, CA 95831
  "Image of women in TV"
  ($1.50).

Flexible Careers
Loop Y.W.C.A. Center
37 S. Wabash Ave.
Chicago, IL 60603
312-263-2488
  Susan Schwein, Coord.

Florida State University
Media Services
Tallahassee, FL 32306
904-224-0221

Flying Dutchman--Atco Records
1841 Broadway
New York, NY 10023

Folkway Records
701 7 Ave.
New York, NY 10036

Folkways/Scholastic Records
906 Sylvan Ave.
Englewood Cliffs, NJ 07632

Ford Associates, Inc.
701 S. Federal Ave.
Butler, IN 46721
  Dr. Lee Ellen Ford, publisher & editor. Women's Legal Rights Series. Small publishing company specializing in legislative/law re rights of women, minorities, animals. See BBC #462

Ford Foundation Faculty Fellowships for Research on the Role of Women in Society
320 E. 43
New York, NY 10017
  "Direct applications are not accepted. Nominations must be submitted by department heads or deans to whom the necessary forms are supplied by the Foundation. Each department or professional school is limited to one nominee. Payment is made by a grant to the nominating institution." Candidates may be male or female!

Forfreedom, Ann, ed. & publisher
Box 25514
Los Angeles, CA 90025
  "Women out of history..." ($3.50).

Forgotten Women
Box 1001
Palo Alto, CA 94302
  Radical history institute for non-violence.

Forum Project
Drawer "E"
Clinton, NJ 08809
  Speakers. Re prisoners. Contact Priscilla Linsley, 609-921-9000.

Frances McLaughlin Gill Productions, Inc.
49 E. 86
New York, NY 10028
  Filmmaker, distributor.

Francis A. Countway Library of Medicine
Boston Medical Library, Harvard Medical Library
10 Shattuck
Boston, MA 02115
  Phrenology, witchcraft, gynecology, obstetrics, etc.

Free Woman's Press
2828 Benvenue
Berkeley, CA 94705

Freeman, Jo
c/o SUNY
Purchase, NY 10577
914-253-5000
  Speaker. Women's Studies. Resource person.

Freewheeling Women's Press
414 N. Park--Women's House
Bloomington, IN 47401
812-336-8691

Fremont Woman's Clinic
6817 Greenwood Ave. N.
Seattle, WA 98103

Friendly House
347 S. Normandie
Los Angeles, CA 90020
213-386-9464
  For women alcoholics.

La Fronde
605 Hudson
New York, NY 10014
212-989-3023
  Feminist restaurant. Owned/operated by women.

- G -

GOP Women for Political Effectiveness
775 Ridge. Candace Olson
St. Paul, MN 55116

Directory of Sources   331

Gale Research Co.
Beok Tower
Detroit, MI 48226

Galleries see Audiovisuals

Gallery 707 see Woman's
 Building

Galt Toys
PO Box 5521
Mt. Carmel Station
Hamden, CT 06518
 Marjorie Wolfe, owner.

Gay Awareness Women's Kol-
 lective (GAWK)
325 Michigan Union
Ann Arbor, MI 48104

Gay Community Services
2314 Elliot Ave. S.
Minneapolis, MN 55403
612-335-5337
 Lesbian Mothers'-group.
 Counseling.

Gay House--women's group
216 Ridgewood Ave.
Minneapolis, MN 55403
612-333-6088
 Straight women also welcome.

Gay Liberation Front
Box 92, Village Station
150 Christopher
New York, NY 10014
212-864-6487

Gay Liberation of Louisville
416 Belgravia Ct.
Louisville, KY 40408

Gay Rights Legislative Committee
34 Spruce, #4
Minneapolis, MN 55403
612-336-3875

Gay Women's Caucus
1941 W. Fletcher
c/o Colleen Monahan
Chicago, IL 60657

The Lavender Woman peri-
 odical. "Lavender" film.

Gay Women's Coalition
PO Box 1300
Garden Grove, CA 92642

Gellis, Audrey
230 E. 15
New York, NY 10003
 "Call Me Ms." weekly femi-
 nist column syndicated by
 Copley News Service.

General Federation of Women's
 Clubs
1734 N St. N.W.
Washington, DC 20036
 Supports ERA.

Genesis Films, Ltd.
1040 N. Las Palmas
Los Angeles, CA 90038
 Also 40 W. 55, New York,
 NY 10019.

Genesis Press
PO Box 866
Ben Lomond, CA 95505
 "Birth Book" by Raven Lang
 ($6).

Gentle Giant Witch
157 Waterloo
Kitchener, Ontario
 Publishes non-sexist children's books.

Georgia State College for Wo-
 men
Library
Milledgeville, GA 31061
 Published-writings of Georgia
 women.

Gill, Frances McLaughlin, filmmaker see Frances Mc-
 Laughlin-Gill Productions

Glass Mountain Pamphlets
PO Box 238
Oyster Bay, NY 11771
 Deirdre English. "Witches,

(cont.) Midwives & Nurses; a history of women healers" their first pamphlet.

Glide Publications
330 Ellis
San Francisco, CA 94102
"Publishes for the community most in need of help--the old, the poor, the homosexual, women, and Third World."

Goldberg, Joan
370 Lexington Ave.
New York, NY 10017
212-725-5970
Feminist attorney of Kunstler, Kunstler, Hyman & Goldberg.

Good Taste Productions
PO Box 1564
Santa Monica, CA 90406

Goodman, Emily Jane
1414 6 Ave.
New York, NY 10019
212-838-4500
Woman attorney. Major part of work in re women in prison.

Goodman, Kelly, Ross, Stanley, Blank, & Bellamy
36 W. 44
New York, NY 10036
212-869-0020
Janice Goodman, Mary Kelly, Susan Ross, Nancy Stanley, Diane Blank, Carol Bellamy. Women lawyers.

Gore, Rea
Charlottesville, VA 22202
Carpenter.

Goteberg University Library: Women's History Collection
Sweden

Grailville Art & Bookshop
Loveland, OH 45140

Grandview 1 & 2 see Woman's Building

Granma Books
2509 Telegraph Ave.
Berkeley, CA 94704

Grant, Marilyn
23 Calumet Ave.
Rockaway, NJ 07866
201-625-1860
Principal of Grant Associates, consultants to industry in solving the problems relating to affirmative action for women.

Graphic Communications Herald
1126 HiPoint
Los Angeles, CA 90035
Feminist tapes, jewelry, posters.

Graphics for Women
PO Box 800
Bristol, CT 06010

Gray Panthers
3700 Chestnut
Philadelphia, PA 19104
Convenor, Maggie Kuhn. Old people's liberation.

Great Expectations (program)
Myra Fisher, 4805 Dunman Ave.
Woodland Hills, CA 91364
Developed to reach junior and senior high school girls. Leader's Guide ($1).

Greater Indianapolis Women's Political Caucus
5947 Carvel
Indianapolis, IN 46220
Buttons, Labels.

Greaves, Wm. Productions, Inc.
254 W. 54
New York, NY 10019

Greenpoint Print Shop Women's Collective

Directory of Sources

(cont.) 573 Metropolitan Ave.
Brooklyn, NY 11211
212-EV8-6916
    Offset, free printing instruction.

The Group
42 1/2 St. Marks Pl.
New York, NY 10003
    Redstockings c/o The Group Center.

Guidance Center
2330 Westwood Blvd., Suite 200
Los Angeles, CA 90064
213-879-3841
    Abortion counseling.

Gulch Stickers
128 W. Davis
Yellow Springs, OH 45387
    Bumper stickers.

Gynecological Self-Help presentation see Lolly & Jeanne Hirsch, New Moon Communications

- H -

Halifax Gay Alliance for Equality
1585 Barrington, #207
Halifax, Nova Scotia

Halifax Women's Bureau
PO Box 3596
Halifax S. Postal Sta.
Nova Scotia

Handbook Collective
PO Box 1000, Station G
Montréal, 130, Quebec
    Birth control and VD handbooks.

Harbor Free Clinic
6736 Los Verdes
Palos Verdes Peninsula, CA 90274

Harragan, Betty & Associates
541 E. 20
New York, NY 10010
212-777-0831
    Consultant on planning and implementing goals/timetables of affirmative action programs, especially re career development of long-term women employees.

Hartley Productions
Cat Rock Rd., Elda Hartley
Cos Cob, CT 06807

Hartmann, Nora
72-11 110
Forest Hills, NY 11375
    Autographs, documents, letters of historical women. Send for free list.

Hathaway, Virtue
    "Fuck housework," "Fuck office work" posters and cards. From KNOW.

Health & Abortion Information Collective. Washington Area Women's Center
1736 R St. N.W.
Washington, DC 20009

Health Organizing Collective
N.Y. Women's Health & Abortion Project
36 W. 22
New York, NY 10010

Health Policy Advisory Center (Health PAC)
17 Murray
New York, NY 10007
    Purpose to expose inequities of the health system and monitor new developments in health reform. Health-PAC Bulletin.

Health Sciences Publishing Corp.
451 Greenwich
New York, NY 10013
212-966-6658

Hearst Metronome News

(cont.) 4 W. 58
New York, NY 10019

Hearts & Struggles Publishing Co.
Under Women's Music Network umbrella, starting summer 1974 to publish songbooks and educational materials.

Her Own Press
79 Isabella
Pleasant Hill, CA 94523
"Train one: moon and shadow" stories and poems by Zel Latner.

Herald Press
Scottdale, PA 15683
412-887-8500
Division of Mennonite Publishing House.

Herstory Films, Inc.
137 E. 13
New York, NY 10003
212-260-0324

Herstory Indexing Task Force
Jean Barnett/Ann Pettingill, Coordinators
c/o Kennedy Library Ref. Dept.
5151 State University Dr.
California State Univ.
Los Angeles, CA 90032
213-224-2251, 2255
Volunteer librarians creating Author/Subject Index to HERSTORY, microfilm collection of women's periodicals published by Women's History Research Center.

Hesse-Rabinovitch, Isa
8700 Kusnacht
Schiedhaldenstrasse 75
Switzerland
Filmmaker, source.

Higher Education Resource Service for Academic Women in New England (HERS)
Box 1901, Brown University
Providence, RI 02912
Dr. Lilli S. Hornig, Exec. Dir. Official name chosen for the Concerns of Women Project. Ford Foundation-supported project.

Highland Community Women's Retreat
Praradox, NY 12858
518-585-7556
Can accommodate children of women attending. Sliding scale. See Women's Retreat.

Hijas de Cuauhtemoc
PO Box 735
San Fernando, CA 91341

Hiltz Publishing Co.
6304 Hamilton Ave.
Cincinnati, OH 45224

Hoban, Tana
2219 Delancey Pl.
Philadelphia, PA 19103
Filmmaker, source.

Hogan, Betsy & Associates
222 Rawson Rd.
Brookline, MA 02146
617-232-0066
Publishes Womanpower.

Homosexual Community Counseling Center
921 Madison Ave.
New York, NY 10021
212-834-1159
Professional therapists who view homosexuality as a viable lifestyle.

Homosexual Women's Hotline
Philadelphia, PA
215-SA9-2001

Hoppin, Ruth
15 Portola Ave.
Daly City, CA 94015
Speaker. "Games Bible-translators play." Religion/Bible resource person

Directory of Sources

(cont.) (SEE #20, Basic Book Collection).

Hotdog
Richfield, UT 84701
   Stands for "humanitarians opposed to degrading our girls." National organization to stop R- and X-rated movies from appearing on TV and anything else that is degrading and demoralizing to "our girls." Petitioning to stop ERA.

House of L.I.B.
PO Box 3239
Santa Monica, CA 90403
   Sculpture, jewelry.

Housewives for Collective Action
c/o Houston Health Dept.
Houston, TX 75001
   Publishes a mini newspaper.

Housewives for ERA
125 Custer Ave.
Evanston, IL 60202

Hughes, Marija Matich
2116 F St. N.W., #702
Washington, DC 20037

Human Genetics Unit, State Health Dept.
717 Delaware St. S.E.
Minneapolis, MN 55414
612-269-5269
   Genetic counseling and testing for people worried about drugs/diseases that might be passed on to unborn.

Human Service Press
4301 Connecticut Ave. N.W.
Washington, DC 20008

- I -

ICI, A Woman's Place
College Ave.
Berkeley, CA 94705
415-654-9920
   Bookstore and women's center. Posters.

I.S. Women
6 Cottons Gardens
London E2, England
   "Women fight back" by Kate Ennis.

Illinois Drug Abuse Program
Office of Women's Affairs
57 St. & Lake Shore Dr.
(Museum of Science & Industry East Pavillion)
Chicago, IL 60637
   Carolyn Gioia, Dir. of Office.

Illinois Men for ERA
Jordan Miller c/o Newsclip
176 W. Adams
Chicago, IL 60690

Impact Films
144 Bleecker
New York, NY 10012
212-674-3375, 2760

Imperial Films
4404 S. Florida Ave.
Lakeland, FL 33803

Imperial International Learning Corp.
Box 548
Kankakee, IL 60901

Independent Bar Assoc. of America
Box 187
Islamorada, FL 33036

India Consulate General
3 E. 64
New York, NY 10021
212-879-7800

Indiana State Teachers Assoc.
312 Rambler Rd., Paula Carter
Muncie, IN 37404
   Women's Caucus

Information Center, Inc.; A
Woman's Place (Bookstore)
5251 Broadway
Oakland, CA 94618
415-654-9920
"Starting a bookstore; non-
capitalist operation within a
capitalist economy" ($.25
for postage).

Inforwomen
PO Box 1727
Chicago, IL 60690
Contact: Jeanne Weimann or
Susan Koester, 312-528-8834.
"Chicago Women's Directory"
($2.25/mail order). Non-
profit collective organized to
produce the Guide. Spanish
women's groups included and
all essays translated into
Spanish.

Ingluvin
Box 994, Place d'Armes Station
Montréal 126, Quebec
Women's Press.

Institute for Administrative Ad-
vancement
Univ. of Michigan
435 Hutchins
Ann Arbor, MI 48104
Virginia Davis Nordin, Dir.

Inst. for Family Research & Ed.
760 Ostrom Ave.
Syracuse, NY 13210
Say it so it makes sense.

Inst. for Sex Education
18 S. Michigan Ave.
Chicago, IL 60603
Pamphlets on VD.

Inst. for Sex Research
Indiana University
Bloomington, IN 47401

Inst. for Teaching Politics. Women Involved, Inc.
c/o Everywoman's Center
Univ. of Mass.
Amherst, MA 01002
The Center has outline of
how the institute was put together.

Inst. of Women Today
125 N. Craig, Mary Dennis
Donovan, Coord.
Pittsburgh, PA 15213

Interagency Council for Family
Planning
2348 7 Ave.
Upper Harlem Medical Assoc.
New York, NY 10030
212-283-9607

Inter-American Commission of
Women
19th St. & Constitution Ave.
N.W.
Washington, DC 20006

Intercollegiate Assoc. of Wo-
men Students
2401 Virginia Ave. N.W.
Box 2
Washington, DC 20037
Feminine focus.

Interdepartmental Committee
on the Status of Women
U.S. Dept. of Labor, Rm. 2131
Washington, DC 20210
202-961-3791
President's Commission on
the Status of Women became/
joined with Interdept. Committee on Status of Women.

International Assoc. of Personnel Women
358 5 Ave.
New York, NY 10001
Has placement Roster.

Internat. Assoc. of Women
Police
100 N. LaSalle, Suite 1410
Chicago, IL 60602

Internat. Childbirth Education
Assoc.

Directory of Sources

(cont.) 208 Ditty Building
Bellevue, WA 98004

Internat. Council of Social
  Democratic Women
88A St. John's Wood High St.
London NW8, England
  Formerly Women's Conference of the Socialist International.

Internat. Credit Women
611 Olive
St. Louis, MO 63101

Internat. Federation of Business
  & Professional Women
Chansitor House
37/38 Chancery La.
London WC2, England

Internat. Federation of Business
  & Professional Women's Clubs
2012 Mass. Ave. N.W.
Washington, DC 20036
202-293-1100

Internat. Federation of University Women
17a King's Rd., Sloane Sq.
London SW3, England

Internat. Federation of Women
  Lawyers
150 Nassau
New York, NY 10038
  Also known as Federación internacional de abogadas and Federation internationale des femmes juristes.

Internat. Feminist Task Force
1736 R St. N.W.
Washington, DC 20009
  Interested in translating articles re Women's Movement.

Internat. Film Bureau
332 S. Michigan
Chicago, IL 60604

Internat. Film Foundation
474 5 Ave.
New York, NY 10017

Internat. Publishers
381 Park Ave. S.
New York, NY 10016

Internat. Toastmistress Clubs
11301 Long Beach Blvd.
Lynwood, CA 90262

Internat. Women's Fishing
  Assoc.
PO Box 2025
Palm Beach, FL 33480

Internat. Women's Hall of Fame
Harriet Holland
Newport, RI 02840
  Being planned, June 1974.

Internat. Women's Year--Canada
Mary Gusella, Dir., Secretariate for...Office in the Privy Council. For information in the U.S.A. re Canada's program, contact U.S. Center of IWY and/or Freda Pelletier, Special Adviser, Status of Women, Health & Welfare Dept., Government of Canada.

Internat. Women's Year--U.S.A.
U.S. Center for International Women's Year
1630 Crescent Pl. N.W.
Washington, DC 20009
202-332-1029 x61
  Yvonne A. Lewis, Staff Asst.; Ruth Bacon, Dir.
  See also SPEAKERS.

Interstate Assoc. of Commissions on the Status of Women
14 & E Streets N.W.
Washington, DC 20004
202-363-7280
  Endorses ERA.

Interval House
173 Spadina Rd.
Toronto, Ontario

Iota Tad Tau Legal Sorority
Supports ERA.

Iowa City Women's Press Collective
Women's Center, 3 E. Market
Iowa City, IA 52240

Isaacs, Barbara
333 E. 43
New York, NY 10017
Filmmaker and source.

Island Industries, Inc.
Box 55
Vashon, WA 98070
Multi-printing services provided by a women's shop.

It's About Time Bookstore
5502 University Way N.E.
Seattle, WA 98105
206-LA5-0999
Posters.

It's All Right to Be a Woman Theatre
318 W. 101, Apt. 2
New York, NY 10025
212-477-1439
  Kathy Stillson. "Our Faces Belong to Our Bodies" song. Part of each performance's proceeds to Women's Bail Fund.

Ivy Films
165 W. 46
New York, NY 10036
212-765-3940

- J -

Jackson Memorial Hospital Rape Treatment Center
1000 N.W. 17
Miami, FL 33136
Dial 325-RAPE
  Roxcy Bolton, Dade County feminist. Dorothy Hicks, medical dir. Dr. Hardat Sukhedo, gives police academy course.

Jacqueline Ceballos Productions
1 Lincoln Plaza
New York, NY 10023

James, Alice Books see Alice...

Janice LaRouche Associates
333 Central Park W
New York, NY 10025
212-663-0970
  Speaker. Founder-partner in "Options, Career workshops for women." Affirmative action consultant, speaker

Jason Films
2621 Palisade Ave.
Riverdale, Bronx, NY 10463

Jewish Family Service
65 E. Kellog
St. Paul, MN 55101
612-227-8086
Also 404 S. 8, 333-6193.
Unmarried parent service.

Jewish Feminist Organization:
West: Diane Gelon, 5553 1/2 Costello Ave., VanNuys, CA 91401.
MidWest: Maralee Gordon, PO Box 60142, Chicago, IL 60660.
East: Cheryl Mach, c/o Network, 36 W. 37, New York, NY 10018.
Canada: Brana Brown, 4 Old Park Rd., Toronto, Ontario.

Joan of Art Seminars
Held by June Wayne, artist-author of The Tamerind Report
Los Angeles, CA

Jobs for Women
PO Box 840
Berkeley, CA 94701

Joesting, Joan
Route 6, Box 154a

Directory of Sources

(cont.) Chapel Hill, NC 27514
Womanmade male chauvinist pig cushion or stuffed toy ($5) by woman who needs money for legal costs.

Johns, Norris Associates
5720 Aylesboro Ave.
Pittsburgh, PA 15217
412-422-7887
Jody R. Johns, a partner. Consultant, trainer specializing in development of women, workshops for business and industry.

Johnson County Council on the Status of Women
108 Potomac Dr.
Iowa City, IA 52240
Affiliate of Iowa Commission on the Status of Women. Has newsletter.

Joint Committee of Organizations Concerned with the Status of Women in the Church
Contact: Elizabeth Farians, PhD
6125 Webbland Pl.
Cincinnati, OH 45213
Co-chairpersons: Bernice McNeela, 1600 Sunset Ave., Waukegan, IL 60085; Patricia Bruner, 3901 Livingston St. N.W., Washington, DC 20015. Member organizations: Deaconess Movement; National Assoc. of the Laity, Women's Rights Committee; Natl. Coalition of American Nuns; Natl. Organization for Women, Ecumenical Task Force on Women and Religion, Catholic Caucus; St. Joan's International Alliance, U.S.A. Section; and Women Theologians United.

Jonas, Joan
66 Grand
New York, NY 10013
Filmmaker, source.

Jones, Laura

Baldwin Street Gallery
23 Baldwin
Toronto, Ontario M5T 1L1

Journalists for Professional Equality
Contact: Vera Glaser 202-638-2844, 244-8787; Eileen Shanahan 202-293-3100, 362-8471. Men and women journalists in press, TV, and radio.

Joyful World Press
468 Belvedere
San Francisco, CA 94117
Shirley Boccaccio & children. Publish contemporary, feminist children's books.

Julie & Shirley
PO Box 633
Portland, OR 97210
T Shirts.

- K -

KDKA
1 Gateway Center
Pittsburgh, PA 15222

KPFA Radio Station
2207 Shattuck Ave.
Berkeley, CA 94704
415-981-7730

KNOW see Know, Inc.

KPIX, TV outlet in San Francisco
Belva Davis: station's first female anchorperson; also has female producer; Roxanne Russell
VanNess Ave. & Greenwich
San Francisco, CA 94109
415-766-5100

KQED, Channel #9
1100 Bryant
San Francisco, CA 94103

K-W Woman's Place
25 Dupont St. E.
Waterloo, Ontario

Kalamazoo Public Schools, Committee to Study Sex Discrimination in the
732 Garland
Kalamazoo, MI 49008
Jo Jacobs, Chairperson.

Carolyn Kane, sports column in Long Island Press
92-24 168
Jamaica, NY 11433
212-OL8-1234
N.Y. correspondent for WomenSports.

Kennikat Press
90 S. Bayles Ave.
Pt. Washington, NY 11050

Kent Gay Liberation Front
University Center, Room 233
Kent, OH 44242
Shout It Loud.

Kentucky University
Margaret I. King Library
Lexington, KY 40506

King Screen Productions
320 Aurora Ave. N.
Seattle, WA 98109

Kinlein, Lucille
9002 Locust Spring Rd.
College Park, MD 20740
301-474-3677
First known independent nurse-practitioner in U.S.A.

The Kitchen
240 Mercer
New York, NY 10012

Kleckner, Susan
117 Waverly Pl.
New York, NY 10011

Know, Inc.
PO Box 86031

Pittsburgh, PA 15221
"Freedom of the press belongs to those who own the press!" KNOW News Nonprofit, tax-exempt corporation, a collective. Storefront, mail-order.

Kraning, Suzan Pitt
897 18 Ave. S.E.
Minneapolis, MN 55414
Filmmaker, source.

Kreps, Bonnie
47 Parkview Hill Crescent
Toronto, Ontario

- L -

Labyris
Ann Arbor, MI 48106
Union women's group participating in Chicago coalition, March 1974.

Labyris Books
33 Barrow (@ 7th Ave. S.)
New York, NY 10014
212-741-3460
Feminist bookstore. Also mail order. Works in Spanish and English, non-sexist children's books, art works. Newspapers from all over the world.

Lacota Indian Women's Assoc.
Lantry, SD 37636
Newsletter.

La Fronde see Fronde

Lady Carpenter Enterprises
405 W. 37
New York, NY 10018
212-239-4283
Joyce Hartwell. "How-to" lessons on tool use, interior design and building.

Lakewood Task Force for Equality in Education

Directory of Sources

(cont.) 1261 W. Clifton Blvd.
Lakewood, OH 44107
Annette Power Johnson, Co-ord. "Report" ($1 donation).

La Leche League see Leche League

Lalor Foundation
Professional publications, films. Program of Research Grants, currently bearing on: (1) early amniocentesis in fetal development and (2) cervical and uterine physiology relevant to pregnancy interruption.

Lambert, Marie, attorney
160 Broadway
New York, NY 10038
212-BE3-8110
Feminist lawyer interested in cases of women vs the medical establishment.

Last Gasp-Eco Funnies
1274 Folsom
San Francisco, CA 94103
415-626-5036
Comics, cartoons. Handles sales for Women's Cartoonist Collective. Comic books by Liberated Women: Wimmen's Comix No. 1 and 2, Abortion Eve, It ain't me babe, Facts o'life funnies, Girl fight comics, Illuminations, and Further fattening adventures of Pudge, $.65 each.

Laughlin, Kathleen
2324 Grand Ave. S.
Minneapolis, MN 55405
Filmmaker, source.

Lavendar Press
PO Box 60206
1723 W. Devon
Chicago, IL 60660
"Thunder from the earth," a lesbian anthology of poetry and photographs ($1.95).
Also: 411 Lathrop, River Forest, IL 60305. Rebecca Hunter.

Lavender
3716 S.E. Belmont
Portland, OR 97214
Posters.

Lavender Brush
New Haven, CT 06510
203-562-2793
Interior-exterior painting.

Lavender Jane Productions
Under Women's Music Network umbrella.

Lawren Productions
4233 Wooster Ave.
San Mateo, CA 94403

Lawyers' Committee for Civil Rights Under Law
733 15 St. N.W., Suite 520
Sarah C. Carey, Asst. Dir.
Washington, DC 20005
202-628-6700

League for Socialist Action (Canada)
c/o Vanguard Books
1208 Granville
Vancouver, British Columbia
"The status of women in Canada."

League of Women Voters
1730 M St. N.W.
Washington, DC 20036
202-296-1770
Also: 131 E. 23, New York, NY 10010, 212-OR7-5050.
SEE "Encyclopedia of Associations" for outlets in all states, Washington, DC and Puerto Rico.

Learn Me
642 Grand Ave.
St. Paul, MN 55105
Local bookstore specializing

(cont.) in non-sexist, non-racist materials.

La Leche League International
9616 Minneapolis Ave.
Franklin Park, IL 60131
"The womanly art of breast-feeding," "Mothers in the kitchen--cookbook." La Leche League News.

Lefcourt, Kraft & Libow
640 Broadway
New York, NY 10012
212-677-1552
All-women law firm, including Clerk Ann Teicher. Carol Lefcourt, Veronika Kraft, Carol Libow.

Legal Aid Society, Women's Division
42 W. 44
New York, NY 10036
212-MU7-8433

Lenox Hill Publishing & Distribution Corp.
235 E. 44
New York, NY 10017

Lesbian Drop-In
31 Dupont
Toronto, Ontario
929-3125

Lesbian Feminist Liberation
67 Terrace Ave., Apt. AZ
Hempstead, NY 11550
516-483-2341
   Martha & Lucy Wilde.

Lesbian Feminist Liberation Activities
PO Box 243, Village Sta.
New York, NY 10014
   Jean O'Leary 212-387-5151.

Lesbian Grapevine
373 N. Western Ave., #202
Los Angeles, CA 90004
   The national Lesbian communications network; Jeanne

Cordova, Secretary.

Lesbian Liberation
c/o Women's Center
46 Pleasant
Cambridge, MA 02139

Lesbian Resource Center
710 W. 22
Minneapolis, MN 55405
612-374-2345
   Speakers' Bureau. So's Your Old Lady.

Lesbians Speak Out
1018 Valencia
San Francisco, CA 94110
   A collective and a series (V. 2 $1.75).

Lib Men-Lib Women
First Unitarian Church
2125 Chestnut
Philadelphia, PA 19103

"Liberated Woman" Column
Irene Davall, writer.
   Contact: George Candreva, The Yorktowner, Front St., Yorktown Hts., NY 10598. 26 cols. a year, available for local newspapers.

Liberation Enterprises
Box 1888, GPO
Brooklyn, NY 11202
   T Shirts, graphics, posters, jewelry. Mail-order house.

Liberation News Service
160 Claremont Ave.
New York, NY 10027
212-749-2200
   Collective, supplies news articles, graphics, LNS packets twice a week.

Liberation School for Women
3179 Dundas St. W.
Western Area YWCA
Toronto, Ontario M6P 2A5
762-8169

Librairie des femmes (Bookstore)
68 Rue des Sts. Pères
Paris 7e, France

Librarians for Social Change
35 Hardy Rd.
London, SW19 1JA, England
Anne Colwell.

Lima Bean Records, Inc.
["a women's record co."]
217 12 St. S.E.
Washington, DC 20003

Lindfors, Viveca
172 E. 95
New York, NY 10028
  Contact: Bob MacDonald, 303 W. 42, New York, NY 10036, 212-765-0900. Speaker; film and lecture program. "I am a Woman" one-woman show.

Lindh, Patricia, Spec. Asst. to Counsellor to The President, in Charge of Women's Programs
White House
Washington, DC 20500

Literature and Education Collective of Women's Health & Abortion Project
36 W. 22
New York, NY 10022
  "Women and their bodies," a course. Bibliography for the course ($.05).

Little, Brown
34 Beacon
Boston, MA 02106
  Barbara Allen Babcock. "Sex discrimination and the law."

Long Island Feminist Coalition
500-168B Peconic
Ronkonkoma, NY 11779
516-585-2316
  (Ms.) Lynn Libros, Coord.

Lonnquist, Judith A.
201 N. Wells
Chicago, IL 60606
312-FR2-1646
  Feminist attorney.

Los Angeles Council of Women Artists
c/o Womanspace
11007 Venice Blvd.
Los Angeles, CA 90534
213-838-9668

Los Angeles Feminist Women's Health Center
746 S. Crenshaw Blvd.
Los Angeles, CA 90005
213-936-7219

Los Angeles Jewish Feminist Coalition
1390 11 St., #C
Sharon Silverman Zipperstein
Santa Monica, CA 90404

Los Angeles Public Access Project
213-791-1686, 734-9911
  Trying to gain access to time on cable TV for feminist projects. Meets every Tuesday, 8 PM in Venice on Ocean Front Walk between Dudley and Sunset in a storefront called H.M.S. Pantaloon (90291).

Los Angeles Women's Abortion Action Committee
2936 W. 8
Los Angeles, CA 90005
213-487-7696

Lucina Speakers Bureau
746 S. Crenshaw Blvd.
Los Angeles, CA 90005
213-396-7219
  Anti-rape. Self-help clinics. Herstory. Lesbianism. Nonsexist childraising. Also: 218 S. Venice Blvd., 90015, 213-823-4774

Lutheran Deaconess Clinic
2314 14 Ave. S.
Minneapolis, MN 55404
612-721-2933 x344
  Contraception, VD testing &
  treatment.

- M -

MOMMA Organization, Inc.
PO Box 5759
Santa Monica, CA 90405
  "How to start a MOMMA
  Chapter" ($.50). Organiza-
  tion for single mothers.

Ms. Books-by-Mail
370 Lexington Ave.
New York, NY 10017
  E.g. "Ira Sleeps Over."

Ms. Corp.
370 Lexington Ave.
New York, NY 10017
  Gloria Steinem, Pres. (Nov.
  1972).

McCaysville Industries
McCaysville, GA 30555
  Women's sewing factory.
  Need help marketing their
  products.

McCormick, Pat
445 Michigan Ave.
Berkeley, CA 94707
  "Volunteerism--what it's all
  about" ($.50).

Macmillan Audio Brandon
34 MacQueston Pky. S.
Mt. Vernon, NY 10550
913-664-5051

Maendeleo ya Wanawake (Progress
  for woman)
Kenya
  Cooperative organized by
  African women permitted traditional modes of expression
  through pottery, batik, jewel-
  ry-making, straw-weaving,
  etc. probably one of the few
  groups whose members,
  representatives of different
  tribes, are able to work
  peacefully together.

Magic Circle Press
31 Chapel Ln.
Riverside, CT 06878
203-637-3875
  Valerie Harms.

Magus Films, Inc.
777 3 Ave.
New York, NY 10017

Mainstream Women
342 Madison Ave.
New York, NY 10017
212-687-3255
  A division of The ManEdCo.
  Group, Inc. Ms. Joan
  Rome, Mg. Dir., seminars.

Maison des femmes
63, Avenue des Gobelins
Paris 75013
Phone 331·70·58
  For correspondence, mms.,
  etc.: Editions 'des femmes'
  2, Rue de la Roquette,
  Paris 75011, 805·17·45.
  Women from the group, Pol-
  itics and Psychoanalysis, in
  Paris WL have started this
  publishing house.

Male Switchboard
2700 Bancroft Wy.
Berkeley, CA 94704

Mama's Press
2500 Market
Oakland, CA 94607
415-653-5033
  "Alta;true story" ($.85),
  Monstor coloring book ($.50).

Mana Workshop
3800 Trailwood Ln.
Ft. Worth, TX 76109
  Bumper stickers.

Directory of Sources

Management Services Division
Remer--Ribolow Employment
  Agency
2 W. 45
New York, NY 10036
212-867-6080
  Management Services (M.S.)
  --Adele Ribolow, Dir.

Manhattan Counseling Center
285 West End Ave.
New York, NY 10023
212-TR4-7846
  Nonsexist psychotherapists.

Margaret Sanger Research
  Bureau
17 W. 16
New York, NY 10011
212-929-6200
  Outpatient vasectomy clinic.

Marriage & Divorce Law Reform League
8940 Lauder
Detroit, MI 48228

Martel's Ms. You
3 Ave. corner 83
New York, NY 10028
212-861-6110
  "Come Lib it up!" restaurant.

Martini, Anita and Nelda Pena,
  Sportcasters
Creative Concepts Co.
Memorial Dr.
Houston, TX 77007
713-869-6494
  Fun in Houston.

Maryland. University. Women's Information Center
  Project
College Park, MD 20742
301-454-4877
  Melora Zeisberg, Asst. Dir.

Maryland. University.
McKeldin Library
College Park, MD 20742
  Susan Cardinale, Special
  Collections Librarian, developing collection of relevant ephemera.

Mass Media Associates
2116 N. Charles
Baltimore, MD 21218

Massachusetts Committee for
  ERA
22 River
Boston, MA 02108

Massachusetts Institute of Technology
Cambridge, MA 02139
  The Libraries: Humanities
  Library, Room 14 S-234,
  617-253-5684. Human
  Studies Collection includes
  materials re "Women's
  Movement and Men's Movement." A guide to the collection is "Human Studies
  Bibliographies" ($1.50).

Massachusetts State Dept. of
  Commerce Library
150 Causeway
Boston, MA 02114

Maternal Information Services,
  Inc.
46 W. 96, 1E
New York, NY 10025
212-865-2563
  The Working Mother.

Maternity Center Assoc.
48 E. 92
New York, NY 10016
212-369-7300
  One of 11 midwifery schools.
  "Preparation for childbirth"
  (donation).

Maud Gonne Press
Berkeley, CA
415-648-2850, Betsy
  Offset printing in a women's
  shop.

Maverick Press
889 Ellis

(cont.) San Francisco, CA 94109
  Publishes "Legal First Aid,"
  and "Legal Awareness."

May, Antoinette, columnist:
  "Single by Choice"

Meaningful Bumpers
1217 Giltspur Rd.
Richmond, VA 23233
  ERA bumper stickers ($1.25).

Media Workshop Tours
311 W. 24, Irene Davall
New York, NY 10011

Medical Committee for Human
  Rights
1520 Naudin
Philadelphia, PA 19146

Men's Anthology Collective
  (MAC)
149 Lexington Ave.
New York, NY 10016
  Also PO Box 9083, Berkeley,
  CA 94709. Redefining stereo-
  typed masculine roles. In-
  cludes Warren Farrell.

Men's Awareness Network
  (M.A.N.)
PO Box 3392
Beverly Hills, CA 90212
213-652-6661
  Lee Christie, founder.

Men's Center
Jones Library
Amherst, MA 01002

Men's Liberation, Inc.
153 E. 18
New York, NY 10003

Methodist Peace Fellowship
5123 Truman Rd.
Kansas City, MO 64127
  "Abortion; a human choice"
  ($.50).

Meuli, Judy
1125 HiPoint

Los Angeles, CA 90035
  Compiling directory of feminist products.

Michigan State University
Alliance to End Sex Discrimination
537 Lexington, Vicki Neiberg
East Lansing, MI 48823

Michigan State University
School of Labor & Industrial
  Relations
402 S. Kedzie
East Lansing, MI 48823

Michigan. University
Center for Population Planning
Ann Arbor, MI 48104

Michigan Women for Medical
  Control of Abortion
Box 272, Route 4
Petoskey, MI 49770
616-347-4511

Michigan Women's Political
  Caucus
1169 Sabron Dr.
East Lansing, MI 48823

Michigan Women's Task Force
  on Rape
508 Packard, Jan BenDor
Ann Arbor, MI 48104
  Packet ($2).

Middle Class Values and Other
  Bargains, Inc.
180 9 Ave.
New York, NY 10011
  Also: 5105 Main, Kansas
  City, MO 64112. Women's
  crafts, domestic/imported
  gifts. Feminist owned and
  operated.

Midwest Academy
600 W. Fullerton
Chicago, IL 60614
312-935-4100
  Heather Booth, dir. "Direct action organizing; a

Directory of Sources

(cont.) handbook for woman."
Course-related. Feminist
training school for organizers.

Midwest Assoc. for the Study of
Human Sexuality
100 E. Ohio
Chicago, IL 60611
312-467-1290

Midwest Family Planning Assoc.,
Inc.
5952 W. Addison
Chicago, IL 60634
312-725-0200
   Also: 2952 N. Milwaukee
60618, 342-8383, 2111. Nonprofit counseling. Abortion
information. Safe and legal.

Midwest Population Center
100 E. Ohio
Chicago, IL 60611
312-644-3410
   Nonprofit licensed clinic.
Counseling. Testing. Followup care.

Midwest Women's Historical
Collection
Univ. of Ill. at Chicago Circle
Library
Box 8198
Chicago, IL 60680

Miller-Brody Productions, Inc.
342 Madison Ave.
New York, NY 10017
   Newbery-awarded books in
AV form.

Minneapolis Health Dept.
250 S. 4
Minneapolis, MN 55401
612-348-2782
   For maternity clinic 348-2782.
Health care for children
348-2963.

Minnesota Organization for the
Repeal of Abortion Laws
(M.O.R.A.L.)
549 Turnpike Rd.

Golden Valley, MN 55416
612-473-1911

Minnesota Speakers Bureau
PO Box 4256, St. Anthony Fall
Sta.
Minneapolis, MN 55414
612-338-3452

Minnesota. State Dept. of Human Rights, State Office
Building, Women's Div.
St. Paul, MN 55101
612-296-2931

Minnesota. University. Council for University Women's
Progress
Minneapolis, MN 55455
   Mabel Powers, 612-373-5115.

Minnesota. Univ. Women's
Center
301 Walter Library
Minneapolis, MN 55455
   "Life styles of educated
American women" evaluation
of a Women's Studies course
presented by the Center includes comparisons with
others.

Minnesota. Univ. Women's
Programs
200 Westbrook Hall, Edith Mucke
Minneapolis, MN 55455
612-373-9743
   Continuing education, extension.

Minnesota Women's Abortion
Action Coalition
100 University Ave. S.E.
Minneapolis, MN 55414
612-332-1812

Minnesota Women's Action Coalition
250 Coffman Union, Univ. of
Mn.
Minneapolis, MN 55455
612-373-2511
   Peggy Peterson. Coalition

(cont.) supports ERA; includes NOW, WEAL, Women's Advocates, University WL, Minnesota Women's Center.

Minnesota Women's Political Caucus
1130 Nicollet Ave.
YWCA, Rm. 100
Minneapolis, MN 55403
612-890-6847
   Mary Ziegenhagen, Metropolitan coord.

Minority Women Employment Program
2626 Calumet, Ms. Beverly Lyle, Dir.
Houston, TX 77004
713-526-3495

Mississippi State College for Women
John Clayton Fant Memorial Library
PO Box E, College Sta.
Columbus, MS 39701

Missoula Women's Health Collective
   Contact: Via Women's Action Center, Venture Center, University of MT, Missoula, MT 59801.

Modern Languages Assoc. (MLA)
MLA Commission on the Status of Women in the Profession.
   Contact: Dr. Carol Ohmann, Wesleyan Univ., Middletown, CT 06457.
   Women's Caucus of the MLA.
      Contact: Dr. Verna Wittrock, Dept. of English, Eastern Ill. Univ., Charleston, IL 61920.

Model Cities--Chicago Committee on Urban Opportunity
640 N. LaSalle
Chicago, IL 60610
   "Child development and early childhood education; a guide for parents and teachers" ($5).

Model City Women's Task Force
2649 Park Ave.
Minneapolis, MN 55407
612-341-2801
   Frankie Quade. Seminar on how to make affirmative action work for women in federally-contracted businesses and industries or under-employed.

Modern Times Book Store
3800 17
San Francisco, CA 94114

More for Women, Inc.
52 Gramercy Park N.
New York, NY 10010
212-674-4090
   Also: 663 5 Ave., 10022, 757-6454. Career center by women for women--workshops, lectures, other services.

Morris, William Agency
1350 6 Ave.
New York, NY 10010
212-586-5100

Mother Courage Restaurant
342 W. 11
New York, NY 10014
212-924-9728
   "First feminist restaurant in New York City." Owned, operated by women.

Mother Jones Press
19 Hawley
Northampton, MA 01060
   Incorporated with Women's Film Coop. "Voices of new women" ($1.25).

Mother Lode
PO Box 40213
San Francisco, CA 94140
   Posters.

Directory of Sources

Mother Truckers
215 W. 14
New York, NY 10011
212-475-2421
    Also: 301 W. 13, 10011,
    741-3380. Furniture mover,
    Bernice Crabtree.

Multi-media Productions
PO Box 5097
Stanford, CA 94305

Multi-Media Resource Center,
  Inc.
540 Powell
San Francisco, CA 94108
415-521-5035

Municipal Women's Project
140 Clarendon, YWCA Bldg.
Boston, MA 02116
    Rosalind Pollan, Ann Wolpert,
    Betty Gittes, attorney: found-
    ers. "Sex discrimination ..."
    pamphlet. Affirmative action
    in action.

Murray, Jessica
Brown University
Providence, RI 02912
    Theater. Painting. Feminist
    studies.

My Sisters' Song
Box 90475
Milwaukee, WI 53202

Myth America: Women's Film
  Educational Project, Inc.
Sandra Shevey
2043 N. Beachwood Dr.
Hollywood, CA 90068
213-465-6741
    Foundation involved in film
    quarterly, film retrospective
    to honor women; movie
    critic for KPFK-FM.

Mythology Unlimited, Inc.
370 Columbus Ave.
New York, NY 10024
    T-Shirts.

- N -

NBC Educational Enterprises
30 Rockefeller Plaza
New York, NY 10020

NCR Microcard Editions
901 26 St. N.W.
Washington, DC 20037

NIP Rape Center
2617 Hennepin Ave.
Minneapolis, MN 55405
612-374-3125

NTL Institute
1815 N. Ft. Myer Dr.
Arlington, VA 22209
703-527-1500
    Has "Women's Develop-
    ment Programs."

National Abortion Rights Action
  League
250 W. 57 St., Room 401
New York, NY 10019

Nat. Action Committee on the
  Status of Women
PO Box 927
Adelaide St.
Toronto, Ontario M5C 2K3
    <u>Status of Women News.</u>

Nat. Advertising Review Board
850 3 Ave., New York, NY 10022
212-832-1320
    Send complaints re truth and ac-
    curacy of national advertising.
    Has "Advertising and women; a
    report on advertising portraying
    or directed to women."

Nat. Advisory Committee on
  Women
350 W. 51
New York, NY 10019
212-757-4927
    "... charged with informing
    the U.S. Secretary of Labor
    concerning needs of women
    in the U.S. and how the La-
    bor Dept. can best help
    them."

Nat. Amer. Women Suffrage Assoc. Carrie Chapman Catt, Pres., thought suffrage fight should be waged with patience and dignity and trust in Pres. Wilson--that energies should be concentrated for duration on War, defense work, franchise work in states. Opposite view: National Woman's Party.

National Archives & Records Service
Audiovisual Archives Division
Washington, DC 20408

Nat. Assoc. for Better Broadcasting
373 N. Western Ave.
Los Angeles, CA 90004

Nat. Assoc. for Women Deans, Administrators & Counselors
1028 Connecticut Ave. N.W., Suite 922
Washington, DC 20036
202-659-9330
 Joan M. McCall, Exec. Dir. & Man. Ed. Journal, Bulletin (its newsletter), and other publications. Operates placement service, continuing education.

Nat. Assoc. of College Women
4620 Kossuth Ave.
St. Louis, MO 63115
 National referral source for women with specific skills. "An association of Black college graduates."

Nat. Assoc. of Media Women, Inc.
157 W. 126
New York, NY 10027

Nat. Assoc. of Minority Women in Business
906 Grand, Suite 500
Kansas City, MO 64106

Nat. Assoc. of Parliamentarians
116 W. 47, Suite 217
Kansas City, MO 64112
 Get practice, instruction.

Nat. Assoc. of Railway Business Women, Inc.
50 E. Broad
Columbus, OH 43215
 Supports ERA. Also: 3763 N.W. 4 Ave., Boca Raton, FL 33432

Nat. Assoc. of the Laity, Women's Rights Committee
 see Joint Committee of Organizations Concerned with the Status of Women in the Church

Nat. Assoc. of Women Deans & Counselors see National Assoc. for...

Nat. Black Feminist Organization
370 Lexington Ave., Rm. 601
New York, NY 10017
212-685-0800
 Spokeswoman: Marge Sloan. "Statement of NBFO." "Standard questions you might be asked--suggested answers that might work." "Reading list."
 MA: Brookline 02146, Suzanne Lipsky, 42 Brighton Rd.; Boston 02118, Barbara Smith, 26 E. Springfield.
 CT: Bloomfield 06002, Beth Rawles, 6 Wedgewood Dr., # F.
 MD: Silver Spring 20910, Ida Clark, Summit Hill #306; 8500 16 St., Washington, DC area contact.
 GA: Atlanta 30314, Sandra Hollin Flowers, 528 Beckwith Ct., S.W.
 IL: Harvey 60426, Linda Johnston, 262 W. 148 Pl. Chicago area contact.
 MI: Detroit 48221, Jeanette Salters, Chairwoman, De-

(cont.) troit Metropolitan Chapter, 10524 W. McNichols, 313-341-9832. Media Task Force Chairwoman: Dorothy Eugenia Robinson.

National Cancer Institute
National Institutes of Health
Washington, DC 20014
> Inst. is setting up 5 testing sites to test 5000 of the approximately 3,000,000 daughters born of DES pregnancies.

Nat. Center for Family Planning Services
5600 Fishers Ln., Rm. 12A-33
Rockville, MD 20852
> Family Planning Digest mailing list.

Nat. Chicana Businesswomen's Assoc.
1801 Lomas N.W., c/o Anna Muller
Albuquerque, NM 87102

Nat. Chicana Foundation
507 E. Ellingbrook Dr.
Montebello, CA 90640
213-723-5949

Nat. Chicana Institute
(1:) PO Box 7306
San Antonio, TX 78207
(2:) PO Box 50155
Dallas, TX 75250

Nat. Chicana Welfare Rights Organization
PO Box 33286
Los Angeles, CA 90033
SEE ALSO Comisión...; Chicana Welfare Rights...

Nat. Civil Service League
1825 K St. N.W., Suite 508
Washington, DC 20006
> Conference Desk.

Nat. Clergy Consultation Service on Abortion
55 Washington Square S.
New York, NY 10012
212-477-0034

Nat. Coalition for Research on Women's Education & Development, Inc.
(1:) c/o Alice K. Smith, The Radcliffe Institute
3 James
Cambridge, MA 02138
(2:) 160 Harper Hall
Claremont, CA 91711
714-626-8511

Nat. Coalition of American Nuns see Joint Committee of Organizations Concerned with the Status of Women in the Church

Nat. Commission on Accrediting
1 Dupont Circle N.W.
Washington, DC 20036
202-296-4196
> For information on caucuses, task forces, rosters, employment registries, etc. within various regions and fields. Affirmative action.

Nat. Committee for Responsible Family Life & Sex Education
c/o SIECUS
1855 Broadway
New York, NY 10023

Nat. Committee for the Day-Care of Children see Day Care & Child Development Council of America

Nat. Committee on Household Employment
1625 Eye St. N.W., #323
Washington, DC 20006
202-872-1056
> Nonprofit service organization. NCHE News. Also: 8120 Fenton. Suite 300, Silver Spring, MD 20910. Edith Barksdale-Sloan, Exec. Dir.

National Conference of Puerto
  Rican Women
PO Box 4804, Cleveland Park Sta.
Washington, DC 20008
  Newsletter editor, Carmen
  Monroe.
  Paquita Vivó, 2510 Virginia
  Ave. N.W., Washington, DC
  20037.
  Miriam Cruz, 1450 E. 55 Pl.,
  #730, Chicago, IL 60615.
  Esther Jiménez, 13 Burnham
  Dr., West Hartford, CT
  06110.
  Carmen L. Pérez, 253 W. 72,
  #610, New York, NY 10023.
  Each chapter has autonomy:
  they are non-profit, non-partisan. SEE ALSO Women's
  Liberation Groups/Centers,
  Washington, DC.

Nat. Conference on Conservation
  and Voluntary Sterilization
c/o Assoc. for Voluntary Sterilization
14 W. 40
New York, NY 10018

Nat. Congress of Neighborhood
  Women
c/o Ann Smith, Nat. Center for
  Urban Ethnic Affairs
4408 8 St. N.W.
Washington, DC 20017

Nat. Council of Administrative
  Women in Education
1815 Ft. Myer Dr. N.
Arlington, VA 22209
703-528-6111
  Eleanor F. Dolan, C. Fern
  Ritter. NCAWE News.
  "Wanted--more women"
  ($2.50).

Nat. Council of Negro Women,
  Inc.
  Contact: Constance M. Carroll, Assoc. Dean, College
  of Liberal Arts, University
  of Maine at Portland-Gorham,
  Portland, ME 04103.

Nat. Council of Teachers of
  English
1111 Kenyon Rd.
Urbana, IL 61801
  "Guidelines for Publications."
  Committee on the Role &
  Image of Women in the
  Council and the Profession.

Nat. Council of Women Chiropractors. Supports ERA.
c/o American Chiropractic
  Assoc.
PO Box 1535
DesMoines, IA 50306

Nat. Council of Women of the
  U.S., Inc.
345 E. 46
New York, NY 10017
  Supports ERA. Ask for list
  of affiliates. Clearinghouse.

Nat. Council on the Aging
1828 L St. N.W., Suite 504
Washington, DC 20036
  Gerontology. Non-profit
  corp.

Nat. Data Use and Access Labs.
1601 N. Kent
Rosslyn, VA 22209
703-525-1480
  Robert Gignilliat. Have
  county/state summary-files
  of socio-eco and fertility
  characteristics for noninstitutionalized women of childbearing age.

Nat. Education Assoc.
Women's Rights Task Force.
  Also, Resource Center on
  Sex Roles in Education
1201 16 St. N.W.
Washington, DC 20036
  Contact Jean Heflin at NEA.
  Task force members include
  Lithangia Robinson, Louise
  Jones, Elaine Marks, Virginia Paul, Connie Nyieto de
  Sandoroff, Hank Harrison.

National Educational Television
10 Columbus Circle
New York, NY 10019
212-262-4200
 NET Training School at same address. A division of Educational Broadcasting Corp. Frederick Jacobi, Dir. of Information Services.

Nat. Federation of Press Women
R.R.1 Peneg Park
St. Clair, MO 63077

Nat. Federation of Republican Women
1625 Eye St. N.W.
Washington, DC 20006
 Supports ERA.

Nat. Film Board of Canada
 Operational headquarters and mailing address: PO Box 6100, Montreal 101 Quebec, 514-333-3333. USA: Suite 819, 580 5 Ave., New York, NY 10019, 212-586-2400.

Nat. Foundation for the Improvement of Education, Center to Counter Sex Bias in Elementary and Secondary Schools
1507 M St. N.W.
Washington, DC 20036
202-833-4404

Nat. Free Clinic Council
1304 Haight
San Francisco, CA 94117
 Lists free clinics.

Nat. Gay Student Center
2115 S St. N.W.
Washington, DC 20008
 "Student Gay groups" ($.25).

Nat. Historical Publications Commission. Advisory Committee on Women's Papers. c/o U.S. Library of Congress see their Report recommending publication of the papers of 70 women (LC Information Bulletin: Appendix v. 33, #23, June 7, 1974).

Nat. Institute of Education
Dept. of Health, Education & Welfare
Washington, DC 20208
202-254-7908
 Their "Grants for Research in Education" claims to be focusing funds on research areas including third area: diversity, pluralism, etc., which in turn includes "racial, cultural, sex-role, or religious stereotyping or discrimination in institutions." Dr. Jean Lipman-Blumen, Dir., Women's Research Program.

Nat. Institutes of Health
Self-Help for Equal Rights Committee
Washington, DC 20014

Nat. Lawyers Guild
23 Cornelia
New York, NY 10014
 Regional offices. Periodicals. "Welfare fair hearings; rights and procedures" (gratis). Also: Box 673, Berkeley, CA 94701.

Nat. Lesbian Information Service
PO Box 15368
San Francisco, CA 94115
 Publishes monthly newsletter.

Nat. Operation Venus Program
1620 Summer
Philadelphia, PA 19103
 Toll-free hot line in Philadelphia: 800-523-1885. VD Control Centers.

Nat. Order of Women Legislators (OWI)
Route 5
Laconia, NH 03246

National Organization for Non-
   Parents (NON)
220 Miramonte
Palo Alto, CA 94306
   Also: 515 Madison Ave.,
   New York, NY 10022.

Nat. Organization for Women
   KNOW distributes "List of
   current NOW officers and
   task force coordinators, with
   addresses and phone numbers"
   (#26301 $.10). Task forces
   on the national level relate to
   volunteerism, compliance,
   ageism, religion, Women's
   Studies, Gay women, and
   numerous other areas relating
   to the Liberation of Women.
   National NOW office: 5 S.
      Wabash, Suite 1615, Chica-
      go, IL 60603, 312-332-
      1954.
   Public Information office:
      527 Madison Ave., Suite
      1001, New York, NY 10022,
      212-755-4587.
   Legislative Office, 1266 Na-
      tional Press Bldg., Wash-
      ington, DC 20004, 202-
      347-2279
   Legal Defense & Education
      Fund, 9 W. 57, New York,
      NY 10019, 212-688-1751.

Nat. Prison Project
American Civil Liberties Union
   Foundation
1424 16 St. N.W. #303
Washington, DC 20036
202-234-9345
   Barbara M. Milstein, Staff
   attorney. Project involved in
   working with women in prisons
   as well as men. Has filed
   suit against Women's Detention
   Center, Washington, DC and
   also working re conditions at
   Federal Reformatory for Women, Alderson, WV.

Nat. Technical Information Service

Springfield, VA 22151
   "Women in apprenticeship;
   why not?" ($6).

Nat. Woman's Christian Tem-
   perance Union
Frances E. Willard Memorial
   Library for Alcohol Research
1730 Chicago Ave.
Evanston, IL 60201
   Includes history and archives
   of WCTU.

Nat. Women's Book Assoc.
124 Church
Mary Gaver, Bro-Dart Industries, Inc.
New Brunswick, NJ 08901
201-828-1555

Nat. Women's Health Coalition
222 E. 35
New York, NY 10016
   Speakers. Merle Goldberg,
   dir. and women's health advocate. Send SASE for information.

Nat. Women's History Center
   1 of 3 projects receiving ap-
   proval at Dec. 7, 1973 meeting of 40 national women's
   organizations re Bicentennial
   commemoration.

Nat. Women's Political Caucus:
1302 18 St. N.W., Ste 703
Washington, DC 20036
202-785-2911
   Sissy Farenthold. News-
   letter. Speakers' Bureau
   202-347-9658, Jane Mc-
   Michael.
   CA: Los Angeles 90019,
   5899 W. Pico, 213-936-
   0236.
   IA: Des Moines 50306, PO
   Box 1941, Roxanne Conlin.
   MA: Auburndale 02166,
   Priscilla M. Leith, 1831
   Washington. "Politics is
   for women; all you need to
   know about being a candidate,

Directory of Sources

(cont.) but were afraid to ask (because you are a woman)" ($1.95). Published by Newton, MA Women's Political Caucus; contact Ms. Leith.
MT: Great Falls 59403, Box 694, Geraldine Travis.
NY: Hewlett 11557, Sylvia Pines, 1007 Wateredge Pl., 516-374-2550. South Hauppage 11722, Sandra Rosalia, 179 Sunflower, 516-234-0900.
WA: Seattle 98133, Box 7536, Sells tote bag.

National Women's Suffrage Assoc. Headed by Elizabeth Cady Stanton and Susan B. Anthony. One of "the most prominent organizations devoted to women's rights--the militant.... The more respectable was American Woman Suffrage Assoc."

Nat. Youth Alternatives Project
1830 Conn. Ave. N.W.
Washington, DC 20009
202-234-6664
 Nonprofit organization. Current publications include: "National directory of runaway centers," "Stalking the large green grant; basic manual on methods of obtaining funds for alternative social service projects." ($1 each.)

Native Alliance for Redpower
Box 6152
Vancouver 8, British Columbia
Native Movement.

Native American Women's Action Council
4339 California
San Francisco, CA 94118
Has newsletter.

Natural Homebirth (course)
Shoshanna Margolin
1122 Beach 12
Far Rockaway, NY 11690

$20 minimum of 10 women.

Nevada Women's Health Collective
12585 Jones Bar Rd.
Nevada City, CA 95959

New Council on Women's Concerns
Univ. of Wisconsin, Milwaukee
Union East 331, Student Govt.
2200 E. Kenwood
Milwaukee, WI 53211

New Day Films
PO Box 315
Franklin Lakes, NJ 07417
201-891-8240
 Deals exclusively with films by/about women. A distribution coop.

New Dynamics Associates
Box 92, RFD #5
Laconia, NH 03216
603-524-1441
 CR for men and women.

New Earth Bookstore
24 E. 39
Kansas City, MO 64111

New England Consortium for Women in Higher Education
See Also HERS. Contact: Sheila Tobias, Asso. Provost, Wesleyan University, Middletown, CT 06457.
Lilli Hornig, Dir., Brown Univ., Providence, RI 02912.

New Environments for Women Associates
44 Bartwell Rd.
Lexington, MA 02173
617-862-0663
 Consultants. Newsletter.

New Feminist Talent Associates
250 W. 57, Suite 1318
New York, NY 10019
 Feminist speakers bureau. Newsletter.

New Haven Women's Film Co-op.
66 2
New Haven, CT 06519

New Jersey Educational Media
  Consortium
240 High
Newark, NJ 07102
201-624-1460
  Ellen Morgan, Program Consultant. Women's Studies Committee.

N.J. Talent Bank for Women
State Office on Women
New Jersey Dept. of Community
  Affairs
Trenton, NJ 08625

N.J. Women on Employment
PO Box 2163
Princeton, NJ 08540

New Moon Communications, Inc.
2 Hemlock Dr.
Stamford, CT 06902
203-348-8529
  Lolly & Jeanne Hirsch. Monthly Extract. Also: Box 3488, 06905. "Proceedings of the 1st Intnatl. Childbirth Conference, 1973" ($2), "The witch's Os" ($2). A communications network of feminist gynecological self-help clinics. Speakers. Buttons, gynecological self-help presentation. Speculum ($2).

New Morning Bookstore
110 High, PO Box 1765
Hartford, CT 06103

New Options, Inc.
1844 Oakman Blvd.
Detroit, MI 48238
313-882-7015
  Jacquelin Washington. New company of women affirmative action consultants. Speciality in mass media.

New Orleans Gay Feminists
1024 Jackon Ave.
New Orleans, LA 70130
  Personal and political raps.

New Orleans Hotel
63 Spring
Eureka Springs, AR 72632
501-253-8630
  On the National Historical Register.

New Press
84 Sussex Ave.
Toronto 179, Ontario
416-964-7654
  Not a feminist press. Published feminist works, however, e.g. Stephenson's "Women in Canada."

New Seed Press
PO Box 3016-A
Stanford, CA 94305
  Has Bulbul's cartoons "Dissecting Doctor Medi-Corpse." Publishes non-sexist books.

New Woman in New China
PO Box 77632
Los Angeles, CA 90007

New Woman's Clinic
Washington, DC
202-872-8070
  Call collect. Contraception, abortion help.

New Words. Women's Book
  Center
419 Washington
Somerville, MA 02143

New World Resource Center
2546 N. Halsted
Chicago, IL 60614

New York. City. Chancellor's Advisory Commission to Promote Equal Opportunity and Eliminate Sex Discrimination
Board of Education, rm. 703
65 Court

Directory of Sources

(cont.) Brooklyn, NY 11201
Nonsexist education commitment in city schools.

New York Consultation & Referral Service
130 W. 57
New York, NY 10019
212-246-5756
Psychotherapist-locator at moderate fees. "Facts you should know about choosing a psychotherapist; a public service pamphlet" (gratis).

New York Filmmakers Co-op.
175 Lexington Ave.
New York, NY 10016

New York Poets' Co-op.
c/o Robert Kramer, 240 E. 240
Bronx, NY 10470
Group '74 anthology of this co-op, which opened up the poetry scene in New York--non-sexist, non-cliquest.

New York Psychological Consultation & Referral Service
see N.Y. Consultation & Referral...

New York Public Library
5th Ave. & 42nd St.
New York, NY 10018
The Berg Collection. Acquired from Leonard Woolf by Drs. Albert A. and Henry W. Berg. Schwimmer-Lloyd [feminist] Collection: Rosika Schwimmer and Lola Maverick Lloyd documents (women's suffrage leaders). Housed in Manuscripts & Archives Division. Permission must be obtained. Manuscripts & Archives Div.: Papers of Catherine Curtis.

New York Radical Feminist Speakers Bureau
Judy Sullivan, Apt. H. 961
463 West St.
New York, NY 10014

212-242-7471

New York. State. Dept. of Labor Library
80 Center
New York, NY 10005

New York State TALENT BANK
270 Broadway, c/o Norma Kraus, 3d fl.
New York, NY 10007

New York. State. Women's Unit
State Capitol
Albany, NY 12224
Virginia Cairns. Also: 22 W. 55, New York 10019. Evelyn Cunningham.

Newfoundland Status of Women Council
PO Box 5021
St. John's, Newfoundland
Newsletter.

Newsreel
NY: New York 10001, 332 7 Ave.
CA: San Francisco 94102, 1232 Market.
Also: Yellow Springs Newsreel, Antioch Union, Antioch College, Yellow Springs, OH 45387. Milwaukee Newsreel, 1618 W. Wells, Milwaukee, WI 53233. Lawrence Newsreel, 815 Vermont, Lawrence, KS 66044. (Another New York City address: 26 W. 20, 10011, 212-243-2310.)

Nielsen, Joyce
850 S. Detroit
Los Angeles, CA 90036
213-933-2876
Jewelry.

Niles, Fred A. Communications Centers
1058 W. Washington Blvd.
Chicago, IL 60607

"9 to 5"
YMCA, 140 Clarendon
Boston, MA 02116
   Ellen Cassedy, Spokesperson, for office workers organizing for better treatment. Newsletter.

Nochlin, Linda
Vassar College
Poughkeepsie, NY 12601
   Art Professor. "Why there have been no great women artists." Women & Art course.

Non-Parents see National Organization for...

Non-sexist Child Development Project see Women's Action Alliance

Nordstrom, Kristina see Festival of Women's Films, First International

North American Indian Women's Assoc.
3201 Shadybrook
Midwest City, OK 73110
   Marie Cox represented the Assoc. at BiCentennial planning meeting.

North Carolina. University.
Woman's College Library
100 Spring Garden
Greensboro, NC 27412

Northern Interrelated Library System
Lincoln Public Library
Lincoln, RI 02865
   Permanent information on women's rights need led to setting up a regional cooperative collection of materials about/by women, including AV. Contact: Librarian Earleen McCarthy.

Northern Women
415 Victoria Ave., Rm. 19
Thunder Bay, Ontario
807-344-2712
   Has newspaper.

Northwestern University Libraries. Special Collections
Evanston, IL 60201
   Bonnie Jo Sedlak, Dir., Women's Collection. One of the largest current Women's Movement collections. Has newsletter.

Not-in-New York Gallery
314 W. 4
Cincinnati, OH 45202

Nurses for Political Action
Molloy College. Marjorie Stanton
Rockville Center, NY 11570
   (Nurses NOW is a task force.)

- O -

Off Our Backs
1724 20 St. N.W.
Washington, DC 20009
   Feminist collective.

O'Hair, Madalyn Murray
4203 Medical Pky.
Austin, TX 78756
   Speaker: contact American Atheist Speakers Bureau, PO Box 2117, Austin 78767. SEE ALSO "Madalyn" in Audiovisual part of Non-Book Resources section.

Ohio Affirmative Action Officers Assoc.
   Contact: Beverly Price, 103 McGuffey Hall, Ohio University, Athens, OH 45701. AA officers in academia.

Older Women's Liberation
OWL Studio 29, 222 Central Park S.
New York, NY 10019
   Also: Women's Center, 243

Directory of Sources

(cont.) W. 20, New York, NY 10003, c/o Schwartz, 91 Bedford, New York, NY 10014.

Olivia Records
Box 1784, Main City Station
Washington, DC 20013
 New feminist, national women's recording company. SEE "Lady" in Audiovisual part of Non-Book section.

Ombudswoman
PO Box 22135
San Francisco, CA 94122
 "Mayhem on women" by Dorothy Shinder ($2.95).

Ontario Council on the Status of Women
Laura Sabia, Social Development
Parliament Buildings
Queen's Park, Ontario

Ontario Institute for Studies in Ed.
Marion Royce Collection
252 Bloor St. W.
Toronto 181, Ont.
416-923-6641
 File of articles, letters, pamphlets, etc. re status of women in both Canada and U.S.A.

Operation Venus
800-523-1885
 Nationwide toll-free VD information. Addresses of clinics.

Options for Women
8419 Germantown Ave.
Philadelphia, PA 19118
215-242-4955
 Nonprofit licensed employment agency placing women in full and part-time jobs.

The Oracle
1024 B St., #6
Hayward, CA 94541
 Feminist books center for feminist literature. Nonsexist children's books, posters, etc.

Oral History Library see Women's History Research Center

Order of Women Legislators
 Supports ERA.

Organization of American States
Inter-American Commission of Women
Washington, DC 20006
 News Bulletin.

Osteopathic Women's National
 Supports ERA.

The Other Woman, Ltd.
153 E. 18
New York, NY 10003

Our Catalogue Co.
6504 Pardall Rd., #3
Isla Vista, CA 93017
 Planning nation-wide feminist directory.

- P -

Pace Services
 Elaine Gordon, Suite 1003, Dupont Plaza Office Bldg., Miami, FL 33131, 305-358-3018. SEE ALSO Nikki Beare. A consulting firm of contract and employment compliance and Affirmative Action programs.

Pacifica Program Service
Pacifica Tape Library
5316 Venice Blvd., Lucy Robins
Los Angeles, CA 90019
213-931-1625
 Also: 2217 Shattuck Ave., Berkeley, CA 94704, 415-848-3785. Sells outstanding tapes. Has catalog of Feminist Movement tapes and brochure, "Women." A non-

(cont.) profit educational foundation incorporated in California.

Painted Women Ritual Theater
178 5 Ave., Jerianne Badanes
New York, NY 10010
212-989-4007
  Write 155 Sheafe Rd., Wappingers Falls, NY 12590.

Pan-African Women's Center. Proposed at regional seminar on integration of women in development, with special reference to population factors in Addis Ababa, June 1974. Assisting the Center would be: African Women's Volunteer Task Force, African Women's Development Fund. Contact UN Economic Commission for Africa.

Pan American Liaison Committee of Women's Organizations, Inc.
1432 Aspen
Washington, DC 20012

Pan American Medical Women's Alliance
1019 W. 50 St. N.
Wichita, KS 67204

Pan American Women's Assoc.
20 W. 40
New York, NY 10018

Pan Pacific & Southeast Asia Women's Assoc. of the U.S.A.
225 E. 46
New York, NY 10017

Pap Smear Clinic
Ramsey County Hospital
640 Jackson
St. Paul, MN 55101
612-222-4260
  1 free pap smear a year to any woman.

Paper Tiger Press
334 N. Vassar
Wichita, KS 67208
  Women's poetry.

Parents Committee for Nonsexist education
Peoria Parents School System
824 W. Stratford Dr.
Peoria, IL 61614

Parents Without Partners
80 5 Ave.
New York, NY 10011

Part-time Feminist Book Center
151 S. Lincoln
Spokane, WA 99202

Peabody Institute Library
15 Sylvan
Danvers, MA 01923
  Witchcraft.

Pena, Nelda see Martini, Anita

Penelope & Sisters
603 S. 4
Philadelphia, PA 19147
  Gallery, posters.

Pennsylvania Program for Women and Girl Offenders
1530 Chestnut, #711
Philadelphia, PA 19102
215-563-9386
  News Resources & Research series.

Pennsylvania Women's Studies Planners
3601 Locust Walk
Philadelphia, PA 19174

Pennsylvanians for Women's Rights
230 W. Chestnut
Lancaster, PA 17603
  PWR Newsletter. Speakers' Bureau.

People's Bicentennial Commission

Directory of Sources

(cont.) 1346 Conn. Ave. N.W.
Washington, DC 20036
202-833-9121
"Nationwide citizen organization dedicated to restoring the democratic principles that shaped the birth of this Republic." Posters, kit ($7), newspaper, study guide & syllabus. Sheila Rollins, Noreen Banks.

People's Press
2680 21
San Francisco, CA 94410
415-282-0856
Records, posters, non-sexist kid lit.

People's Town Hall
488 New York Ave.
c/o Gillian Booth
Huntington, NY 11743
516-423-8330

Pepsi-Cola Co.
500 Park Ave.
New York, NY 10022

Philadelphia Task Force on Women in Religion
PO Box 24003
Philadelphia, PA 19130

Philadelphia Women's Collective
4506 Springfield Ave.
Philadelphia, PA 19143
"The Philadelphia story; another experiment on women." (For postage.) Abortion information.

Phyllis Kind Gallery
226 E. Ontario
Chicago, IL 60611

Physician's Training Program in Early Abortion Techniques see Feminist Women's Health Center(s), Los Angeles

Picture Post Gallery

PO Box 8137
Philadelphia, PA 19101

Planned Parenthood
515 Madison Ave.
New York, NY 10022
Alan F. Guttmacher, Pres.
212-541-7800. Operates clinics for vasectomy in various states.

Planned Parenthood--for abortion information
New York # for abortion info.: 212-777-4504 & 2015;
Colorado # for abortion info.: 303-388-4125 (2025 York, Denver 80205).

Planned Parenthood--New York City:
Planned Parenthood, 300 Park Ave. 10022, 212-777-2002.
Planned Parenthood Federation of America, Inc. Executive office, 810 7 Ave., 10019, 212-541-7800.
Planned Parenthood World Population, 515 Madison Ave. 10019, 212-752-2100; 810 7 Ave. 10019, 212-541-7800; 545 Madison Ave. 10022, 212-826-0947.
Planned Parenthood of New York City, Inc., Executive Office, 300 Park Ave. S. 10022, 212-777-2002.
Planned Parenthood's Thrift Shop, 324 E. 59, 10022, 212-371-1580.

Planned Parenthood--by State
CA: San Francisco 94115, 2340 Clay, 415-567-0870.
MA: Newton Centre 02159, 93 Union, 617-332-8750; Springfield 01107, 103-105 Division, 413-732-0350.

(cont.) MN: Minneapolis 55403, 803 Hennepin Ave., 612-336-8931; St. Paul 55102, 408 St. Peter, 612-224-1361; Midway Shopping Center, 1562 University, Minneapolis, 612-646-9603, multi-media library resource center.
PA: Philadelphia 19102, 1402 Spruce. Has "Techniques" for leading group discussions on human sexuality, by Winifred Kempton, A.C.S.W. ($.60).
TX: Houston, 713-522-3976. For abortion information.

Planned Parenthood--Library
Katherine Dexter McCormick
  Library
515 Madison Ave.
New York, NY 10022

Planned Parenthood--World Population
515 Madison Ave.
New York, NY 10022
(Planned Parenthood--World Population for Europe and Africa-south of Sahara: headquarters in London, England.) Request "Planned Parenthood Publications." Posters, pamphlets, books, audiovisuals.
Planned Parenthood--World Population, 810 Seventh Ave., New York, NY 10019. Pamphlets on birth control, family planning, infertility, marriage and family life, research, religion, etc.; curriculum materials, posters, exhibits, film catalog.

Pluto Press, Ltd.
Unit 10 Spencer Ct.
7 Chalcort
London, NW1 8LH
01-722-0141
Publishers of left-wing books on women, workers, and homosexuality. Canadian distributor: Spartacus Books, PO Box 2881, Vancouver, B.C.

Polay, Nita
666 West End Ave.
New York, NY 10025
Information on how to form a Jewish women's CR group ($.25).

Polymorph Films
331 Newbury
Boston, MA 02115
617-262-5960
Award-winning films about women.

Poppler & Barz
Billings, MT 49103
Believed to be the state's first woman's law firm.

Population Planning (Associates)
105 N. Columbia
Chapel Hill, NC 27514
"Contraceptives through the privacy of the mail" says their ad. Has sampler assortments. "Dr. Timothy R. L. Black, founder."

Powerhouse Gallery
1210 Greene Ave.
Montreal, Quebec

Pregnancy Counseling Service
Washington, DC
202-298-7995
Abortion information, birth control, vasectomy, free pregnancy test. Information and referral, no fee.

Preterm Institute
430 Lexington
Auburndale, MA 02166
Also in Boston. Contraception, abortion, VD, sterilization information.

Directory of Sources

Prime Time Speakers Roster
945 West End Ave.
New York, NY 10025
212-864-7541
   Esther Labovitz, Coord.

Probation Plus
1130 Nicollet (Y.W.C.A.)
Minneapolis, MN 55401
612-332-0501
   Federally-funded agency offering service to women ages 13-18 on probation.

Problem Pregnancy Information Center
Box 9090
Stanford, CA 94305
   Dial A B O R T I O N.

Professional Skills Roster
410 College Ave., Rm. 210
Ithaca, NY 14850
607-256-3758
   Charlotte Shea, Co-ordinator.

Project Equality
1307 S. Wabash Ave.
Chicago, IL 60605
312-341-1530, 786-1530
   Aiding nonprofit institutions to put into practice their EEO programs, offices throughout U.S.A.

Project for Academic Affirmative Action Training ("PAAAT")
1625 K St. N.W., 10th fl.
Washington, DC
202-347-3687
   A joint project of the Project on the Status and Education of Women of the Assoc. of American Colleges and The International Assoc. of Official Human Rights Agencies.

Project on Equality in Education
Women's Equity Action League
1201 S. Scott, #608
Arlington, VA 22204
   Arlene Horowitz.

Project Repair
PO Box 3942, Joyce Nower
San Diego, CA 92103
714-234-2521
   Non-profit group in cooperation with Neighborhood Services, training women for carpentry, electric systems, plumbing, etc.

Project on the Status and Education of Women see Association of American Colleges

Public Action Coalition on Toys (PACT)
Suite 503, 2000 P St. N.W.
Washington, DC 20036
   Formed in 1973 by several women's and consumer groups including N.O.W. and Ralph Nader's Citizen Action Group.

Public Affairs Council
1601 18 St. N.W.
Washington, DC 20009
   "Affirmative Action Programs for Women," a monograph for corporate urban affairs and equal opportunity officers developed by P.A.C. ($10; $5 for nonprofit groups).

Public Broadcasting Service
955 L'Enfant Plaza S.W.
Washington, DC 20024

Pyramid Films
PO Box 1048
Santa Monica, CA 90406
213-828-7577

- Q -

Queen Silver
1632 Lemoyne
Los Angeles, CA 90026
   T-Shirts.

Queensborough Community College of CUNY
Women's Research & Resource Center
222-03 Garland Dr., Audrey Silva
Bayside, NY 11364
212-424-0666, 7

Quest Productions
630 9 Ave.
New York, NY 10036

- R -

Radical America
1878 Massachusetts Ave.
Cambridge, MA 02140
"Women in American Society" pamphlet.

Radical Feminists 28
PO Box 7064
Powderhorn Sta.
Minneapolis, MN 55407

Radical Lesbian Feminists
2828 N. Bristol, #59
Santa Ana, CA 92706
Political activists.

Radical Lesbians
PO Box 1943
Philadelphia, PA 19105

Radical Women
3815 5 Ave. N.E.
Seattle, WA 89105
Numerous pamphlets re lesbiana, race, socialism, class struggle, e.g. "Lesbianism; a socialist-feminist perspective" ($.15), "Race and sex, 1972: Collision or comradeship?" ($.25).

Radio free people
133 Mercer
New York, NY 10012
212-966-6729
Collective of women and men. Tapes.

Radio Free Women see Feminist Radio Network

Radio Free Women
PO Box 413, Station D
Toronto 9, Ontario
416-536-1717
Nonprofit community organization working to establish a non-commercial, nonprofit FM band community radio station in Metropolitan Toronto. Currently aired on Radio Varsity, Univ. of Toronto (96.3 FM). Office space at 1079 Bloor St. W. Meetings held at Gladstone Place, 1089 Bloor St. W. Contact Flo Woods, 96 Chelsea Ave., 416-537-9742.

Randolph-Macon Woman's College
Lipscomb Library
Lynchburg, VA 23304
Published-writings of Virginia women.

Rape Crisis Center
PO Box 20015
Washington, DC 20009
202-333-RAPE
"How to start a rape crisis center" ($1.25 donation). Newsletter. "Protection tactics" (free for SASE) "If you have been raped or sexually attacked, call us for free legal, medical, and psychological assistance, referrals and alternatives. Also free housing with women, escort groups, self-defense and discussion groups."

Rape Crisis Line
3433 Tulane Ave., Y.W.C.A.
New Orleans, LA 70119
504-486-6041
Mary Capps, Coordinator.

Rape Prevention Center

(cont.) Nashville, TN 38102
Donna Pence.

Rebis Press
5806 Lawton Ave.
Oakland, CA 94618
Non-sexist children's stories.

Red Book
91 River
Cambridge, MA 02139

Redactron Corp.
100 Parkway Dr.
South Hauppauge, NY 11787
516-543-8700
"FREE The Secretary" labels.

Redstockings
The Group Center
42 1/2 St. Marks Pl.
New York, NY 10003

Rembrandt Films
59 E. 54
New York, NY 10022

Reporters Committee for Freedom of the Press
1750 Pennsylvania Ave. N.W., Rm. 1310
Washington, DC 20006
202-298-7460
Press Censorship Newsletter.

Reprise Records
4000 Warner Blvd.
Burbank, CA 91505

Republican National Committee
Women's Division
1625 I St. N.W.
Washington, DC 20006
Republican Campaign Committee's "Wives' manual" is noteworthy.

Research Center on Women
Alverno College
3401 S. 39, Mary Austin Doherty
Milwaykee, WI 53215

Research Center on Women in Higher Education and the Professions
c/o Dr. Irene Tinker, A.A.A.S.,
1776 Mass. Ave. N.W.
Washington, DC 20036
&/or Dr. Mary Lefkowitz,
Wellesley College, Wellesley, MA 02181. A research center to be located at Wellesley College.

Research for Social Change, Inc.
44 Coolidge Ave., Lynn Slavitt
Cambridge, MA 02138
Help combat the 'Catch 22' for women in academia via research financing for women without university affiliation.

Resource Center for Women in Higher Education (HERS)
Brown University
Providence, RI 02912
Placement and referral service working with women faculty and university administrators to implement affirmative action for women.

Resource Center on Sex Role Stereotyping
National Education Assoc.
1201 16 St. N.W.
Washington, DC 20036

Resource Center on Sex Roles in Education. National Foundation for Improvement of Education
1156-15 St. N.W., Suite 918
Washington, DC 20005
Research Action Notes.

Response
PO Box 1496, 415 South
Waltham, MA 02154
"The Jewish woman; an anthology" ($2).

Response & Associates
PO Box 333

(cont.) Chicago Heights, IL
  60411
  312-758-4600
   "Emerging woman in management" confidence and skills-building workshops.

"Right to Die"
Maggie Kuhn
c/o the Grey Panthers (q.v.)

Rip-Off File (in art)
Nancy Spero, 171 W. 71
New York, NY 10023
   Also Joyce Kozloff, 225 W. 106, New York 10025. A great idea with application to other fields.

Rock of Ages
   A group concerned with problems of older women. For information contact People's Librarian Task Force of the American Library Assoc.'s Social Responsibility Round Table.

Rockland County Feminists
24 DeBraun Ave.
Suffern, NY 10901
   Aurora.

Rosenberg, Marie B.
Institute of Governmental Affairs & School of Business. Univ. of Wisconsin
Eau Claire, WI 54701
   Projects in progress: "History of Affirmative Action and Equal Employment Policy and Legislation," with bibliography; review of the literature on women in politics for Polity.

ROSTERS: see concluding portion of Directory of Sources section (i.e., "Rosters for Employment Action") for listings of employment rosters, women's caucuses, etc. associated with professional and occupational groups.

Rush Publishing Co.
Box 1, Sara Stauffer Whaley, Pres.
Rush, NY 14543
716-533-1376
   Publishers of bibliographies, Women Studies Abstracts, reviews, etc.

- S -

SCUM Stands for Society for Cutting up Men. Valerie Solanis' name is often associated with SCUM.

SHARE
Contact: Carole Leita
555 Duboce
San Francisco, CA 94117
415-863-8819
   Sisters Have Resources Everywhere: a Directory of Feminist Librarians.

SOHO 20 (gallery)
99 Spring
New York, NY 10012

SOS (Save Our Sisters)
4224 University Way N.E.
YWCA
Seattle, WA 98105
206-ME3-3550
   Feminist organization which began with 2 women taking calls in their homes and providing housing; now provide emergency housing, transportation, legal counsel, medical exams, etc. A model?

SRRT see American Library Assoc.

STOP ERA
   National chairman = Phyllis Schlafly. In Florida, Shirley Schellenberger.

SUNY Caucus on Status of Wo-

Directory of Sources

(cont.) men
Contact: Francine Frank
41 Orchard
Delmar, NY 12054
SEE ALSO CUNY Caucus....
There are sections of the SUNY Caucus at Albany, Binghamton, Buffalo, Stony Brook; Down- and up-state Medical Centers; Colleges at Brockport, Buffalo, Cortland, Fredonia, Geneseo, New Paltz, Oneonta, Oswego, Potsdam; College of Ceramics, Alfred; College of Agriculture, Cornell; College of Human Ecology, Cornell; A&T Colleges at Alfred, Morrisville; Community Colleges at Corning, Erie, Genesee, Hudson Valley, Monroe, Niagara, Onondaga, Queensborough, Rockland, Ulster.

Sagaris
Burlington, VT 05401 .
Joan Peters, spokeswoman. Feminist institute intended as feminist-humanist alternative to existing patriarchal society schools of higher education. Tuition on sliding scale; child care included.

(College of) Saint Catherine Library
2004 Randolph Ave.
St. Paul, MN 55116
Marie Inez, Head Librarian. Slides. Emphasis on psychological liberation of women in 20th century.

St. Christopher's Hospice
London, England
Founder-director, Dr. Cicely Saunders. Private institution pioneering new approaches to relieving both the medical and spiritual suffering of the dying. "The dignity of death" --ABC News' characterization, June 1974.

St. Joan's International Alliance: U.S.A. Section
435 W. 119
New York, NY 10027
212-MO3-3555
Supports ERA. SEE ALSO Joint Committee of Organizations Concerned with the Status of Women in the Church.

San Francisco Mime Troup
450 Alabama
San Francisco, CA 94110
"Guerilla theater essays" ($1.50).

San Francisco Woman's Health Center
3789 24
San Francisco, CA 94114

San Francisco Women's Media Group
225 Corbett
San Francisco, CA 94114
Tapes.

Sanders, Phyllis
29 Old Mill Rd.
Chappaqua, NY 10514
914-238-9031
"The changing world of women" WNYC TV #31 and WNYC AM radio (830 KC). Municipal Building, New York, NY 10007, 212-566-3385. Also feminist travel tours.

Sands, Alan Production
565 5 Ave.
New York, NY 10017

Sanger, Margaret Research Bureau Clinic see Margaret...

Santa Clara County Commission on the Status of Women
1401 Wolfe Rd.
Sunnyvale, CA 94087
408-738-1071
Gloria Guenther, Commis.

Sapphire Publishing Co.
Box 15072
San Francisco, CA 94115
  First publication is Carolyn J. Greene's "70 soul secrets of Sapphire." A publishing partnership in Bay Area of Black women.

Saunders, Pat
685 West End Ave.
New York, NY 10025
  Filmmaker and source.

Save Women's Image
Dept. M, PO Box 4236
Arcata, CA 95521
  Debunking myths!

Schlesinger, Arthur & Elizabeth Library on The History of Women in America; The manuscripts inventory and the Catalogs of the manuscripts, books and pictures. Radcliffe College, Boston. G. K. Hall (70 Lincoln, Boston, MA 02111) has published a "book-catalog" of this collection covering up to Summer 1973, with supplement(s) planned ($215), contact: Diane Baden.

Schloat, Warren Productions
Palmer Ln. W.
Pleasantville, NY 10570

Schneider, Rosalind
40 Cottontail Ln.
Irvington-on-Hudson, NY 10533
  Filmmaker and source.

Scholastic Audio-visual Materials
906 Sylvan Ave.
Englewood Cliffs, NY 07632

School of Living--West
442 1/2 Landfair Ave.
Los Angeles, CA 90024
  Formerly Alternatives Foundation. Distributes "Communes worldwide" ($10), "Directory of free schools, social change & personal growth centers, with bibliographies" ($4), "Commune directory" ($1).

Schulder, Diane B.
351 Broadway
New York, NY 10013
212-966-7110
  Matrimonial and family lawyer. (SEE #132 Basic Book Collection). Has taught women-and-the-law type courses.

Science & Behavior Books, Inc.
PO Box AJ
Cupertino, CA 95014

Scott Education Division
Holyoke, MA 01040

Seattle Radical Women
3815 5 Ave.
Seattle, WA 98105
  Send SASE for inquiries. Packet ($3.50).

Second Story Bookstore
34 Rossmore Rd.
Jamaica Plain, MA 02130

Second Wives Are People
1536 Harvey
Berwin, IL 60402

Seiden, Anne, M.D.
Neuropsychiatric Institute
Univ. of Illinois
913 S. Wood
Chicago, IL 60612
312-996-7380
  Women's Mental Health Task Force.

Selective Buying Campaign
c/o E. N. Kaw
2004 Lexington Ave. N.
Roseville, MN 55113
  "Suzy Baker Story" pamphlet shows up General Mills.

Self Help for Equal Rights (SHER)

Directory of Sources

(cont.) National Institutes of Health
PO Box 30044
Washington, DC 20041
   Has newsletter.

Self Protection Media for Women
c/o Film Fair Communications
10820 Ventura Blvd.
Studio City, CA 91604

Sense and Sensibility Collective
57 Ellery
Cambridge, MA 02138
   Virginia Rankin, Ann Kantzman, Peggy Kornegger. "Women and literature" annotated bibliography of women writers. Seminar in feminist studies.

Serena/Société pour la regulation de natalité
55 Parksdale
Ottawa, Ontario
   Sympto-Thermal-Rhythm is used widely in Quebec as it is the only method of birth control the (Catholic) government will support. Has a clinical-use failure-rate of 0.8 to 6.6% compared to 14.4 to 34.5% for calendar-rhythm. English and French-language materials.

Sexism in Textbooks Committee
Scott, Foresman & Co.
1900 E. Lake Ave.
Glenview, IL 60025
   "Guidelines for improving the image of women in textbooks" (gratis). SEE ALSO Women at Scott, Foresman.

Shameless Hussy Press
PO Box 424
San Lorenzo, CA 94580
   Women publishers. "Remember our fire" Series. Alta, printer and poet.

Sherr, Lynn & Jurate Kazickas
c/o Universe Books

381 Park Ave. S.
New York, NY 10016
   "The liberated woman's appointment calendar."

Shevey, Sandra
2043 N. Beachwood Dr.
Hollywood, CA 90028
   Speaker. Developed first course on Women-in-Film. Editor-publisher of <u>Myth America Magazine</u>. Movie critic for KPFK-FM. Involved in Women's Film Educational Project.

Show of Hands (Gallery)
240 W. 72
New York, NY 10023

Siegel, Lois
5028 St. Urbain
Montreal 151 PQ
   Filmmaker and source.

Siegel, Marian
333 E. 30
New York, NY 10030
   Filmmaker and source.

Silver(wo)man, Sandy
Millstone River, Apt. E-5
Rt. 1
Princeton, NJ 08540
609-452-8721
   Feminist seals, fundraisers, plaques. Consultant on sexism in textbooks and training manuals.

"Single by choice" Column
   Antoinette May, free-lancer
Centurion Press Internatl.
Box 14456
Las Vegas, NV 89114

Sir George Williams University
Center for Interdisciplinary Studies
Joanne Morgan, 2010 MacKay
Montreal, Quebec H36 1M8
   Summer institute in Women's Studies, 1974.

Sisterhood Bookstore(s):
1351 Westwood Blvd., Los Angeles, CA 90024,
1915 3/4 Westwood Blvd., Los Angeles, CA 90025. Mail-order catalog, browing, non-sexist children's books (Westwood).
743 S. Grandview, The Woman's Building, Los Angeles (downtown), CA 90057.
13716 Ventura Blvd., Sherman Oaks (San Fernando Valley), CA 91403, 213-986-3020.

Sisters for Liberation
PO Box 263
Brooklyn, NY 11217

Sisters Have Resources Everywhere see SHARE

Sisters in Solidarity
1428 Lafayette, c/o Alice Turner
Denver, CO 80218
  Posters.

Sisters in Struggle see "Women's Liberation Groups" section: California: Berkeley

Sisters of the Palette
J. J. Wilson & Jeanne Hirsch, Calif. State College, Sonoma Women's Studies
Rohnert Park, CA 94928
  History of women and art. Audiovisuals.

Sloane, Pat
79 Mercer
New York, NY 10012
  Filmmaker and source.

Sophia Smith Collection
Mary Elizabeth Murdock, dir.
Smith College
Northampton, MA 01060
  Mms. catalog ($1). Pictures catalog ($6). Selected bibliographies, e.g. "Women in the medical field" and "The Civil War," compiled by Susan L. Boone (gratis).

Social Welfare Archives
University of Minnesota Library
Minneapolis, MN 55455
612-373-4420
  Andrea Hindling. Source of listings of volunteer groups, feminist publications.

Society for Visual Education, Inc.
1345 Diversey Pky.
Chicago, IL 60614

Society of Future Single Parents
2402 Spruce, Hal Davidson
Philadelphia, PA 19103
  "Females who would like all the benefits of marriage: social, economic, sexual, biological (childbearing) but without its legal entanglements, hangups, hassles, and without its menial household tasks and subservience to male dominance, and without being slaves to sexism. Contact the Society..."

Society of Women Engineers
United Engineering Center, Rm. 305
345 E. 47
New York, NY 10017
  Also: LeEarl Bryant, 639 Downing, Richardson, TX 75080.

Society of Women Geographers
1619 New Hampshire Ave.
Washington, DC 20009

Sojourner Truth Learning Exchange
220 E. Union
Olympia, WA 98502
206-352-0593
  Also: Eileen Lemke Meconi, 2938 Kaiser Rd., N.W. Olympia 98502.

Sojourner Truth Press

Directory of Sources

(cont.) 449 Euclid Ter. N.E.
Atlanta, GA 30307
  "Sleeping beauty; a lesbian fairy tale" by Vicki ($.70).

Solidarity Films
2490 Channing Wy., Rm. 207
Berkeley, CA 94707
415-843-7888
  Group of women with experience in distributing and producing films in Bay Area.

Sommerschield, Rose Neiditch
333 E. 30
New York, NY 10016
  Filmmaker and source.

Soul Survivor
143 Woodland Ave.
New Rochelle, NY 10805
  Women-owned business: Tailor-made blouses. Free catalog with fabric swatches, mail-order.

Southeastern Psychological Assoc.
Commission on Status of Women
Contact: Dr. Annette Brodsky
Dept. of Psychology
University of Alabama
Box 2968
University, AL 35486
205-348-5000
  "Visiting Woman (psychologist) Program." Brochure, "Register of volunteers in Visiting Woman Program '73-4."

Spalding, Shirley
3014 E. Falmouth
Louisville, KY 40205
  Feminist buttons, bumper stickers, etc.

Spanish-language materials--sources see Pamphlets title, "Suppliers of Spanish-Language Materials." Emanuel Molho at French & European Publications, Inc. (610 5 Ave., New York, NY 10020) also advertises recordings and audiovisuals.

Spanish American Feminists
Box 773
New York, NY 10023

Spanish Speaking Women's National Caucus
c/o Irma Santaella
State Human Rights Appeal Board
250 Broadway
New York, NY 10007
212-488-2377

SPEAKERS AND CONSULTANTS AVAILABLE: contact (if no address see main Directory sequence):
Abramson, Joan, 3044 Kiele Ave., Honolulu, HI 96815; 808-923-1019
Assoc. for Voluntary Sterilization
Assoc. of Feminist Consultants
Bantam Lecture Bureau
Barton, Jane
Barufaldi, Linda, 15 Chestnut, Waltham, MA 02154; 617-899-8349 (church & religion)
Benton, Suzanne
Bjorklund, Edi, c/o Univ. of Wisconsin, Milwaukee Library, Milwaukee, WI 53201 (sexism in children's media)
Cheda, Sherrill
Culpepper, Emily, 801 Somerville Ave., Somerville, MA 02143; 617-625-5892 (church & religion)
Daly, Mary
Diamond, Irma, 640 W. 231, Bronx, NY 10463; 212-549-7433 (advertising, media, industry)
Emma Willard Task Force on Education
Fasteau, Brenda and Marc
Federal Women's Program
Feminist Art Journal

(cont.) Feminist Press
The Feminists
Forum Project, Drawer E,
Clinton, NJ 08809 (prisoners/NJ)
Fox, Muriel, 40 E. 83, New York, NY 10018, apt. 4S; 212-988-1124 (business)
Freeman, Jo, SUNY at Purchase, Purchase, NY 10577 (academia)
Guttman, Helene Nathan, PhD, Prof., Dept. of Biological Sci., College of Liberal Arts & Sciences, Univ. of Ill. at Chicago Circle, Box 4348, Chicago, IL 60680; 312-996-2111
Hammerstein, Gretchen, Co-ord., Midstate Libraries & SRRT/CWILS, Toad Ridge Rd., Middlefield, CT 06455; 203-349-3135 (sexism in children's media and librarianship)
Hirsch, Lolly and Jeanne, c/o New Moon Communications (health)
Hogan, Betsy, 222 Rawson Rd., Brookline, MA 02146; 617-232-0066 (fair employment practices)
Hoppin, Ruth
IWY Speakers Bureau at United Nations, 605 3 Ave., BR 4004. Att. Anne Heller, New York, NY 10017; 212-754-1234 x 5234, 5
Keedick Lecture Bureau, Inc., 475 5 Ave., New York, NY 10017; 212-683-5627 (Barbara Loden, Susan B. Anthony, Lucy Komisar, Barbara Walters, Bella Abzug, et al.)
Koontz, Elizabeth Duncan, 1287-F Schaub Dr., Raleigh, NC 27606; 919-829-4534. Asst. State Sec., Dept. of Human Resources, State of North Carolina. Former Pres., National Education Assoc.; former U.S. Dept. of Labor Dep. Sec.; former Dir., U.S. Dept. of Labor Women's Bureau
Kreisberg, Lois Ablin, 247 Kensington Pl., Syracuse, NY 13210. Assoc. Prof., SUNY Upstate Medical Center; 315-472-2155
LaRouche, Janice, 333 Central Park West, New York, NY 10025; 212-663-0970 (affirmative action)
Laura X [X, Laura]
Lesbian Feminist Speakers Bureau, Berkeley, CA, 415-548-2870
Lesbian Resource Center
Lindfors, Viveca
Lucina Speakers Bureau
Macleod, Jennifer S., 4 Canoe Brook Dr., Princeton Junction, NJ 08550; 609-799-0378 (women's status and rights)
MacRae, Jean, 153 Lexington Ave., Cambridge, MA 02138; 617-493-1034 (church & religion)
Marieb, Joyce, 15 Chestnut, apt. 1, Waltham, MA 02154; 617-899-8349 (church & religion)
Medea, Andra, c/o Farrar, Straus & Giroux, 19 Union Sq. West, New York, NY 10003 (rape)
Merriam, Eve, 10 Water, Stonington, CT 06378; 203-535-2635 (sexism in children's media)
Minnesota Speakers Bureau
Minnesota Women's Center, Minneapolis
NOW Long Island Speakers' Bureau
National Women's Health Coalition
National Women's Political Caucus
New Feminist Talent Associates
New York Radical Feminist Speakers Bureau

Directory of Sources

(cont.) Norman, Eve. Ina Dittfeld, agent, Lordly & Dame, Inc., 51 Church, Boston, MA 02116; 617-482-3493

Pennsylvanians for Women's Rights

Prime Time Speakers Roster

Raymond, Janice, 109 Warren, Newton Centre, MA 02159; 617-244-1378 (church & religion)

Rudy, Michelle, 401 Waldron, West Lafayette, IN 47906; 317-434-5771 (women in management, sexism in librarianship, affirmative action in academia)

Schramm, Sara Slavin, 731 Fulton St., Cherry Hill, NJ 08034

Shevey, Sandra, 2043 N. Beachwood Dr., Hollywood, CA 90028 (film)

Silverwoman, Sandra T., Millstone River, apt. E-5, Rt. 1, Princeton, NJ 08540; 609-452-8721 (sexism in school media)

Sisters of the Palette see Audiovisual part of Non-Book Resources section

Speaking of women...

Stone, Janet, 702 Green, #3, Cambridge, MA 02139 (affirmative action)

Theodore, Athena Rentoumis, 27 Turning Mill Rd., Lexington, MA 02173; 617-862-8902 (sexism in academia)

Thompson, Kathleen, c/o Farrar, Straus & Giroux, 19 Union Sq. West, New York, NY 10003 (rape)

Trobec, Maureen, 824 Lawrence Dr., Lake Villa, IL 60046; 312-356-3171 (publishing industry)

VD Information Program

VanVuuren, Nancy, Box 8150, Pittsburgh, PA 15217; 412-421-7925

Viewpoint

Wahlberg, Rachel Conrad

Wheeler, Helen Rippier, #215, 7940 Jefferson Hwy., Baton Rouge, LA 70809; 504-921-2477

Women's Centers: New York City; Philadelphia (Speakers' collective), etc.

X, Laura see Laura X

Speaking of Women..., Inc.
5612 Sonoma Rd.
Bethesda, MD 20034
301-530-9091
   Washington, DC-based feminist speakers' agency. Workshops, seminars, panels designed. Lecture bureau.

Split Infinitive
581 Portland Ave.
Minneapolis, MN 55415
612-325-0006
   Woman-run advertising agency with feminist leanings, i.e. non-sexist advertising objective, although hires men, Marlene Johnson, Jeanette Wagner.

Spoken Arts
301 North Ave.
New Rochelle, NY 10801

Sport LaFemme [store]
2 Haymarket Mall
Sacramento, CA 95821

Spottswood, M.
217 12 St. S.E.
Washington, DC 20003
202-547-5878
   Ms. S. is a womanger, e.g. for Casse Culver.

Stanton Project
10 Garden
Cambridge, MA 02138
   Films about American women. Mary Feldhaus-Weber, Exec. Prod.

STATUS-OF-WOMEN COMMISSIONS, COUNCILS, etc.: see subsection of "Directory of Sources" immediately following this one

Stellman, L. M. see Suddenly Single

Stewardesses for Women's Rights
82 Ohio Ave.
Long Beach, NY 11561
   Jan Fulsom & Sandra Ashworth, co-founders. PO Box 3235, Alexandria, VA 22302.

Stockholders Action Program (SAP)
Box 1267
San Francisco, CA 94101
   Nationwide association of women pressing for representation on corporate boards of directors. Handbook (SASE).

Stop Rape Task Force
Box 65037
Baton Rouge, LA 70806

Store Front
406 Washington
Wausau, WI 54401
   Posters.

Struggling Woman
PO Box 2852
West Palm Beach, FL 33602
   Jewelry for feminists by feminists. Mary Lundin, designer.

Student Coalition for Relevant Sex Education
300 Park Ave. S., 5th fl.
New York, NY 10010
   "Resource booklet on sex education materials" ($.25).
   "How-to handbook on organizing a student sex information project" ($.50).

Student Lawyer
1155 E. 60
Chicago, IL 60637
   "Women and the law" ($.50).

Studio Museum
2033 5 Ave.
New York, NY 10035
212-427-5959

Suddenly Single
1131 W. State
Milwaukee, WI 53233
414-276-4580
   Seminar. L. Mandy Stellman, attorney, conducts seminars with sociologist husband. Re judges using Women's Liberation against women who have spent years in traditional role.

Sudsofloppen. Defunct

Summit Medical Center(s)
   (Abortion information)
   GA: Atlanta 30305, 3098 Piedmont Rd. N.E., 404-262-3000.
   MI: Detroit 48235, 15800 W. McNichols Rd., 313-272-8450.
   DC 20037, 2311 M. St. N.W. 202-337-7200.

Super Samantha & Her Gang Publishing Co.
128 Hwy. 2
Ancaster, Ontario
   "Two Nincompoops" liberated colouring book.

Superscope Library of the Spoken Word
455 Fox
San Fernando, CA 91340

Sussex Films
29 Washington Sq. W.
New York, NY 10011

Sword, Betty
Male chauvinist pig calendar see Colorado Democratic Women's Caucus

Directory of Sources

Sydney Women's Film Group
Contact: Sydney Filmmakers
 Co-op
St. Peter's Ln.
Darlinghurst, NSW, Australia
 Mailing: PO Box 217, Kings
 Cross, NSW 2011; Phone:
 31-3237.

- T -

Talent Bank (Women/libraries)
4248 Anna Ave., Jo Ann Malina
Lyons, IL 60534

Task Force on Women's Rights
 & Responsibilities Appointed
 by Pres. Nixon, 1969

Task Force to Document Governmental Intimidation of the
 Press
Carol Ward, 2032 Spruce
Philadelphia, PA 19103

Taubin, Amy
70 Riverside Dr.
New York, NY 10024
 Filmmaker and source.

TeleKetics
1229 S. Santee
Los Angeles, CA 90015

Texas Woman's University Library
Box 3715, TWU Station
Denton, TX 76204

Texture Films, Inc.
1600 Broadway
New York, NY 10019
212-586-6960
 Sonya Friedman, president.

That Uppity Woman
873 N. A-One-A
Indialantic, FL 32903
305-724-2580
 Company owned and staffed
 by women. Feminist jewelry.

Third Press/Joseph Okpaku
 Pub. Co., Inc.
444 Central Park West
New York, NY 10025

Third World Cinema
62 W. 45
New York, NY 10036
212-972-9300

Third World Communications
330 Ellis
San Francisco, CA 94102

Third World Newsreel
16 W. 20
New York, NY 10011
212-243-2310

Third World Women's Alliance
346 W. 20
New York, NY 10011
212-929-2390
 Also: PO Box 3065, Berkeley, CA 94703. Triple
 Jeopardy newspaper.

Third World Women's Committee
PO Box 3065
Berkeley, CA 94703

Tide Collective
373 N. Western Ave., #202
Los Angeles, CA 90004
 Publishes "The Lesbian
 Tide" Also: 1124 1/2 N.
 Ogden Dr., 90036; 213-656-
 1049.

Times Change Press
Penwell Rd.
Washington, NJ 07882
 Posters, pamphlets.

Today's Woman Placement
 Service
21 Charles
Westport, CT 06880
203-226-4451

Tomorrow's Secretary Workshop packages

(cont.) Johns, Norris Associates
5720 Aylesboro Ave.
Pittsburgh, PA 15217
  Leader's Guide & materials
  for 20 participants = $225.

Toy Lending Library
2311 18 St. N.W.
Washington, DC 20018
202-387-2467
  A project of the National
  Institute of Mental Health, attempting to encourage mothers
  to play with children to prepare them for school.

Tree Toad Graphics
2406 Grant
Berkeley, CA 94710
  Posters.

Triangle Women's Radio
909 Green
Durham, NC 27701

Tulane University
Rudolph Matas Medical Library
1430 Tulane Ave.
New Orleans, LA 70112
  Weinstein Collection includes
  Elizabeth Bass collection of
  women doctors as authors
  and in fiction.

Twin Cities Rape Crisis Center
621 W. Lake, Women's Counseling Service
Minneapolis, MN 55408
612-827-RAPE(7273)
  Speakers. Courses. Aid,
  support, advocacy.

Twin Cities Women's Film Collective
3555 Hamilton Ave., Darlene
  Marvy, Coord.
Wayzata, MN 55391
612-473-2373
  Video tapes, films for CR.

Two Windows Press
2644 Fulton
Berkeley, CA 94704
  Effie's Book Series.

- U -

UNITAR (UN Institute for
  Training & Research)
801 UN Plaza
New York, NY 10017

USSU Women's Directorate
Rm. 14, MUB, University of
  Saskatchewan
Saskatoon
306-343-3747 x4

UW System Ethnic Center
University of Wisconsin
Stevens Point, WI 54481

Underground Press Syndicate
Box 26, Village Station
New York, NY 10014

Union Women's Alliance to
  Gain Equality (Union WAGE)
2137 Oregon
Berkeley, CA 94705
  Also: 2325 Mariposa, San
  Francisco, CA 94110; 415-
  431-1290.
  Publications, pamphlets,
  cassettes, amicus briefs,
  debates, etc. UNION
  W.A.G.E. Anne Lipow,
  415-841-2933, Berkeley;
  Luella Hanberry, 415-935-
  3841, Diablo Valley area;
  Joyce Maupin, 415-431-1290,
  San Francisco.

Unitarian Universalist Assoc.
Dept. of Education & Social
  Concern
25 Beacon
Boston, MA 02108
  "Rev. ed. About your sexuality; multimedia curriculum, junior high and up."

Unitarian-Universalist Women's
  Federation
777 UN Plaza, Room 7D
New York, NY 10017

Directory of Sources 377

United Artists Records, Inc.
729 7 Ave.
New York, NY 10019

United Artists 16
729 Seventh Ave.
New York, NY 10019

United Church of Christ Task Force on Women
Washington Square United Methodist Church
133 W. 4
New York, NY 10012
 Sponsored a "Sistercelebration." "Racism and sexism..." by Russell, available from KNOW.

United Feminist Organization
5 Williams Blvd., Michele Scott
Lake Grove, NY 11743
 Also: Grace Renda, 1575 Roosevelt Ave., Bohemia, NY 11716.

United Methodist Church--source of audiovisuals, literature:
Board of Global Ministries
Women's Div.
475 Riverside Dr., Rm. 1331
New York, NY 10027
212-947-0700
 Ms. Beverly Chain, Assoc. Dir. of AV Resources. Div. of TV, Radio & Film's all-woman crew responsible for "Women, Amen" (SEE Audiovisuals).
 Board's Service Center
  7820 Reading Rd.
  Cincinnati, OH 45237
 Board of Education, Div. of the Local Church
  1001 19 Ave. S.
  Nashville, TN 37212.

United Ministries in Higher Education
PO Box 187
Women's Caucus, Dayton View Sta.
Dayton, OH 45406
 Packet of materials ($1.50).

United Presbyterian Church Task Force on Women, Marriage & Divorce Cmt.
225 Varick
New York, NY 10014
 "Your marriage, the law and you in New York State" pamphlet ($.25) from Varick St. address: Presbyterian Distribution Service.

United Sisters (US)
4213 W. Bay Ave.
Tampa, FL 33616
 Feminist publishing and typesetting concern; works of interest to feminists; low-cost services to feminist enterprises; publishes US; poetry contest.

U.S. Commission on Civil Rights: Office of Federal Civil Rights Evaluation #606. 202-254-6654.
 Individuals trying to work within the system may send experiences and suggestions to: David Pales re Wage & Hour, Victor Sterling re EEOC, Jeanette Binstock re HEW.
 Office of Information & Publications "Statement on affirmative action for equal employment opportunities" (gratis).
 Women's Rights Program Unit, 1121 Vermont Ave. N.W., Washington, DC 20425.

U.S. Dept. of Health, Education & Welfare
 Region I--John G. Bynoe, Dir.
 RKO General Bldg., 5 fl.
 Bulfinch Pl.
 Boston, MA 02114
 Region II--Joel Barkan, Dir.
 26 Federal Plaza, Rm. 3908
 New York, NY 10007
 Region III--Dewey Dodds, Dir.

(cont.) Gateway Bldg.
3535 Market
Philadelphia, PA 19101
Region IV--William Thomas, Dir.
50 7 St. N.E., Rm. 404
Atlanta, GA 30323
Region V--Kenneth A. Mines, Dir.
309 W. Jackson Blvd., 10 fl.
Chicago, IL 60606
Region VI--Dorothy D. Stuck, Dir.
1114 Commerce
Dallas, TX 75202
Region VII--Taylor D. August, Dir.
12 Grand Bldg., 12 & Grand Ave.
Kansas City, MO 64106
Region VIII--Gilbert D. Roman, Dir.
Rm. 11037, Federal Bldg.
1961 Stout
Denver, CO 80202
Region IX--Floyd L. Pierce, Dir.
760 Market, Rm. 700
San Francisco, CA 94102
Region X--Mariana Kiner, Dir.
6101, Arcade Plaza Bldg.
1321 2 Ave.
Seattle, WA 98101.

U.S. HEW Commission on the Rights & Responsibilities of Women
Rm. 3062, HEW North
330 Independence Ave. N.W.
Washington, DC 20201
202-962-0996

U.S. HEW Office for Civil Rights
330 Independence Ave. S.W.
Peter E. Holmes, Dir.
Washington, DC 20201
  Has materials, if not action, on sex-discrimination:
  "Sex discrimination" DHEW Publ. no. (OCR) 74-6.
  "HEW & Civil Rights" DHEW Publ. no. (OCR) 73-1.
  "Executive order 11246" Non-discrimination under federal contracts. DHEW Publ. no. (OCR) 72-4.
  An absolute basic basic in academia.
  "Federal laws & regulations concerning sex discrimination in educational institutions, Oct. 1972" Chart compiled by Project on the Status & Education of Women of Assoc. of American Colleges, with copies available from HEW!

U.S. HEW Women's Action Program
330 Independence Ave. S.W., Rm. 3059
Washington, DC 20201
  "Report of..."

U.S. Dept. of Justice
Constitution Ave. & 10 St. N.W.
Washington, DC 20530
202-737-8200
Director of Bureau of Prisons, Norman A. Carlson.
Female: Connie Springman 202-739-4602.
Prisons:
  Female Reformatory for Women, Alderson, WV 24910, Virginia McLaughlin 304-343-1800
  Robert F. Kennedy Youth Center, Morgantown, WV 26505, (co-ed) J. Flamm 304-296-3556
  Federal Correctional Institution, Ft. Worth, TX 76119, (co-ed) Charles Campbell, 817-535-2230
  Federal Correctional Institution, Terminal Island, CA 90731. 2 separate units, Paul Walker, 213-833-5261.

U.S. Dept. of Labor Women's Bureau
Washington, DC 20210
  Dir., Carmen Maymí. A few titles:

Directory of Sources 379

(cont.) "Women workers in ___state___, 1970."
"Women workers today." 1973
"Economic role of women." 1973
"Who are the working mothers?" 1972
"Careers for women in the 70's." 1973
"State hours-laws for women; changes in states since the Civil Rights Act of 1964." 1974
"Laws on sex discrimination in employment; Federal Civil Rights Act, Title VII, State Fair Employment Practices Laws, Executive Orders." 1973.

U.S. Dept. of Labor Women's Bureau
Citizen's Advisory Council on the Status of Women, Rm. 4211
14th & Constitution Aves. N.W.
Washington, DC 20210
202-961-3791

U.S. Equal Employment Opportunity Commission
1800 G St. N.W., #1134
Washington, DC 20506
202-343-5621, 8005
  John H. Powell, Jr., Chairman
  Sidney A. Wexler, Dep. Dir. of Congressional Affairs
  Eduardo Pena, Jr., Dir. of Compliance
  Helen P. Rivera, Talent Search Coord., Rm. 1217.
The EEOC was set up under Civil Rights Act of 1964 provisions and charged with investigating complaints of discrimination in employment and seeking to conciliate them. It has posters and some brochures:
"The equal employment opportunity act of 1972, together with the text of Title VII of the Civil Rights Act of 1964 as amended by the EEO Act of 1972. Subcommittee on Labor...."
"Affirmative Action and equal employment; a guidebook for employers" (gratis in very limited quantities. Write EEOC, PO Box 1612, Springfield, VA 22151).

_____. Atlanta Regional Office (includes AL, Canal Zone, FL, GA, KY, NC, MS, SC, TN)
Citizens Trust Bldg., Ste. 1150
75 Piedmont Ave. N.E.
Atlanta, GA 30303
404-526-6991

_____. Chicago Regional Office (IL, IN, MI, MN, OH, WI)
600 S. Michigan Ave., Rm. 611
Chicago, IL 60605
312-353-1223

_____. Dallas Regional Office (AR, LA, NM, OK, TX)
1100 Commerce, Rm. 5A4
Dallas, TX 75202
214-749-1841
  New Orleans District Office:
  333 St. Charles, 70130,
  504-589-6817*

_____. Kansas City Regional Office (IA, KS, MO, NE)
601 E. 12, Rm. 113
Kansas City, MO 64106
816-374-2781

_____. New York Regional Office (CT, ME, MA, NH, NJ, NY, PR, RI, VT)
Federal Office Bldg., Rm. 4000
26 Federal Plaza
New York, NY 10007
212-264-3640

*only 2 district offices have been listed here; check your phone book under "E" and "U.S."

U.S. Equal Employment Opportunity Commission (cont.)
Philadelphia Regional Office (DE, DC, MD, PA, VA, WV)
Jefferson Bldg., 1015 Chestnut
Philadelphia, PA 19107
215-597-7784

———. San Francisco Regional Office (AK, AZ, CA, CO, GU, HI, ID, MT, NV, ND, OR, Samoa, SD, UT, Wake Island, WA, WY)
300 Montgomery, Ste. 740
San Francisco, CA 94104
415-556-1775
   Los Angeles District Office:
   1543 W. Olympic Blvd., 90015,
   213-688-3400.*

U.S. Govt. Advisory Committee on the Economic Role of Women. Council of Economic Advisors
White House
Washington, DC 20500
202-395-3000

U.S. Library of Congress
Division for the Blind & Physically Handicapped
Washington, DC 20453
   Has taped the August 1973 issue of Ms. and plans to tape all issues. Free taped copy for any blind or physically handicapped person. Contact regional library for the blind or write LC.

U.S. President
Advisory Committee on the Economic Role of Women
c/o Council of Economic Advisors
Executive Office
Washington, DC 20506

U.S. President
Anne Armstrong, Special Counselor
Washington, DC 20500

U.S. Women's Curling Assoc.
410 Grove
Glencoe, IL 60022

U.S. Women's Lacrosse Assoc.
20 E. Sunset Ave.
Philadelphia, PA 19118

U.S. Women's Squash Racquets Assoc.
Mustin Ln., Ruth Ruddy
Villanova, PA 19085

United Women of Tanzania
c/o Tanganyika African National Union
PO Box 9151
Dar Es Salaam, Tanzania

United World Films
1445 Park Ave.
New York, NY 10029

Universal Kinetic
221 Park Ave. S.
New York, NY 10017

University & College Women of Illinois
Helen Curley, 609 W. Penn. Ave.
Urbana, IL 61801

University Feminist Organization (of the Univ. of Chicago)
c/o 5519 S. University, 1st fl.
Chicago, IL 60637

Up Haste Bookstore
2506B Haste
Berkeley, CA 94604
415-838-6359
   Women's bookstore with all current periodicals, novels, literature about women past and present.

Urban Institute
2100 M St. N.W.
Washington, DC 20037
202-223-1950

---
*only 2 district offices have been listed here; check your phone book under "E" and "U.S."

Directory of Sources

(cont.) "Policewomen on patrol; major findings" The Institute has decided to let this report of 'major findings' go out of print!

- V -

VD Information Program (Mpls. Health Dept.)
250 S. 4
Minneapolis, MN 55401
612-348-2304
 Provides information, referral, printed materials, audiovisuals, speakers.

Valley Women's Center
200 Main
Northampton, MA 01060

Varda One (Varda Murrell)
c/o Everywoman Bookstore

Venereal Disease Control Centers
 For phone numbers (multilingual) and organizations, SEE page 91 of the June 1974 issue of *Ms.* magazine.

Vermont Women's Health Center
PO Box 29
Burlington, VT 05401

Video Nursing, Inc.
2834 Central
Evanston, IL 60201
 Film source.

Videowomen
Minda Bikman, 535 Hudson
New York, NY 10014

ViewPoint; Speakers for Radical Change
PO Box 220, Old Chelsea Station
New York, NY 10011
212-255-9229

Violet Press
PO Box 398
New York, NY 10009
 A collective--"lesbian/feminist press." Has list ($.10) of publishers and periodicals which want lesbian poetry. "We are all Lesbians; a poetry anthology" ($2), Fran Winant's "Looking at women; poems" ($1). Into food and health systems.

Virago Limited
27 Smith
London SW3 4EW
01-352-6634, 5
 Cables and telegrams: Caterwaul, London SW3. "to publish books which emanate from the British Women's Movement." Directors: Andrea Adam, Rosie Boycott, Carmen Callil, Marsha Rowe.

Vision Quest
 Western: 389 Ethel Ave., Mill Valley, CA 94941, 415-388-9094.
 Central: 7715 N. Sheridan Rd., Chicago, IL 60626, 312-388-1116.
 Eastern: 325 W. 86, New York, NY 10024, 212-877-0932.
 Audiovisuals.

Vocations for Social Change
4911 Telegraph Ave.
Oakland, CA 94609
 Workforce. Tax-exempt anti-profit collective.

Voice Over Books
200 Park Ave. S.
New York, NY 10003
212-674-8666
 Best-sellers, abridged, recorded on standard tape cassettes. 90 min. Read by "well known actors." Fiction and non-fiction. Has a few titles relevant to W.M., e.g. "Flying," "Billie Jean," "Buried Alive."

- W -

WAIT (Women Artists, It's Time)
Barbara Farrell, 3617 Coconut Grove
Miami, FL 33133
Art organization for Florida women. Slide registry. Newsletter.

WATCH (Women Act To Control Healthcare)
2058 N. Clifton
Chicago, IL 60614
312-348-6225
Laura Newman. Also: 1318 W. Newport, Chicago 60657. Chicago-based women's group composed of healthcare workers and consumers concerned about the institutional healthcare services available to women.

WE @ CPL (Women Employed at the Chicago Public Library)
2326 Sheffield
Chicago, IL 60614
Organizing committee: Nancy Archer, Lyda Carter, Nancy Harvey, Roberta Luther, Mattye Nelson, Leah Rowton, Kathy Weibel. Women working at all levels in the library, promoting research and discussion on women's issues, believe in principle of collective action.

WEAL Educational & Legal Defense Fund
Ellen Dresselhuis
1625 Park Ave. S.
Minneapolis, MN 55404

WEB (West/East Bag)
International network of women artists' groups with chapters worldwide. The Bay area and Northern California chapters have slide registry. Contact via Cindy Nemser, Univ. of California, Berkeley Art Museum, 94720. Chicago and Boston also have active chapters. WEB Newsletter.

WHPK-FM
University of Chicago student radio station
Chicago, IL 60637
Has broadcast a women's radio show weekly, 88.3 FM.

WIN see Women's International Network

WOMAN
145 W. Alenandrine
Detroit, MI 48201
Women's Organization to "MAS" Alcoholism and Narcotics. Downtown drug project.

WUHY-FM
4548 Market
Philadelphia, PA 19139

Wahlberg, Rachel Conrad
Austin, TX 78757
512-465-0309
Speaker on changing image of women in church and society.

Waking Woman Press
1637 N.W. Kings Blvd., Marjorie W. Hackmann
Corvallis, OR 97330
"Practical sex information" pamphlet ($.50) for all ages.

Walsh, Deidre
1957 N. Bissell
Chicago, IL 60614
Filmmaker, producer, source.

Washington, D.C. Area Feminist Theater (WAFT)
Mailing address:
6205 Cromwell Dr.
Washington, DC 20016
Betsy Toth, lighting dir.

Directory of Sources

(cont.) Sponsoring playwriting contest.

Washington Opportunities for Women (WOW)
1111 20 St. N.W., Rm. 101, Vanguard Bldg.
Washington, DC 20036
202-872-8095
 Christine Nelson. "Non-radical and non-political group aiming at finding women part-time work," by helping the Washington, DC Employment Service. Its methods will be applied in 6 other cities, Atlanta, Richmond, Baltimore, Boston, Providence, Montpelier. Nonprofit, tax-exempt, community service agency supported by the District of Columbia Manpower Administration. Housed in free space in DC. Professional Placement Center.

Washington. University
Office of Women's Continuing Education
Seattle, WA 98105
 Dorothy R. Strawn, Dean of Women & Dir. of Women's Continuing Education. Other feminists and aware persons at UW: (Ms.) Lynne Rhoads, Library faculty. ('73-4 Coord., National Task Force on Status of Women in Librarianship Coord.)
 Dr. Pepper Schwartz, Asst. Prof., Dept. of Sociology.
 Katie Thom, EEO Office staff member.

Weinstein, Miriam
27 Seymour
Concord, MA 01742
617-369-5791
 Filmmaker.

Wells-Christie Associates
PO Box 3392, Theodora Wells
Beverly Hills, CA 90212
213-652-6661
 Consultants in changes in organizational and human relationships. SEE #564 in Basic Book Collection.

West Coast Women Artists
Diane Rumah, Laney College
Oakland, CA 94607
 Slides.

West Coast Women's Design Conference
Contact: School of Architecture & Allied Arts
University of Oregon
Eugene, OR 97403

West/East Bag (WEB)
Women's Artists' CR groups
Box 1984
San Francisco, CA 91301
 Newsletter.

West Glen Communications
565 5 Ave.
New York, NY 10017

West Publishing Co.
50 Kellogg Blvd.
St. Paul, MN 55102
 Publish legal tools for the layperson, although seemingly nothing available re women! Supply is based on demand.

West Side Women's Video Collective
Contact The Kitchen, 240 Mercer
New York, NY 10012
 Video tapes, e.g. "Eeyore's birthday," "Women on sex; a conversation."

Westbrook Junior College Library
Portland, ME 04103
 Grace A. Dow, Curator. Writings of Maine women: first editions, manuscripts, rarities.

Westinghouse Broadcasting Co.
90 Park Ave.
New York, NY 10016

Weston Woods Studios
Weston, CT 06880

Westphal, David
Film Dept., Brandeis Univ.
Waltham, MA 02154
   Film source, e.g. "Diane."

"Where We At"
762 Halsey, Kay Brown
Brooklyn, NY 11233
   Ms. Brown predicts more unity among Black women themselves and "hopefully a coming together of all women in the arts." Staged first known Black women artists' show in history.

White House Talent Bank
Nola F. Smith, Staff Assistant to the President
The White House
Washington, DC 20500

Whole Woman Clearinghouse
Box 1171
Portsmouth, NH 03801

White River Co.
35 Bellevue Ave., Dept. 674
Elmwood Park, NJ 07047
   T-Shirts, Bumper stickers, etc.

Widow-to-Widow Program
Dr. Phyllis Rolfe Silverman, Dir.
Contact at Laboratory for Community Psychiatry
Harvard Medical School
Cambridge, MA 02138

Willett, Roslyn
441 West End Ave.
New York, NY 10024
   Consumer consultant.

Wisconsin Education Assoc. Council
222 W. Washington Ave.
Madison, WI 53703
   Linda Roberson, Legal asst. Involved in sex-discrimination in athletic programs in state and especially related to Wisconsin Interscholastic Athletic Assoc.

Wisconsin Feminists Project Fund, Inc.
5 Waupaca Ct.
Madison, WI 53705
   Judy Kaufman, VP.

Wisconsin Personnel & Guidance Assoc.
Caucus for Women
5917 Old Middleton Rd.
Madison, WI 53705
   Joan Pedro, co-ordinator; especially involved in physical education.

Wisconsin. University. Extension (UWEX)
430 & 433 Lowell Hall
610 Langdon
Madison, WI 53706
   Women's Education Resources. Sells literature, slides, etc. Kathryn F. Clarenbach, 608-262-2576.

Wohali Traders
Box 45 A
Cherokee, NC 28719
   "America's first feminists" pamphlet ($1).

Wollstonecraft, Inc.
6399 Wilshire Blvd., Suite 815
Los Angeles, CA 90048
213-643-1745
   Annette Welles, Pres. Women book publishers.

Woman Book Club
Columbia University Press
New York, NY 10027

Woman Consultants, Inc.
869 Osceola Ave.

Directory of Sources

(cont.) St. Paul, MN 55105
612-224-3871

Woman Talent Productions
508 N. Alta Vista
Los Angeles, CA 90036

WomanArt
31 W. Longview
Columbus, OH 43002
   Photo-shirts.

Womancraft (gallery)
407 W. Franklin, #2
Chapel Hill, NC 27514

Woman's Building
743 S. Grandview
Los Angeles, CA 90057
213-389-6241
   Feminist Studio Workshop.
Grandview One & Two (gallery cooperative). Womanspace has been dissolved. Woman's Building Community Gallery. Anait's Gallery 707. Women's Improvisation Workshop. Sisterhood Bookstore. NOW Chapter of Los Angeles. Ede Gross, building manager.

Woman's Health Clinic
3537 S.E. Hawthorne Blvd.
Portland, OR 97214

Woman's Institute
4180 N. Marine Dr.
Chicago, IL 60613
   Adrienne Smith, spokeswoman. A group of Chicago women including psychiatrists, psychologists, educators, students established this new center to provide alternatives to sexist psychotherapy. Includes research exchange program, workshops, drop-in center.

Woman's National Democratic Club
1526 New Hampshire Ave. N.W.
Washington, DC 20036

Woman's Own Name
261 Kimberly
Barrington, IL 60010
   "Fact sheet for women who wish to retain their own name after marriage" ($.50).

Woman's Place
Princeton, NJ
   Contact: Sandy Silverwoman, Millstone River, Apt. E5, Rt. 1, Princeton, NJ 08540. A service center-meeting place for women.

Woman's Place Agency
1901 Avenue of the Stars
Los Angeles, CA 90067
213-553-0870
   Employment agency.

Woman's Place: Women's Health Center
146 E. 18 Ave.
Vancouver, BC
873-3984

Woman's Soul Publishing
PO Box 5476
Milwaukee, WI 53211
   Publishes Paid My Dues--a magazine forum for women to write about music and about women in music as well as original songs. Planning feminist comic book and coloring book.

Woman's voice (bookstore)
673 Pearl
Denver, CO 80209
303-733-1178
   Posters. CR gifts. $.25 for catalog.

Womanspace (gallery)
743 S. Grandview
Los Angeles, CA
   Has been dissolved, with functions being taken over by other groups within the Woman's Bldg. at that address.

Women
PO Box 187, Dayton View Station
Dayton, OH 45406
: "Women; collection of international articles" ($1.50).

Women Abortion Project of New York
243 W. 20
New York, NY 10011
212-691-3396

Women Administrators Program
Claremont Colleges, Office for Continuing Education
Harper Hall 160
Claremont, CA 91711
714-626-8511
: Mary Ellen Mead, project coord.

Women Against Rape
16141 Marlowe Ave.
Detroit, MI 48235
: "Stop rape handbook" ($.25).

Women Against Rape
Boston, MA
617-492-RAPE
: 24-hour crisis center: legal information, discussion groups, counseling, self-defense, referrals. Staffed by women volunteers having relevant experiences. Other centers planned in New York, Chicago, DC.

Women & Film, International Festival '74
4 Maintland
Toronto, Ont. M4Y 1C5
: Media van touring Ontario.

Women & Smoking
Bethesda, MD 20852

Women and Video
C109A Charles St. W.
Toronto, Ont. M4Y 1R4
: Video Women Catalogue.

Women and Work
Shelley Nopper, c/o U.S. Dept. of Labor, Office of Information, Publications & Reports
Washington, DC 20210
: Monthly news service. Nopper is editor and has mailing list.

Women Artists' Collective
Fresno, CA 93721
: Begun in 1970 by Judy Chicago.

Women Artists in Revolution (WAR)
549 W. 52
New York, NY 10019
212-246-6570

Women Artists, It's Time
see WAIT

Women at Scott, Foresman
1900 E. Lake Ave.
Glenview, IL 60025
: SEE ALSO Sexism in Textbooks Committee. Chicago women in publishing surveyed in 1972 (questionnaire results from M. Weintraub, 7638 E. Eastlake Ter. 60626, $1). 2 caucuses formed: Lyons & Carnahan; Scott, Foresman.

Women Employed
37 S. Wabash
Chicago, IL 60603
312-372-7822
: Darlene Stille, founder. Dedicated to improving women's working conditions in Loop area, where women represent 45% of work force but earn 25% of the wages. Women Employed newsletter.

Women Enterprises
242 E. 50
New York, NY 10022
: Feminist wristwatch. CR gifts, cards, jewelry, posters.

Directory of Sources

Women for a Peaceful Christmas
Box 5095
Madison, WI 53705

Women for Armed Revolution
c/o WL, PO Box 5203
Oakland, CA 94605
   Women's collective
   Printed 3 pamphlets in anti-
   imperialist women's movement ($.25).

Women for Changing the Times
   Coalition including NOW, Manhattan WPC, WEAL, the National Black Feminist Organization, Women's Media Alliance, Feminist Party.
   Nicole Dunn, spokeswoman.
   Picketed New York Times
   June 1972.

Women for Peace
50 Oak
San Francisco, CA 94102
415-863-7146

Women for Political Action
Box 1213, Station Q
Toronto 7, Ontario

Women for the Free Future
Berkeley, CA
   Defunct.

Women for Women--Psychother-
   apy Institute & Educational
   Center
4220 California
San Francisco, CA 94118
415-668-7111

Women Health & Abortion Project
   of New York
243 W. 20
New York, NY 10011
212-691-3396

Women-Health PAC (collective)
17 Murray
New York, NY 10007
   Health Pac Bulletin.

Women Honor Women
Astrid Myers
163 Old Stone Hwy.
Easthampton, NY 11937

Women in Construction
Washington, DC Chapter:
   7603 Georgia Ave. N.W.,
   20012, 202-291-4800.
Chicago, IL Chapter:
   307 N. Michigan, 60601,
   312-782-9410.

Women in Apprenticeship Program see Advocates for
   Women

Women in Cable, Inc.
Suite 2217, Sterick Blvd.
Memphis, TN 38103
   Lynn Yellin, 4241 Park Ave.,
   Memphis 38117.

Women in Communications
8305-A Shoal Creek Blvd.
L. G. Taylor-Pierlot
Austin, TX 78758
   Women in Communications,
   Inc.; American Women in
   Radio & TV, Inc.; National
   Federation of Press Women.
   Formerly Theta Sigma Phi.

Women in Community Activi-
   ties Program
Sarah Lawrence College
Bronxville, NY 10708
   Amy Swerdlow, Women's
   Studies.

Women in Community Service,
   Inc.
1730 Rhode Island Ave., N.W.
Washington, DC 20036
202-293-1343

Women in Distribution, Inc.
Box 8858
Washington, DC 20003
   Cards, posters, publications
   of small presses and independent publishers' works
   by today's women authors,

(cont.) musicians and artists. Wholesale and retail.

Women in Media Collective
University Art Museum
Berkeley, CA 94720
   Includes Joan Levinson, who has report of March 1974 Women in Media festival.

Women in Print
c/o KNOW

Women in Prison
3077 24
San Francisco, CA 94110
415-285-3100

Women in Progress (WIP)
Louisiana State University, New Orleans
New Orleans, LA 70122

Women in Research
1210 E. 48
Chicago, IL 60615
   Alice Dan. Plan a "consulting exchange." Papers, bibliography. "Women in science; working together to vitalize research" ($1 donation).

Women in the Arts
PO Box 4476
c/o Cynthia Navaretta, GC. PO
New York, NY 10017

Women in Transition, Inc.
4634 Chester Ave.
Philadelphia, PA 19143
201-SA4-9511
   Published "Women's survival manual; a feminist handbook on separation and divorce" ($3 from KNOW). Philadelphia-based program providing emotional, legal and therapeutic help for women struggling with the problems of separation and divorce.

Women in Working Class Communities United
4408 8
c/o Natl. Center for Urban Ethnic Affairs
Washington, DC 20017

Women, Inc.
501 Madill, Marjorie Hart
Antioch, CA 94509

Women Involved, Inc.
1572 Mass. Ave.
Cambridge, MA 02138
   Contact for training sessions covering lobbying, organizing local campaigns, caucuses, coalitions. Also 4 Irving Ter.

Women Liberation Abortion Project of N.Y.
243 W. 20
New York, NY 10011
212-691-3396

Women Make Movies, Inc.
257 W. 19
New York, NY 10011
212-929-6477
   Nonprofit tax-exempt educational corporation formed by co-directors Ariel Dougherty and Sheila Paige. Works out of neighborhood church basement to teach women of all ages how to say what they want through filmmaking. SEE for example, "The women's happy time commune" in audiovisual collection. Chelsea Picture Station. Distribution from 43 W. 16. Provides professional training in 16mm film, 1/2" video tape, 1/4" audio tape production through the operation of a prototype media center. Includes Spanish-speaking women, prisoners, teenagers, "working women."

Women Mobilized for Change
37 S. Wabash, YWCA

Directory of Sources

(cont.) Chicago, IL 60603
"Freeing ourselves" ($1).

Women News Service
c/o National Feature Syndicate
2717 N. Pulaski Rd.
Chicago, IL 60639
   Also: Jenny Pevoy, c/o
   Drawer NN, Santa Barbara,
   CA 93101.

Women of La Raza
Dorinda Moreno
69 Campus Circle
San Francisco, CA 94132
   "¡La mujer--en pie de lucha!
   y la hora es ya!" by Moreno
   ($7).

Women of the Free Future see
   WL: CA: Berkeley

Women of Youth Against War &
   Fascism
46 W. 21
New York, NY 10011

Women Office Workers (WOW)
PO Box 439, Planetarium Station
New York, NY 10024
   New York City clerical work-
   ers. Literature kits ($1.50
   + postage $.56).

Women on the Move (WOM)
Redwood High School
Larkspur, CA 94939
   Lisa Lucheta, Candace Boyer.
   Energetic group of high school
   women eager to share ideas
   and activities (Tamalpais High
   School District, Marin County).

Women Poets of the Twin Cities
612-333-8580 Penny Suess
612-227-5314 Mary Ellen Shaw
   Most are feminists.

Women Strike for Peace
799 Broadway
New York, NY 10003
212-254-1925
   National headquarters: 1 Union
   Sq.

Women Strike for Peace Am-
   nesty Clearing House
1363 Pine, Irma Zigas
East Meadow, NY 11554

Women, Students, and Artists
   for Black Art Liberation
   (WSABAL)
   Defunct. For information,
   contact Michelle Wallace,
   345 W. 145, New York, NY
   10031, 212-862-5876.

Women Theologians United
   see Joint Committee of Organizations Concerned with
   the Status of Women in the
   Church

Women Today
Today Publications & News
   Service
245 W. 107
New York, NY 10025
212-222-8947
   News Service. Also in
   Washington, DC.

Women Together
113 W. Mulberry
Baltimore, MD 21201

Women Unite
280 Bloor St. W., Suite 305
Canadian Women's Educational
   Press
Toronto
   Anthology of the Canadian
   Women's Movement ($3).

Women United for Action
58 W. 25
New York, NY 10010
212-989-1252
   Consumerism.

Women United for United Na-
   tions
415 Lexington Ave., Suite 701
New York, NY 10017
   Also known as Women's
   Committee to Support the
   UN.

Women VS Connecticut
Box 89, Yale Law School
New Haven, CT 06520

Women's Abortion & Contraception Campaign
3 Belmont Rd., Margot Pearson
London SW4, England

Women's Abortion & Contraception Group
105 Musters Rd.
c/o Rose Knight
West Bridgford, Nottingham, England
Newsletter.

Women's Abortion Referral see Feminist Women's Health Centers, Los Angeles

Women's Action Alliance
370 Lexington Ave.
New York, NY 10017
212-685-0800
 Contributions tax-deductible. Pamphlet source. John Kenneth Galbraith and Gloria Steinem on Board. Nonsexist Child Development Project. Workshops packet ($.25). Non-sexist curriculum for early childhood education. "How to organize a child-care center," "How to hassle your local government," "How to organize a multi-service women's center." CR guidelines booklet ($.50).

Women's Action Training Center
434 66
Oakland, CA 94609
 Tish Sommers' "The not-so-helpless female" ($7.95).

Women's Advocates
20 W. 6 (Legal Assistance/Ramsey County), PO Box 553
St. Paul, MN 55102
612-225-2504
 Kathy Merfeld, Sue Ryan. Has newsletter.

Women's Aid
London, England
 Originally a house in residential suburb, Chiswick. A small voluntary body with little funds. Came into being because of the battered woman syndrome. A house serving as an advice center. Erin Pizzey's experiment in practical WL.

Women's American ORT
5028 Wisconsin Ave. N.W.
Washington, DC 20016
202-244-2280

Women's Anti-RAPE Group
243 W. 20
New York, NY 10011
212-255-9802

Women's Art Center (and gallery)
7587 Olive St. Rd.
St. Louis, MO 63130

Women's Art Registry
PO Box 539, Canal St. Station
New York, NY 10013
 Agnes Denes 212-966-0288. Maintained by Ad Hoc Women's Committee. International catalog of slides representing work of more than 700 artists.

Women's Bail Fund
PO Box 637, Cooper Station
New York, NY 10003
212-868-3330

Women's Bar Assoc.
84 William
New York, NY 10038
212-WH3-1090
 Harriet Gaier. Also: Sue Wimnershoff Kaplan, 745 5 Ave., New York, NY 10022, 212-PL2-0740. Heads EO and EE Section. Supports ERA.

Directory of Sources

Women's Bookstore/A Woman's Place
706 S.E. Grand Ave.
Portland, OR 97214

Women's Broadcasting Corp. (WBC)
4628 Batavia Pl.
Denver, CO 80220
303-333-2176
 Women's radio station. Also: 2420 S. Quebec, c/o Camilla L. Barnett 80231.

Women's Campaign Fund
2721 O St. N.W.
Washington, DC 20007
202-338-3685
 Congresswomen Yvonne B. Burke, Margaret M. Heckler, Patricia Schroeder. Purpose to raise funds to elect highly qualified, progressive women to federal and state offices.

Women's Campus Ministry Caucus
1145 Mass. Ave.
Cambridge, MA 02138
 Kit.

Women's Career Caucuses
656 N. Michigan Ave.
Chicago, IL 60611

Women's Cartoonist Collective
830 Gilman
Berkeley, CA 94710
 "an informal and fluctuating group of women artists who put out women's comic books" Contact Last Gasp-Eco Funnies for distribution. Adults only: Wimmen's Comix #1 edited by Pat Moodian--showcase for 10 outrageous cartoonists. #2 Lee Marrs. #3 Fun & Games issue, by Sharon Rudahl. #4. $.50 each + $.15 handling.

Women's Caucus
Arlington St. Unitarian Universalist Church
Boston

Contact: Kathryn Lemmel,
107 Westbourne Ter., Brookline, MA 02146.

Women's Caucus for Political Science
3626 Broadway, #4
Boulder, CO 80302
 Newsletter. Jobs section.

Women's Caucus for the Modern Languages
Verna D. Wittrock
Eastern Illinois University
Charleston, IL 61920
 WCML Bulletin. Leonora Woodman, 1100 N. Grant, West Lafayette, IN 47906. Concerns. Has established Florence Howe Award for essays by women scholars concerned with feminist criticism. Those interested in American, English or Canadian literature or pedagogy should write Susan Cornillon, 16896 Sand Ridge Rd., Bowling Green, OH 43402.

Women's Center Abortion Referral Service
Los Angeles, CA
213-936-7466

Women's Centre & Bookstore
804 Richards
Vancouver, B.C.

Women's Center Speakers Collective
4634 Chester Ave.
Philadelphia, PA 19143
215-SA2-1717
 Nancy Friedman: 215-BA2-2066.

Women's Choice Clinic
 "For years, women demonstrated for the right to abortion under the banner of gaining control of our own bodies. But for centuries we, as wo-

(cont.) men, have been denied even such simple knowledge of our bodies as being able to see our own cervix! A change in the law certainly does not give us this knowledge, nor did the legalization of abortion mean that we would receive good abortion care. We saw that only by women controlling the facilities and technology of abortion would we be assured excellent medical care, in a sisterly, supportive environment, and ultimately gain real control of our bodies and our sexuality. So we started the Women's Choice Clinic--run by women, for women, employing women and recycling money and energy back into the women's community." SEE Feminist Women's Health Centers [in this Directory of Sources] and "Women controlled abortion" [in "Audiovisual" part of Non-Book Resources section].

Women's Clearinghouse
1507 University Ave. S.E.
Experimental College
Minneapolis, MN 55414
612-373-9782, 9906
 Objectives: change the accessibility of media to women and content/perspective of news re women.

Women's Clinic
Evergreen State College
Olympia, WA 98505
206-866-6238

Women's Coalition
2211 E. Kenwood Ave.
Milwaukee, WI 53211

Women's Coalition for Positive Action
c/o Cecile Boatright (founder)
Harlem Hospital
Lenox Ave. & W. 136
New York, NY 10037
 Female employees at Harlem Hospital. Supported by National Black Feminist Organization.

Women's Coalition for the Third Century
c/o Rev. Patricia Budd Kepler, Pres. (at) Harvard Divinity School
Cambridge, MA 02138
617-646-9397
 Also 617-495-4536. Wilma Scott Heide, Vice Pres. Celebration of our nation's 200th anniversary--all per-sons are created equal with inalienable rights....

Women's Consultants, Inc.
Minneapolis, MN
 "a sexism consultation service." See Women's Advocates.

Women's Cooperative & Craft Store
1314 N.E. 43
Seattle, WA 98105
 Gallery.

Women's Correctional Assoc.
The Correctional Institution for Women
Clinton, NJ 08809
 Marilyn Davenport, Supt. Affiliate of the American Correctional Assoc.

Women's Counseling Service
San Francisco, CA
415-392-0400
 Feminist alternative.

Women's Counseling Service
621 W. Lake, 3 fl.
Minneapolis, MN 55408
 Abortion and birth control counseling and referral. Checks on clinics and hospitals. Some legal help. Seminars. Pamphlets: "A

Directory of Sources

(cont.) poke in time," "The diaphragm," "Physical facts of sexual intercourse," "Men and women living together," "Pregnancy" ($.20 each).

Women's Counseling Service of New York
527 Madison Ave.
New York, NY 10022
212-832-1170

Women's Crisis Center
306 N. Division/505 Catherine
Ann Arbor, MI 48108
"Freedom from rape" ($.10 + postage), "How to organize a women's crisis center" handbook ($1.50).

Women's Culture
c/o Radio Free People
Tapes and filmstrips made by/about women, from Rena Hansen, 395 Riverside Dr., #141, New York, NY 10025, 212-864-2693. Purpose: to explore, express, share with others women's unique and formerly hidden culture.

Women's Design Program
c/o Sheila Bretteville
2901 Waverly Dr.
Los Angeles, CA 90039

Women's Detention Center
Dept. of Corrections
1010 N. Capitol
Washington, DC 20002
202-629-4301

Women's Economic Development Project REPAIR
PO Box 3942
San Diego, CA 92103
Project-skills training for vocation and in-home repairs.

Women's Educational Equality Act
Contact: Rep. Patsy Mink, DC 20515. Dr. Joan Duval, Dir. of the Women's Program Staff, U.S. Office of Education, 400 Maryland Ave., Rm. 3121, SW Washington, DC 20202, wants suggestions on "how to implement equality education for women."

Women's Equity Action League (WEAL)
799 National Press Bldg., NW
Washington, DC 20045
202-638-4560
"Credit kit," "Divorce kit" ($1.50)
CA: Los Angeles 90048, Marion Marshall, 659 N. Edinburgh Ave.; Whittier 90608, Doris K. Seward, PO Box 182, Bailey Station.
LA: New Orleans 70118, Melissa K. Barr, 6440 S. Claiborne, #720.
MA: Lexington 02173, Dr. Athena Theodore, 27 Turning Mill Rd.
MN: Minneapolis 55417, 5124 18 Ave. S., 612-721-1201.
SC: Columbia 29250, Margaret Young, PO Box 5853.
SEE ALSO Project on Equality in Education; WEAL Educational & Defense Education Fund.

Women's Exchange Employment Office
2421 Penn. Ave. N.W.
Washington, DC 20037
202-FE8-4381

Women's Experimental Studies Project
Rt. 3
Clinton, AR 72031
Send 2 good-quality cassette tapes and they will send you 1 back filled with music from the woods.

Women's Film Collective
1507 University Ave. S.E.
Minneapolis, MN 55414
612-473-2373

Women's Film Co-op
Valley Women's Center
200 Main
Northampton, MA 01060
413-586-2011
   Catalog is much more than a catalog!

Women's Film Crew
San Francisco Newsreel
451 Courtland
San Francisco, CA 94110

Women's Film Educational Project
Sandra Shevey
2043 N. Beachwood Dr.
Hollywood, CA 90028
   Launching new film magazine, Myth America. Plans film archives on women's role in film and series of film retrospectives to honor efforts women have made.

Women's Film Project
c/o Melanie Maholick
2127 California St. N.W.
Washington, DC 20008
   Project did "The emerging woman" (SEE AV) as a collective. Helena Solberg-Ladd and Lorraine Gray, 1735 New Hampshire Ave., DC 20009, also members.

Women's Free Press
2828 Benvenue Ave.
Berkeley, CA 94705
415-848-3502

Women's Free Press
PO Box 8341, Lake St. Station
Minneapolis, MN 55404
   Publishes Goldflower. Shirley Hyer.

Women's Free School
Missoula, MT
   Contact via Women's Action Center, Univ. of MT, Missoula 59801.

Women's Graphics Collective
c/o Chicago WL Union
852 W. Belmont Ave.
Chicago, IL 60657
   Posters, graphics, videotape.

Women's Health & Abortion Information
1736 R. St. N.W.
Washington, DC 20009
202-483-4632

Women's Health & Abortion Project
36 W. 22
New York, NY 10010
   Literature & Education Collective is a part. Contraception and abortion information.

Women's Health & Information Project
Box 110, Warringer Hall
Central Michigan Univ.
Mt. Pleasant, MI 48859
517-774-3762, 0355 x57

Women's Health Center
Women's Place, 146 E. 18 Ave.
Vancouver, BC
873-3984

Women's Health Clinic
2339 Durant Ave.
Berkeley, CA 94704

Women's Health Collective
3789 24
San Francisco, CA 94114
415-282-6999

Women's Health Forum
156 5 Ave., Suite 1228
New York, NY 10010
   Series of pamphlets on sexuality, health.

Women's Health Information Service of North Suburban Chicago
261 Kimberly Rd.
Barrington, IL 60010

(cont.) Terri Tepper, Women's Health Information Center.

Women's Health Project
715 N. Dodge
Iowa Icity, IA 52240
319-338-3289

Women's Health Project
18700 Woodward
Detroit, MI 48203
313-892-7161

Women's H E L P
New Jersey area: 201-567-0425, 0758
Free information on abortion, menstrual extraction, voluntary sterilization.

Women's History Library
2325 Oak
Berkeley, CA 94709
415-524-7772
Laura X, founder. Because of lack of operating funds, collection being dispersed. Microfilm Project will continue, depending on tax-deductible contributions.... See also Herstory, in "Audiovisuals" part of Non-Book Resources section. (A complete rundown of the distribution of the components of the Women's History Research Center appears in C&R News Feb. 1975:49-50.)

Women's Hot-Dog Skiing Assoc.
2890 20, Cindy Scott, Exec. Dir.
Boulder, CO 80302

Women's Information & Referral Center
3595 St. Urbain
Montreal 131, Quebec
514-842-4781

Women's Information Service (WISE)
38 S. Main
Hanover, NH 03755
Elaine Selle, founder. Counseling service. Raising money for network of women's centers in New Hampshire.

Women's Institute for Freedom of the Press
3306 Ross Pl. N.W.
Washington, DC 20008
202-363-0812
Dr. Donna Allen, dir. Media Report to Women. Feminist media group to influence the mass media 'to make both content and employment more representative of all people.'

Women's Institute of Chicago
312-649-9767, 528-8319
Sponsored feminist literature conference.

Women's Interart Center
549 W. 52
New York, NY 10019
212-246-6570, 362-7457
Gallery. Join us to learn to teach, to exhibit, to perform....

Women's Interests & Services East, Inc. see WISE

Women's International League for Peace & Freedom
CA: San Francisco 94102, 50 Oak, 415-863-7146.
NY: New York 10011, 201 W. 13, 212-242-4610.
PA: Philadelphia 19107, 1213 Race.

Women's International Network (WIN)
187 Grant
Lexington, MA 02173
Fran P. Hosken, Coord. "International Women's Di-

(cont.) rectory" project. Send names & addresses.

Women's Involvement Programme
341 Bloor, Suite 309
Toronto, 181
921-6591
   Series of video tapes on women.

Women's Issues in Librarianship
24 Fulton
Medford, MA 02155
   Carole Wilson. Boston-area local organization working to expose discriminatory employment practices, to combat unflattering stereotypes of female librarians, to evoke awareness of how literature provided patrons presents an unfair portrayal of women in society.

Women's Job Corps Information
541 E. Colorado Blvd.
Pasadena, CA 91101
213-449-1620

Women's Job Rights Project
620 Sutter, #318
San Francisco, CA 94102
415-771-1092
   "Women's job rights advocate handbook" ($1.25).

Women's Joint Congressional Committee
1430 Rhode Island Ave. N.W.
Washington, DC 20005

Women's Law Caucus
2500 Red River
Austin, TX 78705

Women's Law Center
351 Broadway
New York, NY 10013
212-431-4074
   Publishes booklets and factssheets on various legal problems common to many women, in an attempt to demystify the law; does not practice law, give legal advice, nor recommend lawyers. Sponsors workshops re how New York divorce laws and courts function.

Women's Law Fund, Inc.
17210 Parkland Dr.
Shaker Heights, OH 44120
   In 1973 received 2-year Ford Foundation grant to finance program in Ohio. Jane M. Picker, Project Dir. Also: 1621 Euclid Ave., Cleveland 44115.

Women's League for Peace and Freedom
120 Maryland Ave. N.E.
Washington, DC 20002
202-546-8644

Women's Legal Center
558 Capp
San Francisco, CA 94110
415-285-5066

Women's Legal Defense Fund
1624 16 St. N.W.
Washington, DC 20009
   Nan C. Bases, member, Screening Committee. Participating attorneys practice only in Washington, DC, Maryland, and Virginia.

Women's Legal Education Fund
1624 Crescent Pl. N.W.
Washington, DC 20009

Women's Liberation Library Collective
492 Putnam Ave.
Cambridge, MA 02139

Women's Liberation Movement
PO Box 1284, Stuyvesant Station
New York, NY 10009
   "Woman's World" packet of 5 back issues of discontinued feminist quarterly, Redstockings ($2).

Directory of Sources

Women's Lobby, Inc.
1345 G St. S.E.
Washington, DC 20003
202-547-0022
    Also 95 Madison Ave., New York, NY 10016, Rm. 200, 212-889-2244.

Women's Media Center
Michigan Union, Rm. 337
Ann Arbor, MI 48104
    Project challenging male control of communications by developing a network among women.

Women's Media Group
905 Diamond
San Francisco, CA 94114
    Tapes.

Women's Media Project
PO Box 4235
Memphis, TN 30104
901-278-3046, 323-0981
    Collective of women working on different aspects of the media--challenging TV stations on their hiring and programming in re women; working with video-tape and with the women's cable channel in Memphis; promoting women's albums, journals, literature; challenging large newspapers on their coverage of women and minorities, etc. Newsletter. Contacts: Martha Allen, Angelika Bammer.

Women's Medical Assoc. of New York City
1740 Broadway
New York, NY 10019
212-586-8683

Women's Medical Center of Washington
1712 I St. N.W.
Washington, DC 20006
202-298-9227

Women's Middle East Study Collective
PO Box 134
West Newton, MA 02156
    "Women in the Middle East; the continuing struggle" ($.50).

Women's Music Network
215 W. 92, #1H
New York, NY 10025
212-799-0020
    "Lavender Jane Loves Women," LP ($5.25). Founded by Alix Dobkin, Kay Gardner, Patches Attom, an umbrella encompassing Lavender Jane Productions, which handles live concerts; Women's Wax Works, the record company; and Hearts & Struggles Publ. Co.

Women's National Abortion Action Coalition
3417 Spruce
Philadelphia, PA 19104

Women's National Democratic Club
1526 New Hampshire Ave. N.W. #676
Washington, DC 20036

Women's National Health Coalition
222 E. 35
New York, NY 10016
212-684-0217

Women's National Press Club
505 National Press Bldg.
Washington, DC 20004

Women's National Republican Club
3 W. 51
New York, NY 10019

Women's Need Center
448 Clayton
San Francisco, CA 94117
415-621-1003

Women's Network Referral System (on jobs)
Wisconsin Dept. of Administration
  Publishes bi-weekly vacancy bulletin.

Women's News Service
  (at) Stanford University
Stanford, CA 94305
  Wendy Quinones, graduate student in Communications, organized. Amy Sabrin, staff member.

Women's Office
Box 85, Rm. 230
Student Union Bldg.
University of British Columbia
Vancouver 8, BR
  Tape Library.

Women's Organizations for Employment
593 Market, Rm. 223
San Francisco, CA 94105
415-495-0923
  "Women's job rights handbook" ($1.50). Buttons ($.25). Stickers.

Women's Photo Co-op
23 Baldwin
Toronto, Ontario
  Laura Jones. Image Nation Eleven.

Women's Political Caucus see National...

Women's Press
280 Bloor St. W., Suite 305
Toronto, Ontario
416-962-3904

Women's Press
Box 562
Eugene, OR 97401
  Catherine Waechter. Goes beyond the scope of a local women's paper.

Women's Press Collective

5251 Broadway
Oakland, CA 94618
  "Lesbians speak out II; a Lesbian autobiography." Coloring book ($.85). Feminists, print-shop, publisher, Posters.

Women's Prison Assoc.
110 2 Ave.
New York, NY 10003
212-674-1163

Women's Psychotherapy Referral Service
NOW New York City Chapter
  Psychotherapy Committee
212-WO4-0400

Women's Radio Workshop
Station WDET, 5035 Woodward
Detroit, MI 48202

Women's Refuge
2134 Allston Wy., YWCA
Berkeley, CA 94704
415-845-8854

Women's Research Center of Boston
123 Mount Auburn
Cambridge, MA 02138
  "Who rules Massachusetts women" ($1.16).

Women's Research Project
404A Yale Station
New Haven, CT 06520
  Slide-show rental on women's image in advertising.

Women's Retreat
Highland Settlement
Paradox, NY 12858
  Marie Deyoe. Using facilities of a residential school: 600 acres in Adirondack forest preserve. Can accommodate children part of the year. Charge on sliding scale.

Women's Revolutionary Art Co-

Directory of Sources

(cont.) op
La Dolores Center, 1250 Halsted
Chicago, IL 60607

Women's Right, Inc.
60 E. 42
New York, NY 10017
212-682-8120

Women's Rights, Athletic Progress (WRAP)
4610 Marble N.E. #B
Albuquerque, NM 37110

Women's Rights Center
351 Broadway
New York, NY 10013
212-431-4074

Women's Rights Project
American Civil Liberties Union
156 5 Ave.
New York, NY 10010
212-725-1222
SEE ALSO American Civil Liberties Union.

Women's Rights Task Force on Education
549 Lenox Ave.
Westfield, NJ 07090
Bibliography of 67 positive female image books in American history and related biography and fiction for junior high school ($.25). "Women's directory" (New Jersey women employed in non-traditional occupations, i.e. resource persons for colleges and schools, $.50.)

Women's Room
2490 Channing Wy., #504
Berkeley, CA 94704
Clipping service for/about women.

Women's School
Twin Cities Women's Union
612-374-9242, 823-3534, 636-4879
Classes include anything women can teach or want to learn about or do together.

Women's Sculpture Assoc.
22 E. 17
New York, NY 10003
212-242-9203

Women's Self-Help Clinic
Saskatoon, Sask.
Clinic, classes, pamphlets.

Women's Services, Inc.
424 E. 62
New York, NY 10021
212-758-7310, 6110

Women's Social & Political Union
From inception in 1903, the strongest women's organization in England; included many workingclass women. Emmeline and Cristabel Pankhurst began organized leadership in Lancashire and Yorkshire. SEE Dictionary of National Biography.

Women's Soul Publishing, Inc.
Box 5476
Milwaukee, WI 53211
Publishes Paid My Dues.

Women's Store
4157 Adams Ave.
San Diego, CA 92116
Feminist.

Women's Strike Coalition
360 W. 28
New York, NY 10001
"Women of the world, unite" symbol with UN leaves.

Women's Studies see Feminist Press; p. 405ff.

Women's Studies Library
Box 7211
Baltimore, MD 21218
Has newsletter.

Women's Studies Program
Instructional Media Center
1720 Oregon
Berkeley, CA 94703
> Susan Bement, dir. Berkeley public schools curriculum development program for correction of racial and sexual stereotypes in schools. Susan B. Anthony kit. Attitude Questionnaire for students. Report to the Board of Education. Report on sex-role stereotyping among intermediate school children. Handbook on developing a Black girls' club. Single copies minimal charge.

Women's Switchboard
San Francisco, CA
415-771-8212

Women's Talent Corps
201 Varick
New York, NY 10014
> Chartered provisionally as 2-year A.A. degree-granting College for Human Services. Audrey C. Cohen, President.

Women's Television Project
> For information, write Bonnie Klein, founder of Portable Channel, 308 Park Ave., Rochester, NY 14607. Project teaches women how to produce videotapes for and about women.

Women's Theater Council
1 Sheridan Sq.
Marie Irene Fornes
New York, NY 10014
212-YU9-7216

Women's Training & Resources Corp.
142 High, Suite 512, Congress Bldg.
Portland, ME 04101
207-772-5482
> "Breaking barriers through speech" workshops.

Women's Transit Authority
919 Spring
Madison, WI 53706
> Debby Swayne, coord. Volunteers, radio-dispatched routes. Counter-rape!

Women's Veterinary Medical Assoc.
Deer Park Veterinary Clinic
4380 E. Galbraith
Cincinnati, OH 45236
> Dr. Helena J. Constantine.

Women's Wax Works
> Record company under Women's Music Network umbrella.

Women's Work [employment agency]
JoAnne Roslansky
820 First National Bldg.
2d & Main Sts.
Davenport, IA 52801
319-326-6249

Women's Year see International Women's Year

Woodrow Wilson Doctoral Dissertation Fellowships in Women's Studies
Box 642
Princeton, NJ 08540
> Nomination by dean of one's graduate school is necessary; he has the forms. Open to men and women.

Working Group on Women & Religion
American Academy of Religion see American Academy...

World View Publishers
46 W. 21
New York, NY 10010
> "Feminism and Marxism" by Dorothy Ballan ($1). "Women workers; their stories

Directory of Sources

(cont.) and struggles" ($.25). Battle Acts.

-X-Y-Z-

Y.W.C.A. of Canada
571 Jarvis
Toronto, Ontario
 Series of mimeo'd reports of women's issues. Published "Guidelines for problem-pregnancy counselling" and "Guide for a study program in abortion."

Yellow Springs Radical Lesbians
c/o Women's Center, Antioch College Union
Yellow Springs, OH 45387

YWCA Loop Center (of Metropolitan Chicago)
37 S. Wabash
Chicago, IL 60603
312-372-6600
 Many feminist projects initiated by the Center.

YWCA Women's Advocacy Center
1130 Nicollet Ave.
Minneapolis, MN 55403
612-332-0501

Youth Film Distribution Center
43 W. 16
New York, NY 10011
212-989-7265
 Nonprofit organization. Deals exclusively with films made by young people.

Yuzuro, Tenno
c/o Japan Library Assoc.
55-11, 1-Chrome
Taishido, Setagoya-ku
Tokyo, Japan
 Once one of the few female members of Japan's professional Storytellers Assoc., has been kicked out of the group for telling sexy stories.

Zero Population Growth
1111 E. Franklin Ave., Suite 210
Minneapolis, MN 55404
612-336-8500

Zero Population Growth
Free Abortion Referral Service, 40 W. 40
New York, NY 10018
212-354-8688

Zeta Phi Beta
1734 New Hampshire Ave. N.W.
Washington, DC 20009
202-387-3103
 EEOC describes this as "Negro sorority/service group which can provide some placement referrals."

Zion Research Library
120 Seaver
Brookline, MA 02146

Zipporah Films
54 Lewis Wharf
Boston, MA 02110
617-742-6680
 Sole distributor for Frederick Wiseman's documentary films.

Zizi Press
525 W. 125
New York, NY 10027
 "The little prick, 2nd ed." (1973 $1.20).

Zonta International
59 E. Van Buren
Chicago, IL 60605

(DIRECTORY OF SOURCES,* cont.)

STATUS-OF-WOMEN COMMISSIONS, COUNCILS, ETC. (GOVERNMENTAL)

Commission on the Status of Women
UN Economic and Social Council
United Nations
New York, NY 10017
"UN Report on women and media in all member nations."

Commission on the Status of Women
UNESCO 25th Session
"Influence of mass communication media on the formation of a new attitude...." SEE Pamphlets.

U.S.A.**

49 states have commissions (Texas alone missing); also Puerto Rico, Washington, DC, cities and counties. Representative are:

District of Columbia
Commission on the Status of Women
District Building, Room 204
Washington, DC 20004
"Free women of VD!" Free mimeo sheets, lists of clinics, prevention ways.

Illinois Commission on the Status of Women
1166 Debbie Ln.
Macomb, IL 61566
309-833-4282
Susan Catania, Chairwoman.

Governor's Commission on the Status of Women
Commonwealth of Mass.
Rm. 2108, 100 Cambridge
Boston, MA 02202
617-727-6693
Ann Blackham, Chairwoman.

Puerto Rico. Governor's Commission for the Improvement of Women's Rights'
Silma Gonzalez, Exec. Dir.
Garraton Building
1608 Ponce de Leon
San Juan, PR

Governor's Commission on the Status of Women
1 W. Wilson
Madison, WI 53702
Kathryn F. Clarenbach, Chairperson.

CANADA

National Action Committee on the Status of Women
Laura Sabia, Pres.
29 Edgedale Rd.
St. Catherines, Ontario
Helen Tucker, Sec., 1524 Douglas Dr., Mississauga,

Status-of-Women Commissions

(cont.) Ontario
Grace Hartman, Treas., 233 rue Gilmour, Suite 800, Ottawa
Moira Armour, Ed., Status of Women News, PO Box 927, Adelaide St., Toronto M5C 2K3

Alberta Status of Women Committee
c/o Shirley Gifford
6628 123
Edmonton, Alberta

Alberta Action Committee on the Status of Women
Ms. J. A. Durand, Pres.
14532 106A Ave.
Edmonton
Jean Marchton, Acting Sec., 9214 117 St., Edmonton.

British Columbia Status of Women
1045 W. Broadway
Vancouver 9, BC
733-1421

Vancouver Status of Women
2049 W. 4 Ave.
Vancouver 9, BC

Victoria Status of Women Action Group
1556 Mileva Ln.
Victoria, BC

West Kootenay Status of Women Council
c/o Susan Charlton
Box 621
Rossland

Manitoba Committee on the Status of Women
Elizabeth Feniak, Chairwoman
437 Don Ave.
Winnipeg, RCL OS5
June Menzies, Research Dir., 715 Fisher St., Winnipeg.
Kathleen Morrison, 2009 Rosser Ave., Branton

Newfoundland Status of Women Council
Shirley Goundry, Pres.
8 Riverview Ave.
St. Johns'
Mary Walsh, Treas., 2 Regina Pl., St. Johns'
Also: 203 Water St., Woman's Place, St. Johns', 709-722-4533.
Has newsletter.

Northwest Territories Status of Women Action Committee
Alison J. McAteer, Coord.
PO Box 1225
Yellowknife, XDE, 1HO
Also: Eileen Binder, PO Box 1057, Inuvik.

Halifax Status of Women
6124 Pepperell
c/o Barbara Harris
Halifax, Nova Scotia

Advisory Council on the Status of Women
Box 1541, Station B
Ottawa, Ontario KIP 5K5

Ontario Committee on the Status of Women
Lorna Marsden
41 Spadina Rd., #7
Toronto

Ontario Status of Women Council
Parliament Buildings
Queen's Park, Toronto, Ont.
Laura Sabia, Chairperson, Secretariat for Social Development.

Prince Edward Island Status of Women Study Group
Martha Pratt, Acting Sec.
57 Newland Cres.
Charlottetown, PEI

Le Conseil du Status de la Femme au Québec
2375 Laurier Blvd.

(cont.) Québec City, Québec
    Laurette Robillard, Pres.

Saskatchewan Action Committee
    on the Status of Women
Linda Tate, Chairwoman
2900 Argyle
Regina
    Jane Graham, Vice Chairwoman, 1191 Simcoe, Moose Jaw
    Emily Sippola, Sec., 329 Whitney Ave., Saskatoon.

Saskatchewan Status of Women
    Committee
Marion Younger
2217 Ewart Ave.
Saskatoon

Yukon Territory Status of Women
    Council
Joyce Hayden, Pres.
10 Tutshi Rd.
Whitehorse

---

* See also entries throughout Directory.
**Check with Interstate Association of Commissions on the Status of Women.

(DIRECTORY OF SOURCES, cont.)

WOMEN'S LIBERATION GROUPS AND CENTERS

The proliferation of Women's Liberation groups and centers, and of Women's Studies has been impressive; the three often overlap, but a general definition of each might be:

WOMEN'S LIBERATION GROUP   It may start with a few women whose collective consciousness has been raised to some aspect of the inequitable position of woman. Their degree of feminism may continue to grow as they meet and develop more formally and become aware of such facts of life as the generalized condition of <u>all</u> women and as they unite and organize to <u>change</u> the status quo and end all discriminatory practices--although they may concentrate on such specifics as rape, health, laws in general, or the Equal Rights Amendment.

Until women discover that, like virginity, there is no such thing as partial equality, the potential power of sisterhood unity will produce no substantial change, however.

WOMEN'S CENTER   Often a center begins when a local Women's Liberation group or coalition of groups realizes the potential power of their unity, or they may have discovered that without "a room of one's own," they cannot begin to implement some of the things about themselves which they are just discovering.

A Women's Center may literally serve as a refuge. It may be a store or a house; on some campuses it may be a token office or room misnamed in fact and spirit, with the administration retaining considerable control. It is possible for a Women's Center to be a place where women can unite and gather their resources and selves for recovery and action. But in the long run, they must realize that although a change is gonna come, they have got to <u>go</u> <u>forth</u> and make it.

WOMEN'S STUDIES   Depending on its organization [see Ruth Crego Benson's "Women's Studies: Theory and Practice," <u>AAUP Bulletin</u> 58, 3 (Sept. 1972), 283-6] and institutional administrative commitment, power structure, etc. a Women's Studies <u>program</u> can provide genuine academic learning experiences, respectable "majors" or interdisciplinary programs, opportunity for exploration for both women and men, continuing education, ad infinitum. It is ludicrous to encounter Black (or Chicano, depending on the locale) Studies without Women's Studies in an American academic institutional curriculum.

A good exercise in consciousness-raising and coping is to prepare oneself to respond to the proposition, "How can it be equitable to have a Women's Studies but not a Black (or African or Afro-American) Studies program?" Intellectual analysis of male and female roles in society is basic to any change in the status of women that would later effect goals of hiring and promotion.

Without knowledge of themselves, women will not question their inferior status and will thus be channeled into appropriate "women's" jobs, disciplines, roles.

Womanhood Media (the 1972 volume) listed some Women's Studies programs at the conclusion of the Directory of Sources (pages 309-10). Since then, so many programs have come into existence that, rather than attempt to assemble a list, information is now provided in the "Pamphlets" part of the Non-Book Resources section (under WOMEN'S STUDIES) and in the Basic Book Collection.

* * * * *

The Project on the Status and Education of Women of the Association of American Colleges publishes a list of women's centers. The list of Women's Liberation groups and centers that follows does not duplicate those included in the 1972 Womanhood Media (pages 297-309), except where a change of data is known. It is of course incomplete.

Note that foreign countries (Canada through Vietnam) are listed, and then US. Canada is subdivided alphabetically by province (or territory), and then city; and the U.S., alphabetically by state and then city/town. Known NOW Chapters are provided at the beginning of each community. Ms. January 1975:91f provides a list of groups/centers abroad.

FOREIGN

Canada

Alberta (AB):
Edmonton Women's Centre
9723 103 Ave., Edmonton

Women's Center
11812 95th St., Edmonton

British Columbia (BC):
Women's Resource Center
2961 272d, Aldergrove

Women's Center
Kamloops

Women's Center
Box 521, Nelson

Women's Center
Prince George

Women's Liberation Groups

A Woman's Place
1766 W. Broadway, Vancouver

Women's Centre
511 Carroll, Vancouver

Women's Center & Bookstore
804 Richards, Vancouver
604-255-0436, 684-0523

Woman's Place
146 E. 18 Ave., Vancouver
604-873-3984

Women's Center
130 W. Hastings, Vancouver 4

Women's Center, #414
1029 Douglas, Victoria
604-385-3843

Manitoba (MB):
Winnepeg Women's Center
377 Agnes, Winnepeg

WL c/o Millie Lamb, #10
813 Wolseley, Winnipeg

300 Victor: A Women's Place
Winnipeg
786-4581

New Brunswick (NB):
Women's Center
386 Priestman, Fredericton

c/o Linda Gow, YWCA
27 Wellington Row, St. John

Newfoundland (NF):
The Woman's Place
203 Water, PO Box 5021
St. John's East
709-722-4533

Northwest Territories (NT):
Women's Group
c/o Nellie Cournoyea
Inuvik

Nova Scotia (NS):
c/o Women's Bureau
PO Box 3596
Halifax S. Postal Station

Women's Centre
c/o Judy Wonk
6299 Yale, Halifax

Ontario (ON):
Women's Center
63 King, Guelph

Open Arms Haven for Women
290 James St. N., near Barton
Hamilton

Women's Centre
306 Herkimer, Hamilton
528-4583

Kingston WL
Kingston

Women's Place, #3
205 47 VanOrder Dr.
Kingston

Women's Resource Center
284 Dufferin Ave., London
432-2344

Ottawa Women's Center Assoc.
136 Lewis, Ottawa
613-233-2560

Women's Place
366 Water, Peterborough

WL
Box 461, Sudbury

Women's Centre
c/o Lakehead Univ.
Thunder Bay

Women's Center
c/o L. Silvonen
318 Marks, Thunder Bay

Toronto Women's Center
1267 Queen St. W., Toronto

WL
c/o Ramsey
51 Maple Ave., Toronto 287

Toronto WL
c/o Ryerson Student Union
325 Church, Toronto

Humber College Centre for Women
Toronto
671-681-0403

The Women's Place
31 DuPont, Toronto 5
416-929-3185

Interval House
173 Spadina Rd., Toronto

Women's Collective
300 Erb, Waterloo

K-W Woman's Place
25 Dupont St. E., Waterloo

Woman's Place
968 University Ave. W.
Windsor
519-252-0244

Women's Place
327 Oullette Ave., #202
Windsor

WL
76 University Ave., W.
Windsor

Prince Edward Island (PE):
Joanne Opperman
Wellington RR#1
Women's Centre
Grand River

Quebec (PQ):
Centre de Femmes/Women's Center
4319 St. Denis, Montréal 131

Women's Information & Referral Center/Centre d'Information et de Référence pour Femmes
3595 St. Urbain, Montréal 131
514-842-4781
   Also: Feminist Communications Collective.

Women's Counselling Service
3650 Hutchison, Montréal 112

Women's Mobile Information Unit
3641 St. Lawrence Blvd.
Montréal

Woman's Place/Place des Femmes
3764 Boul. St. Laurent
Montréal
514-845-7146

Emma Goldman Women's Center
3694 Ste. Famile, Montréal 130

Women's Center, YWCA
1355 Dorchester W., Montréal

WL
3777 St. Urbain, Montréal

Quebecoises Deboutte
3908 Rue Mentana, Montréal

(Note: Montreal Women have produced an anthology of writings, "Mother was not a person"--from Content, Suite 404, 1411 Crescent, Montreal 107, $3.95)

Saskatchewan (SK):
Women's Group
Box 549, Battleford

Campus Women's Center
Student Service Center
Regina
584-5454

Women's Centre
1136 Athol, Regina

YWCA Women's Centre
1940 McIntyre, Regina
525-0151, x06

Community Women's Centre
2505 11 Ave., Rm. 203
Regina
525-6216

Women's Liberation Groups

Women's Centre
1 Angus, Regina

Women's Centre
147 2 Ave. S., Saskatoon
306-242-5830, 343-3747, x4

Women's Group
1622 Ashley Dr.
Swift Current

Yukon (YT):
Women's Group
10 Tutshi Rd., Whitehorse

Czechoslovakia

Czechoslovakian Union of Women is participating in International Women's Year.

Denmark

Barbara Robin, free-lance journalist living in Denmark, has a regular column in the Danish daily, Berlingske Tidende.

Femogruppen
c/o Kvindehuset, Abendra 26
1124 Copenhagen K
  Also has information re Women's Island Camp.

England

New Opportunities for Women
Ruth Michaels
Hatfield Polytechnic
Hatfield, Hertfordshire

AWARE
14 Radnor Ter., London SW 8

Fawcett Library
Fawcett House, 14 Wilfred
London SW1

Ms. Gill Tew
#1 Gunyah Ct., Spencer Rd.
Chiswick, London W4

WL Workshop

3 Shavers Pl., London W1
38 Earlham, London WC2

France

League for the Full Rights of
  Women. Chaired by Simone
  de Beauvoir.

Mouv. de libération des femmes.
  SEE #629 Monique Witting's
  "Les guérrilleres," novel
  published in France just before the first action of the
  Movement, in which she has
  been totally involved since
  its inception.

Jeanne D'Eaubonne
Eco-Féminisme Centre
26, Rue Lécluse, 75017, Paris

Bibliothèque Féminine
Place du Panthéon, Paris 5
  (Good source of information.)

Germany

Women's International Democratic Federation
Unter den Linden 13
108 Berlin
German Democratic Republic
  [East Ger.]

Monica Jaeckel
Königwarterstr 12
6 Frankfurt am Main
Federal Republic of Germany
  [West Ger.]

Vera Stefan
Wilmderdorferstr 81, Berlin
Fed. Rep. of Germany

Italy

Julienne Travers, free-lance writer and translator, is active in Italian Women's Movement.

Portugal

SEE #630 in Basic Book Collec.

Scotland

Scottish Minorities Group
214 Clyde, Glasgow

Sweden

Sandbergs Bokhandel
Box 5702, S-11487
Stockholm 5
(Bookseller.)

Riksforbundet for sexuelit lika-
  berättigande (RFSL) (Swedish
  Union for Sexual Equality)
Box 850, 101 32 Stockholm

Switzerland

Marie Louise de Roulet
Friesenbergstr 112
Zurich 8055

Tunisia

SEE "Women Up in Arms" (mo
pic) in Audiovisual part of Non-
Book Resources section.

Vietnam

Women of VietNam
VietNam Women's Union
39-Hang-Chuoi, Hanoi

UNITED STATES OF AMERICA

(Note: Names/addresses of
chapters, task forces, etc.,
which are parts of the National
Organization for Women (NOW)
are not generally included; SEE
note in "Directory of Sources"
collection under National Organization for Women. Where oc-
casional reference is made to a
NOW group, it is usually provided
as one source for media elsewhere cited, and it precedes
other listings in the community.)

Alabama:
Women's Center

Office of Women's Affairs
Miles College, 5500 Ave. G.
Birmingham 35208

Assoc. for New Women
PO Box U-27, 307 Gaillard Dr.
Mobile 36688

Alaska:
WL
7801 Peck Ave.
Anchorage 99504

Fairbanks Women's Co-op
University of Alaska
Fairbanks 99701

Arizona:
NOW: Victoria Brown
Box 7003
Phoenix 85001

Associated Women Students
Arizona State University Memorial Union 252-C
Tempe 85281
602-965-3438

Tempe Women's Center
1414 S. McAllister
Tempe 85281
602-968-0743

Tucson's Women's Center
838 N. 4 Ave.
Tucson 85705

Women's Collective
829 N. 5 Ave.
Tucson 85705
602-792-1890

Women's Center
912 E. 6
Tucson 85719
602-792-1929

Arkansas:
Women's Center
University of Arkansas
902 W. Maple
Fayetteville 72701

Women's Liberation Groups

California:
Women's Studies Program
California State University,
  Humboldt
Arcata 95521

NOW: Peggy Hora
3690 7 Hills Rd.
Castro Valley 94546
  "Berkeley NOW." Also, Box
  7024, Berkeley 94707, and
  415-548-0379.

Female Liberation
University of California
516 Eshelman Hall
Berkeley 94720
  (Also Berkeley Women's Collective.)

Men's Center
2700 Bancroft Wy.
Berkeley 94704
415-845-4823

Women's Center
Graduate Theological Union
2378 Virginia Ave.
Berkeley 94709

Women's Coffee House
Unitas House, 2700 Bancroft
Berkeley 94704

Berkeley Gay Women's Liberation
2134 Allston Wy.
Berkeley 94704
415-845-8854

Women's Refuge
2134 Allston Wy. (YWCA Bldg.)
Berkeley 94704
415-845-8843, 548-4343
  (Women's Center.)

WL Center
1126 Addison, PO Box 4399
Berkeley 94714
415-843-9403

Gay WL
2828 Benvenue Ave.
Berkeley 94705

Center for Continuing Education
  of Women & Women's Center
University of California
Bldg. T9, Room 1000
Berkeley 94720
415-642-4786

Sisters in Struggle
2713 Ellsworth
Berkeley 94704

Women of the Free Future
PO Box 5399
Berkeley, CA 94714

Bay Area Women's Liberation
PO Box 4137
Berkeley, CA 94704

University of California
Berkeley 94720
  Various caucuses and groups.
  (Contact Center for Continuing Education for information.) E.g. School of Social
  Work, Haviland Hall, Political Science Dept., 210 Barrows Hall, Tolman Hall
  #4511.

Sisters of Sappho
Lesbian Feminist Alliance
PO Box 783
Campbell 95008
408-378-7665

NOW: San Fernando Valley
  NOW Education Cmt.
PO Box 20
Canoga Park 91303

Chico Women's Center
932 Alder
Chico 95926

Women's Studies Center
California State Univ., Chico
Chico 95926

NOW: Box 1975
Costa Mesa 92626

Women's Center
Orange Coast College
2701 Fairview Rd.
Costa Mesa 92626

Women's Center
1926 Placentia #15
Costa Mesa 92627

Women's Forum--WL Center
University of California, TB-124
Davis 95616

Women's Educational Center
California State College
1000 E. Victoria
Dominguez Hills 90246

Women's Task Force
Ohlone College, PO Box 909
Fremont 94537

Fresno NOW
2934 E. Ashland
Fresno 93727

Women's Center
Fresno City College
1101 University Ave.
Fresno 93741
209-262-4721

NOW: Orange County
Box 4035
Fullerton 92634

Women's Center
California State University
Fullerton 92634

Women's Education Program
Gavilan Community College
5055 Santa Teresa
Gilroy 95020

Women's Center
Glendale Community College
1500 N. Verdugo Rd.
Glendale 91208

NOW: Santa Barbara NOW
PO Box 931
Goleta 93017

Media Task Force, 162 Alpine Dr.

Isla Vista Women's Center
6504 Pardell Rd. #2
Goleta 93017
805-968-5774

Women's Center
University of California
Irvine 92664

Women's Opportunities Center
University of California, Irvine, Extension
Irvine 92664
714-833-7128

Women's Programs, Extension
Univ. of California, San Diego
PO Box 109
La Jolla 92037

NOW: Pomona Valley Chapter
2751 Mt. View Dr., Apt. E
LaVerne 91750

NOW
1819 Edgewood Dr.
Lodi 95240

NOW: 733 Termino
Long Beach 90804

Women's Center
Long Beach City College
4901 E. Carson Blvd.
Long Beach 90815

Women's Center
California State University
6407 Bayard
Long Beach 90815

NOW: 8864 W. Pico Blvd.
Los Angeles 90035
213-278-0680, 0286

Center for Women's Studies
Pepperdine University
1121 W. 79
Los Angeles 90044

Women's Liberation Groups

Womanspace
11007 Venice Blvd.
Los Angeles 90034
  See "Woman's Building" in
  Directory of Sources section.

Women's Resource Center
UCLA Powell Library, Rm. 90
405 Hilgard Ave.
Los Angeles 90024
213-825-3945

Los Angeles Women's Union
PO Box 3934, Terminal Annex
Los Angeles 90051

Women's Center
1027 S. Crenshaw Blvd.
Los Angeles 90019
203-937-3964, 5

Los Angeles Women's Center
  SEE Westwood. SEE ALSO
  Woman's Building in "Directory of Sources" section.

NOW: Box 205
Merced 95340

Modesto see Oakdale

NOW
Box 1661 (Also 735 Filmore)
Monterey 93940

Women's Center
Box 1501
Monterey 93940

YWCA of Los Angeles
East Valley Center
4903 Laurel Canyon Blvd.
North Hollywood 91607

NOW: Stanislaus County
Oakdale

WL
PO Box 5203
Oakland 94605

ICI: A Woman's Place (center)
5251 Broadway at College

Oakland 94618
415-654-9920

NOW: 2293 Francis Dr.
Palm Springs 92262

NOW: South Bay Chapter
91 Roosevelt Circle
Palo Alto 94306
  Also 1050 Newell Rd., c/o
  Davis.

Women's Studies Research Institute
Stanford University Graduate
  School of Business
Palo Alto 94305

Stanford Women's Center
Women's Clubhouse
Old Union Courtyard
Stanford University
Palo Alto 94305
415-321-2300

Women's Information & Counseling Center
Contra Costa College
405 Santa Fe Ave.
Point Richmond 94801

NOW. South Bay NOW
1029 Portola Rd.
Portola Valley 94025

NOW: San Bernardino/Riverside
616 E. Citrus
Redlands 92373

Women's Center
4200 Farm Hill Blvd.
Redwood City 94061

Riverside Women's Center
3122 Panorama
Riverside 92506

Women's Center
4459-2 Orange Grove
Riverside 92501

Women's Survival Center
California State Univ.--Sonoma

1801 E. Cotati Ave.
Rohnert Park 94928

NOW: 1446 38
Sacramento 95816

Women's Studies
California State University
6000 J
Sacramento 95819
　　Also Continuing Education.

Women's Center
1221 20
Sacramento 95814

Monterey County Peace Center:
　　Women's Center
Box 1364
Salinas 93901

Valice
205 Laurel Ave.
San Anselmo 94960

Woman's Way
412 Red Hill Ave., Suite 9
San Anselmo 94960

NOW: San Diego Education Task
　　Force
PO Box 22264
San Diego 92122
　　Also Textbook TF. Also
　　Image of Women TF. Another
　　address: 3969 Kenosha Ave.,
　　92117.

Center for Women's Studies &
　　Services
California State University, 908 F.
San Diego 92101

WL
Aztec Center, San Diego State
　　College
San Diego 92105

Center for Women's Studies &
　　Services
805 9
San Diego 92105
714-233-3088

Women's Center
10 & C Sts.
San Diego 92103
714-423-0276

NOW: Box 1267
San Francisco 94101
　　Also 6353 Ascot Dr., Piedmont 94611.

American Indian Women's
　　Center
277 Valencia
San Francisco 94103

Bay Area Consortium of Continuing Education of Women
Lone Mountain College
San Francisco 94118

Haight-Ashbury Women's Center
10 Ryan
San Francisco 94117

Intersection Women's Night
756 Union
San Francisco 94133

San Francisco Women's Switchboard
c/o YWCA, 620 Sutter
San Francisco 94102
415-771-8212

Women's Center for Creative
　　Counseling
San Francisco
415-648-1509
　　Also: San Mateo 342-0278,
　　Daly City 756-4736

Women's Legal Center
558 Capp
San Francisco 94110

Women's Need Center
558 Clayton
San Francisco 94117

Shirley Boccaccio
468 Belevedere
San Francisco 94117
415-566-2787

Women's Liberation Groups

DOB
1005 Market, #208
San Francisco 94103
415-861-8689 (24-hours)

WL
1380 Howard
San Francisco 94103
415-861-2114

YWCA Interchange--Santa Clara
  Valley
1066 W. Hedding
San Jose 95126
408-243-4303
  "Men Against Rape" group.

Women's Alliance: WOMA
1460 Koll Circle
San Jose 95112
408-998-3020 x510

Women's Center
San Jose State University
177 S. 10th
San Jose 95112
408-294-7265

Women's Center
College of San Mateo
1700 W. Hillsdale Blvd.
San Mateo 94402

NOW: Marin County
PO Box 2925
San Rafael 94902

Women's Center & Emergency
  Housing, YWCA
1618 Mission
San Rafael 94901
415-456-0782

PO Box 1412
San Rafael 94902

NOW: (Fresno NOW)
114 N. Wood Duck Dr.
Sanger 93657

Feminist Women's Health Center
  of Orange County

429 S. Sycamore
Santa Ana 92701
714-836-1212, 3

Orange County Women's Center
108 Russell (Off Main, between
  McFaddin & Edidger)
Santa Ana 92707
714-836-1931

Continuing Education for Women
University of California
Santa Barbara 93107

Assoc. Students
University of California
Santa Barbara 93106

Women's Center
314 Laurel
Santa Cruz 95060

428 Escalona
Santa Cruz 95060
415-427-1494

Stanford Women's Center
Box 2633
Stanford 94305
415-321-2300 x314

NOW: San Joaquin NOW
2717 Rutledge Wy., PO Box 4073
Stockton 95207

Sunnyvale--South Bay Chapter,
  NOW
PO Box 2304
Sunnyvale 94087
408-733-5480

West SideWomen's Center
218 W. Venice Blvd.
Venice 90291
213-823-4774

Women's Center
2914 Grand Canal
Venice 90291

Via Torrence Women's Center
16007 Crenshaw Blvd.
El Camino College
Via Torrence 90506

NOW: Contra Costa County
906 Alford Ave.
Walnut Creek 94506

Westwood Women's Center
Westwood (Los Angeles) 96137
213-823-4774

Colorado:
Resource Center for Women
Adams State College
San Luis Ranch
Allamosa 81101

NOW: Denver
1289 Newark
Aurora 80010

Univ. of Colorado Women's Center
Boulder 80302
303-443-2211 x7523

Women's Center
1520 Euclid
Boulder 80302

NOW: Denver see Aurora, Golden

Gay Women's Center
2460 S. Ogden
Denver 80210

Research Center on Women
Loretto Heights College
3001 S. Federal Blvd.
Denver 80236

Virginia Neal Blue Center
Colorado Women's College
1800 Pontiac
Denver 80220

Women's Center
1452 Penn. #17
Denver 80202

Woman's Resource Center
Univ. of Denver, University Park
Denver 80210

Women's Studies Program
Metropolitan State College
Denver 80210

NOW: 1924 Forest Ave.
Durango 81301

Women's Crisis & Information Center
Colorado State University
629 S. Howes
Ft. Collins 80521
303-493-3888

Women's Research Center, Ofc. of Women's Relations
Colorado State University
Ft. Collins 80521
303-491-6383

NOW: Denver
12916 W. 24 Pl.
Golden 90401

Center for Women
Mesa College
Grand Junction 81501

Virginia Neal Blue Women's Resource Center
Southern Colorado State College
Pueblo 81001

Connecticut:
Every Woman's Center
968 Fairfield
Bridgeport 06606
203-334-6154

Asnuntuck Community College
PO Box 68
Enfield 06082

Women's Center
87 Ridgefield
Hartford 06112

WL Center of Greater Hartford, Inc., 11 Amity
Hartford 06106
203-523-8949

Wesleyan Women's Center
High Middletown 06520
203-347-9411

Women's Liberation Groups

Women's Center
115 College
Middletown 06457
203-346-4042

New Britain Women's Movement
375 Farmington Ave.
New Britain 06053

Union Theological Women's
  Center
3438 Yale Station
New Haven 06520

New Haven Women's Liberation
  Center
215 Park
New Haven 06520
203-436-0272

Women's Center, Yale Univ.
Divinity School, Bacon Bldg.
New Haven 06520

Women's Liberation Center
Box 3438, Yale Station
New Haven 06520

Counseling Center for Women
33 Wilson Ave., Norwalk Community College
Norwalk 06851

WL Center
PO Box 844, 11 N. Main
Norwalk 06552

WL Center
11 N. Main
South Norwalk 06856

Women's Center
Univ. of Connecticut
Storrs 06268

Storrs Women's Center
Commons 312
Storrs 06268
203-486-4738

Continuing Education for Women
Univ. of Conn., University Dr.
Torrington 06790

Delaware:
Education Services for Women
Univ. of Delaware
Newark 19711
302-738-2211

Women's Resource Center
57 W. Park Blvd.
Newark 19711

NOW
11 Clermont Rd.
Wilmington 19803

District of Columbia:
NOW: 1736 R St., N.W.
Washington, DC 20009
202-387-6895

Black Women's Institute
Natl. Council of Negro Women
1346 Conn. Ave. N.W.
Washington, DC 20036

Institute for Continuing Education for Women
Federal City College
1424 K St., N.W.
Washington, DC 20001
202-727-2824

Continuing Education for Women, George Washington
Univ. College of General
  Studies
2029 K St. N.W.
Washington, DC 20006

Trinity College Women's Center
Michigan Ave. N.E.
Washington, DC 20002

Washington Area Women's
  Center, Inc.
1736 R St. N.E.
Washington, DC 20009
202-232-5145

Women's Center, Catholic Univ.
Michigan Ave. N.E.
Washington, DC 20017

Women's Phone

(cont.) c/o Community Bookstore
2028 P St. N.W.
Washington, DC 20036

Washington Feminists
609 21 St. N.W.
Washington, DC 20006
202-DI7-3776

D.C. WL
Box 13098 T St. Station
Washington, DC 20009

Multi-Service Center (to serve
  socio-economically deprived
  Hispanic women)
Contact: Isabel C. Lee
2149 30 St. N.E.
Washington, DC 20018
202-LA6-5813

Florida:
NOW: Dade County
Box 276
Coconut Grove 33133

Women's Commission
Univ. of Miami
Coral Gables 33124

Career Planning for Disadvantaged Women
SantaFe Community College
3000 NW 83
Gainesville 32601

NOW
Box 8590
Jacksonville 32211

Options. Women's Center
1825 Hendricks Ave.
Jacksonville 32207
904-398-7728

Council for Continuing Education
  for Women
Miami-Dade Jr. College
141 N.E. 3 Ave.
Miami 33132

Institute for Women, Florida
  International Univ.
Tamiami Trail
Miami 33144

NOW
1057 E. Anderson
Pensacola 32503

Women's Information Center
6255 S.W. 69
South Miami 33143

Women's Center
2554 1 Ave. N.
St. Petersburg 33713
813-822-8156

Tallahassee Women's Educational & Cultural Center
Florida State University
212 Mabry Heights
Tallahassee 32306
904-599-4049, 3281, 3317

Tampa Women's Center
Box 1350
Tampa 33601
  (2205 W. Platte.)

Tampa Women's Center
214 Columbia Dr. #3
Tampa 33606

Women's Center
3215 Walcraft Rd.
Tampa 33611

Women's Center
405 Grand Central Ave.
Tampa 33604

Women's Center
Univ. of South Florida
Tampa 33620

Florida Feminists
4213 W. Bay Ave.
Tampa 33616

Georgia:
Woman's Place
140 Marion Dr.
Athens 30601

Women's Liberation Groups

NOW: YWCA
72 Edgewood Ave. N.E.
Atlanta 30303
 (Also PO Box 54045, 30308.)

Atlanta Woman's Center
1315 Stillwood Dr. N.E.
Atlanta 30306

Women's Center
45 11, Atlanta 30303

Hawaii:
Women's Center
1820 University Ave.
Honolulu 96822
808-947-3351

Women's Studies
University of Hawaii
Manoa, Spalding 252
Honolulu 96822 (Defunct?)

CEW, Univ. of Hawaii
931 University Ave., #205
Honolulu 96914

Akami Sister
PO Box 11042
Honolulu 96814

Idaho:
NOW: 216 W. 14
Idaho Falls 83401

Univ. of Idaho Women's Center
108 Administrative Bldg.
Moscow 83843
208-885-6616

Women's Center
Idaho State Univ.
Pocatello 83201

Illinois:
Women's Center, Aurora College
Aurora 60507

Carbondale Women's Center
1202 W. Schwartz
Carbondale 62901

Continuing Education for Women
Southern Illinois Univ.
Carbondale 62901

Women's Center
404 W. Walnut
Carbondale 62901

NOW: 809 S. 5
Champaign 61820

Student Personnel Office for
 Continuing Education for
 Women, Univ. of Illinois
610 E. John
Champaign 61820
217-333-3137

University YWCA Women's
 Center
1001 S. Wright
Champaign 61820

Chicago Ecumenical Women's
 Center
5751 S. Woodlawn, #111
Chicago 60637

Chicago WL Union
852 W. Belmont
Chicago 60657
312-348-4300, 2011

Ecumenical Women's Center
Northside Center
1653 W. School
Chicago 60657

YWCA Loop Center
37 S. Wabash
Chicago 60603
312-372-6600

M.O.R.E. for Women
5465 South Shore Dr.
Chicago 60615

Sister Center, United Church
 of Rogers Park
Morris at Ashland
Chicago 60626

Sisters Center, Northside WL
7071 Glenwood
Chicago 60626

Women's Center, North Area
1016 N. Dearborn
Chicago 60610
312-337-4385

Women's Center, Southwest Area
3134 W. Marquette Rd.
Chicago 60629
312-436-3500

Women's Center Uptown
4409 N. Sheridan Rd.
Chicago 60640
312-561-6737

Women's Center, West Side
5082 W. Jackson Blvd., 2 fl.
Chicago 60644
312-379-8332

Women's Center
6200 S. Drexel
Chicago 60637
312-955-3100

Women's Center
3322 N. Halsted
Chicago 60657
312-935-4270
  Also 3523 N. Halsted.

Women's Center
436 E. 39
Chicago 60653
312-285-1434

Women's Studies Center
535-3 Lucinda
Chicago 60625

Women's Studies Committee
Mundelein College
6363 N. Sheridan Rd.
Chicago 60620

Women's Institute
20 E. Jackson, Rm. 902
Chicago 60657
312-922-6749

University (of Chicago) Women's
  Assoc.
6031 S. Kimbark
Chicago 60637

Women's Studies Center,
  Northern Illinois Univ.
540 College Ct.
DeKalb 60115
815-752-0110

Women at Northwestern
Northwestern University
619 Emerson
Evanston 60201

WL Center of Evanston
2214 Ridge
Evanston 60201
312-471-4480

Kendall College Women's
  Center
2408 Orrington
Evanston 60201

Prelude, Knox College
Galesburg 61401

Student Services, College of
  Lake County
19351 W. Washington
Grayslake 60030

Women's Center, West Suburban
1 S Park
Lombard 60148
312-629-0170

Assoc. of Women Students
Monmouth College
Monmouth 61462

Women's Center, South Suburban
45 Plaza
Park Forest 60466
312-748-5660

Black Maria Collective
Box 230
River Forest 60305

NOW: 122 S. 4
Springfield 62701
217-523-3523
  (Storefront of several

Women's Liberation Groups

(cont.) groups, including ERA.)

A Woman's Place
401 W. California
Urbana 61801

404 Skokie Ct.
Wilmette 60091

Indiana:
Office for Women's Affairs
Indiana Univ. Memorial Hall-East
Bloomington 47401
812-337-3849

Women's Center
414 N. Park
Bloomington 47401
812-366-8691

Continuing Education for Women
Univ. of Evansville, Box 329
Evansville 47701

Ft. Wayne Feminists
PO Box 2796
Ft. Wayne 46808
219-742-1241

Mayor's Task Force on Women
2501 City-County Bldg.
Indianapolis 46204

Indianapolis WL
PO Box 88365
Indianapolis 46208

Purdue University, Office of
 Dean of Women, Span Plan
Lafayette 47907

South Bend Women's Center
1125 Thomas
South Bend 46625

Purdue Women's Caucus
Purdue Univ., Krannert Graduate
 School of Industrial Admin.
West Lafayette 47906
317-463-1736

Iowa:
Women's Coalition
Univ. of Iowa, Union
Ames 50010

Mt. Mercy College
1330 Elmhurst Dr. N.E.
Cedar Rapids 52402

NOW: 2002 Motley
Des Moines 50315

Continuing Education for Women Section, Drake Univ.
Des Moines 50311

Women's Information Center
8th & Grand
Des Moines 50309
515-244-8961

Univ. of Iowa Women's Center
3 E. Market
Iowa City 52240
515-353-6265

Ain't I a Woman. WL Front
PO Box 1169
Iowa City 52240

Women's Committee
Central College
Pella 50219

Kansas:
Lawrence Women's Center
1314 Oread
Lawrence 66044

Univ. of Kansas Commission
 on the Status of Women
Dean of Women's Office
Lawrence 66044

Women's Resource Center
Kansas State Univ.
Manhattan 66506

NOW: Kansas City NOW
9900 Camino Royal #92
Merriam 66203

A.W.A.R.E., Wichita State Univ.
Wichita 67208

Kentucky:
Women's Center
Brescia College, 120 W. 7
Owensboro 43201

Lexington Women's Center
120 Kentucky Ave.
Lexington 40502

Louisiana:
NOW.
PO Box 65162
Baton Rouge 70806

New Orleans Women's Center
1422 Felicity
New Orleans 70130
504-522-5298

WL Center
PO Box 19001
New Orleans 70119

Maine:
Women's Center
Univ. of Maine
University Heights
Augusta 04330

Women's Center
Box 914, Bangor 04401

Brunswick/Bath Women's Center
136 Main
Brunswick 04011
207-725-2512

NOW, PO Box 534
Kennebunkport 04046

Maryland:
Women's Center, Univ. of Maryland
9010 Riggs Rd., Apt. 205
Adelphi 20783

NOW: 903 W. University Pkwy.
Baltimore 21210

Baltimore WL
101 E. 25, Ste. B2
Baltimore 21218
301-366-6475

Continuing Education for Women, Morgan State College
Baltimore 21239

Women's Center, Towson State College
Box 2013
Baltimore 21204
301-824-7500

Women's Center, Essex Community College
PO Box 9596
Baltimore 21237

Women's Center, Johns Hopkins Univ.
Box 1134, Levering Hall
Baltimore 21218
301-235-3637

Women's Center
St. Mary's College
Baltimore 21210

Women's Law Center
PO Box 1934
Baltimore 21203
301-547-1653

Women's Union, Univ. of Maryland, Baltimore County
5401 Wilkens Ave.
Baltimore 21203
301-455-3446

Women's Center, Catonsville Community College
800 S. Rolling Rd.
Catonsville 21228
301-747-3220 x355

Women's Center, Univ. of Maryland
1127 Student Union
College Park 02742
301-454-5411

Women's Information Center
4110 School of Library & Information Services
College Park 20742
301-454-5441

Women's Liberation Groups

Women's Resource Center
8905 Footed Ridge
Columbia 21045
301-454-5411

Women's Center, Essex Community College, Rm. 17 Red Temporaries
Essex 21221
301-682-6000

NOW: Box 2301
Rockville 20852

Women's Center
Montgomery College
Rockville 20830

St. Mary's Women's Center
St. Mary's College
St. Mary's City 20686

Towson Women's Center
Towson State College
Baltimore 21204
301-823-7500 x826

Women's Center
Goucher College, Box 1434
Towson 21204

GYN Clinic
Western Maryland College
Westminster 21157

Massachusetts:
Men's Center, Jones Library
Amherst 01002

Southwest Women's Center
Univ. of Mass. John Quincy Adams Lobby
Amherst 01002
413-545-0626

Third World Women's Center
Univ. of Mass.
Amherst 01002

Women's Caucus, Univ. of Mass.
School of Education
Amherst 01002

Everywoman's Center, Univ. of Mass.
Munson Hall, Pat Sackrey
Amherst 01002
413-545-0883
(Also Continuing Education for Women.)

Andover Women's Center
224 Lowell
Andover 01810
617-475-6960

Women's Opportunity Research Center
Middlesex Community College
Div. of Continuing Education
Springs Rd.
Bedford 01730

NOW: Eastern Mass. Chapter
45 Newbury
Boston 02116

Arlington Street Women's Caucus
355 Boylston
Boston 02159

Boston Univ. Female Liberation
775 Commonwealth
Boston 02215

Boston Univ. Women's Center
211 Bay State Rd.
Boston 02215
617-353-4240

Pregnancy Counseling Service
3 Joy, Boston 02108

Women's Center
Boston State College
174 Ipswich
Boston 02115

Women's Center
PO Box 286, Prudential Center
Boston 02199

Women's Center
Simmons College, 300 The Fenway
Boston 02115

Boston Women's Collective, Inc.
490 Beacon
Boston 02115
617-261-1561

Crittenston Hastings House
10 Perthshire Rd., Brighton Sta.
Boston 02135

NOW: Box 346
Cambridge 12038

Library Collective
492 Putnam Ave.
Cambridge 02139

Radcliffe Institute
Radcliffe College
3 James
Cambridge 02138
617-495-8211

Women & Work, M.I.T.
Cambridge 02139

Women's Center
46 Pleasant
Cambridge 02139
617-354-8807

Women's Research Center
123 Mt. Auburn
Cambridge 02139

The Second Wave, Box 344
Cambridge 02139

Dorchester Women's Center
1880 Dorchester Ave.
Dorchester 01422
617-288-0770

NOW: 15A Memorial Dr.
East Weymouth 02189

Women's Center, Bristol Community College, 64 Durfee
Fall River 02720

Simon's Rock Early College
Great Barrington 01230

Community Women's Center

208-310 Main
Greenfield 01301
413-773-7519

Greenfield Women's Center
Federal
Greenfield 01301

Women's Caucus
1 Kennedy Dr.
Hadley 01035

Berkshire WL, PO Box 685
Lenox 01240
617-736-3219

Lowell Women's Center
50 Elm
Lowell 01852
617-445-5405

Continuing Education for Women, Jackson College
Tufts Univ.
Medford 02155

YWCA Women's Resource Center
Natick Hall
Natick 01760

New Bedford Women's Center
241 Reed
New Bedford 02747

Women's Resource Center
Andover-Newton Theological School, 215 Herrick Rd.
Newton Center 02159

Southeastern Mass. Univ. Women's Center
North Dartmouth 02747
617-997-9321 x698

Sophia Sisters. Smith College
Lesbian Liberation, Clark House
Northampton 01060

Valley Women's Center
200 Main
Northampton 01060
413-586-2011

Women's Liberation Groups

Women's Center
6 Goswald
Provincetown 02675
617-487-0387

Lower Cape Cod Women's Center
Box 712
Provincetown 02657
617-487-5045

Eastern Nazarene College
23 E. Elm
Quincy 02170

North Shore Women Center
58 High
Rockport 01966

Women's Center, Salem State
   College
Salem 01970
617-745-0556

Somerville Women's Health
   Project
326 Somerville Ave.
Somerville 02143

Women's Center, Mt. Holyoke
   College, 3 Brigham
South Hadley 01075

Women's Health Counseling
   Service, 115 State
Springfield 01103

Springfield Women's Center
451 State
Springfield 01101
413-732-7113, 6734

Brandeis Univ. Women's Center
20 Stanley Rd.
Swampscott 01907
617-598-2188

Lowell Women's Center
90 10
Tewsbury 01876
617-658-5045

NOW: c/o Debbie Volmer
Clark University, Box 1406
Worcester 01610

Women's Center, Clark Univ.
51 Downing
Worcester 01610
617-793-7711

Worcester Pregnancy Counseling
52 Burncoat
Worcester 01603

Worcester Women's Center
905 Main
Worcester 01610
617-753-9622

Worcester Women's Resource
   Center, 2 Washington
Worcester 01608
716-791-3181

Michigan:
Office of Women's Programs
Albion College
Albion 49224

Center for Continuing Education
Univ. of Michigan, 330 Thompson
Ann Arbor 48108

Feminist House
225 E. Liberty, Rm. 203
Ann Arbor 48104

Gay Advocate Office
Michigan Union, 530 S. State
Ann Arbor 48104
313-763-4186

1000 Cedar Bend Dr., Marcia
   Federbush. Committee to
   bring about equal opportunity
   in athletics for women &
   men at the Univ. of Michigan
Ann Arbor 48105

Women's Crisis Center
306 N. Division
Ann Arbor 48108

Women's Resource Center
Kellogg Community College Library
Battle Creek 49016

Women's Center
Lake Michigan College
Benton Harbor 49022

NOW: Metropolitan Detroit Chapter, Box 1455
Detroit 48231

Alternative Resource Center
16261 Petoskey
Detroit 48221

Detroit WL
415 Brainard
Detroit 48201

Women's Action & Aid Center
103 W. Alexandrine
Detroit 48201

Women's Resource Center
18700 Woodward Ave.
Detroit 48203
313-892-7161
 Includes: Feminist Federal Credit union.

WL Coalition of Michigan
2230 Witherell, Rm. 516
Detroit 48201

East Lansing Women's Center
223 1/2 E. Grand River
East Lansing 48823

Michigan State Univ. Women's Center
547 East Grand River
East Lansing 48823

ENCORE Program, Aquinas College
Grand Rapids 49506

Women's Resource Center
Western Michigan Univ.
Kalamazoo 49001

Kalamazoo Drop-in Center & Services for Women
211 S. Rose
Kalamazoo 49006
616-343-1223

Women's Center for Continuing Education, Holly Greer, Dir.
Northern Michigan Univ.
Marquette 49855

Continuum Center for Women
Oakland University
Rochester 48063

Chrysallis Center
Saginaw Valley College
University Center 48710

Women's Center, Delta College
University Center 48710

Minnesota:
Duluth Women's Center, Univ. of Duluth Medical School
EPIC Rm. 5
Duluth 55812

Woman to Woman Center
Univ. of Minnesota
101 Kirby Student Center
Duluth 55812

Grace High School Women's Center
1350 Gardena Ave. N.E.
Fredley 55432

Mankato Women's Center
Mankato State College
426 1/2 N. 4
Mankato 56001

NOW: Twin Cities NOW
5612 34 Ave. S.
Minneapolis 55417
 Also: 192 Seymour Ave. S.E. 55414, 612-336-9726, 459-2826, 333-6870, 377-0549.

Lesbian Resource Center
710 W. 22
Minneapolis 55405
612-374-2345

Minnesota Women's Center
Univ. of Minnesota

Women's Liberation Groups

(cont.) 301 Walter Library
Minneapolis 55455
612-373-3850

Women's Clearinghouse
c/o Experimental College
1507 University Ave. S.E.
Minneapolis 55414
612-376-7449

Women's Counseling Service
621 W. Lake
Minneapolis 55408

Univ. of Minnesota Commission
on Status of Women Students,
operates from Minnesota Women's Center

Twin Cities Women's Union
2953 Bloomington
Minneapolis 55407
612-729-6200, 823-1720

Univ. of Minnesota WL
Rm. 203 Union
Minneapolis 55455

Women's Center
Concordia College
Moorhead 56560

St. Olaf Women's Resource
Lounge, St. Olaf College
Northfield 55057

NOW: PO Box 80065
Como Station
St. Paul 55108
(Also: Roberta Pettit, 1767
Blair Ave. 55104.)

West Suburban Council for Women
16609 Cottage Grove
Wayzata 55391

Mississippi:
Jackson Women's Coalition
Box 3234
West Jackson Station 39507
Also: 622 N. Jefferson,
Jackson 39202, 601-355-8030.

Gay Counseling & Education
Projects, Mississippi Gay
Alliance, Box 4470
Mississippi State Union
State College 39762

Women's Action Movement
Mississippi State Univ., Box 1328
State College 39762

Missouri:
CEW, Univ. of Missouri, Coop.
Extension Services
Carthage 64836

Women's Center
501 E. Rollins
Columbia 65201

Women's Liberation Union
5138 Tracy
Kansas City 64110
816-333-4155

Women's Resource Service
Univ. of Missouri, Div. of
Continuing Education
1020 E. 63
Kansas City 64110

Women's Resource Center
Wm. Jewel College
Liberty 64068

NOW: PO Box 16132
St. Louis 63105

CEW, Washington Univ.
Box 1095
St. Louis 63130

St. Louis Univ. Women's
Center
3801 W. Pine
St. Louis 63108

St. Louis Women's Center
Univ. of Missouri
8001 Natural Bridge Rd.
St. Louis 63121

St. Louis Women's Center
1411 Locust
St. Louis 63103

Women's Center, Florissant
  Valley Community College
3400 Pershall Rd.
St. Louis 63135

Women's Resource Center
Washington Univ.
St. Louis 63130
314-863-0100 x4848

Montana:
NOW: 36 Birch
Great Falls 59405

Women's Center
Great Falls 59403

Women's Resource Center
Univ. of Montana
Missoula 59801
406-243-4153

Nebraska:
Women's Study Group
Dr. Evelyn Haller
Doane College
Crete 68333
402-826-2161

Women's Resource Center
Nebraska Union
Rm. 116, 14 & R
Lincoln 68506

Nevada:
NOW: 2280 Mohican
Las Vegas 98109

Women's Resource Center
Univ. of Nevada
Reno 89507

New Hampshire
Concord Women's Center
130 N Main
Concord 03101
603-244-3412

Dartmouth Women's Center
Dartmouth 03755

Franconia Women's Center

Franconia College
Franconia 03580
603-823-8460, 8045

Women's Center of the Upper
  Valley, 19 S. Main
Hanover 03755
603-643-5981

Keene State Women's Center
Keene State College
Keene 03430
603-352-1909

Laconia Women's Center
21 Shore Dr.
Laconia 03246

Manchester Women's Center
Unitarian Church
Myrtle & Union
Manchester 03106

(The) Women's Center
104 Middle
Manchester 03102
603-622-9721

Women's Center
North Hampton 03862

Portsmouth Women's Center
40 Merrimac
Portsmouth 03801
603-436-0162

Women's Center
Box 172, Warner 03278

New Jersey:
NOW: Essex County NOW
388 Belleville Ave.
Bloomfield 07003

YWCA Women's Center
Upsala College
East Orange 07019
201-266-7213

Together
7 State, Glassboro 08028

Women's Center of Bergen

Women's Liberation Groups

(cont.) County
166 Main
Hackensack 07601
201-342-8958

NOW: Middlesex County NOW
Box 94, Iselin 08830

Women's Center
Brookdale Community College
Newman Springs Rd.
Lincroft 07738

Center for Women's Studies
Fairleigh Dickinson Univ.
285 Madison Ave.
Madison 07940
201-377-4700 x369
   Dr. Mara Vamos, Dir.

Drew Women's Collective
Drew University
Madison 07940

Women's Center
Ramapo College, PO Box 542
Mahwah 07430

AWE Women's Center
PO Box 583
Maple Wood 07040
201-467-1422

Women's Center
15 W. Main
Moorestown 08057
609-235-9297

Women's Center
159 Glenridge Ave.
Montclair 07042

Center for the American Woman
  & Politics, Rutgers Univ.
Eagleton Institute of Politics
New Brunswick 08901
201-247-1766

Women's Center
Douglass College
New Brunswick 08903

Women's Center of New Brunswick

2 Easton
New Brunswick 08901
201-246-9637

NOW: Monmouth County NOW
11 Aberdeen Ter.
New Monmouth 07748
201-671-3123

YWCA Women's Center of the
  Oranges, 395 Main
Orange 07052
201-674-1111

NOW: Morristown Area NOW
3379 Rte. 46, Apt. 16-E
Parsippany 07054
201-334-6135

NOW: Central New Jersey
  Chapter, Box 2163
Princeton 08540
    Also Employment Task Force.

Princeton Seminary Women's
  Center
Princeton Theological Seminary
Princeton 08540

Woman's Place
14 1/2 Witherspoon
Princeton 08540
609-924-8989

NOW: Monmouth County NOW
PO Box 823
Red Bank 07701

NOW: Somerset County NOW
147 Stony Brook Rd.
Somerville 08876
201-722-3866

NOW: Summit Now
34 Canoe Brook Pky.
Summit 07901
201-277-0135

EVE, Kean College
Union 07083

Women's Center
Montclair State College
Upper Montclair 07405

NOW: Passaic County NOW
PO Box 0151, Valley Station
Wayne 07040
201-274-5042

Women's Center
Tombrock College
West Patterson 07424

NOW: N.J. Women's Rights
  Task Force on Education
Jean Ambrose, 549 Lenox Ave.
Westfield 07090

NOW: Northern N.J.
Box 435
Westwood 07675

New Mexico:
NOW: La Voz de la Mujer
111 Laguna Pl. N.W.
Albuquerque 87104
  Also: PO Box 26262, 87125.

Albuquerque Women's Center
Univ. of New Mexico
1824 Las Lomas
Albuquerque 87106
505-277-3716

Santa Fe WL
Santa Fe 87501
505-982-1225

Santa Fe Women's Caucus
Box 292
Santa Fe 87501

NOW: c/o Kay F. Reinharte
General Delivery
Taos 87571

New York (State):
Gay Community House
332 Hudson Ave.
Albany 12210
  "Lesbians for Liberation."

Astoria Women's Center
44-03 28 Ave.
Astoria 11102
212-932-5130

Queensborough Community College Women's Research & Resource Center
222-03 Garland Dr., Audrey Silva
Bayside 11364
212-423-0666

Islip Women's Center
46 Orchard Dr.
Brightwaters 11718
516-665-6378

Women's Center
Sarah Lawrence College
Bronxville 10708

NOW: c/o Park Slope United Methodist Church
6th Ave. & 8
Brooklyn 11215

Women's Center
915 Washington Ave.
Brooklyn 11225

NOW: 610 B. Allenhurst
Buffalo 14226

Women's Studies College, SUNY, Buffalo, 108 Winspear Rd.
Buffalo 14214
716-831-3405

Cedarhurst Women's Center
136B Cedarhurst Ave.
Cedarhurst 11516

NOW: South Shore NOW
67 Scotch Pine Dr.
Central Islip 11722
516-234-4747

Kirkland College Women's Center
Clinton 13323

Women's Information Center
PO Box 268
Dewitt 13224

South Fork Women's Coalition
c/o Judith Hope, George Rd.

Women's Liberation Groups

(cont.) East Hampton 11937
516-324-0856

Queens Women's Center
153-11 61 Rd.
Flushing 11367

Women's Task Force for Affir-
mative Action, SUNY College
Union Box 39, Barbara Britten
Geneseo 14454

NOW: Long Island NOW (Nassau)
116 Brookville Rd.
Glen Head 11545
516-MA6-0253
(Also Ruth Witkin, 5 Patricia,
Plainview 11803, WE5-2805.)

NOW: Long Island Chapter
PO Box 1158, Old Village Station
Great Neck 11023
516-627-0023

Westchester WL Coalition
Box 9
Hartsdale 10530
914-761-1606

Hofstra Women's Center
Hofstra University
Hempstead 11550
516-421-0982

Women's Center, Nassau County
14 W. Columbia
Hempstead 11550
516-292-8106

Hewlett Women's Center
1007 Broadway
Hewlett 11557

Nassau Community College Women's Faculty Assoc.
15 Alan Crest Dr.
Hicksville 11801
516-IV1-7457

Adelphi Women's Rights Committee
c/o Beverly Lawn, RD3
Huntington 11743
516-AR1-3857

Islip Women's Center
1 Grant Ave.
Islip 11751
516-581-2680

Ithaca Women's Center
140 W. State
Ithaca 14850
607-272-6922

Women's Center, Cornell Univ.
Willard Straight Hall
Ithaca 14850

Women's Studies Program
Cornell Univ., 431 White Hall
Ithaca 14850

Nassau Women's Center
104 Greenbelt Ln.
Levittown 11756

Suffolk Right to Choose
179 Church Dr.
Mastic Beach 11951

Suffolk Community College Women's Group II
190 Wavecrest Dr.
Mastic Beach 11951
516-281-8576

NOW: Long Island NOW's Wo-
men's Talent Bank
PO Box 176
Merrick 11566

NOW: New York
47 E. 19
New York 10003
(NOW Center.)

AIR Gallery
97 Wooster
New York 10012

Barnard Women's Center
Barnard College, 606 W. 120
New York 10027
212-280-2067

Career Information Center

Baruch College, CUNY
17 Lexington Ave.
New York 10010

New York Theological Seminary
  Women's Center, 235 E. 49
New York 10017

New York Women's Center
36 W. 22
New York 10010
212-691-1860, 2067

New York Women's Law Center
351 Broadway
New York 10013
212-431-4074

Resource Center on Women
YWCA, 600 Lexington Ave.
New York 10022
212-753-4700

Upper East Side Women's Center
359 E. 68
New York 10021

West Side Woman's Center
210 W. 82
New York 11024

Women's Center (WL Center)
NYC Firehouse, 243 W. 20
New York 10011
212-255-9802

Women's Center for Occupation
  & Educational Development
167 E. 67
New York 10021
212-861-0931

Women's Inter-Arts Center
549 W. 52
New York 10019
212-246-6570

Women Photographers, The Midtown Y Gallery, 344 E. 14
New York 10018

Uptown Women's Center
627 Amsterdam
New York 10024

New York Radical Women
799 Broadway, Room 412
New York 10003

Radical Feminism
Box AA, Old Chelsea Station
New York 10011

WITCH New York Covens
Box 694, Stuyvesant Station
New York 10009

Lesbian Feminist Liberation:
  212-691-5460
Lesbian Switchboard: 212-741-2610

NOW: Suffolk NOW
c/o Nikki Hightower
50 Norwood Rd.
Northport 11768
516-757-1336

Northport Women's Center
  (Suffolk County)
144 Bayview Ave.
Northport 11768
516-757-6564

Dowling College WL
Oakdale 11769
516-OA1-5795

Women's Information Center,
  Oyster Bay
Old Westbury 11771

Women's Awareness Center
Hartwick College
Oneonta 13820

Women's Center
286 Washington Blvd.
Oswego 13126

Rockland County WL. Women's
  Center
St. Stephen's Episcopal Church
Pierce Hwy. & Eberhardt Rd.
Pearl River 10965
914-354-7442

Women's Liberation Groups

Stony Brook Women's Center
23 Old Post Rd.
Port Jefferson 11777
516-HR3-9209

Mid-Hudson Women's Center
27 Franklin
Poughkeepsie 12601
914-473-1538

Poughkeepsie Women's Center
96 Market
Poughkeepsie 12601
914-454-9487

Rochester Women's Center
139 Raleigh
Rochester 14620

Suffolk Community College Women's Group
533 College Rd.
Selden 11784

Staten Island Women's Center
121 Van Duzen
Staten Island 10301

Women's Center, SUNY at Stony Brook
Stony Brook 11790

Rockland County Feminists
24 DeBaun Ave.
Suffern 10901

Women's Center for Continuing Ed., University College
610 E. Fayette
Syracuse 13202

Women's Information Center
104 Avondale Pl.
Syracuse 13210

Syracuse Women's Center
914 S. Crouse
Syracuse 13210
315-478-8558

Nassau Women's Center
25 Melvin Ave.
West Hempstead 11552
516-536-7897

NOW: Queens
162-11 9 Ave., Donna Loercher
Whitestone 11357

Women's Center, Seton College
1061 N. Broadway
Yonkers 10701

North Carolina:
Female Liberation
Box 954
Chapel Hill 27514

Women's Center
1616 Lyndhurst Rd.
Charlotte 28203
704-334-9655

Disadvantaged Women in Higher Ed., 1 Incinerator Rd.
Durham 23824

Durham Women's Assoc.
1001 Carolina
Durham 27705

Women's Center
Guilford College
Greensboro 27410

Women's Center, Chowan College
Murfreesboro 27855

North Dakota:
North Dakota WL
Minot Women's Collective
PO Box 235
Minot 58701

Ohio:
NOW: 5793 Juvene Wy.
Cincinnati 45238
513-831-2725

Continuing Education Group
Univ. of Cincinnati
Raymond Walters College
Cincinnati 45236

Xavier Women's Center

(cont.) Breen Lodge, Victory Pky.
Cincinnati 45209
513-745-3322

Univ. of Cincinnati Women's
 Center
412 Tuc Woman Affairs Council
Cincinnati 45521
513-475-8000

Women Helping Women & Rape
 Crisis Center
2699 Clifton Ave.
Cincinnati 45220
513-861-5933

Women's Center
6728 Alpine Ave.
Cincinnati 45236

NOW: Box 7147
Cleveland 44128

Case Western Reserve Univ.
 Thwing Study Center Women's
 Center
11111 Euclid Ave.
Cleveland 44106

NOW: PO Box 5053
Columbus 43212

Columbus WL
38 E. 12 Ave.
Columbus 43201

Columbus/OSU WL
315 Ohio Union
Columbus 43210
614-422-0833

Dayton Women's Center
1203 Salem Ave.
Dayton 45406

Office of Special Programs for
 Women, Wright State Univ.
Dayton 45431

Women's Center, Univ. of Dayton
Box 612
Dayton 45469

Dayton WL
1721 Burroughs Dr.
Dayton 45406

Cleveland Women's Center
PO Box 2526
East Cleveland 44112

Women's Center
Kent State Univ., Women's Proj.
Kent 44242

Women's Center
Oberlin College
Oberlin 44074
216-774-1221

NOW: Butler County
PO Box 15
Oxford 45056

AWS Women's Resource Center
Miami Univ., 225 Warfield Hall
Oxford 45056

Miami Univ. Women's Informa-
 tion Center, Miami Univ.
Box 123, Bishop Hall
Oxford 45056

WL--USN Center
410 E. High
Oxford 45406

Women's Center, Wittenberg
 Univ., 966 Pythian Ave.
Springfield 45504

Women's Programs
Univ. of Toledo
2801 W. Bancroft
Toledo 43606

Black Women United
Box 421
Wilberforce 45384

Antioch College Women's Center
Yellow Springs 45387
513-767-7331 x311
 (Also information for Dayton
 and Cincinnati.)

Women's Liberation Groups

Oklahoma:
Women's Resource Center
Univ. of Tulsa, 600 S. College
Tulsa 74104

Oregon:
Ofc. of Women's Studies
Oregon State Univ.
Corvallis 97331

NOW: Box 3171
Eugene 97403

University Feminists
Rm. 306, EMU, Univ. of Oregon
Eugene 97403

The George House, Western Baptist Seminary
5511 S.E. Hawthorne
Portland 97215

Women's Institute & Resource Center, Portland State Univ.
Portland 97207

Women's Union at Portland State Univ.
450 Smith Center
Portland 97207
503-229-4459

Woman's Place
706 S.E. Grand
Portland 97214
503-234-8703

Pennsylvania:
NOW: Philadelphia Chapter
PO Box 84
Bala Cynwood 19004

NOW: Pittsburgh Chapter
423 Fox Chapel Rd.
Bethel Park 15102

Career-Counseling Center for Adult Women
Villa Maria College
2551 W. Lake Rd.
Erie 16505

Women's Center
230 W. Chestnut
Lancaster 17603

Bucks County Community College Women's Caucus
Hicks Art Center
Newton 18940

NOW: Philadelphia
Box 15505
Philadelphia 19131

Continuing Education for Women
Temple Univ., Mitten Hall, Rm. 207
Philadelphia 19122

Women's Center
Temple Univ., Mitten Hall
13 & Montgomery Ave.
Philadelphia 19122
215-787-7990

Center for Women in Medicine
Medical College of Penn.
3300 Henry Ave.
Philadelphia 19129
215-849-0400

Philadelphia WL Center
PO Box 19826
Philadelphia 19143

Women's Center
Univ. of Penn., 3533 Locust Walk
Philadelphia 19104

Women's Center
4634 Chester Ave.
Philadelphia 19143
215-729-2001
    Speakers Collective: 215-BA2-2066

Women's Resource Center
YWCA, Kensington Branch
174 W. Allegheny Ave.
Philadelphia 19133
215-RE9-1430

Philadelphia WL Center
928 Chestnut
Philadelphia 19107

NOW: 700 Penn Center Blvd.
Pittsburgh 15235
   Also Greater Pittsburgh Area
   Chapter, 726 St. James,
   15232. Also Southwestern
   Pennsylvania Chapters, PO
   Box 86024, 15221. Addition-
   al Pittsburgh Chapter address:
   PO Box 5156, 15206; also
   South Hills, 403 Hi Tor Dr.,
   15236.

Women's Center Community Col-
   lege of Allegheny County
Allegheny Campus
Pittsburgh 15212

WL House, Penn State Univ.
245 E. Hamilton Ave.
State College 16801

Swarthmore Gay Liberation
Swarthmore College
Swarthmore 19081

Rhode Island:
Kingston WL
Univ. of Rhode Island
Kingston 02881

Resource Center for Women in
   Higher Education
Brown University
Providence 02912

WL Umbrella
59 Olive
Providence 02906

WL Union of Rhode Island
Box 2302, East Side Station
Providence 20906

YWCA Women's Center
Jackson
Providence 02903

South Carolina:
NOW: PO Box 3005
Columbia 29230

Women's Center
1106 Hagwood Ave.
Columbia 29205

Women's Center
Winthrop College, Winthrop
   Coalition Group, PO Box 6763
Rock Hill 29730

Tennessee:
NOW: 370 Wallace Rd., E4
Nashville 37211

Nashville Tennessee Women's
   Center
1112 19 Ave. S.
Nashville 37212
615-327-1969

Women's Center
1929 21 Ave. S
Nashville 37212
615-269-5118

Women's House
Univ. of the South
Sewanee 37375

Texas:
WL
1106 W. 22
Austin 78705

Austin Women's Center
1208 Baylor, West Austin Station
Austin 78103
512-474-1798

WL
Box 7491, University Station
Austin 78712
   Also Box 8011

NOW: 1604 Kindred
Dallas 75221
214-245-6201, 690-8418

Women's Center
3118 Fondrell Dr.
Dallas 75205

Women's Center
Southern Methodist Univ.
Dallas 75275

Women's Liberation Groups

Women-for-Change Center
20001 Bryan Tower, Suite 290
Dallas 75201
214-741-2391

Women's Center
North Texas State University
Denton 76203

NOW: Ft. Worth NOW Education Task Force
3800 Trail Wind Ln.
Ft. Worth 76109

NOW: Box 384
Houston 77401

Women's Resource Center
1521 Texas Ave., YWCA
Houston 77002

Women's Center
3602 Milam
Houston 77002

Utah:
Women's Environ Institute
Weber State College
Harrison Blvd.
Ogden 84403
801-399-5941

Women's Center
Brigham Young Univ.
Provo 84601

Women's Resource Center
Univ. of Utah, 293 Union Bldg.
Salt Lake City 84112
801-581-8030

Vermont:
Women's Center
217 N. Winooski
Burlington 05404
802-863-9133

Women's Union
Middlebury College
Middlebury 95753

Goddard Women's Center
Goddard College
Plainfield 05667
802-454-8311
   Also Feminist Studies.

Women's Center
Windham College
Putney 05346

Virginia:
NOW: Northern Virginia NOW
1923 Shiver Dr.
Alexandria 22307
   Also 2310 Barbour Rd.,
   Falls Church 22043.

Women's Center
Box 7025
Richmond 23220
804-649-2211

Washington [state]:
Women's Center, Women's
   Commission & Occupational
   Resource Center
Western Washington State College
Bellingham 98225

Elizabeth Blackwell Brigade
1409 E. Maplewood
Bellingham 98225
206-733-6344
   (Also Women's Clinic.)

NOW: 4039 9 Ave. N.E.
Seattle 98105
206-632-0559
   Also 5508 S. Orcas, 98118.

Lesbian Resource Center
4224 University Wy., N.E.
Seattle 98105
206-632-4747 x3

Seattle Counseling Center for
   Sexual Minorities
1720 16 Ave.
Seattle 98134
206-329-8737, 8707

Women's Center
Univ. of Washington
Seattle 98195

Women's Guidance Center
1209 N.E. 41
Seattle 98195

Radical Women
3815 5 Ave. N.E.
Seattle 98105
206-632-5160

Feminist Coordinating Council
2207 E. McGraw
Seattle 98112

Tacoma Women's Center
1108 N. Fife
Tacoma 98406

Women's Center
Univ. of Puget Sound
Tacoma 98416

Women's Center
Tacoma Community College
Tacoma 98465

Women's Center, Office of Women's Programs
Spokane Falls Community College
W. 3410 Ft. George Wright Dr.
Spokane 99204

Women's Center, Whitman College
Walla Walla 99362

West Virginia:
Women's Center
Beckley College, S. Kanawha
Beckley 25801

Women's Center
Appalachian Bible Inst.
Bradley 25818

Women's Information Center
West Virginia University
221 Wiley
Morgantown 26506

Wisconsin:
Women's Action Group
Northland College
Ashland 54806

Women's Center
University of Wisconsin
Green Bay 54302

Center for Women's & Family Living Education
430 Lowell Hall, 610 Langdon
Madison 53706

Scarlett Letter Collective
Univ. of Wisconsin YWCA
306 N. Brooks
Madison 53715

Women's Center
836 E. Johnson
Madison 53703
608-255-7447

Research Center on Women
Alverno College, 3401 S. 39
Milwaukee 53215

Women's Center
2110 W. Wells
Milwaukee 53208

Women's Coalition
2211 E. Kenwood Blvd.
Milwaukee 53211
414-964-7535

Women's Information Center
Univ. of Wisconsin, Box 189
Milwaukee 53201

Oshkosh Women's Center
Wisconsin State Univ.
Oshkosh 54900

Women's Center
Univ. of Wisconsin
312 Dempsey Hall
Oshkosh 54901

(DIRECTORY OF SOURCES, cont.)

ROSTERS FOR EMPLOYMENT

The employer who defends a recruitment-promotion process resulting in employment of male after male should be challenged to document open advertising, which includes listing all jobs for the benefit of special sources of qualified women. In order to communicate news of specialized employment opportunities to qualified women, a non-discriminatory affirmative action employer will list all positions, with salary range, application-deadlines, and minimum qualifications declared with all of the women's task force-type groups (caucuses, commissions, etc.) in that field. These groups usually endeavor to maintain placement-related rosters, directories, talent banks, bulletins, placement lists, registries, etc. Because the groups are, of necessity, often staffed by volunteers, their womanpower, addresses, even existence, fluctuate. An employer committed to non-discriminatory affirmative action needs an up-to-date list of such resources in each field and specialization in which s/he has or anticipates staff.

Since female-sex discrimination cases, seemingly, are not being investigated equitably by HEW, EEOC, Wage & Hour, etc., women must form action, rather than service, groups. Equal employment opportunity is at best a passive condition. The "affirmative action" envisioned by the Office for Civil Rights as a better alternative does not require employment of unqualified personnel nor quotas; it does usually involve goals and time-tables. An organization claiming to be (only) an equal opportunity employer or claiming to have an affirmative action plan without goals and time-tables (and in academia, Women's Studies) is suspect.

While women with all the accoutrements of full professorship and top administration as defined on some campuses and by some organizations may not be as numerous as men, it is no longer possible to claim they do not exist, although affirmative action may well be required to reach, attract and retain them. Experience has shown that rosters of names, placed in the hands of personnel workers, are sometimes misused for statistical reportage to document non-existent non-discriminatory affirmative action. Thus, one task-force roster was recently converted to a bulletin periodically distributed to these women, with the choice thus removed from the

Womanhood Media Supplement

employers. Some specialized associations and accreditation bodies have made efforts on behalf of other minorities (considering women as an employment minority), but have done nothing for women yet. In fields where the task force with placement roster structure does not yet exist, contact might be made with women of the task forces, caucuses, and commissions.

* * * * *

"Rosters" are given under broad job titles, arranged alphabetically. The first entry under a job title relates to a feminist group, often having a roster. In addition, professional associations and accrediting agencies are listed indented at the conclusion of each section. The job-titles are:

Adult Education see EDUCATORS
ARCHAEOLOGISTS
ARCHITECTS (see also PLANNERS)
AREA STUDIES PERSONNEL (see also HISTORIANS)
ARTISTS, ART EDUCATORS
ASTRONOMERS
Attorneys see LAWYERS...
BIOLOGISTS (see also SCIENTISTS)
BOTANISTS (see also SCIENTISTS)
CHEMISTS (see also SCIENTISTS)
CLASSICISTS
COMMUNICATIONS PERSONNEL (incl. media, libraries, archives, bibliography)
DENTISTS & DENTAL PERSONNEL
Doctors see PHYSICIANS
ECONOMISTS
EDUCATORS & EDUCATIONAL ADMINISTRATORS
ENGINEERS
English Teachers see EDUCATORS...; LINGUISTS
FORESTERS
GEOGRAPHERS & GEOLOGISTS
Guidance Personnel see PERSONNEL...
HISTORIANS (see also AREAS STUDIES...; CLASSICISTS)
HOME ECONOMISTS

HOSPITAL ADMINISTRATION, MEDICAL RECORDS PERSONNEL
JOURNALISTS
LANDSCAPE ARCHITECTS (see also PLANNERS)
Languages see LINGUISTS
LAWYERS & LEGAL PERSONNEL
Librarians see COMMUNICATIONS PERSONNEL
LINGUISTS
MANAGERS (see also EDUCATORS...); HOSPITAL ADMIN...
MATHEMATICIANS
MUSICIANS & MUSICOLOGISTS
NURSES & NURSING PERSONNEL
OCCUPATIONAL & PHYSICAL THERAPISTS
OSTEOPATHS
PERSONNEL WORKERS (incl. guidance)
PHARMACISTS
PHILOLOGISTS (see also LINGUISTS)
PHILOSOPHERS (see also EDUCATORS...)
Physical Therapists see OCCUPATIONAL...
PHYSICIANS (see also SCIENTISTS)
PHYSICISTS (see also SCIENTISTS)
Physiologists see PHYSICIANS
PLANNERS

Rosters for Employment 441

POLITICAL SCIENTISTS
Psychiatrists see PHYSI-
 CIANS
PSYCHOLOGISTS
Public Administrators see
 MANAGERS; EDUCATORS...
RELIGION, RELIGIOUS
 STUDIES, & THEOLOGIANS
SCIENTISTS
SOCIAL WORKERS
SOCIOLOGISTS
SPEECH & HEARING PERSON-
 NEL
STATISTICIANS
VETERINARIANS
WOMEN'S STUDIES STAFF

The Project on the Status and Education of Women of the Association of American Colleges publishes Recruiting Aids: "Rosters, registries and directories of women in the professions" periodically.

There are also placement lists and services encompassing groups of women in terms of race, location, and other characteristics. See for example the following, listed in the "Directory of Sources":

Advocates for Women
Alpha Kappa Alpha
American Association of University Women Talent Bank
Black Women Employment Program
CA Univ., B.W.C. Talent Bank
Catalyst
Delta Sigma Theta
Distaffers, Inc.
Federation of Organizations for Professional Women
Higher Education Resource Service
Minority Women Employment Program
National Association of College Women
National Federation of Business & Professional Women's Clubs, Inc. Talent Bank
New Jersey Talent Bank
 for Women
New York State Talent Bank
Professional Skills Roster
Professional Women's Caucus newsletter
Resource Center for Women in Higher Education
Roster of Women Scholars (Barnard College's proposal to American Council on Education)
Talent Bank...
Today's Woman Placement Service
Washington Opportunities for Women
White House Talent Bank
Woman's Place Agency
Women's Work
Zeta Phi Beta

ADULT EDUCATION see EDUCATORS

ANTHROPOLOGISTS
Roster of Women Anthropologists. Ernestine Friedl, Dept. of Anthropology, Queens College, Flushing, NY 11367. 212-445-7500.

Committee on Status of Women in Anthropology. (American Anthropological Assoc.) Prof. Shirley Gorenstein, Dept. of Anthropology, Columbia Univ., New York, NY 10027. 212-621-2541. Profs. Carol Vance and Lucie Wood, Dept. of Anthropology, Lehman College, Bronx, NY 10467. 212-960-8881.

American Anthropological Assoc., 1703 N.H. Ave. N.W., Washington, DC 20009. Edward J. Lehman, Exec. Director, 202-232-8800.

ARCHAEOLOGISTS
Archaeological Institute of America, 260 W. Broadway, New York, NY 10013. Mary K. Brown, Exec. Director, 212-925-7333.

ARCHITECTS (see also PLANNERS)
Alliance of Women in Architecture, 41 E. 65, New York, NY 10021.

Women Architects, Landscape Architects, & Planners, 39 Marin, Cambridge, MA 02138.

Assoc. of Women in Architecture. Betty Lou Custer. PO Box 1, Clayton, MO 63105. Dorothy Gray Harrison, 2115 Pine Crest Dr., Altadena, CA 91001.

Assoc. of Collegiate Schools of Architecture, 1785 Mass. Ave., Washington, DC 20036 (women architects).

Society of Architectural Historians, 1700 Walnut, Rm. 716, Philadelphia, PA 19103. Rosann S. Berry, Exec. Secretary. 215-735-0224.

National Architectural Board, 1735 N.Y. Ave. N.W., Washington, DC 20036. 202-833-1180 (accrediting agency).

AREA STUDIES PERSONNEL (see also HISTORIANS)
ASA Committee on Women. (American Studies Assoc.) Joanna Schneider Zangrando, 501 Mineola Ave., Akron, OH 44320. Lois P. Rudnick, Roster editor, 1 Logan Hall, Univ. of Penn., Philadelphia, PA 19174.

Committee on the Status of Women. (Assoc. of Asian Studies). Prof. Joyce K. Kallgren, Center for Chinese Studies, 2168 Shattuck Ave., Berkeley, CA 94705.

Women's Coalition of Latin Americanists (Latin American Studies Assoc.) Dr. Elsa M. Chaney, Dept. of Political Science, Fordham Univ., Bronx, NY 10458. 212-956-7100. Dr. Asunción Lavrin, 8501 Manchester Rd., Silver Spring, MD 20901.

Women's Committee (Latin American Studies Assoc.). Dr. Nancie L. Gonzalez, Dept. of Anthropology, Boston Univ., 232 Bay State Rd., Boston, MA 02215.

American Oriental Society, 329 Sterling Memorial Library, Yale Station, New Haven, CT 06520. Hugh M. Stimson, Secretary-Treasurer. 203-436-1040.

American Assoc. for the Advancement of Slavic Studies, 190 W. 19 Ave., Rm. 254, Columbus, OH 43210. George Kalbouss, Exec. Secretary. 614-422-1105.

Hispanic Society of America. B'way & 156, New York, NY 10032. Theodore S. Beardsley, Jr., Director. 212-926-2234.

Assoc. for Asian Studies, 1 Lane Hall, Univ. of Michigan, Ann Arbor, MI 48104. Richard L. Park, Secretary-Treasurer. 313-665-2490. Has Roster for distribution (715 women).

American Studies Assoc., Box 1, Logan Hall, CN. Univ. of Pennsylvania, Philadelphia, PA 19104. Allen F. Davis, Exec. Secretary. 215-594-6252.

Assoc. for the Study of Afro-American Life & History, 1401 14 St., N.W., Washington, DC 20005. J. Rupert Picott, Exec. Director. 202-667-2822.

African Studies Assoc., 218 Shiffman Center, Brandeis Univ., Waltham, MA 02154. James E. Duffy, Exec. Secretary. 617-899-3079.

ARTISTS, ART EDUCATORS
Commission on the Status of Women in Art & Women's Caucus. (College Art Assoc.) Prof. Ann Harris, 560 Riverside Dr., #17P, New York, NY 10027. 212-360-5566. Dr. Norma Broude, Placement Coordinator, 1175 York Ave., New York, NY 10021. #12M.

College Art Assoc. of America, 16 E. 52, New York, NY 10022. Rose R. Weil, Exec. Secretary. 212-755-3532.

American Society for Aesthetics. c/o Cleveland Museum of Art, 11150 East Blvd., Cleveland, OH 44106. James R. Johnson, Secretary-Treasurer. 216-421-7340.

National Assoc. of Schools of Art. William Lewis, Director. Commission on Accrediting. College of Architecture and Design, Univ. of Michigan, Ann Arbor, MI 48104. 313-764-1302.

ASTRONOMERS (see also SCIENTISTS)
Working Group on the Status of Women in Astronomy. (American Astronomical Society.) Dr. Anne P. Cowley, Research Associate, Astronomy Dept., Univ. of Michigan, Ann Arbor, MI 48103. Dr. B. T. Lynds, Roster information, Kitt Peak Observatory, 950 N. Cherry Ave., Tucson, AZ 85717.

ATTORNEYS see LAWYERS & LEGAL PERSONNEL

BIOLOGISTS (see also SCIENTISTS)
Women in Cell Biology (Society for Cell Biology). Virginia Walbot, Dept. of Bio-chemistry, Univ. of Georgia, Athens, GA 30601.

Professional Opportunities for Women of the Biophysical Society: Caucus of Women Biophysicists. Dr. Daphne Hare, School of Medicine, SUNY, Buffalo, NY 14215.

Biophysical Society Placement Service. Julia T. Apter, Director. Rush Medical College, 1753 W. Congress Pkwy., Chicago, IL 60612.

Committee on the Status of Women Microbiologists. (American Society for Microbiology). Dr. Mary Louise Robbins, School of Medicine & Health Sciences, G. Washington Univ., 2300 Eye St. N.W., Washington, DC 20037.

> American Institute of Biological Sciences, 1401 Wilson Blvd., Arlington, VA 22209. Richard Trumbull, Exec. Director. 703-527-6776.

BOTANISTS (see also SCIENTISTS)
> Botanical Society of America. N.Y. Botanical Gardens, Bronx, NY 10458. Patricia Holmgren, Exec. Secretary. 212-933-9400, ext. 360.

CHEMISTS (see also SCIENTISTS)
Women Chemists Committee. (American Chemical Society). Dr. Susan Collier, Research Laboratories, Eastman Kodak Co., Rochester, NY 14650. Helen M. Free, Ames Co. Miles Laboratories, Inc., Elkhart, IN 46514. (In the past, the Committee has had a "Talent Bank.")

Subcommittee on the Status of Women. (American Society of Biological Chemists). Dr. Loretta Leive, Bldg. 4, Room 113, National Institutes of Health, Bethesda, MD 20014.

> American Chemical Society, 1155 16 St. N.W., Washington, DC 20036. Robert W. Cairns, Exec. Director. 202-872-4600.

> American Chemical Society Committee on Professional Training, John H. Howard, Secretary, 343 State, Rochester, NY 14650. 716-325-2000, ext. 56289 (accrediting agency).

CLASSICISTS
> American Classical League. Miami University, Oxford, OH 45056. Joan Myers, Administrative Secretary. 513-529-4116.

COMMUNICATIONS PERSONNEL (incl. Media, Libraries, Archives, Bibliography)
Women in Communications, L. G. Taylor-Pierlot, 8305-A Shoal

Rosters for Employment

Creek Blvd., Austin, TX 78758. Margot Sherman, 1 Stoneleigh Plaza, Bronxville, NY 10708.

National Assoc. of Media Women, Inc., 157 W. 126, New York, NY 10027. 212-850-1886.

Broadcast Education Assoc. does not have a women's caucus, but has lent support to compilation by K. Sue Foley and Leeda Marting of "Directory of Women in Media Education." SEE "Pamphlets" part of Non-Book Resources, which also includes "Directory of Women in Media." Contact Dr. Mary Jean Thomas, Loyola University of Chicago, 820 N. Michigan Ave., Chicago, IL 60611. 312-670-3000.

Bulletin Board of the Task Force on Women's job roster (Social Responsibilities Round Table--SRRT--of the American Library Assoc.), Liz Dickinson, Barbara Carlson, co-eds. $5 donation/6 months/12 issues. Contact Ms. Dickinson, Technical Services Division, Hennepin County Library, 7001 York Ave. S., Edina, MN 55435. 612-830-4980. News of administrative and specialist positions which are listed with the editors by affirmative action employers; does not provide resumes to employers, preferring to place women in the position of choice (power). Formerly Job Roster of Task Force on Status of Women in Librarianship.

Black Librarians. Dorothy M. Haith, Dept. of Library Science, Virginia State College, Petersburg, VA 23803.

Sherrill Cheda, Seneca College Library, 1750 Finch Ave. E., Willowdale 428, Ontario. 791-5050.

Ad Hoc Committee on the Status of Women in the Archival Profession. (Society of American Archivists). Dr. Mabel Deutrich, Director, Military Archives Div., National Archives & Records Service, Washington, DC 20408.

Phoenix NOW Media Job Bank. 1020 E. Orange, 4E, Tempe, AZ 85281.

> Bibliographical Society of America, 185 Salisbury, Worchester, MA 01690. Marcus A. McCorison, Director. 617-755-5221.

> American Library Assoc. Committee on Accreditation, 50 E. Huron, Chicago, IL 60611. Agnes L. Reagan, Secretary. 312-944-6780.

> See also #252, Basic Book Collection.

DENTISTS & DENTAL PERSONNEL
Assoc. of American Women Dentists. Dr. Fae T. Ashlstrom, 2950 S. Maryland Pkwy., Las Vegas, NV 89109.

Association of American Women Dentists, another address: 33 Ponce de Leon Ave. N.E., Suite 204, Atlanta, GA 30308.

> American Dental Assoc. Council on Dental Education. Thomas J. Ginley, Secretary, 211 E. Chicago Ave., Chicago, IL 60611. 312-944-6730 (accrediting body; also accredits dental assisting, hygiene, & technology).

ECONOMISTS
Committee on the Status of Women in the Economics Profession (American Economic Association). Dr. Carolyn Shaw Bell, Wellesley College, Wellesley, MA 02181.

> American Economic Assoc., Suite 809, Oxford House, 1313 21 Ave. S., Nashville, TN 37212. Rendig Feis, Secretary-Treasurer. 615-322-2595.

> Economic History Assoc., 22 S. 18, Allentown, PA 18104. Herman E. Krooss, Secretary-Treasurer. 215-434-4742.

EDUCATORS & EDUCATIONAL ADMINISTRATORS
Women's Caucus (National Education Assoc.) Helen Bain, NEA, 1201 16 St., N.W., Washington, DC 20036. 202-833-4000.

American Council on Education has been in the process of setting up a Women's Roster for some time. 1 Dupont Circle N.W., Washington, DC 20036.

Women's Caucus (and) Committee on the Status of Women. (Philosophy of Education Society.) Dr. Elizabeth Steiner Maccia, Dept. of History & Philosophy of Education, Indiana Univ., Bloomington, IN 47401.

Commission on the Status of Women in Adult Education. Yvonne Rappaport, Consortium Bldg., G. Mason Univ., Fairfax, VA 22030. Also: Dr. Beverly Cassara, 10421 Courthouse Dr., Fairfax, VA 22030.

Committee on Women. (American Assoc. for Health & Physical Education). Prof. Ione G. Shadduck, Drake Univ., Des Moines, IA 50311.

Committee on the Status of Women in the Profession (American Assoc. of University Professors). Formerly Committee W. Dr. Mary Gray, Dept. of Mathematics, American Univ., Washington, DC 20016.

Women's Caucus (American Educational Research Assoc.) Noele Krenkel, Researcher, San Francisco Unified School District, 135 VanNess, San Francisco, CA 94102.

Women's Rights Committee (American Federation of Teachers). Marjorie Stern, 1012 14, Washington, DC 20004.

Rosters for Employment

National Assoc. for Women Deans, Administrators & Counselors. Joan McCall, Exec. Director, 1028 Conn. Ave. N.W., Washington, DC 20036.

National Council of Administrative Women in Education. Fern Ritter, 1815 Ft. Myer Dr., N. Arlington, VA 22209.

Women's Committee (National Council of Teachers of English). Dr. Janet Emig, Dept. of English, Rutgers Univ., New Brunswick, NJ 08903.

Division of Women's Education Ad Hoc Committee on Concerns of Women. (National University Extension Assoc.) Betty Siegal, Dean of Continuing Education, Univ. of Florida, Gainesville, FL 32601.

> National Institute of Education, Department of Health, Education, & Welfare, Washington, DC 20202.
>
> American Assoc. for Higher Education, 1 Dupont Circle N.W., Suite 780, Washington, DC 20036. 202-293-6440. Ann London Scott, Assoc. Exec. Director.
>
> American Assoc. of University Professors, AAUP Contact: Margaret Rumbarger, Associate Secretary, 1 Dupont Circle N.W., Washington, DC 20036. 202-466-8050. Western Regional Office: Suite 1406, 582 Market, San Francisco, CA 94104. 415-989-5430. Northeastern Regional Office: Suite 2107, 155 E. 44, New York, NY 10017. 212-986-9096.
>
> Philosophy of Education Society, Dept. of Education, G. Peabody College for Teachers, Box 49, Nashville, TN 37203. Jack Willers, Secretary-Treasurer. 615-327-8171.
>
> Accrediting Commission of the National Home Study Council, William A. Fowler, Exec. Secretary, 1601 18 St. N.W., Washington, DC 20009. 202-234-5100.
>
> National Council for Accreditation of Teacher Education, 1750 Pennsylvania Ave. N.W., Washington, DC 20006. Rolf W. Larson, Director. 202-298-7118.

ENGINEERS

Society of Women Engineers. Winifred D. White, Exec. Secretary, 345 E. 47, New York, NY 10017. 212-752-6800, ext. 551. Career Information Clearinghouse helps link members seeking jobs and employers looking for women engineers.

Vivian G. Cardwell, College of Engineering, Univ. of Illinois at Chicago Circle, Box 4348, Chicago, IL 60680. 312-996-3000, 3463.

Task Force on Women in Engineering. (American Society for Engineering Education). 1 Dupont Circle, Suite 400 N.W., Washington, DC 20036.

Institute of Electrical & Electronics Engineers, Inc. SEE Biophysical Society Placement Service in BIOLOGISTS section.

> American Institute of Chemical Engineers, 345 E. 47, New York, NY 10017. F. J. VanAntwerpen, Exec. Secretary. 212-752-6800.

> Engineers' Council for Professional Development. (Engineering & engineering technology accrediting agency). David Reyes-Guerra, Exec. Director, 345 E. 47, New York, NY 10017. 212-752-6800.

ENGLISH TEACHERS see EDUCATORS; LINGUISTS

FORESTERS
> Society of American Foresters. Donald R. Theoe, Director of Professional Programs, 1010 16 St. N.W., Washington, DC 20036. 202-296-7820 (accrediting agency).

GEOGRAPHERS & GEOLOGISTS
Society of Women Geographers, 1619 N.H. Ave., Washington, DC 20009. Benita S. Harris.

Committee on Women in Geography. (Assoc. of American Geographers). Dr. Ann Larrimore, Dept. of Geography, Univ. of Michigan, Ann Arbor, MI 48104.

> American Geographical Society, Broadway at 156 St., New York, NY 10032. Robert B. McNee, Director. 212-234-8100.

> Assoc. of American Geographers, 1710 16 St. N.W., Washington, DC 20009. J. Warren Nystrom, Exec. Director. 202-234-1450.

> Geological Society of America, 3300 Penrose Pl., Boulder, CO 80301. John C. Frye, Exec. Secretary. 303-447-2020.

GUIDANCE PERSONNEL see PERSONNEL...

HISTORIANS (see also AREAS STUDIES PERSONNEL; CLASSICISTS)
Committee on Women Historians. (American Historical Assoc.) Dr. Jane deHart Matthews, Univ. of North Carolina, Greensboro, NC 27412. Prof. Patricia A. Graham, Barnard College, New York, NY 10027. 212-280-2031, 2067.

Coordinating Committee on Women in the Historical Profession (American Historical Assoc.) Dr. Sandi Cooper, Richmond College, Staten Island, NY 10301. Dean Adele Simmons, Univ. of Maine, Portland-Gorham, Portland, ME 04103. Berenice A. Carroll, Dept. of Political Science, Univ. of Illinois, Urbana, IL 61801.

Rosters for Employment 449

    American Historical Assoc., 400 A St. S.E., Washington, DC 20003. Mack Thompson, Exec. Director. 202-544-2422. Dr. Eleanor Straub, Staff Liaison.

    Organization of American Historians, 112 N. Bryan, Bloomington, IN 47401. Richard S. Kirkendall, Exec. Secretary.

HOME ECONOMISTS
    American Home Economics Assoc., Doris E. Hanson, Exec. Director, 2010 Mass. Ave. N.W., Washington, DC 20036. 202-833-3100. (Accrediting agency.)

HOSPITAL ADMINISTRATION, MEDICAL RECORDS PERSONNEL
    Accrediting Commission on Graduate Education for Hospital Administration, Gary L. Filerman, Exec. Director, 1 Dupont Circle N.W., Washington, DC 20036. 202-659-4354.

    American Medical Assoc. Council on Medical Education, C. H. William Ruhe, Secretary, 535 N. Dearborn, Chicago, IL 60610. 312-751-6000. (Accrediting agency in collaboration with the American Medical Record Assoc.)

JOURNALISTS
Ad Hoc Committee on the Status of Women in Journalism Education. (Assoc. for Education in Journalism). Ramona R. Rush, College of Journalism & Communications, Univ. of Florida, Gainesville, FL 32601.

National Federation of Press Women, RR #1, Peneg Park, St. Clair, MO 63077.

Fran Harris (member of Theta Sigma Phi, national society for journalism/communication). WWJ Stations, Detroit, MI 48231.

    American Council on Education for Journalism. Baskett Mosse, Exec. Secretary, Accrediting Committee, Fisk Hall, Room 215, Northwestern Univ., Evanston, IL 60201. 312-492-5662.

LANDSCAPE ARCHITECTS (see also PLANNERS)
    American Society of Landscape Architects. Gary O. Robinette, Associate Exec. Director for Research & Education, 1750 Old Meadow Rd., McLean, VA 22101. 703-893-5171 (accrediting agency).

LANGUAGES see LINGUISTS

LAWYERS & LEGAL PERSONNEL
Dr. Lee Ellen Ford, 336 Hickory, Butler, IN 46721. SEE ALSO "Directory of Women Attorneys in USA, latest revision," #461 in Basic Book Collection.

Committee on Women in Legal Education. (Assoc. of American Law Schools). Prof. Ruth B. Ginsburg, Columbia Univ. Law School, 435 W. 116, New York, NY 10027. 212-280-2640. Prof. Shirley R. Bysiewicz, Univ. of Conn., School of Law, 1800 Asylum Ave., W. Hartford, CT 06117.

Women in the Legal Profession. (Assoc. of American Law Schools). Prof. Ginsburg.

National Lawyers Guild, PO Box 673, Berkeley, CA 94701; 23 Cornelia, New York, NY 10014. 212-255-8028, 989-3222, New York City Chapter. Has List of Women.

NEW Women Lawyers. Carol Bellamy, 36 W. 44, New York, NY 10036. 212-869-0020.

> American Society of International Law, 2223 Mass. Ave. N.W., Washington, DC 20008. John L. Hargrove, Acting Exec. Director. 202-265-4313.
>
> American Society for Legal History. School of Law. Univ. of Pittsburgh, Pittsburgh, PA 15260. William F. Schulz, Jr., Secretary. 412-624-6212.
>
> American Bar Assoc., James P. White, Consultant on Legal Education, Indianapolis Law School, Indiana University-Purdue Univ. at Indianapolis, 735 N.Y. St., Indianapolis, IN 46202. 317-264-4908 (accrediting body).
>
> Assoc. of American Law Schools, Millard H. Ruud, Exec. Director. 1 Dupont Circle N.W., Washington, DC 20036. 202-296-8851 (accrediting body).

See also #461 Basic Book Collection.

LIBRARIANS see COMMUNICATIONS PERSONNEL

LINGUISTS
MLA Commission on the Status of Women in the Profession (Modern Language Assoc.) Dr. Elaine Reuben, 364 Bascom Hall, Univ. of Wisconsin, Madison, WI 53706. Dr. Nancy Hottman, 4 Rollins Pl., Boston, MA 02114. Carol B. Ohmann, Assoc. Prof. of English, Wesleyan Univ., Middletown, CT 06457. 203-347-9411.

Women's Caucus of the MLA (Modern Language Assoc.) Dr. Ruth Altman, 444 E. 84, New York, NY 10028. Dr. Verna Wittrock, Dept. of English, Eastern Illinois Univ., Charleston, IL 61920.

SEE ALSO The MLA's "Directory of women scholars in the modern languages" in Pamphlets: Directories.

Women's Caucus (Linguistic Society of America). Lynette Hirschman, Georgette Ioup, 162 W. Hansberry, Philadelphia, PA 19144.

Rosters for Employment

    Modern Language Assoc. of America, 62 5 Ave., New York, NY 10011. William David Schaefer, Exec. Secretary, 212-741-5588.

    Linguistic Society of America, 1611 N. Kent, Arlington, VA 22209. John Hammer, Assoc. Secretary, 703-528-2314.

    American Dialect Society, 1611 N. Kent, Arlington, VA 22209. A. Hood Roberts, Exec. Secretary. 703-528-4312.

MANAGERS (see also EDUCATORS...; HOSPITAL ADMINISTRATION...)
Women's Talent Bank, PO Box 176, Merrick, NY 11466. All levels of management positions, training, data processing openings. Metropolitan, New York, Long Island.

Committee on the Status of Women in the Management Profession. (Academy of Management). Dr. Kathryn M. Bartol, Dept. of Management, School of Business Administration, Univ. of Massachusetts, Amherst, MA 01002.

Women's Caucus (American Society for Training & Development). Dr. Shirley McCune, Center for Human Relations, National Education Assoc., 1201 16 St., N.W., Washington, DC 20036. Althea Simmons, Director of Training, NAACP, 200 E. 27, New York, NY 10016.

Standing Committee on Women in Public Administration. (American Society for Public Administration). June Martin, Legislative Standing Committee, New York State Legislature, 830 Legislative Bldg., Albany, NY 12224.

Task Force on Women in Public Administration. (American Society for Public Administration.) Joan Fiss Bishop, Director of Career Services, Wellesley College, Wellesley, MA 02181.

Women Academic Administrators in Higher Education. (Institute for College & University Administrators, American Council on Education), 1 Dupont Circle, Washington, DC 20036.

Academic Administrators' Talent Bank. University of California, Berkeley, Women's Center, Bldg. 100 T-9, Berkeley, CA 94720.

MATHEMATICIANS
Assoc. for Women in Mathematics. Prof. Mary Gray, Dept. of Mathematics Chairperson, American University, Washington, DC 20016.

    American Mathematical Society, PO Box 6248, Providence, RI 02940. Gordon L. Walker, Exec. Director. 401-272-9500.

    Mathematical Assoc. of America, 1225 Conn. Ave. N.W., Washington, DC 20036. Alfred B. Willcox, Exec. Director. 202-223-1977.

MUSICIANS & MUSICOLOGISTS
College Music Society Women's Caucus. Dr. Carolyn Raney, Peabody Conservatory of Music, Baltimore, MD 21202. Dr. Adrienne F. Block, Dept. of Performing & Creative Arts, Staten Island Community College, Staten Island, NY 10301.

>American Musicological Society, 201 S. 34, Philadelphia, PA 19104. Alvin H. Johnson, Treasurer. 319-353-3797.

>Society for Ethnomusicology, 4521 Humanities Bldg., 455 N. Park, School of Music, Univ. of Wisconsin, Madison, WI 53706. Lois A. Anderson, Secretary. 608-263-1936.

>National Assoc. of Schools of Music. Robert Glidden, Exec. Secretary, 1 Dupont Circle, N.W., Washington, DC 20036. 202-296-4925 (accrediting body).

NURSES & NURSING PERSONNEL
>National League for Nursing, Dorothy Ozimek, Dept. of Baccalaureate & Higher Degree Programs, 10 Columbus Circle, New York, NY 10019. 212-582-1022 (accrediting agency).

>National League for Nursing, Gerald J. Griffin, Director, Dept. of Associate Degree Programs, 10 Columbus Circle, New York, NY 10019. 212-582-1022 (accrediting agency).

OCCUPATIONAL & PHYSICAL THERAPISTS
>American Medical Assoc. in collaboration with the American Occupational Therapy Assoc., C. H. William Ruhe, Secretary. Council on Medical Education, 535 N. Dearborn, Chicago, IL 60610. 312-751-6000 (accrediting agency).

>... in collaboration with the American Physical Therapy Assoc. ... (accrediting agency).

OSTEOPATHS
>American Osteopathic Assoc., Albert E. O'Donnell, Secretary. Bureau of Professional Education, 212 E. Ohio, Chicago, IL 60611. 312-944-2713 (accrediting agency).

PERSONNEL WORKERS (incl. Guidance)
Commission on the Occupational Status of Women (National Vocational Guidance Assoc.), Thelma C. Lennon, Director, Pupil Personnel Services, Dept. of Public Instruction, Raleigh, NC 27602.

Women's Task Force (American College Personnel Assoc.), Dr. Mary Howard, Hostos Community College, 475 Grand Concourse, Bronx, NY 10451. 212-993-8000. Dr. Jane McCormick, Penn. State University, University Park, PA 16802.

International Assoc. of Personnel Women. Mary Jane Kay, Detroit Edison Co., 2000 2 Ave., Detroit, MI 28226. Also: 358 5 Ave., New York, NY 10001. 212-695-0679.

Rosters for Employment 453

Women's Caucus (American Personnel & Guidance Assoc.), Beverly Clark, 10649 Weymouth, Bethesda, MD 20014.

Women's Caucus (American Society of Training and Development), Dr. Shirley McCune, Center for Human Relations, N.E.A., 1601 16 St., N.W., Washington, DC 20036; Althea Simmons, Director of Training, NAACP, 200 E. 27 St., New York, NY 10016. Steering Committee.

PHARMACISTS
American Council on Pharmaceutical Education, Fred T. Mahaffey, Secretary/Treasurer, 77 W. Washington, Chicago, IL 60602. 312-263-6540 (accrediting agency).

PHILOLOGISTS (see also LINGUISTS)
Women's Caucus (American Philological Assoc.), Prof. Sarah B. Pomeroy, Hunter College, Box 1264, 695 Park Ave., New York, NY 10021. 212-360-5566.

Committee on the Status of Women (American Philological Assoc.), Prof. Mary R. Lefkowitz, Dept. of Greek & Latin, Wellesley College, Wellesley, MA 02181.

American Philological Assoc., 431-432N Burrowes Bldg., Pennsylvania State Univ., University Park, PA 16802. Robert W. Carrubba, Secretary-Treasurer. 814-865-7851.

PHILOSOPHERS (see also EDUCATORS...)
Women's Caucus (American Philosophical Assoc.), Prof. Mary Mothersill, Dept. of Philosophy, Barnard College, New York, NY 10027. Dr. Margaret D. Wilson, Dept. of Philosophy, 1879 Hall, Princeton University, Princeton, NJ 08540.

Society for Women in Philosophy. Prof. Connie C. Price, Dept. of Philosophy, Tuskegee Institute, AL 36088.

American Philosophical Assoc., Hamilton College, Clinton, NY 13323. Norman E. Bowie, Exec. Secretary. 315-859-4188.

American Philosophical Society, 104 S. 5, Philadelphia, PA 19106. George W. Corner, Exec. Officer. 215-925-3606.

PHYSICAL THERAPISTS see OCCUPATIONAL AND PHYSICAL THERAPISTS

PHYSICIANS (see also SCIENTISTS)
Committee on the Status of Women (American Assoc. of Immunologists), Dr. Helene C. Rauch, Dept. of Medical Microbiology, Stanford Univ., School of Medicine, Stanford, CA 94305. The AAI has list of Women Members.

American Medical Women's Assoc., 1740 Broadway, New York, NY 10019. 212-586-8683.

Biophysical Society Placement Service. See BIOPHYSICISTS Section.

Task Force on Women in Physiology. (American Physiological Assoc.) Dr. Elizabeth Tidball, Dept. of Physiology, G. Washington Univ. Medical Center, 2300 Eye St. N.W., Washington, DC 20037.

Women's Caucus (American Public Health Assoc.), Mary Plaska, 1015 16 St. N.W., Washington, DC 20036.

> American Psychiatric Assoc., 1700 18 St. N.W., Washington, DC 20009. Melvin Sabshin, Medical Director. 202-232-7878.
>
> Liaison Committee on Medical Education (representing the Council on Medical Education of the American Medical Assoc. and the Executive Council of the Assoc. of American Medical Colleges), C. H. William Ruhe, Secretary, AMA Council on Medical Education, 535 N. Dearborn, Chicago, IL 60610. 312-751-6000. Or John A. D. Cooper, Assoc. of American Medical Colleges, 1 Dupont Circle N.W., Washington, DC 20036. 202-466-5100 (accrediting bodies).

PHYSICISTS (see also SCIENTISTS)
AIP Placement Service, 335 E. 45, New York, NY 10017. "Roster of Women in Physics."

Committee on Women in Physics. (American Physical Society). Prof. Mildred Widgoff, Physics Dept., Box 1843, Brown Univ., Providence, RI 02912. Dr. Vera Kistiakowski, Nuclear Physics Laboratory, Mass. Institute of Technology, Cambridge, MA 02139. Dr. Elizabeth Baranger, Physics Dept., MIT.

Professional Opportunities for Women of the Biophysical Society. Caucus of Women Biophysicists. Dr. Daphne Hare, School of Medicine, SUNY, Buffalo, NY 14215.

> American Geophysical Union, 1707 L St. N.W., Washington, DC 20036. A. F. Spilhaus, Jr., Exec. Director. 202-293-1144.
>
> American Physical Society, 335 E. 45, New York, NY 10017. W. W. Havens, Jr., Exec. Secretary. 212-685-2014.
>
> American Institute of Physics, 335 E. 45, New York, NY 10017. Sidney Millman, Director. 212-685-1940.

PHYSIOLOGISTS see PHYSICIANS

Rosters for Employment

PLANNERS
Women's Rights Committee. (American Institute of Planners). Diana C. Donald, 1776 Mass. Ave. N.W., Washington, DC 20036.

Women Architects, Landscape Architects, & Planners, 39 Martin, Cambridge, MA 02138.

POLITICAL SCIENTISTS
Committee on the Status of Women in the Profession (American Political Science Assoc.), Carole Parsons, 2400 Virginia Ave. N.W., #1102, Washington, DC 20037. Roster. Also: Josephine E. Milburn, Univ. of Rhode Island, Kingston, RI 02881. Dr. Rutha Silva, Penn. State Univ., University Park, PA 16802.

Women's Caucus for Political Science. Dr. JoAnn Aviel, California State Univ., San Francisco, CA 94132. Permanent Caucus address: Mt. Vernon College, 2100 Foxhall Rd. N.W., Washington, DC 20007. Dr. Evelyn P. Stevens, 14609 Woodland Rd., Shaker Heights, OH 44120. Carol Barry, 3223 Broadhead Rd., Bethlehem Twp., PA 18017.

> American Academy of Political & Social Sciences, 3937 Chestnut, Philadelphia, PA 19104. Marvin E. Wolfgang, 215-386-4594.

> American Political Science Assoc., 1527 N.H. Ave. N.W., Washington, DC 20036. Evron M. Kirkpatrick, Exec. Director. 202-483-2512. Central Office Contact: Dr. Walter Beach.

PSYCHIATRISTS see PHYSICIANS

PSYCHOLOGISTS
Assoc. for Women in Psychology. Leigh Marlowe, 189 West End Ave., New York, NY 10023. Jo-Ann Evans Gardner, 726 St. James, Pittsburgh, PA 15232. Dr. Dorothy Camara, 70012 Western Ave., Chevy Chase, MD 10023.

Ad Hoc Committee on Women in Psychology (American Psychological Assoc.). Dr. Martha Mednick, Dept. of Psychology, Howard Univ., Washington, DC 20001.

Task Force on the Status of Women in Psychology (American Psychological Assoc.). Dr. Helen Astin, Director of Research, Univ. Research Corp., 4301 Connecticut Ave., N.W., Washington, DC 20008. Roster.

> American Psychological Assoc., 1200 17 St. N.W., Washington, DC 20036. C. Allen Boneau, Acting Exec. Officer. 202-833-7660. Staff Liaison: Dr. Brenda Gurel. (Accreditation: Ronald B. Kurz, Associate Educational Affairs Officer.) Committee on Equality of Opportunity in Psychology (minorities and women).

PUBLIC ADMINISTRATORS see MANAGERS; EDUCATORS...;
HOSPITAL ADMINISTRATORS

RELIGION, RELIGIOUS STUDIES, THEOLOGIANS...
Women's Caucus--Religious Studies, Box 6309, Station B, Vanderbilt University, Nashville, TN 37235.

Task Force on the Status of Women. (American Academy of Religion). Mary Wakeman, Univ. of North Carolina, Greensboro, NC 27412. Margaret M. Earley, Alverno College, Milwaukee, WI 53215. Elizabeth Schussler Fiorenza, 1223 N. Lawrence, South Bent, IN 46617.

Task Force on Women, United Presbyterian Church in the U.S.A., Patricia Doyle, Elaine Homrighouse, 730 Witherspoon Building, Philadelphia, PA 19197; also Rev. Patricia Kepler.

Women Theologicans United, Sr. Janice Raymond, Box 138, Andover Newton Seminary, Newton Center, MA 02159.

Women's Institute & Placement Service, Boston Theological Institute. Elizabeth Dempster, (Ms.) Jean L. Williams, 45 Francis Ave., Cambridge, MA 02138. Placement Service for Teachers, Data Bank, etc.

Farians, Elizabeth. SEE "Directory of Sources."

Church Employed Women. Mildred G. Lehr, Westminster Press, 900 Witherspoon Bldg., Philadelphia, PA 19107.

Coalition Task Force on Women & Religion, 4759 15 Ave. E., Seattle, WA 89105.

Women in Religion Task Force. Rev. Imagene Stewart, Washington, DC. 202-343-2766.

> Society of Biblical Literature, Harvard Divinity School, 45 Francis Ave., Cambridge, MA 02138. George W. MacRae, Exec. Secretary. 617-495-2041.

> American Academy of Religion, Florida State Univ., Tallahassee, FL 32306. Walter Moore, Acting Director. 904-644-3849.

> American Assoc. of Theological Schools in the US & Canada. Jesse H. Ziegler, Exec. Director, PO Box 396, Vandalia, OH 45377. 513-898-4645 (accrediting body).

SCIENTISTS (see also under specific science)
Assoc. of Women in Science. Dr. Estelle Ramey, 1346 Connecticut Ave. N.W., Washington, DC 20036. Dr. Judith G. Pool, Stanford Medical School, Stanford, CA 94305. Dr. Neena B. Schwartz, Dept. of Psychiatry, College of Medicine, Univ. of Illinois Medical

Rosters for Employment

Center, PO Box 6998, Chicago, IL 60680. Anne M. Briscoe, Dept. of Medicine, Harlem Hospital Center, New York, NY 10037. Biophysical Society Placement Society. See BIOPHYSICISTS.

Dr. Marion Webster, 2226 Broadbranch Terrace, Washington, DC 20008.

Biophysical Society Placement Service, Rush-Presbyterian-St. Luke's Hospitals, 1753 W. Congress Pkwy., Chicago, IL 60612. Information available at cost with and without vitae.

Women's Caucus. (American Assoc. for the Advancement of Science). Virginia Walbot, Dept. of Biochemistry, Univ. of Georgia, Athens, GA 30601, or at Dept. of Biology, Yale Univ., New Haven, CT 06520.

Graduate Women in Science (Sigma Delta Epsilon). Dr. Hazel Metz Fox, 1231 N. 38, Lincoln, NE 65503. Hope Hopps, 1762 Overlook Dr., Silver Spring, MD 20903.

> History of Science Society. School of Physics & Astronomy, Minnesota Center for Philosophy of Science, Univ. of Minnesota, Minneapolis, MN 55455. Roger H. Stuewer, Secretary. 612-376-7023.
>
> American Assoc. for the Advancement of Science, 1515 Mass. Ave. N.W., Washington, DC 20005. Philip Abelson, Acting Exec. Director. 202-467-4400. 1776 Mass. Ave. N.W., Washington, DC 20036. Dr. Janet Brown, Office of Opportunities in Science. 202-467-4496. Has roster.
>
> National Register of Scientific and Technical Personnel. National Science Foundation, 1800 G St., N.W., Washington, DC 20506. (Register is by sex, field, work.)

SOCIAL WORKERS
Council on Social Work Education, Alfred Stamm, Director, Division of Education Standards & <u>Accreditation</u>. 345 E. 46, New York, NY 10017. 212-697-0467.

SOCIOLOGISTS
Ad Hoc Committee on the Status of Women in Sociology (American Sociological Assoc.). Cora B. Marrett, Dept. of Sociology, Western Michigan Univ., Kalamazoo, MI 49001. Dr. Elise Boulding, Behavioral Science Institute, Univ. of Colorado, Boulder, CO 80302.

Sociologists for Women in Society. Dr. Joan Huber, Dept. of Sociology, Univ. of Illinois, Urbana, IL 61801.

Committee on Social Injustice for Women. (National Council for the Social Studies). Dr. Dell Felder, Univ. of Houston, Houston, TX 77004.

Task Force on Women's Rights & Responsibilities. (National Council on Family Relations). Dr. Rose Somerville, Sociology Dept., San Diego State University, San Diego, CA 92115.

Women's Caucus (Population Assoc. of America). Prof. Nancy E. Williamson, Brown Univ., Providence, RI 02912. Prof. Ruth B. Dixon, Dept. of Sociology, Univ. of California, Davis, CA 95616.

Dr. Athena Theodore, Professor/Sociology, Simmons College. 27 Turning Mill Rd., Lexington, MA 02173.

AWS, Shari Etzkowitz, Box 1113, Dept. of Sociology, Washington Univ., St. Louis, MO 63130.

> American Sociological Assoc., 1722 N St. N.W., Washington, DC 20036. Otto N. Larsen, Exec. Officer. 202-833-3410.

SPEECH & HEARING PERSONNEL
Subcommittee on the Status of Women. (American Speech & Hearing Assoc.). Dorothy K. Marge, 8011 Longbrook Rd., Springfield, VA 22152. (Caucus on Status of Women in ASHA.)

Commission for Women. (Speech Communication Assoc.) Bonnie Ritter Patton, County Office Bldg., Rockville, MD 20850.

> American Speech & Hearing Assoc., Gene R. Powers, Chairman, Education & Training Board, 9030 Old Georgetown Rd., Washington, DC 20014. 202-530-3400 (accrediting body).

STATISTICIANS
Caucus for Women in Statistics (American Statistical Assoc.). Dr. Marie Wann, Statistical Policy Div., OMB, Washington, DC 20503.

Committee on Women in Statistics (ASA). Dr. Jean D. Gibbons, College of Commerce & Business Administration, Univ. of Alabama, University, AL 35486.

> American Statistical Assoc., 806 15 St. N.W., Washington, DC 20005. Fred C. Leone, Exec. Director, 202-393-3253.

VETERINARIANS
Women's Veterinary Medical Assoc. Dr. Helena J. Constantine, Deer Park Veterinary Clinic, 4380 E. Galbraith, Cincinnati, OH 45236.

> American Veterinary Medical Assoc., W. Max Decker, Director. Scientific Activities, 600 S. Michigan Ave., Chicago, IL 60605. 312-922-7930 (accrediting body).

WOMEN'S STUDIES STAFF see "Who's who and where in Women's Studies," #653 Basic Book Collection.

INDEX TO
"A BASIC BOOK COLLECTION"

Numerous books are referred to within the annotations of the Basic Book Collection in this <u>Supplement</u>; they are cited because of their relevance in some way to the main title or to the subject. Although they are not necessarily "basics," these titles and their authors have been included in the index that follows, as references.

Abbott, S. Sappho was a right-on woman 374
Abortion. Gutcheon, B. 542
Abortion and the unwanted child. Calif. Committee on Therapeutic Abortion 485
Abortion bibliography for 1970. Floyd, M.K. 323
Abortion controversy. Sarvis, B. 495
Abortion II. Lader, L. 466
Abzug, B.S. Bella! 438
Adam Smith's daughters. Thomson, D.L. 457
Adams, E. Up against the wall, mother 375
Adams, F. I took a hammer in my hand 557
Adburgham, A. Women in print 611
Adjustment to widowhood... Strugnell, C. 332; see also 384
Affair of Gabrielle Russier. Gallant, M. 711
Affirmative action for women. Jongeward, D. 464
African women in towns. Little, K. 406
Against rape. Medea, A. 491
Aird, E.M. Sylvia Plath 705
Akhmatova, A.A. Poems 631

Aldous, J. International bibliography of research in marriage and the family, 1900-1964 319
Aldrich, A. Take a Lesbian to lunch 345
Alexander, J. Venture of form in the novels of Virginia Woolf, see 612
Alexander, R. Shortchanged 446
Alinsky, S. Rules for radicals, see 427
All said and done. Beauvoir, S. 660
All she needs. Lerner, E. 571
Allen, H. Bread game 478
Alternatives in print, 1973-4. ALA SRRT Task Force on... 320
Amazon expedition. Birkby, P. 593
Amazon odyssey. Atkinson, T. 658
America through women's eyes. Beard, M.R. 378
American Black women in the arts and social sciences. Williams, O. 335
American Civil Liberties Union handbooks series 468

459

American dilemma. Myrdal, G. 410
American health empire. Health Policy Advisory Committee 489
American heroine. Davis, A.F. 655
American Indian women. Girdley, M.E., see 687
American Library Assoc. Social Responsibilities Round Table. Task Force on Alternatives in Print. Alternatives in print, 1973-4 320
American woman... Chafe, W.H. 387
American woman. Riegel, R.E. 514
American woman in sport. Gerber, E.W. 576
American women; images and realities 343
Amir, M. Patterns in forcible rape 479
Anaïs Nin. Franklin, B.V., see 703
Analysis of "Human Sexual Inadequacy." Robbins, J. 549
And perhaps... Dayan, R. 738
Angela Davis. Davis, A.Y. 670
Anne Royall's U.S.A. James, B.R. 710
Anthony, C.P. Textbook of anatomy and physiology 524
Aphrodite at mid-century. Rivers, C. 707
Approaching Simone. Terry, M. 609
Arisian, K. New wedding 370
Ash, L. Subject collections 336
Astin, H.S. Women 321
Atkinson, L. Famous American athletes of today, see 575
Atkinson, T. Amazon odyssey 658
Atwood, M.E. Surfacing 753
Austen, J. Emma 754
Authors' Collective. Storefront day-care centers 480
Autobiography of Miss Jane Pittman. Gaines, E.J. 768
Awake and aware. Chabon, I., see 527

Awful rowing toward God. Sexton, A., see page 63

Babcox, D. Liberation now! 376
Bachelor fatherhood. McFadden, M. 355
Backward child and his mother. Mannoni, M. 357
Ballou, M.M. Notable thoughts about women, see 744
Bambara, T.C. Gorilla, my love 804
Banks, O. Feminism and family planning in Victorian England 377
_____. Prosperity and parenthood, see 377
Barrer, M.E. Women's organizations and leaders 340
Basil, D.C. Women in management 560
Bazin, N.T. Virginia Woolf and the androgynous vision 612
Bean, C.A. Methods of childbirth 525
Beard, M.R. America through women's eyes 378
_____. On understanding women 379
Beatrice Webb's American diary. Webb, B.P. 730
Beauvoir, S. All said and done 660
_____. Belles images 755
_____. Coming of age 380
_____. Very easy death 626
Becoming partners. Rogers, C.R. 417
Bed/time/story. Robinson, J. 708
Beecham, J. Olga 686
Before honor. Schweitzer, G. 794
Before the Supreme Court. Dunnahoo, T. 691
Bella! Abzug, B.S. 438
Belles images. Beauvoir, S. 755
Benedictis, D.D. Legal obli-

Index to Basic Book Collection

gations and rights of married men, see 458
Benet, M.K. Secretary 561
Bengis, I. Combat in the erogenous zone 346
Benson, R.C. Women in Tolstoy 632
Beresford-Howe, C. Book of Eve 756
Bernard, J. Journey toward freedom, see 724
Bernard, J.S. Future of marriage 381
———. Future of motherhood 382
Bernstein, R. Helping unmarried mothers 481
Bessera, S.S. Sex code of California 458
Best circles. Davidoff, L. 389
Between myth and morning. Janeway, E.H. 399
Beyond conception. Willing, M.K. 435
Beyond God the father. Daly, M. 362
Bhatia, K. Indira Gandhi 676
Bibliography of the works of Katherine Anne Porter... Waldrip, L. 333
Bickner, M.L. Women at work 322
Billie Jean. King, B.J. 579
Billie Jean King's secrets of winning tennis. King. B.J., see 579
Billings, V. Womansbook 383
Bing, E.D. Six practical lessons for an easier childbirth 527
Bird, C. Everything a woman needs to know... 562
Birkby, P. Amazon expedition 593
Bittersweet. Ford, L.M. 674
Black woman in America. Staples, R. 428
Black women in White America. Lerner, G. 746
Blackberry winter. Mead, M. 699
Blackett, M. Mark of the maker 727
Blackwell, A.S. Lucy Stone 720

Blais, M-C. Day is dark... 627
———. Manuscripts of Pauline Archange, see 627
———. Season in the life of Emmanuel, see 627
Bluemel, E. Florence Sabin 712
Blues book for blue Black magical women. Sanchez, S. 604
Bluford, R. Unwanted pregnancy 528
Bogan, L. What the woman lived 661
Böll, H. Group portrait with lady 624
Bonham, B. Willa Cather, see 665
Book of Eve. Beresford-Howe, C. 756
Boslooper, T. Femininity game 574
Boston Women's Health Book Collective. Our bodies, ourselves 529
Bostonians. James, H., see 616
Bowen, E. Eva Trout 757
Boys and girls. Merriam, E., see 643
Braxton, B. Women, sex and race 512
Bread game. Allen, H. 478
Breakthrough. Loring, R. 564
Breitbart, V. Every mother's child 482
Bridgman, R. Gertrude Stein in pieces, see 719
Bright eyes. Wilson, D.C. 687
Bring me a unicorn. Lindbergh, A.P.M. 690
Brontës and their background. Winnifrith, T., see 663
Brown, R.M. Hand that cradles the rock, see 758
———. Rubyfruit jungle 758
Browning, E.B. Sonnets from the Portuguese 613
Brownmiller, S. Shirley Chisholm, see 666
Bryant, D. Ella Price's journal

759
Buchanan, C.D. Maiden 760
Bullough, V.L. Subordinate sex 741
Burack, R. New handbook of prescription drugs 530
Buried alive. Friedman, M. 681
Burkhart, K.W. Women in prison 483
By a woman writt. Goulianos, J. 587
By and about women. Schneiderman, B.K. 820
By prescription only. Mintz, M., see 536
Byron's daughter. Turney, C. 688

CWLA Standards for child protective service 484
Cables to rage. Lorde, A., see 599
Caine, L. Widow 384
California Committee on Therapeutic Abortion. Abortion and the unwanted child 485
Cameras and courage. Noble, I. 662
Canadian women and the law. Zuker, M.A. 476
Canary. Conn, C., see 701
Carden, M.L. New feminist movement 385
Career women of America, 1776-1840. Dexter, E.W.A. 640
Carpenter. Cook and the carpenter 761
Carson McCullers. Graver, L. 695
Carter, C.F. Wedding day in literature and art, see 744
Case against having children. Silverman, A. 425
Caserta, P. Going down with Janis, see 681
Casler, L. Is marriage necessary? 386
Cast for a revolution. Fritz, J. 728
Catalog. Indiana University. Institute... 326
Cather, W.S. Lost lady 763
Celebration! Nin, A., see 703
Chabaud, J. Education and advancement of women 499
Chabon, I. Awake and aware, see 527
Chafe, W.H. American women... 387
Chamberlin, H. Minority of members 439
Chandler, E.W. Women in prison, see 483
Changing women in a changing society. Huber, J. 397
Changing years. Gray, M. 539
Charmed circle. Mellow, J.R. 719
Chesler, P. Women and madness 531
Chester, L. Rising tides 594
Chicago women's directory, see 437
Child care--who cares? Roby, P. 494
Children of violence. Lessing, D.M. 778
Chisholm, S. Good fight 440
Church and the second sex; 1975 edition with a New postchristian introduction. Daly, M., see 362
Civilization in transition. Jung, C.G. 352
Clarke, R. Ellen Swallow 721
Cleverdon, C.L. Woman Suffrage Movement in Canada 459
Closer look at Ariel. Steiner, N.H., see 705
Cohen, S.J. Sampler of Women's Studies 500
Colby, V. Yesterday's woman 614
Cole, D. From tipi to skyscraper 570
Colette. Crosland, M., see 667
Colette, S.G. Evening star 667
_____. Retreat from love 764
Collected stories. Parker, D.R.

818
Colonial days and dames. Wharton, A.H. 751
Colonial women of affairs. Dexter, E.W.A. 641
Combat in the erogenous zone. Bengis, I. 346
Coming of age. Beauvoir, S. 380
Complete book of breastfeeding. Olds, S.W. 548
Complete poetical works. Lowell, A. 600
Conception, birth and contraception. Demarest, R. 534
Conception, contraception. Loebl, S. 544
Conn, C. Canary, see 701
Constance DeMarkievicz. VanVoris, J. 697
Conundrum, Morris, J. 701
Cook and the carpenter. Carpenter 761
Cooper, A.J. Voice from the South... 669
Cooper, E. Harim and the purdah, see 744
Cornillon, S.K. Images of women in fiction 584
Corporate lib. Ginzburg, E. 563
Corporate wives. Seidenberg, R. 567
Corsets and crinolines. Waugh, N. 517
Cott, N.F. Root of bitterness 742
Courage to divorce. Gettleman, S. 395
Crane, L. Ms. Africa 638
Crary, M. Susette LaFlesche, see 687
Crawley, E. Mystic rose, see 744
Creative approach to sex education... Schiller, P. 508
Crile, G. What women should know about the breast cancer controversy 532
Crimes without victims. Schur, E.M. 477
Crosland, M. Colette, see 667
Csida, J.B. Rape 486

Cut of men's clothes... Waugh, N., see 517
Cut of women's clothes... Waugh, N., see 517

DaCosta, M.V. Three Marias... 630
Dalton, K. Menstrual cycle 533
Daly, M. Beyond God the father 362
———. Church and the second sex; 1975 ed. with a New postchristian introduction, see 362
Dannett, S.G.L. Profiles of Negro womanhood 639
Dash, J. Life of one's own 388
Daughter of earth. Smedley, A. 797
Daughter of earth and water. Gerson, N.B. 715
Davidoff, L. Best circles 389
Davis, A.F. American heroine 655
Davis, A.Y. Angela Davis 670
———. If they come in the morning 390
Davis, R.H. Life in the iron mills 765
Day is dark... Blais, M-C. 627
Dayan, R. And perhaps... 738
Daycare for infants. Evans, E.B. 487
Dear-bought heritage. Leonard, E.A. 745
Death's single privacy. Phipps, J. 416
DeCastillejo, I. Knowing woman, see 352
DeCrow, K. Sexist justice 460
Decter, M. Liberated woman..., see 391
———. New chastity... 391
Deep throat. Perkins, D.M. 365
Defoe, D. Roxana 766
Degen, M.L. History of the Woman's Peace Party 363

Deiss, J.J. Roman years of Margaret Fuller 675
Demarest, R. Conception, birth and contraception 534
Descent of woman. Morgan, E. 521
Designing a day care center. Evans, E.B. 488
Dexter, E.W.A. Career women of America, 1776-1840 640
———. Colonial women of affairs 641
Dial 577-R A P E. O'Donnell, L. 786
Diary. Nin, A. 703
DiCayan, E. Without prescription 536
Dickinson, P. Fires of autumn 535
Dinesen, I. Seven gothic tales 805
Directory of minority media. U.S. Dept. of Commerce, see 506
Directory of special programs for minority group members, 1974. Johnson, W.L. 506
Directory of women attorneys in the U.S. Ford Associates 461
Discrimination against women. Stimpson, C.R. 471
Divine woman. Schafer, E.H. 515
Diving into the wreck. Rich, A.C. 603
Do with me what you will. Oates, J.D. 784
Doctor's case against the pill. Seaman, B. 551
Don't wear your wedding ring. O'Donnell, L., see 786
Dorothy Thompson. Sanders, M.K. 722
Dorsen, N. Rights of Americans..., see 468
Dreifus, C. Woman's fate 392
Dunn, N. Talking to women 767
Dunnahoo, T. Before the Supreme Court 691
Dworkin, A. Woman hating 393
Dykeman, W. Too many people, too little love 696

Early childhood directory. LaCrosse, E.R. 507
Eckley, G. Edna O'Brien 615
Economics and the public purpose. Galbraith, J.K. 447
Economics of sex discrimination. Madden, J.F. 451
Edna O'Brien. Eckley, G. 615
Education and advancement of women. Chabaud, J. 499
Eleanor Marx. Kapp, Y. 698
Elizabeth Barrett Browning. Lupton, M.J. 664
Elizabeth Cady Stanton. Oakley, M.A.B. 718
Ella Price's journal. Bryant, D. 759
Ellen Swallow. Clarke, R. 721
Ellet, E.L.F. Women of the American Revolution 743
Emily Elizabeth Dickinson. Wood, J.P. 671
Emma. Austen, J. 754
Encyclopedia of the American woman 337
Enigma of the Brontes. Peters, M. 663
Ennis, B.J. Rights of mental patients, see 468
Enormous changes at the last minute. Paley, G. 817
Escape from the doll's house. Feldman, S.D. 501
Eternal bliss machine. Seligson, M. 516
Eva Trout. Bowen, E. 757
Evans, E.B. Daycare for Infants 487
———. Designing a day care center 488
Every mother's child. Breitbart, V. 482
Everything a woman needs to know... Bird, C. 562
Evening star. Colette, S.G. 667
Executive suite. Lynch, E.M. 566

Faber, D. Oh, Lizzie!, see 718

Index to Basic Book Collection

Falling bodies. Kaufman, S. 773
Family guide to children's television. Kaye, E. 511
Family ties. Lispector, C. 810
Famous American athletes of today 575
Famous American belles of the 19th century. Peacock, V.T. 648
Fanny Kemble. Wise, W., see 683
Fanny Kemble and the lovely land. Wright, C. 683
Fanny Kemble's America. Scott, J.A., see 683
Farewell to fear. Freeman, L. 347
Farrell, W. Liberated man, see 394
Fasteau, M.F. Male machine 394
Fear of flying. Jong, E. 772
Feldman, S. Escape from the doll's house 501
Female woman. Stassinaopoulos, A., see 391
Feminine fix-it handbook. Ward, K.B., see 557
Feminine forever. Wilson, R.A. 556
Feminine image in literature. Warren, B., see 585
Feminine plural. Spinner, S. 822
Femininity game. Boslooper, T. 574
Feminism. Schneir, M. 591
Feminism and family planning in Victorian England. Banks, O. 377
Feminism and socialism. Jenness, L. 400
Feminist English dictionary. Todasco, R.T. 518
Feminist papers. Rossi, A.S. 418
Ferguson, M.A. Images of women in literature 585
Fernhurst, QED. Stein, G. 823
Fetherling, D. Mother Jones 680
Fight against fears. Freeman, L., see 347

Fires of autumn. Dickinson, P. 535
First and last notebooks. Weil, S. 628
First cities. Lorde, A., see 599
First Ms. reader. Klagburn, F. 598
Fisher, A. We Dickinsons, see 671
Fitzpatrick, E. Maternity nursing, see 524
Five for freedom. Wagner, G. 622
Flexner, E. Mary Wollstonecraft 732
Florence Sabin. Bluemel, E. 712
Floyd, M.K. Abortion bibliography for 1970 323
Flying. Millett, K. 700
Flynn, E.G. I speak my own piece 673
――――. My life as a political prisoner, see 673
Fogarty, M. Sex, career and family 634
Folk-lore of women. Thiselton-Dyer, T.F., see 744
Foolproof birth control. Lader, L., see 538
Forced labor. Shaw, N.S. 423
Ford, L.M. Bittersweet 674
Ford Associates. Directory of women attorneys in the U.S. 461
――――. Women's legal handbook series... 462
Forman, L. Getting it together, see 395
Forty women poets of Canada. Livesay, D. 618
Foster, J. Sex variant women in literature 586
Fowler, W.W. Woman on the American frontier 744
Fragment from a lost diary. Katz, N. 808
Frankfort, E. Vaginal politics 537
Franklin, B.V. Anaïs Nin, see 703

Frazier, N. Sexism in school and society 502
Free and female. Seaman, B. 422
Freely female. Kochansky, H. 354
Freeman, L. Farewell to fear 347
_____. Fight against fears, see 347
Freeman, M.W. Revolt of mother... 806
Friday, N. My secret garden... 348
Fried, J.J. Vasectomy 538
Friedman, M. Buried alive 681
Fritz, J. Cast for a revolution 728
From a land where other people live. Lorde, A. 599
From man to man. Schreiner, O. 793
From reverence to rape. Haskell, M. 578
From tipi to skyscraper. Cole, D. 570
Frosty. Weaver, H.E. 729
Furniss, W.T. Women in higher education 503
Future of marriage. Bernard, J.S. 381
Future of motherhood. Bernard, J.S. 382
Futz.... Owens, R. 816

Gager, N. Women's rights almanac, 1974 341
Gaines, E.J. Autobiography of Miss Jane Pittman 768
_____. Of love and dust, see 768
Galbraith, J.K. Economics and the public purpose 447
Galenson, J. Women and work 448
Gallant, M. Affair of Gabrielle Russier 711
Garnett, E. Madam Prime Minister, see 676
Garskof, M.H. Roles women play 349

Gemini. Giovanni, N. 679
General guide to abortion. Sloane, R.B. 552
George, M. One woman's situation, see 733
Gerber, E.W. American woman in sport 576
Gerson, N.B. Daughter of earth and water 715
Gersoni-Stavn, D. Sexism and youth 504
Gertrude Stein. Greenfeld, H., see 719
Gertrude Stein in pieces. Bridgman, R., see 719
Gertrude Stein is Gertrude... Rogers, W.G., see 719
Getting clear. Rush, A.K. 550
Getting it together. Forman, L., see 395
Getting married. Strindberg, A. 625
Gettleman, S. Courage to divorce 395
Ghost stories. Wharton, E.N.J. 825
Gilder, G. Sexual suicide, see 394
Gilman, C.P.S. Man-made world 449
_____. Yellow wallpaper 678
Ginzburg, E. Corporate lib 563
Giovanni, N. Gemini 679
Girdley, M.E. American Indian women, see 687
Girl through the ages. Stuart, D.M., see 744
Girls' Christian names. Swan, H., see 744
Give me one good reason. Klein, N. 774
Glimpses of fifty years. Willard, F.E. 731
Going down with Janis. Caserta, P., see 681
Goldreich, G. What can she be?, see 570
Goldstein, R.L. Indian women in transition 396
Good fight. Chisholm, S.A.S. 440

Index to Basic Book Collection

Goode, S.H. Venereal disease bibliography, 1966-1970 324
Gorilla, my love. Bambara, T.C. 804
Gould, L. Necessary objects 769
Goulianos, J. By a woman writt 587
Grants index, see 478
Grau, S.A. Wind shifting west 807
Graver, L. Carson McCullers 695
Gray, M. Changing years 539
Greed. Wakoski, D. 610
Green, T.H. Gynecology 540
Greenfeld, H. Gertrude Stein, see 719
Greenhill, J.P. Office gynecology, see 540
Greygallows. Mertz, B. 779
Group for the Advancement of Psychiatry. Humane reproduction 541
Group portrait with lady. Böll, H. 624
Growing older. Huyck, M.H. 398
Growing up female in America. Merriam, E. 643
Guerilleres. Wittig, M. 629
Guide to sources of consumer information. Thomas, S.M. 456
Gutcheon, B. Abortion 542
Guttmacher, A.F. Pregnancy, birth, and family planning 543
Gynecology. Green, T.H. 540

Habit of loving. Lessing, D. 809
Hadley. Sokoloff, A.H. 702
Half-lives. Jong, E. 597
Hamilton, C.M. Marriage as a trade, see 744
Hand that cradles the rock. Brown, R.M., see 758
Haney, L. Lady is a jock 577
Hardin, G. Mandatory motherhood 463

Hardwick, E. Seduction and betrayal 588
Hardwick, M. Mrs. Dizzy 672
Hardy, T. Tess of the d'Urbervilles 770
Harim and the purdah. Cooper, E., see 744
Harper, I.H. Life and work of Susan B. Anthony 441
Harris, T.A. I'm ok--you're ok..., see 464
Harrison, B.G. Unlearning the lie 505
Harrison, M. Kitchen in history 558
Haskell, M. From reverence to rape 578
He! A contribution... Johnson, R., see 352
Health Policy Advisory Committee. American health empire 489
Hegeler, I. XYZ of love 350
Heilbrun, C.G. Toward a recognition of androgyny 595
Helping each other in widowhood. Silverman, P.R., see 384
Helping unmarried mothers. Bernstein, R. 481
Henderson, N. Out of the curtained world 367
Henry, A. Trade union woman 450
_____. Women and the labor movement, see 450
Herstory... Sochen, J., see 749
Hicks, N. Honorable Shirley Chisholm 666
Hidden from history. Rowbotham, S., see 420
Higher education guidelines. U.S. Dept. of HEW 474
Hillbilly women. Kahn, K. 402
History of sexual customs. Lewinsohn, R. 513
History of the Woman's Peace Party. Degen, M.L. 363
History of women's education in the U.S. Woody, T. 509
Hite, S. Sexual honesty 351

Hochman, S. Walking papers 771
Holliday, C. Woman's life in colonial days, see 744
Home. Mortimer, P. 781
Honorable Shirley Chisholm. Hicks, N. 666
Horos, C.V. Rape, see 486
Hostile sun. Oates, J.C., see 777
Hour of gold... Lindbergh, A.S.M., see 690
House of good proportion. Murray, M. 590
How to return to work in an office. Ralston, M. 453
How to talk back to your television set. Johnson, N. 510
How women can make money. Penny, V. 452
Howe, F. No more masks 596
Huber, J. Changing women in a changing society 397
Hughes, M.J. Sexual barrier 325
_____. Women's rights in employment, see 325
Human liberation in a feminist perspective. Russell, L.M. 368
Human sexual inadequacy. Masters, W., see 549
Humane reproduction. Group for the Advancement of Psychiatry 541
Hustling. Sheehy, G. 496
Huyck, M.H. Growing older 398

I am Mary Dunne. Moore, B. 780
I can sell you anything. Stevens, P. 568
I speak my own piece. Flynn, E.G. 673
I took my hammer in my hand. Adams, F. 557
Iconographia gyniatrica. Speert, H. 553
If they come in the morning. Davis, A.Y. 390
I'm ok--you're ok... Harris, T.A., see 464
Images of women in fiction. Cornillon, S.K. 584
Images of women in literature. Ferguson, M.A. 585
Improper Bostonian. Goodall, M.M. 659
In calico and crinoline. Sickels, E.M. 651
In love and trouble. Walker, A. 824
In no man's land. Parker, T. 493
Indecent exposure. Quist, S. 789
Indian women in transition. Goldstein, R.L. 396
Indiana University. Institute... Catalog 326
Indira Gandhi. Bhatia, K. 676
International bibliography of research in marriage and the family, 1900-1964. Aldous, J. 319
Is marriage necessary? Casler, L. 386
Isak Dinesen's aesthetics. Whissen, T.R. 623

Jacobs, S-E. Women in perspective 327
James, B.R. Anne Royal's U.S.A. 710
James, H. Bostonians, see 616
_____. Portrait of a lady 616
_____. Speech and manners of American women, see 616
Jane Addams... Peterson, H.S., see 655
Janeway, E.H. Between myth and morning 399
Jaquette, J.S. Women in politics 442
Jeanette Rankin. Josephson, H. 706
Jenness, L. Feminism and socialism 400
Jest of God. Laurence, M.W. 776
Jewish family... Schlesinger, B., see 329

Index to Basic Book Collection

Johnson, D. True history of the first Mrs. Meredith 617
Johnson, N. How to talk back to your television set 510
Johnson, R. He! A contribution..., see 352
Johnson, W.L. Directory of special programs for minority group-members, 1974 506
Johnston, C.H.L. Famous American athletes of today 575
Johnston, J. Lesbian nation 401
Jones, E.H. Mrs. Humphrey Ward 656
Jong, E. Fear of flying 772
———. Half-lives 597
Jongeward, D. Affirmative action for women 464
Josephson, H. Jeanette Rankin 706
Journey toward freedom. Bernard J., see 724
Julie. My nights and days 682
Jung, C.G. Civilization in transition 352

Kaese, H. Famous American athletes of today, see 575
Kaeth Kollwitz. Kearns, M. 685
Kahn, K. Hillbilly women 402
Kane, P. Sex objects in the sky 635
Kanowitz, L. Sex roles in law and society 465
Kapp, Y. Eleanor Marx 698
Kathe Kollwitz. Klein, M.C., see 685
Katz, N. Fragment from a lost diary 808
Kaufman, S. Falling bodies 773
Kaye, E. Family guide to children's television 511
Kaye, H. Male survival 353
Kearns, M. Kaeth Kollwitz 685
Kelley, A.V. Novels of Virginia Woolf..., see 612
Kempf, B. Woman for peace 726
Key, M.R. Male/female language 517a
Kids' own XYZ of love and sex.

Widerberg, S., see 529
King, B.J. Billie Jean 579
———. Billie Jean King's secrets of winning tennis, see 579
———. Tennis to win, see 579
Kitchen in history. Harrison, M. 558
Kittrie, N.N. Right to be different, see 477
Klagburn, F. First Ms. reader 598
Klasner, L. My girlhood among the outlaws 684
Klein, C. Single parent experience 403
Klein, M.C. Kathe Kollwitz, see 685
Klein, N. Give me one good reason 774
Knowing woman. DeCastillejo, I., see 352
Kochansky, H. Freely female 354
Koedt, A. Radical feminism 404
Krichmar, A. Women's Rights Movement in the U.S., 1848-1970 328

LaBarre, H. Life of your own, see 384
Labor's defiant lady. Weisstein, I., see 680
Lace ghetto. Nunes, M. 411
LaCrosse, E.R. Early childhood directory 507
Ladders to fire. Nin, A. 783
Lader, L. Abortion II 466
———. Foolproof birth control, see 358
Ladies of horror. Manley, S., see 811
Ladner, J. Tomorrow's tomorrow, see 428
Lady is a jock. Haney, L. 577
Lagerloff, S. Treasure 775
Land of our own. Meir, G.M. 739
Lange, D. To a cabin 572

Langhorne, E. Nancy Astor and her friends 657
Last rights. Mannes, M. 364
Laurence, M.W. Jest of God 776
Law and order. Uhnak, D. 801
Lawrence, D.H. Women in love 777
Lebeson, A. Recall to life 372
Legal obligations and rights of married men. Benedictis, D.D., see 458
Legman, G.A. Rationale of the dirty joke 589
Leighton, M. Shelley's Mary, see 715
Lemons, J.S. Woman citizen 405
Leonard, E.A. Dear-bought heritage 745
Lerner, E. All she needs 571
Lerner, G. Black women in White America 746
Lesbian nation. Johnston, J. 401
Lesbian/Woman. Martin, D. 407
Lessing, D.M. Children of violence 778
———. Habit of loving 809
Levi-Strauss, C. Tristes tropiques 520
Levine, A. Rights of students, see 468
Levy, H.H. What every woman should know about investing..., see 452
Lewinsohn, R. History of sexual customs 513
Liberated man. Farrell, W., see 394
Liberated woman. Decter, M., see 391
Liberation now! Babcox, D. 376
Lichtenstein, G. Long way, baby 580
Life after marriage. Singleton, M.A., see 395
Life and death of Mary Wollstonecraft. Tomalin, C. 733
Life and times of my mother and me. Rose, M.B. 709
Life and work of Susan B. Anthony. Harper, I.H. 441
Life in the iron mills. Davis, R.H. 765
Life is for living. Morse, T.A., see 384
Life of Ivy Compton-Burnett. Sprigge, E. 668
Life of one's own. Dash, J. 388
Life of your own. LaBarre, H., see 384
Lindbergh, A.S.M. Bring me a unicorn 690
———. Hour of gold..., see 690
———. Locked rooms and open doors, see 690
Lispector, C. Family ties 810
Little, K. African women in towns 406
Lives of girls and women. Munro, A. 782
Livesay, D. Forty women poets of Canada 618
Locked rooms and open doors. Lindbergh, A.S.M., see 690
Loebl, S. Conception, contraception 544
Long division. Roiphe, A. 791
Long way, baby. Lichtenstein, G. 580
Lorde, A. Cables to rage, see 599
———. First cities, see 599
———. From a land where other people live 599
Loring, R. Breakthrough 564
Lost lady. Cather, W.S. 763
Loud, P.R. Pat Loud 692
Love between women. Wolff, C. 436
Love, morals, and the feminists. Rover, C. 419
Loving her. Shockley, A.A. 795
Lowell, A. Complete poetical works 600
Lucy Stone. Blackwell, A.S. 720
Lupton, M.J. Elizabeth Barrett Browning 664
Lutzker, E. Women gain a

Index to Basic Book Collection

place in medicine 545
Luxemburg, R. Reform or revolution 693
———. Rosa Luxemburg speaks, see 693
Lyle, J.R. Women in history 565
Lynch, E.M. Executive suite 566
Lytle, N.A. Maternal health nursing, see 524

McCarthy, A. Private faces, public places 694
McFadden, M. Bachelor fatherhood 355
Madam prime minister. Garnett, E., see 676
Madden, J.P. Economics of sex discrimination 451
Maiden. Buchanan, C.D. 760
Majors, M.A. Noted Negro women 642
Male/female language. Key, M.R. 517a
Male machine. Fasteau, M.F. 394
Male myth. Ruitenbeek, H.M. 421
Male survival. Kaye, H. 353
Mama. Martinez Sierra, G. 519
Mama doesn't live here anymore. Sullivan, J. 431
Man-made world. Gilman, C.P.S. 449
Man who loved children. Stead, C. 799
Mandatory motherhood. Hardin, G. 463
Manley, S. Ladies of horror, see 811
———. Mistresses of mystery 811
———. O, those extraordinary women! 619
Mannes, M. Last rights 364
Mannoni, M. Backward child and his mother 357
Mansfield, K. Short stories 812
Manuel de bibliographie et d'iconographie des femmes célèbres. Ungherini, A. 652
Manufacture of madness. Szasz, T.S. 555
Manuscripts of Pauline Archange. Blais, M., see 627
Mark of the maker. Blackett, M. 727
Marriage as a trade. Hamilton, C.M., see 744
Marriage and infidelities. Oates, J.C., see 813
Married women v. husbands' names. Stannard, U. 470
Martin, D. Lesbian/Woman 407
Martinez Sierra, G. Mama 519
Mary Shelley. Walling, W., see 715
Mary Wollstonecraft. Flexner, E. 732
Masters, W. Human sexual inadequacy, see 549
Maternal health nursing. Lytle, N.A., see 524
Maternity nursing. Fitzpatrick, E., see 524
Maxtone-Graham, K. Pregnant by mistake 490
Mead, M. Blackberry winter 699
Measure filled. Sergio, L. 704
Medea, A. Against rape 491
Meir, G.M. Land of our own 737
Mellen, J. Women and their sexuality in the new film 581
Mellow, J.R. Charmed circle 719
Memoirs of an ex-prom queen. Shulman, A.K. 796
Men and masculinity. Pleck, J.H. 358
Men in groups. Tiger, L. 433
Menstrual cycle. Dalton, K. 533
Merriam, E. Boys and girls, see 643
———. Growing up female in

America 643
———. Mommies at work, see 643
Mertz, B. Greygallows 779
Methods of childbirth. Bean, C.A. 525
Middleton, T. Women beware women 620
Miller, J.B. Psychoanalysis and women 546
Millett, K. Flying 700
Minority of members. Chamberlin, H. 439
Mintz, M. By prescription only, see 536
Mrs. Dizzy. Hardwick, M. 672
Mrs. Humphrey Ward. Jones, E.H. 656
Mistresses of mystery. Manley, S. 811
Mitchell, J. Psychoanalysis and feminism 356
———. Woman's estate 408
Mode, H. Woman in Indian art, see 569
Moffat, M.J. Revelations 644
Moffett, T. Nobody's business 443
Mommies at work. Merriam, E., see 643
Monster. Morgan, R. 601
Moore, B. I am Mary Dunne 780
Moreno, D. ¡La mujer--en pie de lucha! 409
Morgan, E. Descent of woman 521
Morgan, R. Monster 601
Morris, J. Conundrum 701
Morse, T.A. Life is for living, see 384
Mortimer, P. Home 781
Mother Jones. Fetherling, D. 680
Motor cycle betrayal poems. Wakoski, D., see 610
Ms. Wonder woman, see 598
Ms. Africa. Crane, L. 638
¡Mujer--en pie de lucha! Moreno, D. 409
Munro, A. Lives of girls and women 782
Murphy, I.L. Public policy on the status of women 444
Murphy, Y. Women of the forest 522
Murray, M. House of good proportion 590
My fight for birth control. Sanger, M.H. 714
My girlhood among the outlaws. Klasner, L. 684
My life as a political prisoner. Flynn, E.G., see 673
My nights and days. Julie 682
My secret garden... Friday, N. 348
Myrdal, G. American dilemma 410
Mystic rose. Crawley, E., see 744

Nadelson, R. Who is Angela Davis?, see 670
Nana. Zola, E. 803
Nancy Astor and her friends. Langhorne, E. 657
Nason, J. Famous American athletes of today, see 575
Nathan, D. Women of courage 645
Nature and evolution of female sexuality. Sherfey, M.J. 424
Necessary objects. Gould, L. 769
Neumann, H.H. Straight story on VD 547
New chastity... Decter, M. 391
New feminist movement. Carden, M.L. 385
New handbook of prescription drugs. Burack, R. 530
New Pamela. Stannard, U., see 470
New Portuguese letters see Three Marias (630)
New way to become the person you'd like to be. Sorensen, J. 361
New wedding. Arisian, K. 370
New woman. Sochen, J. 426
New woman series, see 411

New York woman's directory. Womanpower Project 437
Nicolson, N. Portrait of a marriage 737
Night. O'Brien, E. 785
Nin, A. Celebration!, see 703
―――. Diary 703
―――. Ladders to fire 783
Nine women. Serebriakovna, G. L. 736
No-fault divorce. Wheeler, M. 475
No more masks. Howe, F. 596
Noble, I. Cameras and courage 662
Noble, J. R. Recollections of Virginia Woolf 734
Nobody's business. Moffett, T. 443
Norman, E. Rape 492
North American Reference Encyclopedias: Reference encyclopedia of abortion, 1972 339
―――. Reference encyclopedia of Women's Liberation, 1972 338
Not in God's image. O'Faolain, J. 636
Not-so-helpless female. Sommers, T. 427
Notable thoughts about women. Ballou, M. M., see 744
Noted Negro women. Majors, M. A. 642
Novak, E. R. Textbook of gynecology, see 540
Novels. Radcliffe, A. 790
Novels of Virginia Wolff... Kelley, A. V., see 612
Noyes, E. J. R. C. Women of the Mayflower... 747
Nunes, M. Lace ghetto 411
Nursing your baby. Pryor, K., see 548

O, those extraordinary women! Manley, S. 619
Oakley, M. A. B. Elizabeth Cady Stanton 718
Oakley, A. Sex, gender and society 412
Oates, J. C. Do with me what you will 784
―――. Hostile sun, see 777
―――. Marriages and infidelities, see 813
―――. Scenes from American life 813
―――. Wheel of love..., see 813
O'Brien, E. Night 785
―――. Scandalous woman... 814
O'Brien, P. Woman alone 413
O'Donnell, L. Dial 577-R A P E 786
―――. Don't wear your wedding ring, see 786
―――. Phone calls, see 786
Of love and dust. Gaines, E. J., see 768
O'Faolain, J. Not in God's image 636
Office gynecology. Greenhill, J. P., see 540
Oh, Lizzie! Faber, D., see 718
Olds, S. W. Complete book of breastfeeding 548
Olga. Beecham, J. 686
On being female. Stanford, B. 607
On the psychology of women. Sherman, J. A. 360
On understanding women. Beard, M. R. 379
One-parent family. Schlesinger, B. 329
One woman's situation. George, M., see 733
Oneida Community. Robertson, C. N. 748
O'Neill, N. D. Open marriage 414
O'Neill, W. L. Women at work 815
Open marriage. O'Neill, N. D. 414
Orchid boat. Rexroth, K. 633
Ortiz, V. Sojourner Truth, see 724
Osen, L. M. Women in mathematics 646

Other men's daughters. Stern, R.   800
Our bodies, ourselves. Boston Women's Health Book Collective   529
Our Soviet sister. St. George, W., see 432
Out of the curtained world. Henderson, N.   367
Oven birds. Parker, G.   602
Overton, G. M. Women who make our novels   647
Owens, R. Futz...   816

Paley, G. Enormous changes at the last minute   817
Paolucci, A. Personal perspectives   559
Parker, D. R. Collected stories   818
Parker, G. Oven birds   602
Parker, T. In no man's land   493
Pat Loud. Loud, P. R.   692
Patterns in forcible rape. Amir, M.   479
Peacock, V. T. Famous American belles of the 19th century   648
Peck, E. Pronatalism   415
Penny, V. How women can make money   452
Perkins, D. M. Deep throat   365
Personal perspectives. Paolucci, A.   559
Peters, M. Enigma of the Brontes   663
Peterson, H. S. Jane Addams..., see 655
Phelan, M. K. Probing the unknown, see 712
Phillips, D. G. Susan Lennox   787
Phipps, J. Death's single privacy   416
Phone calls. O'Donnell, L., see 786
Pictures out of my life. Pitseolak   637
Piercy, M. Small changes   788
Pitseolak. Pictures out of my life   637
Plath, S. Winter trees, see 705
Plays, by and about women. Sullivan, V.   592
Pleck, J. H. Men and masculinity   358
Poems. Akhmatova, A. A.   631
Politics of rape. Russell, D. E. H., see 486
Popcorn Venus. Rosen, M.   582
Portrait of a lady. James, H.   616
Portrait of a marriage. Nicolson, N.   713
Position of women in the U. S. S. R. Serebrennikov, G. N.   740
Pregnancy, birth, and family planning. Guttmacher, A. F.   543
Pregnant by mistake. Maxtone-Graham, K.   490
President's wife. Ross, I.   689
Previously uncollected writings. Stein, G.   608
Prime of Miss Jean Brodie. Spark, M.   798
Private faces, public places. McCarthy, A.   694
Probing the unknown. Phelan, M. K., see 712
Professional woman. Theodore, A. R.   473
Profiles of Negro womanhood. Dannett, S. G. L.   639
Pronatalism. Peck, E.   415
Prosperity and parenthood. Banks, O., see 377
Pryor, K. Nursing your baby, see 548
Psyche. Segnitz, B.   605
Psychoanalysis and feminism. Mitchell, J.   356
Psychoanalysis and women. Miller, J. B.   546
Psychology of women. Walstedt, J. J.   334
Public citizen's action manual. Ross, D. K.   454
Public policy on the status of women. Murphy, I. L.   444

Quist, S. Indecent exposure 789

Race, marriage, and the law. Sickels, R.J. 469
Radcliffe, A. Novels 790
Radical feminism. Koedt, A. 404
Ralston, M. How to return to work in an office 453
Randall, M.M. Improper Bostonian 659
Rape. Csida, J.B. 486
Rape. Horos, C.V., see 486
Rape. Norman, E. 492
Raphael, D. Tender gift, see 548
Rascoe, J. Yours, and mine 819
Rationale of the dirty joke. Legman, G.A. 589
Recall to life. Lebeson, A. 372
Recollections of Virginia Woolf. Noble, J.R. 734
Reference encyclopedia of abortion, 1972. North American reference encyclopedias 339
Reform or revolution. Luxemburg, R. 693
Reid, I.S. "Together" Black women 445
Religion and sexism. Reuther, R.R. 373
Renaissance woman. Sachs, H. 569
Retreat from love. Colette, S.G. 764
Revelations. Moffat, M.J. 644
Revolt of mother. Freeman, M.W. 806
Rexroth, K. Orchid boat 633
Reyher, R.H. Zulu woman 716
Rich, A.C. Diving into the wreck 603
Richardson, B. Sexism in higher education, see 501
Riegel, R.E. American woman 514
Right to be different. Kittrie, N.N., see 477
Rights of Americans. Dorsen, N., see 468
Rights of mental patients. Ennis, B.J., see 468
Rights of prisoners. Rudovsky, D., see 468
Rights of servicemen. Rivkin, R.S., see 468
Rights of students. Levine, A., see 468
Rights of teachers. Rubin, D., see 468
Rights of women. Ross, S.C. 467
Rising tides. Chester, L. 594
Rivers, C. Aphrodite at midcentury 707
Rivkin, R.S. Rights of servicemen, see 468
Road past Altamont. Roy, G. 792
Robbins, J. Analysis of "Human Sexual Inadequacy" 549
Robertson, C.N. Oneida Community 748
Robinson, J. Bed/time/story 708
Roby, P. Child care--who cares? 494
Rogers, C.R. Becoming partners 417
Rogers, W.G. Gertrude Stein is Gertrude..., see 719
Roiphe, A. Long division 791
Roles women play. Garskof, M.H. 349
Roman years of Margaret Fuller. Deiss, J.J. 675
Root of bitterness. Cott, N.F. 742
Rosa Luxemburg speaks. Luxemburg, R., see 693
Rosaldo, M.Z. Woman, culture and society 523
Rose, M.B. Life and times of my mother and me 709
Rosen, J. Popcorn Venus 582
Ross, D.K. Public citizen's action manual 454
Ross, I. President's wife 689
Ross, N.W. Westward the women 649
Ross, P. Young and female 650

Ross, S.C. Rights of women 467
Rossi, A.S. Feminist papers 418
Rover, C. Love, morals, and the feminists 419
Rowbotham, S. Hidden from history, see 420
_____. Women, resistance, and revolution 420
Roxana. Defoe, D. 766
Roy, G. Road past Altamont 792
Royall, A.N. Sketches of history, see 710
Rubenius, A. Woman question in Mrs. Gaskell's life and works 677
Rubin, D. Rights of teachers, see 468
Rubyfruit jungle. Brown, R.M. 758
Rudovsky, D. Rights of prisoners, see 468
Ruether, R.R. Religion and sexism 373
Ruitenbeek, H.M. Male myth 421
Rules for radicals. Alinsky, S., see 427
Rush, A.K. Getting clear 550
Russell, D.E.H. Politics of rape, see 486
Russell, L.M. Human liberation in a feminist perspective 368

Sachs, H. Renaissance woman 569
St. George, W. Our Soviet sister, see 432
Sampler of Women's Studies. Cohen, S.J. 500
Sanchez, S. Blues book for blue Black magical women 604
Sanders, M.K. Dorothy Thompson 722
Sanger, M.H. My fight for birth control 714
Sappho was a right-on woman. Abbott, S. 374
Sarvis, B. Abortion controversy 495
Scandalous woman. O'Brien, E. 814
Scenes from American life. Oates, J.C. 813
Schafer, E.H. Divine woman 515
Schiller, P. Creative approach to sex education and counseling 508
Schlesinger, Arthur & Elizabeth, Library on the History of Women in America 344
Schlesinger, B. Jewish family..., see 329
_____. One-parent family 329
Schneiderman, B.K. By and about women 820
Schneir, M. Feminism 591
Schreiner, O. From man to man 793
_____. Track to the water's edge 621
_____. Undine, see 793
Schulman, L.M. Woman's place 821
Schur, E.M. Crimes without victims 477
Schweitzer, G. Before honor 794
Scott, J.A. Fanny Kemble's America, see 683
Seaman, B. Doctor's case against the pill 551
Seaman, B. Free and female 422
Season in the life of Emmanuel. Blais, M-C., see 627
Secretary. Benet, M.K. 561
Seduction and betrayal. Hardwick, E. 588
Segnitz, B. Psyche 605
Seidenberg, R. Corporate wives 567
Seligson, M. Eternal bliss machine 516
Serebrennikov, G.N. Position of women in the U.S.S.R. 740
Serebriakova, G.L. Nine women 736
Sergio, L. Measure filled 704

Seruya, F. Sex and sex education 330
Seven gothic tales. Dinesen, I. 805
Sex and sex education. Seruya, F. 330
Sex, career and family. Fogarty, M. 634
Sex code of California. Beserra, S.S. 458
Sex, gender and society. Oakley, A. 412
Sex objects in the sky. Kane, P. 635
Sex roles in law and society. Kanowitz, L. 465
Sex variant women in literature. Foster, J. 586
Sexism and youth. Gersoni-Savn, D. 504
Sexism in higher education. Richardson, B., see 501
Sexism in school and society. Frazier, N. 502
Sexist justice. DeCrow, K. 460
Sexton, A. Awful rowing toward God, see page 63
Sexual barrier. Hughes, M.M. 325
Sexual honesty. Hite, S. 351
Sexual suicide. Gilder, G., see 394
Shaw, N.S. Forced Labor 423
―――. "So you're going to have a baby," see 423
Sheehan, V.H. Unmasking 359
Sheehy, G. Hustling 496
Shelley's Mary. Leighton, M., see 715
Sherman, J.A. On the psychology of women 360
Shirley Chisholm. Brownmiller, S., see 666
Shockley, A.A. Loving her 795
Short stories. Mansfield, K. 812
Shortchanged. Alexander, R. 446
Shulman, A.K. Memoirs of an ex-prom queen 796
Sickels, E.M. In calico and crinoline 651
―――. Twelve daughters of democracy, see 651
Sickels, R.J. Race, marriage, and the law 469
Sidel, R. Women and child care in China 497
Silverman, A. Case against having children 425
Silverman, P.R. Helping each other in widowhood, see 384
Single parent experience. Klein, C. 403
Singleton, M.A. Life after marriage, see 395
Situation of women in the UN. Szalai, A. 432
Sitwell, E. Taken care of 717
Six practical lessons for an easier childbirth. Bing, E.D. 527
Sketches of history. Royall, A.N., see 710
Sloane, R.B. General guide to abortion 552
Small changes. Piercy, M. 788
Smedley, A. Daughter of earth 797
Smith, S. Women who make movies 583
"So you're going to have a baby." Shaw, N., see 423
Sochen, J. Herstory..., see 749
―――. Movers and shakers 749
―――. New woman 426
Sojourner Truth. Truth, S. 724
Sojourner Truth. Ortiz, V., see 724
Sokoloff, A.H. Hadley 702
Soltow, M.J. Women in American labor history, 1825-1935 331
Sommers, T. Not-so-helpless female 427
Sonnets from the Portuguese. Browning, E.G. 613
Sorensen, J. New way to become the person you'd like to be 361
Spark, M. Prime of Miss Jean

Brodie 798
Speech and manners of American women. James, H., see 616
Speert, H. Iconographia gyniatrica 553
Spinner, S. Feminine plural 822
Sprigge, E. Life of Ivy Compton-Burnett 668
Spruill, J.C. Women's life and work in the Southern colonies 750
Stanford, A. Women poets in English 606
Stanford, B. On being female 607
Stannard, U. Married women v. husbands' names 470
——. New Pamela, see 470
Staples, R. Black woman in America 428
Stassinaopoulos, A. Female women, see 391
Staying on alone. Toklas, A.B. 723
Stead, C. Man who loved children 799
Stein, G. Fernhurst, QED 823
Stein, G. Previously uncollected writings 608
Steiner, N.H. Closer look at Ariel, see 705
Steinfels, M.O. Who's minding the children 498
Stephenson, M. Women in Canada 429
Stern, R. Other men's daughters 800
Stevens, P. I can sell you anything 568
Stimpson, C.R. Discrimination against women 471
——. Women and the ERA 472
Storefront day-care centers. Authors' Collective 480
Straight story on VD. Neumann, H.H. 547
Strindberg, A. Getting married 625
Strouse, J. Women and analysis 554
Strugnell, C. Adjustment to widowhood... 332; see also 384
Stuart, D.M. Girl through the ages, see 744
Subject collections. Ash, L. 336
Subordinate sex. Bullough, V.L. 741
Subversion of women as practiced by churches... Van-Vuuren, N. 371
Sullerot, E. Woman, society and change 430
Sullivan, J. Mama doesn't live here anymore 431
Sullivan, V. Plays, by and about women 592
Sunshine. Klein, N., see 774
Superstar. Viva 725
Surfacing. Atwood, M.E. 753
Susan Lennox. Phillips, D.G. 787
Susette LaFlesche. Crary, M., see 687
Swamp angel. Wilson, E. 802
Swan, H. Girls' Christian names, see 744
Sylvia Plath. Aird, E.M. 705
Szalai, A. Situation of women in the UN 432
Szasz, T.S. Manufacture of madness 555

Take a Lesbian to lunch. Aldrich, A. 345
Taken care of. Sitwell, E. 717
Talking to women. Dunn, N. 767
Tavard, G.W. Woman in Christian tradition 366
Teitz, J. What's a nice girl like you doing in a place like this? 455
Tender gift. Raphael, D., see 548
Tennis to win. King, B.J., see 579
Terry, M. Approaching Simone 609
Tess of the d'Urbervilles. Hardy, T. 770

Textbook of anatomy and physiology. Anthony, C. P. 524
Textbook of gynecology. Novak, E. R., see 540
Theodore, A. R. Professional woman 473
They named me Gertrude Stein. Wilson, E., see 719
Thiselton-Dyer, T. F. Folk-lore of women, see 744
Thomas, S. M. Guide to sources of consumer information 456
Thompson, P. Personal perspectives 559
Thompson, R. Women in Stuart England and America 737
Thomson, D. L. Adam Smith's daughters 457
Three Marias. DaCosta, M. V. 630
Tiger, L. Men in groups 433
To a cabin. Lange, D. 572
Todasco, R. T. Feminist English dictionary 518
"Together" Black women. Reid, I. S. 445
Toklas, A. B. Staying on alone 723
Tomalin, C. Life and death of Mary Wollstonecraft 733
Tomorrow's tomorrow. Ladner, J., see 428
Too many people, too little love. Dykeman, W. 696
Toward a recognition of androgyny. Heilbrun, C. G. 595
Track to the water's edge. Schreiner, O. 621
Trade union woman. Henry, A. 450
Treasure. Lagerlof, S. 775
Tristes tropiques. Levi-Strauss, C. 520
Trotsky, L. Women and the family 434
True history of the first Mrs. Meredith. Johnson, D. 617
Truth, S. Sojourner Truth 724
Tucker, A. Woman's eye 573
Turney, C. Byron's daughter 688
Twelve daughters of democracy. Sickels, E. M., see 651

Uhnak, D. Law and order 801
Undine. Schreiner, O., see 793
Ungherini, A. Manuel de bibliographie et i'iconographie des femmes célèbres 652
U. S. Dept. of Commerce. Directory of minority media, see 506
U. S. Dept. of HEW. Higher education guidelines... 474
Unlearning the lie. Harrison, B. G. 505
Unmasking. Sheehan, V. H. 359
Unwanted pregnancy. Bluford, R. 528
Up against the wall, mother. Adams, E. 375

Vaginal politics. Frankfort, E. 537
VanDerMeer, H. Women priests in the Catholic Church? 369
VanVoris, J. Constance de-Markievicz 697
VanVuuren, N. Subversion of women as practiced by churches... 371
Vasectomy. Fried, J. J. 538
Venereal disease bibliography, 1966-1970. Goode, S. H. 324
Venture of form in the novels of Virginia Woolf. Alexander, J., see 612
Very easy death. Beauvoir, S. 626
Virginia Woolf and the androgynous vision. Bazin, N. T. 612
Viva. Superstar 725
Voice from the South by a Black woman of the South. Cooper, A. J. 669

Wagner, G. Five for freedom 622

Wakoski, D. Greed 610
_____. Motor cycle betrayal poems, see 610
Waldrip, L. Bibliography of the works of Katherine Anne Porter... 333
Walker, A. In love and trouble 824
Walking papers. Hochman, S. 771
Walling, W. Mary Shelley, see 715
Walls. Zassenhaus, H. 735
Walstedt, J.J. Psychology of women 334
Ward, K.B. Feminine fix-it handbook, see 557
Warren, B. Feminine image in literature, see 585
Waugh, N. Corsets and crinolines 517
_____. Cut of men's clothes..., see 517
_____. Cut of women's clothes..., see 517
We Dickinsons. Fisher, A., see 671
Weaver, H.E. Frosty 729
Webb, B.P. Beatrice Webb's American diary 730
Wedding day in literature and art. Carter, C.F., see 744
Weil, S. First and last notebooks 628
Weissler, A. Woman's guide to fixing the car, see 557
Weisstein, I. Labor's defiant lady, see 680
Wenig, S. Woman in Egyptian art, see 569
Westward the women. Ross, N.W. 649
Wharton, A.H. Colonial days and dames 751
Wharton, E.N.J. Ghost stories 825
What can she be? Goldreich, G., see 570
What every woman should know about investing... Levy, H.H., see 452
What the woman lived. Bogan, L. 661

What women should know about the breast cancer controversy. Crile, G. 532
What's a nice girl like you doing in a place like this? Teitz, J. 455
Wheel of love... Oates, J.C., see 813
Wheeler, M. No-fault divorce 475
Whissen, T.R. Isak Dinesen's aesthetics 623
Who is Angela Davis? Nadelson, R., see 670
Who's minding the children. Steinfels, M. 498
Who's who and where in Women's Studies 653
Widerberg, S. Kids' own XYZ of love and sex, see 529
Widow. Caine, L. 384
Willa Cather. Bonham, B., see 665
Willa Cather. Woods, L. 665
Willard, F.E. Glimpses of fifty years 731
Williams, O. American Black women in the arts and social sciences 335
Willing, M.K. Beyond conception 435
Wilson, D.C. Bright eyes 687
Wilson, E. Swamp angel 802
_____. They named me Gertrude Stein, see 719
Wilson, R.A. Feminine forever 556
Wind shifting west. Grau, S.A. 807
Winnifrith, T. Brontës and their background, see 663
Winter trees. Plath, S., see 705
Wise, W. Fanny Kemble, see 683
Without prescription. DiCayan, E. 536
Wittig, M. Guerilleres 629
Wolff, C. Love between women 436
Woman alone. O'Brien, P. 413
Woman citizen. Lemons, J.S.

405
Woman, culture and society. Rosaldo, M.Z. 523
Woman for peace. Kempf, B. 726
Woman hating. Dworkin, A. 393
Woman in art series 569
Woman in Christian tradition. Tavard, G.H. 366
Woman in Egyptian art. Wenig, S., see 569
Woman in Indian art. Mode, H., see 569
Woman on the American frontier. Fowler, W.W. 744
Woman question in Mrs. Gaskell's life and works. Rubenius, A. 677
Woman, society and change. Sullerot, E. 430
Woman Suffrage Movement in Canada. Cleverdon, C.L. 459
Womanpower Project. New York woman's directory 437
Woman's estate. Mitchell, J. 408
Woman's eye. Tucker, A. 573
Woman's fate. Dreifus, C. 392
Woman's guide to fixing the car. Weissler, A., see 557
Woman's life in colonial days. Holliday, C., see 744
Woman's place. Schulman, L.M. 821
Woman's Rights Convention, Seneca Falls... 752
Womansbook. Billings, V. 383
Women... 826
Women. Astin, H.S. 321
Women and analysis. Strouse, J. 554
Women and child care in China. Sidel, R. 497
Women and madness. Chesler, P. 531
Women and the ERA. Stimpson, C.R. 472
Women and the family. Trotsky, L. 434
Women and the labor movement. Henry, A., see 450

Women and their sexuality in the new film. Mellen, J. 581
Women and work. Galenson, M. 448
Women at work. Bickner, M.L. 322
Women at work. O'Neill, W.L. 815
Women beware women. Middleton, T. 620
Women gain a place in medicine. Lutzker, E. 545
Women in American labor history, 1825-1935. Soltow, M.J. 331
Women in Canada. Stephenson, M. 429
Women in higher education. Furniss, W.T. 503
Women in industry. Lyle, J.R. 565
Women in love. Lawrence, D.H. 777
Women in management. Basil, D.C. 560
Women in mathematics. Osen, L.M. 646
Women in perspective. Jacobs, S-E. 327
Women in politics. Jacquette, J.S. 442
Women in print. Adburgham, A. 611
Women in prison. Burkhart, K.W. 483
Women in prison. Chandler, E.W., see 483
Women in Stuart England and America. Thompson, R. 737
Women in Tolstoy. Benson, R.C. 632
Women of courage. Nathan, D. 645
Women of the American Revolution. Ellett, E.L.F. 743
Women of the forest. Murphy, Y. 522
Women of the Mayflower... Neyes, E.R.J.C. 747
Women poets in English. Stanford, A. 606

Women priests in the Catholic Church? VanDerMeer, H. 369
Women, resistance, and revolution. Rowbotham, S. 420
Women, sex and race. Braxton, B. 512
Women; their changing roles 342
Women who make movies. Smith, S. 583
Women who make our novels. Overton, G.M. 647
Women's legal handbook series... Ford Associates 462
Women's life and work in the Southern colonies. Spruill, J.D. 750
Women's organizations and leaders. Barrer, M.E. 340
Women's rights almanac, 1974. Gager, N. 341
Women's Rights Convention, Akron, Ohio, May 18, 1851, see 752
Women's rights in employment. Hughes, M.M., see 325
Women's Rights Movement in the U.S., 1848-1970. Krichmar, A. 328
Wonder woman. Ms., see 598
Wood, J.P. Emily Elizabeth Dickinson 671
Woods, L. Willa Cather 665
Woody, T. History of women's education in the U.S. 509
World who's who of women 654
Wright, C. Fanny Kemble and the lovely land 683

XYZ of love. Hegeler, I. 350

Yellow wallpaper. Gilman, C.P.S. 678
Yesterday's woman. Colby, V. 614
Young and female. Ross, P. 650
Yours, and mine. Rascoe, J. 819

Zassenhaus, H. Walls 735

Zola, E. Nana 803
Zuker, M.A. Canadian women and the law 476
Zulu woman. Reyher, R.H. 716

Z
7961
W48
Suppl.

NOV 1 1976